Hipster Culture

Hipster Culture

Transnational and Intersectional Perspectives

Edited by
Heike Steinhoff

BLOOMSBURY ACADEMIC
NEW YORK • LONDON • OXFORD • NEW DELHI • SYDNEY

BLOOMSBURY ACADEMIC
Bloomsbury Publishing Inc
1385 Broadway, New York, NY 10018, USA
50 Bedford Square, London, WC1B 3DP, UK
29 Earlsfort Terrace, Dublin 2, Ireland

BLOOMSBURY, BLOOMSBURY ACADEMIC and the Diana logo are trademarks of Bloomsbury Publishing Plc

First published in the United States of America 2021

Cover design: Eleanor Rose
Cover image © Getty Images

Library of Congress Cataloging-in-Publication Data
Names: Steinhoff, Heike, editor.
Title: Hipster culture : transnational and intersectional perspectives / edited by Heike Steinhoff.
Description: New York : Bloomsbury Academic, 2021. |
Includes bibliographical references and index.
Identifiers: LCCN 2021007665 (print) | LCCN 2021007666 (ebook) |
ISBN 9781501370427 (hardback) | ISBN 9781501370410 (paperback) |
ISBN 9781501370403 (ebook) | ISBN 9781501370397 (pdf)
Subjects: LCSH: Counterculture. | Bohemianism. | Subculture.
Classification: LCC HM647 .H55 2021 (print) | LCC HM647 (ebook) |
DDC 306/.1–dc23
LC record available at https://lccn.loc.gov/2021007665
LC ebook record available at https://lccn.loc.gov/2021007666

ISBN: HB: 978-1-5013-7042-7
PB: 978-1-5013-7041-0
ePDF: 978-1-5013-7039-7
eBook: 978-1-5013-7040-3

Typeset by Newgen KnowledgeWorks Pvt. Ltd., Chennai, India

CONTENTS

List of Illustrations ix
Acknowledgments x

1 Hipster Culture: A Definition 1
Heike Steinhoff

Hipster Places, Identities, and Transformations

2 (Re-)Dressing the Naked City: Hipsters, Urban Creative Culture, and Gentrification in New York City 27
Annabel Friedrichs and Florian Groß

3 Glocal Hipsterification: Hipster-Led Gentrification in New York's, New Delhi's, and Johannesburg's Cultural Time Zones 47
Melissa Tandiwe Myambo

4 Hipsters in Central and Eastern Europe: From Domesticated Nostalgia to *Manele* and Protests 67
George Alexandru Condrache

5 Pastiching the Pastoral: Hipster Farmers and the Commodification of American Agriculture 85
Katje Armentrout

Hipster Fashion, Porn, and Body Politics

6 Hipsters and (Anti-)Fashion 105
Catharina Rüß

7 The Irony of Hipster Beards 129
Christopher Oldstone-Moore

8 The Politics of Hipster Porn/ography 145
Alexandra Hauke and Philip Jacobi

Hipster Literature and Self-Fashioning

9 Twenty-First-Century Hipster Fiction and Postindustrial Revitalization 167
Brandon McFarlane

10 Choosing Marginality: White Entitlement in Dave Eggers's Hipster Fiction 183
Stephanie Li

11 The Line, the Niche, and the Bathrobe: The White Male Writer as a Hipster Trope 199
Katharina Scholz

12 "The Straight Queer": Hipster Appropriation in the Work of James Franco 215
Ben Robbins

Hipster Media, Aesthetics, and Identity Politics

13 The Female Hipster in *Girls* and *Frances Ha* and the Potential of Emancipated Spectatorship 235
Heidi Lucja Liedke

14 "Fem the Future" of Hipness: Female Hipster Performers in Twenty-First-Century Popular Music 253
Lena Gotteswinter

15 Art Hipsters: Postmodern Proclamations 273
Wes Hill

16 Hipster Post-Communities and Digital Nostalgia Design 289
Marek Jeziński and Łukasz Wojtkowski

Hipster Foodways and Cultural Politics

17 The Pursuit of Culinary Capital in *Portlandia* and *Master of None* 305
Justine Gieni

18 Pabst Blue Ribbon: The Hipster Experiment with Critical Anti-Consumerism in Beer and Beyond 321
Daniella Gáti

19 The Paradox of the Hungry Hipster: The Representation and Cultural Politics of Hipster Foodways 339
Kathleen LeBesco and Peter Naccarato

Hipsters as Intersectional Identities

20 Mipsterz: Cultural Capital, Racialization, and the Emergence of Muslim Cool 357
Anwar Ouassini and Mostafa Amini

21 Skinny Jeans in the Sanctuary: The Hipster Christian Subculture 373
Caroline Barnett

22 The Hipster Animal: Human–Animal Interactions in Hipsterdom 391
Jayson Scott Grimes

List of Contributors 403
Index 409

ILLUSTRATIONS

Figures

2.1 Carol Hummel's installation *Hand-Stitched Hamlet* in Oyster Bay, New York, 2014 (photo by Carol Hummel) 39
3.1 Father Café in Braamfontein, Johannesburg, 2017. Photo by author 54
3.2 Extraction Lab, Industry City, Sunset Park, Brooklyn, 2018. Photo by author 54
6.1 Illustration of Allen Ginsberg by Johannes Siegmund, 2020 119
6.2 Illustration of Gavin McInnes by Johannes Siegmund, 2020 119

Tables

3.1 Typology of Hipster Design Aesthetic 53
16.1 Features of Hipster Digital Nostalgia Design 297

ACKNOWLEDGMENTS

First ideas to this book took hold of me in the summer of 2016, when teaching a cultural studies class on American hipsters at the English Department of Ruhr-University Bochum, Germany. While hipster culture had always fascinated me, I was struck by the lack of scholarly literature on the topic. In particular, there was no study that critically investigated hipster culture from interdisciplinary, intersectional, and transnational perspectives. This seemed striking given the omnipresence of the hipster label in the contemporary culture of the United States, Germany, and beyond, and the attention hipster culture has received in the (social) media. Inspired by the research my students and I conducted in the seminar, I began analyzing hipster culture more closely and eventually set out to conceptualize this book. I am grateful to all colleagues, students, and friends who have contributed ideas to this volume by drawing my attention to the myriad facets of hipster culture.

In particular, I would like to acknowledge my colleague Eric C. Erbacher, whose contributions of expertise on hipster culture were significant in shaping this project in its early stages. Many fruitful discussions of hipster culture that we had in hipster cafés of the Ruhr area informed the conceptualization of the book and my own reflections on the phenomenon.

I am deeply indebted to all the contributors for their excellent chapters and their great collaboration. It was a pleasure to work with you, and I thank you for your scholarly expertise, hard work, and patience that made this volume possible.

I thank my student research assistants Claudia Eugenie Laube, Deniz Yilmaz, and Maike Doll for their careful labor of editing and proofreading. This book could not have been completed without you.

Many thanks to Katie Gallof and her team at Bloomsbury for their invaluable support and editorial work. Thanks are also due to the anonymous reviewers for supporting the project and thus paving the way towards publication.

My heartfelt gratitude goes to my family for their tireless love, care, and support.

1

Hipster Culture: A Definition

Heike Steinhoff

Enter the Hipster

Twenty-first-century popular culture has given birth to a peculiar cultural figure: the hipster. Stereotypically associated with nerd glasses, beards and buns, boho clothing, and ironic T-shirts, hipsters represent a (post-)postmodern (sub)culture whose style, aesthetics, and practices have increasingly become mainstream. In the edited volume *What Was the Hipster? A Sociological Investigation* (2010), Mark Greif describes the American hipster as young, white, urban, college-educated, and middle-class. According to his definition, hipsters are "rebel consumers" who define, acquire, and possess ever new insider knowledge of goods and styles to continually distinguish themselves from the mainstream ("Positions"). Vintage style and retro design, urban gardening and organic food, DIY entrepreneurship and cafés or vegan restaurants marked by a nostalgic industrial chic are only some of the cultural trends that have been linked to hipster culture. At the same time, they have become key components of a dominant popular culture of hip, giving support to Greif's claim that the hipster "aligns himself *both* with rebel subculture *and* with the dominant class, and opens up a poisonous conduit between the two" ("Positions" 9). Their eclectic cultural appropriations and their frequent association with gentrification processes implicate hipsters in some of the most contentious phenomena of contemporary Western urban culture, and they have been held responsible for the commodification and appropriation of past and marginalized cultures. The hipsters' seemingly constant search for "authenticity" and difference from the mainstream has frequently turned them into figures of public ridicule at the same time as they have been increasingly charged with selling out. Yet, whereas some have declared the death of the hipster, hipster culture seems to be very much alive in global urban centers and in the popular cultural imagination.

In striking contrast to the hipster's omnipresence in popular culture, the academic discussion of the (sub)culture has, however, been sparse and limited. With few exceptions, the scholarly publications about the hipster have mostly followed Greif, Ross, and Tortorici's 2010 volume in taking a primarily sociological approach to the hipster. Hipster culture as a whole, however, has largely been ignored by academic studies and remained a topic of feuilletons and blog entries.[1] This book seeks to fill this research gap by providing a collection of original articles that approach hipster culture from a variety of cultural perspectives, including urban studies, food studies, gender studies, queer studies, ethnic studies, art history, literary studies and media studies. A decade after *What Was the Hipster* implied that the hipster, born at the turn to the twenty-first century, had already become a figure of the past, this volume sheds light on the ways in which the hipster and hipster culture have indeed persisted, transformed, and diversified over the last twenty years of their existence. Rather than reflecting on the hipster as a primarily sociological figure, *Hipster Culture* foremost conceives of "hipster" as a powerful cultural discourse that takes shape in representations in movies, novels, TV shows, music, literature, and social media and as a lifestyle and aesthetic that informs and shapes many contemporary cultural practices, economic products, and popular places, such as barber shops, restaurants, urban gardens, arts and crafts products, or fashion.

While all of us well versed in global urban cultures and online media most likely share some idea of what hipsters and hipster culture look like, the hipster, despite frequent stereotypification, has indeed been linked to a diversity of styles, practices and cultural issues.[2] More a sliding signifier than a signifier with a clear referent, "hipster" ultimately remains a nebulous cultural figuration that needs to be examined in the specific cultural, historical, economic, and political context of its (re)production. In the following, I will illuminate some of the features of contemporary hipster culture and hipster identities, suggesting that the hipster presents a liminal figure. At the beginning of the third decade of the twenty-first century, hipster culture sits at the borders between subculture and post-subculture,

---

[1]For scholarly articles that address hipster culture as culture, see, e.g., Maly and Varis as well as Schiermer. Also, these studies primarily apply sociological research methods and theories. For a study of the development of the hipster as discourse and marketplace myth cf. also Arsel and Thompson. The German essay collection *Destruktive Charaktere: Hipster und andere Krisenphänomene* by Wilpert and Zwarg takes the phenomenon of the (German) hipster as starting point for a number of reflections on contemporary society, approaching the hipster as social type from a variety of different philosophical and cultural perspectives.

[2]As also Maly and Varis have argued, the term "hipster" itself is rarely defined: "[I]t seems to be used as if its meaning was universally fixed and transparent, while in reality its meaning is opaque and fluid" (637).

postmodernism and post-postmodernism, irony and sincerity, and political as well as environmental engagement and apoliticism. Moreover, hipster culture oscillates between the promotion of cultural, racial, ethnic, sexual, and gender diversity on the one hand and cultural exploitation and the reassertion of white middle-class privileges on the other hand. Whereas the mainstreaming of hipster culture bespeaks of an appreciation of the hipster as a figure of inspiration and imitation, the dominant mode of hipster criticism constitutes the hipster as object of ridicule and cultural blame. The hipster as cultural figure is produced by discourses about the hipster as well as by practices of hipster self-fashioning. In some cases, as I will argue, hipster criticism and hipster self-fashioning do not even collide but are actually the same.

Hipster: A (Trans)National History

The contemporary hipster—thus runs the dominant narrative—has emerged in urban centers of the United States in the late 1990s, most prominently in Williamsburg, Brooklyn, New York. Hipster culture emerged out of 1990s indie youth culture (cf. Greif, "Positions" 5), predominantly white middle-class youths interested in alternative music and art. Greif specifically dates the emergence of the contemporary American hipster in 1999 with the Iraq War and World Trade Organization protests and thus in the context of anti-war and anti-globalization movements ("Positions" 6). Historically, the roots of the hipster have been traced to the culture of 1940s African-American jazz and the 1950s white counterculture closely associated with the Beat Generation. In his 1948 article "Portrait of the Hipster," Anatole Broyard defines the hipster as a Black subcultural figure. Displaced and marginalized in American society, the hipster expresses himself through the language of jazz, a language of "a priorism" (Broyard 722), that is, of superior and exclusive knowledge. The contemporary hipster shares this emphasis on apriorism as a main source of (sub)cultural capital and main mode of cultural distinction (cf. Bourdieu's theory of cultural capital and Sarah Thornton's theory of subcultural capital; cf. Greif "Positions" 8). It is expressed, for instance, in the ironic prints on their T-shirts, in their foodways, or their consumption—and in case of hipster filmmakers, their production—of idiosyncratic movies. However, the hipster's apriorism is perpetually haunted by its commodification and integration into mainstream culture, now as much as in the mid-twentieth century. Whereas Broyard mourns the hipster's demise through the wider cultural recognition of jazz and its appropriation into white American culture,[3] contemporary critical

---

[3]Significantly, Broyard himself passed as white for most part of his life, cf. e.g., Hill, *Art after the Hipster* 50-3.

discourses about the "death of the hipster" carry a reproachful or outright hateful tone, often suggesting that the twenty-first-century hipster never carried any "true" sub-cultural potential at all.

The recognition of jazz and Black hipster culture by a white avant-garde, in fact, presents the next step in dominant hipster history. In opposition to Broyard's hipster, the contemporary hipster, after all, is imagined as white and middle-class, often less marginalized than self-consciously choosing positions and signifiers of marginalization. It is in this respect that contemporary hipster culture is indebted to Norman Mailer's adoption of this label in his 1957 article, "The White Negro: Superficial Reflections on the Hipster." Implicitly drawing on the Black hipster culture identified by Broyard in his essay, Mailer (re)defines hipsters as a contemporary white American counterculture that formed in American cities where "the bohemian and the juvenile delinquent came face-to-face with the Negro." According to Mailer this cultural encounter gave birth to the hipster, a social outcast and rebel, whose being hip is opposed to the conformist, that is, "square," tendencies of American mainstream culture. In response to the horrors of World War II and the conformity of 1950s American society, Mailer's "white Negro" is an existentialist and non-conformist, characterized by a childlike clinging to the present, a longing for sexual freedom, and a desire to remove all social constraints. Contemporary hipster culture retains some of these features, most prominently the desire for authentic experience, the tendency to appropriate marginalized (life)styles, and the desire to defy (specific) social conventions.

The different and similar ways in which Broyard and Mailer defined the hipster as a rebellious cultural identity are symptomatic for a history of hip as a "story of black and white America" (Leland 6). As John Leland writes in *Hip: The History*, "At its best, it [hip] imagines the racial fluidity of pop culture as the real America ... At its worst, hip glosses over real division and inequity" (6). While Mailer's essay explicitly opposes segregationist and discriminatory racial politics, his claiming of Black culture as the source of the white hipster's non-conformity romanticizes the marginalization of African Americans and reproduces racial stereotypes of Black people as "primitive" or "over-sexualized."[4] As this volume shows, this ambiguity continues to shape twenty-first-century hipster culture and identity both in terms of its racial politics and beyond. The hipster's ambivalent cultural politics take shape in the ways in which the hipster's attempts to be "hip," "cool," and distinct from mainstream culture is coupled with the appreciation, appropriation, and exploitation of the marginalized, be it in terms of race, ethnicity, class, or sexuality.

[4]For some of the various criticisms of the racial and sexual politics of Mailer's essay, cf., for instance, Baldwin and Millett.

Most obviously, at the turn of the twenty-first century, the source of the hipsters' stylistic appropriation shifted from race to class. In allusion to Mailer's "white Negro," Greif has referred to these hipsters as "white hipsters" ("What Was the Hipster?"). White hipsters did not so much copy Black cultural styles, but white hipsters "fetishized the violence, instinctiveness, and rebelliousness of lower-middle-class suburban and country whites" ("Positions" 10). This appropriation of signifiers of what is derogatorily called "white trash" was evident in the white hipsters' adoption of "truckerhats; undershirts called 'wifebeaters', worn as outwear; the aesthetic of basement rec-room pornography, flash-lit Polaroids, fake wood paneling; Pabst Blue Ribbon; 'porno' or 'pedophile' mustaches; aviator glasses, Americana T-shirts for church socials, et cetera" ("Positions" 10). According to Greif's periodization, in 2003 the "white hipster" was replaced by the "green hipster" or the "Hipster Primitive," characterized by references to "animals, wilderness, plus the occasional Native American" ("What Was the Hipster?"). This is the hipster associated with urban gardening, lumberjack beards, and female hipsters in rubber Wellingtons, as well as a (renewed) appropriation of the styles of the "ethnic Other." Mocking popular cultural (stereo)typifications of hipster identities such as Robert Lanham's *The Hipster Handbook* (2003), Joe Mande's *Look at This F*cking Hipster* (2010), based on a popular website by the same name that collected photos of people identified as hipster by the one posting the picture, or the comedy television series *Portlandia* (2011–18) offer numerous additional, most often parodic, categorizations of hipster identities. Toward the end of the first and beginning of the second decade of the twenty-first century, voices in the American media increasingly proclaimed the death of the hipster, and numerous other terms, such as "normcore" or "yuccie" have come up to describe what the hipster has been replaced by or turned into. The articles in this volume suggest that the hipster has not vanished from the cultural landscape.[5] Rather the articles testify to the diversification of hipster identity and culture in terms of nationality, place, race, ethnicity, gender, and sexuality.

Whereas hipster history has predominantly been written as an American history, some critics have suggested that the hipster is also rooted in nineteenth-century European urban culture. Both the mid-twentieth and the early twenty-first-century hipster after all share key features with two nineteenth-century figures, most prominently associated with nineteenth-century Paris and London, namely the bohemian and the dandy (cf., e.g., Kinzey 10–16; Schiermer 176–7). With their rejection of the bourgeoise

[5]Significantly, Wes Hill, in one of his articles on the hipster, refers to "twee," "health goth," "normcore," "lumbersexual," and "yuccies (young urban creative yuppies)" as "hipster subgroups" ("Hipster Aesthetics" 1).

lifestyle, their detached attitude and their desire to turn their life into a work of art, the bohemian artist and the aristocratic dandy can be linked to the contemporary hipster. Significantly, the moment the twenty-first-century American hipster was proclaimed dead, the twenty-first-century European hipster was on the rise or at least gained wide media attention, for instance in German media at the beginning of the 2010s. European hipster culture shared features with its American counterpart, yet European hipster culture has also been culturally distinct. One of the most striking features of recent hipster gentrification processes in Germany, for instance, is the gentrification of the *Schrebergärten* (garden colonies). Once the stereotypical weekend destination of Germany's urban lower and middle classes, *Schrebergärten* are now increasingly taken over by a younger generation of ethnically diverse and eco-friendly couples, and families intent on planting their own vegetables and green oasis in the city. Over the past two decades, hipster culture and style have, indeed, developed into a global and transnational, yet locally distinct, phenomenon that characterizes neighborhoods in major cities worldwide, including not only New York, Portland, Los Angeles, San Francisco, London, Paris, or Berlin but also New Delhi, Sao Paolo, St. Johannesburg, or Tokyo. In all of these places, hipster culture functions both as a motor of globalization and an expression of local particularities and concerns, becoming what could possibly best be described as a glocalized culture.[6]

Though born in the city and closely linked to metropolises, hipster culture has not only spread globally but has come to characterize also rural areas. Or rather, hipster culture blurs the boundaries between the constructed categories of the urban and the rural. Fashion styles and identities closely associated with hipster culture, such as the "green hipster," the so-called lumbersexual, young men sporting lumberjack shirts and long beards, the integration of signifiers of nature and rural life in urban hipster places such as restaurants or shops, so well exemplified by the wooden-paneled stores of the now mainstream brand Urban Outfitters, and practices such as urban gardening, all point to this dissolution of the hipster as a purely urban phenomenon. The emergence of the image of the hipster farmer, explored by Katje Armentrout in this volume, epitomizes this embrace of the "rurban."

The global and urban-rural spread of hipster culture has much to do with hipster culture being not only a physically located phenomenon but also very much a virtual one and one that is (re)produced through the global mediascape. Globally accessed social media platforms like Pinterest, Etsy or Tumblr feature images, fonts, and objects that are closely associated with hipster aesthetics and lifestyle. They testify to the importance of new media

[6]Cf. also Maly and Varis's characterization of hipster culture as a translocal phenomenon (642–4).

technologies for the construction and dissemination of hipster culture and identities (cf. also Clayton 27), alongside more "traditional" media like movies, novels, or TV shows. New technologies are fused with the nostalgic aesthetics of retro technologies, such as the Polaroid or cassette tape/recorder. Digital nostalgia (cf. Jeziński and Wojtkowski in this volume) as well as the pastiche of old and new technologies—such as the resurgence of vinyl in recent years, going hand in hand with the widespread use of iPhones and tablets—point toward hipster culture's eclectic identity, not only in terms of space and place but also in terms of temporality. Hipster culture seeks to fuse past, present, and future.

Though rooted and often located in a twenty-first-century urban American environment, all of these developments suggest that we need to rethink the hipster and hipster culture today as a transnational phenomenon that reproduces and destabilizes spatial and historical boundaries of the national and transnational, the urban and the rural, the physical and the virtual, the past and the present. In the course of this process and as already several times throughout hipster history, hipster identity and hipster culture are transformed and re-signified.

Hipster Culture as (Post-)Postmodern (Post-)Subculture

Hipster culture seems to be a postmodern subculture par excellence. Born out of the moment of late capitalism and marked by irony, bricolage, pastiche, parody, as well as the blurring of "high" and popular culture, hipster culture appears quintessentially postmodern. Moreover, the hipster's quest for distinction from mainstream culture can be perfectly captured by Dick Hebdige's famous 1979 definition of subcultures as cultures that "represent symbolic challenges to a symbolic order" (92). As stylistic bricoleurs who appropriate particularly the styles of the past and the culturally marginalized, hipster culture expresses its challenge to hegemonic culture at the level of style and consumption choices (cf. Hebdige's definition of subculture 17). In its subcultural quality, hipsters have been linked to millennials and Generation Y, terms equally contested as the hipster label itself, but roughly identifying young people born between the early 1980s and late 1990s. Similar to the hipster, Gen Y—if positively cast—has been represented as creative, flexible, as well as socially and environmentally aware, or more often and largely critical, Gen Y and the hipster have seen themselves confronted with being narcissists ("Generation Me"), apolitical, tech-savy, and characterized by an extended adolescence. Critics have claimed that especially the early twenty-first-century hipsters were unproductive, "mere" consumers, engaged in a "hip consumerism," always in search of the "right" and most unconventional product to consume (cf. e.g., Greif, "Positions" 12). Hipster style seems to be perpetually shifting, drawing on ever new sources of marginalized cultures or past decades in its maybe ultimately futile attempt to resist dominant trends and its own incorporation into dominant culture. In the words of Michael Z. Newman, "Hipsters thus comprise a culture in pursuit of hip rather than a hip culture" (72). As "rebel consumers" hipsters are caught up in what Thomas Frank in *The Conquest of Cool* has described as the conundrum of a cultural moment in which rebellion presents the heart of consumer capitalism (cf. Frank 11; cf. also Greif, "Positions" 12). As Bjørn Schiermer has pointed out, hipster culture differs from traditional definitions of subcultures as it "has no cause; hipster culture possesses no manifestos; it has no instituted leaders; it has no clear borders; it is more inclusive and less uniform than the traditional subculture; it does not promote drug use; it does not battle the police or the authorities; (and) it does not market itself discursively as a distinct alternative or rebellious lifestyle" (170). "Hipsters are superficial. They think they are different and individual, but they are actually totally mainstream"—a criticism that I have been encountering perpetually when discussing hipster culture.

While its "failure" as "true" counterculture is one of the major criticisms of contemporary hipster culture *as* subculture, we might, however, also conceive of this impasse as an indicator to shift our perspective from a subcultural to a post-subcultural one, that is, a perspective which recognizes that "the potential for style itself to resist appears largely lost, with any 'intrinsically' subversive quality to subcultures exposed as an illusion" (Muggleton and Weinzierl 5). As Muggleton and Weinzierl point out with reference to Angela McRobbie's work on subcultures, "subcultures of today are also complicit in the (niche) marketing of their own identities. There is a vivid role for subcultural-related practices as an entrepreneurial engine for the new media, fashion and cultural industries, while many of these young producers themselves have subcultural origins (McRobbie 1989, 2002)" (8). This is true for the many cafés, restaurants, boutiques, and creative industries that characterize global hipster neighborhoods or sell their goods and services online. The contemporary hipsters' involvement in DIY culture and entrepreneurship link them to the emergence of what Richard Florida in his debated theories about "creative cities" has called the "creative class" a group "of people who add economic value through their creativity" (68) and share "a common creative ethos that values creativity, individuality, difference and merit" (8). In his ethnographic study of Wicker Park in Chicago, Richard Lloyd coined the term "neo-bohemia" to refer to the ways in which "the population of artists and lifestyle aesthetes abets residential gentrification as well as the concentration of entertainment outlets and design intensive media enterprises" (518) and thus contributes to the redevelopment of formerly industrial areas in the post-Fordist city. Hipsters are part of this urban renewal in quite ambivalent ways, complicit with gentrification processes and simultaneously often critical about these processes (cf. Friedrich and Groß in this volume). Rather than only condemning hipster culture for not presenting a functional counterculture, we should examine the specific and often ambivalent cultural discourses that constitute hipster culture, its particular structures, styles, products, and practices. According to Schiermer,

> the traditional sociological focus on "rebellious youth," on alternative "ways of life" carrying broader emancipative potentials, or on a critique of capitalism is doomed to fail in the case of the hipster. Polemically speaking, this quest for critical potential may only see a lack of resistance or demarcation and thus only access what is really new about the hipster negatively: What may be a sound conservatism is interpreted as a lack of protest. (168)

In its search for individuality, distinction and authenticity, contemporary hipster culture resorts to the past and culturally marginalized, yet it does so not always ironically, but often in a sincere effort for authenticity and an alternative lifestyle. This points toward hipster culture's dissolution not only of conventional conceptualizations of subculture but also towards hipster culture's liminal status between the postmodern and the post-postmodern.

Apparently running counter to hipster culture's postmodern characteristics such as irony, pastiche, nostalgia, and "dephtlessness" (cf. Jameson and Ihab Hassan's definiens of postmodernism), hipster culture is marked by a post-postmodern impetus, expressed in an emphasis on and longing for authenticity, uniqueness, and sincerity. As R. Jay Magill Jr. has suggested, hipster culture, especially post-9/11, partakes of a sensibility of "new sincerity," that is, an oscillation between irony and sincerity. Longing for a more authentic life and yet being mostly well versed in postmodern theory and aware that this ideal is a cultural construct, hipsters "chase[d] the ideals of sincerity and authenticity with a wink" (Magill 198). Across hipster culture and hipster history this sensibility is more or less pronounced. As a sensibility that shapes media culture, it finds expression through the penchant for nostalgia and sentimental representations of childhood and social outcasts, captured by the movies of Wes Anderson, often named as one of the major hipster auteurs (cf. Newman). According to Eric C. Erbacher, "While stylistic celebrations of childhood have usually been treated with irony mocking the naïve refusal to grow up, they are signs also of the search for more emotionality and immediacy in individualistic late-capitalist society" (11). Such a longing is also articulated in the quirky literature of hipster authors such as Miranda July, whose fiction can be classified as "hipster literature" not so much because July herself performs hipster identity and so do her characters, but because her texts appeal to hipster tastes by expressing hipster sensibility through content and style.

The short story "Mon Plaisir," for instance, tells the story of a couple that pursues a hipster lifestyle in quest of distinction and authenticity, and yet, as the first-person female narrator indicates, they perpetually search for, yet cannot reach, a life of meaningful existence. At the heart of the story and the narrator seems to be a void, the regret for not having a child, for not having a fulfilling relationship, for not finding meaning in their life. According to the narrator, her husband and herself seek to be different from the mainstream by only doing meaningful things, their favorites being "Buddhism, eating right and the internal landscape" (148). Beginning with the narrator's initial declaration that "[i]t's the first day of the rest of my life" (148), the story ends with the ironic, yet tragic, revelation that in the end the only moment when the couple can truly connect is when they act as extras for a movie. Hipster sensibility emerges out of this melancholy with a wink. The narrative tone oscillates between irony and sincerity, self-reflexivity, and a yearning for authenticity. July's fiction, published in 2007, indicates a shift or at least a tendency in hipster literature to move from the postmodern and ironic towards the post-postmodern or metamodern. As defined by Timotheus Velmeulen,

> [w]ithin and from practices and artists whose starting point might have been postmodern, sensibilities emerge that no longer fit its framework: sincerity, hope, the inexplicable, the prediscursive ... This development is the development of the metamodern, rediscovering within the postmodern the modern, within apathy hope, within irony sincerity, within distrust (of grand narratives) belief, within the representative presence.

Beyond media culture, the hipster's longing for authenticity and hope manifests in hipster culture's environmentalist interests, its appreciation of the local, the artisanal, the organic, the self-made, the simple, which are reflected in its aesthetics as well as in its consumption and production choices. Contemporary hipsters, at least at the less commodified end of the cultural spectrum, seem to be longing to be producers rather than mere consumers of alternative lifestyles.[7] Selling self-grown food or living a completely self-sufficient, communal, or even nomadic life have all become associated with hipsterism, aligning hipster culture with environmentalist ideas and pointing towards its link to 1970s hippie culture. Minimalism as both aesthetic and lifestyle—with its suggestion of a focus on the "essential"—has come to be a kind of "hipster signature." Simultaneously, minimalism in its many

[7]Cf. also Michael Scott, who argues that "rather than seeing the hipster through the lens of consumption and identity, there is a need for seeing the hipster also as the neoliberalised entrepreneurial figure at the forefront of urban cultural production promoting the art of living well" (72).

facets has turned into a widespread commodified middle-class "trend," once again, highlighting the intricate relation of hipster and mainstream culture. In their definition of metamodernism, Robin van den Akker and Timotheus Vermeulen argue, "Metamodernism is a structure of feeling that emerges from, and reacts to, the postmodern as much as it is a cultural logic that corresponds to today's stage of global capitalism" (5). Likewise, and in accordance, I suggest that hipster culture is as much a product of the neoliberal and postmodern condition as it is a reaction to this cultural moment. Hipster literature as an expression of hipster culture showcases this conundrum and hence hints at hipster culture's self-reflexive awareness of its own nostalgic and melancholic longing for authentic experiences and alternative lifestyles in an age of postmodern irony and neoliberal consumption. Aware that its yearning for individualism and authenticity is caught up in the hegemonic condition that it seeks to resist, hipster culture is still marked by a persistent unwillingness to give up on searching for ruptures in the structure of mainstream neoliberal culture.

The (Trans)Formations of American Hipster Cultural Identities

The cover illustration of the February 11 and 18, 2013, issue of the *New Yorker* epitomizes the image of the American hipster. Called "Brooklyn's Eustace" and created by Simon Greiner, the illustration was submitted through the 2013 Eustace Tilley Contest, in which the magazine asked its readers to reinterpret the Regency dandy who appeared on the cover of the *New Yorker*'s first issue in 1925. Greiner's reinterpretation of the dandy shows a blonde bearded man, wearing nerd glasses, a red beanie, white wifebeater paired with a green duffle coat, and sporting a bricolage of ironic tattoos that point towards his pastiche-like embrace of working class and sailor culture—anchor, romanticized notions of nature and childhood innocence—cute bird, as well as his love for simple, environmentally friendly, and yet stylish and often expensive technologies—fixie bike. The hipster's expression is slightly haughty and his head turned away, signaling the hipster's stereotypical intellectual aloofness and pointing towards his dandy lineage. In the background is the New Yorker skyline as seen from Brooklyn, *the* urban neighborhood associated with hipster culture, and a food truck on pastoral green signifies the hipster's penchant for nature and alternative lifestyles within the city. Most pointedly and at the same time most invisible is the way in which the cover showcases the norm of hipster identity and the hipster label as used in American and global(ized) media discourses: hipsters are white, male, young, middle-class and—as another the *New Yorker* cover from March 2015, "Hipster Stole" by Ricardo Liniers, featuring a Brooklyn hipster couple suggests—at least when depicted in mainstream media, the hipster is also constructed as heterosexual. As critics, including a number of authors in this volume, have pointed out, the hipster's conventionally privileged background provides their lifestyle, their consumption preferences, and their creative expressions with a specific social, ethnic, and cultural perspective. Thus, while an author like Miranda July challenges the hegemonic image of the hipster author as male, narrating her story from a female perspective, the characters in her story "Mon Plaisir" are white, just like the author herself. On closer inspection, rather than reproducing whiteness as invisible norm, July's narrative, however, seeks to make whiteness visible by self-consciously mocking the characters' appropriation of nonwhite cultural practices in their search for a meaningful authentic existence (cf. July 149–50). This results in contradictory and ambivalent representational and identity politics that are emblematic for the way hipster culture reflects, and at the same time self-reflexively addresses larger social structures and hierarchies of hegemonic American culture.

As predominantly white middle-class culture, hipster culture often turns to non-middle-class and nonwhite ethnicities as sources of cultural inspiration or appropriation. To use bell hooks's characterization of the commodification of Otherness in commodity culture, ethnicity in hipster culture "becomes spice, seasoning that can liven up the dull dish that is mainstream white culture" (366). Hipster food culture quite literally uses ethnicity as spice, evident in the ways that hipster foodways appropriate both ethnic dishes and places (cf. LeBesco and Naccarato). Likewise, the incorporation of ethnic styles in hipster fashion and their mainstreaming by companies such as Urban Outfitters or American Apparel function as exploitations of ethnic and racial Otherness that often reproduce colonialist and essentialist ideas about these "Others."[8] Similar arguments can be made about the hipster's appropriation of working-class styles or the aesthetics of queer culture as well as its adaptation of various cultural items and signifiers conventionally considered "not hip" because they are associated with cultural "Others" and outsiders. The popularization of the net bag, for instance, suggests that hipster culture not only turns to "other(ed)" classes, ethnicities, or sexualities but also to different age groups in its search for hip(ster) style. Whereas hipster culture has always turned to romanticized notions of childhood, net bags have been typically associated with elderly women. Upcycled and redesigned, these items have been turned into the latest statement of hipness at a time when the stereotypical hipster tote bag has already become widely mainstream. Significantly, net bags have also

[8]These processes received particular media attention during the legal dispute between Urban Outfitters and the Najavo Nation (2012–16), after the company had used the tribe's name to sell a line of their products.

been popularized by social media "fashionistas" and appeared on runways as high fashion accessories—pointing towards the blurry boundaries of what constitutes "hipster style" or a "hipster trend" in the first place. While it uses "other(ed)" cultural groups as sources of hipness, hipster culture itself has been appropriated, commodified, and turned into a "spice" of American mainstream culture.

Exploring the cultural processes of appropriation, exploitation and depoliticization involved in hipster culture is central to a critical cultural assessment of its cultural and identity politics. Recent developments and a nuanced perspective, however, also bring to light the emergence and oft-ignored existence of hipster identities and cultural facets that challenge the notion of the hipster as white, male, heterosexual, and apolitical. At the beginning of the 2020s, within the United States and beyond, hipster culture is more than a white middle-class phenomenon. The emergence of blipsters, that is, Black hipsters, and mipsterz, that is, Muslim hipsters, complicates common notions about the intersections of such categories as class, ethnicity, and/or religion in the formation of hipster identity. Mipsterz and blipsters challenge both the inherent whiteness of the hipster category as well as prominent understandings of hipsterism, while the inflection of the term hipster in both labels still points toward the *h*ipsters invisible ethnic bias. Defying the widespread notion that hipsters do not self-identify as such, American Muslim youth self-consciously embrace the mipster label and identity to claim their position in mainstream American society (cf. Ouassini and Amini in this volume). Moreover, whereas the hipster has predominantly been imagined as male, the mipster is closely associated with the image of the *hijabista*, that is, young fashionably veiled Muslim women (cf. Ouassini and Amini in this volume).

Women are, in fact, central to hipster culture. Despite their invisibility in most popular and critical discourses, I argue alongside some of the authors in this volume that hipster culture has been shaped by women and has (re)produced particular notions of femininity. Key definiens of hipster culture such as its clinging to certain features of childishness, the self-made, or the quirky are indeed intricately linked to the image of the white female hipster. They are linked to her fashion choices, such as the messy bun or the cute vintage dress, as well as to her involvement in the production of artisanal fashion, arts and crafts, in particular as manifested on social media. The figure of the female hipster is closely related to what has recently been called "mumpreneurship,"[9] at the same time that it is personified by such artists and writers like Miranda July. These gendered cultural manifestations and practices suggest that hipster culture (re)produces rather "conventional" notions of femininity. In one of the few articles dealing with the existence

[9]Cf. Luckman's discussion of hipsters and mumpreneurs.

of the female hipster, Dayna Tortorici observes "an unsatisfying partial-truth: that the female hipster's privileged knowledge is not subcultural, intellectual, or even pseudo-intellectual, but the familiar 'female' knowledge of how to look" (123). This points toward hipster culture's reproduction of rather conventional and sometimes outright sexist and, in other contexts, also racist ideologies under the guise of irony, which has given rise to terms like "hipster sexism" and "hipster racism" (cf. e.g., Quart, Gotteswinter).

However, contemporary hipster culture is also closely aligned with feminist, queer, and anti-racist agendas (cf. Gotteswinter and Liedke in this volume). In accordance with the diversity and broad range of hipster cultures, these range from postfeminist re-significations of stereotypical feminine practices and styles as signs of female agency and creative economies[10] to the promotion of outright political causes associated with so-called third and fourth wave feminisms,[11] with which hipster culture shares not only its penchant for certain aesthetics, such as retro, but also its media channels such as Instagram. As debates about the mumpreneur, the re-evaluation of women's crafts such as crochet and knitting, the TV series *Girls* or the musical performances of female musicians such as Solange indicate, the lines between postfeminist and third or fourth wave feminist hipsterism are more often blurry than clear-cut.

Hipster masculinity is equally characterized by shifting and ambivalent gender performativities, oscillating between an apparent longing for some form of "rugged" masculinity and an incorporation of signifiers coded as feminine or queer. This manifests itself in the male hipsters' fashion style, as well as in their choice of particular forms of literature, music, or art. Whereas the skinny jeans of the male hipster as well as his close attention to style and grooming challenge heteronormative hegemonic notions of masculinity, the beard, particularly associated with the style of the "lumbersexual," expresses longings for a "natural" rough masculinity, associated with outdoorsmanship ("lumberjack"; cf. Oldstone-Moore and Rüß in this volume). This yearning for an idealized "traditional" masculinity is, once again, challenged by the emergence of barber shops and a variety of male beard grooming products that emphasize consumption and body care ("metrosexual").

Hipster culture's ambivalent relation to queer culture can been traced back to the mid-twentieth century counterculture's blurring of the hetero- and homosexual. These roots resurface in the embrace of hipster fashion styles by both straight and gay youths as well as the use of hipster aesthetics

[10]Cf. e.g., Banet-Weiser, Gil, and Rottenberg for a recent overview of the debates about postfeminism. Cf. also Luckman for a discussion of mumprenuerialism in the light of Angela McRobbie's arguments about postfeminism.

[11]For a discussion of third wave feminism and the slippages between the third wave and postfeminism cf. e.g., Gillis, Howie, and Munford. For a definition of fourth wave feminism and its slippages, cf. e.g., Rivers.

in both heteronormative and queer media productions. The appropriation of queer aesthetics in hipster culture as well as the appropriation of hipster aesthetics in queer culture, or rather the blurring of these two processes, expose the ambivalent and highly problematic cultural politics of hipster culture as well as the variety of its cultural expressions. Queer and hipster culture have also been conflated in discussions about the gentrifying impulses of people associated with one or both of these groups.[12] Hipster neighborhoods are not only located in ethnic neighborhoods, but often also deeply entangled with queer spaces, such as gayborhoods and LGBTQIA+ areas in places like Brooklyn, New York, or Malasaña, Madrid. Whereas critical discussions of hipster culture of the 2000s have, however, largely ignored hipster culture's gender and sexual politics, predominantly focusing on aspects of class and race, chapters in this volume pay attention to the intersection of these various and interrelated identity categories.

Though hipster culture lacks any coherent political agenda, from a cultural studies perspective, hipster culture just like any cultural discourse and identity performance is inherently political. Rather than constituting a coherent political and cultural movement, hipster culture oscillates between leftist ideals and more conservative tendencies. Most recently, within a US-American and European context, the adaptation of hipster style and leftist rhetoric by right-wing political groups, such as parts of the American alt-right or the Identitarian Movement in Europe, has complicated matters even more. In the cycle of appropriations that constitutes hipster culture, hipsters take the role of both appropriator and appropriated.

The cultural and political heterogeneity of hipster cultures that this volume identifies is as much the result of historical developments as of studying hipster culture(s) through a variety of intersectional perspectives. Hence, chapters in this volume draw attention to hipster cultures' reproduction of existing social inequalities as well as to the ways in which hipster cultures challenge these very structures. Focusing on North America and Western Europe—areas (still) most strongly associated with hipsterism in the global mediascape—yet also shedding light on hipster cultures beyond these regions, the chapters collected here explore the intricacies of the various politics of hipster cultural representations.

(Re)Defining Hipster Culture: Hipster Criticism and Hipster Self-Fashioning

If hipsterism is a discursive construction, one of the most dominant discursive formations framing contemporary hipster culture is the critical media

[12]Cf. e.g., Florida's theories about the "creative class" and the debates surrounding his theses.

discourse about it.[13] In line with my suggestion that we need to take into account the ways in which hipster culture is intrinsically diverse, I argue that hipster culture only emerges as a homogenous subculture through its critical media representations. As Sarah Thornton has argued in her ethnographic study of clubbing: "communications media create subcultures in the process of naming them and draw boundaries around them in the act of describing them" (162). Critical representations of hipster culture range from the sympathetically mocking to the outright hateful and typically construct the hipster as cultural Other. Hipsters are mocked for their style, taste, and supposedly futile search for distinction and criticized as the harbingers of gentrification and global exploitation processes. Hipster criticism thus often functions as a conduit to express concerns about larger cultural processes of (post-)postmodernity, late capitalism, and neoliberalism, including its gendered, racial, sexual, and class inequalities. In his analysis of hipster criticism in the media, Philipp Ikrath concludes that hipster criticism is not so much a criticism of the hipster, but rather of the cultural logic of neoliberal society, embodied by the hipster (103). Neither a figure of cultural conservatism nor progressiveness, the hipster is a powerful cultural dispositif that is mobilized by various groups for different ends. Significantly, by positioning the hipster as Other, popular criticism often constructs the critic as not responsible for or implied in the processes the hipster is criticized for, thus, ultimately, turning hipsters into "scapegoats" for what is perceived to be wrong with contemporary culture (cf. also LeBesco and Naccarato and Hill in this volume). As Wes Hill puts it, "[c]aught up in the power of taste and the power of its denunciation the hipster presents a kind of spectre in contemporary culture, a figure of hate through which we can identify the politics of taste in neoliberalist culture while distancing ourselves from our place in its system" ("Hipster Aesthetics" 16).

The boundaries between "othering" the hipster and performing hipster identity or "doing" hipster—in the sense of Judith Butler's notion of gender performativity—are, however, often blurry: hipster criticism is also a powerful discourse of hipster self-fashioning. This is most evident in the large number of popular critical publications that, since the early 2000s, claim to provide definitions and explanations of hipster culture. These include such pseudo-academic writings on hipster culture like Robert Lanham's *The Hipster Handbook* (2003), one of the first and few attempts to systematically define the hipster and thus frequently referred to also in this volume, Brenna Ehrlich's and Andrea Bartz's *Stuff Hipsters Hate: A Field Guide to the Passionate Opinions of the Indifferent* (2010), or Kara Simsek's *So You Think You're a Hipster? Cautionary Case Studies*

[13]Cf. also Rob Horning's claim that "[h]ipster hatred may actually precede hipsters themselves" (81).

from the City Streets (2013). Impostors of academically informed studies, these publications engage in aesthetic generalizations, sweeping scientific categorizations, and anecdotal explorations of hipster identities that in their pointed exaggerations and ironic mockery betray the same strategies of distanciation and satire they ascribe to the hipster. Due to their abundance, these fake-scientific publications can thus be regarded as a unique literary genre of self-reflective and mocking hipster self-descriptions that aim to distance themselves from hipster culture while at the same time promoting its styles and values.[14] Neither serious academic criticism nor clearly part of popular hipster bashing, these texts function as forms of literary self-fashioning that constitute hipster culture from within *and* without.

Publications of critical hipster self-fashioning adopt biological, anthropological, or sociological terms and forms to purport that they treat hipsters as an object of scientific study. Their academic framing with a wink suggests that hipsters can be classified as a species, ethnicity or subcultural group with distinct characteristics and personality types. Lanham's *The Hipster Handbook*, for instance, poses as an anthropological field guide to hipster culture. Besides a brief historical contextualization and a list of features allegedly related to hipster culture, such as indie music, queer kissing, and gentrification, the book includes a description of ten hipster personality types and a vocabulary guide to hipster language. Similarly, Simsek presents "case studies" and "personality types," relying heavily on illustrations that function like photos in anthropological or biological handbooks to provide evidence and construct the subject positions of researcher/observer and object of study. The analogy of hipster handbooks and biological field guides is epitomized by Dyna Moe's *Hipster Animals: A Field Guide* (2015) that portrays various animals as hipster characters or rather caricatures various hipster types as animals. Ehrlich and Bartz's *Stuff Hipsters Hate: A Field Guide to the Passionate Opinions of the Indifferent* divides its first chapter into "abstract," "introduction," "method," "results," to then explore the "social habits" and "habitats" of hipsters in the following chapters. In all of these publications, the hipster is positioned as Other and the books pose as windows or tour guides to the unfamiliar and non-normal.

Significantly, these publications use fake scholarly language not only to prove their distance to but also their own in-depth knowledge of contemporary hipster culture. Their illustrations replicate visual aesthetics typically identified as hipster, their content functions like a bricolage and they display their authors' apriorism. Ultimately, their ironic rhetoric and visual pastiche turn these publications into products of the very (sub)culture that they purport to study. Literary distanciating self-representations are part of hipster culture's self-understanding and positioning. Lanham's

[14]These arguments were developed in discussion with Eric C. Erbacher.

Hipster Handbook, in fact, explicitly indicates that his book is for those who want to learn more about hipsters as well as "for those among you who want to become hipsters yourselves" (2). Moreover, in their mocking self-descriptions, authors like Lanham implicitly self-identify as hipsters. As Rob Horning put it in his reaction to *n+1*'s panel discussion "What Was the Hipster?": "It's impossible to obtain objective distance from hipsterism; if you are concerned enough about the phenomenon to analyse it and discuss it, you are already somewhere on the continuum of hipsterism and are in the process of trying to rid yourself of its 'taint' " (80). This is true for contemporary writings about hipsters as well as about historical sources such as Broyard and Mailer, whose texts are equally embedded in the subcultural context that they are writing about. One can also find traces of hipster style and rhetoric in the essayistic and bricolage-like style of the contributions to Greif, Ross, and Tortorici's *What Was the Hipster*. On the one hand, this might mean that we need to re-evaluate parts of the scholarly work on hipsters for not having adequately questioned the self-reflective nature of the (fake-)scholarly publications on hipster culture. On the other hand, the broad popularity and continuing relevance of these writings is symptomatic for the ongoing negotiation of hipster culture between mainstream commercialization and avant-garde progressivism, as well as between hipster criticism and hipster self-fashioning. Most likely some form of involvement with hipster culture also characterizes this volume.

Hipster Culture: A Cultural Study

This volume aims to contribute to an assessment and critical discussion of hipster culture from a variety of perspectives. Contributions have been grouped into six sections in accordance with some of the central features of hipster culture as defined in this introduction. The chapters collected in the first section, "Hipster Places, Identities, and Transformations," are dedicated to a critical (re-)examination of hipster culture's spatial and identity politics. Annabel Friedrichs and Florian Groß devote their contribution to one of the most prominent processes and places associated with contemporary hipster culture: urban gentrification in New York City. Through a study of yarn bombing, they discuss the role of hipster culture as a subform of contemporary creative culture, whose relation to processes of urban gentrification is more complicated than most critical assessments have suggested. Focusing on the oft-ignored group of female creatives, their article moreover explores the specifically gendered features of spatial practices associated with hipster culture. Going beyond the American context, Melissa Tandiwe Myambo takes a transnational approach to investigate the design and cultural function of hipster places in the cities of New York, New Delhi, and Johannesburg in their respective cultural contexts. Her comparative study highlights the ways in which hipster culture is both global and locally specific. Likewise, George Alexandru Condrache goes beyond the discussion of hipster culture as a Western phenomenon, shifting our focus to Eastern Europe. Taking his cue from the centrality of nostalgia as a key feature of global hipster culture, the author argues that particularly in Romanian hipster culture nostalgia has a locally specific form and signals an acceptance of the region's communist past and a concern for marginalized social groups. Katje Armentrout's contribution directs our attention to the ways in which hipster culture is more than a purely urban phenomenon. In her analysis of the figure of the hipster farmer, she explores the various interrelations of hipster culture and farming, shedding light on the role of rural nostalgia and rural gentrification in contemporary American culture. While taking up key concerns of existing critical discourses on hipster culture, all four contributions thus highlight the importance of taking into account the national, cultural, and political specificities of global, yet heterogenous hipster cultures.

The articles assembled in the section on "Hipster Fashions, Porn, and Body Politics" zoom in on the body politics of contemporary American and European hipster culture. Exploring the discursive and stylistic linkages of the proto-hipster, associated with the 1950s Beat Generation, and the dot-hipster of the 2000s, Catharina Rüß examines how fashion theories and media representations of styles construct the hipster as a figure of both fashion and anti-fashion. As she discusses the polysemy of styles, her contribution also offers insights into the phenomenon of contemporary alt-right groups, who appear in hipsterish looks, with a particular focus on "nipsters" in the context of German history. Christopher Oldstone-Moore traces the historical lineages of the hipster beard. As his contribution reveals, the male hipster's turn to the beard is situated in a long history of cultural discourses about masculinity and facial hair. Since the eighteenth century, beards have repeatedly been used to express a "return" to "authentic masculinity," of which the hipster beard only constitutes a most recent manifestation. Hipster porn and pornography is the focus of Alexandra Hauke and Philip Jacobi's contribution. Taking their cue from the works of Catalan filmmaker Noel Alejandro and American photographer Ryan McGinley, they examine the aesthetics and cultural politics of what they call hipster "porn/ography." Hipster porn/ography, they suggest, is a political-cultural discourse within and beyond the erotic.

The section "Hipster Literature and Self-Fashioning" turns to the mediality and representational politics of hipster culture. In his literary study of Canadian hipster literature, Brandon McFarlane observes a shift from postmodern irony, characteristic of hipster literature in the 1990s, to romantic and Dadaist forms and aesthetics in more recent publications. As McFarlane shows, these newer works imagine romantic models of community building and urban revitalization. From the perspective of critical race studies, Stephanie Li in her contribution alerts us to the racial politics of American hipster literature and its reproduction of white entitlement in particular. Focusing on the literary work of Dave Eggers, Li shows how Eggers's books bespeak of racial awareness, yet ultimately fail to incite social changes. Katharina Scholz reflects on the gendered and racial implications of the white male novelist as hipster trope. Focusing particularly on *VICE* magazine, often considered a key source of early hipster culture, she suggests that the magazine's journalistic style is characteristic of a tradition of white men writing about and for white men. Ben Robbins's case study of the literary self-representation of actor, artist, author, and "hipster straight queer," James Franco, turns to the entanglement of hipster culture and queer culture, pointing specifically toward hipster culture's exploitative tendencies. As Robbins argues, in his literary works Franco appropriates queer aesthetics and subcultural symbols as a rebellious pose, while erasing the experiences of marginalization "originally" connected with them.

The section "Hipster Media, Aesthetics and Identity Politics" continues the focus on the aesthetics and representational politics of hipster culture. In her contribution on the TV series *Girls* and the movie *Frances Ha*, Heidi Lucja Liedke challenges the critical focus on male hipsters. In her reading of the two media texts, Liedke shows how the female hipster's marginality functions as a source of her empowerment. Hipness as female empowerment, however, appears to be only a transitory state connected to youth and whiteness. The intersection of hipster identity, gender, and race is also the focus of Lena Gotteswinter's study of twenty-first-century female hipster musicians. Focusing specifically on Asian American and Black hipsters ("blipsters"), her contribution shows that artists like Karen O, Janelle Monáe, and Solange embrace hipness in music and performances that challenge both sexism and racism. Wes Hill's contribution bridges the focus on identity politics and aesthetics as it explores the hipster as trope of aesthetic distinction. In his chapter, Hill discusses hipsters in the context of artistic and economic developments of the postmodern. In particular, his contribution reflects on the art hipster as neo-avant-garde figure and critical-postmodern accusation. Approaching hipster culture from a post-subcultural and communication studies perspective, Marek Jeziński and Łukasz Wojtkowski focus on the function of digital nostalgia, that is, nostalgia expressed in and through new media, for the constitution of hipster culture as a post-community. In their study of prominent social media platforms, they outline central visual codes and narrative frames formative of hipster digital nostalgia design.

The three chapters of the section "Hipster Foodways and Cultural Politics" shed light on one of the most visible and popular identifiers of hipsterism: its culinary culture. Justine Gieni analyzes the representation of hipster foodways in the two popular TV series, *Portlandia* and *Master of None*. As her close reading shows, though both series to different degrees use the representation of hipster foodways as sources of humor and (self-)mockery, they also tend to inscribe these with ethical ideals and longings for cultural change. Turning from media representations to consumption patterns, Daniella Gáti in her contribution reflects on the affective significance of Pabst Blue Ribbon (PBR) beer in hipster culture. Suggesting to understand hipster culture as an internally conflicted and heterogenous culture, she reads the American hipsters' turn to PBR and its working-class connotations as a reaction to larger consumer cultural structures as well as a self-aware reaction to hipster culture's attempt to counter these structures. In case of the hipster's affinity for PBR, she argues, the culture's capitalist-critical impulse ultimately turns into a nostalgic-conservative and (white-)nationalist ideology. The section's final contribution by Kathleen LeBesco and Peter Naccarato is unique in that it shifts the perspective on the relation of hipsters, foodways, and media discourses by elucidating how popular representations of hipster foodways in soft news and social media representations function to turn hipsters into cultural scapegoats. As the authors reveal, hipsters and their foodways are often blamed for structural inequalities, diverting attention away from the critic's own role in these processes.

The final section "Hipsters as Intersectional Identities" collects three articles that study intersections of hipster identities thus far completely neglected in scholarly publications on hipster culture. Anwar Ouassini and Mostafa Amini offer the first comprehensive study of the mipster subculture. As the authors argue, mipster identity is central to American Muslim youths' attempt to express a sense of self in mainstream American culture. Based on their analysis of a broad range of media representations, the two authors provide insights into the symbolic, ideological, and economic processes of mipster culture. Caroline Barnett explores the link between hipsters and evangelicalism in the United States. Hipster Christianity, she argues, blurs the boundaries between the religious and the secular, yet retains the racial and class structures as well as the conservative gender and sexual ideologies that have been characteristic of evangelicalism in the United States. Jayson Scott Grimes offers reflections on the function of non-human animals in hipster identity constructions. His contribution suggests that nonhuman animals function to reinforce particular notions of "humanness" and "hipness."

The last section's title "Hipsters as Intersectional Identities" could indeed function as heading for all contributions collected in this volume. An intersectional perspective is central to the overall aim of this book, and thus most papers could have been placed under more than one heading as their topics, analytical approaches, and results intersect with one another in myriad ways. While the recurring topics and motifs hopefully help to define hipster culture, the overlaps and contradictions in this volume should point towards the fluidity of the hipster label and hipster culture. Rather than reducing hipster culture to a fixed set of features or cultural politics, I hope that this volume offers a variety of perspectives and new paths to investigate hipster culture *as* cultural discourse.

Works Cited

Arsel, Zeynep, and Craig J. Thompson. "Demythologizing Consumption Practices: How Consumers Protect Their Field-Dependent Identity Investments from Devaluing Marketplace Myths." *Journal of Consumer Research*, vol. 37, no. 5, 2011, pp. 791–806.

Baldwin, James. "The Black Boy Looks at the White Boy Norman Mailer." *Esquire*, May 1, 1961, pp. 102–6, classic.esquire.com/article/1961/5/1/the-black-boy-looks-at-the-white-boy-norman-mailer. Accessed March 13, 2018.

Banet-Weiser, Sarah, Rosalind Gill, and Catherine Rottenberg. "Postfeminism, Popular Feminism and Neoliberal Feminism? Sarah Banet-Weiser, Rosalind Gill and Catherine Rottenberg in Conversation." *Feminist Theory*, 2019, pp. 1–22. journals.sagepub.com/doi/full/10.1177/1464700119842555. Accessed June 2, 2019.

Bourdieu, Pierre. *Distinction: A Social Critique of the Judgement of Taste*. Harvard University Press, 1984.

Broyard, Anatole. "A Portrait of the Hipster." *Partisan Review*, vol. 15, no. 6, 1948, pp. 721–7.

Butler, Judith. *Gender Trouble: Feminism and the Subversion of Identity*. Routledge, 1990.

Clayton, Jace. "Vampires of Lima." *What Was the Hipster? A Sociological Investigation*, edited by Mark Greif, Kathleen Ross, and Dayna Tortorici. n+1 Foundation, 2010, pp. 24–30.

Ehrlich, Brenna, and Andrea Bartz. *Stuff Hipsters Hate: A Field Guide to the Passionate Opinions of the Indifferent*. Ulysses Press, 2010.

Erbacher, Eric C. "Hip or Square? Pop Cultural Negotiations of Hipster Lifestyles between Commodification and Subversion." Manuscript, 2011, pp. 1–19. Published in a shortened version with the same title in *Hidden Cities: Understanding Urban Popcultures*, edited by Leonard R. Koos, Inter-Disciplinary Press, 2012, pp. 13–22.

Florida, Richard. *Cities and the Creative Class*. Routledge, 2004.

Frank, Thomas C. *The Conquest of Cool: Business Culture, Counterculture, and the Rise of Hip Consumerism*. University of Chicago Press, 1997.

Gillis, Stacy, Gillian Howie, and Rebecca Munford, eds. *Third Wave Feminism: A Critical Exploration*. Palgrave Macmillan, 2007.

Gotteswinter, Lena. "Hipster Racism—What's Irony Got to Do with It?" *ForAP*, vol. 3, no. 3, 2020, pp. 9–26, doi:10.5283/forap.44. Accessed December 18, 2020.

Greif, Mark. "Positions." *What Was the Hipster: A Sociological Investigation*, edited by Mark Greif, Kathleen Ross, and Dayna Tortoici, n+1 Foundation, 2010, pp. 4–13.

Greif, Mark. "What Was the Hipster?" *New York*, October 22, 2010, nymag.com/news/features/69129/. Accessed September 30, 2019.

Greif, Mark, Kathleen Ross, and Dayna Tortorici, eds. *What Was the Hipster? A Sociological Investigation*. n+1 Foundation, 2010.

Greiner, Simon. "Brooklyn Eustace." Cover illustration. *The New Yorker*, February 11 and 18, 2013.

Hassan, Ihab. "Pluralism in Postmodern Perspective." *Critical Inquiry*, vol. 12, no. 3, 1986, pp. 503–20.
Hebdige, Dick. *Subculture. The Meaning of Style*. Routledge, 1979.
Hill, Wes. *Art after the Hipster: Identity Politics, Ethics, and Aesthetics*. Palgrave Macmillan, 2017.
Hill, Wes. "Hipster Aesthetics: Creatives with No Alternative." *Emaj: Online Journal of Art*, vol. 9, 2016, pp. 1–19, emajartjournal.com/past-issues/emaj-9/. Accessed March 13, 2018.
hooks, bell. "Eating the Other: Desire and Resistance." *Black Looks: Race and Representation*, South End Press, 1992, pp. 21–39.
Horning, Rob. "The Death of the Hipster." *What Was the Hipster? A Sociological Investigation*, edited by Mark Greif, Kathleen Ross, and Dayna Tortorici, n+1 Foundation, 2010, pp. 78–84.
Ikrath, Philipp. *Die Hipster: Trendsetter und Neo-Spießer*. Promedia, 2015.
Jameson, Frederic. *Postmodernism, or, the Cultural Logic of Late Capitalism*. Duke University Press, 1991.
July, Miranda. "Mon Plaisir." *No One Belongs Here More Than You*. Scribner, 2007.
Kinzey, Jake. *The Sacred and the Profane: An Investigation of Hipsters*. Zero Books, 2012.
Lanham, Robert. *The Hipster Handbook*. Anchor Books, 2003.
LeBesco, Kathleen, and Peter Naccarato. "Distinction, Disdain, and Gentrification: Hipsters, Food People, and the Ethnic Other in Brooklyn, New York." *A Place-Based Perspective of Food in Society*, edited by Kevin M. Fitzpatrick and Don Willis, Palgrave Macmillan, 2015, pp. 121–39.
Leland, John. *Hip: The History*. Harper Perennial, 2004.
Liniers, Ricardo. "Hipster Stole." Cover illustration. *New Yorker*, March 16, 2015.
Lloyd, Richard. *Neo-Bohemia: Art & Commerce in the Postindustrial City*. 2nd ed. Routledge, 2010.
Luckman, Susan. *Craft and the Creative Economy*. Palgrave Macmillan, 2015.
Magill, R. Jay. *Sincerity: How a Moral Ideal Born Five Hundred Years Ago Inspired Religious Wars, Modern Art, Hipster Chic, and the Curious Notion That We All Have Something to Say (No Matter How Dull)*. W. W. Norton, 2012.
Mailer, Norman. "The White Negro (Fall 1957)." *Dissent Magazine*, www.dissentmagazine.org/online_articles/the-white-negro-fall-1957. Accessed March 13, 2018.
Maly, Ico, and Piia Varis. "The 21st-century Hipster: On Micro-Populations in Times of Superdiversity." *European Journal of Cultural Studies*, vol. 19, no. 6, 2016, pp. 637–53.
Mande, Joe. *Look at This F*cking Hipster*. St. Martin's Griffin, 2010.
McRobbie, Angela. "Clubs to Companies: Notes on the Decline of Political Culture in Speeded up Creative Worlds." *Cultural Studies*, vol. 16, no. 4, 2002, pp. 516–31.
McRobbie, Angela. "Second-Hand Dresses and the Role of the Rag Market." *Zoot-Suits and Second-Hand Dresses: An Anthology of Fashion and Music*, edited by Angelia McRobbie. Macmillan, 1989.
Millett, Kate. *Sexual Politics*. 1970. Columbia University Press, 2016.
Moe, Dyna. *Hipster Animals: A Field Guide*. Ten Speed Press, 2015.

Muggleton, David, and Rupert Weinzierl, eds. *The Post-Subcultures Reader*. Berg, 2003.

Newman, Michael Z. "Movies for Hipsters." *American Independent Cinema: Indie, Indiewood and Beyond*, edited by Geoff King et al., Routledge, 2013, pp. 71–82.

Quart, Alissa. "The Age of Hipster Sexism." *The Cut*, October 30, 2012. www.thecut.com/2012/10/age-of-hipster-sexism.html. Accessed March 13, 2018.

Rivers, Nicola. *Postfeminism(s) and the Arrival of the Fourth Wave: Turning Tides*. Palgrave Macmillan, 2017.

Schiermer, Bjørn. "Late-Modern Hipsters: New Tendencies in Popular Culture." *Acta Sociologica*, vol. 57, no. 2, 2014, pp. 167–81.

Scott, Michael. "'Hipster Capitalism' in the Age of Austerity? Polanyi Meets Bourdieu's New Petite Bourgeoisie." *Cultural Sociology*, vol. 11, no. 1, 2017, pp. 60–76.

Simsek, Kara. *So You Think You're a Hipster?: Cautionary Case Studies from the City Streets*. Dog n Bone, 2013.

Thornton, Sarah. *Club Cultures: Music, Media, and Subcultural Capital*. Polity Press, 1995.

Tortorici, Dayna. "You Know It When You See It." *What Was the Hipster? A Sociological Investigation*, edited by Mark Greif, Kathleen Ross, and Dayna Tortorici, n+1 Foundation, 2010, pp. 122–35.

Van den Akker, Robin, and Timotheus Vermeulen. "Periodising the 2000s, or, the Emergence of Metamodernism." *Metamodernism: Historicity, Affect and Depth after Postmodernism*, edited by Robin van den Akker, Alison Gibbons, and Timotheus Vermeulen, Rowman & Littlefield, 2017, pp. 1–20.

Vermeulen, Timothy. "Hard-boiled Wonderland, Blue Velvet and the End of Postmodernism." *Metamodernism*, September 23, 2010. www.metamodernism.com/2010/09/23/hard-boiled-wonderland-from-pomo-to-metamo/. Accessed March 13, 2018.

Wilpert, Chris. W., and Robert Zwarg. *Destruktive Charaktere: Hipster und andere Krisenphänomene*. testcard zwergobst, 2017.

Hipster Places, Identities, and Transformations

2

(Re-)Dressing the Naked City: Hipsters, Urban Creative Culture, and Gentrification in New York City

Annabel Friedrichs and Florian Groß

When, in the early 2010s, street artist and "yarn bomber" London Kaye O'Donnell entered the urban scene and began to create colorful crochet pieces around various street elements in New York City, initial reactions in the news media were positive: "London Kaye O'Donnell has taken to the streets of NYC, adding a bit of crocheted flair to the otherwise industrial aesthetic of neighborhoods like Bed-Stuy. Her yarn bombing endeavor began as a 30-day beautification challenge ... with her yarn creations adorning lamps, tree trunks, mailboxes and fences around the BK area" ("Meet the Artist"). Yet, this celebrated instance of urban creativity soon had its share of detractors as well, and the following quote might serve as a preview for the negative reactions the artwork evoked: "Not everyone was charmed. ... Anti-gentrification activists took their frustrations against her to social media. ... [O]ne aggrieved person equated Ms. Kaye and her work to 'colonizers who claim indigenous lands for themselves.' 'I was the perfect scapegoat,' said Ms. Kaye" (Miller). In-between these two vastly different reactions by locals and media alike, London Kaye and her public crochet art had become the subject of a conflict that revolved around the question of the role of young, urban artists and their relation to processes of gentrification.

What had happened? In 2015, Kaye had installed "Moonshine Kingdom," a fifteen-foot crochet mural, on the wall of a building abutting a flea market in Brooklyn's Bushwick neighborhood. The giant artwork showed the twins from Stephen King's *The Shining* holding hands with Sam Shakusky, the boy scout character from Wes Anderson's film *Moonrise Kingdom*. It was Kaye's biggest project to this point, whose prominent reference to a film by a quintessentially "hip" director seemed to signify a common aesthetic and social bond with hipster culture. While being officially commissioned by Bushwick Flea's owner Rob Abner, it was put up without the permission of the adjoining building's owner, a long-term inhabitant of the neighborhood. As a consequence, Bushwick-native Will Giron, nephew of the Latina owner, tenant advocate, and legal coordinator for an anti-gentrification non-profit organization, was enraged by Kaye's project. Venting his frustration with what he perceived as "[a] small piece of a much greater social epidemic" and yet another intrusion by a "hipster transplant," he posted on Facebook that "[g]entrification has gotten to the point where every time I see a group of young white millennials in the hood my heart starts racing and a sense of anxiety starts falling over me" (qtd. in Whitford). After a heated on- and offline discussion between Giron and Abner, who merely claimed that they had "covered up nasty graffiti with nice graffiti," Kaye eventually retracted her artwork and promised to be more careful and more sensitive to the kind of community she "beautifies" with her projects in the future: "now I understand that just because it's an unintrusive form of art doesn't mean that it's invited" (qtd. in Whitford; cf. Voon, "Artist Will Remove").

The question arises: Is Kaye, taken here as one representative of her chosen woolen street art, only an innocent protagonist in a story of a female craft-artist-turned-media-star who "beautifies" postindustrial New York City by using colorful—and temporary—crochet creations to "dress" the streets of a city that Sharon Zukin has proclaimed "naked" due to its supposed lack of authenticity?[1] Or is she rather yet another racially and economically privileged white hipster figure, epitomizing the commodification of urban spaces by outsiders and hipster culture's aestheticized "colonization"[2] and

---

[1]In *Naked City*, her 2010 study of six gentrifying New York City areas, urban sociologist Sharon Zukin laments the trend towards a "soulless" (1), i.e., socially homogeneous (31), naked city. Zukin updates Jane Jacobs's legendary 1961 urban study *The Death and Life of Great American Cities* with a look at what she refers to as an aura of "authenticity." Once a "quality of people" (3), that is, a characteristic of a heterogeneous resident structure, "authenticity" has turned into the driver behind escalating real estate prices and as such not only into "a quality of things" (3), but most of all into "a consciously chosen lifestyle and a performance, and a means of displacement" (4).

[2]Another example for this use of the metaphor of gentrification as a modern form of white urban colonialism is also present in an anti-gentrification rant by Spike Lee, in which he refers to a "Christopher Columbus syndrome" through which high-income arrivals displace predominantly Black residents from their homes (cf. Michael and Bramley).

economic exploitation of "diverse" and "authentic" neighborhoods? In what follows, our answer is decidedly in-between: We read yarn bombing in relation to hipster culture and processes of urban change to show how the confluence of all three aspects—woolen art forms, the hipster, and gentrification—factor into creative culture's ambivalent impact on twenty-first-century cities. Through a comparative analysis of female yarn artists London Kaye, Magda Sayeg, and Carol Hummel, as well as their projects and installations in New York City, this contribution aims to find more nuanced answers to the complex question of hipster culture's impact on local neighborhoods. Moving beyond either celebration or condemnation of hipster culture, we argue that it is necessary to read hipsters as a specific subform of contemporary creative culture and yarn bombing as a form of creative expression congruent with and sometimes identical to hipster culture. The yarn artists analyzed here negotiate questions of agency and their complex middle-position vis-à-vis gentrification processes in a specific manner that goes beyond simplistic descriptions along the lines of "colonizing" hipsters. Rather, their projects and responses to possible connections to processes of economic displacement oscillate between complicity, confrontation, and, most importantly, the possibilities of (re-) constructing urban spaces affected by gentrification.

While the Bushwick Flea-incident raises important questions about race and class (Voon, "Anarchist Protest"), Miller's reference to Kaye's gender is equally striking: "There may be a double standard here. Few would call Banksy's work gentrifying, but Ms. Kaye's genre of street art, known as 'yarn bombing,' has been widely derided as a hipster fad or dismissed as cutesy, mere 'women's work.'" While Miller seemingly defends Kaye's gender, she also sheds new light on the role of "hip" creatives in processes of gentrification. Through a focus on the rather neglected group of female creatives/hipsters and their employment of (supposedly "feminine") yarn-based craft, we analyze how and to what ends these projects may also attempt to gender space through practices that quote femininity, domesticity, and acts of "taking care" in the public sphere. This particular focus helps to get a grasp on the specific potentials of this creative process, yet also highlights the limitations and contradictions of yarn art as activist practice within the creative culture that has become dominant in Western societies in the twenty-first century and also central to a proper understanding of hipster culture.

Hipster Culture = Creative Culture?

Much has been said and written about the hipster, this ubiquitous-yet-elusive (sub)cultural figure that first entered the cultural scene in 1950s urban America. From its earliest incarnations epitomized by

Norman Mailer's essay "The White Negro" to more recent, often far less celebratory instances connected to heavily stylized urbanites living in trendy neighborhoods such as Williamsburg, New York City, "hipster" has become a kind of catchall term to describe overtly stylish urban consumers of conspicuously anti-mainstream, niche products. While our understanding of the term draws on the vast history of the phenomenon,[3] we propose to go beyond stereotypical clichés as well as too-narrow knee-jerk descriptions of certain people as "hipsters" and rather read the kind of individualistic, subculturally stylized, culturally productive, and often (and least symbolically) young urbanites in the broader context of twenty-first-century creativity culture. Drawing on Andreas Reckwitz's study *The Invention of Creativity* and the idea of creativity as an increasingly dominant "dispositif" in Western societies, we understand the individual's ability to come up with something new and live an expressive, rewarding life as *the* culturally desired feature of postindustrial life and work and one of the main nodal points where economic imperatives and aesthetic desires have become interwoven in unprecedented ways (5). Much more than a simple consumption pattern, creative culture has pervaded the middle classes of Western postindustrial societies in many more fields, most importantly the sphere of work, which has transformed in two ways: First, work has become increasingly defined in terms of self-expression, authenticity, and innovation—in short, creativity. Second, this transformed understanding of work has increasingly merged with the desire of large groups of consumers to move beyond the supposedly passive and mindless consumption of industrialized goods and exploitative services by "the mainstream" (Jacobs).

The rather general term "creativity" obtains a much more specific meaning in the context of hipster culture. Several critics have described how ideas and elements from hipster culture have become hegemonic within an aestheticized popular culture that symbolically defies uniform mainstream culture, promotes individual expression in work and (leisure) life, and symbolically rewards attempts to actively shape rather than merely consume cultural products in the passive fashion assumed by critics of mass culture (McGuigan; Heath and Potter; Frank, *Conquest*). Especially Thomas Frank's description of "hip consumerism" as a capitalist phenomenon that has made disgust with homogeneous mass culture one of the principal driving forces of a superficially diversified popular culture and his thesis that this development has its roots in the confluence of counter- and business culture since the 1960s forms the basis for our theoretical understanding of the link between creative urban cultures and increasing urban inequality as a

[3]For an extensive historical account of the term, see Leland.

corollary of upscale consumption practices that emphasize difference and individual expression (*Conquest* 1–33).

Hipster culture is a broad and diverse epiphenomenon of twenty-first-century creative culture, a contemporary subset of popular culture that attracts large numbers of people, yet addresses them as highly individualized subjects that seek to move beyond a perceived mainstream, beyond the norm, and beyond the supposed blandness of "mass culture." While not all creatives are necessarily "hip," both hipster culture and creative culture are obviously characterized by the ostentatious desire—and maybe illusory attempt—to combine cultural productiveness, difference from the mainstream, and an emphasis on individuality and individual experience—an observation that furthermore characterizes the hipster as a downright discursive formation. This desire is expressed in a variety of (increasingly stereotypical) ways ranging from, say, the purchase of trendy clothes, vintage furniture, or organic/local/artisanal food to alternative and seemingly more rewarding ways of working in the cultural and creative sectors—and also a crucial element in the culture of yarn bombing and its ambivalent impact on urban neighborhoods.

The Hipster as Gentrifier?

Coined by Ruth Glass in 1964, the term "gentrification"—the widespread displacement of existing households by more affluent newcomers—has come to define a central characteristic of twenty-first-century urbanity and is certainly "one of the most vigorously discussed phenomena of the post-Fordist city" (Erbacher 245). Particularly the image of artist-led gentrification has become a recurrent topic in urban studies and a central element of anti-gentrification literature (Moskowitz, *Kill*; Moss, *Vanishing*; Busà). While artists and creatives—understood here in the broadest terms—are certainly not the sole culprits, they nevertheless play a facilitating role in this process (Deutsche and Ryan; The Public). Consequently, in an analysis of pervasive rent-hikes in "creative" NYC neighborhoods, Zoe Rosenberg speaks of "an old refrain" where "[a]rtists move into a neighborhood, make it cool, get pushed out by rising housing costs as area desirability increases, … find another place to settle—and on that cycle goes."

Many anti-gentrification activists and commentators specifically identify hipsters as the most notorious agents in this specifically urban development, which might have just entered a new phase of "hyper-gentrification," described by Jeremiah Moss as

> gentrification on speed, shot up with free market capitalism—[that] is a global pandemic, a seemingly unstoppable virus attacking much of the world. … And in every afflicted city, the story is the same: luxury condos,

> mass evictions, hipster invasions, a plague of tourists, the death of small local businesses, and the rise of corporate monoculture. (*Vanishing* 6–7)[4]

Thus, to continue with Moss's curious echo of Will Giron's biological idiom: While the "pandemic" of (hyper-)gentrification is perceived as a global plague, hipsters are supposed to be among its most important carriers, and New York City represents one of its major hotbeds.[5] Here, we do indeed find a distinct and particularly potent connection between gentrification and hipster culture. During the last decades, and especially following the city's economic downturn and subsequent renaissance in the 1970s and 1980s,[6] postindustrial New York City has been at the forefront of cities that experience the influx of a group of professionals, tourists, and residents that urbanist Richard Florida has popularly called the "creative class." This affluent stratum of urban subjects covets a city's "authenticity" and "diversity"—in New York City, for instance, ethnic neighborhoods and (post)industrial areas such as Bushwick—in its creative/hip emphasis on individuality and non-conformist difference from a perceived mainstream. While Florida celebrates this creative class, many critics argue that this group represents the root cause or at least motor for many instances of gentrification.[7] In turn, the urban hipster, one of the most visible representatives of this creative class, is often routinely identified as one of the main gentrification culprits in popular and critical accounts of urban inequality.[8]

This might explain many of the hate comments on Kaye's Instagram account underneath a picture of her mural. The amount of vitriol directed at her supposed hip harbinger of gentrification especially soared after Kaye replied in an admittedly naïve manner that her artwork is just showing

---

[4]Accounts such as this abound; for instance, Alessandro Busà opens his book with a foreword that situates New York City as one among many cities afflicted by "hypergentrification" (xv). Other recent examples are, for instance, Calhoun and her account of St. Mark's Place or Moskowitz, *Kill*.

[5]While the text was written well before it, final revisions of this paper took place during the 2020 Covid-19 pandemic, which changed the connotations of Moss's metaphor considerably. Since Moss's book was written and published in 2017, we decided to retain it without any further qualification and not reflect on its new, and considerably more troubling meaning with respect to New York City.

[6]Cf. Phillips-Fein, who describes how New York City used to be a working-class friendly city with a diversity of real estate value and how it has become a hotbed of rising real estate value since the 1970s.

[7]See for instance Frank, "Dead End" or Peck. For a less optimistic view by Florida himself, see the *New Urban Crisis*.

[8]Not without irony, the aforementioned phenomenon of "hypergentrification" has furthermore resulted in the economic displacement of many creatives who had previously settled in what they appreciated as an inspirational urban environment of mixed uses and a diverse residential structure.

"three [kids] standing together and finding love in unexpected ways. … The last thing I was thinking about was making somebody upset with my art. The whole thing I wanted to do was make people happy" (qtd. in Jewell). Herself a Bushwick resident, Kaye acknowledged that certainly "things are happening here, and people aren't happy about it," but that she still did not understand how "[o]ne wall [is] being the sole example of [gentrification]" in a neighborhood "filled with street art" (qtd. in Whitford). The conflict was aggravated when Kaye hesitated to take down her work and Instagram users like not_your_girl_friday called Kaye's (non-)reaction a "shrugging 'tee-hee' of white girl privilege"; Kaye's assumed act of "claiming" a wall in order to "express herself," also sounded to Instagram user _sarinaca@invinculis like a form of "new age colonialism" by the hands of "white people" (qtd. in Madebylondon). Indeed, Giron's original Facebook post also prompted accusingly: "Consider the fact that it's art when white people put up murals on private property but when we create our own art in Bushwick it's considered 'vandalism'" (cf. user CharloChaplin's copy of the original post on Reddit). Quite ironically, though, for ethnically mixed Bushwick "natives," the only act of vandalism present here is the one created by those urban subjects identified as white hipsters, who supposedly disrupt the neighborhood in more than one sense. For people like Giron, hipsters' subculturally inflected consumption patterns and non-conformist self-stylization are a central component of processes that turn "gritty" neighborhoods into hip real estate objects and contribute to the displacement of long-term residents and businesses (cf. Zukin 51).

While we do not question the importance and severity of the process, we take one step back from the frequent and rather indiscriminate scapegoating of stereotypical "hipsters." Rather, we use the example of London Kaye in order to look for more general cultural and socioeconomic trends. Furthermore, we will take a closer look at the ways how urban creatives reflect upon their own position in this development, and how they also (fail to) acknowledge that they are part of structural urban processes of change that go beyond individual—or, for that matter, collective—agency and intentions. Moreover, we move beyond yet another overgeneralization frequently found in popular and critical discourse: Next to aspects such as whiteness, one central aspect of the increasingly clichéd imaginary of the hipster is the essential maleness of this cultural figure.[9] In many stereotypical accounts and representations, it seems as if the "hipster crowd" consists of nothing more than urban lumberjacks with bushy beards, pretentious glasses, and a keen sense for alternative forms of upscale niche consumption. Yet, next to aspects of race and class, gender also plays a complex role in

[9]Take for instance Greif's seminal anthology *What Was the Hipster?*—only Dayna Tortorici's contribution considers female hipsters.

hipster culture—and the example of yarn bombing constitutes an example worth looking into for the cultural work of female hipsters.

Knitting Social Webs

The initial *Huffington Post* article describes the yarn project by Brooklyn-based London Kaye as "a 30-day beautification challenge" ("Meet the Artist"), and the arts journalist Chloe Veltman claims that these artworks "playfully criticize the soullessness of our cities and make the impersonal streets seem slightly more approachable." For these commentators, yarn art is a form of gendered, post-domestic art in the public sphere that uses warm, "maternal" (Wollan) gestures of (re)dressing Sharon Zukin's "naked city."

As Emma Sheppard notes, next to providing "an aesthetic comment" on the urban landscape as "the cosies are usually brightly-coloured and decorative," yarn art is also "an act of reclamation in the same way that 'tagging' by graffiti artists is an act of claiming a part of a landscape." Read this way, the yarn art by London Kaye, Magda Sayeg, and Carol Hummel emerges as a distinctively feminine (while not necessarily female) form of street art.[10] For many of its practitioners, yarn art is more than a hip new form of individual creative expression, though. For these people, "craftivism," described by American knit activist Betsy Greer as a "practice of engaged creativity, especially regarding political or social causes," rather becomes a part of the panacea to the urban blight hip creatives ostensibly help to create in the first place. As a craft-based form of urban activism, practitioners ascribe to yarn art the potential to take up a complex middling position between the visibly "hip" aestheticization (Reckwitz) and concomitant gentrification of (parts of) the city and the (re)appropriation of urban spaces by "the people."

The activist element particularly lies within distinctively visible acts of "caring"—for public spaces or for other people, by way of a social group solidarity. According to the creatives and those who interpret their art presented here, this constitutes a feminine-connoted form of resistance against an urban policy in which socially minded, bottom-up community approaches fall behind the neoliberal city's financial imperatives.[11] For the

---

[10]Kaye views her art as a feminine or even feminist addition to (male) street art. Justifying her sales to Starbucks or GAP, she announced, "In a male-dominated art form [...] I like being able to have my two cents. I hope I can inspire people to do something daring. Ladies, get out there!" (qtd. in Miller). Miller writes, "In [Kaye's] hands, crochet is both an outlet of creative feminist expression and a lucrative career."

[11]As becomes apparent from a historical glance at the past sixty years, not only knitting, but also urban criticism seems to be a traditionally female "task." The present female urban artists' works stand in a long tradition of female-led urban criticism of (often) male-led, technocratic urban development plans. Next to Sharon Zukin, Jane Jacobs is a prime example of a woman

photographer and author Gale Zucker, who observes the subculture through her portraits of yarn bombers, especially yarn art's emphasis on community building and "caring" has the potential to criticize gentrification:

> [T]he way … actions like yarn bombing can have an effect in counteracting, or slowing down gentrification, is by creating community. Organizing a group effort such as yarn bombing can help bond a group of activists who might be able to collectively counter real estate investors by demanding some affordable housing—and certainly call attention to the issue. It's not exactly a counter-force—but it is something.

Zucker's insight into the craftivist community highlights a central, and especially self-reflective, point: that yarn bombing needs to be more than an individual act of urban creativity. From this point of view, the fiasco Kaye experienced in Bushwick demonstrated that she may have succeeded in putting up a spectacular work of urban creativity, but that she had ignored the central tenet of "taking care": to personally interact and to listen. Kaye may see herself as a member of the creative yarn-bombing community that covers places and objects in yarn, but the alienated reactions from the urban communities that call her an "outsider" and "white colonizer" indicate that she did not properly reflect upon her own position within the city and only insufficiently interacted with the local community she imposed her highly individualized art upon. Done this way, her yarn art, rather than "mak[ing] people happy," as she claims, is seen as a typically individualistic expression of hip creativity that threatens people afraid of becoming displaced in yet another instance of artist-led gentrification. From this perspective, public yarn art becomes structurally synonymous with top-down urban renewal approaches that likewise attempt to impose well-intended "improvement measures" onto long-established neighborhoods and destroy them through this process.

This line of thought is also exemplified by artist-activist Dina Elkan's reflections on the subject of artistic responses to gentrification:

> However, if artists feel moved to do work that is meant to confront or address the subject, then I think the first question should be, "How does this work tangibly help the communities that are threatened or being displaced? How can the voices of marginalized people be made more prominent as a result of this threat to the survival of their communities

who advocated organic bottom-up approaches to urban planning and who, whether through writing or active protest, raised her voice against the controversial, car-centered urban planning approaches by Robert Moses whose LOMEX threatened to destroy close-knit, mixed-use urban communities and the city's social fabric in New York City's 1960s.

> in places that are suddenly being 'discovered' by real estate and monied interests[?]"

Fittingly, this emphasis on community is also one of the lessons seemingly "learned" by Kaye. After removing her crochet mural, she acknowledged that "she should have created something that would 'have brought the community together,' but says that at the time she was focused more on a work that would fill the large wall nicely" (Voon, "Artist Will Remove").[12] In a more recent article in the *New Yorker*, Kaye reflects on putting up "three huge white children" as a "painful memory" that has taught her the "lesson" that "[i]t was the wrong piece on the wrong building" (Fry)—a point confirmed by social worker and Los Angeles-based knit artist Christina Tafoya in an Email interview:

> We all have to be aware of the space we take. … When you do public art in a specified community, you have to be aware of what you can do to benefit that society. We can't take a backseat in life, we need to dig our heels down and possibly get a little dirty. … Art can no longer be selfish. It has to provoke change, trust and a universal love.

As hinted at by Tafoya, close identification with a community, or at least careful attention to its needs, form therefore the core of yarn bombing's potential to "make people happy," to re-quote Kaye's original, well-meant intention.[13] While urban yarn bombers may therefore not always immediately recognize that they are pawns in the game, they also start to acknowledge their art's potential for the urban community, as Kaye's lesson-learned intimates above. In this line, yarn artists' specific link of feminine craft with political, activist street art in their attempt to "dress" the city in yarn installations goes beyond either a celebration as creative "beautifiers" of the city or a vilification as hip harbingers of gentrification—and leads towards potential ways out of the conundrum. This, however, depends on the way how emphasizing community becomes more than just lip service

---

[12]Similar advice is given to artists in a so-called primer published by activist design studio The Public that seeks to sensitize artists for the issue of gentrification: "Key to this dilemma [of creatives' displacement of long-standing residents in gentrifying areas, our addition] is recognizing what effect your presence may have on communities who do not have a choice in terms of their accommodations" (11).

[13]The role that (personal) identification can play with knit art's public perception became apparent in a survey by Tafoya on the public reception of her crocheted hearts with overleaf affirmations. Her survey revealed that she as an artist had automatically been perceived as a "white person or Colonizer," thus echoing the reception of Kaye in Bushwick. Indeed, it was not until Tafoya "took to forums and identified as a person of color, [that she] received better feedback" from the Latino communities in which she is active.

and is indeed taken as a central element *and* potential of this creative form of expression.

Along these lines, yarn bomber Carol Hummel, who creates knitting installations worldwide, emphasizes in a strikingly energetic and uplifting tone:

> I believe our streets are our canvases, our creativity our brushes. Using color, imagination and joy, communities are reclaiming ownership of their public spaces from corporate and civic control. I believe it's time to playfully restructure the commonplace through artwork—the peoples' artwork—in our streets, our neighborhoods, our cities, our lives.

However, how does this work? How exactly does yarn bombing express values of community building? Indeed, the potential for communication, but also the art's inherent ephemerality, prove useful gestures to reanimate "soulless" social structures where one group of residents feels ignored by the other, and vice versa. Taking up Hummel's positive diction, Guerilla knitter Magda Sayeg says,

> [T]emporary or semi-permanent art is so essential and so relevant to bring communication with it. It is much better than putting up a permanent statue. … If I put out my work, people come out because they want to see and talk about it. They are engaging with their own environment, which otherwise they wouldn't be doing. … It's revitalizing a community.

To provide one vivid example, this "engagement" became apparent in (predominantly female) knitting activists taking to Washington Square Park on May 23, 2006 during an event called "Massive Knit NYC." This public event was held in honor of Jane Jacobs, who had died the previous month, and her 1950s efforts to protect the park from destruction by Robert Moses's LOMEX, but also to criticize recurring remodeling plans. New York's "Anarchist Knitting Mob" describes it as follows: "Using individual sensibilities, we plan to create an open structure in the park, connecting various elements of the park together. By the end of the evening we should have a string of material connecting the park together" (Massive Knit NYC). The activist group emphasized the "conven[tion] as a community in a loving and subtle way" through a "knitting circle" that "allows one to be social with this solitary art" in the city, that "likewise, is a solitary place to live" ("Event"). The knitting activists further pointed out "that public spaces … are processes under construction" where "construction does not have to be geared toward redevelopment as capitalist venture" (Bratich and Brush 247). In Zukin's terms, the knitters therefore attempt to literally (re)dress and therefore reclaim the "soulless" and "naked" city by knitting a social "web" that invites for community building, to take care of urban policy, and to invite for communication within an otherwise anonymous cityscape and homogenous residential structures where one group of residents is discouraged from talking to another.

However, doing this in Washington Square Park may already be an indicator of the precariousness of this communal activity. While the aims are certainly noble, the blurry confluence between creativity and capitalism we have outlined above makes it inherently difficult to neatly distinguish between creative activities that strengthen a community and creative activities that are part of artist-led gentrification processes that displace people and/or disrupt existing communities (or even remain a photographic souvenir for city tourists and street-style bloggers). Female-led and supposedly caring acts run danger of remaining on a merely ideational level—one pervaded by a romanticized nostalgia for a supposedly better past where knitting was a domestic task, not an art form practiced on the streets—as they play into or even converge with what the artists perceive as (at least symbolically male-led) capitalist processes.

This also throws into sharp relief idealistic and seemingly innocent claims such as Hummel's idea of "art as a universal language" to overcome ethnic or socioeconomic divisions within communities. In words that seem slightly ironic in light of the reactions to Kaye's mural, Hummel claims that "art 'by the people, for the people' encourages ownership of the neighborhoods by people of all economic levels, not just the middle- and upper classes. It gives residents a point of pride—and delight!—in their neighborhoods." In line with this idea of literally "tying" community bonds, Hummel also maintains that, even though not everybody will always like these installations, they still

> provide an ideal platform upon which people—ALL people or every class—can discuss their opinions and ideas about art and their community. They give voice to ALL classes of people within communities, not just those "in power." ... These projects bring together segments of the population that might never speak to each other. ... I think this does hinder gentrification because it prevents one category of people from speaking for all categories of people.

As the Bushwick-incidence shows, knitting installations with the idea to evoke a community-spirit that hinders the prevalence or isolation of only one class within gentrifying neighborhoods may also fail to account for possible conflicts when the art itself is perceived to be the agent of gentrification. The irritation caused by Kaye's highly individualistic artwork can then be perceived as a result of the absence of this very community-spirit and the ignorance of the Bushwick community's needs, fears, and interests. Her artwork, rather than "bring[ing] together," brought up "segments of the population" against one another.

FIGURE 2.1. *Carol Hummel's installation* Hand-Stitched Hamlet *in Oyster Bay, New York, 2014 (photo by Carol Hummel)—more than 150 volunteers were involved in the artwork that uses a bright color combination of green, blue, purple, and yellow to represent a landscape.*

That residents' irritation is not only restricted to processes of gentrification can be shown by another example. During her community-created[14] art installation *Hand-Stitched Hamlet* (cf. Figure 2.1) in Long Island's Oyster Bay in May 2014, Hummel experienced how knit art can also be perceived as the opposite of "aesthetic" or "beautiful": "there was a group of people who were really negatively outspoken about the project. ... They didn't like the colors, it was 'tacky,' they didn't think the project 'fit' in Oyster Bay, and

[14]Hummel's project involved "[m]ore than 150 volunteers [who] created 500 panels ..., often after taking crochet lessons in 'boot camps' offered at local businesses" and relied upon donations from "[r]esidents and businesses ... that, after expenses, [would] be given to a local youth and family counseling agency" (Jacobson).

they like Oyster Bay 'just like it is.' ... I do think they thought it made their town less genteel, for sure."

Similar to Kaye, Hummel's project caused considerable controversy related to the appropriation of urban space. Unlike London Kaye, however, Hummel placed her project in an "old-moneyed" rather than newly (or potentially) gentrifying neighborhood. Local residents may have been reliable donors for her project and quite likely did not suffer from immediate effects of gentrification, such as displacement, but still objected on grounds of real-estate value.

This inherent ambiguity is the reason why yarn art's activist side must be approached in a nuanced way. For example, considering craft activists' emphasis of community and the fact that displacement predominantly affects communities of color (cf. Moskowitz, "What Role"), it is particularly striking that all yarn artists from New York we have mentioned here represent the white middle class, which confirms previously mentioned perceptions of predominantly white hipster culture.[15] Further reservations against using yarn bombing to actually "mend" the "fabric of [the] streets" (Moss, "Take Back") lie in the very effects of aestheticization and the commodification of hip forms of creativity—as the conflicts around London Kaye highlight. This is illustrated by Zucker: "Once a neighborhood is at the point that there are artists and people doing craft activism and things like yarn bombing, it is like there are also real estate investors." Elkan continues that, especially "in the age of the selfie," urban art is therefore turning into a mere "aesthetic backdrop for one's own self-presentation in a way that's much more self-centered than was ever before possible" so that activist messages threaten to recede behind this "aesthetic backdrop."

London Kaye, with her sixty-one thousand (and counting) Instagram followers, for example, gets frequently tagged in the photos of fashion bloggers who pose in front of her crochet butterflies and the likes. When knit-artist Sayeg reports how she experiences the development of a distinctive "commodity to be cool" where real-estate investors specifically look for "a packaged cool" to insert into areas of urban development, urban yarn art

---

[15]While there are a number of Black knitting groups and Black fiber artists, the Black Lives Matter movement brought to the foreground the activities of various Black yarn activists. The St. Louis based Yarn Mission provides an example of a group of POC knitters who aim to "use knitting to support and contribute to the achievement of Black Liberation. Pro-Black, Pro-Rebellion, Pro-Community" according to the group's Facebook page ("The Yarn Mission"). Not too dissimilar from the artists' strategies presented in this chapter, the members of the Yarn Mission employ knitting as a conversation-starter. An online article quotes group member Taylor Payne's explanation of the group's underlying activist idea: "As a black woman, you're invisible ... But knitting makes people stop and have a conversation with you. If someone asks me what I'm doing, I say, 'I'm knitting for black liberation.' Sometimes they respond and sometimes I just get 'Oh, my grandma knits,' like the person didn't hear me. But at least it opens the door to talking about my experiences" (Payne qtd. in Kendzior).

suddenly becomes more than this "aesthetic backdrop."[16] Therefore, even within their own creative community, makers and activists feel threatened by the very combination of consumerism and real-estate processes they supposedly engender and are afraid of ending up with Zukin's "soulless" city, or with what Sayeg refers to as a city that lost its "vibe":

> [Developers] take everything that's cool about [the neighborhood] and suck it out. They reconstruct the neighborhood … because they still want that vibe. But the vibe cannot be recreated. It's like recreating Venice. … I wished developers understood that, when you destroy something, it will never come back. It is always something missing from the original creation.

On the other hand, particularly places of creative attention attract the urban hipster and eventually lead to the influx of affluent residents, who may also represent a potential target group for buying art. Greif claims that hipsters are no artists themselves, but mere "copycats" imitating the displaced artists' work (142–3) and romanticizing a given neighborhood's ethnic history (cf. Erbacher).

Conscious of her position between complicity and creative confrontation, though on a more critical level, knit-artist Sayeg describes her artwork's development[17] as resembling a tightrope walk, or, as she calls it, "a love-hate relationship." Whereas she criticizes the displacement of lower-income residents, among them artists, and the destruction of established infrastructures, she also benefits from collaborations with galleries in gentrified areas: "I stand in the middle. I'm opposed to gentrification, but I also benefit from it." In this scheme, hip creatives are simultaneously agents and victims of economic processes largely beyond their control and can do little more than rely on their own means to alleviate what is left and do their best to attempt to curb the commercial potential of their craft by emphasizing the aspect of community building and involvement.

These remarks exemplify how creatives self-reflexively engage with their role in relation to hipster culture's facilitating role in processes of gentrification. It is also the point where even the most well-meant attempt to

---

[16]This insertion of a "packaged cool" becomes apparent in the irony around the developments of a former-graffiti-mecca-turned-high-rise in gentrifying Queens: after the 2015 demolition of the 5Pointz building that was extensively used by graffiti artists, the developer announced plans to include "handball court-sized art walls" on the finished condominium complex "that would be built and painted by street artists"—which certainly capitalizes on aspects of "street-cred" and "authenticity," and, according to New York journalist Bucky Turco, provides a distinctively "perverse homage to 5Pointz."

[17]Whereas her early work "used to be done graffiti-style" and was considered "vandalism," Sayeg now receives invitations from cities and large-scale corporations to knit in parking meters or products, as she stated in an interview.

properly interact with urban communities affected by the creative projects has its limits. From the perspective proposed here, selling out, that is, the easy co-optation of yarn art into economic processes of gentrification, is less the result of individual greed or carelessness and rather a structural affinity within creative culture and hip consumerism (cf. Frank, *Conquest* 7–9, 235). Moreover, while community-orientation may in fact be a crucial potential of "feminine" yarn art, not only the desire to express one's individual creative potential but also the way creative culture rewards these kinds of individual aesthetic expressions as "hip" commodities will, symbolically and economically, always counteract communal practices.

To a certain extent, hip creatives depend on capitalizing on the potential of creative consumption that Bishop and Williams read into a gentrified neighborhood, which, thanks to "the cluster of creative producers [,] evolves into a place for creative consumption" (164). Thus, even when creatives criticize the capitalist mechanisms in gentrified neighborhoods, it is evident that the latter provide economically advantageous hotbeds for an affluent "artsy" customer base where the artist can thrive on affluent residents' "hip consumerism," that is, the acting out of differentiation from the norm by consuming perceived "artistic," "creative," and innovative products in order to defy mainstream culture. Rather than for any other street artists, however, this twofold positioning also feeds into hipster artists' self-reflexivity that is informed by a combination of economic imperatives, thrive for authenticity, and aesthetic desires.

Creative urban art therefore seems to find itself in an increasingly complex middling position that negotiates between commercial interests and artists' (alleged) thriving for "authenticity" and (activist) "street-cred."[18] The publicly soaring London Kaye, whose home décor and totes nowadays sell for up to $225 on her web shop, who collaborates with international fashion designers, runs a *Vogue* live knitting project during the Covid-19 pandemic, has established her own yarn line, crochet hooks, and even written her own yarn-bombing book, may then present only one extreme where urban DIY creativity turns into a "hip" commodity and where the lines between yarn art's creative or confrontational appropriation of the city and its complicity with the city's commercial upgrading blur.

Conclusion: Enmeshed in the Middle

In a blog post on knit activism, knitter Karie Westermann argues "that all acts of making are by their very definition acts of resistance, and they

[18]As Banksy himself announced, "commercial success is a mark of failure for a graffiti artist" (qtd. in Lavelle).

are political. Even if you don't think so" (Westermann qtd. in Prain). This reminder can also be read like a hindsight admonition of London Kaye's sociopolitical responsibility: As Kaye learned in a tough lesson from the repercussions, her own "acts of making" were indeed highly "political. Even if [she didn't] think so." Therefore, what is needed here is a self-reflective focus on a community's needs and interests, as well as the encouragement of communication and interaction with a community, that were sounded by fellow knit artists as only some of the threads for yarn artists to take up in processes of making in order not to unravel close-knit communities.

As this contribution has shown, (the activist side of) knitting can be hard, and knit activists can easily stitch themselves with their needles, since both yarn artists take up complex middle roles between (un)consciously collaborating with or critically countering the financial interests of real-estate developers and thereby complicate arguments of urban creativity and criticism. Still, in light of the inexorable process of gentrification, even community-oriented DIY practices, such as knit activism, can at best alleviate the malady's symptoms by encouraging a better coexistence among different socioeconomic and ethnic groups and by giving a voice to marginalized and displaced communities—for which feminine-connoted yarn art (with its associations of creative authenticity, community involvement, and ephemerality) can lend itself ideally as this contribution demonstrated. While yarn artists and other hip creatives are certainly pawns in the game, it nevertheless makes sense to look closer at their specific cultural work and see how they have at least the potential to be more than gentrifying agents. Indeed, by de-emphasizing the individual expressive creativity of certain subjects and emphasizing the importance of the individual's creation within a wider network of community, several yarn artists try to find a way out of the hip-creativity-gentrification conundrum and Zukin's vicious circle where signs of authenticity and creativity seem to fuel a neighborhood's upgrading (4–5). While yarn artists are not always successful or welcome (cf. Hummel's Oyster Bay experience), and while some artists such as London Kaye build an entire literally "self-made" (Luckman 112) public career around the idiom without any particular regard to community building or gentrification resistance, other yarn bombers such as Sayeg seem to consciously take into account their role and potentials in this pattern as the interview with her revealed. Thus, whether hipsteresque practices of yarn art criticize or collaborate with the aestheticization of urban areas also depends upon the individual artist's attitude towards community building.

Works Cited

Bishop, Peter, and Lesley Williams. *The Temporary City*. Routledge, 2012.

Bratich, Jack Z., and Heidi M. Brush. "Fabricating Activism: Craft-Work, Popular Culture, Gender." *Utopian Studies*, vol. 22, no. 2, 2011, pp. 233–60. *Project Muse*, muse.jhu.edu/article/451893. Accessed May 11, 2016.

Busà, Alessandro. *The Creative Destruction of New York City: Engineering the City for the Elite*. Oxford University Press, 2017.

Calhoun, Ada. *St. Marks is Dead: The Many Lives of America's Hippest Street*. Norton, 2016.

CharloChaplin. "Brooklyn Artist Decides to 'Claim [a] Wall for Her Self,' Illegally Installs Mural on Family Home (Story in Comments)." *Reddit*, 2015, www.reddit.com/r/Brooklyn/comments/3l8i7d/brooklyn_artist decides_to_claim_a_wall_for_her/. Accessed July 17, 2018.

Deutsche, Rosalyn, and Cara Gendel Ryan. "The Fine Art of Gentrification." *October*, vol. 31, 1984, pp. 91–111. *Jstor*, www.jstor.org/stable/778358. Accessed July 3, 2018.

Elkan, Dina. "Re: Interview Questions Gentrification in NYC." Received by Annabel Friedrichs, September 4, 2017. Email interview.

Erbacher, Eric C. "(Re-)Constructing the Ethnic Neighborhood—Gentrification in the U.S. and the Longing for a Unique Identity." *Selling Ethnicity: Urban Cultural Politics in the Americas*, edited by Olaf Kaltmeier. Ashgate, pp. 245–60.

"Event." *Massive Knit NYC*, May 8, 2006, massiveknit.blogspot.de. Accessed July 22, 2017.

Florida, Richard. *The New Urban Crisis: How Our Cities Are Increasing Inequality, Deepening Segregation, and Failing the Middle Class—and What We Can Do About It*. Basic, 2018.

Florida, Richard. *The Rise of the Creative Class*. 2002. Basic, 2004.

Frank, Thomas. *The Conquest of Cool: Business Culture, Counterculture, and the Rise of Hip Consumerism*. University of Chicago Press, 1997.

Frank, Thomas. "Dead End on Shakin' Street." *No Future for You: Salvos from The Baffler*, edited by John Summers, Chris Lehmann, and Thomas Frank. MIT Press, 2014, pp. 109–22.

Fry, Naomi. "Crochet for a Cause." *New Yorker*, February 10, 2020, www.newyorker.com/magazine/2020/02/17/crochet-for-a-cause. Accessed July 9, 2020.

Greer, Betsy. "Craftivism Definition." *Craftivism*, 2007, craftivism.com/definition/. Accessed November 29, 2020.

Greif, Mark. "Epitaph for the White Hipster." *What Was the Hipster? A Sociological Investigation*, edited by Mark Greif, Kathleen Ross, and Dayna Tortorici, translated by Avner Davis. n+1 Foundation, 2010, pp. 136–67.

Heath, Joseph, and Andrew Potter. *The Rebel Sell: How the Counterculture Became Consumer Culture*. Capstone, 2006.

Hummel, Carol. "Gentrification." Received by Annabel Friedrichs, June 5, 2014. Email interview.

Jacobs, Ruben. *Everyone is an Artist: On Authenticity, the Position of the Artists, and the Creative Industries*. V2, 2016.

Jacobson, Aileen. "A Hamlet Wrapped in Yarn." *New York Times*, June 7, 2014, www.nytimes.com/2014/06/08/nyregion/a-hamlet-wrapped-in-yarn.html. Accessed October 12, 2017.

Jewell, Nicole. "Crochet Art Mural Unravels Wicked Gentrification Debate in Brooklyn." *Inhabitat*, September 23, 2015, inhabitat.com/nyc/crochet-art-mural-unravels-wicked-gentification-debate-in-brooklyn/. Accessed July 17, 2018.

Kendzior, Sarah. "Ferguson's Radical Knitters: 'If Someone Asks Me What I'm Doing, I Say, "I'm Knitting for Black Liberation."' " *Guardian*, August 6, 2015, www.theguardian.com/us-news/2015/aug/06/ferguson-radical-knitters-talk-justice-race-issues. Accessed September 14, 2020.

Lavelle, Ciara. "Banksy on Sales of His Art: 'Commercial Success is a Mark of Failure for a Graffiti Artist.' " *Miami New Times*, October 10, 2013, www.miaminewtimes.com/arts/banksy-on-sales-of-his-art-commercial-success-is-a-mark-of-failure-for-a-graffiti-artist-6513239. Accessed September 20, 2017.

Leland, John. *Hip: The History*. Ecco, 2004.

Luckman, Susan. *Craft and the Creative Economy*. Palgrave Macmillan, 2015.

Madebylondon. "Welcome to Moonshine Kingdom." *Instagram*, July 27, 2015, www.instagram.com/p/5plnKknf6_/?utm_source=ig_embed. Accessed July 18, 2018.

Mailer, Norman. "The White Negro." *Dissent*, 1957, pp. 276–93.

Massive Knit NYC. *Massiveknit*, 2006, massiveknit.blogspot.de. Accessed July 22, 2017.

McGuigan, Jim. *Cool Capitalism*. Pluto Press, 2009.

"Meet the Artist That Is Yarn Bombing Brooklyn This Month." *Huffington Post*, September 5, 2013, www.huffingtonpost.com/2013/09/05/london-kaye-odonnell_n_3869065.html. Accessed May 25, 2014.

Michael, Chris, and Ellie Violet Bramley. "Spike Lee's Gentrification Rant—Transcript: 'Fort Greene Park is Like the Westminster Dog Show.' " *Guardian*, February 26, 2014, www.theguardian.com/cities/2014/feb/26/spike-lee-gentrification-rant-transcript. Accessed July 18, 2018.

Miller, Jennifer. "Yarn Bombing Hits the High Street." *New York Times*, December 2, 2016, www.nytimes.com/2016/12/02/fashion/london-kaye-yarn-crochet-artist-starbucks-gap-valentino.html. Accessed June 25, 2017.

Moskowitz, Peter. *How to Kill a City: Gentrification, Inequality, and the Fight for the Neighborhood*. Nation, 2017.

Moskowitz, Peter. "What Role Do Artists Play in Gentrification?" *Artsy*, September 11, 2017, www.artsy.net/article/artsy-editorial-role-artists-play-gentrification. Accessed July 2, 2018.

Moss, Jeremiah. "New Yorkers, Take Back Your City." *New York Times*, April 13, 2014, www.nytimes.com/roomfordebate/2014/04/13/the-pros-and-cons-of-gentrification/new-yorkers-need-to-take-back-their-city. Accessed May 25, 2014.

Moss, Jeremiah. *Vanishing New York: How a Great City Lost Its Soul*. HarperCollins, 2017.

Peck, Jamie. "Struggling with the Creative Class." *International Journal of Urban and Regional Research*, vol. 29, no. 4, 2005, pp. 740–70.

Phillips-Fein, Kim. *Fear City: New York's Fiscal Crisis and the Rise of Austerity Politics*. Metropolitan, 2017.

Prain, Leanne. "Using Art to Resist." *Leanne Prain*, January 30, 2018, www.leanneprain.com/2018/01/using-art-remain-optimistic/. Accessed July 25, 2018.

The Public. *Art, Design & Gentrification: A Primer*. Creative Resistance How-To Series. *The Public Studio*, December 6, 2017, issuu.com/thepublicstudio/docs/no11_art__design_and_gentrification. Accessed July 18, 2018.

Reckwitz, Andreas. *The Invention of Creativity*. 2012. Translated by Steven Black, Polity Press, 2017.

Rosenberg, Zoe. "Where Do New York City's Artists Live?" *New York Curbed*, July 13, 2017, ny.curbed.com/2017/7/13/15964650/where-do-new-york-citys-artists-live. Accessed August 12, 2017.

Sayeg, Magda. Interview. June 12, 2014. Received by Annabel Friedrichs. Telephone interview.

Sheppard, Emma. "'It's Not a Hobby, It's a Post-Apocalyptic Skill': Space, Feminism, Queer, and Sticks and String." *Bad Subjects: Political Education for Everyday Life*, vol. 84, 2013, bad.eserver.org/issues/2013/84/notahobby. Accessed June 20, 2017.

Tafoya, Christina. "Aw: Interview Questions: Yarn Art and Gentrification." Received by Annabel Friedrichs, July 27, 2018. Email interview.

Turco, Bucky. "NYC Real Estate: Where the Worlds of Gentrification and Urban Art Collide." *Animal*, July 20, 2015, animalnewyork.com/2015/nyc-real-estate-worlds-gentrification-urban-art-collide/. Accessed August 26, 2017.

Veltman, Chloe. "A Movement in Museums and on the Street." *New York Times*, July 8, 2010, www.nytimes.com/2010/07/09/us/09bcculture.html?_r=0. Accessed May 25, 2014.

Voon, Claire. "Artist Will Remove Bushwick Crochet Mural that Sparked Community Protest." *Hyperallergic*, September 23, 2015, hyperallergic.com/238626/artist-will-remove-bushwick-crochet-mural-that-sparked-community-protest/. Accessed July 18, 2018.

Voon, Claire. "Wes Anderson-Inspired Crochet Mural Sparks Anarchist Protest in Bushwick." *Hyperallergic*, September 28, 2015, hyperallergic.com/240303/wes-anderson-inspired-crochet-mural-sparks-anarchist-protest-in-bushwick/. Accessed July 18, 2018.

Whitford, Emma. "This Wes Andersony Crochet Graffiti Is Causing Extreme Bushwick Gentrification Anxiety." *Gothamist*, September 18, 2015, gothamist.com/2015/09/18/bushwick_crochet_gentrification.php. Accessed July 27, 2018.

Wollan, Malia. "Graffiti's Cozy, Feminine Side." *New York Times*, May 18, 2011, www.nytimes.com/2011/05/19/fashion/creating-graffiti-with-yarn.html. Accessed May 25, 2014.

"The Yarn Mission." *Facebook*, www.facebook.com/theyarnmission. Accessed September 14, 2020.

Zucker, Gale. "Craft Activism: DIY as a Counter-Force against Gentrification." Received by Annabel Friedrichs, June 2, 2014. Email interview.

Zukin, Sharon. *Naked City: The Death and Life of Authentic Urban Places*. Oxford University Press 2010.

3

Glocal Hipsterification: Hipster-Led Gentrification in New York's, New Delhi's, and Johannesburg's Cultural Time Zones

Melissa Tandiwe Myambo

In our contemporary moment, there are at least two types of global gentrification highly visible in global(izing) cities around the world (Smith; Rofe; Davidson; Lloyd; Proud; Bridge). Both types often lead to the displacement of more low-income populations and both are inexorably tied to the branding of the "global" city (Busà) and the emergence of the "corporate city of transnational headquarters" (Zukin, *Naked City* 222). The more well-known variety is what I call "corporate-mainstream" gentrification which has greatly intensified in the era of post-Cold War globalization. This includes but is not restricted to built forms such as skyscrapers, office parks, American-style malls, big box stores like IKEA, retail outlets like Zara and H&M, culinary chains like Starbucks, Costa Coffee, and the ever-ubiquitous McDonald's, global gym franchises like Fitness First and Gold's, five-star hotels like the Marriott and Four Seasons, and so on. The second type of gentrification emerging in the twenty-first century in the global North and increasingly in the global South is "creative-conformist" gentrification, which refers to the kind of spaces that people known as knowledge workers, the "creative classes" (Florida), or "highly-skilled" professionals might demand in the city increasingly dominated by service sector employment rather than manufacturing or light industrial jobs. While this class also benefits from corporate-mainstream gentrification, they also demand different types of infrastructure and amenities (Clark et al.; Lloyd; Dowling) which appear unique or less cookie-cutter than a McDonald's but generally do conform to a "creative," "curated" aesthetic (Zukin, *Naked City*) which is nevertheless hyper-commodified (Busà 58–89).

The growth of Design Districts in cities like Miami, Dubai, London, and Johannesburg (for example the shopping area, 44 Stanley, near two of Johannesburg's universities) are good examples of this type of creative-conformist, amenity-driven urban development (De Monchaux), but the distinction between mainstream-corporate and creative-conformist is not impermeable and can often blur over time. Williamsburg, previously the archetype of the hipsterification model, or the hipster-led gentrification in Brooklyn, is now in a crossover phase from creative-conformist as it transitions into ever more corporate-mainstream gentrification. Global hipsterification as one form of creative-conformist gentrification cannot be entirely separated from the corporate-mainstream type consistent with the "two-step economic process of gentrification" which begins with "a change, first, to 'creative' consumption spaces and then, to chain stores" (Zukin and Kosta 113). These categories are not mutually exclusive, so also Hauz Khas Village in New Delhi, for example, is hipsterified and Design District-like but also boasts a corporate-mainstream Starbucks café.

In this chapter, I am concerned with hipsters as a discursive formation that can at times act as a loosely affiliated social grouping with real world consequences. Hipsterification is the most visibly and aesthetically distinctive form of creative-conformist gentrification today (Wasielewski). Its distinction results in the creation of highly stylized, self-conscious cultural time zones (CTZs). A CTZ is defined as a micro-space and at this particular historical juncture, typical hipsterified CTZs as evidenced by their similarities on the level of architecture, design, aesthetics, furnishings, aural soundtrack, and so on, include but are not limited to the hipster café, the microbrewery, the wine bar, the vintage clothing boutique, the tattoo parlor, the barbershop, the loft-style apartment, creative coworking spaces as well as those temporary "zones" created by music and food festivals, comic book/graphic novel exhibitions and farmers' markets. Similar culinary offerings—see the ubiquity of avocado toast and single-origin coffee—are often available in hipsterified CTZs around the world, but the goal of CTZ theory, and indeed of this chapter, is to both account for the similarities of their "global" elements and search out their "local" connotations, contexts, and particularities.

CTZ theory was developed in the course of my research on migration and globalization as a way to comprehend the increasing homogeneity of global urbanscapes without allowing what is different, or "local," to be completely obscured. I rely implicitly on the theory of space proposed by philosopher Henri Lefebvre, whose notion of space is conceived of as producing social relations and also being a product of those relations.[1] Once the theorist has identified the CTZ to study, for example, a café, a neighborhood, a beauty salon, or a market, there are two primary elements that must be accounted for: firstly, the "cultural times" that pertain within the theorist's chosen borders and which refer to the religious/cultural/social customs, (time-keeping) traditions, histories and calendars present, for example, the Hindu and Muslim calendars form part of the cultural times of most CTZs in Delhi. Secondly, it is incumbent upon the theorist to identify the forms of "cultural capital," in an expanded sense of Bourdieu's formulation (Bourdieu; Myambo, "Frontier Heritage"), necessary for those "cultural times." Hipsters around the world, as part of a "global tribe" (Proud), display many similar forms of cultural capital as they partake in the same fashions, foodstuffs, and (social) media-saturated, middle-class lifestyles. Their shared forms of cultural capital often move from the marginal to the mainstream which in some cases also makes hipsters quite typical of the larger millennial generation (Wasielewski). Hipsters also display many parallels in terms of their complex, contradictory hipster ethos which attaches certain values to consumption, for example, their preference for eco-friendly products, and they can also be socially progressive.

One of the driving forces behind the mainstreaming of hipster culture and indeed its globalization is the internet (Maly and Varis; Alfrey). Thus, along with physical CTZs, there are also virtual CTZs created on digital platforms that establish a network of images and media that both cocreate and interconnect the hipster community across the globe, impacting taste, fashion and lifestyle, and the desire for like-minded hipsters to find desirable spaces that suit these dispositions. Thanks to internet-enabled (social media) platforms, particular aesthetic choices can now be seen across the world simultaneously in real time and can be rapidly emulated. The existence of virtual CTZs which correlate with physical CTZs ("zones" identifiable on the world map) and vice versa forms a global web of startlingly similar micro-spaces on the level of architectural feature, color schema, design aesthetic, furnishings, décor, etcetera. Hipsterified CTZs, both in cyber and "real" space, are the socio-spatial manifestation of virtual-physical representations.

The similarity of the CTZ of the hipsterified café in so many countries around the world is quite paradoxical. One expects a café that is part of a global chain like Starbucks or Le Pain Quotidien to have similar culinary

---

[1]CTZs invoke spatio-temporality as opposed to just space or just temporality. Time zones are a reference to one of the most dominant constructions of time which stem from imperial times. For a more extended discussion of cultural time zones and cultural time zone theory, cf. my articles: Myambo, "Class Identity"; "Spatial Politics of Chick Lit"; "Red Velvet."

offerings and a recognizable design aesthetic. But global hipsterification, epitomized by the extraordinarily similar although individually owned hipster café, is presently a phenomenon visible in geographically disparate neighborhoods from Shahpur Jat and Hauz Khas Village in New Delhi (Lahiri), to Maboneng, Braamfontein, and Victoria Yards in Johannesburg (Burocco), to Dadar in Mumbai (Karkare) and Woodstock in Cape Town ("Not in my Neighbourhood") and of course, Brooklyn's Crown Heights, Bed-Stuy, Bushwick, and Morgantown (Wasielewski). Kyle Chayka argues in an article entitled "Welcome to Airspace" that Silicon Valley sites like Foursquare and Airbnb (virtual CTZs) have "spread the same sterile aesthetic across the world" and begins with the example of Igor Schwarzmann, a Berlin-based strategy consultant, who expresses this strange paradox of geographically ubiquitous sameness:

> Over the past few years, something strange has happened. "Every coffee place looks the same," Schwarzmann says. The new cafe resembles all the other coffee shops Foursquare suggests, whether in Odessa, Beijing, Los Angeles, or Seoul: the same raw wood tables, exposed brick, and hanging Edison bulbs ... they have all *independently decided* to adopt the same faux-artisanal aesthetic. Digital platforms like Foursquare are producing "a harmonization of tastes" across the world, Schwarzmann says. "It creates you going to the same place all over again." (my emphasis)

My aim in this chapter is threefold: to lay out a typology of the hipster aesthetic, to explore how global hipsterification is providing hipsters with their own particular world-straddling habitus, and then finally to use qualitative research data and CTZ theory to illustrate that this habitus is not only global but bears traces of the "local," thus rendering it "glocal" (Swyngedouw).

While it is quite easy, indeed too easy, to identify the distinctive hipster aesthetic in CTZs around the globe, it is much more difficult to pin down a satisfactory and globally accurate definition of hipster. Infamously, hipsters often reject the label hipster (Greif; Maly and Varis; and Wasielewski 38–50). Although they emerged in their current incarnation as a (sub)cultural group in the late twentieth-century United States, today "hipster culture is ... best seen as a translocal and layered phenomenon" whose global growth is highly correlated not only to internet penetration but other globe-spanning infrastructures, especially "the neoliberal structure of the world economy" with which their "ethos of consumption ... is perfectly aligned" (Maly and Varis 642, 643, 645). For the purposes of this chapter, I define hipsters as a global class formation which can be identified by their eclectic, deliberate accumulation of cultural capital and their particular consumption choices (of victuals, commodities, cultural events, spaces). They must be understood relationally, as in relation to other "local" and "global" socioeconomic classes (Liechty), as well as in relation to temporality, spatiality, and paradox. Hipsters create and seek out certain spaces in order to express their hipster ethos and identity, but their (self)definition is always related to a processual moment temporally located (Maly and Varis 638, 645) just before their cultural capital (e.g., fashions, trends, music, art, and so on) has moved from somewhat alternative/countercultural to thoroughly commodified/mainstream (Wasielewski 45). While they are largely middle class, in different countries they may be mostly upper or middle or lower-middle class, and they are inexorably paradoxical because they are perceived to be, by themselves and others, as both countercultural and mainstream (Greif 213), both victims and perpetrators of gentrification and displacement (Eror), as anti or pro-capitalist, embracing repurposing/recycling/upcycling/DIY and/or conspicuous consumption, being more affluent or impoverished, being collectively all the same yet claiming to be uniquely individual and while the hipster ethos embraces causes like climate change and queer/metro/LGBTQI (Lesbian, Gay, Bisexual, Transgender, Queer, Intersex) identities, they also display a pronounced nostalgia for the colonial, especially the Victorian era (Higham; Bridge), and employ many tropes of hyper-masculinity such as beards and plaid flannel lumberjack shirts (Greif 218).

These tensions between contradictory traits, processes, and ethoses mirror the tensions globalization scholars often have to grapple with: one of the original questions asked about the post-1990 world is whether globalization is making the world more homogeneous or more heterogeneous (Barber). There is no simple answer to that question, just like it is not easy to define the hipster. In short, it depends on your (spatiotemporal) scale, and while on the macro-scale, city skylines increasingly exhibit the same type of skyscrapers, on the micro-scale there are sometimes more "layers" to be excavated and often "glocal" is the appropriate adjective to begin to define these composite CTZs and this complex world (Swyngedouw). The concept of a CTZ is an attempt to provide a theory agile enough to zoom in and out as needed in order to accurately identify the paradoxical tangibles and intangibles of different spatiotemporal "zones" and also map them in terms of the cultural, rather than physical, distance that separates one from the other (Gupta and Ferguson 23). Although hipsterified CTZs may be geographically far apart, if one charts their respective distances in terms of cultural kilometers, how culturally different are they? Is a homogenized global hipster habitus possible in this heterogeneous world?

One of the hallmarks of globalization is rapid change, and thus with that caveat, I begin with a typology of globally recognizable hipsterified CTZs as discernible in the second decade of the twenty-first century and then move on to a discussion of how this network of similar spaces can be indexed as a global/glocal habitus. To concretize the complexities of CTZ theory and the paradoxical nature of the hipsterified habitus, global hipsterification, and globalization, I will in the final part of this chapter draw on an interview with an American woman who has lived the hipster life in New York and New Delhi to illustrate local specificities at the level of lived experience.

The Global Hipster Café: A Typology of Hipsterified CTZs

In the twenty-first century, increasing homogeneity is carved into the global urbanscape to the point that some middle-class people who frequent middle-class CTZs in cities around the world, especially those who travel by air and navigate the city in a private vehicle, constantly experience a sense of déjà-vu. This is not, of course, mere happenstance. There are powerful forces at work that are vigorously creating fairly homogeneous physical-virtual CTZs, further facilitated by digital platforms and smart phones.

One of the afore-stated paradoxes of globalization and the postindustrial chic aesthetic that has come to be associated with hipsters is the emergence of strikingly homogeneous hipsterified CTZs which display this same aesthetic around the world. Certainly, hipsterification produces a particular (nostalgic) visual language with a "common set of aesthetic codes" (Bridge 39). Reverberating globally as these physical CTZs appear in Instagram posts, Foursquare, Zomato, and other social media, they form a virtual echo chamber of worldwide, stylistic sameness, "the neutered Scandinavianism of HGTV" (Chayka 2016). The aforementioned culprit, the internet, along with other forms of new and "old" media such as TV, film, magazines, and newspapers, is responsible for causing so many to "independently" adopt a same globally omnipresent design language, but this style also reflects a certain dialectical relationship to space. It bespeaks an ideology, a class identity, a socioeconomic positionality, and the hipster ethos. To paraphrase Lefebvre's formulation of space, the typology of hipster design elements both produce and are produced by the hipster ethos.

Table 3.1 can be read horizontally from left to right, but it is merely evocative of certain hipster elements. It is by no means a comprehensive list, and different architectural spaces can contain a mixture of the elements as there is a lot of crossover. This typology is based on today's features of hipsterification but in a few years may change as the hipster "look" is increasingly adopted into mainstream-corporate urban spaces. When this reaches a tipping point, a new design aesthetic will be developed. Globalization and the global hipsterification it enables does indeed spawn strange paradoxes. On one hand, an article entitled "How Ikea's Billy bookcase took over the world" reflects on the popularity of "[Ikea's] Billy [which] is surprisingly well-accepted by the type of people you might expect to be sniffy about mass-produced MDF [Medium-density fibreboard]" (Harford). Depending on the cultural context, some hipsters might be expected to disdain Ikea as too mainstream, but Ikea dinner plates and furnishings and bed covers are to be found in many a hipsterified space. Indeed, the hipster aesthetic as evidenced in Airbnb and other social media platforms is, according to Chayka's reporting on New York-based Laurel Schwulst, produced by, "the

TABLE 3.1. *Typology of Hipster Design Aesthetic.*

Architecture	Design/Aesthetic	Furnishings	Décor/Ambience/ Detail
Colonial-era, e.g., Victorian	Original features (e.g., pressed tin ceiling), minimalist, open, clean lines, uncluttered	Antique, Etsy, artisanal/rustic/ handmade/ vintage	Everyday (tech) objects from earlier eras repurposed as objets d'art, e.g., nineteenth-century telephones
Former industrial, e.g., warehouses, factories	"Scandinavian," blonde/raw/ reclaimed/ salvaged/ distressed wood, graffiti, screed, cement floors	Communal worktables, farmhouse dining tables and sinks, repurposed materials, Ikea/ modular/DIY	Style: deliberate pastiche, extreme attention to detail, evocative, epigraphic, intertextual, ironic, authentic. Décor: twentieth-century typewriters, rickety chairs
Loft-ceilinged spaces; large windows	Metal, (exposed) brick, accent walls, exposed air ducts/pipes, rope, murals, graffiti, crochet/macramé hangings	Industrial track lighting, Edison bulbs in metal cages, pendant lamps	Interiors: air conditioned/ temperate, Wi-Fi, plugs for devices, neutral color scheme, aural soundtrack—music, "indie"/ eclectic
Shipping containers	Vintage/Persian/ natural fabric area rugs	Butterfly/rattan/ Hammock chairs, farmhouse bench	Jars instead of mugs, wooden boards instead of plates

FIGURE 3.1. *Father Café in Braamfontein, Johannesburg, 2017. Photo by author.*

FIGURE 3.2. *Extraction Lab, Industry City, Sunset Park, Brooklyn, 2018. Photo by author.*

prevalence of mass-produced but tasteful furniture … 'Kind of an extension of Ikea showrooms.' … The ideal Airbnb is both unfamiliar and completely recognizable: a sprinkling of specific cultural symbols of a place mixed with comprehensible devices, furniture, and decoration" (Chayka). Can the Ikea-ization or the Etsy-ization or the Airbnb-ization of the global urbanscape be simultaneously generic and authentic? These processes all have minor differences, but they all point to one of the most fundamental paradoxes that undergirds hipsterification: the contradictory desires for the familiar and the exotic that also play out in hipsters' "foodie" impulses towards certain paradigmatic foods and beverages. The similar design aesthetic and menu available in hipsterified cafés means they can both look the same and sometimes smell and sound and taste the same way—coffee, the espresso machine, aural soundtrack. Figures 3.1 and 3.2 show two cafés, one in Braamfontein, Johannesburg, and the other in Industry City, Brooklyn.

The global habitus formed by this network of hipsterified CTZs with their distinct aesthetic also shares another commonality. Many of them have "unique" products for sale which again reflect the hipster ethos. This abundance of carefully curated, artisanal, crafty, bespoke, "unique" artefacts, objets d'art and consumer goods is bought and sold, all the time speaking the language of local "authenticity" but often uncannily similar to those in other locales. Paradoxically, once again, hipsters are making the same "systematic choices [in a class-defined space] … of which the choices commonly regarded as aesthetic are … [reflected] in the space of life-styles" (Bourdieu 257), except now this takes place on a global scale. Hipsterdom is "enacted through consumption practices and relations with material objects" (Dowling 835) everywhere and it is the same different objects everywhere. Alongside one's flat white, one also wants a T-shirt with an ironic Zulu phrase on it in Johannesburg or a Brooklyn Bridge-shaped egg holder in New York. These objects may be manufactured in China or Vietnam or somewhere else but they symbolize the local.

The tension between the homogeneity of the architectural and design language of the CTZ and the heterogeneity of the objects for sale within the CTZ is also noted in an article in the *Travel and Lesisure* magazine which describes Johannesburg's most hipsterified "hood," the Maboneng Precinct. Maboneng, which means "Place of Light" in the indigenous language of SeSotho, is located in Jeppestown in Johannesburg's Central Business District and has branded itself as quintessentially "African." Yet, its creator, a millennial South African man, specifically based it on a neighborhood in Brooklyn called DUMBO (cf. Myambo, "Africa's Global City?" and Myambo, "Red Velvet"). The magazine's article lists Maboneng as containing many of the all-too-familiar hipster CTZs, including

> galleries, food trucks, sidewalk cafés, street art, cool cars, an artisanal craft market, the David Adjaye-designed Hallmark House hotel, and the

> Museum of African Design (located in a former auto-body shop). A sign bearing the name of the neighborhood [Maboneng] swung in a graceful catenary curve, exactly like the famous one in Venice Beach, California. (De Monchaux 2017)

On one hand, Maboneng is homogeneously hipster, invoking Venice Beach but also reminiscent of "a global Brooklyn where the same digitally distributed hipsterish aesthetic is always available for purchase—[causing you to] wonder ... whether you've [even] left one bubble for another" (De Monchaux). Yet the article's author finds diversity and heterogeneity in the products for sale: "Next to the stuff you could find anywhere was stuff you could find only there—especially fashions and fabrics with their own regional vision and vernacular heritage." Thus, does each hipsterified CTZ have to display a few "local" products that are in fact unique to that geographical region in order to claim some kind of "authenticity?" Especially, when one considers that even "local" has become a branding strategy (Wasielewski 105)?

While on the level of design these places are characterized by oft-repeated hipster aesthetic tropes, a uniformity that often extends even to their wares for sale, all these places are not *exactly* the same. Calling this "strange geography created by [Silicon Valley] technology 'AirSpace'," Chayka, for example, claims that "the homogeneity of these spaces means that traveling between them is frictionless ... Changing places can be as painless as reloading a website." In contrast, I argue, frictionless is an overstatement. Although all these places do look very much the same, they are also all CTZs with their own cultural times which distinguish them from each other despite their shared hipster ethos. A global form of hipster cultural capital is necessary to decode these spaces, but there are still other forms of cultural times/capital which shape these places.

Deciphering the Local in the Global Hipster Café?

When considering three hipster cafés—one in Braamfontein, Johannesburg, another in Hauz Khas Village, New Delhi, and the last in Sunset Park, Brooklyn—one will find that each of these places houses multiple cultural times which determine the corollary forms of cultural capital useful or necessary to navigate that zone. Each of these cafés is a "global" CTZ because it adheres to the time on the clocks on the wall and on the various devices of the staff and clientele. This time-keeping method is derived from Greenwich Mean Time, which is itself an imperial social construct established during a period of intense European colonialism in 1884. They all therefore share the culture-time of Western "clock-time" (Thompson) which, along with the Gregorian calendar, represents a certain cultural history and tradition and is a dominant cultural time globally. This is one aspect of what makes hipster locales "global" because other "zones" do not necessarily adhere so fully to the Western "clock-time" of capitalist-modernity (e.g., rural villages). I use the word zones to keep emphasizing how weighty the construct "clock-time" with all of its connotations of capitalist-modernity is for understanding globalization which is also enacted through the coordination of various transportation, logistical and commodity production processes across time zones.

One of the ways in which the "local" makes its presence felt is through language. Each language inherently represents different historicities/temporalities/calendars/ways of marking time/traditions and so on and is also a form of cultural capital. Based on participant observation in these CTZs, there are at least two or more languages present in a café in Braamfontein, Johannesburg. The kitchen staff and some of the local clientele are most likely speaking English, SeSotho, isiZulu and/or Afrikaans and freely mixing some or all of these. Furthermore, there is usually a wide difference in class between those working at the café and those hanging out in it and the clientele may be more fluent or comfortable in English than the workers. In Brooklyn, both Spanish and English are the city's lingua francas and as opposed to Delhi or Johannesburg, many of the baristas are middle-class and college-educated (like the hipster clientele) while the "behind-the-scenes" staff are mostly Latino/Spanish-speaking. In Delhi, the staff and customers communicate in Haryani, Hindi, Punjabi, and/or English. Of course, any number of other languages may also be spoken in these zones, and each of them brings with it a whole history of traditions and sociodynamics around gender, religion, class, ethnicity, etc. which determine the culture-time(s).

However, the dominant culture-time and thus the dominant form of necessary cultural capital required in all of these hipsterified zones in the United States, South Africa and India, and what makes them as global as their corporate-mainstream equivalents like Starbucks or Coffee Bean, is certainly the dominance of English, the language of globalization due to British imperial history. The dominant culture-time is determined by the clientele who are situated on a hierarchical socioeconomic scale in a dominant position vis-à-vis the staff. In multilingual countries like the United States, India, and South Africa, it is striking that in "global" CTZs, the menu, for example, is only written in English and that the waitstaff will be expected to speak English fluently enough to serve the "cosmopolitan" local and international customers who frequent these CTZs. While the cafés' workers might be expected to be multilingual, a monolingual, English-speaking American can navigate all these zones very easily with only one form of linguistic cultural capital: English. This is one of the paradoxes of the heterogeneous-homogeneous tensions both in globalization and global cultures like hipsterdom: the more cultures globalization encompasses, instead of more multilingualism, we see the increasing monopoly of English. Paradoxically, despite the emergence of a global, largely English-speaking/influenced, habitus consisting of a network of CTZs that are geographically disparate but culturally close to each other, I argue that this does not result in totally "frictionless" transitions and that on the level of lived experience there are still subtle, textural, social differences between hipsterified CTZs in different regions produced by (sub)national cultural dynamics.

Global Habitus of the Glocal Hipster Café

Many studies of gentrification and class (Zukin and Kosta; Rofe) draw on "Bourdieu's [notions of] economic, cultural and social capital and their connections to classifying processes and sets of dispositions and practices that might be termed a 'habitus'" (Dowling 834). Habitus propels the individual member of a certain socioeconomic class along a certain class-defined trajectory in which the individual seeks out the types of virtual-physical CTZs which allow her to perform her class identity. These CTZs are necessary for her self-expression and also distinguish her class-determined spatial practices from that of other classes (Liechty 279). The intensification of capitalist-modernity has also changed the scale of habitus to the point where it can be theorized on the scale of the global (Davidson). However, zooming in a little closer and examining the lived experience of a "global" hipster café reveals that it is—*experientially*—quite "glocal" (Swynegedouw).

In December 2016, I interviewed an American woman named Savannah who was living and working in India. We met in a hipster café in Shahpur Jat Village in South Delhi.[2] While the CTZ of this café was extraordinarily similar to the hipster cafés near my home in Brooklyn, New York, the area outside the café was quite different, consisting of Shahpur Jat's charming, winding allies which since the 1980s had become home to emerging fashion designers, NGOs, language schools, and other "creative" occupations alongside the original middle- and working-class residents of this small urban village from a number of different casts (Dhagamwar). Savannah described herself as belonging to a community of international and local millennials who (self-)identified and/or displayed many typical features of hipsterdom. In our wide-ranging interview in the vegan-friendly hipster café with its preponderance of avocado and salted caramel representing an international/cosmopolitan/global selection of food, Savannah reflected on

[2]Interviewee name has been changed, and this interview took place in relation to my broader research project on "frontier migration" (see Myambo, "Frontier Heritage Migration"), not specifically on hipsterdom/hipsterification. These subjects were raised by the interviewee in the course of describing her migration experiences.

the lifestyle, spaces, products, and practices that are shaped by the hipster ethos. In her early thirties, Savannah had grown up in well-to-do Westchester County, north of New York City, and described herself as coming from an "upper-middle class white background." For her first degree, she had studied cultural anthropology and had since lived in big cities and small villages in North and South America, West Africa, and the Indian subcontinent, which made her highly conscious and thoughtful about her lifestyle choices. When Savannah arrived in Delhi, she was surprised to find a familiar habitus, a hipster community in which she easily integrated: "There's this kind of environment that I didn't expect, frankly, the young, activist, designer, creative community that I have found is really easy to enter into. I have a wonderful community here."

Even though she found it "really easy" to enter into this community and she said, "Yeah, the hipsterification of Delhi is a thing that has made it infinitely more sustainable to live [here]," her transition from New York to Delhi was not completely "frictionless." She described Delhi as "challenging" and explained, as multiple white women also mentioned to me during our interviews, that in many "local" CTZs she was stared at, both because she was a woman (in the often male-dominated streets/ public spaces) and because she looked different, visibly a fair-haired foreigner. Hipsterified CTZs then, like other "global" CTZs, with their more "Western" politics of mixed gender and "cosmopolitan," ethnically and racially diverse clientele, did provide her with less friction because they were so familiar: "[these are] spaces that make me really comfortable," she explained, contrasting this to her earlier experience as a Peace Corps volunteer in rural West Africa where she spent more time in CTZs that were more "localized" and where the necessary linguistic cultural capital consisted of indigenous languages.

Interestingly, and perhaps reflective of her own ethos, this earlier experience prevented her at first from "enjoying" her level of comfort in hipsterified, "global," English-language Delhi which felt less "localized" because her class position there aligned her with the local elite. She explained it thus: "The thing about hipster Delhi is [that] for the average Delhiite, [it's] almost going to be out of reach. You do have only the upper echelon of wealthy creatives or foreigners." This reflects how hipsters and hipsterified CTZs may represent different segments of the middle classes depending on the city/country. Ultimately, however, Savannah realistically decided that a habitus consisting of some "global" CTZs was a more "sustainable way to live long-term as … [an] … American" in the rough-and-tumble city of Delhi which is made up of myriad, culturally complex, and dissimilar CTZs. Global CTZs offered a "comfortable and familiar" alternative.

Historically speaking, global CTZs are a fairly new phenomenon in India because these spaces which also include malls, Western franchises, and corporate-mainstream Starbucks arrived in India after the country's economic liberalization which marked its entry into the global economy in 1991. Furthermore, in "globalizing" cities that display the extremes of uneven development, great wealth next to overwhelming poverty, very "modern" lifestyles juxtaposed with much more "traditional" ways, global hipsterification can represent massive cultural dissonance, cultural cleavage, and cultural distance. However, it can also represent some forms of freedom for those with the economic and cultural capital to access such hipsterified CTZs. Hipster CTZs in cities like New York, Jo'burg, and Delhi offer the possibility of various types of freedom for middle-class women, the LGBTQI community, and socially marginalized creatives. These freedoms might be severely impinged upon in other geographically proximate but culturally distant CTZs. For example, when a (local or foreign) woman walks into an air-conditioned, cappuccino-serving café in New Delhi—and to do so she must have the requisite ("global") cultural capital to successfully enter that CTZ, for example, middle-class apparel—she finds herself in a completely different cultural time than when purchasing a cup of hot tea from the chaiwallah at the street corner.[3] She will need different forms of linguistic cultural capital to navigate these two different CTZs. Normally, Hindi language will be required with the chaiwallah. In the "global" café where the menu is in English, signaling that this is a privileged, Westernized, middle-class CTZ, she might feel comfortable enough to remove her jacket or her dupatta and recline in a spaghetti-strap tank top. Within the confines of the CTZ of the café, she may do so with less risk of sexual harassment. To do the same at the chaiwallah's on the open street, however, is to court controversy and possibly even violence. Thus, for the local or foreign middle-class woman in India, the mode of transport she takes to travel to, for example, a hipsterified CTZ, will influence how she dresses. Public transport may require more "modest" forms of dress while traveling in a private car may allow the woman to safely dress in more revealing apparel.

Savanah's relationship with hipsterified CTZs was influenced by all these dynamics and her life was also textured with other types of "friction" because it was not confined to only "global" CTZs. She still enjoyed shopping at the local, open-air market where she would haggle for fruits and vegetables and often took public transport. However, even Savannah's specific habitus of hipster CTZs that provided spaces of leisure and recreation, mostly a network of cafés and music/dance venues which were located in "Hauz Khas Village [like Summerhouse]" and "Satrojan Market ... the Piano Man Jazz bar, Depot 29," were still different from her New York hipster habitus—no "nice dive bars" in Delhi, she said. In

[3]These observations are based on my own experience in Delhi as a woman as well as the qualitative interview data I collected from dozens of immigrant women, mostly from the West. Many of my female Indian colleagues at the Centre for the Study of Developing Societies in Delhi would daily have to negotiate these different dynamics.

the specifics of her experience of her Delhi community within these hipster spaces, there are subtle differences. Savannah described her community as "mixed [Europeans, Africans, Americans, Indian]," but said, "I think the identity point would be young, lefty, creative, international. Most of my Indian friends have either lived abroad or at least spent a bunch of time abroad, so we all have a similar mindset." A similar mindset would equate in this argument to a shared hipster ethos. However, this again does not mean identical experiences are guaranteed. For Savannah, her hipster community in New York was very different from that of Delhi even though they ate and drank the same type of food and beverages, hung out in similar-looking places and posted about them on social media, creating virtual CTZs that interlinked and interconnected that same global experience. The difference resided in her Delhi clique's own communal relations:

Savannah: My community … [is] … this kind of creative, lefty, hipstery, Delhi space or world [which] is wonderful. It's so fun … I don't have to worry about my image as much as I did in New York. I can just be a little more relaxed …

Melissa: Now, why in New York are you worried about your image?

Savannah: Because people move so fast. They just judge you so quickly, and I find it to be a very judgmental place, even or especially in the hipster side of things. Everyone's just really trying hard *not to be identified that way but also to be identified that way*, and it's just *so constructed and it's so prescriptive*. You're just always made to feel like you're not cool enough or you're not doing the right thing, you don't have access to the right thing, and it just … I don't know it's just not fun, it's not natural, it's not nurturing … I think part of it is this place. There's no irony in Delhi. There's nothing ironic about Delhi culture … People are very sincere and very warm and very genuine, and I like that a lot about this culture.

Savannah asserts here that even in the hipsterified CTZs that she and her community of "international" Indians and foreigners occupy, "local" Delhi culture, which she views as lacking irony and being rich in warmth, genuineness, and sincerity, still influences the culture-time of those "global" spaces. By extension, "local" New York (ironic) culture also influences the CTZs of her habitus there. We therefore see that the "global" microspace is impacted by the local and its multiple culture-times which create varying sociocultural dynamics, or, at least, she is (re)producing particular cultural discourses that are already in circulation about these different cultures. If hipsterdom is a discursive formation, this is relevant to its construction.

Thus, these are not empirical observations but Savannah's subjective experiences. She did not experience hipsterification in the same way despite the empirically observable homogeneity of the actual spaces as evidenced by their design aesthetic: "It's just really fun to watch how people *interpret* it [hipsterification] here, the Delhiites and the young Indians, because *it's different*. It's just *appropriated differently everywhere*, right? It's so localized. If you look at any of these products [on sale in the café], it's very cool." Savannah describes hipsterdom in Delhi as an identity that has been appropriated but also interpreted and translated so that it becomes somewhat "localized," but still, like hipsters everywhere, it is an identity that is primarily expressed through consumption practices—consumption of commodities and experiences, such as working on one's MacBook in a café. Nonetheless, locally produced products were an important locus of difference for Savannah because in "all of these spaces and [in] this whole world of Delhi, young, upwardly mobile, international Indians [are] creating tons and tons and tons of these little brands. If you look around this shop [in the café and the boutique directly below it], there's 30 or 40 of them, probably." As interrogated in the previous section, how many of these products were truly local, or locally sourced, or unique to Delhi? Or did they just display the patina of localness (even though they were still housed in a CTZ whose design and layout reflects the "global" paradigm of hipsterification)? This is one of the paradoxes of the hipster experience everywhere. For Savannah, these non-mainstream, "local" brands not only represent the global hipster ethos but also establish a more comfortable glocalness: hipsterdom's valuation of local entrepreneurship and social enterprises defined what she thinks of as ethical consumerism and are a set of values she positively contrasts to mainstream corporate globalization/consumption:

> I feel better about these [hipster values] being the values that are being spread without people questioning them. I can't imagine if hipsters were actually white supremacists or if it was just a cult of baseball globally ... if it was just something lamer than what it is ... Those key pieces of [hipsterification are] a lot of art design, a lot of local stuff, a lot of crafty stuff, but it is a handmade aesthetic at least. The awareness, there's more awareness to the consumption which I like, and it does end up supporting companies that are small, that are local. The fact that we are ethically [sourcing] ... are mostly local sourcing ... and have some code of practice ... I can't say I have a problem with any of that ... It's teaching people how to value values as consumers. I think that in the last decade that that's really become a thing.

In their search for "distinction" in Bourdieu's terms, hipsters like Savannah have adopted a certain set of values or "code of practice" that seeks to avoid or at least outrun for a time the commodification and mass production inherent to this stage of capitalism which they partially reject. This ethos of craftsmanship, buying local and social enterprise, is a reaction to consumer capitalism, but paradoxically, it comes from *within* the restrictive confines of commodity culture. Although hipsterified CTZs form a global habitus which shares a homogeneous typology of design and fosters a certain ethos that cherishes heterogeneity, hipsterdom can neither escape nor reconcile the paradoxes constitutive of globalization. The glocal is a compromise they search out and (re)produce within the structures and narrow strictures of the neoliberal global cultural economy.

Works Cited

Alfrey, Lauren. *The Search for Authenticity: How Hipsters Transformed from a Local Subculture to a Global Consumption Collective*. 2010. Georgetown University, MA thesis, repository.library.georgetown.edu/bitstream/handle/10822/552895/alfreyLauren.pdf?sequence=1. Accessed October 30, 2020.

Barber, Benjamin R. "Jihad vs. McWorld." *The Atlantic*, March 1992, www.theatlantic.com/magazine/archive/1992/03/jihad-vs-mcworld/303882/. Accessed October 30, 2020.

Bourdieu, Pierre. *Distinction: A Social Critique of the Judgement of Taste*. Routledge, 1984.

Bridge, Gary. "A Global Gentrifier Class?" *Environment and Planning A*, vol. 39, 2007, pp. 32–46.

Burocco, Laura. "'The Darker Side of Modernity' in an Illuminated Precinct in Downtown Johannesburg." *Reversing Urban Inequality in Johannesburg*, edited by Melissa Tandiwe Myambo. Routledge, 2019, pp. 56–68.

Busà, Alessandro. *The Creative Destruction of New York City: Engineering the City for the Elite*. Oxford University Press, 2017.

Chayka, Kyle. "Welcome to Airspace: How Silicon Valley Helps Spread the Same Sterile Aesthetic across the World." *The Verge*, August 3, 2016, www.theverge.com/2016/8/3/12325104/airbnb-aesthetic-global-minimalism-startup-gentrification. Accessed October 30, 2020.

Clark, Terry Nichols, et al. "Amenities Drive Urban Growth." *Journal of Urban Affairs*, vol. 24, no. 5, 2002, pp. 493–515.

Davidson, Mark. "Gentrification as Global Habitat: A Process of Class Formation or Corporate Creation?" *Transactions of the Institute of British Geographers*, vol. 32, no. 4, 2007, pp. 490–506.

De Monchaux, Thomas. "The Rise of the Global Design District." *Travel and Leisure Magazine*, March 14, 2017, www.travelandleisure.com/culture-design/architecture-design/international-design-districts. Accessed October 30, 2020.

Dhagamwar, Vasudha, et al. *Shahpur Jat: A Village Displaced: A Study in Self-Rehabilitation*. Multiple Action Research Group, 1998.

Dowling, Robyn. "Geographies of Identity: Landscapes of Class." *Progress in Human Geography*, vol. 33, no. 6, 2009, pp. 833–9.

Eror, Aleks. "In Defence of the 'Shoreditchification' of London." *The Telegraph*, January 14, 2014, www.telegraph.co.uk/men/thinking-man/10571976/

In-defence-of-the-Shoreditchification-of-London.html. Accessed October 30, 2020.

Florida, Richard. *The Flight of the Creative Class: The New Global Competition for Talent*. HarperCollins, 2005.

Greif, Mark. "What Was the Hipster?" *Against Everything: Essays*. Pantheon Books, 2016, pp. 211–24.

Gupta, Akhil, and James Ferguson. "Beyond 'Culture': Space, Identity, and the Politics of Difference." *Cultural Anthropology*, vol. 7, no. 1, 1992, pp. 6–23.

Harford, Tim. "How Ikea's Billy Bookcase Took Over the World." *BBC News*, February 27, 2017, www.bbc.com/news/business-38747485. Accessed October 30, 2020.

Higham, William. "What the Hell is Steampunk?" *Huffington Post UK*, October 17, 2011, www.huffingtonpost.co.uk/william-higham/steampunk-what-the-hell-is-it_b_1015192.html. Accessed October 30, 2020.

Karkare, Aakash. "Is Dadar, Mumbai's First Planned Suburb, Becoming Hipster Cool? (And at What Cost?)." *Scroll.in*, February 20, 2017, scroll.in/magazine/823802/is-dadar-mumbais-first-planned-suburb-becoming-hipster-cool-and-at-what-cost. Accessed October 30, 2020.

Lahiri, Tripti. "Delhi Journal: Hangouts for Delhi Hipsters." *Wall Street Journal*, August 17, 2012, blogs.wsj.com/indiarealtime/2012/08/17/delhi-journal-hangouts-for-delhi-hipsters/. Accessed October 30, 2020.

Lefebvre, Henri. *The Production of Space*. Wiley-Blackwell, 1992.

Liechty, Mark. "Middle-Class Déjà Vu." *The Global Middle Class: Theorizing Through Ethnography*, edited by Rachel Heiman, Carla Freeman, and Mark Liechty. School for Advanced Research Press, 2012, pp. 282–311.

Lloyd, Richard. "Postindustrial Bohemia: Culture, Neighborhood, and the Global Economy." *Deciphering the Global: Its Scales, Spaces and Subject*, edited by Saskia Sassen. Routledge, 2007, pp. 21–40.

Maly, Ico, and Piia Varis. "The 21st-Century Hipster: On Micro-Populations in Times of Superdiversity." *European Journal of Cultural Affairs*, vol. 19, no. 6, 2016, pp. 637–53.

Myambo, Melissa Tandiwe. "Africa's Global City? The Hipsterification of Johannesburg." *New Left Review*, no. 108, 2017, pp. 75–86, newleftreview.org/issues/II108/articles/melissa-myambo-africa-s-global-city.

Myambo, Melissa Tandiwe. "Class Identity, Xenophobia and Xenophilia: Nuancing Migrant Experience in South Africa's Diverse Cultural Time Zones." *Handbook of African Philosophy of Difference: The Othering of the Other*, edited by Elvis Imafidon. Springer, Cham, 2019, doi.org/10.1007/978-3-030-04941-6_22-1.

Myambo, Melissa Tandiwe. "Frontier Heritage Migration in the Global Ethnic Economy." *Public Culture*, vol. 29, no. 2, 2017, pp. 261–86.

Myambo, Melissa Tandiwe. "Red Velvet Cheesecake in Maboneng, Pap and Steak in Jeppestown: Displacement and Global Hipsterification in Downtown Jozi." *Reversing Urban Inequality in Johannesburg*, edited by Melissa Tandiwe Myambo. Routledge, 2019.

Myambo, Melissa Tandiwe. "The Spatial Politics of Chick Lit in Africa and Asia: Sidestepping Tradition and Fem-washing Global Capitalism?" *Feminist Theory*, vol. 21, no. 1, 2020, pp. 111–29. *SAGE Journals*, doi.org/10.1177/1464700119886224.

Not in My Neighborhood. Directed by Kurt Orderson. Documentary film, South Africa/USA/Brazil, Azania Rising, 2018.
Proud, Alex. "Why This 'Shoreditchification' of London Has to Stop." *The Telegraph*, January 2014, www.telegraph.co.uk/men/thinking-man/why-this-shoreditchification-of-london-must-stop/. Accessed October 2020.
Rofe, Matthew. "'I Want to Be Global': Theorising the Gentrifying Class as an Emergent Elite Global Community." *Urban Studies*, vol. 40, 2003, pp. 2511–26.
Savannah. Interview. By Melissa Tandiwe Myambo. December 2016.
Smith, Neil. "New Globalism, New Urbanism: Gentrification as Global Urban Strategy." *Antipode*, vol. 34, no. 3, 2002, pp. 427–50.
Swyngedouw, Erik. "Globalisation or 'Glocalisation?' Networks, Territories and Rescaling." *Cambridge Review of International Affairs*, vol. 17, no. 1, 2004, pp. 25–48.
Thompson, Edward Palmer. "Time, Work Discipline, and Industrial Capitalism." *Past and Present*, vol. 38, 1967, pp. 56–97.
Wasielewski, Amanda. *Made in Brooklyn: Artists, Hipsters, Makers, Gentrifiers.* Zero Books, 2018.
Zukin, Sharon. *Naked City: The Death and Life of Authentic Urban Places.* Oxford University Press, 2010.
Zukin, Sharon, and Ervin Kosta. "Bourdieu Off-Broadway: Managing Distinction on a Shopping Block in the East Village." *City and Community*, vol. 3, no. 2, 2004, pp. 101–14.

4

Hipsters in Central and Eastern Europe: From Domesticated Nostalgia to *Manele* and Protests

George Alexandru Condrache

Hipster subculture is a global phenomenon that has numerous local particularities worldwide, depending on the continent and country (Maly and Varis 638). In this chapter, I will analyze some of such local particularities within Central and Eastern Europe, focusing mainly on the hipsters from Romania.[1] Both in the West and in the East, hipsters are predominantly represented as middle-class urban people who are characterized by a vintage aesthetic, alternative food and drink, their struggle to be original and to appreciate only underground art. In both contexts the hipster is imagined as the ironic figure who criticizes consumerism, gentrifies neighborhoods, and is concerned about the environment (Alecu). In these definitions, local elements of hipster culture seem to be mere nuances that do not decisively differentiate the local hipsters from the worldwide trend. However, these nuances are intriguing and reflect a somewhat different configuration of

[1]This endeavor is quite challenging, as hipsters have not been a topic of interest for Romanian scholars. There are only a few Romanian academic sources that I have found useful, namely the articles written by Ovidiu Solonar and Diana Margarit.

the Eastern European hipster. I will focus on three chief elements: historic hipster bars, hipster music—particularly the Romanian genre called *manele*—and communist pop music known in Romania as *muzică uşoară* (literally, "light music"), as well as the link between hipsters and the recent major political protests that have shaken Romania and Hungary since 2013. These elements showcase what is commonly identified as a hipster aesthetic while also offering a glimpse of hipsters' positions on social issues such as protests and minorities.

Bars and cafés, which are some of the most obvious public displays of the aesthetic and artistic preferences of hipsters from all over the world, their culinary choices, and their type of humor, convey their fascination with vintage culture and the nostalgic perspective that is commonly associated with hipsters. Also, given that bars are hubs where ideas are exchanged, they are linked with the sociopolitical views hipsters hold in Central and Eastern Europe. *Muzică uşoară* also showcases hipsters' assumed preoccupation with the past. *Muzică uşoară* is a pop music genre that was very popular through the seventies to the nineties. Its main characteristics are sentimental lyrics, usually in the form of love songs, and pop rock rhythms. The most representative artists of this genre are Mirabela Dauer, Corina Chiriac, Margareta Pâslaru, and Dan Spătaru. *Manele*, on the other hand, is a genre that reflects not only a preoccupation with provocative aesthetics but also an interest in marginalized communities. *Manele* developed in the years of postcommunist transition in Romania, and it has its roots in oriental, *lăutărească* (fiddlers'), and gypsy music. According to anthropologist and musician Estelle Amy de la Bretèque, *manele* is not only related to other musical genres from the Balkans (such as turbo-folk) but also to genres from beyond the Balkan area, such as the Armenian genre *rabiz* (Bretèque and Stoichita). Usually, *manele* lyrics focus on themes like fortune, success, love, sexy women, and enemies. While most of the *manele* singers, such as Florin Salam, Liviu Guță, Sorinel Puştiu, or Romeo Fantastick, are of Roma descent, this music is popular among marginalized communities and the criminal world of both Romanians and Roma.

The link between hipsters and protests relies on how protesters are labeled by a part of the media, revealing not only how hipsters are perceived but also the connection between hipsters and social activism. Starting in 2013 with the protests against an environmentally destructive mining project by the Roşia Montană Gold Corporation and the corruption associated with this project, there have been numerous rallies in Romania where tens of thousands of people expressed their disagreement with the attempts of the ruling PSD (Social Democratic Party) to change the law. These protests became more than protests against a mining project, for they turned into protests against the endemic corruption of Romania in general. The protests peaked in January 2017, when more than half a million people rallied all over Romania against the ruling party to change the penal code to their advantage.

Nostalgia, reflected in hipster aesthetics, is the starting point of this chapter. On the one hand, nostalgia is one of the elements that connects hipster culture in the West (Western Europe and North America) and East (Central and Eastern Europe) on both aesthetic and axiological levels. On the other hand, as this chapter is going to show, the nostalgia featured by hipster cultures in Central and Eastern Europe reflects a different attitude towards the past than the notions of nostalgia typically associated with hipster culture(s) in Western Europe and North America. The Eastern European hipsters' fondness of the past is well expressed through historic bars. I will offer examples from Romania, Hungary, the Czech Republic, and Poland and focus on the symbolic implication of the decoration of the bars. All the bars that are part of this study display specific elements which make references to the communist past. This specificity has a constructive component as it implies a reconsideration of the relatively recent traumatic history of these countries. Similarly, the Eastern European hipsters' turn to *manele* and *muzică uşoară* shows how the hipsters' general appreciation of marginalized musical tastes assumes locally specific meanings. As I will elucidate, *muzică uşoară* has sparked hipster interest in recent years, expressing the hipsters' sense of irony and nostalgia for a lowbrow sentimental genre. *Manele*, in turn, is a kind of music very popular in Romanian marginal circles, which is embraced by hipsters who also use this music as a political statement against racism and marginalization. The last part of this chapter analyzes the uncomplimentary perception of hipsters. While hipster hatred is common in the East as well as in the West, the local, social, and political contexts offer some particular explanations for this negative perception. The term hipster has been used by Romanian media both in an appreciative and derogative sense to refer to the protestors who participated in the large demonstrations that have been taking place since 2013 in this country.

Hipsters in the East and in the West: Two Forms of (the Same) Nostalgia

The term hipster was first associated with the American Beats counterculture, and it initially referred to the outsider or the outcast (Hill 4). In the fifties and sixties, it defined the Beat perspective of being exclusive and cool. Yet the hipster movement as we now know it emerged in the nineties (Hill 2). In Central and Eastern Europe, especially in countries such as Poland, the Czech Republic, Hungary, and Romania, it became publicly relevant only later around 2010–12 (Solonar 32). During this period, hipster aesthetics became widespread in many major cities in these regions. In Romania, hipsters also became popular because of their supposed link to the major protests that took place in 2013 and were directed against the corrupt gold mining projects in Roşia Montană. These Roşia Montană protests, which formed the biggest anti-corruption and environmental movement in Romania in years, were depicted in the media as a protest of young, nonconformist corporatists, who were also called hipsters.

Their emergence is synonymous with the following cultural preferences, some being imported from the West (Solonar 32): a preoccupation with authenticity (Schiermer 169) and postmodern irony, a fascination with the past, a fixation on the environment—a "back to the basics" or "back to nature" attitude—and an interest in art, especially underground art, indie music, and indie movies. These interests are expressed through elements such as vintage clothing, vintage haircuts, retro style in general, like the curled moustache that is an iconic example of the ironic hipster, organic food, flea markets, fairs featuring handmade products, fixed-gear bicycles, concerts, bars, and cafés. There are several reasons why the hipster trend reached Eastern Europe later than the West. After the movement gained some popularity in Western Europe, the youth who traveled from Eastern Europe were also exposed to hipster aesthetics. Social media also had a decisive role in spreading hipster tendencies from West to East. Moreover, there are political reasons for the spread of hipster culture. For example, Romania was integrated into the European Union in 2007. Only afterwards was it easier for youth, students, and corporate employees to travel throughout Europe and to have more contact with Western trends. In these ways, the hipster is also an expression of Eastern Europe's integration into the West, which came as a cultural integration that preceded the political integration (Solonar 32).

Hipster style often fuses nostalgic aesthetics and technologies with contemporary ones. Thus, new and old create a dialogue; they do not oppose each other. The past fascinates hipsters worldwide: the past of their parents and grandparents (Schiermer 174) and generic forms of the past are perceived with interest or even fascination. Andreas Huyssen argues that interest in the past is not only a reaction against the danger of forgetting the huge tragedies of the twentieth century, but it is also a measure against the chaotic rhythm—and amnesic consequences—imposed by technology (7). This passion for the past is featured by vintage hipster fashion: grandma's dress, papa's Levi Strauss blue jeans or papa's vest, Ray-Ban sunglasses before the company started to promote the vintage designs, which are considered more authentic as they are harder to find (Maly and Varis 645), retro haircuts, old furniture, vinyl discs, typewriters, and other items that can be purchased from thrift stores, flea markets, and antique boutiques. Especially after 2010, the retro trend has caught on with big retail chains, which suggests that this trend broke through into mainstream culture as well. Visiting a thrift store or a flea market transcends a simple economical transaction. The objects that are bought are in a way saved, as they are filled with aesthetic value and used as such. Furthermore, the objects are bought because they represent a different epoch and thus are the carriers of a story of a specific context from the past. Symbols from the recent past are introduced in an eclectic aesthetic[2] that transforms the conservation of the past into a quasi-ideology. As it is difficult to identify a specific past, the quite imprecise formula "the past of the parents and grandparents" makes a useful reference to a period that starts in the nineties and maybe goes back to the forties. Thus, the past is blended, as it does not focus on a specific period, and, most importantly, it is brought as close as possible to the intimacy of the one who strives to revive it. Hipsters use the vintage objects, they wear them, and they use them to decorate their houses or cafés. However, this mix does not always have to lead to, as Fredric Jameson would say, a cannibalization of the past, namely an effaced past, and to the loss of the link with history (18). When collecting and playing with the past, it is not deprived of its meaning, regardless of how random it is evoked. The concept that describes this attitude is coined by Svetlana Boym in *The Future of Nostalgia* as "reflective nostalgia" (15). Reflective nostalgia does not try to recover the past exactly as it was, but it focuses instead on creating an experience of the past. This form of nostalgia does not focus on homesickness but on a playful, fragmentary, and ironic perspective upon the past "that explores ways of inhabiting many places at once and imagining different time zones" (15). When one visits such cafés as Montreal's Eva-B. and finds a vintage radio there, or Szimpla, in Budapest, and finds a Trabant, an East-German, two-cylinder tiny car popular within the Eastern Bloc, there, one gets in contact with the past as a time that cannot be recovered and also with time as an expression of intimacy and as a reflection of something that does not exist anymore and that is accessed through that object. The difference between the two examples is that the Trabant from Szimpla also has a political connotation.

Hipster Historic Bars in Central and Eastern Europe

Hipster historic bars have opened in several countries of Central and Eastern Europe: Scârț and Atelier Mecanic[3] in Romania, Szimpla in Hungary, Café V lese in the Czech Republic, and Pijalnja in Poland are some representative examples. Both women and men who attend these places are generally white people in their twenties or thirties who belong to the middle class, are part

[2]One can "save" objects that represent different countries or different historical moments.
[3]Atelier Mecanic was closed in 2014.

of the majoritarian ethnic group of their country, are college graduates, hold corporate jobs, own small businesses or work in the independent art sector, live in the cities in which the bars are located, have cosmopolitan views, and travel abroad frequently (Ungureanu). Very few of them would identify themselves as hipsters, yet their aesthetic and artistic preferences, and other people's perception as well, justify this label (Ungureanu). For example, they manifest a predilection for vintage or retro clothing, wear moustaches or beards if they are men, have haircuts like a side cut, with "waves," "pompadour," "symmetrical subtle fade," or "pixie fades", own vintage or single speed bicycles, or wear canvas rolltop backpacks or tote bags (Brewer).

The events that are organized in these bars are representative of the underground art scene: concerts, plays, mini-festivals, flea markets, handmade fairs, and local product fairs. Szimpla and Café V lese are known for the underground concerts they put on. Szimpla periodically hosts a flea market and a market for local products. Scârţ serves as an independent theatre. Besides the numerous plays, the owners of the bar periodically organize uncanny events such as David Bowie's *parastas* which is typically an Orthodox Christian wake—at Scârţ it has no religious connotations. These bars and cafés are described in numerous articles from the local press and travel blogs or sites. For instance, the owner of Atelier Mecanic said in an interview that

> Atelier Mecanic (Mechanical Workshop) is a bar made of 1950 to 1970 industrial relics, salvaged leftovers, graphics and original furniture. Romanians have an uncomfortable relationship with their past which usually ends up in simply erasing it: factories were perceived as a symbol of communism and keeping some memories of it was by no means a priority after the Revolution. 50 years of industrialization vanished in no time in the scrapyards. Atelier Mecanic ironically brings them back. (Paulesc 190)

The owner of Atelier Mecanic presents himself as an ironic preserver of the past, as he claims that his bar is a statement that the past cannot be forgotten, nor idolized. The preservation of the past is also very important for Scârţ and the Museum of the Communist Consumer. A blogger who visited the two locations thinks of his experience as a travel back in time:

> Now, my dear reader, be careful because here starts the travel back into the past … That past time of the Cold War, where the world was separated in two, the capitalistic 'West' led by America on one side, and the communist 'East' led by Soviet Union on the other. That past time when Ceausescu was leading Romania. That time that passed, but which however we were experiencing and discovering in our present. (Giampaoletti)

The dialogue between the present and the past is even better featured in a post written by a blogger who visited Pijalnja and who considers the bar to be "half way [*sic*] between soviet and hipster." He also makes an inventory of the elements that contribute to the Soviet atmosphere of the place:

> From the communist times, they have kept the waiters' strict uniform, the red-hair lady ... who won't give a smile or a hug but will sell a shot, and the decoration, which as often in shot bars evokes nostalgia, but here less with old Soviet paraphernalia than elsewhere and more with authentic old TVs and old newspaper articles used by way of wallpaper. (Traveller on a Mission)

The communist past is a fundamental aesthetic element of all these places. This past belongs primarily to the parents and grandparents of those who own the bars. The owners themselves lived their childhood during the communist period and have decorated their bars with objects that are representative of the communist epoch: toys (such as the rubber doll, with an oversized head and members carved in the body, simply known as the plastic doll, or plastic replicas of Eastern European cars and trucks), handbooks (such as the alphabet books with drawings that depict the socialist reality), bicycles (for instance, the Pegas bicycle, which was very popular in the Socialist Republic of Romania), original furniture, industrial objects, and placards with political slogans famous during the epoch. Their bars are transformed into unconventional museums, where fragments of the communist past receive a new "existence." These locations are transformed in what Pierre Nora calls *lieux de mémoire*, places that keep alive memories that otherwise would be forgotten (8). Probably the most relevant example is Scârț, which also hosts the Communist Consumers Museum. The basement is organized as a one-bedroom apartment—a most typical apartment in the Socialist Republic of Romania—and it exhibits numerous objects that were used in daily life before 1989. For instance, in the kitchen there are hundreds of products that one could find in such a place during the communist period: utensils, plates, pots, cans, bottles, all being made in Romania or in other communist countries. These are the objects that recreate how reality looked like in most of the average urban Romanian families; they mirror what people bought and what they used.

The communist past is often perceived in these locations through the lens of irony. The way the objects are "used" in the bar is only one example that confirms this. For instance, at Scârț, a big, framed photo of Ceaușescu finds its spot on the walls among things such as a kitsch broidery that depicts the "Abduction from the Seraglio." Ceausescu's portrait, that was once a mandatory presence in each institution's room, is now nothing but a joke. Its presence in this almost carnivalesque context is the reverse of what such a portrait used to invoke before 1989: fear, respect, admiration. Thus, irony overlaps nostalgia, entailing a postmodern approach of the feeling, which domesticates the nostalgic suffering (algos) by enhancing instead a more critical and less romanticized view of the past (Hutcheon and Valdés 19).

Communism is not only aesthetically recycled, as the objects that define it are used in different contexts, but so is its role for the collective memory. Romania's transition from communism to capitalism employed two antagonistic narratives about the communist regime. The dominant narrative which is disseminated by Romanian authorities and supported by most of Romanian public intellectuals, such as the popular philosophers Gabriel Liiceanu and Andrei Pleşu, depict the communist regime as an atrocious period in Romania's history. Even though their position is correct from a historical standpoint, their perspectives exclusively rely on condemning the regime and pay less attention—if they pay any attention at all—to creating a collective coping mechanism to deal with the trauma of communism. At the opposite pole stand those who regret the fall of the regime. As they mainly belong to the working class, the economic uncertainties that characterized the transition and the collapse of the Romanian economy, the effects of which can still be felt in the present, made them regret and idealize the communist regime (Fati). Both narratives share one common point, namely a dogmatic, humorless, and unironic approach to the past. Some have tried a different approach, however. For instance, Romanian artist Ada Milea made a song in which she ironizes the omnipresent figure of former communist leader Ceauşescu in Romanian's collective consciousness, thus pushing for a more relaxed and humorous understanding of the recent past (Georgescu 157).

Bars such as Scârţ employ a discourse that is placed in between the two antagonistic narratives of damning or romanticizing Romania's communist past, thus pleading for a less dogmatic and more humorous approach to the past. Such places invite their visitors to take a glimpse into the past, as it should not be forgotten, yet they are encouraged to not idealize it. On the contrary, they might as well make fun of it, as the absurdity of characters like Ceauşescu deserve to be made fun of. These bars make a statement that the communist regime should finally be perceived differently, neither through the lens of a rigid nostalgia nor through the filter of collective trauma.

Sacrifices on the Altar of Authenticity: The *Manele* and the *Muzică Uşoară*

Hipster nostalgia is also expressed through music. Romanian hipster culture is characterized by the resurgence of *muzică uşoară* and the *manele*. These two music genres intend to escape the mainstream and challenge its traditions, values, and prejudices. The hipster from Central and Eastern Europe feels the same pressure of being swallowed up by the mainstream as the hipster from the West. For instance, hipster bars have inspired many mainstream bars in areas such as Centrul Vechi (Old Town) in Bucharest. The choice of music represents an attempt to refuse the mainstream, although such efforts run the risk of ending up as no more than a ridiculous bravado.

Irony entails a reevaluation of the musical genres that are popular among hipsters. Their approach includes a dose of humor that also betrays a condescending attitude towards elements such as the lyrics of the songs or the attitude of the singers. This irony transforms art into an unserious game and features hipsters as the unusual, almost exotic personages that shock the world with their choices. This exercise can be linked to the avant-gardes (Hill 8) and to a specific tradition of not taking art and life in general too seriously. The role of irony is important for the reevaluation of the retro pop music that is now listened to by hipsters. The pop rhythms and simple lyrics about love helped Romanian singers such as Angela Similea and Mirabela Dauer to become the iconic voices of mainstream music for the decade before the Revolution. After 1989, they slowly lost their popularity, as other pop, rock, and house figures gained more success. In 2015 and 2016, this music that smacks of kitsch all throughout became increasingly popular in hipster clubs in Bucharest such as Eden and Control. Angela Similea and Mirabela Dauer were even invited to significant music festivals, such as Electric Castle. Whereas irony motivates this artistic choice, a genuine connection was enhanced between the artists and the public during these concerts. This connection was possible not only because of the enthusiasm of the artists who experience an artistic revival, thanks to the young generations, but also because of the youths themselves who obviously enjoy listening to the songs, beyond any sort of irony (Foarfă). The music recreates the same atmosphere as the vintage objects in the historic bars. The communist epoch is not longed for, but its eclectic revival is appreciated. Just like the toys from the Museum of the Communist Consumer, this music refers to the communist period but invokes the ludic and intimate, as it revives some of the moments spent at home among family. Thus, a nightmarish epoch is revisited from a reconciliatory perspective. When irony is made secondary, nostalgia for one's own childhood takes its place, which does not fall into the trap of idealizing the communist regime, as it is a form of nostalgia that focuses on personal experiences which were possible regardless or even against the communist regime, as family was the realm where one would be insulated from the gloomy sociopolitical conditions (Pohrib 144).

Regarding the *manele*, the focus is less on reevaluating the past and more on reevaluating the present. *Manele*[4] is a genre that appeared after

---

[4]The term itself dates from the nineteenth century, yet the music phenomenon I am referring to developed after the fall of the communist regime, when a wild form of capitalism emerged in Romania (Moisil 45). Due to the limits of this chapter, the case of proto-*manele* and neo-*manele*, which are two subgenres related to *manele* and to the hipster culture, cannot be analyzed.

1990 (Bretèque and Stoichita 327). From the very beginning, this music was created to be as popular as possible, and indeed it was, until it lost a part of its public, which reoriented toward other pop-culture genres. The lyrics are very simple, even simplistic, and, although the singers belong to the Roma community, are written in Romanian, and thus address Romanians as well as the Roma community. The *manele* has been approached with disgust by cultural critics, highbrow artists, mainstream intellectuals, and most of the people who consider themselves educated. It is quite common for people to state, "I listen to anything but manele" (*Spirala Colorată*). Its negative reputation is so strong that it created a new slang word in Romanian: *manelar*. A *manelar* is an insult, as it refers to a person associated with *manele* culture, who is also a punk or a redneck, maybe a thief, someone who lacks moral values or manners, lacks education, and even the ability to speak grammatically correct sentences ("manelar"). Such stereotypes have been generated by the fact that *manele* were popular among the working class, in the rural and the less developed communities, especially Roma communities, but also because the genre was commonly associated with the criminal world, members of which would commonly sponsor the artists to praise their success in the artists' songs (Mihăilescu 248). There are only a few Romanian scholars, such as Speranța Rădulescu and Adrian Schiop, who try to better understand this music and to argue that this phenomenon is not anti-artistic. Their opinions have been promoted by a few public figures such as Cătălin Ștefănescu, who is the host of *Garantat 100%*, one of the most important cultural talk shows to appear on public television in Romania.

Hipsters from Romania embraced this music because of its popularity in some marginal or marginalized social layers and its immense unpopularity among intellectuals, which made it the perfect means not only to escape the mainstream but also to shock and ridicule it. There is nothing more underground than a *manele* concert in Ferentari, a rough neighborhood of Bucharest. Such an event is ironic because white, educated individuals, coming from the wealthy neighborhoods of Bucharest, agree to buy tickets to an event in an infamous and unsafe neighborhood. The often simplistic[5] characteristics *manele* has makes it hard to be taken completely seriously, as it oscillates between difference and mediocrity, between undiscovered artistic value and ignorance, between originality and kitsch. As Vintilă Mihăilescu argues, the universe of *manele* praises a world of gangsters (*interlopi*) and people who made it in life while disregarding the law (248). When *manele* are not about social status and money, and they approach other issues such

[5]The lyrics of Florin Salam's song *Vreau să îmi iau un Lamborghini* (*I want to buy a Lamborghini*), for instance, run as follows: Eu pe tata îl iubesc/ Dar m-am plictisit de S/ Și să vadă toți vecinii/ Vreau să-mi iau un Lamborghini (I love my father/ But I got bored of [Mercedes] S/ I want all my neighbors to see/ I'm gonna buy a Lamborghini).

as love or homesickness, they picture a cheesy and sentimental universe.[6] That is why the hipster's approach toward this music entails both curiosity and irony.

However, it would be wrong to interpret this reevaluation of the *manele* only from the perspective of a fight, ironic or not, with the mainstream. According to Speranţa Rădulescu and Adrian Schiop (42), there are *manele* singers (such as Florin Salam) who have impressive artistic potential. Those who are interested in this cultural phenomenon do not consider the artistic creation to be of secondary relevance. Speranţa Rădulescu remarks Salam's ability to improvise when singing live and mix various genres, from *muzică lăutărească* to reggaeton, from folklore to jazz.[7] *Manele* singers usually perform at private events such as weddings or birthday parties or in *manele* clubs and have no link with hipster culture. Before hipsters showed an interest in the genre, *manele* singers would rarely perform in front of a white, educated public or on large stages. In fact, this change of venue led some authors such as Dinu Guţu to argue that hipsters took the *manele* out of their context and gentrified them. This is interpreted as a means to glorify the *manele*, which is suddenly labeled as "world music" in order to fit the standards of a public that would not attend the weddings and funerals where *manele* artists would usually perform (169).

Whether *manele* has been gentrified or not, accepting these artistic creations implies a change of perspective regarding the marginalized people who play and appreciate this music. The first person to organize *manele* events in Bucharest for middle-class white people was Adrian Schiop, a journalist and writer known among hipsters from Bucharest. Hipters' interest in Roma issues was also mentioned in Adrian Schiop's novel *Soldaţii, Poveste din Ferentari*, in which he depicts the character of a hipster who is interested in Roma issues. Hipster bloggers such as Spirala joined the discussion as well: she mentions that one of the reasons why she went to *manele* concerts was due to her interest in the Roma community. Following these appearances of *manele* in popular culture, *manele* singers performed in hipster clubs in Bucharest such as Eden and Control, so the phenomenon gained even more attention. In 2017, Florin Salam sang at the Outernational Days, a world music festival popular among hipsters (Ghenţ). The festival also organized a debate about *manele*, inviting both writers, such as Adrian Schiop, and people representing the *manele* industry, such as the music producer Dan Bursuc. This debate, which the same demographic of the white, middle-class, educated urban youngster attended, was one of the very few occasions when the *manele* culture was the focus of a public

---

[6]For further discussion cf. Condrache, "Between a Harmless Game and a Bittersweet Disease: Forms of Nostalgia in Post-Socialist Central and Eastern Europe."

[7]His talent was also remarked by Goran Bregović with whom he collaborated on the album *Champagne for Gypsies* released by Bregović in 2012.

event in which the phenomenon was reflected on rather than simply rejected. Issues such as the white-collar disdain for *manele* were raised, as one of the causes of this disdain is racism, as *manele* is perceived by many Romanians as a product of Roma culture (Beissinger xxvii). Such efforts to reevaluate a musical genre go beyond mere attempts to consume music that is anti-mainstream but directly link hipsters to a serious problem, namely the way the Roma community is perceived by Romanians.

The "Beautiful People" Who Fight against Corruption

In an article about protests in Romania published in *Dilema Veche*, the most renowned Romanian cultural magazine, Cătălin Ştefănescu states that "at least in our minds if not in the University Square,[8] we should erect a statue for the unknown hipsters!" (my translation). He is only one of the intellectuals who directly links hipster culture to the protests that took place in Romania, starting with the Roşia Montană protests and continuing with the anti-corruption protests in 2016 and 2017. Also Doru Pop, in one of the most important newspapers in Romania, *Adevărul*, writes about the hipster's role in these anti-corruption protests. These journalists consider the hipster to be responsible for the revival of civic engagement in Romania. There are other journalists, such as Mircea Badea and Mihai Gâdea, hired by mass media trusts who support the government, who also label the protesters as hipsters, but they use the word in a derogatory sense. According to them, the hipsters or, as they also call them very depreciatively and superficially, the "beautiful people"[9] (*oameni frumoşi*) are young people who are paid by corporations who do not care about Romania and the poor. Thus, there are two opposite groups of journalists that engage publicly in labeling the protesters hipsters. The first group, who either collaborates with newspapers that have a more liberal political view or who writes for cultural magazines and typically avoid politics, such as Cătălin Ştefănescu, pleads for an understanding of the importance of hipsters in the context of the revival of civic activism in Romania. This group also argues for an understanding of this culture beyond the prejudices that usually follow the word hipster. In their opinion, hipsters are young, educated people, socially active and responsible, who do not deserve to be judged for a specific fashion style they embrace or for

[8]A symbol for social activism in Romania.

[9]The expression was first used by intellectuals who support the protests and who acknowledge the fact that a new generation of people defend the democratic values in Romania. When using the term in a derogatory manner, efforts are made to convince the public opinion of an alleged negative role of the protesters.

the music they listen to (Ştefănescu; Pop). Moreover, hipsters follow the footsteps of the students who protested in Romania at the beginning of the nineties, the so-called *mineriade*.[10] The second group of journalists who label the protestors as hipsters work within media trusts that are controlled by corrupt officials and use the news channels Antena 3 and România TV as well as the newspaper *Jurnalul Național* to propagate anti-justice rhetoric. They make significant efforts to discredit hipsters, as they use the term to label the protesters in a way that becomes a synonym for naive, ignorant, elitist, selfish people whose role regarding Romania's future is toxic.

When used in the context of social activism, the word hipster becomes a generic term that refers to youngsters who are not necessarily part of the hipster subculture. While the participants of the demonstrations were diverse, a significant percentage displayed the following profile: young, riding a bicycle, wearing slightly nonconformist clothing, having a vintage haircut, and having an ironic, humorous attitude. For instance, some wore a tomato in their shirt pocket, as *Roşia* (as in Roşia Montană) means red or tomato in Romanian, while others wore huge fake-gold chains. This specific type of protester was a common presence at all the anti-corruption demonstrations that were organized in Romania, especially those that took place in 2017. Furthermore, bars associated with hipster culture were supportive of the protests. For instance, during the protests in the winter of 2017, Scârț provided free hot tea to the protesters from Timisoara.

Any member of society can adopt more or less of the hipster values and aesthetic, especially if some sociological criteria—such as age, living in a big city, having a minimal interest in art and culture, and being interested in fashion—are met. Their compatibility with hipster subculture is even greater if they are interested in themes like consumerism, ecology, gender equality, minority rights, and the refusal to use certain types of products (Cronin, McCarthy, and Collins 3). However, whereas it is difficult to state how close the protesters truly were to hipster subculture, or if they embraced the hipster aesthetic and values as they gained more popularity in mainstream culture, one thing is for sure: the hipster label was applied to the protesters, and it entailed both positive and negative perceptions. This has been the case in Romania and also in Hungary, where there were massive protests against the restrictions imposed by the Hungarian authorities on foreign universities. The same characteristics found in some of the Romanian protesters can be observed in the Hungarian protesters too: young people, intellectual interests, ironic messages, bicycles, and vintage clothing (Hume).

[10]This is an idea discussed during the debate *Hippies, Yuppies, Hipsters*. The debate took place in 2017, during the film festival *Festivalul de Film şi Istorii Râşnov* (Ştefănescu, Papadima, and Chivu).

The "protester-hipster" becomes a typology that marks some of the most important civic events in Central and Eastern Europe.

Conclusion

Hipster subculture was imported to Central and Eastern Europe from the West, yet it adapted to the local context, as it responded to local needs and to several cultural, social, and political particularities of Eastern Europe. This chapter focused on those local aspects in Romania and the political potential of hipster culture. The hipster aesthetic, as it is reflected by the historic bars, can be understood as the beginning of a process of reconciliation with a traumatic national past. The same bars host or promote events that reevaluate some musical genres that used to be marginalized, just like the ethnic groups that play this music. And finally, the hipster subculture has been associated with the street protests that marked Romania in the last years. Just as in the West, hipsters from Central and Eastern Europe face a series of challenges: they are assimilated by the mainstream, while in some contexts the hipster label represents hypocrisy, snobbery, elitism, or pomposity. The aspects of hipster culture which I have analyzed in this chapter demonstrate that hipsters go beyond the clichés that are often used to characterize them. This does not mean that the hipster reputation is or ought to be predominantly positive (or not) in Central and Eastern Europe. However, this chapter pleads for a complex perspective on what hipsters are.

Works Cited

Alecu, Dana. "Întrebarea zilei: Ce este un hipster?" *Vice*, July 9, 2013, www.vice.com/ro/article/nzv9d7/ce-este-un-hipster. Accessed June 17, 2017.

Atelier Mecanic. *Facebook*, October 17, 2011, www.facebook.com/ATELIER-MECANIC-136056266494733/. Accessed August 12, 2017.

Beissinger, Margaret. "Introduction." *Manele in Romania: Cultural Expression and Social Meaning in Balkan Popular Music*, edited by Margaret Beissinger, Speranța Rădulescu, and Anca Giuchescu. Rowman and Littlefield, 2016.

Boym, Svetlana. *The Future of Nostalgia*. Basic Books, 2001, pp. xxv–xxxiii.

Bretèque, Estelle Amy, and Victor Alexandre Stoichita. "Musics of the New Times: Romanian Manele and Armenian Rabiz as Icons of Post-Communist Change." *The Balkans and the Caucasus: Parallel Processes on the Opposite Sides of the Black Sea*, edited by Ivan Biliarsky and Ovidiu Cristea. Cambridge Scholars, 2012, pp. 321–35.

Brewer, Taylah. "30 Best Hipster Haircuts for Men." *TheTrendSpotter*, www.thetrendspotter.net/hipster-haircuts/. Accessed September 1, 2020.

Café V lese. www.cafevlese.cz/. Accessed September 15, 2017.

Condrache, George Alexandru. *Between a Harmless Game and a Bittersweet Disease: Forms of Nostalgia in Post-Socialist Central and Eastern Europe*. 2020. Western University, PhD dissertation.

Cronin, M. James, Mary B. McCarthy, and Alan M. Collins. "Covert Distinction: How Hipsters Practice Food-Based Resistance Strategies in the Production of Identity." *Consumption Markets and Culture*, vol. 17, no. 1, 2014, pp. 2–28.

Fati, Sabina. "Românii și nostalgia la români." *Radio Europa liberă Moldova*, August 2, 2014, www.europalibera.org/a/24672021.html. Accessed August 13, 2018.

Foarfă, Cristina. "Șase chestii noi și faine la Electric Castle din 2017." *Vice*, July 14, 2017, www.vice.com/ro/article/3kn7pn/chestii-noi-si-faine-la-electric-castle-din-2017. Accessed July 16, 2017.

Georgescu, Diana. "Ceaușescu Hasn't Died: Irony as Countermemory in Post-Socialist Romania." *Post-Communist Nostalgia*, edited by Maria Todorova and Zsuzsa Gille. Berghan Books, 2010, pp. 155–77.

Ghenț, Marius. "Am fost la un festival de manele pentru hipsteri din București, că n-am bani de Salam altfel." *Vice*, July 10, 2017, www.vice.com/ro/article/59pdxk/festival-de-manele-pentru-hipsteri-din-bucuresti. Accessed August 12, 2017.

Giampaoletti, Marcello. "Time Travel is Possible! Back in the Time of Communism." *Zooming Up.Blog*, March 15, 2016, blog.zury.org/2016/03/15/time-travel-possible-back-communist-time/. Accessed August 12, 2017.

Guțu, Dinu, "A venit nebunu' de Salam (la un festival de hipster)." *Hipsteri, bobos și clase creative*, edited by Ciprian State and Dinu Guțu. Cartier, 2019.

Hill, Wes. "Hipster Aesthetics: Creatives with No Alternative." *Emaj*, vol. 1, no. 9, 2016, pp. 1–19, vr2pk9sx9w.search.serialssolutions.com. Accessed August 15, 2017.

Hume, Tim. "Hungarians Take to the Streets to Protest Rising Russian Influence." *Vice*, May 2, 2017, news.vice.com/en_us/article/bjdk55/hungarians-take-to-the-streets-to-protest-rising-russian-influence. Accessed August 12, 2017.

Hutcheon, Linda, and Mario J. Valdés. "Irony, Nostalgia and the Post-modern." Paper presented at the Modern Language Association Conference. San Francisco, December 1997.

Huyssen, Andreas. *Twilight Memories: Marking Time in a Culture of Amnesia*. Routledge, 1995.

Jameson, Fredric. *Postmodernism or the Cultural Logic of Late Capitalism*. Verso, 1991.

Maly, Ico, and Piia Varis. "The 21st-Century Hipster: On Micro-Populations in Times of Superdiversity." *European Journal of Cultural Studies*, vol. 19, no. 6, 2016, pp. 637–53.

"manelar." *Dexonline*: *Dicționarul explicativ al limbii române online*, dexonline.ro/definitie/manelar. Accessed August 21, 2017.

Margarit, Diana. "Ideology and Social Movements: A Comparative Analysis of the 2013 Protests in Bulgaria, Hungary and Romania." *Social Movements in Central and Eastern Europe: A Renewal of Protests and Democracy*, edited by Geoffrey Pleyers and Ionel N. Sava. Editura Universității din București, 2015, pp. 13–27.

Mihăilescu, Vintilă. "Turbo-Authenticity: An Essay on Manelism." *Manele in Romania: Cultural Expression and Social Meaning in Balkan Popular Music*, edited by Margaret Beissinger, Speranța Rădulescu, and Anca Giurchescu. Rowman and Littlefield, 2016, pp. 247–59.

Moisil, Costin. "A History of the Manea: The Nineteenth to the Mid-Twentieth Century." *Manele in Romania: Cultural Expression and Social Meaning in Balkan Popular Music*, edited by Margaret Beissinger, Speranța Rădulescu, and Anca Giuchescu. Rowman and Littlefield, 2016.

Nora, Pierre. "Between Memory and History: Les Lieux de Memoire." *Representations*, no. 26, 1989, pp. 7–24.

Paulesc, Marie-Louise. *Living Relationships with the Past: Remembering Communism in Romania*. 2014. Arizona State University, PhD dissertation, repository.asu.edu/attachments/134781/content/Paulesc_asu_0010E_13626.pdf. Accessed August 7, 2017.

Pijalnia. pwip.com.pl/. Accessed September 2017.

Pohrib, Codruța. "Communist Childhoods and Nostalgia: A Cultural Analysis of Online Remembrance Strategies." *Reinventing Childhood Nostalgia: Books, Toys, and Contemporary Media Culture*, edited by Elisabeth Wesseling. Routledge, 2018, pp. 135–53.

Pop, Doru. "Revoluția hipsterilor." *Adevărul*, January 31, 2017, adevarul.ro/news/politica/revolutia-hipsterilor1_5890fd585ab6550cb8fc10ca/index.html. Accessed August 2, 2017.

Rădulescu, Speranța. "Garantat 100%." *YouTube*, uploaded by Nicu Mâță, January 23, 2015, www.youtube.com/watch?v=5pgkhLv3SYY. Accessed September 12, 2017.

Scârț loc lejer. *Facebook*, October 29, 2013, www.facebook.com/scartloclejer/. Accessed August 12, 2017.

Schiermer, Bjørn. "Late-Modern Hipsters: New Tendencies in Popular Culture." *Acta Sociologica*, vol. 57, no. 2, 2014, pp. 167–81.

Schiop, Adrian. *Șmecherie și lume rea: Universul social al manelelor*. Cartier, 2017.

Schiop, Adrian. *Soldații. Poveste din Ferentari*. Polirom, 2014.

Solonar, Dumitru Ovidiu. "Cultura pop ca ideologie: Hipsterii din România, între anti-corporatism și anti-corupție." *Sfera Politicii*, vol. 23, no. 186/4, 2015, pp. 27–36.

Spirala Colorată. spiralacolorata.ro/2014/03/03/hipsteri-plus-manele-egal-love/. Accessed August 18, 2017.

Szimpla. szimpla.hu/. Accessed September 12, 2017.

Ștefănescu, Cătălin. "Monumentul hipsterului necunoscut." *Dilema Veche*, September 1, 2016, dilemaveche.ro/sectiune/tilc-show/articol/monumentul-hipsterului-necunoscut. Accessed August 2, 2017.

Ștefănescu, Cătălin, Liviu Papadima, and Marius Chivu."Hippies, Yuppies, Hipsters." *Soundcloud*, uploaded by Daniel Secarescu, September 12, 2017, soundcloud.com/danielsecarescu/hippiesyuppieshipsters/s-otbvZ. Accessed September 17, 2017.

Traveller on a Mission. "My Favorite Shot Bar in Warsaw, Half Way Between Soviet and Hipster." *Traveller on a Mission*, May 6, 2015, Wordpress, travelleronamission.wordpress.com/2015/05/06/my-favourite-shot-bar-in-warsaw-half-way-between-soviet-and-hipster/. Accessed August 3, 2017.

Ungureanu, Laurenţiu. "Care-i treaba cu hipsterii? Vintilă Mihăilescu: 'Nonconformişti de duminică.' Aurora Liiceanu: 'Tineri şi rătăciţi de regiment.' " *Adevărul*, January 25, 2014, adevarul.ro/life-style/stil-de-viata/hipster-vintila-mihailescu-aurora-liiceanu-1_52e3b531c7b855ff56c92e0e/index.html. Accessed September 1, 2020.

5

Pastiching the Pastoral: Hipster Farmers and the Commodification of American Agriculture

Katje Armentrout

On the cover of the February 2015 issue of *Acres U.S.A.*, a young woman harvests a luscious bunch of beets by hand. She smiles a perfectly orthodontics-fixed straight-toothed grin, while donning her backwards trucker hat, hiding her eyes is a pair of over-sized aviator glasses. Her cutoff sleeve T-shirt displays her upper-arm owl tattoo. After the Great Recession and even more so since the early 2010s, farming publications that present "pastoral hip" images such as this one have become popular and preserve the myth that agricultural processes can be easily duplicated by anyone. Moreover, when presented with images such as the one described above, it seems that a diverse group of young people have begun to reengage agricultural landscapes, perform rural customs, and take up farming professions after a prior massive out-migration from such places and practices during the most recent farm crisis in the 1980s (Conkin 132).

With this new crop of young farmers in mind, this chapter contrasts cultural representations of traditional family farmers with mainly white, middle-class millennials living in more urban environments to analyze the characteristics of "hipster farmers." More specifically, this chapter defines hipster farmers as young people establishing prosperous food producing operations constructed upon romanticized principles appropriated from past and current agrarian societies and the sustainable lifestyle practices associated with rural places where American farmers stereotypically reside. Their migration stems from their reaction to the modern made possible by seeking out "the simple life" stereotypically associated with rural farm communities, as well as a revolt against industrial failure in metropolitan areas. Their existence challenges the fluid relationship between the urban and the rural and puts into question what personal traits have been historically associated with rural residents in the agricultural profession (i.e., aging, lower socioeconomic class, white men without a college education). Furthermore, while appropriating characteristics of traditional family farmers and commodifying their lifestyle, hipster farmers blur the lines between urban and rural landscapes and create unique spaces for producers and consumers in metropolitan communities. However, the recent introduction of hipster farmers has not only caused a shift in geographical developments. There has also been a changing presence in media discourses and cultural representations surrounding the farming community showing a greater presence of hipster farmers.

By exploring both media representations and real-life examples of hipster farmers in this chapter, I will critically analyze several stereotypes associated with the hipster identity by highlighting their complicated involvement with farming communities. By looking at various forms of print and digital media such as *Acres U.S.A.* magazine, *Modern Farmer* magazine, the website Farmrun, and National Young Farmers Coalition videos, I will show how representations of hipsters have appropriated characteristics typically aligned with the American farmer image by (perhaps unintentionally) reinforcing the importance of rural nostalgia. Additionally, I will reveal how a subgroup of hipsters is prospering across a wide variety of American agricultural settings because they are pastiching the landscape of the traditional family farm and creating sites of pastoral sentimentalism. By turning to Gold Cash Gold and Selden Standard, restaurants in Detroit, Michigan, as examples of places where people gather to enjoy the fruitful labors of thriving hipster farmers, I will examine how the farm-to-table movement has carved out a niche clientele for consumers of artisanal products in an emerging community focused on sustainable agriculture. Ultimately, this chapter illuminates how hipsters have become hipster farmers to grow and generate hipster products for hipster consumers to enjoy hipster food with other hipsters.

Identifying Hipster Farmers

To understand the identity of the hipster farmer, it is first imperative to define the figure of the contemporary hipster. Typically, hipsters have been associated with urban regions. One of the most comprehensive descriptions is put forward in an entry on Urbandictionary.com:

> [A] subculture of men and women typically in their 20's and 30's that value independent thinking, counterculture, progressive politics, an appreciation of art and indie-rock, creativity, intelligence, and witty banter ... Although "hipsterism" is really a state of mind, it is also often intertwined with distinct fashion sensibilities. Hipsters reject the culturally-ignorant attitudes of mainstream consumers, and are often seen wearing vintage and thrift store inspired fashions, tight-fitting jeans, old-school sneakers, and sometimes thick rimmed glasses ... The "effortless cool" urban bohemian look of a hipster is exemplified in Urban Outfitters and American Apparel ads which cater towards the hipster demographic. Despite misconceptions based on their aesthetic tastes, hipsters tend to be well educated and often have liberal arts degrees. (Parasuco)

Quoting this passage at length not only touches on the economic underpinnings which the hipster is geared toward but also explores their personal aesthetic and style based on their geographical environment. Moreover, as the imagery in Cassar's *How to Spot a Hipster* suggests, some popular pastimes for these individuals include playing quirky musical instruments such as the banjo, accordion, or ukulele, knitting, crocheting, writing, blogging, yoga, seeing live bands, and living an unconventional lifestyle. Upon further consideration of the stereotypical characteristics of hipsters, it appears that some of them have recently begun populating environments outside of urban areas and adopted a cliched typecast with an agrarian-like swagger which I will display throughout the remainder of this chapter.

As Mark Greif claims in his book *What Was the Hipster?* co-edited with Kathleen Ross and Dayna Tortorici, the hipster "aligns himself *both* with rebel culture *and* with the dominant class, and opens up a poisonous conduit between the two" ("Positions" 9). In his *New York Magazine* article with the same title, he refers to a "green" transformation occurring among hipsters in the early twenty-first century and notes their shift from "midwestern suburbs to animals, wilderness, plus the occasional Native American" ("What Was the Hipster?"). Describing this subgroup as "the Hipster Primitive," Greif explains:

> [They] recovered the sound[s] and symbols of pastoral innocence with an irony ... the Hipster Primitive feminized hipster markers; one spoke [then] of headdresses and Sally Jesse Raphael glasses, not just male facial hair. Women took up cowboy boots, then dark-green rubber Wellingtons, like country squiresses off to visit the stables. Men gave up the porno mustache for the hermit or lumberjack beard. Flannel returned, as did

> hunting jackets in red-and-black check. Scarves proliferated unnecessarily, conjuring a cold woodland night (if wool) or a desert encampment (if a kaffiyeh). Then scarves were worn as bandannas, as when Mary-Kate Olsen sported one, like a cannibal Pocahontas, hungry enough to eat your arm. ("What Was the Hipster?")

Before the early 2010s, hipsters pursuing agricultural ventures could have easily been described as individuals who were "playing farmer," a pejorative term borrowed from Philip Deloria. Throughout his arguments in *Playing Indian*, Deloria makes it quite clear that Americans have an "unparalleled national identity crisis" resulting from defining themselves by appropriating characteristics from marginalized communities that have been historically unfamiliar to them (3). Linking the hipster-farmer identity with manufactured Native American imagery is powerful because it illuminates how the hipster farmer is not imagined but is a sociocultural constructed performance and alludes to the process of appropriating the style of the marginalized. Paralleling Greif's "Hipster Primitive," I argue that hipster farmers typically embrace the cultures of a variety of settings, simultaneously portraying urban *and* rural material culture attributes, as well as the physical characteristics associated with both regions.

In media and other cultural representations, male hipster farmers usually have facial hair—beards, mustaches, goatees, stubble, etcetera. Flannel shirts, knitted stockings caps, and overalls are commonly popular articles of clothing. Usually, female hipster farmers resemble a modern-day Rosie the Riveter—gender bending conventions with their choice of attire—to focus on functionality and not necessarily on fashion. Recently, these stylistic behaviors have been pushed into the mainstream and become quite trendy fashion selections. Shannon Hayes's *Radical Homemakers*, Emily Matchar's *Homeward Bound*, and Martha Hodgkin's *Letters to a Young Farmer* portray hipster farmers as people who tend to drink Pabst Blue Ribbon (or microbrews), black coffee, and chai tea. Additionally, some of them smoke American Spirit natural cigarettes, pipes, and clove tobacco (Doll). Usually, they attempt to live a more "sustainable" lifestyle by living in greener environments as shown on websites such as urbanexodus.com, outstandinginthefield.com, womenwhofarm.com, femalefarmerproject.org, and youngagrariains.org. Likewise, moving "back to the land" to grow, harvest, raise, butcher, and preserve their own food, while purchasing artisanal goods and wares, as well as producing them for others to consume are perhaps the most important characteristics of hipster farmers actively practicing within agricultural communities. They romanticize the rural environment of family farmers, creating a commodified façade of certain ideas about sustainability.

Hipster farmers share similar characteristics with the white hipster defined by Greif. According to his depiction of contemporary hipsters, they broadly represent upper-middle-class whites who focus on entitled luxury, rather than on the marginalized people laboring for their pleasures ("What Was the Hipster?"). However, he explains they perform largely under the pretext that they are not controlled by capitalism and rely on past rhetoric of countercultural politics as their guiding principles. More specifically, Greif defines hipsters by the tensions created by their "rejection of consumerism" and knowledge "about exclusive things before anyone else," as well as their desire to obtain those specialty goods ("What Was the Hipster?"). This ideology indicates hipsters (and subsequently, hipster farmers) are principally generated by neoliberalism's necessity to privatize goods and redistribute wealth (Greif, Preface xvii).

As Fredric Jameson argues in *Postmodernism, or, the Cultural Logic of Late Capitalism*, the postmodern aspects of late capitalism involve an emergence of a "cultural dominant" (4). While it seems that the cultural dominant in most rural, American agriculture communities is still traditional family farmers, hipster farmers commonly control urban farm environments and the consumers who frequent those markets. Yet, most hipster farmers want to believe they are not actively competing in globalized modes of capitalism but are attempting to create methods of social change based on authentic farming processes which historically resisted domination and exploitation (Chase-Dunn). More specifically, they have developed countless metropolitan neighborhoods to include green spaces in which they practice small-scale farming operations to resist corporatization and distribute agricultural products to other hipsters who share the same interests in food quality, authenticity, aesthetics, and social justice concerns. Likewise, they are captivated by aspects of environmental sustainability and sociopolitical concerns commonly linked to traditional family farmers and ideals of pastoral sentimentalism.

Hipster Farmer Connections to Pastoral Sentimentalism

In the American cultural imagination, the traditional family farm environment has been typically associated with dynamics of familial closeness and nostalgia, environmental stewardship, and personal autonomy, fulfillment, and security. Arguably, all these characteristics enhance the attractive quality that traditional farming lifestyles and their communities have to offer. In *Selling Tradition*, Jane Becker defines tradition as

> the past, of course, but also the way in which the past is transmitted ... the passing down of knowledge from generation to generation [with implied] value and veneration. It represents a lingering of the past in the

> present, a touchstone with those who have gone before and have left behind some of what they held most important for later generations. (1)

She suggests that tradition is a personal experience, filled with learned skills, customs, rituals, and stories that are maintained and performed through generations of community (1). According to several scholarly works such as Wendell Berry's *The Unsettling of America*, Wes Jackson's *New Roots for Agriculture* and *Becoming Native to this Place*, Gene Logsdon's *The Contrary Farmer*, and David Danbom's *Born in the Country*, agriculture is the most traditional occupation in the United States. However, since the 1980s Farm Crisis in America, the traditional family farm is vanishing from the rural landscape (Conkin 132). Younger generations no longer see agriculture as a rich source of economic longevity mainly due to the increase in large agribusiness farming models dominating the industry, with their capacity to purchase more up-to-date technologies and ability to hold greater financial power (Fried).

The USDA's 2012 Census information included on Farm Aid's website showed a loss of about 95,000 farms. According to a 2014 article published in *Stateline*, "Every week, about 330 farmers leave their farms for good ... less than 1 percent of Americans today claim farming as an occupation. The fastest growing group of farmers and ranchers is 65 and older ... but the second-fastest growing group is young farmers and ranchers who are under 35 ... most first-generation" (Wiltz). A report from the National Young Farmer's Coalition states that 78 percent of young farmers did not grow up on a farm ("2015 Annual Report"). This back-to -the-land movement is motivated by a longing for a natural environment different from the (sub)urban life in which these young people have often grown up. It is an expression of what Leo Marx, in his influential work on American literature, *The Machine in the Garden* (1964), refers to as "pastoral sentimentalism."

In his analysis of the symbolism of technology's interruption on pastoral settings during the American industrial revolution and its metaphorical merit within American literature from the same time, Marx suggests, "Wherever people turn away from the hard social and technological realities [pastoral sentimentalism] is likely to be at work" (5). He addresses the nostalgia that hangs over urban landscapes and creates a desire to participate in a greener setting because of the "pursuit of happiness" (6). About nostalgia and pastoral sentimentalism, Marx argues:

> Evidently it is generated by an urge to withdraw from civilization's growing power and complexity. What is attractive in pastoralism is the felicity represented by an image of a natural landscape, a terrain either unspoiled or, if cultivated, rural. Movement toward such a symbolic landscape also may be understood as movement away from an "artificial" world, a world identified with "art," using this word in its

> broadest sense to mean the disciplined baits of mind or arts developed by organized communities. In other words, this impulse gives rise to a symbolic motion away from centers of civilization toward their opposite, nature, away from sophistication toward simplicity, or to introduce the cardinal metaphor of the literary mode, away from the city toward the country. When this impulse is unchecked, the result is a simple-minded wishfulness, a romantic perversion of thought and feeling. (9)

The anxiety caused by the modern culminates in a return to nature and what Marx refers to as the middle landscape, "the ritual marriage at the end of a pastoral landscape" (31). He expresses his idea of the middle landscape as "the best of all human conditions ... the point of transition between the lower and the higher, animal and intellectual forms of being" (100). In his clearest definition, Marx asserts the middle landscape is an "imaginative and complex" cultural symbol derived from the pastoral ideal, "a new, distinctively American, post-romantic, industrial version of the pastoral design" (5, 32). Ultimately, I see Marx's "middle landscape" as a place where hipster farmers reside in both the physical and metaphysical pastoral domains. While hipster farmers are not longing for outright primitivism, they are seeking a mediation between nature and civilization (Segal 138). Again, the hipster farmer is a mixture of rural and urban motifs and lifestyles. Therefore, the image of the hipster farmer and those pursuing such a lifestyle embody the idea of "rurban" in every sense of the word. Yet, there is an obvious separation happening between the agrarian middle landscape that Marx writes of and the rural longing of the contemporary hipster because of neoliberal capitalism. As argued in *The Rise and Fall of Neoliberal Capitalism*, neoliberal policies center on lessening governmental economic regulations in exchange for greater participation in free markets to encourage economic efficiency, economic growth, and technological innovation (Kotz 9). While the reasons for the flight from the city are the same, hipster farmers connect with both the city and the country because of their use of technology in performing agricultural tasks as well as self-promotion, both of which are made most apparent in media representations of hipster farmers.

Media Representations of Hipster Farmers

Most media representations of hipster farmers fuse aspects typically associated with hipster culture such as monochromatic and neutral color schemes, polished, simple, clean, industrial design principles, and repurposed fixtures with characteristics appropriated from rural and farming culture such as clothing, food, tools and equipment, and hobbies to construct a particular "rustic," "vintage," and/or "folksy" aesthetic in the images portrayed, the fonts used in the written content, and the topics that are discussed in the articles. Usually these are targeted at attracting a specific demographic of young, white, middle-class liberals interested in industrial agriculture design, authentic food production, and food policy and sustainable production practices. *Modern Farmer* magazine is no exception. As described on the magazine's website, this quarterly publication exists for people who want to make a connection with what they eat, how they live, and the planet they reside on ("About Us"). Further, "it is for window-herb growers, career farmers, people who have chickens, people who want to have chickens and anyone who wants to know more about how food reaches their plate" ("About Us"). From this description, it appears to be an all-inclusive agrarian periodical. However, a closer look at some of the products advertised in the publication suggests the magazine's exclusivity and its marketing toward the previously defined demographic.

In the Winter 2014/15 issue of *Modern Farmer* magazine, Kaufman Mercantile's advertisement displays a woman nestled in a monochromatic wool blanket, sitting atop an antique wooden bench (7). Similarly, the Dansko Shoes advertisement in the same issue portrays a woman holding a bunch of carrots smiling coyly while harvesting her raised garden beds (16–17). Additionally, Sterling College's ad promotes a class for "Artisan Cheesemaking in Vermont" (42), and there is also a vibrantly colored page presenting Baker Creek Heirloom Seeds to the readership of the magazine (52). Furthermore, there is an entire section devoted to a "Winter Gift Guide" which displays artisanal products such as hand-thrown bowls from Tivoli Tile Works Pottery running for $40 apiece, Gierups wool Boot House Slippers for $99, a "specially made-in-the-U.S., heat-treated, steel mulch fork" prices out at $138, and even a Double Mackinaw Cruiser Jacket manufactured by Filson is advertised for the price of $415. However, there is also the steadfast Carhartt coverall listed in the "practical and classic" section of the gift digest, which only costs $36 (77–80). Based on such advertisements, what type of farmer makes up the readership of *Modern Farmer* magazine? I contend this publication is geared toward hipster farmers (and their hipster consumers) interested in the luxury versions of goods at their disposal in more neoliberal environments.

In an interview with National Public Radio's (NPR's) "The Salt: What's on Your Plate," *Modern Farmer*'s past CEO and editor-in-chief Ann Marie Gardner referred to the publication's readership demographic as "more modern farmers ... hobby farmers" (Charles and Aubrey). Arguably, this could be interpreted as people who are participating in farming processes on a much smaller scale than the large, agribusiness model of family farmers with which so many Americans are familiar. Additionally, she stresses that *Modern Farmer*'s readers frequently produce their goods in rural environments, but the consumers of their products generally reside in urban locations and desire to build relationships with the farmers. Therefore, she considers *Modern Farmer* to be a publication which merges the rural and urban environments, describing it as "'rurban' … where rural, it's cool." Likewise, she suggests the magazine is utilized as an influential tool for people to appropriate material culture aspects of agricultural lifestyles in environments not historically known for farm site developments by positing the question, "If you look at Brooklyn, the hipsters, they're dressing like farmers now, have you noticed?" Gardner asserts agricultural authenticity as a method by which to engage *Modern Farmer* readers when she states, "To be credible with a hipster [the publication] has to be credible with a farmer." Therefore, building rapport with multiple communities is necessary for the longevity of the publication.

Regarding hipster farmers, two parts of Ann Marie Gardner's interview with NPR seem important. First, her inability to claim traditional family farmers as the primary reader of the publication. Throughout the interview she suggests how silly some of the stories are that the magazine reports on which indicates its lack of banality and inclusion of fresh, romanticized articles geared towards non-tenured farmers. For example, articles titled "Inside the Mind of a Turkey" or "Are You Cool Enough to Drink Switchel?" are not stereotypically pieces that traditional family farmers want to read about (Charles and Aubrey). The NPR analysts also refer to *Modern Farmer* as "*The Onion* of farm magazines" thereby alluding to the inexperience and credibility of the magazines' young, agrarian readership (Charles and Aubrey). However, nearing the end of the interview, Gardner relies heavily on the identification of the "authentic farmer" as a matter of measurement to whom the magazine's primary reader is aspiring to be. Consequently, the publication results in a variety of mixed messages to say the very least. Secondly, the use of the term "rurban" is important. Ultimately, I argue this neologism describes how hipsters are embracing romanticized traits of rural and agricultural lifestyles where tradition, nostalgia, and familial closeness are endeared methods of belonging to appear trendy amongst their peers in urban locations. Media images of hipster farmers in the selected American publications evoke notions of the frontier, and other key American mythologies surrounding manifest destiny, the yeoman farmer, and self-sustainability. For example, there are multiple images of hipsters standing in fields amongst the fruits of their hard labors holding up "perfect" specimens of fruits or vegetables which they grew like the one described at the beginning of this chapter. These images are all reminiscently suggestive to passages from Thomas Jefferson's *Notes on the State of Virginia* about the yeoman farmer or Henry David Thoreau's work *Walden* regarding self-sufficiency and sustainability. Likewise, there are numerous photographs depicting someone staring wistfully into the distance to absorb their scenic surroundings not unlike John Gast's iconic allegorical painting *American Progress* and its portrayal of the theme manifest destiny. However, in these contemporary publications, hipster farmers do not always fit the white patriarchal model established in rural, wide-open spaces typically associated with past American agricultural imagery. More specifically, some of these examples proliferating the pages include women, people of color, and a much younger demographic to depict their farm experience in more urban backdrops. Therefore, I contend that while hipsters embrace similar characteristics of past versions of American farmers in their daily lives, they are doing so in more diverse and modern settings. Thusly, they are commodifying interpretations of historical significance to perform authentically as farmers but also breaking away from these past manifestations to establish unique versions of agricultural production. Still, white, middle-class young people seem to predominate the image of hipsters (and subsequently, hipster farmers) beyond these media publications and are therefore the focus of my study of how hipster farmers are appropriating sociocultural attributes from a variety of historical and contemporary landscapes

Essentially, hipster farmers connect with both the city and the country because of their ability to adapt to their environment and portray themselves as an authentic construct in a variety of locations. Similarly, media representations of hipster farmers inspire other hipsters to modify themselves in order to participate in their own versions of agricultural authenticity. For example, Andrew Plotsky is the creator of Farmrun, a website and studio geared towards graphic design, branding, and photography focusing on multiple aspects of the agrarian lifestyle. As narrated on his website, Plotsky was born and raised in the metropolitan area of Washington, DC and is the first member of five generations to leave the city to search for his agrarian roots (Plotsky). Plotsky's original attraction to farming began when he attended college in upstate New York where he detected that something was severely corrupt with the way America grew and delivered food to the people of the country. Upon acknowledging this nationwide corruption, Plotsky became acquainted with the practices of vegetable farming as he worked alongside several area farmers. After graduating college, he set out to jog behind a baby stroller holding all his belongings. His lofty aspirations were to archive traditional farming practices on his cross-country journey. To keep in contact with his family, Plotsky created a blog: *Farmrun*.

Originally, the main content of *Farmrun* contained "empirical knowledge and cultural context about simple, positive, land-based livelihoods" (Plotsky). Furthermore, "[Plotsky] explored photography, writing, and illustration as outlets to synthesize the people, places, theories, and themes he encountered … It eventually became unavoidably apparent that the distinctly creative and agrarian sides of his life presented a marriage so deeply sensible that no other choice was available but to smoosh them together." As *Farmrun* so eloquently describes:

> While the computer is instrumental in the facilitation of our services, Farmrun is principally a function of the earth ... We are farmers ourselves. We work with our hands and live by the sun. We are deeply invested in tradition, we are self-taught, we are aware that perfection is a myth. We worship the forest, connect with our tools, and revere the strength required of a laborful existence. We strive, above all else, to foster the prosperity of the agrarian renaissance.

Since beginning the website, Plotsky has lived full time on a farm, growing a diverse variety of vegetables to sell at his local farmer's market, as well as producing video, print design, identity design, illustration, lettering, and photography for the marketability purposes for other agricultural prospectors across the nation. As the website states, Farmrun is an "agrarian creative studio."

Plotsky's website displays features characteristic of similar representations of hipster farmers. First, visual representations of individuals in agricultural spaces (i.e., working in a barn, interacting with an animal, harvesting vegetables, etc.) are a prominent feature of most of the imagery. These individuals appear to be "hipster farmers" because of their age range (usually in the millennial generation), racial make-up (primarily white), and personal style (simple clothing, bearded, thick frame glasses, stocking caps, flannel shirts), as well as other material culture items (vintage, rustic, industrialized, repurposed, refurbished objects) in the photograph. Photo filters are applied in order to render the images cool and more on trend, deeming them hashtag- and Instagram-worthy; thereby, making them easily recognizable for their duplicability, marketability, and capitalistic potential. More specifically, these images have both environmental elements showing natural beauty in pristine form juxtaposed with an agricultural profession not well known for its clean, aesthetic value. Most long-established farmers recognize agricultural jobs as somewhat dirty and mundane chores which do not necessitate glamourous reproduction opportunities.[1] It seems hipster farmers require proof that these events occurred and that they participate in authentic agricultural experiences. Arguably, these reproductive characteristics suggest the salability of the products, the people, the environment, and the lifestyle included in the image. Similarly, another main component of many of Plotsky's designs is the use of a rustic, vintage, or minimal typeface in combination with agrarian elements. For example, chalkboard style lettering overlays a lot of webpages created for young farmers. Likewise, these websites are adorned with artisanal vegetables, and a handwritten motif is typically used for a video outlining methods of craft

---

[1]See, for example, Rhodes *Farm: A Year in the Life of an American Farm*; Funda *Weeds: A Farm Daughter's Lament*; Hamilton *Deep River: A Memoir of a Missouri Farm*.

butchery, or a san-serif font is utilized in designing a farm-to-table restaurant menu. Farm products and farming experiences are thus aestheticized and valorized. At the same time, all these examples point towards promoting the profitability of agricultural endeavors.

Plotsky's endeavors at *Farmrun* have assisted institutions focusing on agricultural sustainability to connect with younger individuals, thereby allowing hipster farmers to become more culturally aware of the generational wisdom of traditional family farms and interested in what their agricultural lifestyle has to offer. One of the leading alliances in the most recent resurgence of agriculture is the National Young Farmers Coalition (NYFC). In 2013, the NYFC commissioned Andrew Plotsky's company, Farm Run Media to create their "Bootstrap Videos," a series of short films dedicated to chronicling the daily experiences of young dairy farmers (National Young Farmers Coalition). All three NYFC films produced specifically depict dairies that are managed by women (a component that already makes these films extraordinary). However, Ashlee Kleinhammer's roles at North Country Creamery at Clover Mead Farm in the Eastern Adirondacks of New York is a particularly illustrative example.

After earning an undergraduate degree in environmental studies from Lewis and Clark University in Portland, Oregon, Ashlee Kleinhammer moved to upstate New York to learn how to make cheese (Bouvier). Eventually, she took over a creamery operation specializing in a 100 percent grass-fed, non-GMO and Animal Welfare Approved yogurt, cheese, and raw milk (National Young Farmers Coalition). The short NYFC film's opening scene shows Kleinhammer in the winter, wearing Carhartt coveralls, a knitted cap, and a zip-up hoodie nudging cows gently into their pen. Fading into the next shot, her hair is twisted up into a childish style of two buns on each side of her head, and she is wearing muck boots, another hoodie sweatshirt layered with a plaid overcoat, and grimy, mud-covered jeans. Both combinations of garments are stereotypical attire for people working on a dairy farm, but what is completely unusual in the second scene is her pose: lounging leisurely in a pasture surrounded by her dairy cows munching on luscious hay.

Throughout the NYFC film, Kleinhammer speaks in a cheerful, undulating timbre to explain that she became interested in farming while taking a semester off from college to travel to Central America, where she volunteered on a farm in Guatemala. After returning to the United States and upon graduation, she taught children how to milk cows before taking over at Clover Mead Farm. At this location, Kleinhammer has learned from a presumed family farmer the methods of cheese production and now keeps the farm and dairy active. However, the part of the NYFC video that is possibly most interesting is when she references how desirable the artisanal products generated at Clover Mead Farm are because of their proximity to local consumers. Her audible description of this small, agricultural endeavor is dubbed over a scene of her squirting milk directly from a cow's udder into a steaming cup of coffee. Eventually, Kleinhammer admits her luck in the lucrative farm experience when she states near the end of the video, "And, gosh, it was already here" (National Young Farmers Coalition). With the vocal inflection of her exclamation, it seems that she is shocked about the longevity of Clover Mead Farm, as well as the desirability for its products. Likewise, she may be astonished with the prosperity of the farm in its rural location because she has been accustomed to acquiring and experiencing artisanal, small-batch products in more urban environments. Put differently, it seems that hipster farmers are usually inhabitants of urban, green spaces because they typically produce diverse varieties of food on small-scale farms for their consumers.

Locating Hipster Farmers and Their Consumers

Since the beginning of the twenty-first century, many locations across the United States' inner city residential zones have been in a deteriorating state due to industrial decline, white flight, and poverty wrought havoc on the city landscape (cf., e.g., Zukin's *Naked City*, Gibson's *The Edge Becomes the Center*, and Freeman's *There Goes the "Hood"*). Correspondingly, Detroit neighborhoods such as Brush Park and Corktown are becoming revitalized by millennials who find the districts filled with promise. These young, primarily white people are moving into typically impoverished neighborhoods which at one time housed mainly people of color to buy cheap properties and turn them into sites of profitability through the process of gentrification (Moskowitz 6–9). In this process, metropolitan Detroit neighborhoods are also growing greener as the new inhabitants are starting small-scale growing operations, marketing their food products within their neighborhoods, and profiting off artisanal products such as heirloom, organic, and experimental crops, handmade cheeses from grass fed cows or goats, and other cottage industry manufactures, thereby creating systems to pursue greater economic benefits and pastoral sentimentalism as suggested earlier.

Large, vacant lots are evolving into acres of urban gardens: sites of environmental and agricultural prosperity. As described in an article for the journal publication *Geoforum*, "[i]n 2014, approximately 100,000 lots lie 'vacant' in Detroit" but have since been repurposed (Safransky). Cooperative gardens, farmer's markets, and Community Supported Agriculture (CSA) are a trend. For example, urban growing spaces like ACRE, Food Field, and Brother Nature Produce (all located in the metro-Detroit region) allow consumers to purchase a harvest share to receive fresh, local produce distributed throughout the growing season. They also sell produce at the local farmer's market (Haimerl). Most importantly, these farm sites produce artisanal food items such as farm fresh eggs, kale, microgreens, beets, Romanesco, jams, jellies, chutneys, radishes, tatsoi, ossabaw pork, heirloom tomatoes, grass-fed beef, and kohlrabi for neighboring consumers. While all these goods are also being produced by traditional family farmers, hipster farmers demonstrate how the superiority of these items and their authenticity is especially profitable in environments where other hipsters reside.

For example, one of the biggest supporters of ACRE was Gold Cash Gold—a farm-to-table restaurant that was located in Detroit's Corktown district ("ACRE Detroit"). Although, Gold Cash Gold has recently closed its doors permanently for a variety of reasons—one of which being local restaurant industry oversaturation (Selasky)—Josh Stockton, the original chef, described himself and his vision for the restaurant thusly:

> I'm a country boy. Rooted in the South, and with deep respect for the Old World. But, I'm lost and in love with this city. I still make food like they do in the country, on the farm. In my mind, there's no other way … I make use of what's available, what excites my local farmers. The most delicious, seasonal stuff they've got. ("About")

Once a crumbling area of inner-city decline, Corktown has become one of the premiere hot spots for the scene of Detroit's nightlife, its burgeoning community of hipsters, as well as a location increasingly abundant with hipster farmers. One of the neighborhood's major success stories, Gold Cash Gold was housed in a repurposed pawn shop. The very name of the restaurant was due to the exterior appearance of the once deteriorating building and the painted pawnbroker advertisements. Inside, the décor featured shelves of Ball canning jars filled with a myriad of house-made pickled vegetables adorning the walls. Refurbished objects could be noticed everywhere: the ceiling was salvaged from the walls of the former pawn shop, the dining room flooring was reclaimed from a nearby school that had been closing due to the city's economic hardship, stain-glass panels repurposed from a local warehouse were used for dining room partitions, and the benches to sit on were relocated from a nearby community industrial center (Rector). There was an unadulterated dichotomous nature about the restaurant—a younger population was building up the old neighborhood to reestablish an environment that was originally not intended for the purposes of the building, but they were filling it with old, antiqued, repurposed products to exemplify a rustic theme.

Aesthetically, Gold Cash Gold's interior was like many current farm-to-table restaurants on trend amongst hipsters. At Selden Standard, another restaurant in midtown Detroit frequented by young people associated with the hipster lifestyle, industrialized design focused on simplicity appears to be important. Descriptions of menu items are limited to a few words to highlight the exceptional quality of the ingredients. For example, a $15 tomato salad is listed with "melon, Thai vinaigrette, crispy shallots" as the additional ingredients and a $14 offering of "Herbed Flatbread" contains "Stracciatella, roasted garlic, Castelvetrano olives" (Selden Standard). By these straightforward descriptions, it seems the food products used to create dishes at these venues is highly desirable. Similarly, it seems restauranteurs/ chefs, as well as hipster diners, want to know the origin of where their food is coming from, and most farm-to-table restaurants include a list of farms and food production companies on their menu. The monochromatic menu at Selden Standard even includes the number of miles to the growing location, as well as the date and time it was harvested to ensure freshness. Given this uncomplicated aesthetic, it seems that the proprietors of Selden Standard are interested in relaying information regarding the farmers who are producing their ingredients to their diners. Likewise, it appears that the hipster farmers generating these products are also invested in the marketing process and the increasing desire of young people to consume products generated at sustainable agricultural operations. Put differently, hipsters are purchasing food from local farms in order to remain trendy even if that requires them to pay more for artisanal food items. Once again, these exclusionary circumstances point toward the gentrification processes occurring in metropolitan regions.

Conclusion

Analyzing images published in print and digital media sources such as *Acres U.S.A.* and *Modern Farmer* magazine, the website Farmrun, and National Young Farmers Coalition promotional videos helps to explore the ways contemporary agriculture discourses are being represented within a variety of social and cultural frameworks. More specifically, they illustrate how hipsters are constructing a subcommunity of agricultural professionals by commodifying material culture characteristics typically associated with traditional, family farming models. (Self-)Representations of hipster farmers are characterized by a pastoral sentimentalism and nostalgic yearning for a mythological rustic, American farm life. Fundamentally, hipster farmers grow food to assert their understanding of authentic farm life, as well as establish their own personal autonomy. However, going against the agricultural mainstream, hipster farmers produce goods aligned with the palettes of their principal consumers: other hipsters and the increasingly popular farm-to-table restaurant scene. According to census data provided by the United States Department of Agriculture, it seems their introduction to the American agricultural sector has led to an increased production of specialty crops within their own communities, as well as driving the production for local, artisanal crops up in other farming populations ("United States Department of Agriculture"). By recognizing that there is an increasing number of hipster farmers across a wide spectrum of locations, there is an indication of the viability and profitability of agriculture as a profession. Ultimately, by creating a paradigm shift in the economic, social, environmental, and cultural structures of what has been previously understood as American agriculture, hipster farmers may be providing motivation for the longevity of the farming industry in the United States.

Works Cited

"About." *Gold Cash Gold*, www.goldcashgolddetroit.com. Accessed April 27, 2015.

"About Us." *Modern Farmer*, modernfarmer.com/about-us/. Accessed April 25, 2015.

"ACRE Detroit." *Facebook*, www.facebook.com/ACREDetroit. August 22, 2011. Accessed April 20, 2015.

Acres U.S.A. February 2015.

Becker, Jane S. *Selling Tradition: Appalachia and the Construction of an American Folk, 1930–1940*. University of North Carolina Press, 1998.

Berry, Wendell. *The Unsettling of America: Culture and Agriculture*. Counterpoint Press, 1979.

Bouvier, Karen. "A New Generation of Farmers." *Strictly Food for Thought*, www.strictlyfoodforthought.com/articles/265. Accessed April 26, 2015.

Cassar, Jeremy. *How to Spot a Hipster*. Smith Street Books, 2016.

Charles, Dan, and Allison Aubrey. "With Style and Silo, 'Modern Farmer' Melds Agrarian with Urban Hip." *NPR*, November 1, 2014, www.npr.org/blogs/thesalt/2014/10/30/360181799/with- style-and-silo-modern-farmer-melds-agrarian-with-urban-hip. Accessed April 20, 2015.

Chase-Dunn, Christopher. "Dependency and World-Systems Theories." *The Blackwell Encyclopedia of Sociology*, edited by George Ritzer. Blackwell, 2007, pp. 1–3. *Wiley Online Library*, doi:10.1002/9781405165518.wbeosd031. Accessed March 2, 2015.

Conkin, Paul K. *A Revolution Down on the Farm: The Transformation of American Agriculture Since 1929*. University Press of Kentucky, 2009.

Danbom, David. *Born in the Country*. John Hopkins University Press, 2010.

Deloria, Phil. *Playing Indian*. Yale University Press, 1999.

Doll, Jen. "A 'Deconstructed, Purposeful' Cigarette for Hipsters." *The Atlantic*, August 30, 2012, www.theatlantic.com/culture/archive/2012/08/deconstructed-purposeful-cigarette-hipsters/324124. Accessed July 27, 2020.

Freeman, Lance. *There Goes the 'Hood: Views of Gentrification from the Ground Up*. Temple University Press, 2011.

Fried, Kate. "Food for Thought with Dr. Dennis Keeney." *Food and Water Watch*, February 2015, www.foodandwaterwatch.org/blogs/food-for-thought-with-dr-dennis-keeney. Accessed April 26, 2015.

Funda, Evelyn. *Weeds: A Farm Daughter's Lament*. University of Nebraska Press, 2013.

Gibson, D. W. *The Edge Becomes the Center: An Oral History of Gentrification in the Twenty-First Century*. Overlook Press 2015.

Greif, Mark. "Positions." *What Was the Hipster? A Sociological Investigation*, edited by Mark Greif, Kathleen Ross, and Dayna Tortorici. n+1 Foundation, 2010, pp. 4–13.

Greif, Mark. Preface. *What Was the Hipster? A Sociological Investigation*, edited by Mark Greif, Kathleen Ross, and Dayna Tortoici. n+1 Foundation, 2010, pp. vii–xvii.

Haimerl, Amy. "North Corktown CSA Will Be Next Best Thing to Backyard Garden This Summer." *Crain's Detroit Business*, April 21, 2014, www.crainsdetroit.com/article/20140421/BLOG017/140429978/north-corktown-csa-will-be-next-best-thing-to-backyard-garden-this. Accessed April 27, 2015.

Hamilton, David. *Deep River: A Memoir of a Missouri Farm*. University of Missouri Press, 2001.

Hayes, Shannon. *Radical Homemakers: Reclaiming Domesticity from a Consumer Culture*. Left to Write Press, 2010.

Hodgkins, Martha. *Letters to a Young Farmer: On Food, Farming, and Our Future*. Princeton Architectural Press, 2017.

Jackson, Wes. *Becoming Native to This Place*. University Press of Kentucky, 1994.

Jackson, Wes. *New Roots for Agriculture*. University of Nebraska Press, 1980.

Jacobs, Jane. *The Death and Life of Great American Cities*. Knopf Doubleday, 2016.

Jameson, Frederic. *Postmodernism, or, the Cultural Logic of Late Capitalism*. Duke University Press, 1991.

Jefferson, Thomas. *Notes on the State of Virginia*. 1785. Penguin Classics, 1998.

Kotz, David M. *The Rise and Fall of Neoliberal Capitalism*. Harvard University Press, 2015.

Logsdon, Gene. *The Contrary Farmer*. Chelsea Green, 1994.

Marx, Leo. *The Machine in the Garden: Technology and the Pastoral Ideal in America*. 1964. 35th ed. Oxford University Press, 2000.

Matchar, Emily. *Homeward Bound: Why Women Are Embracing the New Domesticity*. Simon and Schuster, 2013.

Modern Farmer. Winter 2014/15.

Moskowitz, Peter. *How to Kill a City*. PublicAffairs, 2017.

National Young Farmers Coalition. *Bootstrap Videos* Series. *Farmrun*, 2013, www.youngfarmers.org/2015/02/bootstrap-dairy-farmer-video-release/. Accessed April 20, 2015.

Parasuco, Trey. "Hipster." *Urban Dictionary*, November 22, 2007, www.urbandictionary.com/define.php?term=hipster. Accessed April 25, 2015.

Plotsky, Andrew. "About Farmrun." *Farmrun*, 2014, farmrun.com/about. Accessed April 20, 2015.

Rector, Sylvia. "Gold Cash Gold to Feature Seasonal 'Farmstead Cuisine.'" *Detroit Free Press*, December 3, 2014, www.freep.com/story/entertainment/dining/sylvia-rector/2014/12/03/gold-cash-gold-restaurant-open/19840005. Accessed April 27, 2015.

Rhodes, Richard. *Farm: A Year in the Life of an American Farmer*. Simon and Schuster, 1997.

Safransky, Sara. "Greening the Urban Frontier: Race, Poverty, and Resettlement in Detroit." *Geoforum*, vol. 56, 2014, abstract.

Segal, Howard P. "Leo Marx's 'Middle Landscape': A Critique, a Revision, and an Appreciation." *Reviews in American History*, vol. 5, no. 1, 1977, pp. 137–50.

Selasky, Susan. "Gold Cash Gold in Detroit's Corktown to Close Feb. 2." *Detroit Free Press*, January 11, 2020, www.freep.com/story/entertainment/dining/2020/01/11/gold-cash-gold-restaurant-detroit-corktown-close/4446508002/. Accessed September 8, 2020.

Selden Standard. 17 June 2020, www.seldenstandard.com/. Accessed April 27, 2015.

"10 Things the 2012 Census of Agriculture Tells Us about Family Farmers and Our Food System." *Farm Aid*, July 8, 2014, www.farmaid.org/site/c.qlI5IhNVJsE/b.9147949/k.D6B7/10_Things_the_new_Census_of_Agriculture_tells_us_about_Family_Farmers_and_Our_Food_System.htm. Accessed April 10, 2015.

Thoreau, Henry David. *Walden*. 1854. Thomas Y. Cromwell, 1910.

"2015 Annual Report." *National Young Farmers Coalition*, www.youngfarmers.org/wp-content/uploads/2014/06/Annual-Report-2015-FINAL-PAGES.pdf. Accessed April 14, 2015.

"United States Department of Agriculture." *USDA*, www.nass.usda.gov/AgCensus/. Accessed April 20, 2015.

Wiltz, Teresa. "Are Hipster Farmers the Future of Farming?" *The Pew Charitable Trusts*, November 7, 2014, www.pewtrusts.org/en/research-and-analysis/ blogs/stateline/2014/11/07/are-hipster-farmers-the-future-of-farming. Accessed April 16, 2015.

Zukin, Sharon. *Naked City*. Oxford University Press, 2010.

Hipster Fashion, Porn, and Body Politics

6

Hipsters and (Anti-)Fashion

Catharina Rüß

"How did the hipster burn his mouth? He ate pizza before it was cool." This joke, which appears in an article titled "Death of the Hipster" (Durham), clearly indicates hipsters are considered anything but cool these days (Michael 163). Their styles are satirized regularly in magazines, memes, and video clips.[1] In these parodies, specific looks are highlighted as identification codes of hipsters, although their aesthetics change continuously over time. What these presentations have in common, however, is that they focus on images of the body. They include a range of haircuts, clothes, and accessories, which can also be associated with different contexts such as Beatniks, indie, skaters or ravers, normcore or millennials (Bassil; Fischer; Hilber 124; Horning; Leland; Limar, "Shit Berlin Fashion Hipsters"). Furthermore, the term hipster also refers to diverse age groups.

Due to this broad spectrum of looks, this chapter shows that hipsters are not a phenomenon characterized by a specific material culture that could be precisely described, nor are they comparable with twentieth-century subcultures such as punk, gothic, or hip-hop (Greif, "Positionen" 23–31). Rather, taking as the main point the fashion discourse,[2] I consider the hipster as a historically and transnationally shaped concept that regularly occurs in media critiques of styles. In particular, I address, how the term hipster is used in the interpretation of outfits and body appearances. Analyzing mediated articulations of styles as part of the fashion discourse, which includes a

---

[1]See the hipster spoofing sketch series *Portlandia* (Flanagan) and the track *Being a Dickhead's Cool* on YouTube (Dangoor).

[2]I conceive of mediated articulations of styles as fashion media, which are a part of the fashion discourse.

discourse on hipsters, this study argues that the performativity of talking and writing about hipsters often appears as a technique to create the hipster as a template of both fashion[3] and anti-fashion. Based on the analysis of historical and contemporary representations of fashion, recurring logics of style narratives, aesthetics, and gender constructions, attributed to hipsters, will be explored. The sources examined range from academic and literary works to articles, blogs, and YouTube videos. The line of argumentation of this chapter is structured as follows. First, I provide a brief overview of the hipster as an umbrella term (Rabe 193) that includes two types of hipster figurations, the proto-hipster and the dot.hipster. These are examined in more detail in the subsequent discussion of typical motifs of hip dress practices. In this context, this chapter sheds light on the hipster's entanglement with anti-fashion, coolness, and masculinity, on the one hand, and the hipster as an expression of fashion and femininity, on the other. Drawing on the fashion theories of Walter Benjamin, Georg Simmel, Nickolas Pappas, and Thorstein Veblen, I demonstrate how the hipster sometimes appears as a synonym for fashion or fashion forerunners, sometimes as a formula for anti-fashion. Based on the examples of selected iconic looks, I problematize the simultaneity of contrary meanings of outfits by showing the adaption of hip (anti-)fashions by different groups. With reference to the German historical context, I will demonstrate how hip styles have been instrumentalized by radical rights to destroy modern society with the means of modernity (C. Schulze 22, my translation), that is, by using (anti-)fashions as propaganda tools and statements of their white-supremacist agenda.

Proto-Hipsters and Dot.Hipsters

In contemporary fashion discourses, the hipster takes shape in form of two, apparently, opposite figurations. These are no rigid opposites, as they show some overlaps, but they symbolize different accentuations in the valuation of dress practices. On the one hand, there is the idea of the historical hipster (Greif, "Positionen" 28), associated with art, American Beat, and counterculture from the 1940s to the 1960s, and anti-consumerism (Hebdige 46–51). This type, whose portrait is codetermined by the frequently quoted essays of Arnold Broyard and Norman Mailer (Gilson 44), tends to be associated with a positive image and is linked to alternative styles. In addition, this figure, as a supposed archetype of the first American subcultures of the twentieth century, often symbolizes subversiveness

[3]Following Georg Simmel, I conceive of fashion not only as clothes, but rather as a dynamic process in which outfits, designs, and aesthetics *change* and are performed, consumed, mediated, and interpreted differently depending on the *zeitgeist*.

associated with many following countercultures, from hippies to punks. In this chapter, this type will be referred to as proto-hipster. On the other hand, many articles picture the contemporary hipster, who is referred to here as dot.hipster.[4] This figuration is usually represented as a degeneration (Rabe 195) or a "far cry" (Quartz and Asp 219) of the "original" hipster (Gilson 44). Although the dress practices of this type sometimes contain references to the proto-hipster's approach to style, this figure holds "a generally pejorative set of connotations—particularly of inauthenticity and superficiality" (McCauley 15). This phenomenon seems to indicate that the dot.hipster is more often used as a "term of abuse" to stigmatize (McCauley 15) styles of people (Michael 66) in the "indie field" of the creative industries (Arsel and Thompson 792–3; Florida 190–211) than to describe a (sub) culture. In publications about hipster outfits in the twenty-first century, the dot.hipster rarely appears in connection with self-descriptions but rather as the figure of the Other (Haddow). Even scientific contributions are hardly based on studies about collectives, who contextualize their clothes as part of their own hipster culture (Greczy and Karamiras; Ikrath; Pountain and Robins; Quartz and Asp). This silence of dot.hipsters can be attributed to the phenomenon that it is "rare, if not impossible, to find an individual, who will proclaim themself a proud hipster" (Haddow). Contemporary hipsters are often accused of being "the darlings of viral marketers" (Lorentzen). Their outfits seem to express the values of the Western "society of singularities" (Reckwitz 275), such as cultural capital, unconventionality, and ironic self-reflection (Arsel and Thompson 794). At the same time, dot. hipsters are stereotyped as blind individualists, who cannot see that they belong to a class of conformist consumers (Haddow; Hilber; Ikrath 47; Kinzey 51). According to Phillip Ikrath, in contrast to the proto-hipster the contemporary hipster functions as an allegory for neoliberalism (93). Not surprisingly, in 2013 "only 16 percent of Americans" had "a favorable opinion of hipsters" (Quartz and Asp 219). This image of the dot.hipster can also be considered as a reverberation of the romanticizing of its predecessor; that is, the icon of the proto-hipster as a cool rebel.

Styles of Self-Exile

Many descriptions of proto-hipsters (cf. MacAdams; O'Brien) focus on portraits of writers of the Beat Generation such as Allen Ginsberg, William Burroughs, and Jack Kerouac. The following passage from the *Time Out*

[4]This differentiation refers in part to Quartz and Asp study, who distinguish the hipster phenomenon between the historical "rebel cool"—consumerism of the twentieth century—and the "dot.cool"—consumerism of the postindustrial age (175–246).

article "Kill the Hipster" (2007) shows how these men are glorified as nonconformists in contrast to their distorted echo of the present: "What distinguishes the zombie hipsters at large today from the 'white Negroes' Norman Mailer described in the 1950s is a lack of menace. The original hipster—Mailer had in mind James Dean and the Neal Cassady who inspired *On the Road*—was a 'philosophical psychopath' who might steal your car and drive it to Mexico" (Lorentzen). This statement demonstrates the tendency of using Beatniks[5] and hipsters as synonyms. Even in academic research on historical hipsters, these two words are hardly distinguished (Hebdige 46–51; MacAdams 14; Pountain and Robins 66–70).[6] Furthermore, despite the close entanglement of the Beatniks with the Black community, the style of the proto-hipster is mostly outlined as a look of an American white man. The dominance of men in the fashion discourse about hipsters is also evident in the academic field. As Jay McCauley Bowstead points out in his 2019 study *Menswear Revolution*, the "image conjured up by the term 'hipster' ... is almost always male and some 80 percent of the results generated by a Google Image search are of men" (15). Particularly, this phenomenon is also mirrored in explorations on menswear such as *Fashion and Masculinities in Popular Culture* (2017), where a chapter is dedicated to the hipster.

Repeatedly, Mailer's concept of the "white negro" (1957) plays a central role in this context. It is mentioned in analyses of style (Hebdige 47; Geczy and Karaminas, *Fashion and Masculinities* 56), in which historical hipsters are presented as loners, who are idealizing African American culture as an exit strategy from bourgeois restrictions (Geczy and Karaminas, *Fashion and Masculinites* 54–5). The proto-hipster personifies the "old bohemian idea" (Frank 13) of an "underground poet" (Broyard 727), who tries to embody an alliance with outlaws. From the point of view of the white bohemian, identification with Black and Hispanic communities symbolizes the rebellion against the Protestant work ethic, linked to White Anglo-Saxon Protestants (WASPs) and entrepreneurs in stiff suits. Thus, the Beatniks are imagined as rebels, who distance themselves from this appearance by questioning the dominant dress code of bourgeois men's fashion.

They wear a bricolage (Hebdige 103) of items from diverse contexts that express proximity to outsiders, especially to "those assigned to the bottom of the hierarchy: the African American, the petty criminal" (Quartz and Asp 176), the working class as well as the gay subculture. Many studies on fashion connect the subversiveness of proto-hipsters with casual outfits

---

[5]The meaning of the word Beatnik is also characterized by fuzziness. Writers rarely differentiate between Beat, Beatniks, or Beat Generation nor different styles of the Beat movement during the years 1944–9, 1950–6, and 1957–63 (Shakouchi 1272).

[6]Taking into account this narrative persistence, the terms Beatnik and proto-hipster are also used as synonyms here.

associated with the "big wide world," as well as with gangs wearing zoot suits and "guerrilla" (Broyard 272) warfare. The hip signature look of the 1940s and 1950s is connected with baggy chinos, jeans, creased unbuttoned gingham shirts, sailor tops, black turtlenecks and leather jackets, berets, desert boots and sandals, crucifix necklaces, sunglasses, and tattoos (Hebdige 48–9; Kerouac 124–33, Welters, "The Beat Generation" 145–68). These styles also appear in poems of Bob Kaufman (11, 26). The Beat style in particular also stands for drugs (Kotynek and Cohassey 175), "sex and dirt and communism" (Johnson 233).

The proto-hipster outfit is also identified as a homage to French existentialists, who were regarded as role models for American bohemians, who traveled to Paris and adapted the "Left Bank café intellectual style—the black beret, the horn-rimmed glasses, the wee goatee" (MacAdams 24) which later became the stereotypical Beatnik look.[7] By moving to "sweet slums of Bohemia" (Johnson 208), Europe, Morocco, or Mexico, the American Beatniks tried "to break out into forms" that seemed to be "unrestricted and new" (162). This attitude of "somewhereness" (Broyard 727) is a crucial motif that is attributed to the informally collaged proto-hipster look. Kerouac, for instance, is portrayed as a man, who went on the trip with only a "canvas bag," wearing a lumberjack shirt and expressing the image of the drifter with "Mexican *huaraches*, the trademark of the New York Bohemian intellectual" (Johnson 22). His self-defined Otherness is regarded not as a stigma but as a style; not as a sign of marginalization but as a choice.

Today, outfits that are associated with this style of self-exile reappear as new trends from time to time. Mostly, those garments that are reminiscent of road dust and shabby workwear, such as plaid shirts, leather jackets, or destroyed denim, suggest the fantasy of vagabondage. They stand less for labor than for a cool outsiderism (Rüß, "Looking Cool"). This motif characterizes the narrative of the "dumpster chic," which takes the idea of ragpickers and migrant workers as models for new looks. Throughout the history of fashion, this approach is transformed into many trends (Cole 25–39) described as boho or bobo, punk, grunge, heroin chic, or white trash. At the beginning of the 2000s, for instance, magazines labeled indie bands—like The *Strokes*, who wore "greasy $200 haircuts" (Martin 89), vintage T-shirts, faded black skinny jeans, and leather jackets[8]—as hipsters (Lifter 39). A similar style, in combination with tousled hair and smokey

[7]For the female Beatniks, it was more difficult to express their cool style, because "women's jeans were not available ... until the 1950s, and universities and businesses could ... legally require women to wear dresses and skirts" (See 2). They protested against these restrictions by buying men's clothing and sewing their own shirts and jeans.

[8]In the late 1990s, Hedi Slimane and Raf Simons brought the "indie boy" look to the catwalk as an alternative fashion (McCauley 115–28; Lifter 43–72).

eyes, has been represented by models like Kate Moss (Lifter 75–7), Cory Kennedy (Tortorici 102) or Erin Wasson (Odell). Wasson was condemned as a "silly hipster" after confessing in an interview: "The people with the best style for me are the people that are the poorest" (Odell). This strategy of aestheticizing poverty repeatedly appears in luxury fashion (Lynge-Jorlén 69) and often leads to scandals.[9]

The proto-hipster's appearance is also associated with self-exoticism, in the sense of suggesting "non-whiteness." This idea refers to the bohemian tradition (Wilson) of representing wilderness as a withdrawal from the establishment and "an alliance with the non-western world" by combining clothing from foreign cultures, subsumed under terms such as gypsy, folk, or oriental (Rüß, "Imagining Cool Fashion" 243). In Western societies these garments are often theorized as fixed costumes of anti-fashion that supposedly do not change (Barnard 34–5), although they modify over time. The Mexican sandals of the proto-hipster, for instance, can be seen as a manifestation of fashion resistance of the bohemian (Lifter 73–4). In the course of student protests during the 1960s, this idea became popular as "hippy" clothing, which has similarities to today's boho look. "American Indian inspired beads ... fringes and feathers" (Miles 103) are combined with ornamental Art Nouveau fabrics. As the fashion historian Valerie Steele points out, in this context the "long ago ... and the far away ... provided inspiration for individualized ensembles" as expressions for "anti-conformity, anti-consumption, and anti-hierachy" (9). Overall, this dress practice is perceived as an expression of a secret knowledge based on travels and cultural capital (Bourdieu). On the one hand, it is seen as a sign of appreciation (Davis 97), on the other, it is criticized as an instance of "hipster appropriation" (Gilson 36). In particular, from 2005 to 2013, with the rise of the popularity of music festivals like Coachella, the hippie look reappeared as a "boho chic" which was connected with dot.hipsters (Lifter 73–104). During these years, the style transformed from an alternative outfit of indie fans into a "mainstream hype" produced by fast fashion companies, which started to launch festival collections promoted by celebrities (73–104). In this context, especially "feathered headdresses" were criticized as signals of "Native appropriations" (Andrews).

Although the styles associated with hipsters came and went, there is a typical narrative attached to many of these looks: When they first appear, they are perceived as demarcations from the mainstream, as something "outsiderish," weird, or exotic. The aesthetic of self-exile is characterized by the principles of "the far away" and "the long ago" in terms of collaging

---

[9]In 1960, Yves Saint Laurent provoked a scandal with his Dior collection inspired by the Beatniks. In 2018, Balenciaga was accused of staging a heroin chic because the company positioned mannequins with hoodies in crouched positions in the window display of Selfridges.

codes that not everyone is supposed to understand (Nagle 108). This dress practice is often associated with the cool (anti-)fashion of those "who are hip and in the know" (Lifter 87).

Anti-Fashion and Masculinities

The proto-hipster is repeatedly imagined as the innovator of cool (Quartz and Asp 177).[10] Overall, coolness in the area of the language of style articulates a "partially resisting play with stylish vocabulary" (Rüß, "Imagining Cool Fashion" 241). This play articulates "distance and autonomy as a whole" (241). Cool appearances are commonly characterized by the embodiment of transgressions in terms of *épater le bourgeois*. They are undermining bourgeois "dress codes and mainstream limits of taste by fluctuating between two poles: the pole of up-dressing and the pole of down-dressing" (241). Therefore, cool personalities occur in different looks, for example, in shabbiness or the elegance of the dandy as well as in flamboyant camp styles (Sontag). The coolness connected with the concept of the proto-hipster is most often associated with a down-dressed appeal, communicating an "I don't care" attitude, a staging of distance from glamourous luxury.[11] This style suggests especially the denial of conventional status badges.

According to Thorstein Veblen's *Theory of the Leisure Class* (1899), the gain in prestige in modern capitalism is connected with conspicuous fashion consumption (Veblen 118–23). Taking this analysis into account, the imagination of the proto-hipster, who shows disdain for the hegemonic system of "commodity fetishism" (Marx 163), can be identified as a representation of anti-fashion (Davis 98; Steele 9). Veblen, moreover, conceptualizes fashion as a terrain of femininity in bourgeois milieus. He refers to the beginning of modernity, when the middle-class woman was assigned to the role of representing her husband's economic success by investing his salary in expensive fashions (Veblen 119). In this sense, the image of the proto-hipster in shabby workwear not only implies a disapproval of bourgeois values but also bourgeois femininity in terms of ostentatious glamour. Despite the emergence of numerous cool women in pop culture (Dinerstein 33–6), many writers imagine coolness, supposedly shaped by proto-hipsters, as a "mode of masculinity" (Fraiman xii). In this vein, the look of female Beatniks with short haircuts and black clothes is interpreted as a cool expression of masculinity, namely gamin style, a French word referring to a woman acting

---

[10]The word "cool" gained popularity in the 1950s (Geczy and Kamarinas, *Fashion and Masculinites* 48). However, coolness is a concept that cannot be fixed to only one specific period, country, or group (Rüß, "Imagining Cool Fashion" 241; Pountain and Robins).

[11]In contrast, the concept of the dot.hipster tends to be connected to a broader range of styles. This type is also associated with bold logos, camp, and kitsch (McCauley 15).

like a boy. As Johnson remembers, Françoise Sagan, who wore a "gamin haircut," made this style popular, when she published her novel *Bonjour Tristesse* in 1955. She embodied "coolness" and served as a role model for female Beatniks (104). Although anti-fashion is a "form of fashion rather than an alternative or showing the way to alternatives" (Pappas 136), hip down dressings are mostly romanticized as manly liberations of "fashion's dictates" and as rejections of the "loss of autonomy" triggered by fashion (131). These styles are seen as cancellations of the "social contract of fashion" (136), regardless of its chances at success (131–2). In particular, anti-fashion suggests longevity in opposition to the transience of trends (Barnard 37). As Nickolas Pappas emphasizes, tattoos, one of the features most often ascribed to hipsters, make this ideal particularly clear. Unlike clothes, they cannot be changed according to the season (144). In keeping with this fantasy of timelessness, also the non-color black is conceived as the anti-fashion shade par excellence. It triggers notions of a superiority above fashion's "hysteria" and color changes. This is why black is considered a mode of coolness. Its darkness suggests a sublime position outside the accelerated "shopping madness." After the French Revolution, black and shades of grey wiped out bright tones in men's clothes (Hollander 131–2). Whereas women still wore colorful dresses, black evolved increasingly into a proclamation for manly sovereignty and the seriousness of the revolutionaries. In this sense, black anti-fashion implies the consistence of not only masculinity but also rebelliousness. Following in this tradition, Parisian avant-gardes and American proto-hipsters elevated black to their signature tone (Shakouchi 1272). Today, especially black hoodies define street styles from protestors and gangsters to hip musicians and designers (Turney; Watzlawik 75–98). Moreover, the idea of anti-fashion as timelessness is traditionally associated with uniforms (Pappas 136) like the breton shirt. Kerouac compared the Beat drifterism with "Popeye the sailor" (127–31). In doing so, he alludes to the subversiveness of the bohemian culture, in which the sailor[12] symbolizes both a "rugged masculinity" and a "queer identity" (Geczy and Karaminas, *Fashion and Masculinities* 67). Especially the breton shirt, known as a French outfit of creatives like Cocteau or Chanel at the beginning of the twentieth century (67), evolved into a key item of the Beatniks. Dressed in blue and white stripes, Bob Kaufman and James Dean expressed their dissatisfaction with the establishment. Later, the shirt was considered a piece of nonconformism, worn by punk and indie scenes (Knee 118–19; Lifter 79), but it was also interpreted as a preppy "fashion classic" (Alexander). Finally, in the 2020s, the proto-hipster motif of maritime finds its expression in the "shipster"-style attributed to the dot.hipster. This look is characterized by

[12]The mariner personifies the anti-bourgeois on the sea, an area where conventional humans do not belong (Geczy and Karaminas, *Fashion and Masculinities* 67).

"a small beanie hat", dark coats with cropped pants "above commando sole boots" (Renwick).

According to Pappas, beside black, tattoos, and uniforms, the most radical expression of anti-fashion is to be the negation of all eye-catching attires (135–50). While in Western societies plain clothes represent male respectability, independence, and intellectuality (Hollander 147), especially outfits characterized by eye-catching fabrics, artistic embellishments and cuts tend to be perceived as products of fashion's commercial dictate (Hollander 258). "There is a long-standing and consistent belief" in Western societies that fashion "can be separated from, and is less serious than ... content. ... This theory about the separability of form and content ... is the root of the common prejudice that fashion" is not only "trivial and unimportant" (Barnard 15) but a terrorizing dictatorship (Hollander 258) which distracts from the "authentic true core of being" by selling "frivolous" glamorous "mask[s]" (Barnard 15). In the twentieth and twenty-first centuries, the attempt to deconstruct this "regime of trend productions" also proves to be a recurring motif of anti-fashion (Hollander 260–1) and dress practices ascribed to hipsters, along with the mode of self-exile. Since the 2010s this is reflected in the unisex normcore aesthetic embodied by "fashion hipsters" (Rabkin). Ironically, this style approach was proclaimed by the trend agency K-Hole in 2013: "The most different thing to do is to reject being different all together" (23). Their credo of pretending fashion indifference was orchestrated from the very beginning by the label Vetements[13] within the fashion industry. From the standpoint of a "bourgeois stability" (Fischer) normcore can be regarded as a down-dressed class appropriation that suggests an "I don't care"-attitude toward "the Chanel logo on cashemere" (Rabkin). The androgynous streetwear of the ordinary "lower middle class" (Tudor) with oversize hoodies combined with an "it's so bad that it's good" humor (Rabkin) popularized the idea of "becoming distinctive by being indistinctive" (Tudor). In contrast to boho, for example, normcore suggests less self-exile uniqueness, but rather stands in the tradition of male French revolutionaries,[14] who wanted to disempower fashion as a status symbol of the effeminate aristocracy.

[13]In this context, one of the brand's founders, Demna Gvasalia, is often described as an "alternative fashion hero" and rebel (Aronowsky Cronberg).

[14]See Anne Hollander's study on the change of men's fashion during the French Revolution. The clothes of the revolutionaries were inspired by the dark Anglo-Saxon men's fashion, which was connoted with democracy, Protestantism, and, of course, the American Revolution. From the eighteenth century onward, London in particular became the capital of men's tailoring as well as the new cotton industry, whereas Paris stood for Catholicism, aristocracy, silk and feminine robes. Since the French Revolution, fashion in the Western world became more and more divided into two styles based on gender: men generally wore plain suits and women wore flashier, colorful dresses (Hollander 132–83).

Overall, it is no secret that, already at the beginning of the twentieth century, the rise of countercultures was determined by entanglements of anti-fashions and fashions through collaborations of artists, the media, and the fashion industry (Davis 99). Kerouac criticized this effect of mainstreamization in his memoir: "They have beatniks routines on TV, starting with satires about girls in black and fellows in jeans with snap-knives and sweatshirts and swastikas tattooed under their armpits" (131–3). But as Valerie Steele emphasizes, alternative styles were "never effectively or for long a form of anti-fashion" (10). Notwithstanding this fact, numerous presentations and exhibitions with titles like *You Say You Want a Revolution* (2017) still create the impression of proto-hipsters as cool innovators of anti-fashion (Quartz and Asp 173–99). These depictions tend to display these "American Rebels" (Kotynek and Cohassey) as mentors of numerous subcultures of the twentieth century.

Fashion Forerunners and Femininities

The reemergence of hipsters in the course of the 2000s is accompanied by an increase of hipster critiques (Ikrath 67). In YouTube clips like "Shit Berlin Fashion Hipsters Say" or blog posts, the term "hipster" functions as a "placeholder for 'whatever young people seem to like' " (Fischer), and it is used to unmask trendsetters, who are accused of pretending to ignore trends, even though they change their outfit if it becomes mainstream. They are typified as "fashion insiders" (Rabkin), who "like things that not many people like ... because not many people like ... them" (Durham). Overall, the narrative about dot.hipster styles is dominated by degradations (Ikrath 68–70). It becomes apparent in the way of how bloggers and cultural critics interpret hipster looks as codes of emptiness. As McCauley states, especially the critiques in "blogs that arose during the late 2000s, including *Hackney Hipster Hate* or *Look at This Fucking Hipster*," set the focus "on male hipster's failure to conform to orthodox masculinity, but it is also significant that accusations leveled at hipsters are so frequently centered upon narcissism, inauthenticity, and pretention" (16). Dayna Tortorici makes a similar argument. However, she emphasizes that especially women, who are considered female hipsters, are not recognized for their work but are reduced to their outward appearance and either praised as "it-girls" or condemned as "fashion victims" (99–101). Typical outfits, like vintage apparels, are identified as "backward looking" (Fischer) purchases of relics from "style tribes" (Polhemus 14) under the reign of retromania (Reynolds). Whereas the dress practice of the Beatnik is imagined as a statement of rebelliousness, art, and creativity, dot.hipsters "seem incapable of doing anything creative beyond borrowing from the past" (Kinzey 41). In "Death of the Hipster," Alex Durham marks hipster styles as a sign of "the dilution of culture," similar to Cecilia Winterhalter who, in her reflections on hipster culture, speaks of a "supermarket style" consisting of materials from "a huge, meaningless depot to plunder" (122) that could express anything and everything. In the fashion discourse, this characterization refers to several looks from bold logos, vintage, pastel colors "of the '80s and '90s" (Fischer) to normcore (Tudor). All these aesthetics, connected with dot.hipsters, are regularly described as a particularly hopeless attempt at suggesting meaning, leading to nothing more than new hypes "becoming the past" (Fischer). For this reason, the death of hipsters is regularly proclaimed (Bassil; Durham; Hilber; Horning; Leszkiewicz; Lorentzen). These obituaries usually refer only to an outdated trend like the lumberjack beard. However, transformed into a new aesthetic, like the shipster style, the immortal figure of the hipster reappears.

This persistence of obituaries and resurrections proves the liveliness of the hipster as a concept characterized by its paradoxical double-folded rhetoric. Not only does it contain two temporally separate meanings—the proto-hipster (figure of the past) and dot.hipster (figure of the present)—but it also contains two stylistic concepts: anti-fashion and fashion, including their dialectical relationship. As described above, the motifs for the dress practices related to the proto-hipster are more associated with anti-fashion and masculinity, whereas the dot.hipsters are more equated with fashion. In this sense, the dot.hipster comes closer to the bourgeois idea of femininity. Hip millennials are, as Molly Fischer argues, "always performing, always watching themselves be [*sic*] watched. Maybe that was once primarily the condition of women, but it seems increasingly to apply to us all." This is the mode, which Tortorici considers to be a female facet of the hipster: a life in quotation marks, always performing acts of self-expression in front of the camera (101).

The dual face of the hipster is comparable to the dialectical quality of fashion, which can be explained with Walter Benjamin's and Georg Simmel's theories: the dot.hipster's affection for vintage conforms to Benjamin's and Simmel's notion of fashion. Both consider fashion as an agent of "captialism's will of change" (Geczy and Karaminas, "Walter Benjamin" 82) which tends to annihilate meanings. This change is described as a process moved by two motifs: destroying mainstream looks and producing new looks by quoting historical references which are staged as the "new anti-mainstream now." Benjamin claims that the "spectacle, the unique self-construction of the newest in the medium of what has been, makes for the true dialectical theater of fashion" (Benjamin 64). Furthermore, Simmel describes fashion as a social process that is based on a dual mode, on the one hand the drive toward imitation and on the other hand the drive toward separation. In this sense, Simmel constitutes material objects, related to fashion, as empty signs in motion. For him, the dynamic of the "in and out" of fashion is not based on content but exclusively on the basal algorithm of distinction, that is, the social practice of demarcation and imitation (15–20). Similar to Veblen, Simmel constitutes fashion as a terrain of femininity. For him, its acceleration is primarily caused by women's fascination with new clothes, which he conceives as an act of compensation (23–4). This notion can be traced back in part to dominant nineteenth-century gender ideologies that ascribed women an affinity for shopping as a signal for their lack of sanity.

Today, this history of imagining fashion, consumerism, and change as feminine is central in order to understand the rhetoric of hipster bashings, which seems to use the word hipster as a metaphor for fashion victims. As McCauley argues, most of these condemnations refer to male "fashionable scenesters" (14), whose outfits reflect nonconformism. In contrast, "female hipsterism" (16) is less the target of attacks, because it seems to be more "difficult to distinguish" it "from other forms of fashionable femininity," "female and fashionable is considered as normal" (16). Especially men, who embody effeminacy in the sense of questioning traditional gender roles, are "stigmatized" in "aggressively phobic hipster discourses" (19). They are condemned as advocates of "castration" and the "lack of masculinity" (Hilber 125). These bashings have the effect of a double victimization. For they seem to be expressions of "fearing femininity" (McCauley 19) and gender fluidities. Male passions for new clothes are criticized as externally controlled by the capitalistic system, as well as non-male (19).

According to Simmel's analysis, an elite regularly demonstrates its capital by wearing new looks that initially appear as ugly anti-fashion in the sense of nonconformist outfits but at some point, automatically lead to new fashions, because these outfits are copied by other groups trying to be part of the "cool scene." In today's fashion discourse, hipsters are often identified with multiple milieus, from precarious baristas to highly paid influencers accused of embodying an alternative look. However, as Veblen notes, fashion, with its emphasis on the special and different, also evokes feelings of envy (20–77). Thus, hipster hatred might also be rooted in a subtle sense of feeling excluded by those privileged creatives, who mark boundaries of hipness by "happily" flaunting their money in designer hoodies (Bassil). However, hipster hatred can presumably also be an expression of demarcation behavior on the part of actors in these milieus who claim to be creative, and elevated above fashion, while at the same time distancing themselves from those who devalue them as inauthentic "copy-cat hipsters" because they supposedly follow a certain lifestyle trend.

Hipster and Nipster—Nature Boys and Proud Boys

As illustrated above, not only the character of the two-faced hipster figure but also the meaning of its clothes seems to be contradictory. This polysemy of styles becomes apparent in the fact that the garments can be read as signs of progressiveness as well as conservatism. Hence, anti-fashion and "nature looks" attributed to hipsters, for example, have a potential to express both left-wing and right-wing ideologies. Since the 2010, particular alt-right movements in the United States and Europe have appeared in hipsterish outfits. In 2014 the *Rolling Stone* described German neo-Nazis, who "try to give hate a stylish face," as "nipsters." By appropriating modern (anti-)fashion, the "nipster may be impossible to distinguish from a regular hipster" (Esculapio). In recent years many scientists have published studies on this topic. Cynthia Miller-Idriss and Christoph Schulze, for instance, show how far-rights in Germany adapt hip streetwear or, to be precise, instrumentalize heritages of proto-hipsterish anti-fashions in order to suggest an aura of "up to date" coolness. This strategy of style confusion as a method of "downplay[ing] the harm" of a "white- supremacist ... agenda" (Gaugele 712) can also be observed in globalized right-wing cultures such as the Proud Boys, an organization with chapters in North America and Europe. They cultivate their rejection of the establishment with "hipster codes" (712). These codes include multiple looks (Miller-Idriss). According to the *Rolling Stone*, in 2014 the nipsters (Rogers) appeared with skinny jeans, beards, and plug piercings which were interpreted as appropriations of the style of the lumberjack hipster, who is mostly associated with the "desire for something pre-industrial" (Fischer).

A historical perspective shows that similar processes of imagination and appropriation have occurred repeatedly throughout history: In the nineteenth century, bohemian critics of modernity wore workwear and beards as signs of their rejection of the industrialization. Especially, Walt Whitman and Henry David Thoreau, "leadfigures" of hip dropouts (Leland 39–56), preached craftmanship and the contemplation of the "primitive intensity of nature" (49). Thoreau condemned Parisian fashion in his book *Walden* (1854): "I say, beware of all enterprises that require new clothes" (Thoreau 22). This "back-to-nature"-idea in connection with the praise of beards, simplicity, and handicraft was also part of the aesthetic agenda of the *lebens reform* movement in Germany at the end of the nineteenth century. This movement can be situated in the context of a broader European constellation of avant-gardists, like the British Arts and Crafts movement, who criticized fashion as an effect of mass production. In particular, they rejected restrictive corsets and shapes of the high white-collar establishment (Bertschik 91–111). In these reform circles loose fittings and loose hair as well as sportified trained bodies symbolized a free mind and healthiness (Mrozek 272–3). Some men of this movement, as Bodo Mrozek has argued, appeared as "jesus figures" (284, my translation)[15] with a style of long hair and Roman sandals, which shows similarities to some contemporary hippies or hipsters (281–7). Their ideal of vegetarianism and athletic bodies (Wedemeyer-Kolwe 182) represents what Fred Davis describes as "fitness naturalism" (90), one of the recurring motifs of anti-fashion. A small group of the German reform members emigrated to California, where they founded a community named Nature Boys and spread their ideas throughout the United States (Kennedy; Marchant). Some aspects of their holistic philosophy and anti-fashion approach of "naturalism" can be found in the Beat Generation of the 1950s, who "embraced non-Western religious ideas" and "avoided spending money on their appearance by purchasing second-hand clothes" (Welters, "The Natural Look" 492). Allen Ginsberg, for instance, propagated "nakedness as the best defense against the world" (qtd. in Johnson 78). Like many nonconformists of New York's bohemian scene, he began sporting a beard in the late 1950s. In the present, their aesthetic finds its echo in a lifestyle of "sustainability, ... DIY aesthetics [and] wellness" (Bigalke 61–86) that Anna Lesziewicz in the *NewStatesmen* describes as characteristic of the hipsters of the late 2010s—mostly associated with left-wing ideologies.

A closer look at the German *lebens reform* movement, however, shows that the "back-to-nature" ideology cannot always be clearly positioned politically. This movement included many heterogenous groups from progressive artists to right-wing oriented conservatives. Nowadays, their lifestyle of healthiness, vegan diet, muscles, and beards is not only reflected in bohemian or left-wing milieus but can also be found in national-conservative and radical-right scenes in Europe and the United States. The credo of "fitness naturalism" is mirrored in the nipsters' "hyper masculinity" (Kutner 1) as an expression of "the survival of the fittest." In fact, the body ideals of the Nature Boys and Proud Boys do not differ as markedly as it might seem at first glance. In particular, the national-conservative actors of the *lebens reform* movement condemned fashion as the opposite of healthiness, an ill artifice of capitalism (Wedemeyer-Kolwe 182–3). They propagated muscles (Theweleit), beards, and wide clothes as a statement against the Parisian feminized decadence and "Jewish capitalism" (Bertschik 302). Their body ideal was based on their "blood and soil" ideology, which included ideas of anti-semitism and anti-fashion, nationalism and naturalism (Bertschik; Mrozek 272–3; Wedemeyer-Kolwe 182). These ideas were partially adopted by the Nazis some years later (Theweleit). After their rise to power,

[15]Some life reformers aligned their appearance with pictures of the Messiah. The long-haired Christ was imagined as a charismatic nonconformist, who paid more attention to the body than to clothing. Reference was made above all to the figure of the image of the half-naked Jesus wearing a loincloth, which was interpreted as a divine legitimation for nudism (Mrozek 283).

FIGURES 6.1 and 6.2. *These illustrations of Allen Ginsberg and Gavin McInnes point out the seeming similarities between their looks. Illustrator: Johannes Siegmund, December 2020.*

Note: The illustration of Ginsberg (Figure 6.1) is based on a photograph of Allen Ginsberg in which he is pictured with Jack Kerouac and other writers. The photo was published in the October 5, 1958, issue of the *San Francisco Examiner* alongside a review of Kerouac's book *The Dharma Bums* by Luther Nichols. The illustration of McInnes (Figure 6.2) is based on a 2017 documentary "Who are the Proud Boys?" showing Gavin McInnes wearing a Fred Perry shirt and giving a speech (CBC News: The National).

the National Socialists referred to the nationalistic reformist Paul Schultze-Naumburg, who compared Parisian fashion with prostitutes (Bertschik 91). According to the fascist ideology, the body of the Germans should above all be hardened and healthy, and the clothes should look modern, not in the sense of "capricious" and "exaggerated" like the Parisian couture but in the sense of functional (292–3) and "down-to-earth" (Kraft 22, my translation). The Nazis called for loose-fitting uniforms in contrast to the "Jewish fashion" that would restrict men (Bertschik 302). Thus, as Kerstin Kraft notes, National Socialist ideology appeared contradictory with regard to clothing. On the one hand, it emphasized naturalness and peasant cult and on the other hand, mechanization (21). On the one hand, the German clothing in the fascist era was characterized by ultramodern, multifunctional cuts; on the other hand, it referred to traditional costumes (21).

With regard to the longue durée of male chauvinism, it is not surprising that Gavin McInnes—once cofounder of the magazine *Vice* (Greif, "Nachruf" 120)[16] and from 2016 until 2018 (Wilson) leader of the Proud Boys—showed his naked torso with tattoos at a conference at the University of California, Los Angeles, in 2010 (Kellogg). Although he seems to sport a similar beard like Ginsberg in the late 1950s, his body performance communicates a different message. The Jewish pacifist Ginsberg tried to express peacefulness, openness, and vulnerability with his appearance, whereas McInnes's body presentation triggers notions of aggression and fight. His performance functions as both an expression of his fascistic fantasy of masculine power[17] and a staging of himself as a rebellious "tough guy" through a gesture that references the practice of violent dancing with naked tattooed upper bodies at punk or hardcore concerts (M. Schulze 277). The suggestion of subcultural subversion contains and simultaneously conceals his fascist rebellion. It is a method of hiding on the one hand and "foster[ing] violent ... racist intentions" (Gaugele 727) on the other. In a similar way, McInnes instrumentalizes the double meaning of iconic styles such as Fred Perry's black and yellow trimmed polo shirt (Iqbal). On the one hand, it stands for British working class and countercultures like rude boys or ska-punks (Iqbal).[18] On the other hand, as a garment that has "a long history of being part of the uniform worn by racist skinheads" (Reid and Valasik 24) and that has not been transformed in its design for almost

---

[16]McInnes was socialized in the punk scene. In 2008 he left *Vice* (Greif, "Nachruf" 131). In 2016 he founded the Proud Boys who share a collective identity that "is one of a hipster persona that uses irony and humor to facilitate far-right arguments that attack the political ... status quo" (Reid and Valasik 24).

[17]The term fantasy refers to Klaus Theweleit's study *Männerphantasien* (engl. *Male Fantasies*) about the fascist ideal of a steel body as a defense against softness (vol. 1, 311).

[18]The shirt was designed in 1952. According to the brand's web page, it has become a "British subcultural uniform since the 1950s, adopted by each generation as their own." The company

seventy years (Iqbal), it can also be interpreted as a symbol of anti-change and anti-fashion. Dressed in this uniform, the Proud Boys embody their "chauvinism" and demand for a return to the "natural order of things" in which women are assigned the role of "housewives" (Kutner 3). Besides subcultural clothes, many far-rights also adapt "hipster styles" like normcore (Gaugele 716). Again, the meanings of these outfits are contradictory, yet rooted in particular historical and cultural contexts and dress practices. Even if normcore implies trendiness in terms of fashionable streetwear in the media, in the context of the far-rights it foremost represents anti-fashion as a rebellion against extravagant designs, dressed-up styles and effeminacy. The polysemic meanings of clothes turn them into perfect tools for the game of propaganda. If far-rights appear in polo shirts, they do not refer to fashion but rather to anti-fashion and its fantasy of a stable masculinity.

Conclusion

An analysis of hipsters and (anti-)fashion shows that the hipster appears as a generic term for various changing outfits, depending on the temporal and spatial background. Differentiating between proto-hipster and dot. hipster, I tried to characterize the double face of this phenomenon. Its subtle duality seems to be the reason for its powerful persistence in the fashion discourse. For it is precisely because of its indeterminacy and ambivalence that the hipster can be used as a template for labeling different styles and their inherent simultaneity of contrary meanings such as nonconformism and conformism, social progressivism and conservatism, and last but not least fashion and anti-fashion. But despite the coming and going of various trends, some stable motifs of dress practices can be identified—such as the style of self-exile—that are regularly associated with the hipster. Especially the dot.hipster is repeatedly linked to insubstantiality and the eternal flight from the mass, ideas that are central to Western ideas about fashion. This is probably one reason why the word hipster is so often used by fashion critics in the context of satires or complains about urban trends, distinctions or imitations, adaptions and appropriations of looks. In conclusion, however, it can be stated that (anti-)fashions always include possible processes of recoding, shift, and change. And yet certain garments carry a nonarbitrary potential of meanings and narratives that makes them attractive for strategic confusions of styles, due to their being interwoven into an international, mobile web of references made up of historical and contemporary stories.

---

has "repeatedly spoken out against its use by far-right groups" (Elan). Its chairman John Flynn said "Fred [Perry] was the son of a working-class socialist MP who became a world tennis champion at a time when tennis was an elitist sport. He started a business with a Jewish businessman from Eastern Europe" (Elan).

Works Cited

Alexander, Ella. "Why the Breton Top Will Never Lose Its Appeal." *Hapers Bazaar*, harpersbazaar.my/fashion/why-the-breton-top-will-never-lose-its-appeal/. Accessed December 20, 2020.

Andrews, Jessica. "How to Avoid Cultural Appropriation at Coachella." *TeenVogue*, April 13, 2018, www.teenvogue.com/story/coachella-cultural-appropriation. Accessed December 20, 2020.

Aronowsky Cronberg, Anja. "The Revolution Will Be Branded Vetements." *Vestoj*, April 17, 2016, vestoj.com/the-revolution-will-be-branded-vetements/. Accessed December 20, 2020.

Arsel, Zeynep, and Craig J. Thompson. "Demythologizing Consumption Practices: How Consumers Protect Their Field-Dependent Identity Investments from Devaluing Marketplace Myths." *Journal of Consumer Research*, vol. 37, no. 5, 2011, pp. 791–806.

Barnard, Malcolm. *Fashion Theory: An Introduction*. Routledge, 2014.

Bassil, Ryan. "How the Early Thirties Hypebeast Replaced the Hipster." *Vice Magazine*, October 25, 2019, www.vice.com/en_uk/article/evjq77/hypebeast-new-hipster-mens-fashion-lifestyle. Accessed December 20, 2020.

Benjamin, Walter. *The Arcades Project*. Harvard University Press, 1999.

Bertschik, Julia. *Mode und Moderne: Kleidung als Spiegel des Zeitgeistes in der deutschsprachigen Literatur (1770–1945)*. Böhlau Verlag, 2005.

Bilgalke, Bernadett. "Healthy, Happy, Holy: 'Yoga' und Selbstverhältnisse um 1900 und 1970." *Lebensreform um 1900 und Alternativmilieu um 1980*, edited by Detlef Siegfried and David Templin. V&R Unipress, 2019, pp. 61–86.

Bourdieu, Pierre. "Ökonomisches Kapital, kulturelles Kapital, soziales Kapital." *Soziale Ungleichheiten, Soziale Welt Sonderband 2*, edited by Reinhard Kreckel. Schwartz, 1983, pp. 183–98.

Breines, Wini. "The 'Other' Fifties: Beats and Bad Girls." *Not June Cleaver: Women and Gender in Postwar America 1945–1960*, edited by Jay Joanne Meyerowitz. Temple University Press, 1994, pp. 382–408.

Broyard, Anatole. "Portrait of the Hipster." *Parisian Review*, vol. 15, no. 6, 1948, pp. 721–7.

CBC News: The National. "Who are the Proud Boys?" *YouTube*, uploaded by CBC News: The National, July 5, 2017, www.youtube.com/watch?v=lWHkfDSQbNo. Accessed December 20, 2020.

Cole, Daniel James. "Dumpster Chic and Haute Homeless: Placing Brother Sharp in a Fashion Industry Continuum." *Critical Studies in Men's Fashion*, vol. 5, no. 1/2, 2018, pp. 25–39.

Dangoor, Reuben, and Raf Riley. "Being a Dickhead's Cool." *YouTube*, uploaded by Reuben Dangoor, September 9, 2010, www.youtube.com/watch?v=lVmmYMwFj1I. Accessed December 20, 2020.

Davis, Fred. "Antifashion: The Vicissitudes of Negation." *Fashion Theory: A Reader*, edited by Malcolm Barnard. Routledge, 2007, pp. 89–102.

Dinerstein, Joel. "The Art and Complexity of American Cool." *American Cool*, edited by Joel Dinerstein and Frank H. Goodyear. Prestel, 2014, pp. 21–41.

Durham, Alex. "Death of the Hipster: Are We Living in a Post-Ironic World?" *Bizarre Culture*, November 16, 2019, bizarreculture.com/death-of-the-hipster-are-we-living-in-a-post-ironic-world/. Accessed December 20, 2020.

Elan, Priya. "Fred Perry Withdraws Polo Shirt Adopted by Far-Right Proud Boys." *Guardian*, September 28, 2020, www.theguardian.com/world/2020/sep/28/fred-perry-withdraws-polo-shirt-adopted-by-far-right-proud-boys. Accessed December 20, 2020.

Esculapio, Alex. "Operation New Balance: How Neo-Nazis Hacked the Mall." *Vestoj*, March 21, 2017, vestoj.com/operation-new-balance/. Accessed December 20, 2020.

Fischer, Molly. "The Tyranny of Terrazzo." *The Cut: Spring 2020 Fashion Issue*, March 3, 2020, www.thecut.com/2020/03/will-the-millennial-aesthetic-ever-end.html. Accessed December 20, 2020.

Flanagan, Andrew. "15 Spot-On Hipster Parodies From 'Portlandia.'" *Billboard*, August 1, 2015, www.billboard.com/articles/news/list/6436288/portlandia-hipster-parody-sketches. Accessed December 20, 2020.

Florida, Richard. *The Rise of the Creative Class*. Basic Books, 2002.

Fraiman, Susan. *Cool and the Second Sex*. Columbia University Press, 2003.

Frank, Thomas. *The Conquest of Cool: Business Culture, Counter Culture, and the Rise of Hip Consumerism*. University of Chicago Press, 1998.

Gaugele, Elke. "The New Obscurity in Style: Alt-right Faction, Populist Normalization, and the Cultural War on Fashion from the Far Right." *Fashion Theory: The Journal of Dress, Body and Culture*, vol. 23, no. 6, 2019, pp. 711–31.

Geczy, Adam, and Vicki Karaminas. *Fashion and Masculinities in Popular Culture*. Routledge, 2019.

Geczy, Adam, and Vicki Karaminas. "Walter Benjamin: Fashion, Modernity and the City Street." *Thinking Through Fashion: A Guide to Key Theorists*, edited by Agnès Rocamora and Anneke Smelik. I.B. Tauris, 2016, 81–96.

Gilson, Duane. "The Revolution in Our Pants: Hipsters, Race and American Fashion." *International Journal of Fashion Studies*, vol. 4, no. 1, 2017, pp. 35–49.

Greif, Mark. "Nachruf auf den weißen Hipster." *Hipster: Eine transatlantische Diskussion*, edited by Mark Greif et al. Suhrkamp, 2012, pp. 112–40.

Greif, Mark. "Positionen." *Hipster: Eine transatlantische Diskussion*, edited by Mark Greif et al. Suhrkamp, 2012, pp. 23–31.

Greif, Mark. "Vorwort zur amerikanischen Ausgabe." *Hipster: Eine transatlantische Diskussion*, edited by Mark Greif et al. Suhrkamp, 2012, pp. 11–19.

Haddow, Douglas. "Hipster: The Dead End of Western Civilization." *The Rag Blog*, August 10, 2008, theragblog.blogspot.com/2008/08/hipster-dead-end-of-western.html. Accessed December 20, 2020.

Hebdige, Dick. *Subculture: The Meaning of Style*. 1979. Routledge, 2007.

Hilber, Regina. "Adieu Hipster." *Lettre International*, 2020, pp. 124–5.

Hollander, Anne. *Anzug und Eros: Eine Geschichte der modernen Kleidung*. Berlin Verlag, 1995.

Horning, Rob. "The Death of the Hipster." *PopMatters*, April 12, 2009, www.popmatters.com/the-death-of-the-hipster-panel-2496026662.html. Accessed December 20, 2020.

Ikrath, Phillip. *Die Hipster: Trendsetter und Neo-Spießer*. Promedia, 2015.

Iqbal, Nosheen. "Fashion ... or Fascist? The Long Tussle Over That Fred Perry Logo." *Guardian*, October 4, 2020, www.theguardian.com/fashion/2020/oct/04/fashion-or-fascist-the-long-tussle-over-that-fred-perry-logo. Accessed December 20, 2020.

Johnson, Joyce. *Minor Characters: A Beat Memoir*, 2nd ed. Methuen, 2012.

Kaufman, Bob. "Collected Poems." *Collected Poems of Bob Kaufman*, edited by Neeli Cherkovski, Raymond Foye, and Tate Swindell. City Lights Books, 2019.

Kellogg, Carolyn. "What Do Hipsters and Pornography Have in Common?" *Los Angeles Times*, October 12, 2010, latimesblogs.latimes.com/jacketcopy/2010/10/hipster-pornography.html. Accessed December 20, 2020.

Kennedy, Gordon. *Children of the Sun: A Pictoral Anthology; from Germany to California, 1883–1949*. Nivaria Press, 1998.

Kerouac, Jack. "The Origin of the Beat Generation." *The Cool School: Writing from America's Hip Underground*, edited by Glenn O'Brien. Library of America, 2016, pp. 124–33.

K-Hole. "Youth Mode: A Report on Freedom." *Box 1824*, 2013, khole.net/issues/youth-mode/. Accessed December 20, 2020.

Kinzey, Jake. *The Sacred and Profane: An Investigation of Hipsters*. Zero Books, 2012.

Knee, Sam. *The Scenes in Between: Tripping through the Scenes of UK Indie Music 1980–1988*. Cida Books, 2013.

Kotynek, Roy, and John Cohassey. *American Rebels: Avant-Garde and Bohemian, Artists, Writers and Musicians from the 1850s Through the 1960s*. McFarland, 2008.

Kraft, Kerstin. "Dirndl, Diva oder deutsches Mädel in Uniform?" *Glanz und Grauen: Mode im "Dritten Reich,"* edited by LVR-Industriemuseum Ratingen. Kettler, 2012, pp. 16–25.

Kutner, Sarah. "Swiping Right: The Allure of Hyper Masculinity and Cryptofascisim for Men Who Join the Proud Boys." *ICCT Journal*, May 2020, pp. 1–33, icct.nl/app/uploads/2020/05/Swiping-Right-The-Allure-of-Hyper-Masculinity-and-Cryptofascism-for-Men-Who-Join-the-Proud-Boys.pdf. Accessed December 20, 2020.

Leland, John. *Hip: The History*. Ecco, 2005.

Leszkiewicz, Anna. "H is for Hipster: The Decade the Dickhead Died." *New Statesman*, December 12, 2019, www.newstatesman.com/2019/12/h-hipster-decade-dickhead-died. Accessed December 20, 2020.

Lifter, Rachel. *Fashioning Indie: Popular Fashion, Music and Gender*. Bloomsbury, 2020.

Limar, Wanar. "Shit Berlin Fashion Hipsters Say." *YouTube*, uploaded by MTV Deutschland, June 26, 2017, www.youtube.com/watch?v=XSLExb8GYio. Accessed December 20, 2020.

Lorentzen, Christian. "Kill the Hipster: Why the Hipster Must Die. A Modest Proposal to Save New York Cool." *Time Out New York*, no. 609, May 30–June

5, 2007, web.archive.org/web/20080725151413/http:/www.timeout.com/newyork/article/4840/why-the-hipster-must-die. Accessed December 20, 2020.

Lynge-Jorlén, Ane. "The Homeless and the Hunchback: Experimental Styling, Assembled Bodies and New Material Aesthetics in Niche Fashion Magazines." *Fashion Stylists: History, Meaning and Practice*, edited by Ane Lynge-Jorlén. Bloomsbury, 2020, pp. 63–82.

MacAdams, Lewis. *Birth of the Cool: Beat, Bebop, and the American Avant-Garde*. Free Press, 2001.

Mailer, Norman. "The White Negro." 1957. *Dissent*, June 20, 2007, www.dissentmagazine.org/online_articles/the-white-negro-fall-1957. Accessed December 20, 2020.

Marchant, Ian. *A Hero in High Times: A Younger Reader's Guide for the Beats, Hippies, Freaks, Punks, Ravers, New-Age Travellers and Dog-on-a-Rope Brew Crew Crusties of the British Isles 1956–1994*. Penguin, 2018.

Martin, Richard A. "The Strokes: Is This It." *CMJ: New Music Monthly*, November 2001, p. 89.

Marx, Karl. *Capital Volume One*. Penguin, 1990.

McCauley Bowstead, Jay. *Menswear Revolution: The Transformation of Contemporary Men's Fashion*. Bloomsbury, 2018.

Michael, Janna. "It's Really Not Hip to Be a Hipster: Negotiating Trends and Authenticity in the Culture Field." *Journal of Consumer Culture*, vol. 15, no. 2, 2015, pp. 163–82.

Miles, Barry. "The Counter-Culture." *You Say You Want A Revolution? Records and Rebels 1966–1970*, edited by Victoria Broackes and Geoffrey Marsh. V&A, 2016, pp. 98–135.

Miller-Idriss, Cynthia. *The Extreme Gone Mainstream: Commercialisation and Far Right Youth Culture in Germany*. Pinceton University Press, 2017.

Mrozek, Bodo. "Walle, walle, nimm die schlechten Lumpenhüllen: Body politics der Langhaarigkeit in Lebensreform um 1900 und alternativem Milieu um 1980." *Leben um 1900 und Alternativmilieu um 1980*, edited by Detlef Siegfried and David Templin. V&R Unipress, 2019, pp. 271–94.

Nagle, Angela. *Kill All Normies: Online Culture Wars From 4chan and Tumblr to Trump and the Alt-Right*. Zero Books, 2017.

Nichols, Luther. "Kerouac as the Savant of the Religious Beat." *The San Francisco Examiner*, October 5, 1958, p. 173, www.newspapers.com/newspage/458637322/. Accessed December 20, 2020.

O'Brien, Glenn. *The Cool School: Writing from America's Hip Underground*. Library of America, 2016.

Odell, Amy. "Erin Wasson: 'Homeless People Have the Best Style.' " *The Cut*, September 15, 2008, www.thecut.com/2008/09/erin_wasson_homeless_people_ha.html. Accessed December 20, 2020.

Pappas, Nickolas. *The Philosopher's New Clothes*. Routledge, 2016.

Polhemus, Ted. *Streetstyle: From Sidewalk to Catwalk*. Thames & Hudson, 1994.

Pountain, Dick, and David Robins. *Cool Rules: Anatomy of an Attitude*. Reaktion Books, 2000.

Quartz, Steven, and Anette Asp. *Cool: How the Brain's Hidden Quest for Cool Drives Our Economy and Shapes Our World*. Farrar, Strauss and Giroux, 2015.

Rabe, Jens Christian. "Gegenwärtigkeit als Phantasma: Über den Hass auf den Hipster." *Hipster: Eine transatlantische Diskussion*, edited by Mark Greif et al. Suhrkamp, 2012, pp. 188–204.

Rabkin, Eugene. "Op-Ed: The Rise of the Fashion Hipster." *Business of Fashion*, April 22, 2016, www.businessoffashion.com/opinions/fashion-week/op-ed-the-rise-of-the-fashion-hipster. Accessed December 20, 2020.

Reckwitz, Andreas. *Die Gesellschaft der Singularitäten*. Suhrkamp, 2019.

Renwick, Finlay. "Why 2020 Is the Year of the 'Shipster.'" *Esquire*, December 23, 2019, www.esquire.com/uk/style/fashion/a30256309/shipster-fashion-trend/. Accessed December 20, 2020.

Reynolds, Simon. *Retromania*. Faber and Faber, 2012.

Rogers, Thomas. "Heil Hipster: The Young Neo-Nazis Trying to Put a Stylish Face on Hate." *Rolling Stone*, June 23, 2014, www.rollingstone.com/culture/culture-news/heil-hipster-the-young-neo-nazis-trying-to-put-a-stylish-face-on-hate-64736/. Accessed December 20, 2020.

Rüß, Catharina. "Imagining Cool Fashion Bodies and 'Exoticism' in the Literature of the Weimar Republik." *Zone Moda Journal*, vol. 10, no. 1S, 2020, pp. 239–54, doi.org/10.6092/issn.2611-0563/10569.

Rüß, Catharina. "Looking Cool in Black Leather." *Fashion Studies Journal*, no. 4, 2017, www.fashionstudiesjournal.org/longform/2017/7/28/cool-poses-with-leather-jackets-bm6ee.

Schulze, Christoph. *Etikettenschwindel: Die Autonomen Nationalisten zwischen Pop und Antimoderne*. Tectum, 2017.

Schulze, Marion. *Hardcore and Gender: Soziologische Einblicke in eine globale Subkultur*. Transcript, 2015.

See, Raven J. "Fashion and Female Beat Identity in the Writing of Jones, Johnson, and di Parma." *CLCWeb: Comparative Literature and Culture*, vol. 18, no. 5, 2016, pp. 1–7, doi.org/10.7771/1481–4374.2905. Accessed December 20, 2020.

Shakouchi, Yuri. "Stereotypes of the Beatniks and Hip Consumerism: A Study of Mad Magazine in the Late 1950s and 1960s." *Journal of Popular Culture*, vol. 48, no. 6, 2015, pp. 1270–86.

Shannon, E. Reid, and Matthew Valasik. *Alt-Right Gangs: A Hazy Shade of White*. University of California Press, 2020.

Simmel, Georg. "Philosophie der Mode." *Die Philosophie der Mode: Die Religion; Kant und Goethe; Schopenhauer und Nietzsche, Gesamtausgabe Bd. 10*, edited by Michael Behr et al. Suhrkamp, 1995, pp. 7–38.

Sontag, Susan. "Notes on Camp." *Susan Sontag: Essays of the 60s and 70s*, edited by David Rieff. Library of America, 2013, pp. 259–74.

Steele, Valerie. "Fashion Futures." *The End of Fashion: Clothing and Dress in the Age of Globalization*, edited by Adam Geczy and Vicki Karaminas. Bloomsbury, 2019, pp. 5–18.

Theweleit, Klaus. *Männerphantasien*. Vol. 1 and 2. Piper, 2005.

Thoreau, Henry David. *Walden*. Penguin, 2016.

Tortorici, Dayna. "Man erkennt sie, wenn man sie sieht." *Hipster: Eine transatlantische Diskussion*, edited by Mark Greif et al. Suhrkamp, 2012, pp. 99–111.

Tudor, Elisabeta. "What the 'New Normcore' Trend Says About Our Fashion Industry." *NowFashion*, nowfashion.com/what-the-new-normcore-trend-says-about-our-fashion-industry-22427. Accessed December 20, 2020.

Turney, Joanne. "The Horror of the Hoodie: Clothing the Criminal." *Fashion Crimes: Dressing for Deviance*, edited by Joanne Turny. Bloomsbury, 2019, pp. 23–32.

Veblen, Thorstein. *The Theory of the Leisure Class*. 1899, edited by Martha Banta. Oxford University Press, 2007.

Watzlawik, Jan. *Gegenstände: Zur materiellen Kultur des Protests*. Kadmos Verlag, 2018.

Wedemeyer-Kolwe, Bernd. "Der Neue Mensch: Lebensreform und Reformkleidung um 1900." *Kleider in Bewegung: Frauenmode seit 1850*, edited by Maren CH. Härtel et al. Michael Imhof Verlag, 2020, pp. 182–7.

Welters, Linda. "The Beat Generation: Subcultural Style." *Twentieth Century American Fashion*, edited by Linda Welters and Patricia A. Cunningham. Berg, 2005, 145–67.

Welters, Linda. "The Natural Look: American Style in the 1970s." *Fashion Theory: The Journal of Dress, Body and Culture*, vol. 12, no. 4, 2008, pp. 489–510.

Wilson, Elizabeth. *Bohemians: The Glamorous Outcasts*. Tauris Parke, 2009.

Wilson, Jason. "Proud Boys Founder Gavin McInnes Quits 'Extremist' Far-Right Group." *Guardian*, November 22, 2018, theguardian.com/world/2018/nov/22/proud-boys-founder-gavin-mcinnes-quits-far-right-group. Accessed December 20, 2020.

Winterhalter, Cecilia. "Recent Gastro-Trends: Food Surfing on the Streets." *Engaging with Fashion: Perspectives of Communication, Education and Business*, edited by Federica Carlotto and Natalie C. McCreesh. Brill Rodopi, 2018, pp. 119–48.

7

The Irony of Hipster Beards

Christopher Oldstone-Moore

For the past two decades, few stylistic features of a male hipster are more commonly recognized than a long beard or mustache. Facial hair is often near the top of the list of defining characteristics of international hipster style. British journalist Ed Cumming offers a typical assessment when he wrote in 2015 that "twenty-first-century hipsterism can be hard to define, but you know it when you see it. Beards, plaid, tattoos, thick glasses, fixed-gear bicycles, artisanal breads (artisanal anything, really), Apple products, cold-pressed juices … these are some of the outward signs." One enterprising blogger determined from a search of more than two hundred Google images of hipster-classified men that 89 percent had beards (Dennis). Indeed, beards are overidentified with hipsters, to the extent that commentators are often too quick to identify bearded men as hipsters and to credit hipsters with inspiring the popularity of beards in the broader culture. In 2016, for example, the *New York Post* declared "the bearded-hipster trend has truly and utterly taken over New York," noting that a survey found that 67 percent of New York City men sported some form of facial hair (O'Neill). Another journalist discussing hipster style referred to a survey indicating that 48 percent of Frenchmen have facial hair, mostly beards (Mansfield-Devine). It is certainly going too far to assume that two-thirds of New Yorkers or half of the French are hipsters, or even hipster imitators. Even so, there is a common assumption among writers on popular culture that the growing popularity of facial hair is a sign of the "hipsterification" of urban society, which is to say the expansion of hipster sensibilities to the wider culture (Crilly; Kurutz; O'Neill; Williams).

This chapter offers an alternative narrative. Hipsters are not the sole source of the trend toward beards. They are participants in a more general cultural discourse involving masculinity and facial hair. To understand the meaning of hipster beards, therefore, it is necessary to consider them in this wider context. An examination of this aspect of hipster style, moreover, will shed new light on hipster culture more generally. Critics find hipster style rife with irony, both intentional and unintentional, because it is an invented tradition ungrounded in, and disconnected from, the hipsters' true social status (Daniels; Greif, "Positions"; Magill; McCracken). To some extent, hipsters participate knowingly in this cultural appropriation, adopting an eclectic assemblage of styles and practices from the past and from other classes and ethnicities. To their strongest critics, such as Mark Greif, R. Jay Magill, and Brett McCracken, however, this cultural montage is worse than ironic; it is morally bankrupt. In their view, the hipsters' anachronistic glasses and bikes, faux lumberjack shirts, expensive artisanal goods, and patriarchal beards are all symbols of a strained effort by young, educated urbanites to pretend not to be the superficial bourgeois consumers that they are. A consideration of beards will help illuminate the extent to which this criticism is justified.

Not surprisingly, hipsters—at least those willing to admit to that label—do not accept their critics' indictment. As will be demonstrated later, hipsters do not see their facial hair as a false or ironic façade, but rather the opposite: a genuine declaration of personal authenticity and cultural nonconformity. In one important respect, both hipsters and their critics are wrong about beards, however. Viewed in the context of history, hipster justifications are neither fraudulent nor unironically genuine. The true irony of the hipster beard is that it is a rather conventional form of rebellion—conventional because it stands within a centuries-long tradition in Western culture of reading facial hair as an assertion of masculine authenticity and autonomy. Hipsters are tapping into this tradition, which is as much theirs as anyone's, and so there is no falseness or irony in the hipster appropriation of these ideas. Since the eighteenth century, when facial hair was banished as superfluous and vulgar, beard-wearing became a self-conscious act of cultural resistance that invoked the countercultural authority of nature and history. Even when facial hair won the endorsement of mainstream society in the mid-nineteenth century, it retained its affiliations with personal independence and resistance to conformity. Indeed, this was the appeal of beards for a society seeking to embrace a fuller expression of masculine individualism. The bearded hipster exists within this tradition in his hopes of asserting a historic, natural, and authentic identity in the face of the anomie and atomization of modern life. Of course, there is irony in modern urban men appropriating "natural" and historic signifiers that stand in remove from urban industrial society. But this irony is also traditional, at least since the eighteenth century. Indeed, this deliberate appropriation of the "natural" is fundamental to modernity itself. All citizens in an industrialized, urban environment, cut off as we are from nature and tradition, must craft, more or less self-consciously, social communities and cultural meaning. All claims of authenticity are therefore precarious, as are all criticisms of others' authenticity.

The traditionalism of bearded hipsters will become evident through a consideration of hipster discourse on beards in comparison with ideas about facial hair in the wider culture, past and present. Finally, this analysis will serve as groundwork for reevaluating criticisms leveled at hipster culture.

The Hipster and His Beard

What does the hipster think of his mustache or beard? Does he see it as comic, ironic, serious, or some combination of all of these? American journalist Luke O'Neil confesses in a 2013 article in *Slate* that he is a hipster, and he also admits that he is a self-conscious cultural consumer who changes his style and affect to suit his needs:

> I play up my working-class roots when the situation calls for it, and my educated media persona when that fits better. I'm a social chameleon, a voracious consumer of culture who knows how to use it as a weapon or as a salve. I studied poetry in school, for Christ's sake. Oh, right, I also write contrarian articles on the internet for hipster media. And yes, I have a pretty intense beard.

O'Neil acknowledges the irony of his self-conscious, derivative, and constructed identity. His rhetoric implies, however, that even though he is a "social chameleon" who changes his affect from day to day, his "intense" beard remains a constant. Rhetorically, O'Neil links his beard with personal autonomy and nonconformity. The modifier "intense" may be in part a jesting boast, but it is more clearly intended to indicate the forcefulness of his contrarian personality and his commitment to think and act freely. A similar sentiment is echoed in blogs on grooming websites catering to hipsters, such as *Hipster Beard Club*. One article on this site offers ten reasons not to shave off one's beard. The final reason is that, "in a world where conformity and uniformity is the norm, your beard stands out as a statement of uniqueness and confidence" ("Ten Reasons").

Harry Cheadle's defense of beards in *Vice* magazine in 2016 follows a similar line. Responding to Jacob Gallagher's *Wall Street Journal* piece denigrating beards as boring and uncool, Cheadle sarcastically thanks Gallagher for revealing to him and his bearded friends that, while they had believed they acted out of "personal preference and shave-laziness," they were in fact craven trend chasers who must return to razors immediately. This snarky riposte implies two things. First, beards are a matter of personal freedom, not trendiness, and second, hipsters like himself have absolutely no interest in being told by anyone what their motives or actions should be. Cheadle's reference to "personal preference" and "shave-laziness" suggests that one needs no justifications for one's grooming choices. He is most interested in denying the accusation that hipsters are trend chasers; they have greater integrity than that. His rejection of Gallagher's criticism also echoes O'Neil's expression of nonconformity and personal autonomy. A "shave-lazy" hipster is a contrarian who resists grooming expectations, including standards set by the fashion and cosmetics industries.

The subgroup of hipsters who are most strongly identified by their beards are the so-called "lumbersexuals," a term coined by Tom Puzak, writing in *GearJunkie* in 2014. He derives it from the term "metrosexual," which designates an urban, heterosexual male whose proclivity for shopping, fashion, and grooming threatens to blur the lines between male and female personalities. According to Puzak, "the metrosexual is a disappearing breed being quickly replaced by men more concerned with existing in the outdoors, or the pseudo-outdoors, than meticulous grooming habits." The lumbersexual, like the metrosexual, is stereotypically a young, straight, urban professional man but, unlike the metrosexual, affects an outdoorsy, rugged look, distancing himself from the sort of gender-ambiguous qualities that had made metrosexuals the object of ridicule. Though the terms "metrosexual" and "lumbersexual" are not particularly well defined, they attempt to describe the increasing importance of fashion and styling for urban professional men. Some hipsters like Harry Cheadle, who claim to be simply shave-lazy, appear to reject fashion, but others are more self-conscious about image, products, and grooming. According to Logan Rhoades, "lumbersexual men have a calculated look with the desire to be (and be seen as) rugged and the heteronormative version of 'manly.' "

Denver Nicks is one of the few willing to admit in print to belong in this category. He explains himself this way in *Time* magazine:

> As a 21st-century man who does not identify with the pickup artist thing or the boobs/cars/abs triad of masculinity on display in most 21st-century men's magazines (Maxim et al), is not particularly fastidious or a member of any clearly identifiable subculture, and who is as attracted to notions of old-timey authenticity as anyone else in my 20s-30s hipster cohort (all of you are hipsters get over it), I guess this is just the fashion sense that felt most natural.

Nicks acknowledges that urban hipsters are not real outdoorsmen, and that they do not even look like present-day lumberjacks but instead like those from a century ago. To him, the primary motive is to find a sensible presentation of manliness. Because the masculine modes on offer in popular culture do not appeal to him, Nicks needed an alternative. He admits that his style choice is trendy but defends it as authentic all the same. He concludes by arguing that "if my beard is a trend-inspired attempt to reclaim a semblance of masculinity in a world gone mad, then so be it." Nicks's comments indicate that a beard is a link to nature for men extracted from nature and also a connection to the past in a time of rapid change. Even if he is only able to acquire a "semblance" of authentic masculinity, he is satisfied with that. At one level, Nicks accepts the irony of his identity as an urban professional in the guise of a rugged outdoorsman. That is not, however, the whole meaning for him. At least he is able to reject what he believes to be the truly false expressions of manliness and indicate his preference for that which was "most natural." In her study of the checkered lumberjack shirt, fashion historian Maria Mackinney-Valentin finds this reasoning at the core of the lumberjack style, noting that "even if only on a symbolic level, the hipster with his full beard, lumberjack shirt, and grandfatherly demeanor proposes a vision of slower life more connected to nature" (152).

Nicks' self-description echoes the findings of anthropologist Margaret Ann Murray in her study of hipster men in Detroit. "Hipsterdom," Murray concludes, "was a useful identity resource that enabled participants to challenge many middle-class norms associated with masculinity" (20). Many of the young men she studied had neither the desire nor resources to live up to social expectations of career, marriage, and "shallow friendships" (20) with other men. Beards, bicycles, vinyl records, and thrift-shop clothes helped them to fashion a liberating, alternate type of manhood that seems, as Nicks puts it, "more natural."

While they acknowledge the irony of their created identities, bearded hipsters such as Nicks, Cheadle, and O'Neil associate their facial hair with authenticity, not irony. They claim to be bearded because they are independent and critical of modern society and wish to assert an alternative manhood founded in nature and history rather than thoughtless convention and conformity.

Western Beard Discourse

One striking aspect of these self-descriptions is how similar they are to narratives of bearded men more generally, even men of radically different subcultures. Tomer Hanuka's drawing for a cover of a 2016 issue of the *New Yorker* presents a striking visual observation of this crosscultural resonance. It features two men riding the L train, which connects Manhattan with the Williamsburg section of Brooklyn. One is a hipster in tight jeans, black muscle shirt, tattoos, and a long beard. The other man is a Hasidic Jew, in a black frock coat, brimmed hat, and similarly long beard. In many respects these two men are opposites. They face away from each other, reflecting the social tensions in Williamsburg between these two groups. They share three things, however: the same section of New York City, similar faces, and identical long beards. The similar beards relate to deeper likenesses of these contrasting communities: their resistance to mainstream culture and their appeal to history.

Ironically, the clash of hipster libertinism and Hasidic conservatism was intensified by these similarities. In his essay on their conflict, Christopher Glazek observes that "at their most extreme, hipsters and Hasids present rival heresies, dueling rejections of bourgeois modernity. That each group selected Williamsburg as the terrain for carving out this secessionist utopia can only be blamed on the cunning of history, plus the L train" (173). One can extend Glezek's observations by noting that in their common desire to stand apart from mainstream society, hipsters and Hasids draw on symbolic historical references, including beards. Like the hipster beard, Hasidic beards are the result of a relatively recent effort to reconnect to a "lost" history, strengthen group identity, uphold male autonomy, and enact cultural resistance to majority society. Though Biblical tradition is certainly favorable to facial hair, premodern rabbinic tradition did not require the maintenance of beards. Most urban Jews living in Western Europe and the Americas over the past three centuries have accommodated themselves to the modes and tastes of a shaven society. Even highly observant and Orthodox Jews of the eighteenth and early nineteenth centuries typically chose to make themselves as smooth-faced as their Christian neighbors (Leiman 197; Horowitz 95–115). For both observant and secular Jews, the mid-nineteenth century was an important turning point. An influential early Jewish fundamentalist, the Hungarian rabbi Moses Sofer, and his even more strident Ultra-Orthodox successors erected a bulwark against the erosion of tradition by stressing the equal importance of every religious stricture found in Jewish law and writings, including Biblical injunctions against trimming the edge of the beard (Silber 48–9).

This consideration of Hasidic beards underscores the fundamental similarity of hipsters and Hasidim when it comes to beards. Though they came to it a century later, hipsters also deploy the historical resonance of facial hair to enhance their social distinctiveness and authenticate their nonconformist culture. The fact that Jewish traditionalists adopted their distinctive look earlier does not make them more authentic than hipsters. Indeed, the checked lumberjack shirt of the hipster and the black frock coat of the Ultra-Orthodox are similarly ironic in their anachronism, and both are derived from the same moment in time, the mid-nineteenth century. Both groups are contemporary New Yorkers, and both grow beards intentionally and self-consciously in their modern milieu.

The triumph of beards from the 1850s to the 1880s in Western societies has been an inspiration to Hasidim and hipsters alike—and also to a wide range of groups and individuals in contemporary society. Understanding the dynamics of this era will shed light on the cultural meaning of facial hair today and underscore the continuities of beard discourse over time.[1] The general fashion for beards in Europe and America in the mid-nineteenth century was rooted in the hopes and fears of a democratic and industrial age. Revolutions in Europe and America at the end of the eighteenth century declared the rights of man, theoretically investing power in sex rather than class. In subsequent decades, the more ardently revolutionary or republican a man was, the more likely he was to grow facial hair because he wholeheartedly embraced this revolutionary ideal of masculine liberation. Leftist students and intellectuals were therefore enthusiastically bearded in the early nineteenth century. The resulting linkage between facial hair and radicalism, however, made beards and mustaches off limits for respectable men, though they pressed the envelope as far as they dared, favoring long and bushy sideburns that stopped just short of the chin.[2] When the republican revolutions across Europe in 1848 failed, however, and the fear of radical beards vanished, facial hair was immediately repurposed as a bravura display of masculine pride. There was a more defensive impulse in this new style as well. Even as more men attained political rights in Europe and America, the changing economic patterns of work and family life in industrial society undermined traditional patriarchal patterns and allowed women to increasingly challenge male dominance in both private and public life. As a matter of collective self-defense, as well as pride, therefore, mid-century beard apologists were united in arguing that God, providence, and/or nature had provided men with the beard to ensure their dignity as men, their autonomy as free individuals, and their authority over women.

For nineteenth-century men, the native masculine virtues of intellect, moral clarity, and decisive will entitled a man to both honor and authority. It was widely believed that a beard served as both the emanation and symbol of these masculine strengths. Beards therefore offered men the comforting sign that some things never change and that nature and history justified and preserved a man's independence and authority. After 1848, American and European journalists, writers, and essayists articulated these principles in countless publications. A contributor to the prestigious English periodical, the *Westminster Review*, expressed the *zeitgeist* by declaring "the beard—identified as it is with sternness, dignity and strength—is only the becoming complement of true manliness" ("The Beard" 33). A true man, it was argued, rejects fashion and superficial convention, founding his character on nature and truth. Shaving, by contrast, was recast as dishonesty. A beard manifesto appearing in Charles Dickens's journal *Household*

[1]This discussion of nineteenth-century beards is based upon my research. See Oldstone-Moore, *Of Beards and Men*, chs. 8–9 and conclusion.

[2]A tradition of military and aristocratic mustaches emerged in early nineteenth-century Europe, especially in Germany, but mustaches were generally discouraged for civilians.

Words put it this way: "How ill does a smooth chin support at any time the character assumed by the remainder of the face, except it be a character of sanctimonious oiliness that does not belong honestly to a man" ("Why Shave?" 561). Because natural honesty and strength of will entitled a man to claim his rights as an individual, a beard was also seen as an affirmation of personal autonomy. Walt Whitman neatly summed up both these themes of authenticity and autonomy in his poem "Song of Myself," declaring "washes and razors for foofoos … for me freckles and a bristling beard" (28). In other words, wimps shave because they fear to act forcefully, honestly, and independently.

Today, in spite of, or rather because of, the reassertion of the shaving norm for conventional masculinity, the rhetoric surrounding facial hair is largely unchanged. Mustachioed Hollywood heroes in the 1930s and 1940s, such as Flynn, Fairbanks, and Gable, as well as the bearded rebels of the 1960s, all drew upon the symbolic autonomy and nonconformity of facial hair. This theme has gained renewed prominence in recent popular culture. Television, especially programs that appeal to hipsters and other young urban professionals, presents an updated version of nineteenth-century ideals. One of the earliest examples is *Star Trek: The Next Generation*. Jonathan Frakes's decision to enhance his character, Commander Riker, with a full, dark beard at the beginning of the second season of the show in 1988 made him appear stronger and coincided with the improvement of the series as whole (Venables). The terms 'Riker's Beard' and 'Riker Syndrome' then entered the American popular lexicon, the first to indicate an improvement of one's appearance and effectiveness ("Riker's Beard"), and the second to describe someone who looks unimpressive without a beard ("Riker Syndrome"). These terms captured the popular imagination because Riker's look was a striking departure in the 1980s and because it was a compelling representation of an old idea that beards imparted strength of character. More recently, realist fantasies such as *Breaking Bad*, *The Walking Dead*, and *Game of Thrones* have all presented bearded protagonists who are paragons of masculine individuality, daring, and fortitude. The protagonist in *Breaking Bad*, Walter White, starts out, before he begins his career as drug dealer, as a washed-out, underpaid, and overlooked schoolteacher with a modest mustache. By the second season, when White becomes a major player in the drug trade, and confronts dangerous competitors, he has shaved his head and grown a goatee. In the concluding episodes of the final season, when his commitment to criminal enterprise entraps him in violence and self-destruction, White has grown a full head of hair and a full beard ("Felina"). His evolving facial hair tracks his development as a daring, defiant, and formidable man.

There is a similar pattern in *The Game of Thrones*, which offers a veritable gallery of bearded heroes and anti-heroes. The enduring virtue of Jon Snow, the main male character, is reflected in his unchanging, natural beard. The facial hair of Tyrion and Jamie Lannister, like White's, is used to indicate the characters' development. Both of these brothers started out as self-absorbed, morally compromised, and clean-shaven. Their gradual attainment of moral depth and sense of purpose over the long arc of the story corresponds with their increasing beardedness. Tyrion's beard appears in the first episode of season five, after he kills his father and flees the capital with Varis, a royal councilor who challenges Tyrion to "decide if the world is worth fighting for" ("The Wars to Come"). Jamie grows a beard temporarily during his captivity in season one but gains a permanent (and trimmer) one much later, in season six. Jamie's chin becomes even more grizzled as his devil-may-care swagger gives way to hardened determination. After he fails to save his daughter from murderous enemies, and as he faces still more ominous threats to come, he swears to Cersei, his sister/lover, at the beginning of season six that "everything they have taken away from us we will take back, and more" ("The Red Woman"). He is not yet a good man, to be sure, but he is resolute. Like Riker's beard, the facial hair of Walter White and the Lannister brothers grows in proportion to their liberation from constraint and their developing strength of will.

The most outspoken champions of facial hair in contemporary society echo these themes. Members of beard clubs, and participants in beard competitions, are not typically hipsters, but like hipsters, they are mainly young professionals who share a pride in their masculinity and their hair, as well as the values they are supposed to represent. Liberation is the prevalent theme. Gary James Chilton, for example, a contestant at the 2003 World Beard and Mustache Championships, describes a bearded man as "open-minded, non-judgmental and a free spirit," whereas a clean-shaven man is "someone who has been told what to do" (Mallozzi 9). As in the nineteenth century, this notion of autonomy is related to natural authenticity. As another beard enthusiast put it, "I think that your face is not your real face if you shave every day" (Nelson 45). Sociologist Paul Roof, longtime president of a beard club in Charleston, South Carolina, draws these twin themes together in a pithy manner, opining that men with "beards and the mustaches are the most interesting men at any party." This is not an idea shared only by men. Fashion writer Maria Del Russo, for example, agrees that "there's just something inherently mysterious and attractive about a dude who lets his beard grow," and this is why "beards were big before they were 'trending,' and I'm sure they'll be big long after."

The self-justifications of bearded hipsters fall in line with these historic and contemporary assertions about bearded manhood. Hipsters speak the same language of integrity and individuality that Western men have employed for centuries. Denver Nicks claims for himself a "semblance of masculinity." Luke O'Neil's "intense" beard reflects his outspoken and contrarian opinions. Harry Cheadle renounces fashionable trendiness and insists on his "personal preference" with regard to grooming. Like Paul Roof and his bearded friends, they aspire to escape the routine and mundane and become the most interesting men at the party.

Critics of Hipster Beards

Criticisms of hipster beards are more plentiful in the media than justifications. The most common objection is that these beards, like other hipster accessories, are simply the slavish pursuit of trendiness. The popular TV sketch comedy series *Portlandia* gave this idea humorous expression during its first season in 2011. In one sketch, Fred Armisen plays a chin-bearded hipster who encounters a shaven, straight-laced, Dockers-wearing man hanging out at the hipster's favorite coffee shop, which leads Armisen's hipster to declare the shop to be "over." Then he sees the same man riding a fixed-gear bicycle and declares that "over" too—and so forth, until finally the imposter adopts a chin beard, forcing the original hipster to declare that "over" as well. In the end, the hipster is reduced to being the shaved, Docker-wearing conformist he had once despised, while the original imposter has morphed into a hipster ("Aimee"). The conceit is that hipsters only care about coolness, which is defined as whatever "mainstream" people do not do.

This belief that hipsters are style snobs has led many cultural observers to assume that the increasing popularity of beards in contemporary society will force hipsters to abandon facial hair in order to remain distinctive (Brooks; Mount; Gallagher). English commentator Harry Mount, for example, declared sarcastically to hipster readers in 2014 that "[i]t's time to get the razor out! You have hit peak beard." The hipsters' countercultural habits, he writes, had gone mainstream and lost their caché. Jacob Gallagher, a fashion writer for the *Wall Street Journal*, repeated this argument in 2016, declaring beards to be too popular to be cool. For similar reasons, Mark Greif prognosticated in 2009 the imminent collapse of hipsterism itself in his provocatively titled book *What Was the Hipster?* (Greif, Preface ix).

These predictions of the demise of beards have not proven accurate. One reason is the persistence of the shaving norm in mainstream society, which bolsters the beard's countercultural credibility. Another reason is stylistic conservatism. Steven Kurutz, a reporter for the *New York Times*, observes that some longtime hipsters he knows remain unfazed by the ubiquity of their style in New York. He reports that a friend of his "used to get embarrassed when a long-cultivated aspect of his personal style became popular with the masses. Now he doesn't care, secure in his own tastes." This attitude is not so surprising if one takes into account the stated motives of hipsters, which is to affirm authenticity and autonomy, not simply trendy coolness. The continuing affinity for beards among hipsters—and men more generally—is best explained by the vitality of a well-established tradition of interpreting facial hair as the signifier of independence. That desirable affiliation remains for all beard-wearers regardless of facial hair's expanding popularity.

In addition to the charge of faddishness, bearded hipsters are mocked for their nonconformist pretensions and wayward individualism. Blogger Nicki Daniels memorably ridiculed hipsters for turning beards into "the padded bra of masculinity" and pretending to be more mature and competent than they really were. A recent trope in television and film comedy involves bearded fools, many of them hipsters, whose willful independence has become ungrounded and chaotic. Characters played by Jack Black and Zach Galifianakis are the most notable recent examples of this "comedy beard" (Engber). There was a profusion of Galifianakis-like characters on TV comedy series that debuted in 2014, such as *Marry Me*, *Manhattan Love Story*, *A to Z*, and *Silicon Valley*. Dubbed by a *Washington Post* critic as the "the Bearded Best Friend," he was the "schlubby, awkward, often delusionally self-confident supporting male" who could be identified by his hipster-geek thatch of facial hair (Stuever). *Silicon Valley* features two bearded characters, Bertram Gilfoyle and Erlich Bachman, who are the oddest personalities in a cast of oddballs. Gilfoyle qualifies as "hipster-geek," while Bachman suffers from a severe case of delusional self-confidence (Stone). Indeed, Bachman's quirky and highly-styled beard takes on increasingly affected forms as his schemes become more grandiose and detached from reality. The message in all these comedies is that men who try too hard to be manly, independent, and willful end up in laughable confusion and that hipsters in particular often demonstrate an insufficient connection to reality.

The most incisive critiques of hipsters, however, are those that acknowledge the hipster quest for autonomy and authenticity but deny its validity. The argument is that hipsters have fashioned a derivative and fundamentally inauthentic identity appropriated from the cultures of other eras, regions, races, and classes. This identity must be expressed ironically because it cannot genuinely be their own. This applies to beards as well as other aspects of hipster culture and style. As Mark Greif put it in one of his proposed definitions of hipsterism, white hipsters from suburban, middle-class backgrounds "fetishized the violence, instinctiveness, and rebelliousness of lower-middle-class suburban or country whites" ("Positions" 10). What Greif objects to most is the falseness of hipsters' appropriation of outsider status. They pretend not to be privileged and self-indulgent consumers in order to escape their moral and political responsibility as members of the elite. The hipster, Greif argues, is someone who "aligns himself *both* with rebel subculture *and* the dominant class and opens up a poisonous conduit between the two" ("Positions" 9).

Cultural historian R. Jay Magill offers a similar analysis. He sees the hipster as attempting to camouflage or escape humdrum bourgeois life. "For this reason," Magill contends, "the uncivilized child, nature, and the antisocial character continue to inspire hipster fashion (childlike sneakers, clothes that are too small, wife-beaters, hillbilly beards, ethnic tattoos). These are the go-to figures because both child and outsider live freely, the Romantics say, unhampered by the pestering superego that hounds the well-to-do" (209–10). According to Magill, the hipsters wear their stylistic identifiers ironically, not only because they are disingenuous but also because the hipster ultimately does not want to be mistaken for these childish or outsider alter egos. For both Greif and Magill, therefore, hipsters refuse to identify with either their actual or appropriated social milieus. They are insiders posing as outsiders who refuse to be honest adults and take responsibility for their moral and social choices.

In line with this perspective, a hipster's beard is found at fault for various reasons. In the first place, it serves to dissociate the hipster from the middle-class values in which he or she was raised. According to Brett McCracken, beards, along with clothing and accessory choices, "purposefully embody styles and behaviors that are nonsense and improper" in order to be a thorn in the side of the boring, conventional world (McCracken 65). Magill spells out a second objection. The hipster beard is a mask that gives the wearer a false appearance of natural manliness: "The hipster beard, for all its surface commentary, reveals something more fundamental about its wearer's inner life: a sense of inauthenticity he has without one. The hipster beard, unlike the non-hipster beard, rides the coattails of manly ruggedness with a degree of cheekiness, saying, *What this beard appears to be, I am not*" (Magill 217). In other words, the beard is one way to hide from the essential inauthenticity of hipster existence. For Magill, however, hipsters have failed even in this conceit. Their beards, he writes, "only look like real-guy beards. Attempting sincere presentation of the brawny, unadorned self, hipsters are weighted down by the transparency of their attempt, preventing them from being what they want to be: unself-conscious outsiders" (217). According to this line of thinking, hipsters are tragically ironic, forced into an uncomfortable awareness of their own contradictions.

A glaring difficulty with Magill, McCracken, and Greif's moral critique is an insufficient conception of what constitutes authenticity. Who, for example, is this "real guy" that Magill presents as the foil to the hipster poser? If hipster style is "nonsense," as McCracken says, what is the "sense" that hipsters should conform to? As for Greif's critique, there is still a need to identify the sort of responsible privilege that hipsters apparently refuse to exercise. As author and critic Greg Jackson points out, all cultural styles are in some measure constructed and derivative, and the virtue of the original hipsters was a recognition that "social life is never wholly separate from performance," a truth "we forget at our peril in an age overconfident of its authenticity" (104). Overconfident or not, critics show more urgency in identifying hipster impostures than in defining the normal or genuine. We might wonder, along with Rob Horning, whether there really are actual hipsters, "or just a pervasive fear of hipsters" (Horning 81). In other words, it may be that critics derive the category "hipster," defined as inauthentic, in order to present themselves as the authentic inverse and thus confirm their own social and cultural validity. Phrased in gendered terms, the bearded hipster is said to be faking manliness so that others (including the critics) can be identified as "real guys."

Insufficient though it is, the criticism of hipster style and attitudes is not without merit. Hipster culture is certainly contradictory and problematic in many respects. It may be that features of hipster style are disingenuously appropriated for superficial or escapist reasons, particularly as hipster style has gone mainstream and lost its countercultural edge (Jackson). The hipster beard is a performance of anti-fashion, partly knowing and partly sincere. As a performance, the beard is ironic but not in any way unique to hipsters, whose appeal to nature and autonomy is part and parcel of a time-honored and reliable cultural strategy. Hipsters have embraced a traditional understanding of the meaning of facial hair, and they have deployed it for the same cultural purposes that it has always served throughout the modern era. Historically, the question of the appropriateness of facial hair hinges on whether individualist assertion is desirable, or whether, by contrast, it is preferable for men to adopt a more disciplined and sociable demeanor, usually indicated by shaving, suits, and other signifiers. In the final analysis, therefore, it seems that male hipsters have had little choice other than to adopt facial hair in order to align themselves on the right side of this equation. The true irony of the hipster beard is that it is conventionally unconventional. It is not simply an affectation, a fashion trend, or a ruse but a social and cultural statement, the meaning of which is well defined in modern Western societies.

Works Cited

"Aimee." *Portlandia*, written by Jonathan Krisel, directed by Fred Armisen et al., performance by Fred Armisen, season 1, episode 3, IFC, February 4, 2011. *Netflix*, www.netflix.com/watch/70222164?trackId=14277281&tctx=0%2C2%2C63e89161-ed3f-4083-a1b4-577de97951ad-12823675%2C%2C%2C. Accessed April 23, 2018.

"The Beard." *Westminster Review*, vol. 62, 1854, pp. 48–67.

Brooks, Rob. "Fear Not the Hipster Beard—for It Too Shall Pass." *Guardian*, April 16, 2014, www.theguardian.com/commentisfree/2014/apr/16/hipster-beard-guys-growing-a-beard. Accessed April 23, 2018.

Cheadle, Harry. "Beards Aren't Cool Anymore." *Vice*, April 13, 2016, www.vice.com/en_us/article/wd7mzb/beards-are-now-uncool. Accessed September 2017.

Crilly, A Woife. "Is 2017 Really the End of the Beard?" *The Sharpe*, February 5, 2017, thesharpe.com/life-style/2017-really-the-end-of-the-beard. Accessed April 11, 2018.

Cumming, Ed. "Can Hipsters Save the World?" *Guardian*, March 8, 2015, www.theguardian.com/uk-news/2015/mar/08/can-hipsters-save-the-world. Accessed April 11, 2018.

Daniels, Nicki. "An Open Letter to Bearded Hipsters: Stop Ruining My Beard Fetish." *Sabotage Times*, February 6, 2014, www.sabotagetimes.com/life/an-open-letter-to-bearded-hipsters-stop-ruining-my-beard-fetish. Accessed April 24, 2018.

Del Russo, Maria. "The Internet Says Beards Are Out—and Hearts Break Everywhere." *Refinery29*, June 11, 2015, www.refinery29.com/2015/06/89005/hipster-beards-over-clean-shaven-men. Accessed April 24, 2018.

Dennis, Brandon M. "How to Tell if You Are a Bearded Hipster." *Growabeard*, 2014, www.growabeardnow.com/beard-hipster. Accessed April 24, 2018.

Engber, Daniel. "Why Beards Have Always Been and Always Will Be Funny." *Slate*, December 3, 2014, www.slate.com/articles/arts/books/2014/12/beards_history_and_theory_of_male_facial_hair_and_comedy.html. Accessed September 2017.

"Felina." *Breaking Bad*, written and directed by Vince Gilligan, performance by Bryan Cranston, season 5, episode 16, AMC, September 29, 2013. *Netflix*, www.netflix.com/watch/70236428?trackId=200257859. Accessed April 24, 2020.

Gallagher, Jacob. "Is the Beard Trend Over?" *Wall Street Journal*, April 12, 2016, www.wsj.com/articles/is-the-beard-trend-over-1460492755?mod=e2fb. Accessed August 2017.

Glazek, Christopher. "South Side Story: Hasidim vs. Hipsters." *What Was the Hipster? A Sociological Investigation*, edited by Mark Greif, Kathleen Ross, and Dayna Tortoici. n+1 Foundation, 2010, pp.168–83.

Greif, Mark. "Positions." *What Was the Hipster? A Sociological Investigation*, edited by Mark Greif, Kathleen Ross, and Dayna Tortoici. n+1 Foundation, 2010, pp. 4–13.

Greif, Mark. Preface. *What Was the Hipster? A Sociological Investigation*, edited by Mark Greif, Kathleen Ross, and Dayna Tortoici. n+1 Foundation, 2010, pp. vii-xvii.

Hanuka, Tomer, "The L Train." [Cover Art] *New Yorker*, April 11, 2016. thanuka.com/#/take-the-l-train. Accessed June 20, 2020.

Horning, Rob. "The Death of the Hipster." *What Was the Hipster? A Sociological Investigation*, edited by Mark Greif, Kathleen Ross, and Dayna Tortoici. n+1 Foundation, 2010, pp. 78–84.

Horowitz, Eliot. "The Early Eighteenth Century Confronts the Beard: Kabbalah and Jewish Self-Fashioning." *Jewish History*, vol. 8, 1994, pp. 95–115.

Jackson, Greg. "Hipster Elegies." *Hedgehog Review*, vol. 21, no. 2, summer 2019, pp. 93–105.

Kurutz, Steven. "Caught in the Hipster Trap." *New York Times*, September 14, 2013, www.nytimes.com/2013/09/15/opinion/sunday/caught-in-the-hipster-trap.html. Accessed September 2017.

Leiman, Shnayer Z. "Rabbinic Openness to General Culture in the Early Modern Period in Western and Central Europe." *Judaism's Encounter with Other Cultures: Rejection or Integration?* edited by Jacob J. Schacter. Rowman and Littlefield, Jason Aronson, 1997, pp. 143–211.

Mackinney-Valentin, Maria. *Fashioning Identity: Status Ambivalence in Contemporary Fashion*. Bloomsbury, 2017.

Magill, R. Jay. *Sincerity: How a Moral Ideal Born Five Hundred Years Ago Inspired Religious Wars, Modern Art, Hipster Chic, and the Curious Notion that We All Have Something to Say (No Matter How Dull)*. Norton, 2012.

Mallozzi, Vincent. "Sideburns to Fu Manchu, the Best and Brightest." *New York Times*, December 28, 2003, Sports 9.

Mansfield-Devine, Patricia. "How the Hipster Beard Trend is Catching on in France." *Cosmetics Business*, December 2, 2016, www.cosmeticsbusiness.com/news/article_page/How_the_hipster_beard_trend_is_catching_on_in_France/123483. Accessed April 4, 2018.

McCracken, Brett. *Hipster Christianity: When Church and Cool Collide*. Baker Books, 2010.

Mount, Harry. "It's Time to Shave That Beard: The Decade of the Hipster Is Over." *The Spectator*, October 25, 2014, www.spectator.co.uk/2014/10/its-time-to-shave-that-beard-the-decade-of-the-hipster-is-over/. Accessed August 2017.

Murray, Margaret Anne. "White, Male and Bartending in Detroit: Masculinity Work in a Hipster Scene." *Journal of Contemporary Ethnography*, February 26, 2020, pp. 1–25, doi.org/10.1177/0891241620907126. Accessed June 2020.

Nelson, Bryan. "My Real Face." *Beard*, edited by Matthew Rainwaters. Chronicle Books, 2011, pp. 44–5.

Nicks, Denver. "Confessions of a Lumbersexual." *Time*, November 25, 2014, time.com/3603216/confessions-of-a-lumbersexual. Accessed August 2017.

Oldstone-Moore, Christopher. *Of Beards and Men: The Revealing History of Facial Hair*. University of Chicago Press, 2016.

O'Neil, Luke. "It's Hip to Be Hip." *Slate*, September 23, 2013, www.slate.com/articles/life/culturebox/2013/09/proud_of_being_a_hipster_one_bearded_indie_rock_loving_contrarian_article.html. Accessed August 2017.

O'Neill, Natalie. "The Bearded-Hipster Trend Has Truly and Utterly Taken Over New York." *New York Post*, April 12, 2016, www.nypost.com/2016/04/12/the-bearded-hipster-trend-has-truly-and-utterly-taken-over-new-york/. Accessed October 2017.

Puzak, Tom. "The Rise of the Lumbersexual." *GearJunkie*, October 30, 2014, gearjunkie.com/the-rise-of-the-lumbersexual. Accessed September 2017.

"The Red Woman." *Game of Thrones*, written by David Benioff and D. B. Weiss, directed by Jeremy Podeswa, performance by Nikolaj Coster-Waldau, season 6, episode 1, HBO, April 24, 2016. *YouTube*, www.youtube.com/watch?v=8SZu-SkkP0g. Accessed April 23, 2020.

Rhoades, Logan. "Introducing the Hot New Trend among Men: 'Lumbersexual.' " *BuzzFeed*, November 13, 2014, www.buzzfeed.com/mrloganrhoades/introducing-the-hot-new-trend-among-men-lumbersexual#.vlVG8Rw3z. Accessed September 2017.

"Riker Syndrome." *Urban Dictionary*, www.urbandictionary.com/define.php?term=Riker%20Syndrome. Accessed April 24, 2018.

"Riker's Beard." *Urban Dictionary*, www.urbandictionary.com/define.php?term=Riker%27s%20Beard. Accessed April 24, 2018.

Roof, Paul. "The Social Significance of Facial Hair." Panel discussion at Ohio Beardcon, October 5, 2012 (quote at 10:25), *YouTube*, www.youtube.com/watch?v=dxhLpODj6jo. Accessed March 7, 2014.

Silber, Michael K. "The Emergence of Ultra-Orthodoxy: The Invention of Tradition." *The Uses of Tradition: Jewish Continuity in the Modern Era*, edited by Jack Wertheimer. Jewish Theological Seminary of America, 1992, pp. 48–9.

Stone, Zara. "What Erich Bachman's Changing Facial Hair Reveals about His Psyche on HBO's 'Silicon Valley.'" *Forbes*, June 27, 2017, www.forbes.com/sites/zarastone/2017/06/27/what-erlich-bachmans-changing-facial-hair-reveals-about-his-psyche-on-hbos-silicon-valley/2/#565c9dcb725a. Accessed October 2017.

Stuever, Hank. "Fall 2014 TV: A Sharp Increase in Bearded Best Friend." *Washington Post*, September 20, 2014, www.washingtonpost.com/entertainment/tv/fall-tv-2014-a-sharp-increase-in-bearded-best-friend/2014/09/18/04304754-3cf9-11e4-b03fde718edeb92f_story.html?utm_term=.1c6d83489166. Accessed October 2017.

"Ten Reasons Why You Shouldn't Shave Your Beard." *HipsterBeardClub*, www.hipsterbeardclub.com/beard-care-tips/10-reasons-shouldnt-shave-beard. Accessed April 25, 2018.

Venables, Michael. "Frakes on Meeting Roddenberry, the Riker Beard, His 'Next Gen' Family and Learning to Direct." *Forbes*, April 22, 2013, www.forbes.com/sites/michaelvenables/2013/04/22/frakes-on-meeting-roddenberry/#23e8d25d1142. Accessed August 20, 2020.

"The Wars to Come." *Game of Thrones*, written by David Benioff and D. B. Weiss, directed by Michael Slovis, performance by Peter Dinklage and Conleth Hill, season 5, episode 1, HBO, April 12, 2015. *YouTube*, www.youtube.com/watch?v=eJ6kclT15z8You. Accessed April 23, 2018.

Whitman, Walt. *Leaves of Grass*. Brooklyn, 1855.

"Why Shave?" *Household Words*, August 13, 1853, 560–3.

Williams, Alex. "The Brooklyn Beard Goes Mainstream." *New York Times*, January 8, 2014, www.nytimes.com/2014/01/09/fashion/the-brooklyn-beard-goes-mainstream.html. Accessed August 2017.

8

The Politics of Hipster Porn/ography

Alexandra Hauke and Philip Jacobi

Introduction: Aesthetic Pleasures and/as Hipsterdom

On April 5, 2010, Tumblr site Fuck Yeah, Ryan McGinley! reblogged a photograph that was captioned "Look at this fucking hipster flipping through Ryan McGinley's *Everybody Knows This is Nowhere* book. Buy your own here and maybe you'll be as cool as this guy! But probably not." The image reveals a tall, slender man with a moustache and a mullet sitting in the sun on a park bench, wearing a white knitted cardigan, a green checkered button-down shirt, pink leopard-print leggings rolled up to above the ankles, black-and-white lace-up shoes, a neon-orange trucker hat, a pair of dark sunglasses, and an assortment of gold jewelry, including bracelets, rings, and necklaces. On his lap rests a copy of New York photographer Ryan McGinley's photo collection *Everybody Knows This Is Nowhere*, the open page showing a black-and-white portrait titled "Sam, 2010 gelatin silver print 18x12 inches, edition of three"—a photograph of an equally thin, Caucasian guy in his mid to late twenties wearing a nose ring, who echoes the youthful aesthetic features of the book holder. While the photo in the publication does not reveal anything below Sam's neck, we can safely assume the model's nudity, in line with the rest of the project—a collection of intimate photographs of young subjects staged in McGinley's downtown New York studio, a neutral space with white walls whose neither-here-nor-there quality fittingly represents the "nowhere" in the title of the book and the spatial and temporal emptiness associated with the "never-gonna-die-mentality of youth" (Vartanian). Both the portrait of Sam and the Tumblr photograph as a whole therefore exemplify very clearly the kind of aesthetic ascribed to "the hipster indie generation" (Raposo).

Cultural products in this vein are informed by a certain "rhetoric of neoliberal creativity, marked by alternative lifestyle, niche markets, … gentrification, and pseudo-bohemianism" (Robertson 186): they celebrate self-referentiality, subcultural aestheticization, and a commitment to both in unabashed excess. In his seminal article "What Was the Hipster?" (2010), later compiled with other essays in *What Was the Hipster? A Sociological Investigation*, Mark Greif aims to define this phenomenon of the hipster, which has drawn substantial public yet little academic attention and remains elusive as to the parametric composition of its exponents: he discusses that hipsters are, above all, aestheticized and aestheticizing creatures who graze the fine line between the mainstream appeal of counterculture and counterculture itself by supporting the very consumerism they are trying to oppose. Greif takes up Thomas Frank's term "rebel consumer" for this purpose, identifying the hipster as "the person who, adopting the rhetoric but not the politics of the counterculture, convinces himself that buying the right mass products individualizes him as transgressive. Purchasing the products of authority is thus reimagined as a defiance of authority." He further understands particularly the white hipster, who emerged in the late 1990s, as a one-dimensional phenomenon submerged in "the aesthetic of basement rec-room pornography" and thus in the kind of porno-chic fashion he claims is associated, for example, with mustaches. This understanding allows the hipster, yet again, to tread along the margins of subculture and mainstream because of the ways pornography comprises a similar inventory of formulaic practices in terms of both form and content: visibility of the body plays a role during intercourse in pornography and also defines a variety of hipster projects, such as the aforementioned McGinley book; an underlying power dynamic that is either gendered in straight pornography or role-related in gay pornography and also lays bare the ambivalent political efforts of hipsterdom; and an inconsequentiality regarding the framed actions and actors, which are geared toward specific forms of closure, such as sexual release in pornography and aesthetic as well as political limits in hipster cultures. Such a comparison fuses two seemingly oblique approaches which have in common that "[n]o one self-identifies as a hipster" (Evans 104), and "it is rare to hear people boast about how much they enjoy porn" (Le Bled).

From this follows that hipsters as putatively rebellious figures and pornography as a fiction of lust occupy a conjoined taboo space, which ultimately converges in aesthetics that promise intellectual, affective, and sensual pleasures including, but not limited to, dimensions of sexual arousal. In this sense, we want to argue that hipsterdom plays with the strategies of pornography, which negotiates the corporeality of sex, and the aesthetic dimension of porn in a larger sense, a set of intersections, according to Helen Hester, that "display an interest in nonsexual or nongenital concerns" and are thus no longer "necessarily required ... to facilitate a state of sexual arousal in the consumer-viewer" (73). While Linda Williams, for example, uses the terms porn and pornography interchangeably in her seminal study *Porn Studies*, Hester, in *Beyond Explicit*, claims that porn, in contrast to pornography, suggests "a cartography that charts a cultural landscape in which sex has been largely displaced as the primary locus of transgression" (189). While we are aware that the discipline that is concerned with the aesthetic representation of sexuality has been theorized under the umbrella term "porn studies," we believe that this nomenclature conflates and thus falls short of the intricacies between pornography (intended for sexual pleasure) and porn (intended for pleasure). The distinctions between pornography and porn we want to foreground in this essay through the marker *porn/ography* are made visible through a countercultural reconsideration of the (visual) practices of aestheticization and the political dimensions of the body as a site of performance and fantasy. By looking at the ways hipsterdom negotiates these ideas, we want to read beyond the commodified and commodifying parameters of hardcore erotica that, more often than not, prescribe the aforementioned monodimensional understanding of pleasure to carve out a multilayered set of ways satisfaction can be derived from cultural, artistic, corporeal, or political products and actions. Laura Kipnis observes that "there's still the issue of what pornography means as a form of culture, and why it's meaningful to our culture" (x); in a similar fashion, this volume attempts to delineate the cultural significance of the phenomenon of the hipster.

Our examinations of Catalan filmmaker Noel Alejandro's short films *Eloi & Biel* (2013), *Bad Medicine* (2016), *Doing Elliot* (2016), and *Trivial* (2017) as well as American photographer Ryan McGinley's collection of images *The Kids Were Alright '98-'03* (1998–2003) show that a conjunct reading of the aesthetics that define hipsterdom and pornography allows for an intersectional vantage ground from which we may observe the oscillation between the "creative pretensions," the "psychological motivations" (Mercer 62), and the "inevitably political questions" (Kipnis 164) of the cultural productions these realms offer and the cultures they emerge from. Taking into account hipsters' pervasiveness as an allegedly "anti-political group" (Greif) and pornography's ascribed "socially destabilizing" potential (Kipnis 163), we are concerned with the phenomenological conventions and transgressions of both the hipster and pornography, that is, with the ways both are invested in and scrutinize the "cultural politics of canon formation" (Hester 163). We argue that reading pornography through hipster aesthetics and practices, and vice versa, thus brings about a reconsideration of the ways the terms "porn" and "pornography" have been used conversely to conflate ways of attraction, pleasure, and enjoyment derived from viewing bodies engaged in sex all the while the former continues to transgress the boundaries of such a straightforward imagination. As we will show, Alejandro and McGinley engage in what we call the politics of porn/ography by making use of the cultural and visual politics of their times, subjects, and media as well as of the aesthetics of hipsterdom as a discursive phenomenon. Their works emerge as palimpsests of the patterns of excessive youth culture, hardcore pornography, and porn photography, pushing the "naked ethereal opus of the hipster indie generation" (Raposo) into "a wholly eroticized realm" (Hester 64). We want to emphasize at this point that the title to the German edition of Mark Greif's seminal study on hipsters and their afterlives, *Hipster. Eine Transatlantische Diskussion* (trans.: *Hipster. A Transatlantic Discussion*), not least suggests that hipster aesthetics can no longer be confined to the cultural formations of their origins and serves as a gateway to our comparison between McGinley and Alejandro. Despite their different national backgrounds, the politics and aesthetics of the hipster and porn/ography in their works symbolize the glorification of reactionary politics against consumer culture on both sides of the Atlantic.

Transforming the Mainstream? Noel Alejandro's Countercultural Pornography

Presently, "[c]ontemporary 'hipster' aesthetics and attitudes" (Mercer 214), which often manifest in a commitment to narratives and aesthetics outside those of mainstream hardcore pornography, that is, pornography recognized as "a set of texts made by producers who are prominent in media reportage, blogs and discussion fora" (Mercer 74), may be found in a variety of works by a multitude of artists. What unites them is an avowal to supersede, counterpoint, or subvert the narrative, performative, and aesthetic standards of the adult entertainment industry while at the same time retaining the explicitness of the sex on display.

Independent Catalan filmmaker Noel Alejandro's short films teeter in between amateur and professional pornography, "ready to give some dignity and quality the gay adult genre deserves" (Simoneau). With a distinctly un-American and intimate aesthetic, Alejandro produces "alternative adult films, aimed to disrupt taboos" (Behrenbeck, our translation); as a pornographic filmmaker, Alejandro self-identifies as having "always been driven by his interest in all kinds of art that break taboos" ("About Noel"). While the argument that transgression is "pivotal to the inner dynamics of pornography" (Paasonen 162) still holds true in a general sense, since pornography relocates a generally private activity to the public, while at the same time the genre itself is paradoxically consumed privately, pornography's transgressive potential is on the decline. Yet in an age when the "forbidden fruit of homosexual sex" has been thoroughly commodified (Anderson 6), sexually explicit materials can be watched "at any time and in almost any place" (Massey, Burns, and Franz), and taboo practices in gay pornography, such as barebacking, have been normalized (Varghese). Alejandro seeks to reintroduce an element of transgression into a genre that "constructs a heteronormative vision of masculinity and sexuality in terms of sexual conduct, body types and settings" (Mercer 119). His efforts speak to the spirit of producing counterculture (Goffman and Joy 232; Newman 74), which has been an ongoing project of feminist and queer pornography.

To problematize pornography's production patterns, let alone any production outside pornography's established formulaic patterns, refocuses and exponentiates its transgressive capability: while "all of pornography's consumers become transgressors of certain cultural codes" (Juffer 2), its creators may become countercultural transgressors by creating or subverting the codes themselves. In his endeavor to "push for a more sensitive way of scriptwriting [and to] push pre-settled boundaries of [pornographic] filmmaking" ("About Noel"), Alejandro lays claim to the political potential of transgressing "mainstream" pornographic filmmaking: "the transgressive," argues Jon Jervis, "is reflexive, questioning both its own role and that of the culture that has defined it in its otherness" (4). Pornography, "as a critical part of our media and cultural practices, understood as a vast matrix incorporating industrial, labour, activist, representational, governmental, and creative performance practices" (Sullivan and McKee 230) and as a culturally transgressive aesthetic text, thus implies both medium and counter-medium framing as fundamentally political. On his website, Alejandro cites feminist pornographer Erika Lust as one of his main influences: Lust's works are part of the growing body of "queer pornography," which strives to question the mechanisms of normalization and identity construction in mainstream pornography. Especially her crowdfunded *XConfessions* series (2013–), which intends to counteract mainstream pornography's "shitty ... values, ethics, and aesthetics" (Lust qtd. in Furness) through an approach that favors quality over quantity, transparent production conditions over anonymity, and diversity over uniformity, can be seen as a vantage point for Alejandro, at least in an aesthetic sense.

Eloi & Biel (2013), Alejandro's first pornographic short film, and *Bad Medicine* (2016), his second, form two polar opposites in terms of aesthetics and content, the former of which does not necessarily read as pornography per se. Although it features hardcore sex, it lacks most of the trappings of hardcore films with Alejandro aiming for "it to be fun and aesthetically pleasing" (qtd. in Simoneau). Although the narrative—lovers discover a deserted finca in the Spanish countryside and decide to stay there overnight—does not necessarily transcend the inventory of porn plots, the sex between the eponymous protagonists—two young men—progresses at a much slower pace than one would expect from mainstream pornography. Penetration is incremental rather than instantaneous; the cinematographic framing is naturalistic rather than gratuitous or exploitative. Moreover, Eloi and Biel do not conform to established and, arguably, compulsory body standards of gay mainstream pornography; and neither does their largely non-verbal lovemaking. While one ejaculation is shown in a close-up, thus retaining the prerequisite "maximum visibility" (Williams, *Hard Core* 49) of male arousal and lust, the director also chooses to show at length the intimate aftermath of sex. With these aesthetic choices, Noel Alejandro and his coproducer Victor Ayala displace common tropes of hardcore pornography into a decidedly hipster aesthetic: a rustic finca next to a seemingly infinite expanse of moonlit forest offsets the conventionally neutral sets of gay mainstream pornography; corduroy pants and a diegetic folk guitar score counterpoint the jockstrap and techno of gay mainstream hardcore as sexual aggressiveness.

Bad Medicine (2016) dispenses with all of this transgressive counter-framing: it is, by and large, a gonzo scene featuring two performers more in line with a stereotypical gay hardcore aesthetic and focuses wholly on the straightforward depiction of hardcore sex. Instead of a similarly invested narrative and/or aesthetic framing as found in *Eloi & Biel*, Alejandro includes but one narrative element: the film ends with one performer casting a wistful glance at the receding silhouette of the man who penetrated him minutes earlier. We may read Alejandro's decision to sharply condense all possible affective potential of a more expansive narrative framing into a singular, somewhat incongruous, shot as a self-referential, ironic nod toward his own agenda to counteract the purported lack of narrative in mainstream pornography, while highlighting that the sex alone in pornography already constitutes a narrative in itself (Dyer 125).

Doing Elliot's (2016) opening sequence is replete with the paraphernalia of hipster aesthetics: Thomas, the scruffy protagonist, sports a checkered shirt and has his latte in a café among countless succulents while doodling in his Moleskine journal. Thomas dutifully returns a gym membership card dropped by a passing runner, the eponymous Elliot, an old school friend. When they later settle around Elliot's kitchen table to catch up, a picture of Elliot's girlfriend receives a laconic "[d]on't worry, she's not here," while a page in Thomas's journal simply says, "To do Elliot." Over the course of the conversation, we learn of their teenage romance and the subsequent drifting apart. The film ostensibly settles into the established canon of gay porn tropes: teenage lust is revisited in an adult context; the now straight man does indeed harbor secret homosexual desires and will act upon them. The narrative inventory of the plot becomes inconsequential and is dropped as soon as clothes come off, revealing that both performers conform to porn body standards (fit, well-endowed), and their lust is rendered palpable in both auditive and visual spectra for the audience. The performers and the sex itself, moreover, rather comfortably follow the established "porn loop" (Dyer 125) of gay mainstream pornography: kissing is followed by mutual fellatio, which leads to penetration and ends in ejaculations. Considering this, we are hard-pressed to conceive of *Doing Elliot* as having the same transgressive impetus as Alejandro's earlier works: it lacks both *Eloi & Biel*'s porn/ographic equilibrium and *Bad Medicine*'s ironic potential. Instead, the film interlinks its transgressive moment with its aesthetics. It is less concerned with the performative tropes of mainstream hardcore in favor of its presentation: the lovemaking appears credible and organic primarily because of soft cuts that work against gay mainstream pornography's compulsive need to depict the fictitious entirety of the sex act and because of the conspicuous amount of close-up shots of faces in ecstasy during the initial moments of penetration and the frequent kissing. Again, the short film's hardcore portion remains nonverbal, except for Thomas urging Elliot to "breathe" and commenting on how "tight" he is when he tries to penetrate him for the first time (*Doing Elliot*). These glaring markers of hardcore vernacular, nonetheless, prove and undermine the hipster's suspected "lack of authenticity" (Horning): it disrupts Alejandro's ambition to produce "no ordinary porn" (*Doing Elliot*) by inserting dialogue tangibly out of place in a scene that otherwise lacks it and diminishes the intended cinematic realism and aesthetic authenticity of *Doing Elliot*. At the same time, however, it re-situates the film in the realm of gay mainstream hardcore, thus awarding it a different kind of authenticity as a (gay mainstream) hardcore product.

Alejandro's repeated claims to offset mainstream pornography's standards by fashioning his films in a different, hyper-stylized "aesthetic [that is] largely missing today in gay porn" (qtd. in Simoneau) ring hollow, especially considering his frequent use of its aesthetic markers. Arguably, Alejandro co-opts the narrative of (potentially) transgressive and thus political media to self-serve a self-fashioning of the Alejandro brand, which embodies hipster aesthetics not only in the products but also in the producer. This is potentially most obvious in one of his recent films, *Trivial* (2017). After a hammy scene, in which three visually similar twenty-something men negotiate a potential flatshare in Brussels—an exercise in the visual lexicon of "hipster retro-bricolage" (Threadgold 177), with vintage furniture, herbal tea, and corduroy trousers—the film immediately cuts to a medium shot of bareback penetration, rimming, and ass-to-mouth. By omitting foreplay and by beginning the hardcore portion of the film with practices considered dangerous and unhygienic but in line with mainstream's "trend towards extreme pornography" (Boyle 57), Alejandro's film not necessarily counterpoints the mainstream. In fact, the film—and certainly all of his later works—bear down on what they initially seemed to avoid. *Trivial*'s omission of sexual negotiation as well as foreplay and its presentation of both bareback penetration and ass-to-mouth in its place may indeed be read in several ways. As a message of sex positivity, it evokes the recent reinvigoration of not only gay hardcore filmmaking but also gay life in general made possible by new HIV prevention drugs like PrEP. This largely frames the essentially political issues surrounding the pathologization of gay sex as newly "trivial" to a generation whose concerns orbit, like the conversation in *Trivial* tells us, topics like "stylish stuff," "e-piano[s]," and "studying and stuff." The three toned, well-endowed, and bearded performers also diminish Alejandro's claims to making films in the spirit of queer pornography itself, which "questions exclusionary practices of identity construction and also normalization" (Fuchs and Jacobi 42, our translation), especially in its presentation of sexual bodies. At the same time, this omission enhances the triviality of the film itself: it is nothing but "a smooth, uncomplicated film" ("Trivial"), akin to mainstream pornography, and thus subscribes, *mutatis mutandis*, to the same politics it set out to subvert or transgress. While we may acknowledge the text's desire to "use ... the pornographic aesthetic to artistic ends" (Newall 212), its artistic—and thus arguably political—ends are problematic, especially considering the way Alejandro uses his platform to proclaim countercultural authorial intent. When asked about his productions' safe sex policies, Alejandro responded:

> The most annoying part of the discussion, for me, doesn't have to do with the safety of the people involved, but in showing to the viewer that using condoms is the right thing to do. Yes, that might be true, but I don't see how a porn director should be entitled to teach this message. *I don't believe that porn has to be educational. I don't think porn needs to tell people what to do.* ("Why")

While attaching himself to feminist and queer pornographers, he communicates a message very much like that of the gay mainstream hardcore industry: despite initial claims to body positivity, the performers' physiques are normative—down to the sailor tattoos—and the sex on display is well within the range of the (gay) mainstream's move toward extreme but, as of now, normalized practices and characterizations remain unable to communicate emotional depths. This is, arguably, the conundrum of hipster pornography, as erotica writer Hannah Wilde notes:

> The vast majority of porn, especially if we're just talking about pictures and videos, is only supposed to be a short little vacation into fantasy; you get in, you get out, you move on. That means that most people would rather look at a guy or girl and see tattoos and instantly think, I relate to that, instead of having a 20-minute intro where the porn star talks about how much they love Jack Kerouac. That's just not the way most people treat their porn, and I think that's totally fine. (qtd. in Pardes)

Trivial exemplifies that Alejandro's works must be perceived as incrementally moving away from something that can be seen as aligned with the aims and attitudes of feminist and queer pornography, while retaining the hipster aesthetic: *Eloi & Biel* comes closer to a form of explicit erotica, where the sex not necessarily takes center stage but borrows heavily from the visual framing of hipsterdom while consciously breaking with both the strategies and aesthetics of hardcore pornography. Alejandro's later works, however, where there is little besides the sex, are ultimately unable to hide the lack of "melodramatic context" (qtd. in Simoneau) at the core of what we conceive of as "porn" under the political veneer of his pornography. Alejandro produces pornography that is also porn in the sense that it provides multidimensional entry points to pleasurable experiences beyond the depiction of explicit sex through the lens of a distinct hipster aesthetic; he fails, nonetheless, to embrace the pleasures that exist in the realm of the uncommodified and political. His films serve instead as a point of departure revealing the complicated relationship between hipster pornography and hipster porn. Asserting this distinction allows for a "re-examination of … sexuality … and the politics of representation" (Attwood qtd. in Hester 2) beyond pornography and in porn.

Toward Hipster Porn: Ryan McGinley's *The Kids Were Alright '98-'03*

Our explorations of the potentials of porn as a multidimensional collection of pleasure-stimulating practices and aesthetics that transgresses the realm of corporeal arousal expose Vanessa Grigoriadis's estimation that Ryan McGinley's art "sometimes falls just *short* of pornography" (emphasis added) as insufficient. Rather, we want to suggest that his work as a "naked hipster photographer" (Helmore), whereby the ambivalence of whether McGinley photographs naked hipsters and/or constitutes a naked hipster himself fittingly characterizes the limitless, fluid essence of his artistic ventures, moves *beyond* the hardcore concerns we discussed with regard to Alejandro and toward narratives in which the human body and its surroundings are framed through the representational strategies of photography as medium and hipsterdom as counterculture. Another look at the opening example of this essay reveals that McGinley's reputation as the creator of a "youthsex brand" stems from his ability to portray "America's flaming youth" (Connor) in settings and ways that appear at once timeless and anchored in a particular present-day moment that cannot be repeated.

The publication of McGinley's volume of photographs entitled *Everybody Knows This Is Nowhere* accompanied an exhibition of the same name at Team Gallery in Soho in 2010 for which he allegedly "shifted his focus away from constructing a youthful sublime within the boundless American landscape" and is no longer the "chronicler of youthful adventure" ("Everybody Knows") he was in earlier projects, such as *The Kids Were Alright '98-'03*. The portrait of Sam in the Tumblr photograph above—the image within the image—does, however, exemplify very clearly why he has been labeled "the most important photographer in America" (Gregory) for his portrayal of the excessive behavior of a seemingly untroubled and debauched subculture. The "hipster" in the Tumblr image is ascribed an attribute of "coolness" for his aesthetic and taste in art, a characteristic which is "always about performances—of body and fashion, habit and attitude, style and changes in style and many more" (Geiger, Schröder and Söll qtd. in Kohlenberger 32)—and which Tumblr claims will be transferred to whoever purchases McGinley's publication. This prospective engagement in the capitalization of the artist's work through the promise of "coolness" thus points to a reading of McGinley's photography as a form of art drawing on, even exploiting, the creative potential of nudity as well as the aesthetic representation, the dubious politics, and the contested hedonism of hipsterdom.

The Kids Were Alright '98-'03 serves as the collection responsible for McGinley's initial fame. It is also an apt representation of the kind of "filtering of popular culture, the celebration of youth, [and] the direct and raw immediacy ... that so characterizes his photographs" (Abrams), wherein he creates extensions of the very hipster aesthetic through a decidedly non-pornographic lens. The large number of portraits, Polaroids, and precursors to the contemporary selfie that make up this extensive project disclose McGinley's obsession with eternalizing every move of his friends, "an expansive, legendary group of wild downtown figures, all of whom he refers to by first name only" (Gregory). His frames thus offer the viewer a window into the intimate moments of relationships and the rebellious antics of a generation dedicated to protesting all aspects of mainstream culture and political authority. The comparatively high number of photos portraying the artist and his exclusive circle of friends half-naked, in the nude, and/or in potentially compromising positions not only speaks to McGinley's interest in the corporeality of anatomy but also raises fundamental questions about the notions of and connections between nudity, sexuality, and porn. McGinley claims that "[his] photos are the least sexual thing" and that instead of posing in an overly sexualized way he instructs his models to "kind of act natural" so that his pieces can become an "investigation of the human body" (Slenske) rather than pornographic content. In line with this, we argue that his approach desexualizes his images but does not present sexuality and nudity as innocent or accidental byproducts of his work. Rather, the subjects' nakedness, the public staging of their debaucherous lives, and their addictions to drugs, alcohol, and aesthetic self-representation define *The Kids Were Alright* as a project that epitomizes the fundamentals of freedom at the heart of both the hipster agenda and "the nonsexual pornographic," that is, "sexually explicit material that engages with nonsexual content, affects, and intentions" (Hester 69).

In this sense, McGinley's collection creates through the medium of photography—the art of capturing moments in time in still images—a fiction of non-explicit pleasure that adds further layers to the complexity of pornography we discussed in Alejandro, pushing what Linda Williams has called "moving-image sex" (*Screening* 122) beyond its textual limits. Thereby, *The Kids Were Alright* approximates a conceptualization of porn as an aesthetic characterized by the occasional exposition of bodies but lacking their engagement in sexual intercourse and pornographic content. McGinley produces a narrative of the hipster (body) in which "the powers of silence and immobility which belong to and define all photography" (Metz 83) merge with the anarchistic freedom of a "gleeful, unfettered subculture" living in "a Neverland where people are thrilled and naked, leaping in front of graffiti on the street, sacked out in heaps of flannel shirts—everything very debauched and drug-addled and decadent" (Levy). In this narrative, McGinley showcases a never-before-seen lack of restraint in the way he portrays the naked bodies of mainly young, male models, exhibiting the most intimate processes between individuals engaged in a variety of pleasurable acts that approximate but never fulfil the expectations of sexual practices. As such, the photographs never allow the viewer to witness entire sexual acts, in part due to the limitations of the medium in comparison with films such as those created by Noel Alejandro. The image *Having Sex (Polaroids), 1999*, for example, shows two young, slender males in bed during an intended sex act, both laughing while surrounded by hundreds of Polaroids stuck to the wall behind and beside them. At first glance, the image immediately raises a variety of questions: Who are the individuals in the picture? Who is behind the camera? Is this a candid image or was it staged? Does the content of this image qualify as pornographic or does it suggest something else? In contrast to other photographs in the collection of couples contemplating or having sex, the title here does not indicate the individuals' names, making it difficult to recognize them in the array of pictures of well-known yet illusive underground artists and party-goers—especially when many of the models resemble each other or when half their faces are concealed, as is the case in this photograph. While from the context of the rest of the project we assume that this is a still of McGinley and his boyfriend at the time, Marc, other images of this couple are explicitly captioned with their names, such as *Ryan & Marc (Red Kiss), 1999*, which shows them engaged in a sensual French kiss lying on what is presumably a red bed sheet.

While *Having Sex* is likely to shock certain viewers due to its somewhat explicit yet mostly insinuated content, its straightforward and unapologetic title takes away from its potential to scandalize and, instead, suggests a narrative in which sex itself as well as sex between men is normalized. Upon second glance, it becomes clear that McGinley offers spectators more of a sensual imaginary than a pornographic reality: the fact that, in contrast to film, there is no movement, no sound, and no temporal or spatial change in *Having Sex* implies that McGinley engages in capturing a single moment in time that offers the viewer the possibility of a variety of fantasies on top of a more common narrative with sexual release as its primary goal. In this sense, the potentially pornographic aspect of the image is not created by its producer, but can be imagined, projected, or translated into a nonsexual account of intimacy by its consumer. *Having Sex* offers no foreplay, main act, or final cum shot; it does not facilitate exclusively sexual arousal in the viewer, it does not expect to be used as an impetus for sexual stimulation, it offers no answer to the question of candidness vs. staging, and it does not dip into the "improbable sexual acrobatics" or the "theatrics" (Kipnis 163, 164) of certain hardcore pornographic narratives. It rather enjoys and employs the kind of timelessness and youthful lawlessness, freedom, and carelessness associated with hipsterdom, eschewing sexual pleasure or practice as its main focus and highlighting instead the pleasures of being young and independent, of (over)using illegal substances, of populating the urban party scene, of disregarding parental expectations, and of deconstructing the hegemony of heteronormativity. The subjects on the images derive these distinctive forms of pleasure from the very culture they occupy while viewers are allowed to watch these radical antics all the while constructing their own fantastic narratives, sexual or not. This is essentially where McGinley's *The Kids Were Alright* transgresses pornography and approaches porn: the artist elicits reactions by aestheticizing everyday practices, thus offering an unlimited space for fantasy on top of the opportunity for a sexual result.

Laura Kipnis proposes that a "culture's pornography becomes, in effect, a very precise map of that culture's borders" (164), exemplified in the way pornography is still equated in oftentimes essentialist and reductive ways with "yesterday's ideology of hate" in terms of race and gender (Bernardi 240) and thus gets caught up in the stigmata associated with the "early stage[s]" of its "invention—that it is by and for men and about women" (Williams, "Motion" 14). In our consideration of McGinley's approach to sex and nudity, these implications are downplayed to the point of elimination because the way the artist photographs his subjects in *The Kids Were Alright* speaks to the varying potentials of pornography and porn. McGinley's images function as a clear indicator of the possibilities and limitations of the hipster ethos, in which everything from food to colors, instruments, real estate, and more is considered "porn," as illustrated by the outstanding number of hashtags found on *Instagram* which are indicative of porn as a practice of looking at and deriving pleasure from highly aestheticized versions of ordinary objects without necessarily sexualizing them.

Taking this even further, McGinley's connection with popular social media platforms such as Instagram is especially apparent in his use of the Polaroid photograph. Examples include *Marc, Polaroids (Dates Variable*

1998–2003) and *Teddy, Polaroids (Dates Variable 1998–2003)*, both of which show nine individual photos of the respective subject, arranged in a three-by-three fashion. Most of them heavily filtered through predominantly pastel color effects, McGinley's Polaroids echo the contemporary appeal of a vintage medium that defines a fundamental hipster shape and emphasizes the significance of framing in the context of hipster aesthetics. The appeal of the Polaroid camera for this and other artistic projects is underlined in the announced discontinuation of the Polaroid camera in 2009, "weighing heavily on many a hipster's soul that one of their favored methods of capturing narcissism" would be no more (Epstein). In response, Urban Outfitters, an essentially American hipster brand, launched "The Impossible Project," a lobbying group who restarted production of Polaroid film in 2010, an effort celebrated in an article fittingly titled "Success! Hipsters Save Polaroid!" The fact that "the film will cost more as it will be imported from Europe" (Epstein) once more plays into the double standard of condemning yet participating in the pitfalls of consumerism Mark Greif and other critics have foregrounded with regard to both the realities and stereotypes surrounding hipster sub/countercultures.

The immediacy of the Polaroid form indicates at once a "friendly snapshot" (Bonanos 162) taken in the heat of the moment, and at the time McGinley created these pictures, "a more private image—no need to send off those potentially embarrassing images to a photo lab," suggesting "the equation of the Polaroid with sex and titillating images (instant ones at that)" (Sturken 102–3). Photography has largely become digital in the twenty-first century, with the Polaroid symbolizing hipster nostalgia; yet, the restrictive frames of this form, that is, the white borders surrounding Marc and Teddy in *The Kids Were Alright*, continue to enclose private moments of Marc in the process of taking off his shirt and Teddy holding his German shepherd into the camera, aestheticizing commonplace processes through artistic filtering and adding even more intimacy to McGinley's already diaristic approach. The spatially limited, cut-out style that defines the Polaroid further accentuates the artist's aforementioned interest in the shapes, sizes, and individual significances of the human body, effectively tracing the edge between on-frame and off-frame by snipping away any aspect of the world outside the photograph and instead offering the viewer the pleasure of experiencing the subject in close detail. In this sense, McGinley's Polaroids serve as metaphors for the borders separating hipster subculture from mainstream; they showcase "an act of cutting off a piece of space and time, of keeping it unchanged while the around continues to change" (Metz 85), highlighting the live-and-let-die mindset of a generation existing in the here and now.

Critics such as Kirsty Robertson observe that the time of McGinley's *The Kids Were Alright* project "was one in which the kids were very much not all right but were taking to the streets in cities around the world in unprecedented numbers to protest the inequitable results of the spread of global capitalism" (172) among other issues. What this suggests on McGinley's part is a potential purposeful disregard of the harsh reality of the politics outside his subjects' allegedly blissful dreamland, pointing toward "an erasure of concerns defining that moment in George Bush-led America—the tumbling economy, the war in Iraq—an erasure so strong that it implie[s] denial" (Robertson 172). While it is true that McGinley does not engage on-frame with the societal outrage that characterized the project's time period off-frame, images such as the famous *Dash Bombing, 2001* or *Dash (Trucktop), 1999* do speak to an investment by McGinley's hipsters in a type of countermovement against prescribed rules and laws. Both show McGinley's close friend and downtown New York cult artist Dash Snow, who died of a drug overdose in 2009, in late-night graffiti sessions dangerously high up on a twenty-story ledge where his work could become part of the "crimes of style" (Ferrell) that define the connection between art and politics: "graffiti is a process, as much as it is a finished product. The philosophy behind this process stems from making private spaces public and challenging the rules of access whether it be physical access or social access. Pure vandalism at its core is a political act as much as it is an artistic image" (Pudl qtd. in Iveson 97). As such, McGinley's efforts may at times seem less politicized than those of some of his contemporaries—such as Nan Goldin, Larry Clark, and Jean-Michel Basquiat (cf. Abrams)—and thus demonstrate less investment in the American political scene of the late 1990s and early 2000s. However, *The Kids Were Alright* does dip into a range of concerns with regard to body and identity politics, and, especially, the politics of aestheticization.

As we have shown, McGinley's hipsters participate in the kind of cultural revolution that seems pretentious at first, but necessary at last. Their laissez-faire attitudes, their openness to the tastes and potentially voyeuristic practices of their viewership, their insistence in the normalization of nakedness and (non-normative) sexual acts, and their willingness to share their aestheticized, intimate hipster utopias with the public are a clear testament not only to their passion for self-fashioning but also to the significant artistic and cultural implications of porn—a set of modes and practices of looking, fantasizing, and appreciating that transcend sexual pleasure. *The Kids Were Alright*—much like the later project *Everybody Knows This Is Nowhere*—is symbolic of these practices: youth cultures will continue to occupy today's nowheres in desperate attempts to find their somewheres all the while protesting any standardized norms along the way. Hipsterdom does not only represent "the fruits of a cultural crisis" (Brainpolice2) but also cultural, political, and artistic opportunity. McGinley's art "stubbornly point[s] to the print of what *was*, but no longer *is*" (Metz 83), but at the same time reminds us that it is in fact alright to reminisce, to dream, and to be naked—not just as kids. Laura Kipnis observes that pornography "insist[s] on a sanctioned space for fantasy," which "is part of its politics" (163).

Hipster porn comments on yet also eludes instances of dissent imposed on pornography as a set of hardcore moving images in the first place and focuses on additional forms of fantasy that are more often than not defined by its aesthetics rather than by its content. McGinley's photographs combine the nostalgia of a generation of anarchy, liberation, and revolution with that of a medium—the Polaroid—associated with that generation's philosophies to achieve this kind of reverie: by staging non-hardcore yet explicit bodies in intimate moments and muted color schemes, hipster porn thus allows for a broad framing of pleasure beyond physical contours.

Conclusion: Politics, Hipsters, Porn/ography

Social media make apparent how hipsterdom is a fundamentally aesthetic phenomenon. Its proponents invest heavily in representational aspects of cultural, transgressive, and subversive strategies that define both porn and pornography, arguably because "pornography isn't just an individual predilection: pornography is central to our culture"; it "is revealing," it is "the royal road to the cultural psyche," and it thus "exposes the culture to itself" (Kipnis x). The hipster's investment in and engagement with the aesthetic potential of sex and sexuality proves that "pornography isn't necessarily corrupting, violent, or oppressive, [and] neither is it always progressive, healing, or liberating" (Hester 16). The case of Noel Alejandro's films, nonetheless, has shown the difficulties in escaping the gravity of genre and the pitfalls of non-politics in a profoundly political medium. Ryan McGinley's works depicting hipsters in their aestheticized habitat counter the necessarily sexualized or supposedly dangerous narrative of hardcore pornography—a potential side effect of the constraints of the still image—through strategies of insinuation. Porn subsequently is able "to satisfy—but also, Foucault reminds us, to further incite—the desire not only for pleasure but also for 'the knowledge of pleasure,' the pleasure of knowing pleasure" (Foucault qtd. in Williams, *Hard Core* 3) and the possibility to derive these pleasures from a variety of things—sexual or not.

Society frames both media, hardcore pornographic film and porn photography as non-political, yet our analyses show that this is not always the case. The cultural-aesthetic discourses at play in Alejandro's and McGinley's projects merge the illusive concepts of the hipster and porn/ography, resulting in a synergy of these phenomena that dissolves the boundaries of sexual and sensual practices, and of mainstream and subculture, ultimately providing insights into twenty-first century hipster aesthetics within and beyond inevitably erotic materials. The prevailing argument is that "[t]he hipster may be disdained for bottoming out politics in favor of stylized, consumer-based ways of occupying public space" (Campbell 49). The eclectic yet aesthetic assortment of images posted to Tumblr archive "That Hipster Porn," however, proves through an affluence of photographs, paintings, and digital artwork—such as a highly filtered photo of slim, denim-clad legs in white tennis socks marked "motherfucker" and Converse shoes or of a seemingly naked and equally slender young girl bathing in blue and pink water, her lips formed to a duckface and an image of a burning Nazi flag—that practicing politics may look different through a hipster-filtered lens.

To echo Helen Hester, not all of hipster porn/ography "will get your dick hard" (67); however, as we have shown, hipster porn/ography calls into scrutiny the regulative processes at play when aesthetics meet politics, laying bare the endless possibilities for pleasure within and beyond the corporeal realm, across textual boundaries, and along the margins between mainstream and counterculture.

Works Cited

Abrams, Nora Burnett. "Downtown." *Ryan McGinley*, 2017, ryanmcginley.com/nora-burnett-abrams/. Accessed October 6, 2017.

Alejandro, Noel. "About Noel." *Noel Alejandro Films*, noelalejandrofilms.com/about-noel/. Accessed October 13, 2017.

Alejandro, Noel. "Doing Elliot." *Noel Alejandro Films*, noelalejandrofilms.com/films/doing-elliot/. Accessed October 13, 2017.

Alejandro, Noel. "Trivial." *Noel Alejandro Films*, noelalejandrofilms.com/films/trivial/. Accessed October 13, 2017.

Alejandro, Noel. "Why I Don't Think Condoms Are Mandatory in Porn." *Medium*, September 27, 2017, medium.com/@noelhortas/why-i-dont-think-condoms-are-mandatory-in-porn-ea2dd60a8a09. Accessed October 13, 2017.

Anderson, Eric. *Inclusive Masculinity: The Changing Face of Masculinities*. Routledge, 2009.

Bad Medicine. Directed by Noel Alejandro, Noel Alejandro Films, 2016.

Behrenbeck, Julian. "NSFW: 'Trivial'—vom Mitbewohnercasting zum Flotten 3er." *Vangardist*, May 26, 2017, vangardist.com/news-article/trivial/. Accessed October 13, 2017.

Bernardi, Daniel. "Interracial Joysticks: Pornography's Web of Racist Attractions." *Pornography: Film and Culture*, edited by Peter Lehman. Rutgers University Press, 2006, pp. 206–43.

Bonanos, Christopher. *Instant: The Story of Polaroid*. Princeton Architectural Press, 2012.

Boyle, Karen. *Everyday Pornography*. Routledge, 2011.

Brainpolice2. "The Problem of Hipster Politics." *Anti-Libertarian Criticism*, Wordpress, July 29, 2014, antilibertariancriticism.wordpress.com/2014/07/29/the-problem-of-hipster-politics/. Accessed October 15, 2017.

Campbell, Miranda. "Creative Entrepreneurship in the Cultural Industries: Rhetoric and Realities of Youth Creative Work." *The Borders of Subculture: Resistance and the Mainstream*, edited by Alexander Dhoest et al. Routledge, 2015, pp. 37–54.

Connor, Tim. "Ryan McGinley: Building a Youthsex Brand." *Tim Connor: Looking at Visual Culture*, Blogspot, May 6, 2007, timconnor.blogspot.de/2007/05/ryan-mcginley-youth-brand-in-art-biz.html. Accessed October 13, 2017.

Doing Elliot. Directed by Noel Alejandro, Noel Alejandro Films, 2017.

Dyer, Richard. *Only Entertainment*. Routledge, 1990.

Eloi & Biel. Directed by Noel Alejandro, Noel Alejandro Films, 2013.

Epstein, Leonora. "Success! Hipsters Save Polaroid!" *The Frisky*, October 14, 2009, www.thefrisky.com/2009-10-14/success-hipsters-save-polaroid/. Accessed October 14, 2017.

Evans, Patrice. "Hip-Hop and Hipsterism: Notes on a Philosophy of Us and Them." *What Was the Hipster? A Sociological Investigation*, edited by Mark Greif, Kathleen Ross, and Dayna Tortorici. Sheridan Press, 2010, pp. 103–11.

"Everybody Knows This Is Nowhere." *Team Gallery*, 2010, www.teamgal.com/exhibitions/171/everybody_knows_this_is_nowhere. Accessed October 1, 2017.

Ferrell, Jeff. *Crimes of Style: Urban Graffiti and the Politics of Criminality*. Northeastern University Press, 1996.

Fuchs, Matthias, and Philip Jacobi. "'Fuck Me for the Revolution!' Transgression und Subversion im Queeren Porno." *Kulturen der Pornographie*, edited by Daniel Schulze and Andrea Stiebritz. Wissenschaftlicher Verlag Trier, 2016, pp. 39–52.

"Fuck Yeah, Ryan McGinley!" *Tumblr*, April 5, 2010, fuckyeahryanmcginley.tumblr.com/page/36. Accessed September 25, 2017.

Furness, Dyllan. "Sex-Positive Porn Director Wants Us to Ask, 'Who Makes My Porn?'" *Vice*, July 27, 2017, www.vice.com/en_au/article/gybeaq/sex-positive-porn-director-erika-lust-berlin-film-society. Accessed August 6, 2020.

Goffman, Ken, and Dan Joy. *Counterculture through the Ages: From Abraham to Acid House*. Villard, 2004.

Gregory, Alice. "Ryan McGinley: The Most Important Photographer in America." *GQ*, April 10, 2014, www.gq.com/story/ryan-mcginley-photographer. Accessed September 28, 2017.

Greif, Mark, ed. *Hipster: Eine Transatlantische Diskussion*. Suhrkamp, 2012.

Greif, Mark. "What Was the Hipster?" *New York Magazine*, October 22, 2010, nymag.com/news/features/69129/. Accessed July 14, 2020.

Grigoriadis, Vanessa. "The Edge of Hip: Vice, the Brand." *New York Times*, September 28, 2003, www.nytimes.com/2003/09/28/style/the-edge-of-hip-vice-the-brand.html. Accessed October 12 2017.

Helmore, Edward. "Ryan McGinley: Nude in New York." *Guardian*, April 13, 2010, www.theguardian.com/artanddesign/2010/apr/13/ryan-mcginley. Accessed September 29, 2017.

Hester, Helen. *Beyond Explicit: Pornography and the Displacement of Sex*. SUNY Press, 2014.

Horning, Rob. "The Death of the Hipster." *Popmatters*, April 13, 2009, www.popmatters.com/post/the-death-of-the-hipster-panel/. Accessed October 13, 2017.

Iveson, Kurt. "Policing the City." *Urban Politics: Critical Approaches*, edited by Mark Davidson and Deborah Martin. Sage, 2014, pp. 85–99.

Jervis, Jon. *Transgressing the Modern: Explorations in the Western Experience of Otherness*. Wiley-Blackwell, 1999.

Juffer, Jane. *At Home with Pornography: Women, Sex, and Everyday Life*. New York University Press, 1998.

Kipnis, Laura. *Bound and Gagged: Pornography and the Politics of Fantasy in America*. Duke University Press, 1999.

Kohlenberger, Judith. *The New Formula for Cool: Science, Technology, and the Popular in the American Imagination*. Transcript, 2015.

Le Bled, Francois. "Hipster Porn: Does It Exist?" *New Heroes and Pioneers*, July 2, 2014, thenewheroesandpioneers.com/magazine/2014/07/hipster-porn/. Accessed October 13, 2017.

Levy, Ariel. "Chasing Dash Snow." *New York Magazine*, November 25, 2007, nymag.com/arts/art/profiles/26288/. Accessed October 7, 2017.

Massey, K., J. Burns, and A. Franz. "Young People, Sexuality and the Age of Pornography." *Sexuality & Culture*, 2020, doi.org/10.1007/s12119-020-09771-z. Accessed July 30, 2020.

McGinley, Ryan. *The Kids Were Alright '98-'03*. *Ryan McGinley*, ryanmcginley.com/the-kids-were-alright-19982003/. Accessed October 15, 2017.

Mercer, John. *Gay Pornography: Representations of Sexuality and Masculinity*. I.B. Tauris, 2017.

Metz, Christian. "Photography and Fetish." *October*, vol. 34, 1985, pp. 81–90.

Newall, Michael. "An Aesthetics of Transgressive Pornography." *Art and Pornography: Philosophical Essays*, edited by Hans R.V. Maes and Jerrold Levinson. Oxford University Press, 2012, pp. 206–27.

Newman, Michael Z. "Movies for Hipsters." *American Independent Cinema: Indie, Indiewood and Beyond*, edited by Geoff King et al. Routledge, 2013, 71–82.

Paasonen, Susanna. *Carnal Resonance: Affect and Online Pornography*. MIT Press, 2011.

Pardes, Arielle. "Inside the World of Hipster Erotica." *Vice*, December 17, 2015, www.vice.com/en_au/article/nn9xxd/hw-meet-the-girl-writing-erotica-for-hipsters-511. Accessed October 13, 2017.

Raposo, Maria. "Ryan McGinley, Photographs 1999–2015." *Kids of Dada*, www.kidsofdada.com/blogs/magazine/34635777-ryan-mcginley-photographs-1999–2015. Accessed October 13, 2017.

Robertson, Kirsty. "This Is What Democracy Looks Like? Or, the Art of Oppression." *Transnationalism, Activism, Art*, edited by Kit Dobson and Aine McGlynn. University of Toronto Press, 2013, pp. 171–91.

Simoneau, Naikee. "Noel Alejandro—An Interview." *Kaltblut Magazine*, June 12, 2016, www.kaltblut-magazine.com/noel-alejandro-an-interview/. Accessed October 13, 2017.

Slenske, Michael. "With Nudes, Ryan McGinley Shoots for History." *BlouinArtInfo*, March 18, 2010, www.blouinartinfo.com/news/story/276522/with-nudes-ryan-mcginley-shoots-for-history. Accessed October 16, 2017.

Sturken, Marita. "Facebook Photography and the Demise of Kodak and Polaroid." *Images, Ethics, and Technology*, edited by Sharrona Pearl and Barbie Zelizer. Routledge, 2015, pp. 94–110.

Sullivan, Rebecca, and Alan McKee. *Pornography: Structures, Agency and Performance*. Polity Press, 2015.
Threadgold, Steven. *Youth, Class and Everyday Struggles*. Routledge, 2017.
Trivial. Directed by Noel Alejandro, Noel Alejandro Films, 2017.
Varghese, Ricky. *Raw: PrEP, Pedagogy, and the Politics of Barebacking*. University of Regina Press, 2019.
Vartanian, Ian. "This Charming Man." *Ryan McGinley*, 2017, ryanmcginley.com/pageh/. Accessed October 6, 2017.
Williams, Linda. *Hard Core: Power, Pleasure, and the "Frenzy of the Visible."* University of California Press, 1999.
Williams, Linda. "Motion and E-Motion: A Feminist Perspective on the 'Frenzy of the Visible.' " Lecture Series *Feminist Idols*. University of Vienna, June 20, 2017.
Williams, Linda. *Screening Sex*. Duke University Press, 2008.

Hipster Literature and Self-Fashioning

9

Twenty-First-Century Hipster Fiction and Postindustrial Revitalization

Brandon McFarlane

One of the anxieties expressed by Canadian hipster fiction originates from the uneasy relationships between creativity and capital in the postindustrial city. The story should be familiar: globalization and new technologies deindustrialize a district, leaving behind a landscape of derelict infrastructure. Artists, students, and hipsters arrive in pursuit of cheap rents. They spawn an artsy scene that attracts hip service industries—bars, cafes, galleries—creative industries—your high-tech start-ups, architecture studios, and design firms—and, lastly, moneyed members of the creative class. Property values increase and rents rise pushing out longtime residents and "first-wave" gentrifiers—the artists, hipsters, and students who made the area "cool." An authentic neighborhood becomes its opposite, the generic streetscape of global capital. Whether you consult Sharon Zukin's *Loft Living* (1982, 1989), Richard Lloyd's *Neo-Bohemia: Art and Commerce in the Postindustrial City* (2005, 2010), or Richard Florida's creative city research, there are ample studies demonstrating hipsters are the harbingers of neoliberal gentrification. Hipster culture plays a role in urban revitalization, a process that hipsters paradoxically resist.

The semantic confusion caused by using "hipster" as a critical term mirrors tensions between bohemia and business. Cultural commentators lambasted hipsters during the years bracketing the millennium. *Adbusters* claimed they represented nothing less than the "dead end of Western civilization": they appropriated the style of politically potent and original subcultures but not their substance (Haddow). More widespread representations presented them as a benign manifestation of urban elitism—culture snobs who fetishized the avant-garde and flaunted their superior knowledge: the pursuit of the new, the misguided attempt to remain one-block ahead of the gentrifying tide of condos and Starbucks or the shill quest to better position oneself for success in the gig economy in which street cred is currency (Greif). Hipster, a term that, back in Norman Mailer's day, signified rebellion against capital's reproduction of homogeneity became a slander for the neoliberal, superficial, and mainstream. Hence the satirical *Onion* headline, "Two Hipsters Angrily Call Each Other 'Hipster.'" What is a hipster, or a theorist of hipster culture, to do? My answer is to pay attention to aesthetics.

An examination of Canadian literature reveals there was an aesthetic and thematic shift in hipster fiction during the years bracketing the millennium from postmodern ex-centricity and comedy to new forms that blend romance and Dadaist-inspired aesthetics. The 1990s fiction used ex-centric irony to flag the hipster's initiation into middle-class, urban culture which they nevertheless critiqued. Twenty-first-century works use romantic motifs to critique neoliberal models for urban redevelopment and imagine inclusive, street-level communities as alternatives. In what follows, I offer a brief history of hipster fiction in Canada to contextualize the aesthetic and thematic shifts, and then analyze representative twenty-first-century examples that imagine romantic models for culture-based community building.

Canadian Hipster Fiction

The hipster is an archetypal figure with a relatively long history in Canadian fiction.[1] Northrop Frye first theorized hipster writing in his influential "Conclusion to *Literary History of Canada*" (1965) which established Canadian literature as an academic field of study. Frye argued the canonical Montreal Poets and Mordecai Richler's fiction expressed a hip sensibility in which protagonists resisted the "repressive morality" of squares that diminished artistic and sexual libido "which are closely aligned" (355). Amy Lavender Harris's literary history of Toronto documented how 1960s and 1970s Yorkville inspired a wave of hippy-lit in which authors celebrated a new form of bohemian life that was emerging in Canada's gritty downtowns (179). A historical irony, of course, is Yorkville's more recent status as Canada's most expensive neighborhood and a playground for the global elite.

---

[1]For an in-depth history of hipster fiction, see McFarlane's *Canadian Literary Urbanism*.

A second wave of postmodern fiction emerged in the 1990s that ambivalently represented what Richard Lloyd dubbed "neo-bohemian" culture: characters are drawn to the party scene in a run-down neighborhood where they find a like-minded community of aspiring artists, cultural workers, and other party-hearty eccentrics. Representative texts include Daniel Jones's *The People One Knows* (1994), Andrew Pyper's *Kiss Me* (1996), Russel Smith's *How Insensitive* (1994), *Noise* (1998), *Young Men* (1999), and *Confidence* (2015), and Michael Winter's *This All Happened* (2000). W. H. New's *A History of Canadian Literature* dubbed the writing style "urban chic"; texts took "sardonic delight in the very superficiality of fad and fashion" (284).[2] Less stodgy critics have demonstrated that the supposed superficiality of "urban chic" reflects characters' ambivalence about living in a neo-bohemia. Lisa Salem-Wiseman's "Divided Cities, Divided Selves: Portraits of the Artist as an Ambivalent Urban Hipster" examined a theme in which the city, paradoxically, nurtures and frustrates the hipster's creativity. Hipster living demands a certain degree of performativity due to the role of reputation in the highly competitive urban environment; one needs to become a member of the network, or scene, in order to gain access to artistic and employment opportunities. Yet, hipsters are often overwhelmed by doubt due to the disparities between reputation and reality and become so hooked to the scene that they never actually make any art.

The thematic conflict is represented through ex-centric irony, in which characters self-reflexively waver between celebration and critique—an aesthetic that Linda Hutcheon argues "almost inevitably" puts postmodern writers (and characters) into an "'ex-centric' position" for they take "pot-shots at the culture of which they know they are unavoidably a part but still wish to criticize" (3). The authors of the 1990s critiqued the pursuit of the avant-garde from the perspective of class and age. Professional and artistic success necessitates building a reputation in the scene which requires regular attendance at cultural events, many of which are designed for upper-class urbanites with substantial disposable incomes; similarly, younger art and cultural workers are only afforded low-paying gig work while Baby Boomers enjoyed substantial support through government grants and full-time, salaried positions. Indeed, hipster critics claimed that influential Boomers conspired to exclude younger, urban authors because

---

[2]A handful of Toronto authors were branded the "Brat Pack" by a national newspaper due to their critique of long-standing Canadian myths that privileged rural and wilderness spaces. They caused a minor scandal by arguing urban writers were marginalized by the literary establishment; in response, established critics dismissively labeled "Brat Pack" writers—Smith, Pyper, Evan Solomon, and Derrick McCormick—hipsters. A female front, the "Book Babes," was similarly branded through a special issue of *Blood & Aphorisms*. For an analysis of the controversies and the non-fiction works of 1990s hipster writers, see McFarlane's "Hipster Urbanism."

they challenge long-standing culture myths that connected gilded, Canadian identity with rural and wilderness spaces. For example, in a polemical about the suppression of hipsters by Boomers, Andrew Pyper contended there was systemic "bias toward a vision of what CanLit *should* be: nice, harmless, and decidedly grey-haired" and concluded the "thinking seems to be that, if the gates aren't buttressed now, they may soon be battered down altogether by the hordes of young literary barbarians gathering outside them, armed with sex, recreational pharmaceuticals, and pop culture references" ("High anxiety" 89). In short, the system was rigged in favor of entitled Baby Boomers who were unwilling to make systemic changes which excluded the younger cohort from participating in and creating culture. In ex-centric fashion, hipsters did not call for radical change—indeed, they championed the country's progressive cultural funding programs—but merely wished to be included within national literary culture and given fair access to funding opportunities in order to earn a living income.

Mirroring the desire for inclusion, 1990s hipster fiction was also comedic: it portrayed a protagonist's struggle to gain membership in a postindustrial community and make creative works. The structure encouraged navel-gazing, a series of episodes where a protagonist's attempts to belong are represented humorously, and ironic attention is directed toward the protagonist's desire to join a community that, despite its glamour, may be superficial.[3] Comedy acknowledges problematic aspects of hipster culture but presents them as episodic gags—novelties to be laughed off. The white hipster's interactions with working-class locals, street-level crime, people of color, and gentrification become ironic rites of initiation rather than symptoms of crisis and inequity. Indeed, such issues are overshadowed by the white hipster's (eventually successful) quest for middle-class comforts: gainful employment, a cool apartment, love, and intellectually pleasing nights out on the town. While Smith and Pyper penned critical articles that celebrated the diversity of neo-bohemia, hipster fiction expresses a profound ambivalence as texts ridicule factors of the scene that prevent *their* entry into the urban middle-class but fall well short of meaningfully representing and contesting barriers to equity and inclusivity facing equity seeking communities.

A different type of hipster fiction emerged in the new millennium. While texts were still set in gritty, postindustrial neighborhoods and featured protagonists pursuing a neo-bohemian lifestyle and a sense of belonging, authors started using romantic motifs that placed hipster culture in ideological conflict with neoliberalism. In contrast to comedy,

[3]There is an odd genre of *bildungsroman* fiction set in 1960s and 1970s bohemian neighborhoods emerging in Canada. Texts include a series of vignettes that not only dramatize the protagonist's struggle to integrate into the community but also take issue with contradictions of hippie culture, especially its misogyny. For a representative example see Meredith Quartermain's *U Girl* (2016).

romance features protagonists who contest the status quo and challenge the corrupt, old guard with a new, idealistic model. The stakes are a lot higher as characters are synecdochic: They are representative of broader ideas, and the conflicts between hipsters and squares dramatize an ideological conflict between progressivism—which values reconciliation, community, beauty, and social justice—and neoliberalism—which reduces everything to its economic value, prioritizes individual profit, and builds low-quality, exclusionary spaces. Indeed, the characters are heroes and villains whose abilities are hyperbolic, often magical; the elevation of characters' talents stresses how ideology produces urban spaces and places and the pertinent need for just alternatives to neoliberalism. In doing so, the fiction updates one of the long-standing myths of Canadian literature, what Frye theorized as the "Quest for the Peaceable Kingdom." Contrasting the United States' revolutionary culture—in which the younger generation rebels against and overthrows the corrupt, old guard—Canadian culture tends to identify with the pastoral myth, in which competing factions build an inclusive culture that facilitates "the reconciliation of man with man and of man with nature" (371). Recent works of hipster fiction reimagine the "Quest for the Peaceable Kingdom" in which characters seek reconciliation of hipster and square and of person with postindustrial places and spaces.

Hipster fiction of the new millennium uses Dadaist strategies to acknowledge the dialectical intersections between hipster culture and neoliberalism when it comes to culture-based development. My use of the term Dadaism as a critical term is influenced by Lloyd's *Neo-Bohemia: Art and Commerce in the Postindustrial City* and Dionne Brand's *What We All Long For* (2005). Lloyd's monograph offers a street-level analysis of Chicago's Wicker Park in the 1990s. He introduced "grit-as-glamour" as a critical term to describe how hipsters reconstituted "elements of the local landscape that many would find as alarming as symbolic amenities" that signified new opportunities for marginal cultures (78). Whereas James Q. Wilson and George Kelling's broken window theory conceptualized urban decay as a threatening manifestation of disorder, incivility, and crime, the hipsters of Wicker Park interpreted elements of the decayed streetscape as symbolic connections to earlier, bohemian districts such as Mont Parness, SOHO, or Greenwich Village. "Grit" became a "glamorous" metaphor for liberty, freedom, diversity, and counterculture. The problem, though, is that Wicker Park also became a global center for the creative industries and culture-based development: corporations seeking to brand themselves as urban, creative, and rebellious strategically exploited the neighborhood's ethos. The global, creative industries appropriated and transformed the images and symbols of Wicker Park's hipster culture into romantic metaphors for neoliberalism.

In her novel *What We All Long For*, Brand imagines hipster culture and neoliberalism as oddly similar because they both find value in what society deems useless. The novel juxtaposes two siblings—Tuyen, an aspiring artist, and Binh, a criminal/business person—who are opposing personifications of Dadaism: "And Tuyen, a little more esoteric but with the same surrealist bent and without the masculinist charm of her brother, but perhaps with a little more intellectual rigor, would become a Dadaist, making everything useful useless and vice versa in her chaotic apartment" (68). Brand romanticizes the ways Tuyen and her diasporic friends use art to transform urban decay and other tragic aspects of the urban environment into inclusive community spaces. In contrast, Binh sees poverty, marginalization, and personal tragedy as exploitable resources for his criminal activities. He exploits the racism of Canadian society, which blinkers Asian bodies and cultures, to hide his criminal activities; his family are Vietnamese "boat people," and he uses that tragic history to invest in human trafficking and forced prostitution. Similarly, he views pretty much everything Tuyen values as useless: art, beauty, community, diversity, and bohemianism. The contrapuntal structure grants both characters near-magical Dadaist abilities to transform the useless into the useful (and vice-versa) but Tuyen uses her talents for the social good whereas Binh only cares about personal profit. The contrast puts a new twist on the archetypal hip vs. square dichotomy, for it foregrounds hipster romanticism and neoliberalism which both participate in the logic of urban revitalization by reconceptualizing decay and other denigrated aspects of the urban environment as valuable. Doing so acknowledges hipster culture shares similar imagery and symbolism as neoliberalism but importantly produces radically different metaphors that uphold oppositional worldviews. While Brand makes her Dadaist aesthetic explicit and self-referential, other authors apply similar aesthetic strategies that inverse the value of the useful and useless but without explicit references to Dadaism.

The romantic motifs further diverge from the comedic hipster fiction of the 1990s by integrating a third, spatial pole that creates a tense trialectic of hip, square, urban.[4] The romantic structure places progressivism and neoliberalism in conflict by dramatizing how the ideologies produce places and spaces. Indeed, the representative texts all feature trialectics where synecdochic characters compete to influence geographies and characters interpret the aesthetics of space. Timothy Taylor's *Stanley Park* (1999) places Jeremy Papier—an experimental chef who cherishes local cuisine—and Dante Beale—an owner of a transnational, demonic themed coffee chain who also looks like the devil—in a battle for control of a restaurant that is

[4]My thinking, here, is informed by Henri Lefebvre's *The Production of Space* and Edward Soja's *Thirdspace*. Both build upon the material-historical dialectic by adding spatiality as a third, critical pole. Hipster fiction tends to collapse grand-scale processes into representative urban spaces. It produces an aesthetic in which characters' interactions with and contemplation of a site evokes how global capital, post-industrialism, and gentrification are modifying local places and cultures.

a metaphor of the future of Vancouver's Crosstown. Michael Christie's *If I Fall, If I Die* (2015) includes a conflict between skateboarding teenagers and criminals over Thunder Bay's abandoned shipping yards: the defeat of the criminals and the transformation of the shipping yards into a skatepark reconciles young and old, native and white. In Brand's *What We All Long For*, artistic and commercial creativity compete to shape Toronto's Kensington Market. And in Matthew J. Trafford's "The Renegade Angels of Parkdale" (2011), hipsters and angels try to preserve Parkdale from intolerant gentrifies. Contrasting the navel-gazing of 1990s fiction, newer works foreground how the actions and ideas of individuals can transform community and city.

Critique: The Useful as Useless

In its critical form, authors use Dadaist aesthetics to criticize neoliberalism as useless. The integration of entrepreneurial characters draws critical attention to how the very processes hipsters cherish play a role in gentrification. Indeed, finding beauty and opportunity in decayed space mirrors the logic of urban redevelopment in which business and government target undervalued land and increase property value through investment and culture-based revitalization. Authors navigate this contradiction through a critical Dadaism that reconstitutes neoliberalism as useless and critiques inequitable and low-quality geographies as undesirable.

The tension between local and global culture is the main theme in Taylor's *Stanley Park*. Economies of scale provide transnational corporations a competitive edge because they reuse the same designs and strategies across the globe, a process that spreads repetitive geographies that elide the relationship between place and culture—"if you're inside a Starbucks, you really can't tell where you are." The antagonist, Dante Beale, pollutes the world with sameness: "Dante was a man by whose efforts a uniform commodity was distributed through identical shops to consumers all over North America. There was no difference in process, design or product between any two locations making the Inferno a brutally efficient, market-researched repudiation of the local" (255). The hipsters hate Inferno because it is an usurper that replaces high-quality uniqueness with low-quality blandness in the pursuit of profit.

What We All Long For offers the most complicated application of critical Dadaism as the experiences of the younger generation is contrasted with their parents: rather than using a young-hip/old-square dichotomy, Brand complicates her story by also contrasting the different forms of racism experienced by the two generations, and how those experiences are etched onto the cityscape. The older generation—immigrants, refugees, and migrants—find few opportunities to belong. Tuyen's family are Vietnamese refugees; her father is an engineer and her mother is a doctor, but they are unable to find meaningful employment in Canada because institutions will not recognize their credentials or tolerate their functional but awkward English. Instead, they become moneyed owning a Vietnamese restaurant; the cash allows them to flee to a suburban mansion and they avoid returning to Kensington Market because it reminds them of their past life. They reject Tuyen's lifestyle because they see her pursuit of art as economically useless—her father keeps trying to convince her to become an architect—and view her bachelor apartment as a repudiation of family and "decent" moral values—Tuyen is a lesbian. Oku, an aspiring spoken-word poet, also sees the city as a place of opportunity whereas his father sees it as a place of wasteful decadence. Oku's ambition to earn a masters in English and write poetry are constantly disparaged by his father as useless: "What good would that do, what the hell kind of job could you get with that, was Oku intending to eat the papers or wipe his ass with them when he got it? Because that is all his 'master's' would be useful for" (87). In contrast, the twenty-somethings see their parents' material success and neoliberal worldview as useless: none of the adults are happy—they are all, in fact, traumatized and miserable—yet they surround themselves with possessions that have no use and provide no enjoyment. Tuyen's parents had a "businesslike readiness to have all the world had to offer by way of things. A voracious getting. They had everything and nothing" (62). Oku's father also fills his home with useless possessions: "Back of the garden was a garage with at least three broken-down cars, parts, anyway, from three broken-down cars. His father threw nothing away. An old muffler, a leaking carburetor, a rusty fender. Fitz filled every minute and every space with work" (84). Following the novel's Dadaist logic, the twenty-somethings inverse their parents' values as ugly, useless, and crass.

If I Fall, If I Die explores how organized crime finds new uses for decayed urban spaces, a theme that is prominent in texts set in smaller cities and rural spaces.[5] The novel's villain is Butler who uses decades-old grain to distill moonshine and hides his operations in the city's abandoned buildings and cars. Decay becomes a valuable resource that provides free commodities and rent and also camouflages his illegal activities. His target market is Thunder Bay's unemployed and native populations, who are dying *en masse* after consuming the toxic but cheap beverage. Butler presents himself as a businessman who is solving community's challenges: he provides jobs for

[5]The "revitalization" of decay in smaller cities and rural spaces by criminals is a prominent theme in recent Canadian fiction, e.g., Kevin Hardcastle's *Debris* (2015), Andrew Battershill's *Pillow* (2015), and James Grainger's *Harmless* (2015). Many of the texts do not feature hipsters, but they do associate revitalization with criminal exploitation, producing a new genre we might tentatively label the postindustrial noir. For an analysis of grit-as-glamour in other postindustrial fiction see McFarlane's "Emergent Fiction 2015."

the homeless and satisfies racist municipal leaders, including the police, by poisoning natives. Christie decolonizes Thunder Bay by presenting Butler's neoliberalism as an extension of Canadian colonialism that exploits racism and poverty as valuable resources for profit.

Reconciliation: The Useless as Useful

In its romantic form, hipster fiction uses Dadaism to imagine inclusive alternatives. In Matthew J. Trafford's "The Renegade Angels of Parkdale," Toronto's speak-easy dance clubs provide a forum where hipsters congregate, build a sense of community, and overcome social exclusion. Renegade angels operate indie dance clubs in hipster districts across the world: they sneak out of Heaven and Hell to reunite, forgive, and forget after Satan's failed rebellion. The protagonist is Zach, a twenty-something homosexual who is mourning his partner's suicide. The ever up-beat Lucky takes Zach out for a night of fun hoping to help Zach overcome his remorse. They, like the angels, come to Parkdale because it is a hotbed of deviance, a place where the marginalized are welcomed and belong: "There was something scattered and untidy about Parkdale, something jittery, uninhibited and bold, and it was that way long before the angels had arrived. Parkdale seethed, breathed, craved. Parkdale shivered, shimmered, bent the light. Parkdale let everyone in: no gatekeepers, no guards, no one barring the way" (87). The dance clubs function as therapeutic spaces where young LGBTs and other outcasts may find a sense of belonging and overcome shared trauma. To enter a Fallen dance club, the angel-bouncer explains, revelers must either perform "E.E.L.S. or Squeals. If you pick E.E.L.S., you must cry out *Eli, Eli, lama sabachthani* as loud as you can. If you pick Squeals, you must tell me the moment in your life which you experienced the most profound despair. Otherwise you don't get in" (90–1). The protagonist is randomly assigned door duty, he becomes responsible for observing E.E.L.S and recording Squeals. The conceit allows Zach to connect with others as he records the trauma experienced by young, LGBT, and straight hipsters. It helps him realize that while he feels alone due to his partner's suicide, he is a member of a broader community who, together, can overcome their collective despair. Parkdale, which was strategically denigrated as a threatening space by developers who gentrified the neighboring Liberty Village, becomes a safe space of belonging and reconciliation.[6]

[6]For analysis of how developers used security infrastructure and marketing to distinguish "safe" Liberty Village from "dangerous" Parkdale, see Catungal and Leslie (2009) and Catungal, Leslie, and Hii (2009).

In Brand's *What We All Long For*, Kensington Market's slum apartments provide a similar sense of community to the artists, LGBTs, and people of color who are excluded from Canada's national culture that has historically privileged the experiences of white Boomers. Tuyen and Carla live in small, rat-infested bachelor apartments. They flee home as high schoolers to live on their own and form a network of like-minded bohemians:

> Tuyen's and Carla's apartments became places of refuge, not just for their immediate circle but for all the people they picked up along the way to their twenties. Like the Graffiti Boys across the alleyway, Tuyen's friends from the gay ghetto, a few hip-hop poets, two girls who made jewellery and knit hats, and an assortment of twenty-somethings who did various things like music and waitering. The two rundown apartments were above a cheap clothing store. Mrs. Chou only made appearances to collect the rents and to say, "No Parties," and other than those predictable visits Carla and Tuyen had free reign of the place. (23)

The hipsters, of course, throw wild, ecstasy-fueled parties and ask revelers to donate funds toward food, rent, and drugs. Paralleling their entrepreneurial buddy Jackie—an Africadian who owns a used-clothing shop—Tuyen and Carla approach locations stigmatized by poverty and filth as "places of refuge" where they can welcome and love diverse people who struggle to find a place within mainstream Canada due to their race, ethnicity, gender, or sexuality.[7]

Characters use art-based practices to revitalize urban spaces. Christie's *If I Fall, If I Die* presents skateboarding as a form of street-art that re-forms the city's industrial ruins. The city's decline traumatizes the native and boomer populations. Will's mother becomes agoraphobic after her lover dies in an industrial accident and her twin brother disappears, ostensibly due to a failed rescue attempt. She shelters Will from the dangerous outside world, but he eventually sneaks out and becomes an avid skateboarder who explores the city's industrial ruins with Jonah, his first true friend. Christie presents their skateboarding as a form of street art:

[7] *What We All Long For* was instantly canonized because its publication corresponded with the cosmopolitan turn in Canadian cultural politics. The novel inspired several publications that outlined how the text moves beyond official multiculturalism, which emphasizes difference via ethnicity, to intersectional modes that find common ground among categories such as ethnicity, class, gender, sexuality, and culture; see Dobson and Rosenthal for examinations of how Brand represents very specific urban spaces that are representative of the city's emerging cosmopolitanism. This article builds upon Dobson and Rosenthal by suggesting the characters' hipster identities are the culmination of intersectionality.

> But when riding his skateboard, even the "rusty ruin" of Thunder Bay sparkled with vitality and potential in Will's eyes. While investigating the map, they happened over perfect skateboard terrain: painted curbs surrounded by smooth concrete and perfect sets of stairs with no cracks at the top, where the boys would return again and again after security guards had shooed them away. Surfers rode waves, which were already beautiful, but skateboarding *made* things beautiful: the ugly, discarded nooks and leftovers of a place, the abandoned, unused architecture that people preferred to ignore. Beneath their wheels, these dead places became sites of wonder. (165–6)

Skateboarding rebuilds the ugly, dangerous cityscape into a site of beauty and reconciliation. The new skateboarding community they find brings the city's whites and natives together (Will is white, Jonah is native), and renews the bond between the old and young. The adults, long defeated by deindustrialization, receive new hope from the younger generation who only see beauty, opportunity, and inclusivity in spaces that Boomers perceive as ugly and tragic.

Taylor's experimental chef mobilizes an extreme Dadaism to usurp Dante's neoliberal worldview and uncritical celebration of globalization. Dante desires to create a restaurant that celebrates newfangled, transnational cuisine that designs recipes based upon sophisticated market research that shows customers crave transnational cuisine that synthesizes exotic ingredients. Papier is philosophically opposed to the idea as he believes food should showcase or make explicit its connection to place; he rejects Dante, and his business model, because it obliterates the local and his near-religious devotion to market research encourages the production of incoherent dishes that uncritically celebrate globalization. Similarly, Dante exclusively targets the wealthy, global elite whereas Papier believes a business should also serve the neighborhood's existing population which is overwhelmingly comprised of low-income residents, students, and homeless people suffering from drug addiction or mental health challenges. In protest, Papier learns how to cook animals and plants from the squatters of Stanley Park. In return, he cooks banquet meals in which all the Park's residents share ingredients that Jeremy synthesizes. He brings these newfound techniques to the city proper: after selling out to Dante Beale, he sabotages the new restaurant's grand opening by substituting exotic, globalized ingredients with materials gathered in the city such as racoons, fish, pigeons, and plants. Indeed, Beale spends months on market research and demands Papier incorporate specific colors and words into dishes that scored well with test audiences. With the exception of a food critic who sneaks into the kitchen, no one knows what they ate as the dish titles and accompanying descriptions are the product of nonsensical marketing discourse designed to fluff the egos of elites who view themselves as "connoisseurs" but are ignorant consumers who purchase things that are marketed to signify membership within the one percent. The restaurant closes after the test run due to a high-profile health code inspection.

Brand's protagonists use art to announce the presence of Toronto's diasporic communities and create a sense of place that reflects their experiences. Tuyen builds a *lubaio*, a work that records the longings of Torontonians, especially those traditionally excluded from official histories. A *lubaio* is a structure that people would post anti-government messages on. Tuyen collects the longings of random Torontonians—some real, others imagined—and carves them on a great structure that slowly fills and eventually transcends the walls of her bachelor apartment. Some longings are playful and happy, while others record experiences of exclusion, racism, and exploitation. The Graffiti Boys also paint a large mural—it synthesizes various blinkered stories about the neighborhood's residents. Carla's family history features prominently: her mother had an affair with a wealthy man who disowned Carla's family after her mother became pregnant. Heartbroken, she commits suicide by jumping off her balcony in a social housing tower. The mural records this loss but also the mother's surrealist dreams of a better future for the family.

Decay facilitates experimentation. Characters are attracted to gritty locals for economic reasons: low rent allows new businesses to find their groove on the cheap while also enjoying access to countercultural customers who tend to support local, independent businesses. Consider Taylor's *Stanley Park*: Jeremy Papier decides to locate his local food haunt, The Monkey's Paw Bistro, in a down-and-out district famed for its homeless and drug-addicted population:

> The neighbourhood offered a shifting multicultural client base that nobody could consciously target. Film school kids in the mid-morning. (It was a financial necessity to open for the coffee trade.) Business lunches for the kind of businesses that embraced neighbourhoods in the earliest stages of gentrification: architects, designers, software developers. After work they had a bike-courier scene. And in the evening, a tantalizing trickle of those foodies and reviewers adventurous enough to dine out deep on the downtown eastside, pushing up against the Hasting Street heroin trade. It was a colourful, kaleidoscopic place. Very Crosstown, very X-town. (52–3)

While the contingent of like-minded hipsters appeals to Papier, economics is the biggest factor influencing his embrace of Crosstown. Every day, his team buys local ingredients at a nearby market and invents new dishes based upon what is fresh and local. The ingredients are expensive, so the low rent allows them to take risks, innovate, and change the sense of place in Vancouver. In *What We All Long For*, Jackie sees similar business potential in Toronto's Parkdale—the neighborhood west of Liberty Village that hosts the country's largest mental health hospital (CAMH) and is a hotbed of anti-gentrification and renters' rights activism. Yet Jackie chooses the neighborhood for her used-clothing store due to its low rents and radical vibe:

> Ab and Zu advertised itself as selling post-bourgeois clothing. The store was just on the border where Toronto's trendy met Toronto's seedy. The rent was cheap, and Jackie had had the foresight to think that the trendy section would slowly creep toward Ab and Zu and sweep the store into money. Next door to Ab and Zu was a greasy spoon—Sam's—recently taken over by other hopeful trendies—a couple of women who were anarchists. There, a mix of the old neighbourhood—the working class, the poor, the desperate—and an increasing number of anarchists—mostly friends of the two women—drank coffee in mutual curiosity. (99)

Both entrepreneurs' approach to gentrification is ex-centric: they are aware that they are participating in the early phases of revitalization and hope to profit from it. Yet both seek to help residents of "the old neighbourhood": Jeremy feeds and learns from the homeless in nearby Stanley Park, and the anarchists help prostitutes leave their pimp and find treatment in a nearby women's shelter. Jackie grew up in a nearby social housing project in Kensington Market, hence her business does not necessarily represent the displacement of equity seeking communities but, perhaps more hopefully, their upward economic mobility through countercultural entrepreneurialism.

Conclusion: The Longings of Twenty-First-Century Hipster Fiction

It may be appropriate to conclude by highlighting the key longings of twenty-first-century hipster fiction as the texts present creative but not overly pragmatic solutions to the critical issues which they explore. My use of the term *longings* is inspired by Tuyen in *What We All Long For*, whose *lubaio* is a bricolage of longings, some real, some imaginary, that she collects during her everyday interactions with the city. Indeed, hipster fiction presents a vision for urban living that is aspirational: it inspires critical readers to reflect upon their everyday lives and how their actions positively or negatively shape urban environments and communities.

This chapter's introduction briefly discussed Northrop Frye's "Conclusion to *A Literary History of Canada*." Frye's essay concludes by proposing that Canadian culture expresses itself through pastoral romances that value reconciliation and the social good. While Frye upheld Western-centric archetypes that associated the pastoral with rural and wilderness spaces, twenty-first-century hipster fiction expresses a similar politics but uses images, symbols, and metaphors of urban decay. Just as older pastoral myths feature characters fleeing to spaces isolated from the corruptions and economics of the court, hipster characters find refuge in decayed urban spaces where they escape the corruptions of neoliberal capital. Indeed, the spaces and places they build are quasi-magical and, often, transgress property law. Tuyen transforms her bachelor apartment into a club-like space where hipsters congress, and her art magically moves beyond the apartment's physical space—it is literally impossible to build a work of that scale and materiality in such a tiny space even though Tuyen tears down walls to make more room. Tuyen destroys the property without consequence. In *If I Fall, If I Die* the teenagers reclaim derelict industrial infrastructure and transform them into a skatepark; Christie never addresses who owns the property or heavy-handed municipal bylaws that would govern appropriate use (and close down the park due to significant safety and environmental risks). In *Stanley Park*, Papier teams up with underground chefs to find a speakeasy in an abandoned heroine den and metaphorically brings the values of the homeless community in Stanley Park, which is also represented as a pastoral space, to the city proper. And Trafford's indie dance club, Fallen, only exists through the divine intervention of angels. All these examples express longings to transcend neoliberal urban planning that prioritizes the rapid increase in property value in order to generate tax revenue for cash-strapped municipalities (Canadian municipalities primarily generate revenue through federal funding, property tax, service fees, and fines; provincial and federal governments have the power to tax income and consumption). The spaces the hipster characters create are not fiscally viable within the existing model, and they contest entrenched, neoliberal policies that prioritize individual and corporate profit over the social good; the spaces present an alternative that showcases what is lost when all facets of life are reduced to their economic value.

Twenty-first-century hipster fiction riffs on earlier themes of belonging by bringing diversity and inclusivity to the foreground. In their critical writing, Smith and Pyper celebrate the diversity of Canadian cities, especially within neo-bohemian culture; however, their fiction tends to relegate diverse characters to the background, thereby producing a gap between theory and practice. Newer works diverge by incorporating diverse protagonists and antagonists, and by developing critiques that consider how class and age intersect with other factors such as race, ethnicity, sexuality, citizenship, gender, and mental health. Indeed, Brand and Trafford implicitly contest earlier hipster fiction by omitting white, heterosexual males. The only white character in *What We All Long For* is Jackie's partner, a punk rocker, who the other characters jokingly refer to as "Nazi Boy" exclusively due to his race. "Nazi Boy" is only mentioned a handful of times, which demonstrates a deliberate choice by Brand to take issue with earlier hipster fiction. Similarly,

Trafford's narrator mentions the presence of white, heterosexual hipsters at Fallen, but they too are relegated to the background. Taylor and Christie also diverge from earlier works: while their protagonists are white, heterosexual males, their novels include fully developed supporting characters who are essential to the texts' poetics and politics. Notably, the protagonists find a sense of belonging by cocreating new communities and spaces with equity-seeking characters who are disadvantaged by systemic racism, mental health challenges, and class-based inequities.

Works Cited

Battershill, Andrew. *Pillow*. Coach House, 2015.

Brand, Dionne. *What We All Long For*. Vintage, 2005.

Catungal, John Paul, and Deborah Leslie. "Placing Power in the Creative City: Governmentalities and Subjectivities in Liberty Village, Toronto." *Environment and Planning*, vol. 41, no. 11, 2009, pp. 2576–94.

Catungal, John Paul, Deborah Leslie, and Yvonne Hii. "Geographies of Displacement in the Creative City: The Case of Liberty Village, Toronto." *Urban Studies*, vol. 45, no. 5/6, 2009, pp. 1095–114.

Christie, Michael. *If I Fall, If I Die*. McClelland and Stewart, 2015.

Dobson, Kit. *Transnational Canadas*. Wilfrid Laurier University Press, 2009.

Florida, Richard. *Cities and the Creative Class*. Routledge, 2005.

Frye, Northrop. "Conclusion to *A Literary History of Canada*." *Northrop Frye on Canada*, edited by Jean O'Grady and David Staines. University of Toronto Press, 2003, pp. 339–72.

Grainger, James. *Harmless*. McClelland and Stewart, 2015.

Greif, Mark. "The Hipster in the Mirror." *New York Times*, November 12, 2010, www.nytimes.com/2010/11/14/books/review/Greif-t.html. Accessed October 1, 2017.

Haddow, Douglas. "Hipster: The Dead End of Western Civilization." *Adbusters*, no. 79, 2008, pp. 4–5.

Hardcastle, Kevin. *Debris*. Biblioasis, 2015.

Harris, Amy Lavender. *Imagining Toronto*. Mansfield Press, 2010.

Hutcheon, Linda. *The Canadian Postmodern: A Study of Contemporary English-Canadian Fiction*. 1988. Oxford University Press, 2012.

Jones, Daniel. *The People One Knows: Toronto Stories*. Mercury Press, 1994.

Lefebvre, Henri. *The Production of Space*, translated by Donald Nicholson-Smith. Blackwell, 1991.

Lloyd, Richard. *Neo-Bohemia: Art and Commerce in the Postindustrial City*, 2nd ed. Routledge, 2010.

McFarlane, Brandon. *Canadian Literary Urbanism*. 2012. University of Toronto, PhD dissertation. *Tspace*, hdl.handle.net/1807/67295.

McFarlane, Brandon. "Emergent Fiction 2015." *University of Toronto Quarterly*, vol. 86, no. 3, 2017, pp. 1–24.

McFarlane, Brandon. "Hipster Urbanism and Glocal Toronto." *Literature and the Glocal City*, edited by Ana Maria Fraile-Marcos. Routledge, 2014, pp. 130–45.

New, W. H. *A History of Canadian Literature*. McGill-Queen's Press, 2003.
Pyper, Andrew. "High Anxiety in the Bush Garden: Some Common Prejudices in Mainstream Canadian Criticism." *Essays on Canadian Writing*, vol. 71, 2000, pp. 88–95.
Pyper, Andrew. *Kiss Me*. Porcupine's Quill, 1996.
Quartermain, Meredith. *U Girl*. Talonbooks, 2016.
Rosenthal, Caroline. *New York and Toronto Novels after Postmodernism*. Camden House, 2011.
Salem-Wiseman, Lisa. "Divided Cities, Divided Selves: Portraits of the Artist as Ambivalent Urban Hipster." *Downtown Canada*, edited by Justin D. Edwards and Douglas Ivison. University of Toronto Press, 2005, pp. 142–65.
Smith, Russell. *Confidence*. Biblioasis, 2015.
Smith, Russell. *How Insensitive*. Porcupine's Quill, 1994.
Smith, Russell. *Noise*. Porcupine's Quill, 1998.
Smith, Russell. *Young Men*. Vintage, 1999.
Soja, Edward. *Thirdspace*. Blackwell, 1996.
Taylor, Timothy. *Stanley Park*. Random House, 2001.
Trafford, Matthew. "The Renegade Angels of Parkdale." *The Divinity Gene*. Douglas and McIntyre, 2011, pp. 85–115.
"Two Hipsters Angrily Call Each Other 'Hipster.' " *The Onion*, March 29, 2006, local.theonion.com/two-hipsters-angrily-call-each-other-hipster-1819568370. Accessed October 1, 2017.
Wilson, J. W., and G. L. Kelling. "The Police and Neighborhood Safety: Broken Windows." *Atlantic Monthly*, 1982, pp. 29–38.
Winter, Michael. *This All Happened*. House of Anansi Press, 2000.
Zukin, Sharon. *Loft Living: Culture and Capital in Urban Change*. 1982. Rutgers University Press, 1989.

10

Choosing Marginality: White Entitlement in Dave Eggers's Hipster Fiction

Stephanie Li

Following the publication of his stunning debut memoir, *A Heartbreaking Work of Staggering Genius* (2000),[1] Dave Eggers was widely heralded as "the voice of his generation."[2] The self-referential text, rife with postmodern antics and comedic asides, movingly expressed the anxieties and desires of Generation X and appealed to American audiences increasingly captivated by confessional texts and reality-based narratives. Eggers's account of his parents' death by cancer months apart and his struggle to care for and raise his 8-year-old brother Toph reflected a widespread disaffection with "adult" institutions from marriage to the office of social services to back-to-school nights. Eggers came from a wholesome, all-American family, but his tragic loss seemed to exile him from any notion of normal life and encapsulated the disaffection of the post-baby boom generation. This paradox of an insider cast adrift became foundational to his hipster appeal; Eggers was familiar but profoundly othered by his experiences. If the hipster is, as Christy Wampole observes, possessed by "nostalgia for times he never lived himself," Eggers was nostalgic for the childhood he could never pass on to Toph, a simultaneously egotistical and altruistic sentiment with important social ramifications. There was touching sincerity to his ironic posturing.

---

[1]Henceforth abbreviated as *AHWOSG*.

[2]See Caroline D. Hamilton's *One Man Zeitgeist: Dave Eggers, Publishing and Publicity*.

With divorce rates spiking, Eggers's story of a shattered family spoke to a nation desperate for narratives of loving resilience. His patchwork but still powerful support system of family and friends suggested that the traditional nuclear family need not be a social cornerstone, or at least not the only social cornerstone. Named the best book of the year by a slew of national newspapers and magazines, *AHWOSG* remains Eggers's most celebrated and resonant text.[3]

Over twenty years since the publication of Eggers's debut, it is hard to imagine any young writer being dubbed the voice of his or her generation. When Eggers bore this moniker, such a description could be made without considerations of race or class. Throughout the 1990s and even at the turn of the millennium, any voice of a generation was assuredly white, heterosexual and middle-class. Twenty years later, there are dozens of exciting young talents on the literary scene, but no single voice identified as representative of an entire generation. In fact, to refer to such a spokesperson is to willfully ignore the workings of social privilege. Hannah Horvath, the lead character of HBO's hit series *Girls* (2012), became an easy object of satire and criticism when she tells her parents in the first episode of the first season that she longs to be "her generation's voice." The swift condemnation of Lena Dunham, the show's creator and director, received for her overwhelming focus on the problems of well-funded white girls attests to Hannah's insularity and the danger of conflating author and character. The more politically savvy Dunham would hardly proclaim herself "her generation's voice" while the fictional and often hapless Hannah cedes to reductive generalizations that erase important markers of race and class. When Hannah describes her ambitions to her parents, the exchange is laughable because twenty-first-century viewers, well-versed in the language, if not the practice of multiculturalism and social difference, know that there are too many forms of identity for a single voice to unite them all. The very phrase "voice of a generation" and Hannah's narrow self-image are an anachronism, a throwback to a time in which whiteness operates as a default subject position, in which whiteness need not question its own primacy.

The shift in how "voice of a generation" signifies in the early decades of the twenty-first century reflects an important evolution in what the hipster has come to mean in the twenty-first century. Neither figure can be meaningfully identified as their generation's voice, but both are recognizable hipsters, edgy and self-conscious, and, perhaps most obviously, white. However, to identify their racial identity seems superfluous since the ironic denizens from Brooklyn to Portland derided as hipsters are predominantly white. And yet

[3]*AHWOSG* was named the best book of the year by the *New York Times*, one of the best one hundred books of all time by *TIME* magazine, as well as the twelfth-best book of the decade by *The Times*.

their whiteness does not necessarily connote blind privilege since key to the hipster mentality is an extreme conscientiousness, an obsessive if not always shrewd understanding of one's image. Moreover, hipsters delight in their own chosen marginality—in fashions that counter the mainstream, in eating habits and recreations that are still underground. The hipster's chosen marginality is in part dependent upon a seeming sensitivity to racial dynamics; after all, as the mainstream is blind to or dismissive of racial dynamics, the hipster by necessity must recognize the abiding significance of race. In the second episode of the second season of *Girls*, Hannah's final argument with her Black boyfriend culminates in her declaration, "I also would love to know how you feel about the fact that two out of three people on death row are black men." Her seeming racial enlightenment is undercut by her final rejoinder, "I never thought about the fact that you were black once." Hannah is both a good white liberal, educated in the racial inequalities of capital punishment, but unable to recognize the delusion of her supposed color blindness. The hipster's seeming racial awareness ultimately occludes a disturbing reification of white entitlement. The quiet racism of a phrase like "voice of a generation" highlights cultural theorist Richard Dyer's contention that "[w]hite power … reproduces itself regardless of intention, power differences and goodwill, and overwhelmingly because it is not seen as whiteness, but as normal" (12). To combat such a dangerous dynamic, Dyer argues, "White people need to learn to see themselves as white, to see their particularity. In other words, whiteness needs to be made strange" (10). Even as Eggers's literary rise has been shaped by a marketplace and critical reception that largely continues to equate whiteness with normalcy, his literary protagonists are uniquely aware of their whiteness. Although they rarely, if ever directly, employ the language of race, these are characters who encounter whiteness as deeply alienating and confounding. Eggers responds to Dyer's provocation by creating characters who are indeed strange and perhaps more importantly strangers to themselves.

A wide array of such characters from Eggers's own literary persona—from Dave in *AHWOSG* to Josie, the dejected mother of two from his recent novel *Heroes of the Frontier* (2016)—share a similar trajectory of racial consciousness. They come to recognize that whiteness does not erase their failures or limitations, and as a result, they must find meaning in alternative modes of identification. Their race repeatedly functions as a manufactured identity, a kind of expectation of normality that they struggle, and quite frequently fail, to fulfil. Throughout his broad oeuvre, Eggers presents us with white individuals who fail at whiteness, that is, individuals who do not wield the privileges and status typically associated with their racial identity. In *AHWOSG*, Dave and Toph are cast out from the middle-class world of two parent homes and good suburban schools. Eggers distinctly racializes their social Otherness by invoking familiar racial tropes as if the loss of their parents has severed their singular claim to whiteness. This opening characterization lays the foundation for later texts which explore how personal and professional failures lead to a paradoxical desire to escape the expectations of whiteness while still depending upon the promise of reinvention made by a deeply racialized form of American exceptionalism. Eggers presents white characters who relish the privileges of whiteness while also adopting an underdog posture with striking racial resonance.

Despite Eggers's striking and sustained engagement with the meanings attached to whiteness, the racial politics of his work are a notably underexplored component of the growing critical attention he has received. Scholars have largely analyzed his work through considerations of genre and the ways in which Eggers's books defy conventional notions of memoir, novel, and testimonial literature.[4] However, whiteness remains an insistent site of anxiety throughout all of his works. While his characters recognize themselves as white, they are eager to present themselves as social others, exceptions to the privileges usually accorded white Americans. This dynamic reflects a hipster impulse to find Otherness or cool cache in the white normal from trucker hats to tube socks. Such recalibration of the white normal allows texts by writers like Eggers to be understood less as white literature than as a kind of hipster literature. By eliding the mainstream label "white," hipster literature threatens to diminish the importance of race to texts by writers like Eggers, Miranda July, David Foster Wallace, or Leanne Shapton. While these authors certainly contribute to a body of work that can be defined as hipster literature, critics must be attentive to how various forms of social difference are often elided or co-opted in these texts.

I focus first on *AHWOSG* and then on one of Eggers's later novels, *Heroes of the Frontier*, because these texts most directly address the anxieties that pervade contemporary concerns about whiteness. The protagonists of both books are outsiders from established notions of whiteness and operate at the margins of acceptable behavior. Dave and Toph are left shocked and unmoored by the death of their parents as they attempt to reestablish some measure of social and personal structure. Similar to the disoriented orphans of *AHWOSG*, Josie of *Heroes of the Frontier* is adrift in the frontier wilderness of Alaska in a chosen isolation that reflects her unrecognized privilege. Estranged from her parents and often disgusted by the father of her children, she is no well-adjusted working mother, but a desperate fugitive from her own life. If whiteness is a privilege, these characters affirm that it is little help in today's ailing economy and litigious culture. Consistent with J. D. Vance's recent *Hillbilly Elegy* (2016) or the reassessment of Tonya Harding as a victim of prejudice, Eggers presents us with portraits of white Americans struggling to fit a racial identity that is less a source of cultural

---

[4]On *AHWOSG*, see Smith and Watson; Nicol; and Widiss. On *What Is the What*, see Peek; Yost; and Eaglestone.

and national affirmation than an impossible and even dubious social ideal.[5] Dave and Josie are indeed white, but they are perhaps best defined by their inadequacies. In some cases, these insufficiencies are cast upon them, but others are deliberately cultivated to separate them from mainstream society. They are white shorn of all the successes usually associated with this racial identity. However, despite their best attempts to other themselves, like contemporary hipsters, they maintain often troubling entitlements of whiteness.

A Heartbreaking Work of Staggering Genius

Though *AHWOSG* is not a novel, the book affirms Toni Morrison's observation that "the readers of virtually all of American fiction have been positioned as white" (*Playing in the Dark* xii). White characters are introduced without reference to race because whiteness functions as the assumed standard. Eggers adheres to this model throughout the memoir, suggesting that he and his friends and family are unmarked by race. However, one of the central concerns of *AHWOSG* is how, as young orphans beset by struggle and tragedy, Dave and his younger brother occupy a new marginalized social identity. Dave suggests that he and Toph have moved beyond the usual parameters of whiteness and are instead more closely aligned with the poor and people of color. When the two move into a house in San Francisco (rented by "a large, middle-aged black woman" (75)), Dave describes the neighborhood as somewhat eccentric because of the diversity of its residents:

> The immediate neighborhood includes an older lesbian couple, an elderly Chinese couple, a black man/white woman pair in their early forties, and Daniel and Boona next door, sandals and beaded, unmarried—and just friends, it seems—both in some kind of social work. Elsewhere on the block are single mothers, divorcees, widows, widowers, single women living with single men, single women living with single women, and, a few blocks away, there is even Barry Gifford. Only here would we blend. Only here, by comparison, would we seem ho-hum. (78)

Dave understands the neighborhood as unorthodox and transgressive, comparable to the new model of family he is creating with Toph. From our twenty-first-century perspective, it also reflects a hipster dream of ungentrified city life—a diverse enclave unaware of its diversity. Like the

---

[5]See Taffy Brodesser-Akner's article "Tonya Harding Would Like Her Apology Now."

lesbians and the interracial couple, Dave and Toph seem part of a brave new world of domestic experimentation. However, there is little that is especially remarkable about an elderly Chinese couple or even unmarried social workers who we know to be white because their racial identity is not specified. Dave envisions bold difference when the only surprising aspect of this neighborhood is his surprise at its inhabitants. Here, as elsewhere in the text, Eggers presents the loss of his parents as a weighty mark of difference. Arriving late to Toph's elementary school open house, Dave imagines that he and his brother are objects of curious scrutiny: "We are disadvantaged but young and virile. We walk the halls and the playground, and we are taller, we radiate. We are orphans. As orphans, we are celebrities. We are foreign exchange people, from a place where there are still orphans. Russia? Romania? Somewhere raw and exotic" (96). While Dave cannot shed the pigmentation of his skin, he imagines himself as from a "raw and exotic" nation. He relies on the ethnic difference embedded in Russia and Eastern European countries to suggest that the loss of his parents destabilizes the purity of his American whiteness. Dave's longing for a community of people similar to himself takes on racial resonance as he envisions a place where his status as an orphan is unremarkable, even common. Like an immigrant, he has been displaced, and this American world of mundane conformity and nuclear families is not his. Significantly, Dave assumes that his difference can be immediately read on his body—"Heads turn. This is our first open house, and people are not sure what to make of us" (95)—and that such difference immediately inspires speculation: "We capture everyone's imagination" (96). Like racial others, they become the site of projection and desire even if only so imagined by Dave. He is an insider transformed by tragedy into a social exile.

However, the only person clearly fantasizing about their identity is Dave, who rhapsodizes for pages on the beauty evident in his and Toph's most casual gestures. He describes their superhuman frisbee throwing: "We take four steps for each throw, and when we throw the world stops and gasps. We throw so far, and with such accuracy, and with such ridiculous beauty. We are perfection, harmony, young and lithe, fast like Indians" (67). Here, Dave and Toph are wondrous, astonishing spectacles who, reigniting the tired stereotype of the noble savage, belong to a mysterious, endangered people. They are fundamentally Other, existing apart from the mundane white middle-class life that once defined Eggers's family. The death of his parents severs Dave from conventional identity categories. He is both mother and father to Toph, both child and adult, both white and no longer a part of the expectations associated with whiteness. In short, he is a hipster's dream, a counterculture renegade who can create his own independent identity.

This transgressive liminality is highlighted in a conversation that is more an exchange between Dave and himself than between Dave and Toph. The latter indicts his older brother for his combative independence: "You've got that single-parent rage, that black-single-mother defensiveness, combined with your naturally ready-to-be-indignant/aggressive tendencies" (117). By racializing Dave's anger as well as his domestic circumstance, Toph's comment suggests that Dave has moved past the boundaries of white masculinity. The emendation that Dave has developed "black-single-mother defensiveness" as opposed to just "single-parent rage" implies that both gender and race are unstable categories for Dave. With his identity thrown into question by the loss of his parents, Dave becomes a repository of all kinds of Otherness. His suffering and grief seemingly justify his appropriation of marginalized subjectivities. Toph, further ventriloquizing Dave's guilty conscience, claims that Dave is using his personal tragedy as a way to transcend his middle-class background and assume a new totalizing authority. Toph explains:

> And now you feel that you have the moral authority to pass judgment on these people, that because of your recent experiences, you can expound on anything, you can play the conquering victim, a role that gives you power drawn from sympathy and disadvantage—you can now play the dual role of product of privilege and disenfranchised Job. Because we get Social Security and live in a messy house with ants and holes in the floorboards you like to think of us as lower class, that now you know the struggles of the poor—how dare you!—but you like that stance, that underdog stance, because it increases your leverage with other people. (118–19)

Dave and Toph are hardly poor. Toph receives Social Security checks because these funds were owed to his parents, and they live in squalid conditions because they refuse to clean the house. As such, their circumstances in no way mimic the lives of the American underclass. At one point Dave explains that while his mother had been a pennypincher, now he always chooses convenience over expense; Dave states, "When it's a matter of expense over convenience, the choice is not a choice. While my mother would have driven forty miles for a half-priced tomato, I'll pay $10 for it if it means I don't have to get in the car" (76–7). If there is poverty in Dave and Toph's life, it is not financial but purely emotional and familial. As recent orphans, they lack stability and the wisdom of elders. The absurd conflation of this loss with the struggles of the poor only showcases Dave's anxiety about the social advantages he previously enjoyed. However, it is important to note that Toph's accusation positions Dave as both the "product of privilege and disenfranchised Job." Dave does not simplistically aim to adopt the identity and perspective of the poor; instead, he combines "the underdog stance" with the entitlements of his race, class, and gender. Rather than being transformed into the disenfranchised Other, Dave is both original self and abject Other. He effectively claims all subject positions. Even as the text reflects on such appropriation through the imagined dialogue with Toph, such totalizing usurpation reflects a staggering degree of white privilege.

Eggers expresses all of these concerns through Toph who, at 9 years old, hardly has the insight and sophistication to levy such charges. The young boy is used as a rhetorical device to articulate genuine concerns. One might argue that by having Toph, a kind of innocent moral center, make these accusations, Eggers is at least acknowledging the problems inherent in trying to pass himself off as part of the struggling poor and disenfranchised. As Toph exposes Dave as a racial and class voyeur, Eggers points to the dangerous consequences of Dave's whiteness. It is useful here to frame Eggers's recognition of his own racial and class slippage against Sara Ahmed's observations concerning "the politics of declaration" in whiteness studies. Ahmed explains, "[D]eclaring whiteness, or even 'admitting' to one's own racism, when the declaration is assumed to be 'evidence' of an anti-racist commitment, does not do what it says. In other words, putting whiteness into speech, as an object to be spoken about, however critically, is not an anti-racist action." Eggers effectively admits his problematic conflation of parental loss with the struggles of the marginalized through Toph's comments. However, as Ahmed notes, to recognize such careless and self-serving acts does not rectify the problem. Rather than engage Toph's accusations, Dave announces that he is tired and then puts his brother to bed. These dynamics are never revisited in the text. Whiteness may be spoken, but anti-racist action remains beyond the purview of the text, a lazy and troublingly complacent move that elides meaningful social change.

Heroes of the Frontier

A wish to escape one's identity also animates Eggers's 2016 novel *Heroes of the Frontier*. It tells the story of 40-year-old Josie who abandons her suburban life in Ohio after losing her dentistry practice to a litigious patient and learning that the father of her children plans to marry another woman. Unlike Dave in *AHWOSG*, Josie is not an obvious example of hipster culture. However, her often solipsistic approach to life and desire for reinvention reflect the same racialized entitlement that animates Dave, suggesting that such an attitude is not limited to hipster figures. Exhausted by her awareness that "the primary response she provoked in others was disappointment" (134), Josie absconds with her two young children, Paul and Ana, hoping to find "someone bold ... someone of substance" amid the "magic and clarity" (5) of Alaska. Josie remains tightly bonded to her children even though many of her parenting choices are dubious at best. She ultimately prevails due to her dedication to her children. The book culminates in her recognition that her search for heroes is best realized by parenting them well: "All along she had been looking for courage and purity in the people of Alaska. She had not thought that she could simply—not simply, no, but still—create such people" (308). Josie finds redemption in cultivating kindness, resilience, and joy in her children. The novel's emphasis on children and caretaking might seem to obviate the more explicit engagement with whiteness and hipsterism that pervade *AHWOSG* and some of Eggers's other works. However, Josie's empowering epiphany about the need to create bold, substantive people is troubled by her often astounding sense of racial entitlement; her children may indeed be adventurous and resourceful but they also further a legacy of white privilege. Like many of Egger's previous protagonists, Josie does not describe herself as white even as her self-perception is inextricable from her racial identity. Eggers presents Josie as an earnest but exasperated woman who, while deeply devoted to her children, longs for the blurry escape of another bottle of wine. The 5-year-old Ana receives more reliable care from her 8-year-old brother Paul, who intuits what his mother knows all too well: "that at every opportunity, she made precisely the wrong choice" (70). Such a hapless protagonist makes for an amusing read, but Josie's intense focus on the promise of a new day, even one soaked in last night's pinot, masks a more disturbing approach to her own sense of history. Though Josie never identifies herself as white, she recognizes herself as uniquely American:

> She had been born a blank. Her parents were blanks. All her relatives were blanks, though many were addicts, and she had a cousin who identified as an anarchist, but otherwise Josie's people were blanks. They were from nowhere. To be American is to be blank, and a true American is truly blank. Thus, all in all, Josie was a truly great American. (20)

Despite a degree of self-aware irony in this passage, Eggers conflates Americanness with a form of ahistorical whiteness. Though Josie had "heard occasional and vague references to Denmark. Once or twice she heard her parents mention some connection to Finland. Her parents knew nothing about these cultures, these nationalities," (20) her family is so far removed from their country of origin that they have become nothing more than "blanks." Josie presents herself as a kind of *tabula rasa* upon which a new story and identity may be cast, operating from a key assumption of American identity that extends back to European settlement. While there is a longing here for a greater sense of rooted identity, this absence makes possible a dangerous invention of self. Josie believes that by driving to Alaska, she can escape the past and become a purer, freer version of herself. The narrator further notes that Josie's parents "cooked no national dishes, they taught Josie no customs, and they had no relatives who cooked national dishes or had customs. They had no clothes, no flags, no banners, no sayings, no ancestral lands or villages or folktales" (20). This is whiteness as absence, tragic perhaps in its lack of a specific cultural heritage but bent toward limitless possibility and, for the purposes of the novel, heroic fulfilment. Such absence is consonant with the hipster appetite for foods, garments, customs, and practices of nonwhite cultures as it makes space for a fetishistic colonizing of the Other. Though Josie is not an obvious hipster, her whiteness links her to key aspects of this figure.

Despite Eggers's wry conclusion that Josie is "a truly great American" because she is "truly blank," she is in no way an absence. Josie may not have family recipes or beloved traditions to pass on to her children, but her history is not an empty slate. To assert such blankness is to willfully deny the complexities and errors of her actual experience. Josie is not a blank, but instead desires blankness as a way to refuse what James Baldwin identifies as the rejection of truth at the heart of white identity. Baldwin explains in his essay "On Being 'White' ... and Other Lies," that whiteness is "absolutely, a moral choice," built upon a refusal to "confront the ravage and the lie of their history" (180). Josie desperately wants to deny her personal history, and the sad backstory Eggers provides for his protagonist only underscores this desire. Josie is the only daughter of former psychiatric nurses in a veterans' hospital. She emancipated herself as a teenager after her parents became ensnared in a scandal involving the overprescription and subsequent suicide of numerous patients. The explanation of the doctor largely held responsible for the deaths, "I only wanted them to live without pain" (108), highlights a broader national failure to confront the violent legacy of the Vietnam War, one of the key tragedies of the baby-boom generation. In a tragic turn of events, Josie's parents become addicted to the very drugs overprescribed by the head doctor, leaving their daughter to fend for herself. Josie is taken in by her dentist, Sunny Kimura, who previously rescued another teenage girl, Samantha. Sunny remains a steady source of support for Josie throughout her life and inspires her to become a dentist.

This detailed history contradicts Josie's easy self-conceptualization as a "blank." She is, in fact, deeply ensnared in a uniquely American story of willed forgetting that mirrors her own desire for erasure. Like the vets they treated, Josie's parents are eager to ignore the past and their own guilt in a wider national tragedy which has a lasting impact on later generations and Josie in particular. The narrator notes that during the fallout from the Candyland scandal— the nickname used by the vets to refer to the VA hospital—"Josie learned the meaning of the word *complicity*" (109). Josie's parents are not entirely to blame for the overprescription and suicide of their patients, but neither are they innocent. They instead demonstrate a quality that Toni Morrison associates specifically with whiteness: willed innocence. In her 1983 novel *Tar Baby*, the first of her books to include developed white characters, Morrison indicts rich, white Valerian Street for his refusal to recognize the abuse his wife inflicted upon their son:

> He thought about innocence there in his greenhouse and knew that he was guilty of it because he had lived with a woman who had made something

> kneel down in him the first time he saw her, but about whom he knew nothing; had watched his son grow and talk but also about whom he had known nothing. And there was something so foul in that, something in the crime of innocence so revolting it paralyzed him. He had not known because he had not taken the trouble to know. He was satisfied with what he did know. Knowing more was inconvenient and frightening. (242)

Like Valerian, Josie's parents are complicit in abuse. They did not instigate the overprescription of the veterans and they certainly did not intend their deaths, but they are guilty of innocence by failing to question or consider the consequences of their actions. Their subsequent addiction to narcotics highlights their refusal to confront their personal histories. Like Josie, they seek escape and a troubling form of historical amnesia. This amnesia provides the breeding ground for powerful but misguided fantasies. Like Dave in *AHWOSG*, Josie imagines herself as the victim of some vague form of oppression. She too takes on a kind of marginalized social status due to her itinerancy even though her "homeless" condition is entirely voluntary. Josie here aligns with the hipster tendency toward usurping already marginalized spaces and viewing personal transgression as a means of creating an original self. Despite being decidedly unhip, Josie shares key aspects of the hipster's troubling approach to race. Looking out upon the majesty of Alaska, she reflects,

> But then again, this home, this property, was evidence of the glory of the land, this country. There was so much. There was so much space, so much land, so much to spare. It invited the weary and homeless like herself, her worthy children. She had the blurry thought that all the world's searching and persecuted could find a home up here. Alaska's climate was warming, was it not? It would soon be a forgiving place, with milder winters and uncountable millions of unpopulated acres, and so many empty homes like this, waiting to take in the desperate travelers of the world. It was a wonderful thought, a numbing notion. (219–20)

Josie ponders these possibilities from the cottage of a bed and breakfast that she and her children have adopted as their own. It is not one of "many empty homes" waiting for wanderers like herself to effectively usurp as their own. In fact, there are no such empty homes, even the one Josie and her children have happened upon. Josie's fantasy reflects a kind of proto-colonialism in which she and other kind but "desperate travelers" make Alaska their own. Her nostalgia-driven appropriation of another person's home reflects a hipster desire for originality. In this disturbing dream, global warming conveniently and ironically softens the challenges of the land, and there are no preexisting inhabitants, only their cozy cottages to stock with snacks. Josie understands the world as structured to cater to her particular needs and desires. Alaska seems to offer a new form of manifest destiny for the perpetually disappointing. Josie and her children arrive at the bed and breakfast while wildfires rage across the countryside, leading to disorienting mass evacuations. Desperate for a place to rest, Josie enters the clean, apparently new cottage and immediately improvises a justification for their stay to her cautious son:

> "The way bed and breakfast work," she said, changing her tone to one of almost blasé authority, "is that often you arrive after the proprietors"—she knew Paul would not know the meaning, but the word would heighten her authority—"go to sleep. And sometimes they live nearby but not on the premises. So the standard thing to do"—now she was really blasé, she considered yawning—"is that you write a note and tape it to the front door." (213)

Josie smoothly lies to her son in order to justify what effectively becomes her usurpation of the cottage. Paul writes a misspelled note that conveys both the charm of his youth ("We saw your Sign. We are sleeping in your wonderful Cabin") and the entitlement of his mother ("Please don't wake us in the morning"), closing with the unfulfilled promise: "P.S. We will pay you for using the Cabin" (215). Paul's note affirms the childish narcissism at the heart of Josie's seemingly benign approach to the world.

Although Josie's actions are not criminal, they betray an astounding sense of self-righteous ownership. Even as she recognizes that "they had more or less broken into" the house, she justifies herself by creating a new protocol of acceptable behavior:

> It was within the bounds of appropriate and even legal behavior for the wayward. There was a time, was there not, when it was right and good to go on a journey, and find an unoccupied cabin in the woods, and spend the night there, and then clean it, leaving it as they found it, ready for the next tired traveler? All this should be allowed. (216)

Josie hearkens back not to a former era of boundless generosity but to a fantasy of her own creation akin to hipster nostalgia for a world not entirely curated by the internet. She imagines an America of benevolent settlers and wanderers when in fact Alaska, like the continental United States, was the site of violent imperial conquest. Moreover, Josie and her children do not leave the cottage as they found it, cleaned and readied for the next fortunate traveler. Instead, they make use of all its provisions until they are eventually discovered by the owner. Rather than explain their actions, Josie flees like the fugitive she is, not the discovering journeywoman she imagines herself to be. Although the owner only calls the police and does not in any way threaten Josie, she refuses to answer his questions and makes a fast break for her RV. She drives off uncertain if he grabbed on by the ladder and is riding on the speeding vehicle. Rather than stop and see about his safety, she drives faster, hoping he will disappear. By the time she stops at a gas station, the man is gone. Is he hurt? Is he lying somewhere on the highway? Is he alive? None of these questions matter to Josie, who is palpably relieved that he is simply gone. The man and his cottage warrant no further mention. Josie may have grievously injured or even killed a man, but this is not part of her heroic journey. This is not a history she ever need remember, and Eggers never returns us to the scene of the crime.

Heroes of the Frontier closes with another remarkable moment of casual usurpation. Josie and her children decide to hike to a mountain lake they mistakenly assume to be close to town. After hours of walking, they are hit by a massive thunderstorm. Without raincoats or protective gear, they stumble through the rain. Ana slips and cuts her leg while Josie runs in a bra after using her shirt to bandage her daughter. They continue to run through the storm which precipitates an avalanche that strews rocks across the trail. Despite these setbacks, the family soldiers on with determined frenzy. After climbing over the fallen rock, Josie and her children arrive at the mountain lake and immediately seek shelter in "a sturdy cabin made of logs and bricks, the straight line of its chimney standing like a beacon" (382). The well-made cabin is the dream of both Alan and Josie, a solid construction welcoming them home. And, in fact, the cabin is ideally prepared for their arrival. Inside, they find all the items necessary for a surprise party: "There were balloons, streamers, a table overflowing with juices and sodas, chips, fruit and a glorious chocolate cake under a plastic canopy." A sign over the porch reads, "Welcome Stromberg Family Reunion," and "[a]ll around the cabin were framed photos from every era, most in black and white, all neatly labeled." Josie promptly announces to Paul and Ana, "Today we are the Strombergs," (432) and wrapped in wool blankets, they feast on the food and warm themselves by the fire.

Josie and her children take not just the food and provisions of the cabin; they implicitly project themselves into a family that spans generations. If they began as blanks, they conclude as appropriators, taking what they believe to be theirs but which rightfully belongs to invisible others. They remain completely oblivious to their theft as Eggers stages the final scene as a triumphant assertion of their power, not a reckoning of the ethics of their actions: "Every part of their being was awake. Their minds were screaming in triumph, their arms and legs wanted more challenge, more conquest, more glory" (383). And yet what has been awakened? They remain blind to their own history, blind to the properties they have used and discarded, and blind to a world that is not made just for them. They have summited a mountain in a bad storm and warmed their bodies with firewood cut by no one they will ever meet, much less thank. The scene concludes as "Josie looked at the bright flaming faces of her children and knew this was exactly who and where they were supposed to be" (433). Although Josie's commitment and love for her children is joyous, she remains firmly circumscribed by the narcissism of her whiteness. Even as she gazes at her children, she sees in them a rosy vision of her own reckless appropriation and disregard of others. For Eggers, this is "a new and untroubled happiness" (384), but it is in fact an old and tired form of willed ignorance and racial blindness.

In both *AHWOSG* and *Heroes of the Frontiers*, Eggers presents protagonists who overcome significant obstacles. Dave and Toph confront the loss of their parents, and Josie struggles for basic survival in the wilderness of Alaska. Both texts conclude with victorious characters who learn important life lessons about independence, resilience, and the bonds of love. However, the simplicity of these narratives belies a more complex set of racial dynamics that assumes white authority and elides white privilege. While these examples of hipster literature eschew the irony and superficial posturing often associated with hipsterism, their sincerity is premised upon a troubling set of assumptions that reify destructive notions of race. Eggers's heartfelt endings betray the casual arrogance of whiteness.

Works Cited

Ahmed, Sara. "Declarations of Whiteness: The Non-Performativity of Anti-Racism." *Borderlands*, vol. 3, no. 2, 2004, www.borderlands.net.au/vol3no2_2004/ahmed_declarations.htm. Accessed October 30, 2020.

Asthana, Anushka. "The 100 Best Books of the Decade." *The Times*, November 14, 2009, www.thetimes.co.uk/article/the-100-best-books-of-the-decade-952h76nd689. Accessed April 23, 2010.

Baldwin, James. "On Being 'White' … and Other Lies." *Black on White: Black Writers on What It Means to be White*, edited by David R. Roediger. Schocken Books, 1998, pp. 177–80.

Brodesser-Akner, Taffy. "Tonya Harding Would Like Her Apology Now." *New York Times*, January 10, 2018, www.nytimes.com/2018/01/10/movies/tonya-harding-i-tonya-nancy-kerrigan-scandal.html. Accessed October 30, 2020.

Dyer, Richard. *White: Essays on Race and Culture*. Routledge, 1997.

Eaglestone, Robert. "'You Would Not Add to My Suffering if You Knew What I Have Seen': Holocaust Testimony and Contemporary African Trauma Literature." *Studies in the Novel*, vol. 40, no. 1/2, 2008, pp. 72–85.

"Editor's Choice." *New York Times*, December 3, 2000, www.nytimes.com/2000/12/03/books/editors-choice.html. Accessed October 30, 2020.

Eggers, Dave. *A Heartbreaking Work of Staggering Genius*. Vintage Books, 2000.

Eggers, Dave. *Heroes of the Frontier*. Knopf, 2016.

Girls. Created by Lena Dunham, performance by Hannah Horvath and Lena Dunham, HBO, 2012–17. *HBO MAX*, July 22, 2019.

Hamilton, Caroline D. *One Man Zeitgeist: Dave Eggers, Publishing and Publicity*. Continuum, 2010.

Morrison, Toni. *Playing in the Dark: Whiteness and the Literary Imagination.* Vintage, 1992.

Morrison, Toni. *Tar Baby.* 1981. Vintage, 2004.

Nicol, Bran. "The Memoir as Self-Destruction: *A Heartbreaking Work of Staggering Genius.*" *Modern Confessional Writing: New Critical Essays*, edited by Jo Gill. Routledge, 2006, pp. 100–14.

Peek, Michelle. "Humanitarian Narrative and Posthumanist Critique: Dave Eggers's *What is the What.*" *Biography*, vol. 35, no. 1, 2012, pp. 115–36.

Smith, Sidonie, and Julia Watson. "The Rumpled Bed of Autobiography: Extravagant Lives, Extravagant Questions." *Biography: An Interdisciplinary Quarterly*, vol. 24, no. 1, 2001, pp. 1–14.

Wampole, Christy. "How to Live without Irony." *New York Times*, November 17, 2012, opinionator.blogs.nytimes.com/2012/11/17/how-to-live-without-irony. Accessed October 30, 2020.

Widiss, Benjamin. *Obscure Invitations: The Persistence of the Author in Twentieth-Century American Literature.* Stanford University Press, 2011.

Yost, Brian. "The Voices of Others: Dave Eggers and New Directions for Testimony Narrative and Cosmopolitan Literary Collaboration." *Ariel: A Review of International English Literature*, vol. 42, no. 1, 2011, pp. 149–70.

11

The Line, the Niche, and the Bathrobe: The White Male Writer as a Hipster Trope

Katharina Scholz

Writing about writers has its pitfalls. In the act of writing and subsequently creating a text of one's own, any author can hardly escape the lineage of creative and academic analysis sparked by works before him. And who really is a writer? Can anyone position themselves along the pantheon of Hemingway et al. by simply proclaiming kinship? Or does only critical anointment by the sanction of peers satisfy the longing for approval? In this way, the writer is similar to the hipster: an insubstantial being, arising from the tensions between attribution and self-identification. Looking at the intersection of "the writer" and "the hipster," this chapter aims to draw a concurrent demarcation of a specific subset of white male writer as a hipster trope.

The central thesis of this chapter can be summarized as follows: contemporary hipster culture gave rise to a creative cohort of white male writers that draw their identity, as well as their creative linage, through the usage of nostalgia, transgression, and niche knowledge, which they reproduce for an audience of white (upper-)middle-class readers who share the same coded knowledge. It must be noted that the aforementioned elements do not necessarily appear in equal measures in the work of the hereafter mentioned writers: some intersect and necessitate each other. This chapter will contrast the role and historic positions of more traditional forms of publishing (print) with digital publishing to establish a cultural framework from which the white male writer emerges as a hipster trope.

What Is the White Male Writer and What Makes Him a Hipster?

Norman Mailer's essay "The White Negro," the cultural critic Mark Greif's 2010 article "What Was the Hipster?" published in *New York Magazine*, and Sabine Broeck's thoughts on male writers in "Grounds of Whiteness: White Male Claims to Authenticity" will be guides to develop a trope that will henceforth be referred to as the "white male writer." This white male writer uses coded knowledge to position himself in relation to his readers, specifically dealing in nostalgia, transgression, and niche knowledge. "Nostalgia," in this case, specifically refers to harkening back to a time unfettered by the restrictions of the modern world—often referencing forms of masculinity that have disappeared or are no longer acceptable in today's world. "Transgression" is another facet of the white male writer's existence: the mores of modern society are ignored, ridiculed, or simply shown to be recent constructs that were not present during the times of nostalgia. Finally, the white male writer and his reader bond through shared niche knowledge: references to places, people, and concepts that form common touchpoints and frame the shared narrative experienced by both white male readers and white male writers.

There are several parameters this chapter will be limited by: first, while hipster culture is (or perhaps was) a global phenomenon, the following analysis focuses exclusively on hipster culture and, more specifically, writing and publishing outlets in the United States and Central Europe. Secondly, the following analysis defaults to the narrow category of privileged white maleness and authorship. The omission of female writers, writers of color, or other intersectionally marginalized writers and their work in this context should by no means be seen as indifference to their work or impact but is simply a matter of pointed focus. Moreover, it has to be stressed at this point that personal essays, cultural criticism, and other types of essay journalism are classed as literature going forward. The hipster as a writer transgresses structure intentionally by offering himself as a mirror of his own anomalous experiences in nonfiction works.

There are several historic and cultural circumstance that enabled the emergence of the white male writer as a hipster trope in the late 2000s and early 2010s. Journalist and writer Norman Mailer describes his hipster's coming-of-age period during the late 1950s as a period of "crisis of accelerated historical tempo and deteriorated values," (283) which is equally valid for the contemporary hipster. For Mailer's white hipster, it was the collective awareness of the Holocaust and the use of the atomic bomb (277); for Greif's hipster, the crisis is the invasion of Iraq and the 1999 WTO protests. For the contemporary hipster, the horrors of concentration camps and atom bombs have yielded to pictures of Abu Ghraib, Guantanamo Bay, and a post-nine-eleven reality of asymmetric warfare and diffuse imminence of terrorist threats. The financial crisis of 2008 and its subsequent fallout, rivalling that of the Great Depression, is another leitmotif contributing to the mirroring of the contemporary hipster's "lessons of disillusionment" (Mailer 278). Said disillusionment and the subsequent experience of loss of material and societal security produces a need to canonize an accelerated societal frame of reference of historic proportions. The white male writer seizes this opportunity to style himself as a maker of meaning who has to balance both tradability and authentic creation. Norman Mailer's hipster—his "white negro"—rebels with showcased transgressive behavior as a means of self-definition and self-liberation from what he sees as a saturated society that revels in post-war prosperity and comfort (278). His hipster appropriates jazz as a cultural practice and subversive art he can consume to find solace from his white middle-class reality (279). His whiteness allows him to move in and out of this sphere with minimal consequences to his life as he by no means faces the same amount of scrutiny, institutionalized racism, and danger to his existence as his African American peers (Taylor). Mailer fails to address said reality and instead only offers a problematically reductionistic portrayal of race, and specifically Black masculinity and bodies (279). To understand the white male writer as a hipster trope, his whiteness has to be understood as a prerequisite of his identity. In the twenty-first century, the hipster is part of "[a] new class of rich young people" (Greif) to be exact. Belonging to the educated, white, (upper) middle class, the hipster "convinces himself that buying the right mass products individualizes him as transgressive" (Greif). He performs said transgression through the acquisition and consumption of coded goods, selected meticulously by a framework of "knowing-in-advance," which he turns into a "heroic practice" (Greif).

This appetite for transgression becomes evident when looked at in relation to publishing. In "Grounds of Whiteness: White Male Claims to Authenticity," Sabine Broeck, writing about Anthony Giardina's novel *White Guys* (2006), identifies a distinct class of novels and their respective authors as part of

> a series of texts which one could call white male post-creative writing novels. With a host of other contemporary novels that have successfully entered the publishing market after a grooming in creative writing classes, the novel shares a certain amount of speculativeness, narcissistic investment in calculated effect, and a premeditated accessibility vis-à-vis prospective readers. (153)

While Broeck's characterization alludes to the prevalence of a wider cultural trope, it does not give a full insight into how said trope developed or how it presents itself in a broader cultural context. The white male writer has to be understood as a creative, aware of an ever-shifting frame of reference for his writing. His own creative output has to be closely interlinked with the ability to judge and adapt to what the "right" transgression is. What Broeck calls "a certain amount of speculativeness" (153) in the novel applies to the cultural practice of the white male writer as a hipster trope. "Speculativeness" allows the writer to create his work from a "what if" perspective, allowing him to perform transgressive actions, be it only in writing or in real life for the purpose of writing about it. Endeavors such as drug usage, sexual adventures, or experimenting with forms of literary publishing that try to smudge the lines between writing and (performance) art are the "creative" vehicles for this transgression. His "what if" is clearly studied and performed as hip practice, outside the mainstream. The transgression is calculated and intended to position the white male writer as a maker of meaning in the sphere of his in-the-know peers.

The first hipster generation of the early 2000s is largely the first generation of digital natives or near-digital natives. For this generation of writers, there is a striking shift from print to online writing and publishing, which has only been accelerated progressively in the first decades of the twenty-first century. The shifting publishing landscape and the resulting need for freelancer's work has given rise to a "Digital Bohème" (Friebe and Lobo): A cohort of educated young people for whom the idea of full-time employee status in their creative field of interest is as unachievable as it is unappealing. Content creation, especially content that was marketable or could vertically integrate brands and products in the style of so-called advertorials, became a sought-after vendible.

Genealogy: From Hemingway to *Vice Media*

The following genealogy is meant to provide a short, cursory set of examples, trying to outline the white male writer as a product of a literary canon that favors his kind. The evolution of the white male writer is by no means a complete or linear process and could easily be expanded by the inclusion of writers like Charles Bukowski or Allen Ginsberg. But when it comes to hipster culture, and subsequently the white male writer, one cannot avoid journalist, writer, and bon vivant Ernest Miller Hemingway. Hemingway is the definition of a man's man: his writing and public personas embody virile masculinity, as do his leisure pursuits (hunting, drinking) along with his distinct writing style and topic choice. His performative self-fashioning, unmistakable personal brand, and concern with niche knowledge are distinct features emulated by the twenty-first-century hipster. Discussing Michael Gold's thoughts on the intended audience of Hemingway's writing, James Penner concludes that "[m]en's literature becomes a collection of masculine wish-fulfilment fantasies, and the assumed audience is male" (2).

There is an unending amount of in-depth research on motifs and meaning in Hemingway's life and work, but for the purposes of this chapter, a brief look will suffice. The deep entanglement of Ernest Hemingway in contemporary hipster culture may warrant its own line of research, but there is little ambiguity over his brand; Hemingway is to literature what Apple used to style itself as in the late 1990s and early 2000s with its "Get a Mac" campaign: a pseudo nonconformist. Hemingway is by his own merit an outsider, a man making his own life, unafraid and uninhibited by the societal standards of the time. From his notes on the Spanish Civil War to small game hunting as a leisure pursuit, war, sex, death, and the eternal struggle for one's own humanity (often by means of near-theatrical performativity of it) are central to his writing.

A few of his works are particularly interesting in this regard. First, his columns for *Esquire* magazine, published during the 1930s, are a collection of notes and anecdotes of Hemingway's personal experiences traveling as a journalist and writer. They range from cocksure nonchalance—"*There are too many supers in these last two sentences. Re-write them yourselves lads and see how easy it is to do better than Papa. Thank you. Exhilarating feeling isn't it?*" ("Notes on a Dangerous Game")—to deeply personal—"All I do is go out and get depressed and wish I were somewhere else" ("A Paris Letter"). The posthumously published *A Moveable Feast* (1964) consists of observations and anecdotes which he penned while trying to become a writer in Paris. Much like in his columns for *Esquire*, the book is filled with specific references to places like restaurants, bars, or even particular dishes and drinks, enabling the reader to gain access to niche experiences beyond the mainstream.[1]

Hemingway inarguably was—and remains—one of the great writers of literary history to such an extent that even mentions of Hemingway alone are enough to ennoble a product to the hipster. From drinking culture with craft beers or cocktail bars named after him (Bottle and Bull or simply Hemingway, a former hipster club in Los Angeles) to smaller and more indirect, possibly even accidental, acts of tribute, such as taxidermy (which are just salvaged stranger's hunting trophies), being displayed in hipster bars and homes and maybe even the big bushy hipster beards grown from Bushwick to Berlin. The white male writer uses history, and in fact even literary history, as a salvage yard for his own identity. What he can create and position as a riff on an original creation (or at least something marginal enough to deem outside mainstream style and taste) he will make use of.

While Hemingway's nonfiction writing features personal introspection combined with observations of his surroundings, by and large they are

[1]Some of the *Esquire* columns even feature specific advice to his readers on how exactly to procure a specific drink or dish.

not fictionalized, unlike Jack Kerouac's roman à clef *On the Road* (1957). The main characters' (and thus Kerouac's) journey through America is an introspective journey through themselves and the promised American Dream the world failed to deliver outside the rigid moral and societal constraints of America's postwar era. For twenty-first-century hipster readers, this potentially resonates with the loss they experienced during the fallout of the 2008 financial crisis. The main character's journey is not simply a transgressive voyage into the unexplored and strange fueled by drugs and sex. "However, headlong their steps into the unknown, Sal and Dean are traditionalists, looking to connect with old forms, not slay them. In their lament for lost fathers, they are creatures of nostalgia as well as New Men," (144) writes John Leland in *Why Kerouac Matters: The Lessons of On the Road* (2007). This shift, from authentic self-creation to the struggle to carve out one's own identity in relation to societal and personal dogma, was furthermore accelerated in the following period of the counterculture movement of the 1960s and 1970s, which gave rise to a new literary form. In this sense, Kerouac's work remains a timeless source for those experiencing themselves as outsiders or desire to be armchair-adventurers.

The following decades—the 1960s and 1970s—gave rise to the New Journalism movement. According to John Hellman's *Fables of Fact: The New Journalism as New Fiction* (1981), "The new journalism is, in my view, most properly understood as a genre of literature. Like realistic fiction or romantic fiction ... it has an aesthetic form and purpose making its final direction inward" (24). The white male writer utilizes this "direction inward" as a tool of self-styling, his inner workings a fountain of meaning and truth. And while the New Journalism movement changed and shaped journalism and writing as a pursuit of the self in the postmodern era, Hunter S. Thompson is credited as the inventor of gonzo-style journalism. Gonzo-style writing destabilizes the conventional narratives and ethos of journalistic work: it is "a vehicle for outrageous semi-autobiographical narrative that did not cloak itself in any pretense of objectivity. It offered a new epistemology of satire, perfectly suited to the image-driven environment of the late twentieth century" (Stephenson 10).

Hunter S. Thompson's works, specifically *Fear and Loathing in Las Vegas: A Savage Journey to the Heart of the American Dream* (1971) and to a lesser degree *The Kentucky Derby Is Decadent and Depraved* (1970), show the fluidity, adaptability, and potential for the republishing of pieces by the white male writer. These pieces follow the above discussed tendency of using introspection as a maker of meaning. Hunter S. Thompson, the boozing, balding, bathrobed eccentric became a token as of himself—a man unencumbered by the pressure and restrictions of society and the "polite society" he found himself writing about. His whiteness is hereby crucial, allowing him to blend with the subjects of his exploration, drawing neither suspicion nor ire. By blurring the lines between fact and fiction, gonzo journalism emerges as its own category of literature, thereby becoming an accessible form of publishing to the white male writer who seeks to break into writing as a career.

Mark Greif's 2010 essay "What Was the Hipster?" engages with one publication in particular, a publication that encompasses the hipster spirit in writing as well as cultural touchpoint: *VICE Magazine* and with it the media publishing empire that sprung from it, *VICE Media*. *VICE Media*'s cofounder and journalist Shane Smith once described himself as "the poor man's Hemingway" (qtd. in Widdicombe). Looking at his bylined pieces (among other work), there is an overwhelming amount of travel to areas of conflict, war zones, or dictatorships like North Korea. Smith clearly coquets with the image of a hard drinking, traveling maverick that goes beyond superficial travel journalism and more in the direction of uncensored embedment. *VICE* itself calls its style of reporting "immersionism" (qtd. in Widdicombe): its writers find themselves at the center of the experience or occurrence they are reporting on.

Looking at examples of journalism as literature, the popularization of gonzo-style journalism is comparable to the rise and diversification of online media that specifically favors the narrative, first-person essay to provide the impression of authenticity. Gavin McInnes (one of the cofounders who since departed *VICE*) describes the self-conception of *VICE*'s work saying, "Understand that we are freaks. We're not delving into the freak world. We live with the dregs of humanity"[2] (qtd. in Heimlich). For the white male writer, this subsequently means evening himself with his peers by being aware of their niche knowledge and tastes: his works need to engage them by means of positioning himself as part of an in-the-know hipster culture, without necessarily having to admit to it. And, in the end, what could be more authentic than the one thing that the hipster is an expert on and that he created so meticulously: himself—his life and experiences.

Much like in the literary world and circles, *VICE Media* is a distinctly knowledge-based domain that is partially hostile and exclusionary to people not familiar with it. The magazine and its digital branches act as tastemakers and an "ever-expanding universe of influence" (*Vice Digital: Media Kit* 5). In an effort to achieve this, *VICE*'s editorial content has been ever-shifting over the years, presumably due to the fact that there is a limited amount of time that "The VICE Guide to Anal Sex" (2000) or "The VICE Guide to Rehab" (2005) will shock its prospective readers when republished. The blurred lines between fact and fiction that the fast-paced environment online publishing cultivates allow the white male writer to traverse the borders between objectivity and subjectivity. Yet, subjectivity is offered as objectivity and thereby becomes an agent of self-creation. The white male writer is not

[2]A statement that reads like a more edgy version of Apple's 1997 "Think Different" campaign.

bound by factuality or reporting guidelines; all that matters is his experience of the world and how he makes sense of it. Recalling Penner's remark on Hemingway (2), *VICE Media* offers their readers an immersive proximity to danger, sex, and drugs. Roughly two thirds of their audience are male, whilst approximately half of the entire readership has graduated college with a degree; nearly 40 percent report an income of over $100K (*Vice Digital: Media Kit* 7). The *VICE* reporter becomes a foil through which the audience is able to see themselves. It is an infinite feedback loop of white men's perspectives for a white male audience sparked from a historic lineage of white men writing about white men.

Cultural Practices of the White Male Writer and His Emergence as a Hipster Trope

The advent of *VICE Media*, and the possibility of tracked digital engagement and reach, gave rise to what could be called a golden age of transgression. Online writing about acts of transgression became more encouraged as the demand for fast and readily available content rose. Specifically, personal transgression or personal takes on wider political topics became increasingly marketable. A push for notoriety, which overlaps with the yearning for authenticity, and the hunt and hunger for "truly" authentic content followed. *VICE Media*'s journalistic output distinctly oscillates between the topics of drugs, sex, danger and, if possible, takes place either in a far-flung place that traditionally does not lend itself to mass tourism (North Korea, Afghanistan, etc.) or is elevated by being accessible in a way similar to locals (VICE Guide to Europe 2014) (Miller). The authors have an unmistakable drive to be makers of meaning. Immersed in a foreign culture—be it "exotic" or accessible—the writer himself becomes a medium through which his reader is able to experience cultural practices (no matter how marginal) himself. Of course, the fact that the medium is not necessarily bound by standards of journalistic integrity, or even factuality, allows the white male writer to act as a stand-in for the reader's disgust, delight, or whatever other emotional reaction is to be evoked. The writer becomes a *pars pro toto* for his reader, giving him a glimpse of self-knowledge through the eyes of one of his peers; someone that lives and exists in the same culture and knowledge system as the reader himself: journalism and writing created by hipsters for hipster consumers. This approach has left outlets like *VICE* open to criticism, challenging its contributors. A comment found under a video titled "The South Korean Love Industry" reads, "VICE has a talent for finding the most judgmental, uncomfortable, uninformed, but attractive journalism students they can get. They always find the most salacious part of a culture, depict it as a freakshow and patronize everyone they interview. It's journalism for white hipsters who don't want to learn anything except vague generalisations" (Price). And while it could be argued that *VICE* furthered a breaking of the mold in regards of digital journalism, while the formats were new, the ideas and ways of engagement (in this case that of colonialist arrogance and (white) superiority, especially "exploring" nonwhite cultures) were not. The comment echoes critiques such as Trinh T. Minh-ha's observation on anthropology:

> Have you ever attended a white man's presentation (often also ours) on a "native" society, be he a photographer, a filmmaker, a choreographer, a musician, a speaker, or a writer? It is as if, unvaryingly, every single look, gesture, or utterance has been stained with anthropological discourse, the only discourse in power when it is a question of the (native) Other. (56)

This transgressive as posturing has taken a turn for the problematic in recent years. The election of Donald Trump gave rise to a multitude of far-right fractions, among them a group called *The Proud Boys*. This men-only neofascist grouping (established by former *VICE Media* cofounder Gavin McInnes) and its members self-describes as "[a] pro-Western fraternal organization for men who refuse to apologize for creating the modern world; aka Western Chauvinists" (The Elders). Inside the group there is a strong focus on "brotherhood," initiation rituals, and in-group practices which are meant to affirm its members' masculinity (physical violence or abstinence from pornography and masturbation). The organization has in recent times tried and failed to distance themselves from the label of "alt-right," with McInnes "reluctantly" (Moynihan) relinquishing his affiliation in November 2018, after a series of arrest and violence charges against members. Of course, this escalation of regression toward an archaic ideal of one-dimensional masculinity presents an outlier in McInnes. And while the white male writer is not a white nationalist, he is drawn to outdated ideas of masculinity which he finds in the texts of the white American canon.

James Penner's analysis of the writer's relationship with his own work and creative praxis reflects this struggle of transgression and masculinity. For example, "Kerouac ... positions himself as the masculine artist/rebel who is struggling against the effeminate cultural authorities, that are trying to repress his work" (126). The white male writer desires the same transgression and struggle against a society that has evolved toward what Penner calls "effeminate culture" over the last decades, becoming more inclusive and self-aware about its class, race, and gender divide. This type of performative masculinity follows a pattern in which "true" masculinity can be acquired by transgressing and a fallback on old concepts and performances of said masculinity. The dangers and thrill of war zones, sexual debauchery, and recreational drug usage blended into a new identity which resembles that of what Mailer calls "Hemingway's categorical imperative": "What made him feel good became therefore The Good" (278). The white male writer embraces, even needs, transgression to create meaning for himself and his peers.

The male author writing for *VICE* finds transgressive space not only in foreign countries but even inside his own mind, by simply altering his brain chemistry. Authenticity can still be easily performed for pieces that hold less shock value but demand a distinct knowledge framework from its readers: Imagine a mundane activity like going to a cat café (Keefe), or a special interest activity like attending a dog show (Smith). Neither activity is in itself transgressive or distinctively hip. The hipness and meaning are injected into the story by transgression—in Keefe's case the taking of psilocybin mushrooms at the cat café and in Smith's case the use of Acid at a dog show. While the gonzo writing of Hunter S. Thompson's era references drug usage in a stark but more casual manner, the experience of drug use (in, for example, an unusual setting) becomes the central focus of these white male writers' work. There is a strong element of irony interwoven with nostalgia in this practice. The venues are chosen either as (nostalgic) backdrop of comfort (cat café) or a specific coded sphere (such as a white middle-class event like the Westminster Kennel Club Dog Show). This engagement toes a thin line between ironic and post-ironic engagement with what the writer deems to be an outlet of bourgeoise or dominant culture. Yet it opens a new way of engaging with said culture. Still, the white male hipster positions himself as a sort of infiltrator, able to thumb his nose at the people attending such events or places unironically. They and their pursuits become easily available scenery in which the male writer can erect his identity as a transgressor.

This "premeditated accessibility vis-à-vis prospective readers" (Broeck 153) is what the white male writer's work comes down to. He is keenly aware of himself and his peers as potential readers. The question if his work is accessible is one that incorporates marketability, knowledge, and specific relevance of his writing. One example is the rise of casual pop culture criticism or outlets such as McSweeney's Internet Tendency, which mainly publishes humorous pieces pegged on cultural or political events, or emulations of literary voices, and makes apparent that the white male writer moves in a field of potentially exclusionary humor and knowledge. Beyond that, the white male writer functions as a cultural critic by means of the essay, which allows him to dignify his opinion as a matter of wider significance. Chuck Klosterman's "low culture manifesto" essay collection *Sex, Drugs, and Cocoa Puffs* (2003) is a good example of how the white male writer's works are specifically coded to appeal to his peers by requirements of nontraditional knowledge. Klostermann's analysis of low culture is not groundbreaking, but by intermingling a semi-academic approach to low cultural phenomena like *Star Wars*, MTV's *The Real World* or pornography, he caters to a highly specific cohort of readers. The white male writer's audience is the white male writer himself. His works are geared toward peers of the same social class and those with a similar horizon of experience and invite his readers to rejoice in a shared reexperience of nostalgia (for television programs, movies, cereals, etc.) enjoyed in childhood and early adolescence. While Mailer's hipster lacks what Greif describes as a sense of "nostalgia for suburban whiteness," this "nostalgia" is the "the source of prior knowledge" (Greif) that enables the contemporary hipster to make and construct his own authenticity by creating and consuming inside a frame which Greif identifies as "the very old dyad of adulthood and a child-centered world." The hipster is in that way an extended version of a teenager's rebellious phase. On the one hand, a craving for the nostalgia and comfort of the known and on the other, a desire for transgressive self-definition and creation. The hipster and hereinafter the white male writer trope emerge from a nostalgic yearning for a glorified past that offered a more clean-cut idea of originality and masculinity.

"I Realized I Was a Cliché: A Drunk Writer Who Couldn't Write Drunk" (2016) by James Wilt for *VICE* is an exemplary piece of the white male writer's praxis. Wilt's contributions to *VICE* oscillate between reporting, cultural criticism, and personal essay, placing him firmly in the tradition of the prior established genealogy: "So while my roommates worked real jobs in construction and data entry, I drank and wrote and spent money I made from writing on drinking, pretending to live out the tortured ideal pioneered by the Holy Drunken Trinity of Hemingway, Hitchens, and Hunter S." (Wilt). The essay meanders between the author's personal struggle with alcoholism and thinly veiled praises (and cautions) to the tradition of drunk writing in a conversational and ironic, self-aware voice. It requires the reader to be aware of the aforementioned tradition and history acquired through prior niche knowledge, as well as a certain amount of fraternization with the author himself. Wilt is thereby able to carve his own identity as a writer from historic tropes and ideas. The author laces the piece with detailed references to his life and social relationships, unimportant for the reader at best, uninteresting at worst:

> Absurdly, my infatuation with shitty sherry—and, if I was feeling fancy, a 750 mL bottle of Copper Moon malbec—was something I'd make subtle quips about in social settings, presumably hoping to rack up some of that esteemed bad boy cred I missed out on by skipping high school prom to play *Star Wars* video games with my friends. It probably never worked. Despite that, my go-to anecdote for nearly a full year was the tale of being unable to complete a cover feature on time because I was stuck in Indiana on a Sunday (when there's a preposterous ban on packaged liquor sales). (Wilt)

Personal authenticity becomes a commodity that can be manufactured from scavenged parts of literary and cultural history. The white male writer makes sense of the world by using his curated self and a constantly changing sphere of shifting knowledge. The memoir or personal essay, be it transgressional, confessional, or using immersive gonzo-style writing to convey his "authentic" truth, serves as a vehicle for the white male writer's narcissistic engagement with himself and his prospective readers who move in the same, or similar, bounds of education and knowledge. Like Broeck's novelist the white male writer utilizes "narcissistic investment in calculated effect" (153) creating a narcissistic effigy of himself in order to bond with readers and thereby prioritizes authenticity of expression over factuality.

The White Male Writer as Content Creator and Consumer

White male writers who have successfully entered the publishing market attain (or retain) a marketable value through the performance of their craft. They are part of a commodified creative class in which they are able to replicate transgression, knowledge, and themselves through their art. The white male writer toes the line between commercial success and niche elitism. As Greif describes, the hipster aligns himself with the dominant societal paradigm while rejecting its current cultural practices as beneath him and so does the white male writer. The only way for the white male writer to embrace said practices is by delving into nostalgic longing for a (possibly imagined) cultural reality of bygone times. The white male writer as a hipster trope emerges from the tension between marketability and authentic content that reflects his curated self and positions him as a consumer himself.

The Moleskine notebook as a coded token showcases how the hipster in general and the white male writer in particular consumes goods and authenticity that are linked to literary and creative genius. The brand was founded in 1997. There is no real brand history, just an idea that, through clever phrasing and repetition, it establishes the brand as (a successor to) notebooks used by artists like Hemingway. *A Moveable Feast*'s genesis is recalled by Hemingway's contemporary A. E. Hotchner: "Ernest had filled them with his careful handwriting while sitting in his favorite café, nursing a café crème. The notebooks described the places, the people, the events of his penurious life." "It's marketing, not science. It's not the absolute truth" (qtd. in Horowitz) is the official line of defense by the company's marketing department when pressed on the matter. The brand itself evokes Pablo Picasso, Ernest Hemingway, and travel writer Bruce Chatwin indirectly as ambassadors despite these artists having used notebooks that seem not be attached to one specific brand (*Moleskine S.p.A* 130). Yet, the brand understands and markets its products to a specific demographic which it describes as "[covering] a wide demographic spectrum and manifested lifestyles characterized by strong mobility and a growing need to identify and recognize themselves through objects whose evocative value corresponded to their own scale of values: individuality, expression of self, mobility, authenticity" (*Moleskine S.p.A* 138, my translation).

The early hipster-mocking blog Stuff White People Like featured the notebooks as distinctive accessories for the creative hipsters (Lander). Moleskine is in its essence a contemporary hipster brand, selling nostalgia in an easily consumable way on the promise of greatness. It allows "the hangers-on" (Greif) to access the same ascription framework as their heroes or more successful peers. The notebook itself is a visual marker, more for the outside world than for the hipster himself. It does not matter what ends up being written in the notebook, what matters is the possible greatness of what could be written in the notebook. The Moleskine notebook offers greatness (or at least the possibility of it) by proxy. The white male writer is able to emulate his role models not in work or success but in performative similitude. Not nursing a café crème in a Parisienne café, but brooding over a Moleskine notebook in a Starbucks or musing at home over a MacBook, the white male writer injects another layer of consumerism into Greif's "heroic practice" by linking his consumption of goods to a lineage of writers that came before him. The notebook's promise of greatness has found its way into parody on McSweeney's Internet Tendency in a satirical piece titled *The History of the Legend of the Myth of the Moleskine* which echoes the exact talking points Moleskine used in its 2013 initial public offering for the Italian stock market.

The white male writer invites not only parodies of his tokens of identification, he himself becomes the object of analytical ridicule, and while there have been many parodies of the hipster per se, the white male writer has sparked his own niche area of mockery: especially in works by writer and journalist Dana Schwartz and writer Daniel M. Lavery. Schwartz operates a Twitter account under the guise of a character, simply named Guy In Your MFA (@GuyInYourMFA) tweeting the stream of consciousness contemplations of a man that is described as "[t]wo re-writes away from finishing the great American novel. Maybe about a 20-something in Brooklyn?" The tweets oscillate between narcissistic self-reflection—"I'm writing a memoir about the struggles of being a 24-year-old writer who came from the suburbs and went to a good college"—"artistic" contemplation—"Oh, I'm working on a novel. Well, not exactly a novel—more of a textual experience" and cultural criticism—"Ugh, stop comparing the Trump administration to Harry Potter. It's infantile. This presidency is much more kafkaesque." The trope is identifiable by its distinct voice, which can be condensed to, "It almost feels like a waste to write fiction when being a white 24-year-old trying to be a writer in New York is so unique and interesting." The tweets reference tokens, pop culture and literary history with a certain nonchalant pomposity that is attributed to a young white male writer's attempts to stylize himself in the manner of his predecessors. Schwartz's character sees himself as a unique voice and attempts to carve his own identity in a contemporary culture awash with white male writers (and wannabe writers) like himself.

Daniel M. Lavery's satirical vignette *Male Novelist Jokes* (2013) works in a similar way by condensing the male novelist's voice into a collection of stereotypical themes (drugs, sex, and the struggle for self-defined authenticity). The piece utilizes the "how many x does it take to screw in a lightbulb" joke format, to which Lavery's novelist responds with excerpts and fragments of his work or musings.[3] The humor is based on a tight frame of reference that is replicated and stylized in an ironic way, thereby demanding previous engagement and awareness of the male writer as a trope itself. The parodies' success shows that the "male novelist," despite his attempts at authentic self-curation, is not as unique and outside the mainstream as he would potentially appreciate. Lavery's work strips the "male novelist's" writing down to a set of sentences, easily recognizable as formulaic, repetitive, and creative within a certain boundary of transgression relating to sex, drugs, and self-perception. The function of Schwartz's and Lavery's parody is reinforced by their self-aware outsider position as writers vis-à-vis the established canon of the American white (cis-)male writer. And while authors like Ben Lerner are recognized for their "genius" (Lerner received a MacArthur Fellowship Grant, often referred to as "Genius Grant," in 2015), Schwartz is able to create a character parody of striking resemblance to Lerner's auto-fictitious character Adam Gordon in *Leaving the Atocha Station* (2011). This ability to create parody of the (self-)celebrated work of the white male writer goes beyond mere hipster- or writer-bashing, leading to a deeper and more rounded challenge to the question of what true artistic authenticity looks like.

Conclusion

The white male writer is a hipster trope that is beholden to self-created cultural practices. He performs masculinity, authenticity, and nostalgia in a set selection of areas of expertise. Niche knowledge, transgression, and the cultural performance of the self vis-à-vis his own peers allows him to

[3]For example, "Q: How many male novelists does it take to screw in a lightbulb? A: [four thousand words about an isolated encounter with a service worker that borders on racist and goes nowhere]" (Lavery).

become a maker of meaning and imagine himself into the genealogy of the white male American literary canon. He emerges from an infinite feedback loop of white men's perspectives for a white male audience sparked from a historic lineage of white men writing about white men.

Works Cited

Broeck, Sabine. "Grounds of Whiteness: White Male Claims to Authenticity." *The Pathos of Authenticity*, edited by Ulla Haselstein, Andrew Gross, and Maryann Snyder-Körber. Universitätsverlag Winter, 2010, pp. 151–62.

The Elders. "Proud Boys: Who Are They?" *Proud Boy Magazine*, August 2017, officialproudboys.com/proud-boys/whoaretheproudboys. Accessed July 15, 2020.

Friebe, Holm, and Sascha Lobo. *Wir Nennen es Arbeit: die Digitale Bohème oder: Intelligentes Leben Jenseits der Festanstellung*. Heyne, 2008.

Greif, Mark. "What Was the Hipster?" *New York Magazine*, October 22, 2010, nymag.com/news/features/69129/index2.html. Accessed October 22, 2017.

@GuyInYourMFA. "I'm writing a memoir about the struggles of being a 24-year-old writer who came from the suburbs and went to a good college." *Twitter*, January 22, 2017, 10:32 p.m., twitter.com/GuyInYourMFA/status/823282212263104512. Accessed October 22, 2017.

@GuyInYourMFA. "It almost feels like a waste to write fiction when being a white 24-year-old trying to be a writer in New York is so unique and interesting." *Twitter*, December 4, 2016, 11:10 p.m., twitter.com/GuyInYourMFA/status/805534662173069312. Accessed October 22, 2017.

@GuyInYourMFA. "Two re-writes away from finishing the great American novel. Maybe about a 20-something in Brooklyn? Repped by @danaschwartzzz." *Twitter*, twitter.com/GuyInYourMFA. Accessed October 22, 2017.

@GuyInYourMFA. "Ugh, stop comparing the Trump administration to Harry Potter. It's infantile. This presidency is much more kafkaesque." *Twitter*, February 22, 2017, 1:42 a.m., twitter.com/GuyInYourMFA/status/834201768829603840. Accessed October 22, 2017.

Heimlich, Adam. "Vice Rising: Why Corporate Media Is Sniffing the Butt of the Magazine World." *New York Press*, web.archive.org/web/20081010201329/nypress.com/15/40/news&columns/feature.cfm. Accessed October 22, 2017.

Hellmann, John. *Fables of Fact: The New Journalism as New Fiction*. University of Illinois Press, 1981.

Hemingway, Ernest. *A Moveable Feast*. 1964. Scribner, 2003.

Hemingway, Ernest. "Notes on a Dangerous Game." *Esquire*, July 1934, pp. 19, 94.

Hemingway, Ernest. "A Paris Letter." *Esquire*, February 1934, pp. 22, 156.

Horowitz, Jason. "Does a Moleskine Notebook Tell the Truth?" *New York Times*, October 16, 2004, www.nytimes.com/2004/10/16/business/worldbusiness/does-a-moleskine-notebook-tell-the-truth.html. Accessed October 22, 2017.

Hotchner, A. E. "Don't Touch 'A Moveable Feast.'" *New York Times*, July 19, 2009, www.nytimes.com/2009/07/20/opinion/20hotchner.html. Accessed October 22, 2017.

Keefe, Stephen. "I Went to Montreal's New Cat Café, on Shrooms." *Vice*, September 12, 2014, www.vice.com/en_us/article/gq8maq/i-went-to-montreals-new-cat-caf-on-shrooms-654. Accessed October 22, 2017.

Kerouac, Jack. *On the Road*. 1957. Penguin Books, 1999.

Klosterman, Chuck. *Sex, Drugs, and Cocoa Puffs*. 2003. Scribner 2004.

Lander, Christian. "#122 Moleskine Notebooks." *Stuff White People Like*, February 24, 2009, stuffwhitepeoplelike.com/2009/02/24/122-moleskine-notebooks/. Accessed October 22, 2017.

Lavery, Daniel M. "Male Novelist Jokes." *The Toast*, November 4, 2013, the-toast.net/2013/11/04/male-novelist-jokes/. Accessed October 2017.

Leland, John. *Why Kerouac Matters: The Lessons of On the Road*. Penguin Books, 2008.

Mailer, Norman. "The White Negro." *Dissent*, 1957, pp. 276–93.

Miller, Alex. "What to Do in Europe—the Vice Guide to Europe 2014." *Vice*, July 2, 2014, www.vice.com/en_us/article/mv5p3b/welcome-to-the-vice-guide-to-europe-2014. Accessed October 22, 2017.

Moleskine S.p.A.: Prospetto Informativo. Borsa Italiana, 2013, www.borsaitaliana.it/prospetti-informativi/1513pros_1_it.pdf. Accessed October 1, 2020.

Moynihan, Colin "'Far-Right Proud Boys' Founder Called 'Hatemonger.'" *New York Times*, August 14, 2019, www.nytimes.com/2019/08/14/nyregion/proud-boys-trial-gavin-mcinnes.html. Accessed July 22, 2020.

Penner, James. *Pinks, Pansies, and Punks: The Rhetoric of Masculinity in American Literary Culture*. Indiana University Press, 2011.

Price, Isabella. Comment on "The South Korean Love Industry." *YouTube*, uploaded by *Vice*, February 5, 2015, www.youtube.com/watch?v=cYcEXCy4izY&lc=z13ogj5yqrzyxlqgu04cf3pobnflfrga1x00k. Accessed October 22, 2017.

Smith, Jonathan. "The Westminster Dog Show … On Acid!" *Vice*, February 15, 2012, www.vice.com/en_us/article/dp47qq/the-westminster-dog-show-on-acid. Accessed October 22, 2017.

Stephenson, William. *Gonzo Republic: Hunter S. Thompson's America*. Continuum, 2012.

Taylor, Douglas. "Three Lean Cats in a Hall of Mirrors: James Baldwin, Norman Mailer, and Eldridge Cleaver on Race and Masculinity." *Texas Studies in Literature and Language*, vol. 52, no. 1, 2010, pp. 70–101.

Thompson, Hunter S. *Fear and Loathing in Las Vegas: A Savage Journey to the Heart of the American Dream*. 1971. Second Vintage Books Edition, 1998.

Thompson, Hunter S. *The Kentucky Derby Is Decadent and Depraved*. Scanlan's Monthly, 1970.

Trinh T., Minh-ha. *Woman, Native, Other Writing Postcoloniality and Feminism*. Indiana University Press, 1990.

Vice Digital: Media Kit. January 2016, upload-assets.vice.com/files/2016/01/15/1452894236compressed.pdf. Accessed October 22, 2017.

Widdicombe, Lizzie. "The Bad-Boy Brand." *New Yorker*, April 8, 2013, www.newyorker.com/magazine/2013/04/08/the-bad-boy-brand. Accessed October 22, 2017.

Wilt, James. "I Realized I Was a Cliché: A Drunk Writer Who Couldn't Write Drunk." *Vice*, January 6, 2016, www.vice.com/en_us/article/5gj4k5/i-realized-i-was-a-cliche-the-drunk-writer-who-couldnt-write-drunk. Accessed October 22, 2017.

12

"The Straight Queer": Hipster Appropriation in the Work of James Franco

Ben Robbins

Hollywood's James Franco has frequently been labeled a "hipster" to draw attention to his alignment with tastes and commercial practices stereotypically associated with this cultural trope. Used in this sense, the label has been applied to Franco to highlight how his fashion choices and creative endeavors can be connected to commonly recognized attributes of hipster identity. Among many examples, he has been called a "celebrity hipster" fashionista due to his unkempt style complete with uncombed hair (Wenger), named "a hipster-nerd" (Howe 20) for cultivating a relaxed aesthetic that incorporates 1950s fashion items, such as horn-rimmed glasses, that are reminiscent of the style of the Beats, and he has been described as working within a vintage, analogue aesthetic to produce "hipster-approved" (Cain) $89 T-shirts with Polaroid images printed on them. Consistent in these assessments of Franco's image as a celebrity hipster is the idea that he is simultaneously part of the Hollywood establishment but an outsider within this cultural group.

This apparent "insider-outsider" status has led to Franco receiving the hipster label not only on the basis of style and image but additionally in relation to the cultural position he is seen to occupy. When used in this way, there is a more overtly pejorative intention since he is dubbed a hipster to challenge his intermediate position between differing constructions of masculinity and sexuality and between mass and subcultural artistic markets. Historically, the hipster epithet has frequently been deployed against (predominantly) white men to criticize their positioning as "middlemen" between mainstream culture and subculture and to expose the forms of appropriation they are alleged to take part in. Rob Horning speculated in 2010 whether "the hipster [is] a kind of permanent cultural middleman in hyper-mediated late capitalism, selling out alternative sources of social power developed by outsider groups …?" (ch. 5). Horning's statement on the commercial exploitation of marginalized groups is part of a tradition of supposedly inauthentic cultural practices being criticized as "hipster." As Wes Hill summarizes, the stereotypical hipster figure "unwittingly stimulates tension between subcultural and mainstream identity, revealing the difficulty of identifying political, critical or ethical authenticity through aesthetic displays alone" ("Hipster Aesthetics" 5). In other words, the derogatory use of the term hipster can be used to call attention to contradictions inherent within subcultural aesthetics that lack a radical dimension.

Franco is particularly vulnerable to such criticism due to his "middleman" position between Hollywood and indie movie production, between hegemonic and alternative masculinity, and between mainstream celebrity culture and the "outsider groups" of queer subculture. By accusing Franco of being a "hipster" in a derogatory fashion, critics have sought to make apparent the ways in which he blurs the boundary between these multiple social and cultural positions as an insider-outsider. In a prominent example, the activist and former actor Rose McGowan posted a tweet after Franco won a series of acting awards for his work in the comedy *The Disaster Artist* (2017). Franco was being honored at award ceremonies at the same time as he was facing allegations of sexual misconduct in the wake of the Me Too movement from several women who had previously worked with or been taught by him. McGowan tweeted that "James Franco is a cuddly guy, but so are bears. Selectively Deaf Hollywood has heard about this asshole for years. His hipster Prince of Hollywood's bro status protected him. Bros before Ho's, amiright?" (@rosemcgowan).[1] McGowan uses the term "hipster" critically to highlight what she sees as a series of contradictions within Franco's persona: he is both part of the mainstream as a "Prince of Hollywood" but is also simultaneously positioned as somewhat outside this culturally dominant group as a "hipster." She additionally alleges that his status as a "bro,"

[1]During an interview on *The Late Show with Stephen Colbert* on January 9, 2018, Franco denied the accusations, deeming them to be "not accurate" (Colbert). In October 2019, two female students of Franco's now-closed acting school, Studio 4, sued him for sexual misconduct. Franco has also denied these claims through his lawyer. A tentative settlement was reached in February 2021 in which the two students agreed to drop their individual claims.

which the Urban Dictionary defines as "an alpha male idiot" (Sanity, def. 2.2), has allowed him to behave with impunity in exploiting women. The relationship between hegemonic and alternative masculinity is crucial here, since McGowan believes Franco uses the latter as a cover for the former; when McGowan ironically asserts that he "is a cuddly guy, but so are bears," she implies that his ostensibly harmless and alternative "hipster" persona serves a mask for the dangerous, alpha male behavior of which she maintains he is actually representative.

This chapter primarily focuses on Franco's literary responses to the charge that he is a "hipster middleman," which, I argue, cement rather than critique negative stereotypes about the white male hipster through the relationship they establish to queer culture. Discourses about the white male American hipster have linked this cultural trope to histories of appropriation across lines of race and class since the mid-twentieth century, and Franco has been accused of the same actions across lines of sexuality. Franco has established himself as one of the most versatile contemporary Hollywood leading actors in mainstream, commercially successful films that run the generic gamut from superhero (*Spider-Man* trilogy, 2002–7) and science-fiction films (*Rise of the Planet of the Apes*, 2011) to the survival drama *127 Hours* (2010), for which he received an Academy Award nomination for Best Actor. Additionally, throughout his career, he has consistently been attracted to queer figures and material, playing the following queer protagonists in largely independent movies: the title role in the television biopic *James Dean* (2001), a gay politician's lover in *Milk* (2008), Allen Ginsberg in *Howl* (2010), an "ex-gay" pastor in *I Am Michael* (2015), and a gay porn producer in *King Cobra* (2016).

Franco's slippage as an actor between straight and queer roles across mainstream Hollywood and independent movies is also apparent in his work as a filmmaker. Franco has directed nineteen films to date. On the one hand, he has produced successful, mainstream Hollywood work, such as the *The Disaster Artist*, which grossed almost $30 million at the box office. On the other, he has directed independent films with queer content, including the following: *The Broken Tower* (2011) about the life of the gay poet Hart Crane; *Sal* (2011), which focuses on the last few hours of Sal Mineo's life, one of the first openly queer major Hollywood actors; and *Interior. Leather Bar* (2013), an attempted reconstruction of the lost forty minutes of sexually explicit footage from the controversial film *Cruising* (1980), which is largely set in New York's gay leather and fetish scene.

This is a remarkable track record for a Hollywood actor and filmmaker and has led to frequent accusations of appropriation, which frame Franco as the maligned cultural intermediary of hipster stereotype. In interviews, Franco has responded to such criticism by performatively adopting the hipster middleman persona and conflating straight and gay identity as a "straight queer." He claimed in an interview with *New York* magazine from 2016 that he is gay in his work, elaborating that "I guess you could say I'm a gay cock tease. It's where my allegiance lies, where my sensibilities lie, how I define myself. Yeah, I'm a little gay, and there's a gay James" (Saltz). Here Franco enacts a separation of gay community and aesthetic taste (his "allegiance" and "sensibilities" respectively) from sexuality (he is merely a "gay cock tease") to the extent that he cannot be fully aligned with gay nor straight identity.

In this chapter, I am particularly interested in Franco's performative responses to the criticism that he is a hipster cultural middleman in his literary works, where he frequently inhabits the persona of the maligned white male American hipster, who in Franco's case appropriates from gay subcultures. In his 2013 book *Actors Anonymous*, the only novel he has published to date, he fashions the role by drawing on artistic techniques and features that have historically been associated with hipsterdom through appropriation (pastiche and acritical irony) or the creation of insider communities among outsiders (participant-observer narration, metonymy, and self-reflexivity). The text is structured as a linked series of prose, dramatic, and poetic vignettes concerning Hollywood and the acting profession. It alternates between sections containing a seasoned pro's general thoughts on Hollywood—narrated in part by a figure who identifies himself as "James Franco" (*Actors* 117)—and sections narrated by struggling actors in Los Angeles. Such narrative alternations establish an insider-outsider perspective on Hollywood, but it is particularly in relation to queer culture that Franco self-consciously performs the hipster middleman persona as a response to accusations of appropriation.

In the novel, Franco explores the contradictions of the white male American hipster trope, in which queer subcultural aesthetics and alternative gay masculinities can be used to bolster mainstream culture and hegemonic, straight masculinity. First, the novel establishes a pattern in which straight-identifying characters pursue supposedly "dangerous" encounters with queer men to grant them outsider cachet that they believe will appeal to women. Second, the novel makes use of aesthetic features derived from queer literary and cultural traditions to distance characters from the hegemonic masculinities of mainstream Hollywood. However, as a form of retort to the pejorative label of being a hipster cultural middleman, or a "straight queer," the novel does not succeed in dismantling negative stereotypes about the white male hipster. By presenting voyeuristic interest in gay sex or culture as beneficial in establishing an aura of rebellion for straight-identifying characters, this activity is never clearly challenged. Additionally, by drawing on queer artistic strategies as a form of subcultural capital to qualify straight masculinities associated with the dominant culture, Franco decouples these strategies from experiences of marginalization, which results in the loss of their intended power as formal devices to challenge processes of social exclusion.

The Hipster, White American Masculinity, and Appropriation

Discourses about the white male American hipster have linked this trope to histories of appropriation and the creation of social exclusivity among outsiders since the late 1940s. Franco's staging of the middleman persona across his creative works is deeply embedded in this history. His performance of a version of the hipster stereotype as a "straight queer" is a type of outwardly alternative masculinity that has roots in forms of appropriation across lines of race, class, and sexuality.

A first account of this cultural trope is provided in the African American writer Anatole Broyard's 1948 essay "A Portrait of the Hipster," which portrays the hipster as a transgressive and culturally marginal figure. For Broyard, hipsters defined themselves against the dominant culture, within which they were accorded little status, but nevertheless became prone to commercial exploitation (727). This hipster figure would increasingly become associated with postwar American counterculture, specifically the work of the Beats. Near the beginning of Allen Ginsberg's "Howl" (1956), the poet refers to "angelheaded hipsters ... floating across the tops of cities contemplating jazz" (9). Such images contributed to the association of this incarnation of the hipster with the transgressive rebellion of a young white generation against the dominant culture, which was frequently expressed through investment in African American culture. As Robert Holton describes, "Beat slang ... laid claim to aspects of African American difference," and the Beats drew on African American language and music (jazz and bebop) in order to assume "inverse symbolic capital" (19). Beat expressions of social alienation were additionally complicated by forms of exclusion within the cultural movement; as the Beatnik writer Joyce Johnson said of the scene, "we fell in love with men who were rebels ... Once we had found our male counterparts, we had too much blind faith to challenge the old male/female rules" (xvii). The subjugated position of women demonstrates that while the Beatniks may have adopted outsider positions in rejection of mainstream culture, systems of oppression may still be transferred into underground environments.

Responding to the Beats, in his countercultural essays Norman Mailer made the racial dynamics at work in the hipster figure's countercultural transgressions explicit. In "The White Negro: Superficial Reflections on the Hipster" (1957), Mailer problematically speculated that the marginalization of the African American man is the source of the white male hipster stereotype's very "[h]ip" quality (278), as he "must live with danger from his first day, and no experience can ever be casual to him" (279). Mailer cemented the idea of hipster figures as "urban adventurers" (279), who tap into a sense of danger to lead a more physical, sensual life. Mailer's language is steeped in the exoticization of the racial Other as a "sexual outlaw" (284), thereby discursively framing white male hipsters as risk-free adventurers, tourists into the lived realities of the historically oppressed and the art of the marginalized. "The White Negro" provided a highly influential definition of the white male American hipster as a cultural persona who has historically mistaken transgression as a goal in itself rather than seeing it as the inevitable result of systems of social oppression that have not worked upon him in the same way.

The hipster trope we can identify in "The White Negro," a figure who appropriates from oppressed groups to pose as an outsider, finds continuity in late twentieth- and early twenty-first-century definitions. As well as laying claim to Black sexuality, the white male hipster has repeatedly been charged with adopting the image of the American lower classes, or the "white-trash-worshipping" (Horning ch. 5) aesthetic, particularly since the 1990s, with the distinguishing features of trucker hats and forearm tattoos, a form of appropriation that has been carried out by both straight and gay men in the search of the "'authentic masculinity' of the lower-class man" (Rehberg, "Hipster-Sex" 218, my translation). In addition, Peter Rehberg asserts that, since the 2000s, the male hipster's presentation of nonnormative masculinity, as part of a strategy to distance himself from the "gestures of aggressive masculinity" ("Gender als Lifestyle," my translation), demonstrates a questioning of gender categories of the kind we would typically associate with queer culture. However, Rehberg argues that this ostensible "queering" of masculinity by the twenty-first-century hipster is without risk. While this hipster figure may, on one level, wish to demonstrate that gender presentations are constructed, and therefore potentially changeable, his "performance" of masculinity still insists on an essential and consistent natural core to male identity, as Rehberg illustrates, "[r]egardless of what he wears, the unavoidable hallmark of the hipster is the beard" ("Gender als Lifestyle"). Rehberg therefore concludes that, from a gender-political perspective, the twenty-first-century hipster is "a conservative figure" ("Gender als Lifestyle").

Tapping into these histories, definitions, and performances, Franco's "straight queer" hipster literary persona can similarly be seen as a figure whose ostensible "queerness" masks an underlying conservatism. Franco may state in a poetic dialogue from his 2015 collection *Straight James/Gay James* that his aim is to make "queer art that destabilizes ingrained ways of being, art that challenges hegemonic thinking" (48). However, within this disparaged persona, Franco immerses himself in and appropriates from subcultural traditions while signaling his distance from them; while he professes to be "queer in [his] art" (*Straight James* 48), he elsewhere states that he is "gay in [his] life up to the point of intercourse" (*Straight James* 45).

Creating the Persona: Aesthetics and the Hipster Middleman

In order to support his performance of the white male American hipster middleman in his art and literature, Franco draws on a range of aesthetic features that have been associated with the hipster within cultural analyses and debates that have sought to define, and usually criticize, the figure since the postwar American countercultural era. Specifically, these discourses have consistently linked the hipster trope to aesthetic strategies that can either be used to create an insider-outsider status or engage in appropriation.

Actors Anonymous is relayed in a series of first-person narratives by different characters on interconnected events. Some of these chapters are narrated by "James Franco" himself, and the author uses the Franco persona as the dominant narratorial perspective in order to adopt the hipster's stereotypical social position as an insider-outsider through participant-observer narration. The Franco narrator provides a wry commentary on the actions of a discrete, elitist group of which he is officially a member (the rich, white, male, heterosexual Hollywood set) but from which he maintains a critical distance. In the novel, the narrator professes to have "an insider's knowledge of how things worked" within the world of celebrity and "from the inside [he] could begin to peek out to the outside and say, 'Hey, look, this is what it's really like, not like they show on TMZ or on Paris Hilton's reality show' " (Franco, *Actors* 212). Franco thus narrates the novel from the stereotypical hipster stance as the floating intermediary between mainstream culture and outsider communities.

Franco also uses figuration to maintain this fluctuating insider-outsider position in his creative projects. Broyard asserts that "[t]he hipster's frequent use of metonymy and metonymous gestures (e.g., brushing palms for handshaking ...) also connoted prior understanding" (722). While Broyard is referring to the specific context of the African American jive scene, such actions are reflected in the characteristic knowingness of both the postwar (Konstantinou 54) and twenty-first-century (Greif 10) incarnations of the hipster. *The Oxford Dictionary*'s definition of metonymy as "the substitution of the name of an attribute or adjunct for that of the thing meant" ("metonymy," def. 1) illustrates how the device depends on preexisting knowledge within a closed system of reference, as the replacement name or term must necessarily be associated with the original. So, when a jive hipster brushes his palms, one has to be "in the know" about the process of substitution involved in this case. Metonymy holds us, as René Wellek and Austin Warren outline, in a "single world of discourse" (195) and is therefore suitable for exclusive communicative codes that can create a sense of being an insider among outsiders.

In his performances of the hipster persona's knowingness in *Actors Anonymous*, Franco demonstrates an attraction to metonymy in order to occupy insider and outsider positions simultaneously. One narrator in the novel fixates on a single body part of The Actor character, who may or may not be synonymous with Franco, in a photo from a magazine article: "I am staring at a photo of The Actor's backside ... it is an ass that has been speculated about more than most, the big question: Is it a gay ass or a straight ass? ... they can be so ambiguous" (141). The Actor's sexuality is metonymously substituted for his ass, and the passage develops with a knowingness that we are not really talking about one bodily feature but the whole of his sexuality. Of course Franco, with a wink to his readers, addresses the extensive media speculation about his own sexuality here, an instance of self-reflexivity that also creates a community of insiders who are "in the know" about Franco's queer personas. As Hill comments, the "hipster's cultural codes" have been recognized "as a knowing wink, communicating cultural relevance with an air of self-consciousness" ("A Hipster History" 47).

While these are examples of gossip circulating around Hollywood celebrity bodies, elsewhere Franco's work also displays subcultural knowledge through metonymy. In his Berlin exhibition *Gay Town* (2013), for example, one of his collages contained the words "MY OWN PRIVATE RIVER." Here the name of the actor River Phoenix replaces the name of a US state in the independent film in which he starred: *My Own Private Idaho* (1991), directed by Gus Van Sant. When taken in connection with the exhibition's title, the name not only references Phoenix's role as a hustler in the film but also flags up Franco's awareness of the late actor's subcultural status as a gay icon; for instance, Phoenix appears as a ghost in the works of two gay writers—Dennis Cooper's graphic novel *Horror Hospital Unplugged* (1996), which focuses on the twenty-something gay lead singer of an LA indie band, and Bret Easton Ellis's novel *Glamorama* (1998).

In addition to creating an insider-outsider status, Franco fashions the hipster middleman persona through creative strategies of appropriation. When cultural products are labeled "hipster," they are often being accused of an alleged parasitic tendency, imitating or reorganizing existing cultural products in an artistic mode that cites without elaboration or extension. Mark Greif, for example, argues that in hipster culture "there is a radicalization and aestheticization of the mode of pastiche" (11). Franco's piece "New Film Stills" (2013) directly mimicked or loosely interpreted several of Cindy Sherman's photographs for her "Untitled Film Stills" series from 1977–80. In those that are close recreations, Franco simply inserts himself into the originals. Where Sherman's photos intended to scrutinize restrictive female stereotypes for women in film, Franco's restaging of the works performs a visual trick by stepping into Sherman's female costumes with his male-presenting body, his beard and hairy legs in clear view. As the art critic

Roberta Smith put it, "[m]aybe he sees what he's doing as reverse feminism ... Mainly, we sense Mr. Franco once more playing himself, dipping a toe simultaneously in the waters of art and demi-drag." If one can consider pastiche an aesthetic strategy of appropriation, then the subcultural artistic practices from which Franco "borrows" here are twofold: those of feminist and queer artists.

Along with pastiche, Franco performs the appropriations for which the white male hipster figure has been derided through the ironic circulation of established art works. Greif, for example, has mocked hipster artists for their supposed "reconstruction of past aesthetics and techniques more perfect than the originals, in an irony without sarcasm, without bitterness or critique" (11). Franco's reconstruction of Sherman's work is indeed neither scathing nor subversive; it lacks the keen, critical bent of the originals and does not build upon Sherman's deft exploration of gender politics. Irony without criticism risks collapsing under its own contradictions. In *Actors Anonymous*, for example, Franco repeatedly attempts to parody unsuccessful forms of art-making, such as when a group creates a tasteless film called *Murder Hospital* at an orphanage for children with learning disabilities in what appears to be a pallid "homage" to both Lars von Trier's *The Idiots* (1998) and Cooper's *Horror Hospital Unplugged*: "The film was terrible. Shaky shots of me acting like a psychotic moron and retarded kids stuck inside their stymied brains, confined to their beds, rolling their animal eyes" (227). The intended irony inherent in Franco's description of such cruel and exploitative artistic practices—namely, that we, along with the author, look down upon inferior, wantonly shocking art—cannot mask the contextual reality that the book itself proceeds through a great number of shocking scenes of exploitation to create its picture of Hollywood.

Among these, the novel describes male celebrities' abuse of power in sex with young women.[2] It also describes instances of rape and child prostitution. In some respects, such descriptions of sexual violence are typical of the postmodern transgressive fiction of Cooper and Ellis. However, rather than providing a wider social commentary through the violation of norms, they have more of a structural function in Franco's work, since sexual exploitation frequently serves as a means to conclude vignettes abruptly in the novel without further examination. For example, a description of a child in the orphanage is completed with the line, "Miles had a mouth that looked like a ragged anus because his father and stepmother had abused him when he was a young child" (*Actors* 216). Such violent images punctuate the narrative as a shocking means to bring episodes sharply to a close. As Jameson Fitzpatrick commented in a review of a poem from *Straight James/*

---

[2]Different sections of the media have commented on how these passages from the novel match aspects of the sexual misconduct accusations that have been raised against Franco (Lopez).

Gay James, which concludes with a terse description of murder and rape, "the violence ... does not seem justified ... by any meaningful commentary on people's capacity for violence." These literary representations are not consistent with transgressive fiction's deep engagement with troubling social phenomena, such as misogyny and violence, by providing "a virtual space for a critical analysis of these developments and the role transgression plays in their evolution" (d'Hont 4). Rather than critically interrogating the sexually violent transgressions of the Hollywood industry, Franco essentially uses the troubling theme to circumvent the need for narrative transitions in his highly fragmentary novel.

The description of sexual abuse in the novel is also consistently characterized by a tone of cynical nonchalance. An Ohio teenager half-admits to raping a woman to his teacher at acting school, hedging that "'I raped a girl once. Well, it wasn't rape, but I guess it was'" (Franco, *Actors* 74). Such episodes fail to offer a critical analysis of a morally bankrupt Hollywood, since the novel appears to invite the reader to pay more attention to the detached, ironic tone in which "vice" is described than to its social implications. In one passage, the novel describes the rape of The Actor's girlfriend Angel when she was 18, but the narrator is markedly less interested in the events themselves than in deciding on the way in which they should be relayed. Apparently these events were so "disturbing" that The Actor "had to write a play about it," but in a footnote the narrator says that he "made up that stuff above about the Angel being raped, because it seemed so close to the play that The Actor wrote" (201). In a surviving extract from the original play, a character wonders whether Angel was "thinking of me while it happened," which the narrator annotates with "It's a little melodramatic, but can you blame him?" (204). Sexual violence is obscured by layers of metafictional irony and relativization as textual experimentation buries the possibility of social analysis through transgression.

Queer Desire and Art as Subcultural Capital in the "Straight Queer" Novel

In tandem with literary and artistic techniques that have been associated with the stereotypical hipster middleman, *Actors Anonymous* further explores the persona by featuring a number of straight-identifying characters who both appropriate from queer subculture and participate in the supposed "danger" of sexually charged encounters with queer men in order to heighten their allure to women as outsiders. In a wider aesthetic strategy, the author also draws on a number of queer subcultural literary traditions and repurposes them in ways that seriously limit their capacity to challenge processes of social exclusion.

References to queer subcultural figures in the novel proceed on the basis of allusion rather than elaboration; we know that "the friend who is the mother of Judith Butler" (Franco, *Actors* 47) is jealous of the Hollywood star narrator's grandmother for having a famous grandson and that another narrator calls William Burroughs "*the master*" (196), but we never get any more detailed sense of the significance of these attachments to or identifications with queer theory or literature; it is principally called upon as subcultural capital. For instance, the Franco narrator also claims that the dominant influence on his craft is the work of a gay writer, "My director? The poet Frank Bidart" (49), with whom Franco collaborated on his 2010 film *Herbert White*, an adaptation of a Bidart poem. However, the reader is given little insight into the aesthetic commonalities between narrator and poet, other than "the human need to create" (49). Indeed, Bidart is primarily named to establish the hipster persona's position between Hollywood and queer subcultures, as the narrator goes on, "[f]uck business. Fuck money. Fuck fame. Fuck coolness. I am in a great position. I *can* say fuck all those things because I am a famous actor and because I *have* money and I can do whatever I want (within a range) and I will look cool" (49).

In several scenes from the novel, queer desire and subcultural aesthetics are drawn upon to signal an air of dangerous rebellion to women. Early in the novel, one "straight queer" narrator goes to a Hollywood café "full of gay men in T-shirts and tank tops" (Franco, *Actors* 38) where he reads Tennessee Williams's *A Streetcar Named Desire*. He seems a little surprised when a man sits next to and begins to talk to him with a "high" voice that had "a slight whiney upswing at the end of his sentences" (39). After showering the narrator with compliments, the gay man leans in to kiss him, which the narrator allows to happen for a second, before the gay man's "stubble pulled [him] out of it" (40) and he pushes him away. He describes the man's "gazelle body" as "full of energy," but he manages to slip away from him to his car, screaming "'Fuck *off*'" (40) over his shoulder. As he drives away, he thinks the following: "The gay kiss made me excited, like life was happening. I drove over to [my female lover's] feeling romantic and wild" (40). The passage demonstrates the narrator's use of a queer person to infuse his straight sexuality with the energy of what he perceives is a transgressive, rebellious life. One could criticize the gay man for pushing himself on the narrator, although the narrator says he was not "scared" (39), but the whole situation feels manufactured to create such excitement. So too the narrator's prejudiced and stereotyped description of the man's "high," "whiney" voice and "gazelle"-like body ensures that he defines himself against the gay man as Other, while also cultivating an encounter of increasing closeness. The narrator takes what he wants from the other man—the energy of rebellion—but extracts himself before his sexual identity could come into question.

Franco apparently aims to ironize the activities of his narrators through exaggeration, but by presenting such voyeuristic interest in gay desire and culture as partly successful in establishing an aura of subversion that may lead to the sexual exploitation of women, the activity is never clearly challenged. In one chapter, a female actor and NYU freshman describes visiting the character "James Franco" at his apartment: "He showed me some pictures on the wall. One of them was an early Warhol, a sketch of a boy's face that looked like James Dean. We watched a little bit of a weird art film called *Scorpio Rising*, gay guys on motorcycles. Then he kissed me" (Franco, *Actors* 81). The cultural capital of queer art—the paintings of Warhol, the likeness of the face in the piece to James Dean, the sexually ambiguous actor, and the underground, experimental films of Kenneth Anger—is used to pique heterosexual desire, and within a hierarchical exchange in which "James" takes the girl's virginity and continues to have sex with her even after she is in pain and bleeding. In another staged seduction, the queer Beats are used as the high-minded backdrop for the Hollywood pro narrator's crude description of an affair with a Columbia undergraduate: "*Some people smell when you bend them over … She lived on Amsterdam, in some old church property that Lucien Carr lived in, Ginsberg's buddy*" (253, italics in original). For the "straight queers" of the novel, whom Franco aligns with the stereotypical hipster middleman persona, queer art and people are called upon to veil hegemonic masculinity.

Any intention to ironize the hipster middleman is further undermined by the presentation of queer sex in the novel. Although the novel abounds with references to queer culture as inverse symbolic capital, actual gay sexual activity is invariably presented as degraded and exploitative, decoupled from subcultural coolness. Among many examples, the novel refers to River Phoenix getting "a blowjob from a fatman" (Franco, *Actors* 54) in the Van Sant film and alleges that Marlon Brando had to "fuck" Tennessee Williams on the beach to get the part in the film of *Streetcar* (85). While the novel does call attention to structural inequalities in Hollywood through these portrayals, it is remarkable that Franco consistently inhabits a straight perspective to portray gay men as repellent and even subhuman. In one account of a meeting with the Broadway playwright William Inge, a character describes a "[f]unny man with a high voice … he went into the bathroom and while he was there I saw this container of Vaseline on the dresser. The cap was off and when I looked in I saw there was a little bit of brown *shit* in it" (85). One narrator is paid by a McDonald's colleague for a blow job in the toilet; the colleague's voice is described as sounding "like a ventriloquist was projecting the voice of a small Mexican girl into his mouth" (100) and having "dumb animal eyes" (128). Although Franco may have hoped to expose sexual exploitation and underlying homophobia within Hollywood through such portrayals, the novel cannot escape the consistent contradiction that his straight queer characters repeatedly invoke gay subculture and assume gay roles to lay claim to an attractive outsider status, but whenever the text actually references gay sex, it is an experience that arouses disgust or is cynically motivated.

In addition to the symbolic recirculation of queer subcultural artefacts, the novel, more broadly, situates itself within several queer aesthetic traditions, namely through the depiction of sexual underworlds, the presentation of subcultural identifications with Hollywood stars, and the encoding of identity in the roman à clef. Queer authors developed these systems of expression with the intention of cementing minority communities and negotiating social marginalization, despite the exclusions that also characterized outsider groups such as the Beats. Literary pastiche is, of course, not synonymous with exploitation. However, by detaching such features from the exploration of social marginalization, they are rendered impotent in contesting exclusion.

The literary group Franco references with most frequency in the novel are the Beats—at one point the novel familiarly calls Jack Kerouac, Ginsberg, Burroughs, and Carr "the boys" (*Actors* 254), most of whom were queer. The Beats' influence is most clearly manifested in the novel's exploration of sexual underworlds. In one chapter, a character organizes a "fuck-train in the bathroom" (166), which is described as "this horrible cement thing with steel toilets, graffiti, and dirty water on the floor" (167) near a beach in Santa Monica. A hundred people turn up to the orgy, which the narrator reflects upon: "I have images of asses, cocks, graffiti, green walls, grime, and cum. It was fucking amazing. And when someone was done, he would just run out across the hot sand and jump in the ocean. I kept thinking about Blake's palace of wisdom and I knew that that cement bathroom was the palace of wisdom!" (167). Franco ironizes the character's sense that sexual transgression is a route to superior knowledge, but these same transgressions are used by the author to generate inverse symbolic capital through his depiction of "dark" queer spaces. The passage is reminiscent of some of the sexual excesses described in Burroughs's *Naked Lunch* (1959):

> The Zone is a single, vast building. The rooms are made of a plastic cement that bulges to accommodate people, but when too many crowd into one room there is a soft *plop* and someone squeezes through the wall right into the next house—the next bed that is, since the rooms are mostly bed where the business of the Zone is transacted. A hum of sex and commerce shakes the Zone like a vast hive. (149)

While both Franco and Burroughs describe cement-clad, sexual hinterlands, the different attitudes to sexual transgression are key here. Franco's novel toys with the idea that "deviant" sexualities, and even sexual violence, can be a source of inverse prestige; in a poem in *Actors Anonymous*, titled "River in Idaho," Franco focuses on Phoenix's filmic performance as a hustler, reflecting back nostalgically on a time "when playing gay was as cool/As getting raped" (54). The sexual transgressions of Burroughs's novel are not intended to shock in the service of "coolness" but instead express the state of being at odds with mainstream culture due to nonnormative sexual desire, and therefore sex in his writing is necessarily depicted in dark or liminal spaces and settings.

Identification with Hollywood stars across the gender divide has historically been an important source of subcultural capital for gays and lesbians seeking to cultivate an alternative relationship to the dominant culture. As Richard Dyer shows, Judy Garland's post-1950 career spoke to male gay subcultures through the "qualities of her image that were homologous" with that culture, namely "ordinariness, androgyny and camp" (151). Prefigured with the Whitmanian line "I am all actors" (Franco, *Actors* 5), Franco's actor persona professes to fluid star identifications with straight male actors (Jack Nicholson, Jimmy Stewart, Steve McQueen) and sexually ambiguous and gay male actors (Marlon Brando, James Dean, Rock Hudson, Montgomery Clift), but the longest section by far is dedicated to female stars of Classical Hollywood: "I am Bette Davis and Barbara Stanwyck and Kathryn Hepburn and Audrey Hepburn and Grace Kelly ... I am Vivien Leigh and fucking Shelley Winters" (6). Such a strong affinity with female stars is taken even further in his poem "Born to Die" from *Straight James/Gay James*:

> In my little apartment I have my pot
> And my wigs, and my make up,
> That I apply slowly, in slow motion,
> In my Marilyn mirror with the star lights. (36)

Here the sense of a shared identity progresses into a desire to *become* the female star, enabled by the queer subcultural practice of drag.

These passages loosely recall the work of Alfred Chester, a postwar queer Jewish writer, who was connected to the Beats through his time in the international subcultural communities of Paris and Tangier. In his novel *The Exquisite Corpse* (1967), he writes, "I am Technicolor movies sprinkling rainbows over the drab streets. I am Marilyn Monroe and Tony Curtis rolled into one. Except that she is dead and he has lost his looks" (153). Chester brings stylistic flair to his subcultural identifications with Hollywood stars, infusing his writing with the theatricality, poise, and ironic humor typical of the queer discourse of camp. Style, therefore, establishes a clear link between queer subculture and mainstream Hollywood culture. In Franco's work, by contrast, the long, unadorned list of actors with whom he identifies—even with a hint of the sardonic—is marked by an absence of subcultural style, meaning that we cannot view Hollywood askance from a minority perspective through his writing.

Instead, we find an author using a persona to position himself within a mainstream cultural group.

If *Actors Anonymous* can most squarely be situated within one literary genre, it is the roman à clef, the "novel with a key" to events and people in objective reality. As Franco has said of the book, "[i]t's not like my book is a memoir by any means, but it's just me embracing what I have that is fairly unique about my life" (Christensen). The genre is situated between fiction and memoir, and consequently, as Sean Latham highlights, it occupies "an ambiguous critical space by seeming to insist on itself as fiction while encoding scandalous and often disturbing facts about real people and events" (13). Many key works in this literary mode have been produced by queer writers, including Truman Capote, Djuna Barnes, and Christopher Isherwood. This is not to say that it is a specifically queer genre, but, as part of its development, it was used to encode real-world, same-sex relationships that were criminalized in the societies through which these texts were circulated.

Franco plays with the genre through a self-conscious use of aliases—"*Your alter ego, 'The Devil' or whatever he may be, is dead on: This roman à clef is as transparent as fuck*" (*Actors* 179–80)—and in one passage, narrated by a figure whose personal history strongly resembles Franco's, he omits the names of promiscuous celebrities: "lots of guys that become actors were shy or nerdy or sensitive when they were younger, so when they become famous they really cash in to make up for those years when they were overlooked and rejected. S_____ N_____ was one that cleaned up, man, he slept with (big time actress), really, and (big time pop star)" (212). Initials are also used to conceal identities by Isherwood in his novel *Prater Violet* (1945), which is narrated in the first person by a "Christopher Isherwood" persona: "J. will pass, the need will remain. The need to get back into the dark, into the bed, into the warm naked embrace, where J. is no more J. than K., L., or M. Where there is nothing but the nearness, and the painful hopelessness of clasping the naked body in your arms" (119). Isherwood uses code to hide the names—and the gender—of his male lovers in the repressive environment of England in 1945. We cannot criticize Franco for the use of a genre that is not *solely* queer in its origins. What is interesting here, in a novel that makes such frequent reference to images and figures from a sexual "underworld" populated by outsiders, is that the device is used to place a veil over the activities of the dominant culture. Where Isherwood finds a way to talk of queer desire among publicly known figures in a society that maligned it, Franco marshals that same genre to dodge libel in a boast about the sexual prowess of major heterosexual Hollywood actors. Franco may wish to ironize male Hollywood actors' exploitation of their powerful position by showing how they compensate for the insufficient performance of hegemonic masculinity by their younger selves. However, the strategy forms part of an unfortunate pattern in which queer symbols and aesthetic features are almost invariably used to shore up hegemonic masculinity, while queer sex is derided.

Conclusion

In his literary performances of the hipster middleman figure, Franco draws on the symbols and aesthetic techniques of queer subculture in his descriptions of the Hollywood industry, but he largely neglects to connect them to a marginal lived reality. In *Actors Anonymous* he creates queer dark underworlds where transgression is elective, his narrators identify with queer icons without establishing their subcultural relationship to them, and he writes within the genre of the roman à clef to create a sense of an illicit dominant culture rather than to evade the censors in documenting an outlaw subculture. The inverse symbolic capital of queer literary culture becomes detached from the "substance" of the queer lives that produced it, and these aesthetic strategies thereby lose their power to challenge social marginalization.

In *Actors Anonymous*, Franco set out to interrogate the persona of the white male American hipster who appropriates across sexual lines, but by simultaneously drawing on subcultural symbols for outsider cachet, mocking queer sex, and rendering queer aesthetics toothless, the novel reinforces many of the negative associations the cultural trope has attracted as an exploitative intermediary. Franco asks in the novel whether there "[i]s … a veridic self underneath? Or are the surfaces what rule?" (251). By assuming the middleman role between Hollywood and queer subculture in the novel, Franco explores the hipster figure as a cultural performance. However, by inhabiting the transgressive "straight queer" persona in his literature, Franco also reduces the minority artistic traditions from which he borrows to pure surface, since subcultural symbols never align with the selfhood of the marginalized.

Works Cited

Broyard, Anatole. "A Portrait of the Hipster." *Partisan Review*, vol. 15, no. 6, 1948, pp. 721–27.

Burroughs, William. *Naked Lunch: The Restored Text*, edited by James Grauerholz and Barry Miles. HarperCollins, 2005.

Cain, Spencer. "James Franco Designs Hipster-Approved Tees for Seven for All Mankind." *Style Caster*, August 21, 2012, stylecaster.com/james-franco-hipster-approved-polaroid-tshirt-line/. Accessed August 13, 2020.

Chester, Alfred. *The Exquisite Corpse*. Black Sparrow Press, 2003.

Christensen, Lauren. "Q&A: James Franco on His First Novel, *Actors Anonymous*, and Why There Is a Character Named 'James Franco.'" *Vanity Fair*, October 15, 2013, www.vanityfair.com/culture/2013/10/James-franco-interview-actors-anonymous. Accessed August 13, 2020.

Colbert, Stephen, creator. *The Late Show with Stephen Colbert*. Spartina Productions and CBS Television Studios, January 9, 2018.

D'Hont, Coco. *Extreme States: The Evolution of American Transgressive Fiction 1960–2000*. Routledge, 2019.

Dyer, Richard. *Heavenly Bodies*. Routledge, 2004.

Fitzpatrick, Jameson. "A Queer Take on James Franco's 'Straight James/Gay James.'" *Lambda Literary*, January 16, 2016, www.lambdaliterary.org/2016/01/a-queer-take-on-james-francos-straight-james-gay-james/. Accessed August 13, 2020.

Franco, James. *Actors Anonymous: A Novel*. Houghton Mifflin Harcourt, 2013.

Franco, James. *Gay Town*. February 9–March 9, 2013, Peres Projects temporary space, Karl-Marx-Allee 87, Berlin.

Franco, James. *Straight James/Gay James: Poems*. Hansen, 2016.

Ginsberg, Allen. *Howl and Other Poems*. City Lights, 1959.

Greif, Mark. "Positions." *What Was the Hipster? A Sociological Investigation*, edited by Mark Greif, Kathleen Ross, and Dayna Tortorici. n+1 Foundation, 2010, pp. 4–13.

Hill, Wes. "Hipster Aesthetics: Creatives with No Alternative." *Emaj: Online Journal of Art*, vol. 9, 2016, emajartjournal.com/past-issues/emaj-9/. Accessed August 3, 2020.

Hill, Wes. "A Hipster History: Towards a Post-Critical Aesthetic." *Critical Studies in Fashion and Beauty*, vol. 6, no. 1, 2015, pp. 45–60.

Holton, Robert. "'The Sordid Hipsters of America': Beat Culture and the Folds of Heterogeneity." *Reconstructing the Beats*, edited by Jennie Skerl. Palgrave Macmillan, 2004, pp. 11–26.

Horning, Rob. "The Death of the Hipster." *What Was the Hipster? A Sociological Investigation*, edited by Mark Greif, Kathleen Ross, and Dayna Tortorici, Kindle ed. HarperCollins, 2010.

Howe, Katherine. *Conversion*. Penguin, 2014.

Isherwood, Christopher. *Prater Violet*. Random House, 2012.

Johnson, Joyce. *Minor Characters: A Beat Memoir*. Methuen, 2006.

Konstantinou, Lee. *Cool Characters: Irony and American Fiction*. Harvard University Press, 2016.

Latham, Sean. *The Art of Scandal: Modernism, Libel Law, and the Roman a Clef*. Oxford University Press, 2009.

Lopez, Ricardo. "James Franco's 2013 Novel 'Actors Anonymous' Describes How Actor Approached Women." *Variety*, January 11, 2018, variety.com/2018/film/news/james-franco-book-seduced-actors-anonymous-1202662019/. Accessed September 2, 2020.

Mailer, Norman. "The White Negro: Superficial Reflections on the Hipster." *Dissent*, 1957, pp. 276–93.

"metonymy." *Oxford Dictionary of English*, 3rd ed., Oxford University Press, 2010, p. 1114.

Rehberg, Peter. "Gender als Lifestyle: Wie Queer ist der Hipster?" *taz*, November 15, 2016, www.taz.de/!5353672/. Accessed August 13, 2020.

Rehberg, Peter. "Hipster-Sex—Postpornografische Erzählungen im schwulen Fanzine BUTT." *Pornografisierung von Gesellschaft: Perspektiven aus Theorie, Empirie und Praxis*, edited by Martina Schuegraf and Angela Tillmann. UVK Verlagsgesellschaft, 2012, pp. 213–21.

@rosemcgowan. "James Franco is a cuddly guy, but so are bears. Selectively Deaf Hollywood has heard about this asshole for years. His hipster Prince of Hollywood's bro status protected him. Bros before Ho's, amiright? @CriticsChoice." *Twitter*, January 11, 2018, 6:08 a.m., twitter.com/rosemcgowan/status/951682279067156480?lang=en. Accessed August 13, 2020.

Saltz, Jerry. "In Conversation: James Franco. The Celebrity Makes a Case for His Art before His Critic." *New York Magazine: Vulture*, April 18, 2016, www.vulture.com/2016/04/james-franco-jerry-saltz-converstaion-c-v-r.html. Accessed August 13, 2020.

Sanity, Counter. "Bro." *Urban Dictionary*, August 7, 2012, www.urbandictionary.com/define.php?term=Bro. Accessed August 13, 2020.

Smith, Roberta. "Everybody is Playing Someone Else Here." *New York Times*, April 22, 2014, www.nytimes.com/2014/04/23/arts/design/james-franco-new-film-stills-arrives-at-pace-gallery.html. Accessed August 13, 2020.

Wellek, René, and Austin Warren. *Theory of Literature*. Harcourt, Brace & World, 1962.

Wenger, Adam. "Celebrity Hipsters: James Franco." *Style Bistro*, www.stylebistro.com/Celebrity+Hipsters/articles/6OYJN15CeBL/James+Franco. Accessed August 13, 2020.

Hipster Media, Aesthetics, and Identity Politics

13

The Female Hipster in *Girls* and *Frances Ha* and the Potential of Emancipated Spectatorship

Heidi Lucja Liedke

Hipsterism is inextricably linked to the millennial identity. While most people have a notion of what a "hipster" is, it is more complicated to provide a clear-cut definition for the purposes of critical analysis. At first glance, hipsters are mainly defined via stylistic markers: for instance, seemingly haphazard yet often quite expensive clothing, "ugly" glasses, a fondness for vintage furniture, and their fashion style. Moreover, hipsters often tend to be regarded as apolitical, aloof, and ironic. In one of the few studies of hipsters and hipsterism in/and movies, "Movies for hipsters" (2013), Michael Z. Newman investigates the post-2000s cultural construction of hipsterism in North America and the connection between indie cinema and generational audience formation. He points out that millennial indie hipsters

> [c]ome of age in a time of allegedly "post everything": post-Fordist, post-industrial, post-consensus society, but also postfeminist, postracial, and postmodern culture. There is a hypersaturated consumer capitalism and also a world of fluid identities and hyperconsciousness of cultural difference, meritocracy, and egalitarianism, especially within the privileged communities of white, elite cosmopolitan culture wherein educational institutions promote such ideals as received wisdom. (75)

Something that Newman does not mention explicitly is that hipsters, at least in the public's perception, seem to be predominantly male. Tellingly, a

Google image search for "hipster" only shows images of men with elaborate beards, sleek haircuts, and wearing plaid shirts. The first couple of women appear next to men. Thinking along these lines of a stereotypically gendered representation of female hipsters, Dayna Tortorici points out that hipsters are usually classified as art students and/or people collecting slogans of past avant-gardes who

> in the case of many women—like *clothes*. It's telling that once adopted or sanctioned by hipster taste, those would-be exemplars of the hipster feminine are not praised for their art, but repurposed as style icons … It points to an unsatisfying partial-truth: That the female hipster's privileged knowledge is not subcultural, intellectual, or even pseudo-intellectual, but the familiar "female" knowledge of how to look. (123)

Thus, in most critical discussions, female hipsters do not come up as agents in their own right. It seems that representations of female hipsters are up against stereotypical and heteronormative takes on them, that is, depictions in which they merely hunt for cool and somewhat random objects to collect and locations which they could share on Instagram, often together with their boyfriend. For instance, the episode "Kimmy Drives a Car!" in the US-American web television sitcom *Unbreakable Kimmy Schmidt* features a hipster couple from Austin, Sue and Bob (played by *Girls*' Shoshanna, Zosia Mamet, and Evan Jonigkeit), as Airbnb lodgers, who represent and reproduce traditional male/female gender roles. In the first shot Sue unpacks her suitcase and puts a purse into one of the drawers; her husband introduces her to their landlady Lilian. Their plan to open a soul food restaurant in Lilian and Titus's neighborhood and their open-mouthed proclamations of how "perfect" and "authentic" everything there is fuel Lilian's fears of gentrification and evoke questions around the authenticity of people's nostalgia. This, apart from their visible stylistic markers, can indeed be regarded as another main characteristic of the culturally constructed hipster: a (sometimes ironic) nostalgia for the look of a time in which one has not even been born yet, which coincides with the rise of Instagram sepia filters. Sue and Bob do not emerge as complex characters, but as shallow hipster signifiers who even blend into one another when wearing almost the exact same red plaid shirts and extravagant fedoras—a gender-bending aspect that is usually noted to a lesser extent as "extravagant" with regard to female hipsters. In her discussion of hipster women as style icons, Tortorici argues that a main reason for the invisibility of women in the millennial discourse on hipsters is that people see "no novelty in women dressing to fit a culture" and "funny style markers" such as fedoras, tight pants, and horn-rimmed glasses would be more noticeable in men (124). The assumption following from this is "that a 'true' hipster female didn't exist: if hipsters were fashion victims, then all women were hipsters, and therefore none were" (124).

In a *New York Times* article from 2013, the female hipster is mentioned several times in her role as a mother (Williams). The article outlines how hipster families are now creating their very own suburbia, or "hipsturbia," twenty-five miles north of Williamsburg in Hastings-on-Hudson, and depicts a very heteronormative image of family life, thus ultimately revealing the hipster microcosm as collapsing into conventionality once a family is started, and youth is over. In a nod to 1960s society, the woman seems to be there as that "Other" whose main purpose is to complement the man. In Mark Greif et al.'s *What Was the Hipster?* Margo Jefferson asks, "What I can't tell ... is how powerful as agents—as artists, as shapers—women are in contemporary hipster culture. Riot grrrls were mentioned. There are female musicians in some of the named bands. But what else? Where else? Who else? In the old days, we were artifacts, consumers, muses, and accessories. How about now?" (101). Jefferson's examples are to the point here and already anticipate the role of the gaze in defining female hipsters that is also relevant for the discussion in this chapter. For centuries women have been passive objects—active only as muses who aid a male artist's work, and it needs to be investigated whether their role is not a similar one in twenty-first-century hipster culture. The female hipster in particular is an enigma, an undefined totality. Why does she escape the radar? As Greif puts it, *What Was the Hipster*? tries out "definitions based on what we've experienced so far" (Preface xiii) and includes assessments of the hipster from different critical angles, but he rightly observes that there is an inability "despite the centrality of women in every sphere of fashion, art, and endeavor touched by hipsterism, to place the 'hipster feminine,' or to think about hipster women beyond the filter of male domination of the category" (Preface xiii).

To initiate an end to this silence, this chapter wants to tease out what makes female hipsters and their depictions noteworthy in two selected media texts, the HBO series *Girls* (2012–17) and the hipster cult movie *Frances Ha* (2012). In particular, this chapter wants to make the case for the potential of female hipsters not as the (less visible) counterpart to male hipsters but as agents in their own right, successfully modifying notions of hipsterism in a postfeminist mainstream cultural context, if only for a transitory period. As Rosalind Gill has convincingly argued, "postfeminism is best understood as a distinctive sensibility, made up of a number of interrelated themes" (147), for instance, the notion that femininity is a bodily property, a focus on individualism, and a shift from objectification to subjectification. To a great extent, the depictions of the female protagonists in *Girls* and *Frances Ha* defy this postfeminist mainstream sensibility and its inherent sexualization and objectification. Their central characters exemplify young, emancipated, strong-minded female hipsters who strive for an individualistic lifestyle that is not dictated by others or a patriarchal society. Yet this is a transitory state, for both at the end of the movie and the series they seem to align with the "profoundly contradictory" constructions of contemporary binary gender relations (Gill 163), thus perpetuating gender binaries rather than reshuffling them.

In its discussion of *Frances Ha*, this chapter links the comparatively marginal figure of the female hipster to another not sufficiently acknowledged female urban agent, namely the *flâneuse*, who has also for a long time been neglected by the dominant critical discourses (cf. Parsons). Much like the hipster, the *flâneur* is primarily imagined as male, white, from the (upper) middle class, and the bearer of his gaze. Most memorably captured by Walter Benjamin, the *flâneur* roams the streets and collects the phantasmagoria of the metropolis (164). For female walkers, however, walking is a tactic to *become* the bearers of the gaze, take in the cityscape and act it out as their own fiction. Walking is a way of stepping out of bounds and embracing the potentiality of a given situation. I am introducing the concept of the *flâneuse* here because the above qualities and self-assertions coincide with those made by female hipsters. Thus, similarly to the figure of the *flâneuse*, I see that of the female hipster as a figure that is in transition and fluid, neglected by the critical discourse.

At its core, the chapter traces this notion of marginality and flexibility as a form of empowerment that is turned into an affirmation of a female hipster persona as represented in *Girls* and *Frances Ha* in the shape of Jacques Rancière's emancipated spectator. I am drawing a parallel between female hipsterism and what Jacques Rancière calls emancipated spectatorship in order to work out the idea that female hipsters play with and reappropriate the gaze. He conceives of spectatorship as an independent and primary activity rather than a secondary or interpretative one that is dictated or controlled by the spectacle itself. Rancière's "emancipated spectator" is an active, individual subject, not the member of an audience. He starts off with a discussion of the necessity to rethink and deconstruct the default dichotomy between theatre/spectacle/actor as active and spectator as passive and uses the analogy of the schoolmaster and the pupil. The schoolmaster's knowledge (and one can extend the "schoolmaster" to stand for society and/or convention) is a position; the pupil (in the following referred to as "she") in this analogy can be any member of society. Thus, a gulf is created between the two, a radical difference; Rancière concludes that the "first thing it teaches her is her own inability" (9). To be confronted with an alleged inability invites a counterreaction, the urge to *en*-able herself—and this is where Rancière locates the beginning of the process of emancipation of the "passive" spectator/pupil:

> Emancipation begins when we challenge the opposition between viewing and acting; when we understand that the self-evident facts that structure the relations between saying, seeing and doing themselves belong to the structure of domination and subjection ... The spectator also acts, like the pupil or scholar. *She observes, selects, compares, interprets*. She links

> what she sees to a host of other things that she has seen on other stages, in other kinds of places. *She composes her own poem with the elements of the poem before her. She participates in the performance by refashioning it in her own way*. (13, my emphases)

Building on this thought in the hipster context, this chapter argues that the female hipster is, much like Schipper has put it with regard to the flâneur, "not just an observer or passive spectator of a finished play," she is "more a co-producer" of her own play (193). Thus, the female hipster, *flâneuse*, and emancipated spectator/pupil are concepts and figures that define each other. Their unifying element is that they have been silenced by the cultural critical discourse, delegated to the sidelines as either nonexistent, that which is not its male counterpart, or that which is the object (of instruction). In order to reify her notion of selfhood, the female hipster takes on the role of the self-contained (non)agent, the emancipated spectator. Their emancipated spectatorship manifests itself in an individualistic stance and a retreat to an own system of values and tastes. In an act of defiance of the gendered gaze on women, the female hipster displays a heightened, refined awareness to live according to her own masterplan. This especially finds its expression in an own language.

Both the series and the movie are millennial versions of a *Bildungsroman*, narrating of the twists and turns in a certain period in their protagonists' lives in their mid- to late 20s. The female hipster persona is presented as a vehicle for a kind of emancipation that is centered on the idea of potentiality. "Emancipation" here is used in the sense of an assertion of the self that is precisely not political, but rather inexpert. This inexpertise may be necessary to disrupt the consensus that Rancière calls "the distribution of the sensible" (qtd. in Ridout 173). This refers "to the entire system of social and cultural processes, codes, values and material realities through which we jointly understand the world, and according to which we make our judgements about what and who belongs where, who has the right to speak and be heard, who counts when it matters, and who gets to be recognized as an expert" (Ridout 172). There is, in fact, a close connection between this distribution of the sensible and the sensibilities characteristic of the postfeminist context as outlined by Gill: values and judgments are, sometimes unwittingly, internalized and copied. By ignoring and playing with expectations they are met with both because of their gender and their age, the female hipsters as represented in *Girls* and *Frances Ha* for great parts of the show and movie, respectively, reject such an internalization of values and judgments.

It is at this junction that I locate the potentially disruptive power of the female hipster. In the following, I will examine the manifestations of emancipated spectatorship through storytelling/verbalization and failing/trying. By taking a step back, the female hipsters as represented in *Girls* and *Frances Ha* emancipate themselves from gendered expectations—they blur the boundaries between "those who act and those who look" (Rancière 19) and speak. The default (male) hipster detachment is turned into a powerful creative emancipation in its female expression that entails the ability of expressing a hope *toward* something. Yet as both the series and the movie come to a close, the plot lines evoke a sense of closure, which coincides with the ending of the previously portrayed hipster potentiality. Female empowerment through hipness presents itself as a transitory phenomenon confined to youth that only creates a realm for female self-assertion for a limited amount of time before having to settle into conventionality.

On Being Gazed at and the Potential of Failing

In his study of indie cinema and hipster audiences, Newman distinguishes between indie films that are "seen as pandering to hipsters, and those seen as models for hipster ethos and style—if not by direct example, then in terms of their *sensibility*" (71, my emphasis). He names *(500) Days of Summer* and Wes Anderson's oeuvre as exemplary of these two. *Girls* and *Frances Ha* are examples for both kinds, not only because of their protagonists but also because of their specific topics and aesthetics. Both are set in or around Brooklyn, New York; the crowds depicted in both media texts live in hip apartments furnished with either improvised or vintage objects and are made up of actors, writers, bartenders, dancers, or start-up founders. *Frances Ha* is even shot entirely in black and white, thus creating an atemporal nostalgia. Yet most importantly, these two films can be considered as hipster films/series because they center on their protagonists' striving for a lifestyle that is both hip *and* their own. That is, they slightly modify Newman's assertion that "[h]ipsters are defined by their *striving* to be hip, but among the crucial components of hipsterism are frequent failure [*sic*] at hipness" (72, my emphasis). While it is unclear whether Newman refers to *all* hipsters or not, with regard to the female hipster this modification of a striving for and failure to achieve a particular desired version of individuality is key, and this is also the case in the two media texts selected for this chapter.

In an analysis of the female hipster in films and TV shows, one notices that her gender puts her to a great extent in the same tradition with non-hipster women on screen. The female hipster figure as depicted on screen is from the outset conditioned by questions of visibility and an exposure to the (male) gaze. As John Berger with regard to art and paintings more generally and Laura Mulvey with regard to cinema specifically have summarized it most succinctly, in a patriarchal society, a "woman must continually *watch* herself. She is almost continually accompanied by her own image of herself" (Berger 49). As Mulvey puts it,

> [in] a world ordered by sexual imbalance, pleasure in looking has been split between active/male and passive/female. The determining male gaze projects its fantasy onto the female figure, which is styled accordingly. In their traditional exhibitionist role women are simultaneously looked at and displayed, with their appearance coded for strong visual and erotic impact so that they can be said to connote *to-be-looked-at-ness*. (60)

While Mulvey refers to classical Hollywood cinema, the notion of female self-surveillance is still topical in the context of postfeminist times. As Gill convincingly argues, one can observe a shift in the way that power operates "from an external male judging gaze to a self policing narcissistic gaze" (151). This, according to Gill, "represents a higher or deeper form of exploitation than objectification—one in which the objectifying male gaze is internalized to form a new disciplinary regime" (151–2).

When turning to the protagonists of *Girls* and *Frances Ha*, who are, as my analysis will show, quirky, idiosyncratic, and, most importantly, very outspoken, the cinematic depiction and emancipation of female hipsters begins with a slippage—the slippage of woman from the role of passive/inactive, from the margins of *to-be-looked-at-ness* to the center of *looking-at*. This slippery, unstable position is problematized by the fact that, as hipsters, women tend to be reduced to being looked at merely for what they are wearing. What follows from this equation is the notion that when hipsterism means visibility, female hipsterism oscillates between invisibility and visibility. On the one hand, to-be-looked-at-ness is women's default state (even more so on screen), yet the female hipster has been rendered invisible in the discourse about hipsters. Thus, the depiction of female hipsters on screen invites enhanced scrutiny and is met with a set of expectations.

Any argument for an emancipation of the female hipster therefore happens against the background of this friction between visibility and invisibility and traces the ways in which she manages to transform the gaze she is exposed to into her own in order to become something like "a muse for herself, and for other women" (Tortorici 125). The detachment that follows from this is also expressed in a celebration of individualism and in a nonchalant approach as far as conventional notions of femininity are concerned, something that stands in contrast to the obsession with the (sexy) female body that is still pervasive in postfeminist media culture. What I am thus tracing in my readings of *Girls* and *Frances Ha* is what role the protagonists' attempts to achieve something (or simply be) play and in what ways this trying is depicted.

The narratives created in *Frances Ha* and *Girls* for a great part introduce powerful counter narratives to those dominant in a (Western) society that is defined through the achievements of its members and gender binaries; something that may seem paradoxical given the consumer capitalist context they have been born into. Both female and male hipsters, in their interest in "snatching failure from history's dustbin" (Newman 75) do indeed manage to defy neoliberalism—temporarily. With regard to female hipsters, this defiance and emancipation take place on the level of narration. Representations of female hipsters can be read as crucial testimonies, "individual poems" of the millennial identity, and constructions of culturally and individually emancipated selves that appear in the shape of storytelling/a verbalization of their stories (in *Girls*) and a daring to try and fail (*Frances Ha*).

The Female Hipster in *Girls*: Verbalizing Your Self

From the time it was first aired in 2012, the show *Girls* has been read as a millennial feminist take that also bears many traces of hipster sensibility (cf. Miller; Harris; Mahdawi). Crucial to my argument, a particular attention to the role of language as a powerful tool plays a central, character-defining role; rather than being used to articulate clichés, emphatic statements and monologues define the representation of female hipsters and turn them into emancipated spectators creating their own "texts." In particular, Hannah's directness and verbal outbursts have gained the character some notoriety. For instance, when she becomes a teacher at a private high school, her unorthodox teaching methods are criticized both by her boyfriend Fran, also a teacher there, and by the schoolmaster (5.4. "Old Loves"; cf. 5.7. "Hello Kitty"). *Girls*, as a hipster cultural text, contains explicit markers of hipsterism such as the protagonists' "precarious and bohemian unconventionality" in choosing their clothing to express their disregard of the "buyers and wearers of mainstream fashion" (Erbacher, "Lifestyle" 132). Yet, more crucially, the show makes an unashamedly sentimental case for the importance of one's individual voice via its portrayal of the emancipated female hipster spectator who participates in the performance before and around her by refashioning it in her own way—with her voice. By doing so, she is engaged in an independent and primary activity rather than a secondary or interpretative one.

The notion that Hannah "has a voice" has not been met with praise only, especially since the character represents a privileged, white person. From the start, the show, which ended in April 2017, has been attacked and celebrated as telling "stories about privilege, by and about women who went to fancy schools": Hannah went to Oberlin, Frances (from *Frances Ha*) to Vassar College (Nussbaum; Cook). Yet it gained considerable attention from feminist and media scholars (cf. Weitz 218) largely because of it being created by a *female* auteur (cf. McCann 91). As Erbacher elaborates, the protagonists are all aspiring members of the "creative class," a term introduced by Richard Florida ("Lifestyle" 122). The creative class is a socioeconomic class of US society and comprises the super-creative core, representing professions in arts, design, and media, among others, and creative professionals whose work is knowledge-based, for instance, in education, the legal sector, and business. According to Erbacher, while part of the relatability especially female viewers feel toward the show is based on its representation of "non-normative, yet attractive women … an even more central element has made the series salient for its audience of well-educated urbanites in their twenties and thirties, namely its obsession with and celebration of creativity and a creative lifestyle" (127).

However, even the most "hipstery" dressing character of *Girls*, Jessa (Jemima Kirke), who usually appears in loose shirts or dresses, torn jeans, and with a decidedly messy bun, is reduced to having "the face of Brigitte Bardot and an ass like Rihanna" by her employer's friend (1.4. "Hannah's Diary"). Instead of being granted her own face, she is immediately turned into a hybrid of two style icons by two male onlookers. The series thus oscillates in both exposing and reproducing the aforementioned shift in power structures in postfeminist media culture expressed in the ways the gaze operates because of the casting and clothes.

Another central factor that is directly linked to notions of millennial female hipsterism is the female characters' obsession with and urge to *articulate* their outlook on life. The specific context of female hipsterism enhances the effect this voice can have and thus creates an enabling context for it. As Hannah Horvath self-reflectively proclaims early on in the show, she is "*a* voice of *a* generation" (1.1). To be precise, one must argue critically that she represents "a subset of millennial women" (Nash and Grant 979) that is white, middle-class, and well educated, thus exemplifying Gill's assertion that the "postfeminist sensibility recentres both heterosexuality and whiteness" (162–3). However, she does represent this group of society as *a* voice, not *the* voice—a small yet crucial difference. Most importantly, she voices the concerns and hopes of *female* hipsters, thus contributing to a hitherto marginal discourse.

The final season of *Girls* has been, in great parts, described as a condensed succession of "a series of outwardly mundane actions: having sex, walking around the city, talking about this and that" yet "[r]unning beneath everything was a current of despair and denial" (Zoller Seitz). Thus, while accusations of the narcissism of the protagonists are apt (Cook), their (and especially Hannah's) rants are more than just dramatizations for drama's sake. They can loosely be grouped into addressing the themes love, friendship, and life/female authorship with the third thematic complex providing the most powerful statements with regard to the millennial hipster identity.

In an analysis of selected rants from the show, one notices that what they have in common is that they oscillate between sentimentality and self-affirmation. They subtly subvert hipster stereotypes, especially those centered on the notion that hipster culture is completely nihilistic (Finston qtd. in Greif, "Discussion" 53). These speeches often occur in the shape of rambling epiphanies and enable the character voicing them to emancipate herself. Early on in their relationship, for example, Hannah tells Adam after he has sent her a picture of his penis:

> I'm really not asking you for anything ... I just want someone who wants to hang out all the time and thinks I'm the best person in the world and wants to have sex with only me. And it makes me feel very stupid to tell you this, because it makes me sound *like a girl who wants to, like, go to brunch*. And I really don't wanna go to brunch, and I don't want you to, like, sit on the couch while I shop or, like, even meet my friends ... And also, I don't want a picture of your dick because I live very near you, so if you wanted me to look at your dick, I could just come over and look at your dick. (1.4. "Hannah's Diary")

She is outspoken in articulating what her boundaries and expectations are, and she especially does not want to resemble the conventional idea of a girl who goes to brunch, with the urban coffee shop as one of the stereotypical hipster meeting places (cf. Chayka), thus rejecting both conventional femininity and stereotypical hipster femininity. Hannah's rejection of the hypothetical idea of brunch and of Adam's message makes her step out of any normative system with which the particular "subset" she represents might be associated.

She continues subtly defying these normative expectations when being interviewed for a position at jazzhate.com (2.3. "Bad Friend"); the exchange is also an example for the witty dialogue typical for *Girls*. When the interviewer suggests that she should have a threesome with some people that she meets on craigslist "or do a whole bunch of coke and then just write about it," Hannah responds, "Okay, re [*sic*] the threesome, that is something that I just I [*sic*] feel like I have enough trouble just figuring out where to place my attention on one person's body, which is something I'd write about for sure" and points out she has never done cocaine before because of her "weird nasal passages." Her interviewer counters her hesitation by hilariously showing her a circle that depicts the "comfort" zone, pointing to a spot right next to it and assuring her that, "[t]his is where the magic happens." Hannah's use of sarcasm combined with her quirky self-consciousness in fact protects her here from doing something she would not feel comfortable doing.

It takes an encounter with a stranger, the doctor Joshua, to make Hannah articulate an explanation for why she refuses to do what others tell or expect her to do:

> I made a promise such a long time ago that I was gonna take in experiences, all of them, so that I could tell other people about them and maybe save them, but it gets so tiring trying to take in all the experiences for everybody, letting anyone say anything to me … I want what they all want. I want all the things. I just want to be happy … If anything, I think I'm just too smart and too sensitive and too, like, not crazy. So that I'm feeling all these big feelings and containing all this stuff for everybody else … I just want to feel it all. (2.5. "One Man's Trash")

Hannah wants to feel it all, but on her own terms: she is coming to terms with her own expectations and aspirations. By proclaiming that she wants "all the things" and "to feel it all," Hannah is articulating her reluctance to be pigeonholed in two regards: On the one hand, this reflection is part of her coming-of-age process that the show traces. On the other hand, when reading her character as a discursive formation of the female hipster, this is also an instance of refusing to be put into the same gender biased box that both women and women hipsters have been put into. By stylizing herself as being guided by a kind of Emersonian transparent eyeball, she takes up one of the perceived obsessions of hipsters, namely, to be "for real," lead authentic lives and have meaningful experiences, as Finston has put it (qtd. in Greif, "Discussion" 53). Finston then asks whether there is not something "useful and productive" in such a commitment to preserving the authenticity of experiences (53). Analogously, this also applies to contemporary hipsters' hunt for "authentic inauthenticity" (Newman 75), for it proves that hipster culture is not nihilistic but actually a "positive protective force of our cultural moment" (Finston qtd. in Greif, "Discussion" 53). In the same way, Hannah can be seen to completely strip hipsterism of its air of constant irony by committing to want to be who she wants to be even if what that entails is not clear to her. She thus preserves a core of her self that is not molded into something else, that is, another image of idealized womanhood, by the postfeminist sensibility. This sentiment is echoed later in the series when she tells her old friend Tally Schifrin (Jenny Slate) about the fact that Adam and Jessa are dating: "And I could do what my instinct is, which is run around and destroy things and scream and try to throw myself in front of a van to make a point, but … that would just be me fulfilling all of their expectations of me, and I would love to surprise someone sometime" (5.9. "Love Stories"). At this point, she is doubtful that much has happened in her life, but Tally assures her that she has had "boyfriends and jobs and moments" and, most importantly, she has "so much to say" (5.9.). Looked at as a whole, the series is not only about "girls" but also comments on hipsters as a cultural construct and, in particular, female hipsters. In *Girls*, the emancipated female hipster is not merely a fashion dummy and/or consumer; she takes part and shapes the discourse around her, trying to disrupt the prevailing sensibility of the mainstream.

Frances Ha—But I Try, I Try

If there is one movie that both depicts (female) hipsters and has acquired cult status among hipsters, it is Noah Baumbach's *Frances Ha*. The story about some days in the life of 27-year-old Frances Halloway (Greta Gerwig), aspiring dancer trying to figure out life, has been met with predominantly positive reviews and holds a rating of 93 percent on Rotten Tomatoes. Romney has referred to it as "mumblecore deluxe: a hip, half-gritty, half-glossy comedy" spiced with a somewhat unfortunate turn to a biographical reading. The connections between Gerwig and the character she portrays and the frequent comparisons to *Girls*, "that touchstone of contemporary cool" (Bradshaw) are manifold (cf. Scott). Usually, critics point out that *Girls* is a more successful, realistic, and therefore convincing depiction of the struggles of young women in their mid-twenties. In contrast, *Frances Ha* has been accused of being too meek, too much of a whitewashed feel-good movie whose protagonist is never actually in a precarious situation, financially speaking. Even though Frances Halloway is portrayed as somebody who fears that "time is running out," some critics claim that the movie is inconsequential in that it suggests that her being broke is "only a temporary boho-chic Adventure in Brokeness" (Romney). Even though her job is not well paid, she is still able to afford a stylistic marker of hipster chic and "show up at dinner parties in an Acne aviator leather jacket" (Jun). This is an aspect that according to Erbacher has made critics of hipsterism condemn this downplayed display of privilege angrily in that hipsters are accused of "slumming in run-down urban neighborhood such as Williamsburg in Brooklyn ..., thus assisting in their eventual gentrification" ("Hip" 17). Crucially, "Frances is neither blandly agreeable nor adorably quirky. Rather ... she is *difficult*. She hogs conversations, misses obvious social cues and is frequently inconsiderate, though more in the manner of an overgrown toddler than a queen-bee mean girl" (Scott), something that makes her represent hipsterism in a typical manner because of hipsters' romanticization of childhood (cf. Newman).

There are scenes which suggest that Frances has internalized the male gaze women tend to be exposed to. For instance, she is scolded by her friend Sophie for constantly looking at herself in the mirror and when on a spontaneous trip to Paris, she manically obsesses over a pimple on her cheek rather than storming out to explore the city at once (even though she has slept for most of the day already). She seems trapped in that vicious circle of having to watch herself. The look she gives herself in the mirror is a skeptical, even insecure one—she seems to wonder whether her outer appearance is in accordance with a dominant societal beauty ideal that presents women with symmetrical faces and never without makeup. While the male ideal spectator is the powerful agent watching things happen, the female is the spectacle.

Some of the expectations *Frances Ha* does not meet are, in fact, inherently gendered. This suggests that, in a postfeminist context, female hipsters are also expected to adhere to conventional gender roles similar to the ones in the 1960s and even more so—or under greater scrutiny—than non-hip millennial women. While *Girls*, according to Jun, hits "that all-in-one, authentically quirky, tragicomic, and adorable note about young women navigating the enigma of postmodern adulthood and intimacy," *Frances Ha* has been termed "a soromance instead of the usual romcom" (Bradshaw) as if to endow it with a cute label from the start. It indeed plays with these expectations by starting off with a succession of "authentically quirky" scenes: The two best friends Frances and Sophie have a mock fight in Central Park. The two are shown exchanging thoughts and empty phrases like, "To praise a work of literature by calling it sincere is now at best a way of saying that it may be given no aesthetic or intellectual admiration," or "I wouldn't eat a domesticated dog."—"You say that just because they're cute," and, later at a party, "I can't get interested in art or books or movies about animals. The animals have to talk or be at war for me to be interested." All of these phrases, following one another rapidly like gun fire show, as Sophie later on in the movie puts it to describe Frances's new flat share, that those using them are indeed "very aware" of themselves. That is, they are uttered to underline that those speaking them know which cultural capital and which stylistic markers define them.

Yet *Frances Ha* then emancipates the female hipster by subverting this kind of stereotypically gendered image of a cute "catfight" between two "girls." What the movie excels at is a nuanced, formal depiction and celebration of trying; it depicts mundanity and is constructed around scenes that portray characters that are in motion, striving toward goals they may not have defined for themselves yet. Frances is a female hipster turned emancipated spectator composing her very own text and thus stepping out of the "sensible" order. The movie unpacks and pinpoints the female hipster persona poignantly through its poetic intertwining between dialogue and the composition of scenes, as an analysis of selected scenes shows.

Perfecting the wish uttered by Hannah to "surprise" people's expectations for once, Frances does not seem to care about or be too aware of conventions or social protocol. She cannot hide her dislike for Sophie's fiancé Patch, basically invites herself to stay with her acquaintance from the dance company, Rachel, and almost joyfully bubbles herself into trouble at a dinner party with Rachel's friends. This is also where her most pronounced moment of emancipated spectatorship occurs, when she, feeling that she forms an apart among this group of people, delivers an epiphanic speech about what she wants in life:

> It's that thing when you're with someone, and you love them and they know it, and they love you and you know it ... but it's a party ... and you look across the room and catch each other's eyes ... but—but not because you're possessive, or it's precisely sexual ... but because ... that is your person in this life. And it's funny and sad, but only because this life will end, and it's this secret world that exists right there in public, unnoticed, that no one else knows about. It's sort of like how they say that other dimensions exist all around us, but we don't have the ability to perceive them. That's—That's what I want out of a relationship. Or just life, I guess.

Having said that, Frances gets up and leaves. It is particularly significant that Frances has this outbreak at the end of an evening during which she was relegated to the margins and *a priori* excluded from the conversation as the only single person at the table without a steady job; she was forced to be a (externally) passive spectator. Yet she demonstrates her emancipated spectatorship by ending the night with this unashamedly unironic story to which the other guests, especially the hostess, can only listen in an enthralled way. She is capable of demarcating the vague outlines of her personal performance space.

More than being a storyteller, however, Frances is a *flâneuse* and the movie celebrates her eternal non-arriving. Most of the time it appears as if she has just fallen out of bed with a "blithe bounce" (Brody) and is carrying all her belongings in her rucksack. The film's episodes are structured according to the addresses of the apartments she lives in, yet these markers do not provide any actual rooting or orientation—"[n]owhere to stay means no status" (Romney)—but not having a status is precisely what turns Frances into an emancipated spectator. Rather than anchoring its protagonist in a "somewhere," the movie captures the flux she is in, this in itself being part of her privileged position as a white woman. The most powerful scene in the movie is a homage to Leos Carax's *Mauvais Sang* from 1986 (cf. Brody): Frances dances and runs down to the street accompanied by David Bowie's "Modern Love." This dance is not a struggle and expression of agony as performed by Denis Lavant in *Mauvais Sang*, but a celebration of potentiality, of a refusal to be pinned down. Frances has just moved into Benji and Lev's apartment in Chinatown, and this scene shows her jog-jumping, laughing to herself, and making pirouettes down the street, always accompanied by a look of slight incredulity on her face. Frances's running resembles an em-dash, traversing the space but being of a completely indefinite nature. She is a twenty-first-century *flâneuse* who moves about at a much faster pace than her nineteenth- and twentieth-century counterparts, but is equally undetermined. The line between running and running away from something is a thin one; yet it is actually a powerful technique to keep oneself afloat, embracing uncertainty as a means to keep trying. Frances sums up this sentiment after the show she has choreographed at the end of the movie when she tells Sophie, "I like things that look like mistakes." What is perceived as a "mistake," of course, lies in the eyes of the beholder. In comparison to *Girls*, *Frances Ha* thus manages to keep some of the potentiality of emancipated spectatorship at the end, while at the same time for the most part capturing the protagonist's return to conventionality.

Conclusion

The main characters in both *Girls* and *Frances Ha* are representations of the millennial female hipster. Both the show and the movie follow the lives of their protagonists when they are in their mid- to late-20s, thus presenting an insight into the female millennial identity and the female hipster as a cultural and gendered construct. More precisely, the setting and stylistic markers turn both story worlds into microcosms of hipsterism. In putting female hipsters at the center of the narratives, both the show and the movie provide an invitation to fill the conceptual gap that surrounds the female hipster in the cultural discourse on hipsters and thus present critical takes on a postfeminist sensibility that reproduces quite conventional notions of femininity. More precisely, as this chapter has shown, they present the female hipster persona as successfully participating in processes of emancipated spectatorship. In *Girls*, this emancipation takes the shape of sincere verbal manifestations of the self that I have referred to as verbalizations and storytelling. These female hipsters make the case for the necessity of speaking up—they reclaim their voices and become the bearers of the gaze—in order to define their positions in life. Not being afraid of sentimentality is also a defining characteristic of Frances Halloway, a twenty-first-century *flâneuse*. Her emancipated spectatorship manifests itself in the shape of a constant pursuing of potentiality; of trying and becoming a poet of her own acts in Rancière's sense. It must be emphasized that both *Girls* and *Frances Ha* present insular worlds: the hipsters these cultural texts explore are almost exclusively white and middle-class. So while they do not represent a universal portrayal of the Brooklyn hipster experience, they do depict a world that exists and are "for better or worse … absolutely realistic" (Harris).

As a whole, these emancipated versions of female hipsters dominate the stories, yet ultimately both the movie and the show refuse their protagonists the right to keep trying. They suggest a transitory nature of this striving and a link between hipsterism and youth. The final scene in *Girls* shows Hannah breastfeeding her baby son, having left New York City to raise him and work at a college upstate. Frances finally settles for an office job at her former dance company and rents her first own apartment—at least she can still live out some of her former aspirations by choreographing shows. Still, in both cases, the protagonists' female hipsterism seems to be dampened, their plots are forced into something very akin to closure. Therefore, the moment life is figured out coincides with the collapse/disappearance of hipsterism, which is reserved for the still striving.

Works Cited

Benjamin, Walter. *Das Passagen-Werk: Erster Teil.* Suhrkamp, 1982.

Berger, John. "Chapter 7: *Ways of Seeing.*" *The Feminism and Visual Culture Reader*, edited by Amelia Jones. Routledge, 2010, pp. 49–52.

Bradshaw, Peter. "Frances Ha—Review." *Guardian*, July 25, 2013, www.theguardian.com/film/2013/jul/25/frances-ha-baumbach-gerwig-review. Accessed July 15, 2020.

Brody, Richard. "'Frances Ha' and the Pursuit of Happiness." *New Yorker*, May 15, 2013, www.newyorker.com/culture/richard-brody/frances-ha-and-the-pursuit-of-happiness. Accessed July 15, 2020.

Chayka, Kyle. "Same Old, Same Old. How the Hipster Aesthetic is Taking Over the World." *Guardian*, August 7, 2016, www.theguardian.com/commentisfree/2016/aug/06/hipster-aesthetic-taking-over-world. Accessed July 15, 2020.

Cook, John. "'Am I Rich Enough?': A *Girls* Recap." *Gawker*, June 19, 2012, gawker.com/5919400/am-i-rich-enough-a-girls-recap. Accessed July 15, 2020.

Erbacher, Eric C. "Hip or Square? Pop Cultural Negotiations of Hipster Lifestyles Between Commodification and Subversion." *Hidden Cities: Understanding Urban Popcultures*, edited by Leonard R. Koos. Inter-Disciplinary Press, 2012, pp. 13–22.

Erbacher, Eric C. "Lifestyle Precarity and Creative Class Affirmation in *Girls*." *Class Divisions on Serial Television*, edited by Sieglinde Lemke and Wibke Schniedermann. Palgrave Macmillan, 2016, pp. 121–42.

Frances Ha, directed by Noah Baumbach, performances by Greta Gerwig and Mickey Sumner, RT Features et al., 2012.

Gill, Rosalind. "Postfeminist Media Culture: Elements of a Sensibility." *European Journal of Culture Studies*, vol. 10, no. 2, 2007, pp. 147–66.

Girls, created by Lena Dunham. Apatow Productions, I Am Jenni Konner Productions, and HBO Entertainment, 2012–17.

Greif, Mark. "Discussion." *What Was the Hipster? A Sociological Investigation*, edited by Mark Greif, Kathleen Ross, and Dayna Tortorici. n+1 Foundation, 2010, pp. 31–77.

Greif, Mark. Preface. *What Was the Hipster? A Sociological Investigation*, edited by Mark Greif, Kathleen Ross, and Dayna Tortorici. n+1 Foundation, 2010, pp. vii–xvii.

Harris, Aisha. "*Girls* Is Still Very White—and That's OK." *Slate*, March 18, 2013, slate.com/culture/2013/03/hbo-girls-diversity-a-black-girls-perspective-on-living-among-brooklyn-hipsters.html. Accessed July 31, 2020.

Jefferson, Margo. "19 Questions." *What Was the Hipster? A Sociological Investigation,* edited by Mark Greif, Kathleen Ross, and Dayna Tortorici. n+1 Foundation, 2010, pp. 97–102.

Jun, Christine Coco. "'Frances Ha' Paints Rather Inaccurate Portrait of Brooklyn Hipster Scene." *HuffPost*, September 22, 2013, www.huffingtonpost.co.uk/christine-cocotte/frances-ha-review_b_3638729.html. Accessed July 15, 2020.

"Kimmy Drives A Car!" *Unbreakable Kimmy Schmidt*, written by Dan Rubin, directed by Shawn Levy, season 2, episode 6. Little Stranger Inc. et al., April 15, 2016. *Netflix*, www.netflix.com/title/80025384. Accessed July 15, 2020.

Mahdawi, Arwa. "Is Lena Dunham's 'Hipster Racism' Just Old-Fashioned Prejudice?" *Guardian*, November 25, 2017, www.theguardian.com/world/2017/nov/25/hipster-racism-lena-dunham-prejudice. Accessed July 31, 2020.

McCann, Hannah. "'A Voice of *a* Generation': *Girls* and the Problem of Representation." *Reading Lena Dunham's Girls*, edited by Meredith Nash and Imelda Whelehan. Palgrave Macmillan, 2017, pp. 91–104.

Miller, Julia. "Watch: HBO's New Hipster Sex and the City." *Refinery29*, March 5, 2012, www.refinery29.com/en-us/girls-trailer-hbo. Accessed July 31, 2020.

Mulvey, Laura. "Visual Pleasure and Narrative Cinema." *The Feminism and Visual Culture Reader*, edited by Amelia Jones. Routledge, 2010, pp. 57–65.

Nash, Meredith, and Ruby Grant. "Twenty-Something *Girls* v. Thirty-Something *Sex and the City* Women." *Feminist Media Studies*, vol. 15, no. 6, 2015, pp. 976–91.

Newman, Michael Z. "Movies for Hipsters." *American Independent Cinema: Indie, Indiewood and Beyond*, edited by Geoff King, Claire Molloy, and Yannis Tzioumakis. Routledge, 2013, pp. 71–82.

Nussbaum, Emily. "Hannah Barbaric: 'Girls,' 'Enlightened,' and the Comedy of Cruelty." *New Yorker*, February 4, 2013, www.newyorker.com/magazine/2013/02/11/hannah-barbaric. Accessed November 17, 2020.

Parsons, Deborah L. *Streetwalking the Metropolis: Women, the City and Modernity*. Oxford University Press, 2000.

Rancière, Jacques. "The Emancipated Spectator." *The Emancipated Spectator*. 2008, translated by Gregory Elliott. Verso, 2011, pp. 1–23.

Ridout, Nicholas. "Mis-Spectatorship, or, 'Redistributing the Sensible.'" *Archaeologies of Presence*, edited by Gabriela Giannachi. Routledge, 2012, pp. 172–82.

Romney, Jonathan. "Even Hipster Goddesses Get the Blues." *Independent*, October 10, 2013, www.independent.co.uk/arts-entertainment/films/reviews/jonathan-romney-frances-ha-even-hipster-goddesses-get-blues-8734791.html. Accessed November 17, 2020.

Schipper, Imanuel. "From Flâneur to Co-Producer: The Performative Spectator." *Performing the Digital: Performativity and Performance Studies in Digital Cultures*, edited by Martina Leeker et al., transcript, 2017, pp. 191–209.

Scott, A. O. "If 27 Is Old, How Old Is Grown Up?" *New York Times*, May 16, 2013, www.nytimes.com/2013/05/17/movies/frances-ha-with-greta-gerwig.html. Accessed July 13, 2020.

Tortorici, Dayna. "You Know It When You See It." *What Was the Hipster? A Sociological Investigation*, edited by Mark Greif, Kathleen Ross, and Dayna Tortorici. n+1 Foundation, 2010, pp. 122–35.

Weitz, Rose. "Feminism, Post-Feminism, and Young Women's Reactions to Lena Dunham's *Girls*." *Gender Issues*, vol. 33, no. 3, 2016, pp. 218–34.

Williams, Alex. "Creating Hipsturbia." *New York Times*, February 15, 2013, www.nytimes.com/2013/02/17/fashion/creating-hipsturbia-in-the-suburbs-of-new-york.html. Accessed July 15, 2020.

Zoller Seitz, Matt. "*Girls*' Final Season Was the Show at Its Saddest, and Best." *Vulture*, April 17, 2017, www.vulture.com/2017/04/girls-review-the-final-season-was-the-show-at-its-best.html. Accessed July 15, 2020.

14

"Fem the Future" of Hipness: Female Hipster Performers in Twenty-First-Century Popular Music

Lena Gotteswinter

Hipsters have been puzzling Western society for quite some time. They are constantly changing, from the turn-of-the-millennium look of wifebeaters and trucker hats (Greif, "Positions" 9) to the current "lumbersexual" (cf. Rademacher and Kelly). Still, in two realms hipsters have appeared one-dimensional: gender and ethnicity. Contemporary hipsters are commonly identified as white, urban, middle-class, anti-mainstream, and flaunting irony (Olopade). They are usually young men wearing idiosyncratic fashion styles, and they are closely associated with indie culture (Greif, "What was the Hipster?" 213), especially the indie music industry. Music is particularly valuable for hipsters as, together with sound, it crucially embodies the hipster sensibility and its immediacy of experience (Ford 6, 9).[1]

This stereotypical understanding of hipsters, however, has shifted, with hipsters of various ethnicities and gender identities moving into the limelight (also in Williamsburg, New York, as a trip in August 2017 made clear to me). While these hipster manifestations historically are not new, they now seem

[1]Indie music is often equated with indie *rock*. In this essay, I refer to indie in a more generic way as "independent music," which is launched on independent record labels, characterized by artistic autonomy, or not necessarily geared toward mainstream audiences.

more visible, claiming their space opposite selective hipster representatives who display sexist and racist inclinations. Gavin McInnes, cofounder of hipster *Vice* magazine, for instance, asserted in 2003 that "Steinem-era feminism did women a lot of injustices, but one of the worst ones was [the claim] that women don't want to be dominated" and declared his "love" for his whiteness (Grigoriadis). But hipness also offers the possibility for progressive social criticism.

In this chapter, I seek to elucidate the multi-faceted character of hipness, with new manifestations reviving this stereotypically white, male-dominated realm and defying sexism and racism through self-assertive performances. To examine the "blind spot" concerning race and gender in the hipster discourse, I focus on female biracial and female Black hipsters or "Blipsters"—a portmanteau of "Black" and "hipsters" (P. Evans 108). While hipsters in the twenty-first century have been identified as apolitical (Greif, "What was the Hipster?" 221), there have also been politically engaged hipsters like Bob Dylan. Contemporary hipsters' politically disinterested reputation may derive from an association of hipness with "the elevation of style and background as narrative and foreground" (Leland 10). I, however, argue that some hipsters in the twenty-first century embody concrete sociopolitical engagement in a parallel strand to apolitical hipsters.

I will be focusing on three contemporary female singers: Karen O (born Orzolek), lead singer of the indie rock band Yeah Yeah Yeahs, soul artist Solange (Knowles), and Prince-protégé Janelle Monáe. These artists represent different music genres, which illustrates that hipsters can also be found in other categories than indie rock. They are "indie" in a wider understanding as largely "independent" from expectations dictated by the mainstream. What connects these artists is their hipster habitus, which is performed in their avant-garde music and their artistic[2] and idiosyncratic fashion styles, fashion being a prime instrument for consolidating hipness (Maly and Varis 640). The three performers are highly self-reliant (e.g., in their music production). They use intertextual references (e.g., to films) to convey subcultural capital—to use Sarah Thornton's term[3]. Moreover, they are marginalized within the predominantly white and male popular music and hipster spheres: Karen O is a rare woman in the indie rock scene of the early 2000s. Incidentally, she is also a rare woman of color (she is Asian American) within this sphere. Solange and Monáe may be well received in R'n'B and soul, but originally, they were not considered mainstream.[4] All three convey individualistic hipster styles via fashion, music, and

[2]I use the term "artistic" to refer to performances which are experimental and innovative. Diligently composed, they are often understood in their entirety as pieces of art.

[3]Cf. Thornton, *Club Cultures*, 11–2. For a discussion of subcultural capital and hipster culture, cf. also Schiermer and Steinhoff in this collection.

[4]Just like hipness, both have recently moved closer to the mainstream.

performance: Karen O performs hedonistic excess, Solange embodies a minimalist, choreographed performance, and Monáe evokes a retro feel through her signature suits. The three performers also produce music that may seem challenging, for example, by using atonal sounds (Karen O on *Fever to Tell*[5]; Solange on *A Seat at the Table*) or including tracks played backwards (on Monáe's *The Archandroid*), thereby interpellating their audiences also as non-mainstream. They provide a glimpse into the ways in which hipness can be used to express individual artistic endeavors and, as I will show, various feminist attitudes.

Female hipsters have questioned hipster patriarchy for decades. While earlier female hipsters (e.g., in the 1950s) grappled with being acknowledged (Leland 249–50), contemporary representatives assert themselves more successfully. Employing hip women's (formerly) marginalized position and the concomitant awareness of marginalizing practices, they defy socially constructed limitations based on gender or ethnicity. Karen O has been negating the male dominance of hip both in her presence in indie rock and in her performances. Combining stereotypically "feminine" characteristics and styles with individualistic ideals of personal (sexual) freedom, she can be aligned with both third wave feminism and postfeminism. Like representatives of the Riot grrrl movement, Karen O embodies Third Wavers' "claim that popular culture can be the site of activism, and that media such as music can be used to communicate political messages" (Pilcher and Whelehan 168). At the same time, her representation can also be linked to postfeminist values. Angela McRobbie identifies postfeminism as a stance which "positively draws on and invokes feminism as that which can be taken into account, to suggest that equality is achieved, in order to install a whole repertoire of new meanings which emphasise that it is no longer needed, it is a spent force" (McRobbie 385–6). Postfeminism is somewhat paradoxical in its "double entanglement" of combining "neo-conservative values in relation to gender, sexuality and family life" with an insistence on personal liberation and freedom of choice, especially concerning sexuality (McRobbie 386). While Karen O conveyed aspects of such a postfeminist ideology in her early career, later in her life she has become more vocal in addressing womanhood (Phillips), seemingly exemplifying what Sarah Banet-Weiser calls a rise in "popular feminism" in recent years. Popular feminism designates a widespread public engagement and promotion of feminist values within popular culture, which, however, also entail the danger of sidelining actual activism against oppressive structures through a mere showcasing of feminism (Banet-Weiser et al. 9). Due to her lack

[5]This album was released on Interscope, a major label instead of an indie label. It speaks to the band's immense subcultural status that they are nevertheless perceived as "indie."

of concrete feminist activism countering oppressive systems, this seems to apply to Karen O.

In contrast, Monáe and Solange exemplify female Black hipsters who have engaged in feminist criticism more openly and (at least in Monáe's case) for a longer time than Karen O. Both highlight their experiences as Black women and build their critical stance on "Black feminist thought" (Collins 6). Black feminism is based on a criticism of white feminists for not taking the experiences of women of all ethnicities and class backgrounds into account (Collins 8). According to Patricia Hill Collins, Black women's oppression in the United States has been manifesting in three dimensions: first, economically through exploitative practices concerning Black female labor; second, politically, in that Black women have not been given equal rights as white American men, for example, with regard to legislation; and third, ideologically, through a proliferation of stereotypes about Black women (6–7). Solange and Monáe address these levels of discrimination in their performances. They can also be associated with third wave feminism, which has developed in various strands in reaction to second wave feminism. The two singers specifically convey a strand in which intersectionality is crucial (E. Evans 22–4). This form of feminism is largely indebted to Black feminism and its focus on addressing various dimensions (like race, gender, and class) of discrimination (E. Evans 29). Through their performances, all three artists exemplify pathways to "Fem the Future" of hipness—to use the name of Monáe's women-focused organization (Spanos 39)—and exemplify a politicization of hipness, updating it to contemporary concerns of diversity.

The Gender Politics of Hipness and the (Indie) Music Industry

Diversity is in fact deeply rooted in the history of hipness. The term "hipness" signifies the "act of being hip" and designates a specific way of life, a habitus. But what is hip? According to Leland's *Hip: The History*, hip starts out in the seventeenth century as a "subversive intelligence" developed among slaves in West Africa (5–6). Specifically, it originated among enslaved Blacks, who had been translocated to the American continent, and in the ensuing intercultural clash with white Americans (17–18, 20–1).[6] This

[6]While some have located the origin of hipness at the middle of the twentieth century (e.g., Greif, "What was the Hipster?" 214), Leland goes further back, using Thompson's essay "An Aesthetic of the Cool" (242). Thompson traces the roots of "coolness"—a concept associated with hipness—back to African traditions. According to him, there are parallels between rites in African communities and communities of the Americas due to the transatlantic slave trade (41, 43).

"subversive intelligence" is what Anatole Broyard in 1948, in one of the earliest definitions of the (Black) hipster, identifies as "a priorism" (722). It describes a specific knowledge that exclusively hipsters had and deployed to counteract the power dominant society had over Black Americans (721–2). In 2010, Greif reutilizes this term to describe contemporary hipsters and their display of this knowledge (Greif, "Positions" 8). This unique intelligence prompted a century-long intercultural exchange between Black and white, specifically also white appropriations of Black knowledge (Leland 6, 10). In his essay "The White Negro" from 1957, Norman Mailer addresses this appropriation of Black hipness by white Americans. His text exemplifies the hipster-specific continuous exchange between Black and white cultures and other seemingly dichotomous categories (Leland 11, 51). Despite the highly performative character of hipness—it relies on an audience (Leland 8)—and its history of "imitation," values such as "authenticity, uniqueness, and individuality"—while remaining nonchalant—are prerequisites for hipsters (Maly and Varis 644).

Although intercultural exchange has been foundational for hipster culture, the hipster and indie music discourse can also be exclusive. Popular music (specifically rock) has for a long time been dominated by men, in particular the (also white-dominated) indie guitar rock genre (Bayton 51, Bannister 77–8).[7] Moreover, indie has come to be associated with whiteness due to an imagined connection between Black music and "commodification and mass deception" (Bannister 88)—thus conflicting with ideals of an allegedly non-materialistic indie culture.[8] The close association of hipness with white male indie music has therefore also fostered a white male image of hipsters. Despite, or maybe even because of their marginal status, female hipsters[9] are standing out as they rearticulate hipness critically from a subaltern position. While they embody similar characteristics as male hipsters, this embodiment is often more complicated for them. Fashion, for example, cannot function as a clear indicator of hipness for the female hipster, since women have stereotypically been connected to sartorial experimentation and men with indifference toward fashion (Tortorici 123–4). Women thus are forced to be more innovative. Among female hipsters, two major strategies become apparent: embracing femininity and the female experience as an asset, informing their hipster performance (Leland 255–6). This may include a transformation of "negative" gender stereotypes into productive ones in a postfeminist move, for example, by wearing a feminine fashion style reminiscent of the 1950s to convey individualism and subcultural

[7]This perception seems to have developed into a more inclusive conception in the twenty-first century.

[8]Indie rock is paradoxically indebted to rock'n'roll, which emerged in Black culture.

[9]Unless stated otherwise, I am using this term to refer to hip women of all ethnicities in this section.

capital in ways that conflict with the "canon" of "cool, masculine" hipster performances. This is exemplified by the actress and singer Zooey Deschanel. The other strategy of embodying hipness is gender-bending or refuting gender stereotypes as exemplified by Patti Smith (Leland 253, 255). It can take the form of a combination of stereotypical femininity and ironic detachment, for example, in performing emotionally charged songs with a detached Rockstar attitude. While both of these strategies may be criticized from a feminist perspective (e.g., as a reinforcement of gender stereotypes or a submission to male prescriptions of hipness), they illuminate gatekeeper mechanisms within hipster culture set to exclude women and forcing them to negotiate their gender identity within this field.

In their critical awareness, many female hipsters seem strongly indebted to their (historic) marginalization within this sphere, embodying bell hooks's understanding of the radical potential of margins as "both sites of repression and sites of resistance" ("Choosing Margin" 151). The knowledge of both the margins of society and its center enables a critical evaluation of both (148–9).[10] hooks identifies "marginality … as a central location for the production of a counter-hegemonic discourse" ("Choosing Margin" 149). Therefore, specifically women and African Americans as sidelined players may productively challenge normative ideals of hipster culture in their performances.

The Blipster and Forms of Double Consciousness

Marginalizing practices in the hipster sphere are not only directed at women and African Americans. Hipsters of other ethnicities (e.g., Asian American or Latino hipsters) are not at all, or only selectively, specifically addressed in the contemporary discourse (cf. Clayton). In this chapter, I will focus on the current example of Black hipsters as exemplifying the marginal status of nonwhite individuals in contemporary hipster society and as positioned within the tension between Blackness, hipness, and contemporary mainstream society.

The complex position of Blipsters in relation to white indie scenes is addressed in Barry Jenkins's independent film *Medicine for Melancholy*, which, as Simon Dickel shows, belongs to the film genre of "mumblecore"—a genre characterized by a focus on relationships and usually foregrounding whiteness (109–10). Jenkins deliberately positions Blackness as central to

---

[10]hooks's thoughts are framed by the Black female experience, but they also ring true for female hipsters of all ethnicities. Leland identifies this marginal, self-reflective position as a "second internal voice," with which hip women offer "both image and commentary" (258–9).

the movie (Dickel 122). The film revolves around the short relationship of two Black representatives of indie culture who negotiate their racial identities and hipness.[11] In discussing the white San Francisco indie scene, they disagree if Blackness is an all-defining category or if it can be considered only one aspect of a many-faceted identity (Dickel 110). While Jo' evokes post-Blackness and "cosmopolitan universalism," Micah insists on Blackness as *the* definitive category of his identity (Dickel 119). In these unresolved discussions, Jenkins's film poignantly touches upon the complexities of identifying as a Black hipster.

These complexities begin with the label itself. The term "Blipster" is highly controversial, adopted, and rejected both by people identifying as and critical of hipsters. It appears problematic because it seems to deal in stereotypes, implying that hipsters are inevitably white. Blipsters have also been accused of assimilating to white cultural values, professing admiration of a cultural sphere which has continuously sidelined Black people (Pressler). Others argue that the term reduces an individual to a cherry-picked racial categorization. However, there are also some who promote hipness while de-emphasizing Blackness (Olopade), thus evoking concepts like post-Blackness. In describing post-Blackness, Dickel refers to Bertram Ashe's essay "Theorizing the Post-Soul Aesthetic" and his argument that post-Blackness includes an unprecedented transgression of conventional racial boundaries in Black pop cultural performances and production. According to Dickel, it is often connected to an ironic attitude (just like hipness) (121–2). In one conception of the term, Blipsters have been understood as refuting limited, racialized spaces. By transgressing socially constructed boundaries, they criticize the hegemony of white hipsters *and* an internalization of racial boundaries, exemplified by African Americans accusing them of assimilation. In a 2016 article, Spencer Simpson, a college student and rare self-identified Blipster, specifies this interpretation:[12]

> Typically a political progressive [*sic*]—though acutely critical of all political ideologies—blipsters are uniquely dressed people of African descent soundly committed to defying a variety of stereotypes imposed upon Black bodies. [Blipsters] are Black people who fashionably mesh various social norms and cultural products in an organic refutation of socially imposed racial boundaries.

---

[11] I would argue that the protagonists Jo' and Micah are both Black hipsters.

[12] Due to the phenomenon's currency, the discourse on Blipsters mostly takes place in a nonacademic and journalistic environment (primarily online), in this case even in a student newspaper. Still, Simpson's account demonstrates the identity policing which Blipsters may encounter.

To Simpson, the term offers a form of assertive self-identification and a repudiation of stereotypes. Notably, he defines Blipsters as politically engaged, contrasting with stereotypical white hipsters. The "socially imposed racial boundaries" (Simpson) here insinuate both the gatekeeper role of white hipsters and a prescriptive understanding of Blackness. Blipsters therefore negotiate sociopolitical dimensions of racial identity and appropriation.

The Blipsters' complex identity politics call up W. E. B. Du Bois's concept of "double consciousness"—a theory also useful for generally approaching the hybrid hipster condition (Leland 354–5). In 1903, Du Bois, one of the earliest institutionally established Black intellectuals promoting an advancement of the African American society and racial equity through education, addresses the particularity of the Black experience in America. In *The Souls of Black Folk*, he identifies "double consciousness" as African Americans' feeling of displacement within the American society, as

> this sense of always looking at one's self through the eyes of others, of measuring one's soul by the tape of a world that looks on in amused contempt and pity. One ever feels his two-ness,—an American, a Negro; two souls, two thoughts, two unreconciled strivings; two warring ideals in one dark body, whose dogged strength alone keeps it from being torn asunder. (11)

Extending this argument, I argue that Blipsters experience a "multiple consciousness," identifying as Americans, Blacks, and hipsters, always running the risk of alienating hegemonic society, white (American) hipster society, *and* Black communities. Having to justify being a hipster while displaying pride in Black heritage demonstrates how hipness is a continuous site of racial identity politics.

While several early essays on Blipsters are written with a focus on men (e.g., Olopade), more recent accounts specifically name, for example, Solange as the epitome of Black hipness (Simpson). For Black female hipsters, multiple consciousness is even more extended, as they already are doubly marginalized due to their gender and race.[13] Janelle Monáe and Solange use this multiple consciousness and awareness of discriminatory mechanisms to challenge hegemonic social dynamics and renegotiate the hipster discourse.

---

[13]I want to emphasize that "hipness" as a *chosen* characteristic is not equal to other aspects of identity such as gender, race, or sexuality, which may be met with marginalization, discrimination, and violence.

"I Manifested That Shit for You!"[14]: Karen O's Edgy Individualism

Karen O started out as one of few female hipster musicians in New York in the early 2000s. She is also a hipster of color, although in contrast to Black hipsters like Solange, she has never been vocal about her Korean roots. There are no explicit references to Asian culture in the music of the Yeah Yeah Yeahs, and in spite of the title of the song "Native Korean Rock" from her solo album *Crush Songs*, the song itself does not entail any lyrical or musical references to her ethnicity. Only in recent years (possibly reacting to an increased public discourse on diversity) she has started to address her heritage (albeit briefly), confessing in 2015 that she had felt like an outsider at school among others because of her ethnicity and shyness—a marginal position which she explicitly suspects to be identity-shaping for rock musicians (Blanning). Then, in a 2018 interview about her songwriting for a project by Japanese fashion brand Kenzo, she explained how Korean music inspired her (Phillips). Still, apart from these selective examples she has primarily conveyed indifference toward ethnicity.

Interestingly and correspondingly, Karen O has often been "overlooked" as an Asian American person, for example, with writers like Ta-Nehisi Coates viewing her as white (Euse), which speaks of the general association of hipness and indie with whiteness. It seems that Karen O has (possibly unconsciously or unintentionally) been passing as white, although her performances seem indifferent toward whiteness (in contrast to other hipsters like McInnes). Her white public image is thus a creation of her audience. It demonstrates that whiteness is a performative and discursively created category which here emerged in the tension between a performer and her audience and certain preconceived ideas. It insinuates the hypocrisy of the hipster discourse, its focus on appearances, and its reproduction of artificially constructed one-dimensional norms conflicting with the multicultural history of hip.

While ethnicity is not vastly addressed by Karen O, (post)feminist ideas constitute a prominent undercurrent in her work. She openly defies gender expectations, but also insists on her femininity, in wild, experimental performances. Although gender-bending is a common practice for male (rock) musicians (e.g., wearing long hair), women within indie culture are confronted with a double standard *forcing* them to masculinize themselves to be taken seriously (Long as qtd. in Goodman 247). Karen O complicates this premise, emphasizing her femininity within a "male" domain after admitting to also having masculinized herself in the past: "One of the biggest

[14]Karen O as quoted in Goodman (566).

challenges for me ... was getting all the men around me to understand that I wasn't one of them" (as qtd. in Ryzik).

She does so by performing aggressively and excessively, screaming and rolling on the floor, while also employing sexualized, fetishized moves emphasizing her androgynous body (cf. Yeah Yeah Yeahs, "Rich"). Questioning the narrowly defined categories of gender in rock music, she advocates postfeminist sexual liberation and individualized freedom (McRobbie 386, 391–2). She further underpins this impression by arguing that she never had a distinct interest in "the whole feminist movement" (as quoted in Jonze), similar to how many postfeminists reject the concept of "feminism" (McRobbie 386). Only later, after she has given birth to a son, Karen O describes a shift in the ideological framework of her music toward an interest in women and their social position (Phillips), seemingly exemplifying how popular feminism has become *en vogue* recently (Banet-Weiser et al. 9).

Karen O performs specifically (post)feminist ideals prominently on stage and in her edgy outfits, which combine leather (a staple in hypermasculine rock), glitter, plastic, and fetish vinyl pieces. She often wears stereotypically feminine (but torn) attire such as tight skirts, dresses, and heavy, smeared makeup, continuously playing with patriarchal ideals of feminine beauty and behavior (e.g., by sprawling on the floor). Her arty costumes, codesigned by her and Christian Joy, have become the singer's trademark (Long, Joy, and Ahmed as qtd. in Goodman 246). They are provoking in that they are deliberately ugly or revealing (Karen O and Joy as qtd. in Goodman 246–7). Karen O uses them to transgress boundaries of propriety and patriarchal expectations, thus using hipster performances to express her artistic individualism *and* sexual freedom. Using the *a priori* knowledge emerging from her marginal status as a woman in a "male" domain, she asserts herself in innovative and uncensored self-staging—which is also evident in her register. When discussing fans thanking her for getting them through difficult times, she admits to thinking, "I manifested that shit for you! I *wanted* to get in there [possibly referring to the rock scene *and* her fans' lives] like a motherfucker and that's what I did" (as qtd. in Goodman 566).

Despite these (post)feminist elements, Karen O's performances also exemplify stereotypical "apolitical" hipster qualities, such as the foregrounding of stylistics as narrative, for example, in the band's obscure and stream-of-consciousness-like lyrics.[15] Combined with strong rhythms, they convey nihilism and transgression. In the video to "Heads Will Roll," this is performed in an ironic and provokingly inappropriate manner. Staged at a small concert in an elegant basement room, the video shows a werewolf killing the band and their audience, with red glitter and confetti instead

[15]Karen O usually takes the lead in the band's songwriting (Zinner as qtd. in Goodman 229).

of blood splattering everywhere. The artistically designed, but grotesque, scene is contrasted with the image of the cool, calm band, who are not at all surprised, implying *a priori* knowledge that the panicked audience in the video does not have. The video further exemplifies pastiche, as the werewolf, styled with a suit, a hat, and white socks, dancing on a lit-up dance floor, evokes Michael Jackson's music videos to "Billie Jean" and "Thriller." The band thus exemplifies the reference cycle of hipness in the intercultural contact of Black and white, using irony (in the video's grotesque character) to adapt an—incidentally also male—mainstream artist's work to a more glamorized and "hipper" version corresponding to Karen O's style.

In contrast to the band's excessive music, Karen O's solo album *Crush Songs* conveys a lo-fi sound and is focused on emotions and vulnerability, resisting the stereotypical (masculine) hipster norm of "playing it cool." Still, similar to Karen O's self-assertive performances with the band, *Crush Songs* conveys autonomy, individualism, and authenticity, as most of the songs were recorded in a demo-like fashion with just Karen O and her guitar (Deusner). This sound is often used to promote the idea of an authentic listening experience, undisturbed by financial aspirations, and to evoke liveness, which is highly valued in the indie music industry (Bannister 83). The sound and the topic of love seem to convey a stereotypically more feminized and internalized hipster identity, illustrating the legitimacy of different facets of hipness and Karen O's refusal to favor one or the other.

By blurring and defying gender expectations in her performances, Karen O illustrates that hipness does not only signify through prescriptions of "masculine" coolness. Rather performing than voicing interpretations of feminism, she makes clear that hipness can be framed through individual negotiations of the female experience to deconstruct essentialist stereotypes about indie culture.

The Electric Lady: Janelle Monáe's Futuristic Feminism

Janelle Monáe's music is an eclectic mix of R'n'B, funk, soul, rock'n'roll, and folk. Her unique music style makes her "one of the [twenty-first] century's most inventive voices" (Spanos 36). Interestingly, Monáe sartorially combines this status as innovator with the past, in particular the dandy aesthetic. The dandy is a historical-cultural figure that—like the hipster—is closely associated with gender-bending (Houk 59). Dandies and hipsters share a tacit association with whiteness as well as an understanding of style as a way of life. By presenting herself as a Black dandy wearing elegant clothes originally designed for men, such as tuxedos, Monáe appropriates the stereotypically white male dandy phenomenon, which Baudelaire in 1863 defined as a diligently orchestrated lifestyle of the idle, elegant, wealthy, and hedonistic (26–7). Dandyism is not just a preference of visual refinements, but in fact "the burning need to create for oneself a personal originality, bounded only by the limits of the proprieties.[16] It is a kind of cult of the self" (Baudelaire 27), which parallels hipsters' strive for uniqueness. Especially in their reverence for retro styles in a digitized world, "the hipster carries out on a popular scale what used to be the prerogative of the aristocratic dandy figure ...: He[17] insists on individuality in the face of homogenization" (Schiermer 176–7). Monáe's dandy style exemplifies an artistic hipster image, being carefully created through pastiche of aristocratic and contemporary fashions and, even more, embodies a strong critical awareness of racial boundaries—which, in true Blipster-fashion, she defies. By laying claim to the dandy aesthetic, Monáe reverses the direction of white appropriation of Black culture anchored in the history of hipness.

Conveying a strong Black feminist attitude, Monáe's stance is particularly prominent in her music. Taking inspiration from Fritz Lang's *Metropolis* from 1927[18] (and thus conveying subcultural capital) she conceptualizes her first albums around her alter ego Cindi Mayweather, an android from 2719 who has illegally fallen in love with a human and is now being chased. Cindi is also "the archandroid," a messianic figure that will lead a revolution to redeem the androids from their status as "the Other." Mayweather's story describes a metaphor for African Americans' struggle against racial discrimination in the United States and embodies Monáe's identification with the Black community. Monáe here addresses Black discrimination through Afrofuturism. Coined by Mark Dery, this term describes "African-American signification that appropriates images of technology and a prosthetically enhanced future" (180). In the discourse of progressivism, African Americans have often been presented as the "Other," which created a "racialized digital divide narrative" (Nelson 6) influencing the public conception of race and technology (Nelson 1, 6). Applying this approach, Monáe defies these assumptions and uses science fiction to embody Blackness.

Although Monáe has not prominently called herself a feminist, her support for gender equality and equal rights for the LGBTQIA+ community, which she has promoted in an interview with *Variety*, implies a feminist framework (Janelle Monáe Defines). This is advanced even more in her performances, in which she promotes intersectional feminist notions. In her song "Q.U.E.E.N." for instance, she refutes economic, social, and political discrimination of Black women, picking up major tenets of Black feminism. In the lyrics, she defies the social policing of (Black) women's failure to

[16]Hipsters are much less concerned with proprieties.

[17]Also, dandies are tacitly identified as male.

[18]Lang's movie revolves around a two-tier society in which the working class operates the machines that support the upper class.

fulfill patriarchal expectations, for example, defying heteronormativity by displaying homosexual interest. She also criticizes economic factors like intellectual theft from women and encourages her female audience to actively fight for equality. On her 2018 album *Dirty Computer*, Monáe, who has come out as queer and pansexual in 2018 (Spanos 36), develops her feminist stance even more toward an intersectional interpretation of third wave feminism. In the video to "Make Me Feel" she is engaged in a three-party relationship with a woman and a man while the lyrics identify her as gender-fluid. Finally, she explicitly engages in politics through her activist organization Fem the Future supporting women (Spanos 39). Monáe thus asserts herself from a (at least initially) marginal position and uses her awareness of discriminatory practices and her innovative performances to demonstrate how a hipster perspective can be utilized to enforce criticism of social inequalities regarding Black women. Although her recent shift toward the mainstream has entailed more sexualized performances (cf. the video to "Make Me Feel"), Monáe's embodiment of feminist thought has only become more prominent in an increasing politicization of her hipster performance.

A Seat at the Table: Solange's Aesthetic Black Rebellion

Black feminism and artistic expression are also integral elements in the music performance of Solange, especially on her 2016 album *A Seat at the Table*. In contrast to Karen O and Monáe, Solange has literally identified as "a proud black feminist" in an interview, asserting, "I'm a feminist who wants not only to hear the term intersectionality, but actually feel it, and see the evolution of what intersectional feminism can actually achieve" (Wilson). Focusing on intersectional currents of third wave feminism, Solange uses a hipster aesthetic to convey individualism as well as *a priori* knowledge and authenticity anchored within feminist ideals. The album artwork to *A Seat at the Table* depicts her with apparently no makeup on, wearing her hair naturally, looking defiantly but calmly into the camera. This image represents both authenticity and coolness. Its bareness implies that the album offers a reliable, unmediated account of Solange's experiences as a Black woman—and her artistic performances reinforce this impression.

In these performances (cf. the music video to "Don't Touch My Hair"), her choreographies seem located in modern dance, a style that is stereotypically associated with the white upper/middle class (although there have been notable African American choreographers like Alvin Ailey). She deploys it to express Black experiences, thus asserting that Black people need to claim their space in areas monopolized by white society, a message the singer also promoted during a secret performance at the Guggenheim Museum in New York in 2017 (Lang). She maintained, "I'm not settling for being allowed in these spaces but for tearing these f—king walls down ... Inclusion is not enough. Allowance is not enough. We belong here. We built this sh—t" (as qtd. in Lang). Alluding to the fact that African Americans have vastly contributed to the US-American national identity and infrastructure, while later being denied access to these, Solange here reclaims what Black people have always also been entitled to in an open political statement.

Specifically the Black female experience and self-assertion are major tenets of Solange's work. The song "Don't Touch My Hair" addresses the unique signifying practices of Black hair and women's (often complicated) relationship with it. These practices have been a contested topic in cultural studies. For example, hooks acknowledges her childhood memories of straightening hair as a bonding ritual between Black women but later has come to understand the supremacist dimensions of this practice ("Straightening" 111–13, 116). Kobena Mercer also addresses the politicization of hair, describing hairstyling as evocative of an individual's personal identity and larger social standards (99–100). He argues that "Black hairstyling may thus be evaluated as a popular *art form* articulating a variety of aesthetic 'solutions' to a range of 'problems' created by ideologies of race and racism" (100, emphasis in original). It is therefore an aesthetic practice with critical potential—a claim which I confer to hipness. Solange's song "Don't Touch My Hair" specifically addresses the ignorance of many non-Black people when it comes to Black hair and the degrading exoticization of African Americans based on hairstyles. Although acknowledging her close connection to hair, Solange also rejects the idea of a related token Blackness and argues that her hairstyle does not influence her identification as Black (Rosen). Like Jo' and Simpson, Solange refuses to be reduced to a category, while at the same time she conveys pride in her Black identity.

Solange's critical approach to racial and gender politics is underscored by interludes between songs on her album. In these, rapper Master P and her parents narrate experiences of racism and Black pride. These interludes embody a derivative of the *a priori* knowledge of early marginalized Black hipsters in that they address specific African American experiences which non-Black listeners may not be familiar with or aware of. Promoting the Black community and a focus on Black women in her performances as a Black hipster, Solange conveys intersectional feminist thought on *A Seat at the Table*. Embodying these values from a marginal position, she reframes hipness in opposition to a white male norm, highlighting the phenomenon's potential to speak to contemporary African American experiences while tracing the original roots of hipster knowledge.

Conclusion: Raising Their Voices

Through their (formerly) marginal status, female hipsters[19] have become aware of the shortcomings of the hegemonic hipster discourse when it comes to diversity. As sidelined figures within this sphere, they are aware of the value of their individual experiences for a renegotiation of hipness according to current standards. They use their liminal status to offer new impulses for hip cultural performances, specifically in more critically engaged manifestations. The examples presented here show how these different female singers embody various, specifically feminist performances of hipness and exemplify how contemporary female hipsters have increasingly more loudly challenged the white, male-dominated hipster discourse from various angles, deconstructing prescriptive limitations of hipsters as ironically detached white men. They offer a glimpse of various contemporary strands of feminism which can be performed in the context of hipness. While Karen O conveys an individualized form of self-assertion and as an "unacknowledged" Asian American hipster has implicitly brought the discursively constructed character of whiteness to the forefront, contemporary female Blipsters are enriching the monotonous discourse on hipsters by highlighting the complex experience of being a Black, hip woman and evoking the (often ignored) long history of Black hipsters. Thereby, they depict hipness as a cultural category steeped in racial and sexist stereotypes. They also illustrate that women (of all ethnicities, sexualities, etc.) are not "insignificant" for hipness, but in fact perfectly embody it, because "[in] gender as in race, hip thrives in the hybrid, the hyphen. It requires the enlightenment of a second voice: the female within the male, the black within the white, or vice versa. In a society that has devalued women and blacks, hip embraces the feminine and the African" (Leland 257). Not only are these artists claiming their space within the hipster discourse, but by emphasizing the valuable potential for socio-critical performances from different viewpoints, they are also normalizing and fostering plurality among hipsters.

Works Cited

Banet-Weiser, Sarah, Rosalind Gill, and Catherine Rottenberg. "Postfeminism, Popular Feminism and Neoliberal Feminism? Sarah Banet-Weiser, Rosalind Gill, and Catherine Rottenberg in Conversation." *Feminist Theory*, vol. 21, no. 1, 2020, pp. 3–24. *Sage Journals*, doi:10.1177/1464700119842555. Accessed September 28, 2020.

[19]Again, unless indicated otherwise, I am using this term to refer to female hipsters of all ethnicities.

Bannister, Matthew. "'Loaded': Indie Guitar Rock, Canonism, White Masculinities." *Popular Music*, vol. 25, no. 1, 2006, pp. 77–95. *Jstor*, doi:10.1017/S026114300500070X. Accessed September 28, 2020.

Baudelaire, Charles. "The Painter of Modern Life." *The Painter of Modern Life and Other Essays*, translated and edited by Jonathan Mayne. Phaidon Press, 1964, pp. 1–40.

Bayton, Mavis. "Out on the Margins: Feminism and the Study of Popular Music." *Women: A Cultural Review*, vol. 3, no. 1, 1992, pp. 51–9.

Blanning, Lisa. "EB Cover Star Karen O Reflects on the Yeah Yeah Yeahs." *Electronic Beats*, February 25, 2015, www.electronicbeats.net/eb-cover-star-karen-o-reflects-on-the-yeah-yeah-yeahs/. Accessed September 28, 2020.

Broyard, Anatole. "A Portrait of the Hipster." *Partisan Review*, vol. 15, no. 6, 1948, pp. 721–7.

Clayton, Jace. "Vampires of Lima." *What Was the Hipster? A Sociological Investigation*, edited by Mark Greif, Kathleen Ross, and Dayna Tortorici. n+1 Foundation, 2010, pp. 24–30.

Collins, Patricia Hill. *Black Feminist Thought: Knowledge, Consciousness, and the Politics of Empowerment*. 2nd ed. Routledge, 2009.

Dery, Mark. "Black to the Future: Interviews with Samuel R. Delany, Greg Tate, and Tricia Rose." *Flame Wars: The Discourse of Cyberculture*, edited by Mark Dery. Duke University Press, 1994, pp. 179–222.

Deusner, Stephen M. "Karen O: *Crush Songs*." *Pitchfork*, September 10, 2014, www.pitchfork.com/reviews/albums/19794-karen-o-crush-songs/. Accessed September 28, 2020.

Dickel, Simon. "Between Mumblecore and Post-Black Aesthetics: Barry Jenkins's *Medicine for Melancholy*." *Understanding Blackness Through Performance: Contemporary Arts and the Representation of Identity*, edited by Anne Crémieux, Xavier Lemoine, and Jean-Paul Rocchi. Palgrave Macmillan, 2013, pp. 109–24.

Du Bois, W. E. B. "The Souls of Black Folk." 1903. *The Souls of Black Folks: Authoritative Text, Contexts, Criticism*, edited by Henry Louis Gates Jr., and Terri Hume Oliver. Norton, 1999, pp. 1–164.

Euse, Erica. "The Defiant Sound of Asian American Women in Indie Rock." *Vice*, June 29, 2017, www.vice.com/en/article/qv4yqq/the-defiant-sound-of-asian-american-women-in-indie-rock. Accessed December 7, 2020.

Evans, Elizabeth. *The Politics of Third Wave Feminisms: Neoliberalism, Intersectionality, and the State in Britain and the US*. Palgrave Macmillan, 2015.

Evans, Patrice. "Hip-Hop and Hipsterism: Notes on a Philosophy of Us and Them." *What Was the Hipster? A Sociological Investigation*, edited by Mark Greif, Kathleen Ross, and Dayna Tortorici. n+1 Foundation, 2010, pp. 103–111.

Ford, Phil. *Dig: Sound and Music in Hip Culture*. Oxford University Press, 2013.

Goodman, Lizzy. *Meet Me in the Bathroom: Rebirth and Rock and Roll in New York City 2001–2011*. HarperCollins, 2017.

Greif, Mark. "Positions." *What Was the Hipster? A Sociological Investigation*, edited by Mark Greif, Kathleen Ross, and Dayna Tortorici. n+1 Foundation, 2010, pp. 4–13.

Greif, Mark. "What Was the Hipster?" 2010. *Against Everything*. Vintage, 2017, pp. 211–21.

Greif, Mark, Kathleen Ross, and Dayna Tortorici, eds. *What Was the Hipster? A Sociological Investigation*. n+1 Foundation, 2010.

Grigoriadis, Vanessa. "The Edge of Hip: Vice, the Brand." *New York Times*, September 28, 2003, www.nytimes.com/2003/09/28/style/the-edge-of-hip-vice-the-brand.html. Accessed September 28, 2020.

hooks, bell. "Choosing the Margin as a Space of Radical Openness." *Yearning: Race, Gender, and Cultural Politics*. South End Press, 1990, pp. 145–53.

hooks, bell. "Straightening Our Hair." *Tenderheaded: A Comb-Bending Collection of Hair Stories*, edited by Juliette Harris and Pamela Johnson. Pocket Books, 2001, pp. 111–16.

Houk, Deborah. "Self Construction and Sexual Identity in Nineteenth-Century French Dandyism." *French Forum*, vol. 22, no. 1, 1997, pp. 59–73. *Jstor*, www.jstor.org/stable/40540408. Accessed September 28, 2020.

Jackson, Michael. "Billie Jean (Official Video)." *YouTube*, uploaded by Michael Jackson, October 2, 2009, www.youtube.com/watch?v=Zi_XLOBDo_Y. Accessed September 28, 2020.

Jackson, Michael. "Thriller (Official Video)." *YouTube*, uploaded by Michael Jackson, October 2, 2009, www.youtube.com/watch?v=sOnqjkJTMaA. Accessed September 28, 2020.

"Janelle Monáe Defines Her Power in Variety's Power of Women." *YouTube*, uploaded by Variety, June 9, 2020, www.youtube.com/watch?v=6zEdAix_7zQ. Accessed December 8, 2020.

Jonze, Tim. "Yeah Yeah Yeahs: They Wear It Well." Guardian, April 13, 2013, https://www.theguardian.com/music/2013/apr/13/yeah-yeah-yeahs-mosquito-interview. Accessed April 1, 2021.

Karen O. *Crush Songs*. Cult Records, 2014.

Lang, Cady. "8 Things to Know about Solange's Super Secret Guggenheim Performance." *Time*, May 19, 2017, time.com/4786319/solange-guggenheim-performance/. Accessed September 28, 2020.

Leland, John. *Hip: The History*. Harper Perennial, 2005.

Mailer, Norman. "The White Negro: Superficial Reflections on the Hipster." 1957, *Advertisements for Myself*. Penguin, 2018, pp. 343–66.

Maly, Ico, and Piia Varis. "The 21st-Century Hipster: On Micro-Populations in Times of Superdiversity." *European Journal of Cultural Studies*, vol. 19, no. 6, 2016, pp. 637–53. *Sage Journals*, doi:10.1177/1367549415597920. Accessed September 28, 2020.

McRobbie, Angela. "Post-Feminism and Popular Culture." *Feminist Media Studies*, vol. 4, no. 3, 2004, pp. 255–64. Rpt. in *Popular Culture*, vol. 2, edited by Michael Pickering. Sage, 2010, pp. 385–96.

Mercer, Kobena. "Black Hair/Style Politics." *Welcome to the Jungle: New Positions in Black Cultural Studies*. Routledge, 1994, pp. 97–128.

Metropolis [Deluxe Edition]. 1927. Directed by Fritz Lang, performances by Brigitte Helm, Alfred Abel, and Gustav Fröhlich, Leonine, 2018.

Monáe, Janelle. *The Archandroid*. Bad Boy/Wondaland, 2010.

Monáe, Janelle. *Dirty Computer*. Bad Boy/Wondaland, 2018.

Monáe, Janelle. *The Electric Lady*. Bad Boy/Wondaland, 2013.

Monáe, Janelle. "Make Me Feel [Official Music Video]." *YouTube*, uploaded by Janelle Monáe, February 22, 2018, www.youtube.com/watch?v=tGRzz0oqgUE. Accessed December 8, 2020.

Monáe, Janelle. *Metropolis: The Chase Suite*. Bad Boy/Wondaland, 2008.

Monáe, Janelle, feat. Erykah Badu. "Q.U.E.E.N." *The Electric Lady*. Bad Boy/ Wondaland, 2013.

Nelson, Alondra. "Introduction: Future Texts." *Social Text*, vol. 20, no. 2, 2002, pp. 1–15.

Olopade, Dayo. "The Rise of the Black Hipster." *The Root*, May 19, 2009, www.theroot.com/the-rise-of-the-black-hipster-1790869385. Accessed September 28, 2020.

Phillips, Lior. "Karen O Explains the Catharsis and Melodrama in Her New Music." *Dazed*, February 20, 2018, www.dazeddigital.com/music/article/39115/1/karen-o-yo-my-saint-kenzo-interview. Accessed September 28, 2020.

Pilcher, Jane, and Imelda Whelehan. *Key Concepts in Gender Studies*. 2nd ed. Sage, 2017.

Pressler, Jessica. "Truly Indie Fans." *New York Times*, January 28, 2007, www.nytimes.com/2007/01/28/fashion/28Blipsters.html. Accessed September 28, 2020.

Rademacher, Mark A., and Casey R. Kelly. "Constructing Lumbersexuality: Marketing an Emergent Masculine Taste Regime." *Journal of Communication Inquiry*, vol. 43, no. 1, 2019, pp. 25–46. *Sage Journals*, doi:10.1177/0196859918796169. Accessed September 28, 2020.

Rosen, Christopher. "Solange Knowles A Seat at the Table Videos Released." *Entertainment Weekly*, October 2, 2016, www.ew.com/article/2016/10/02/solange-knowles-seat-table-videos-released/. Accessed September 28, 2020.

Ryzik, Melena. "Karen O Goes Solo with 'Crush Songs.' " *New York Times*, August 29, 2014, www.nytimes.com/2014/08/31/arts/music/karen-o-goes-solo-with-crush-songs.html. Accessed September 28, 2020.

Schiermer, Bjørn. "Late-Modern Hipsters: New Tendencies in Popular Culture." *Acta Sociologica*, vol. 57, no. 2, 2014, pp. 167–81. *Jstor*, doi:10.1177/0001699313498263. Accessed September 28, 2020.

Simpson, Spencer. "A Blipster Manifesto." *Daily Californian*, April 1, 2016, www.dailycal.org/2016/04/01/a-blipster-manifesto/. Accessed September 28, 2020.

Solange. "Don't Touch My Hair ft. Sampha (Official Music Video)." *YouTube*, uploaded by solangeknowlesmusic, October 2, 2016, www.youtube.com/watch?v=YTtrnDbOQAU. Accessed September 28, 2020.

Solange. *A Seat at the Table*. Saint Records/Columbia, 2016.

Spanos, Brittany. "Janelle Monáe Frees Herself." *Rolling Stone*, May 17–30, 2018, pp. 34–9.

Thompson, Robert Farris. "An Aesthetic of the Cool." *African Arts*, vol. 7, no. 1, 1973, pp. 40–3, 64–7, 89–91. *Jstor*, www.jstor.org/stable/3334749. Accessed September 28, 2020.

Thornton, Sarah. *Club Cultures: Music, Media and Subcultural Capital*. Polity Press, 2003.

Tortorici, Dayna. "You Know It When You See It." *What Was the Hipster? A Sociological Investigation*, edited by Mark Greif, Kathleen Ross, and Dayna Tortorici. n+1 Foundation, 2010, pp. 122–35.

Wilson, Jamia. "Turning the Tables." *BUST*, bust.com/feminism/192922-solange-knowles-digs-deep-and-opens-up-about-life-as-a-woman.html. Accessed December 28, 2020.

Yeah Yeah Yeahs. *Fever to Tell*. Interscope, 2003.

Yeah Yeah Yeahs. "Heads Will Roll." *YouTube*, uploaded by yeahyeahyeahsmusic, November 24, 2009, www.youtube.com/watch?v=auzfTPp4moA. Accessed September 28, 2020.

Yeah Yeah Yeahs. "Rich." *YouTube*, uploaded by Patty Lee, June 24, 2010, www.youtube.com/watch?v=aP3LA5O3kfc. Accessed September 28, 2020.

15

Art Hipsters: Postmodern Proclamations

Wes Hill

The hipster invites analysis across many different fields of research, spanning issues of race, class, gender, gentrification, consumerism, globalization, irony, subcultures, and the political Left. Despite this promiscuity, the trope is primarily an aesthetic one, functioning, by and large, as an embodiment of discerning yet defective taste. As an aesthetic trope, the hipster has close affiliations with visual art, amalgamating a range of nineteenth- and early twentieth-century "sensitive-to-beauty" archetypes. Specifically, the hipster distorts the Western avant-gardist legacy of flâneurs, aesthetes, connoisseurs, and dandies by transplanting them to the sphere of post-Warholian practice, within the ever-shifting parameters of neoliberal global capitalism.

Of course, "art hipsters" might want what hipsters everywhere want: to not be identified as hipsters. Therefore, to name a hipster is to enter into its rhetorical displays of perspicacious appearance. This is essentially what Rob Horning calls the hipster's "taint," whereby "if you are concerned enough about the [hipster] phenomenon to analyze it and discuss it, you are already somewhere on the continuum of hipster and are in the process of trying to rid yourself of [it]" (80). In contemporary art, which notoriously waivers between "hip" and "politically progressive" signaling, the story of hipsters is the story of visually literate creatives who do not think of themselves as hipsters until being named as such by someone assumed to be even more visually literate than them. This one-upmanship is key to understanding the hipster; a circular dispute about critical complexity performed through overdeterminations of aesthetic taste.

Since reaching its zenith point sometime in the late 2000s, hipsters have, of course, been synonymous with artisanal cultural identities. They are known in most places of the capitalist world as the arty cool-hunters whose actions spoil what for others counts as real, resistant, alternative, or distinctive forms of cultural expression. However, for Slavoj Žižek, if we look beyond their specific traits, "hipster," as an utterance and an accusation, functions self-protectively for those who use it, at a time when the burden of identity (the extrapolation of every social media comment, look and like) is acutely felt around the world, spreading entitlement paranoia to almost anyone well-off enough to take such issues seriously.

Žižek thinks we must not disregard the fact that hipsters are largely external, rather than first-person, identifications, whose naming is "an act of individual and group projection" ("L'etat d'hipster" 3). Freud himself refers to this phenomenon as the "narcissism of minor differences," describing, in *Civilization and Its Discontents* (1930), how cultures (and, by implication, individuals) with only a few differences between them, or that share adjoining territories, are more combative and hateful than those that have little in common (61). In Freud's evolutionary-psychological framework, narcissistic conflicts provide "convenient and relatively harmless" (63) forms of satisfaction, appeasing the aggressive tendencies of group identity, or, as Homi Bhabha points out, expressing the "ambivalent identifications of love and hate" constitutive of all communities (149). As Freud writes, "[i]t is always possible to band together a considerable number of people in love, so long as there are other people left over to receive the manifestations of their aggressiveness" (65).

As an accusation, "hipster" is this narcissistic grievance. It is a way for assumed non-hipsters to symptomatically act out their own critical and creative authenticities against the threat of duplication; against other supposedly unique and discerning individuals who look and think too much like the person we do not want to be. This is very different from the definition provided by Mark Greif in *What Was the Hipster?* (2010), who claims that the hipster "aligns himself both with rebel subculture and with the dominant class, and opens up a poisonous conduit between the two" (9). As the object of an accusation, hipsters do not "align" themselves, let alone with a mainstream. Rather, they are put there by discriminating subjects, whose "symbolic and pseudo-ejaculatory utterance[s]" identify (after Freud, in a "convenient and relatively harmless" way) (64) those considered a "danger to the 'scene' and the autonomous self" (Žižek, "L'etat d'hipster" 3).

Greif confuses the hipster as victim and protagonist because its contours are "very specific," compelling us to look beyond its operative role as an accusation and to instead analyze the particular characteristics with which it is associated (8). But, as Daniel Rosenblatt puts it, the hipster is "at once fact and figure: it is an accusation people make about each other and a youth subculture that came into existence at the end of the 1990s" (617).

Rather than attempting to define what, say, a "contemporary art hipster" might look like (requiring the categorizing of all manner of identity-politics significations in the art world, unscrambling their moral fortitude from their virtue signaling), it is more to the point that we should examine the ideological scenes in which hipsterism is weaponized. If the hipster is an intrusion on an in-the-know art scene, what is it about the values of such a scene that he or she does not fit?

The Waning of the Avant-Garde

In contemporary art, the exemplary scene of the hipster is rooted in the critical legacy of "advanced" art forms, entailing the critic who thinks they can out-discern the discerning across all manner of not-for-profit, commercial, and museum sectors. Of course, in art, as opposed to, say, music, fashion, or film, this ideological setting has been fundamentally shaped by the legacy of the avant-garde, especially the avant-garde as mutated through the postmodern lens of the neo-avant-garde. Wherever an avant-garde has gone dominant, wherever a marginality meets its market, the critical mechanisms of hipsterism are rarely too far away.

In a 2003 issue of the US magazine *Artforum* which looked back at the 1980s, the installation artist Mark Dion remembered the decade as a time when there was a "profound sense that the avant-garde was finally dead" (192). For the previous generation of seventies artists, "ideas like 'who did what first' were still important. Who could give a damn today? Nothing feels more irrelevant" (192). Although Dion portrays this newfound distance in positive terms, the death of the avant-garde at the hands of postmodern cultural pluralism proved to be exceptionally problematic, particularly for critics and art writers in America. The redefining of the avant-garde under an emergent postmodern discourse led to impassioned debates about the constitution of "critical" and "complicit" art. For those heavily invested in being able to name and define "advanced" forms of art—those motivated by non-conformity, political ideals, innovation, or the reconstitution of avant-garde disruption—this supposed peak of cultural pluralism was something to resist, something that may actually have ushered in new levels of ambiguity and conformism. Through the concept of the neo-avant-garde, an eighties art world debated what counted as consensus on "advanced," "progressive," "resistant" or even "interesting" art when the very notion of a historical standpoint was itself regularly cast in doubt.

Here, a connection can be made between the cultural pluralism of postmodern art and the pervasiveness of hipster hate some thirty years later: as a liberation from "advanced" culture that culminates in mass paranoia. In other words, the freedom that comes from there being no such thing as someone who is "late" to a scene gives rise to the fear that this once discernible scene will be detrimentally changed forever if it is opened up to all manner of weak human values, to the general indiscriminations of the viewing public. In this scenario, the capacity to name the contours of a scene is the capacity to be perceived as perpetuating the conceits and convictions of a now outmoded elite avant-garde minority. The result is what we might call "the paranoia of perspicaciousness."

On the surface, the hipster trope looks relatively straightforward, largely revolving around the art-critical values of postmodernism: white, left-wing males who argue with each other over who is more entrenched in the superficial registers of society and the market. But, scratch this surface and the hipster can take on the function of a master-signifier, authorizing and reproducing a range of very specific worldviews abstractly. To this end, the hipster stands for almost any neo-avant-garde figure whose fashionable mask the critic sees fit to expose, spanning different genders, cultural backgrounds, urban, and regional settings, and entrepreneurs and luddites alike.

Peter Bürger, in *Theory of the Avant-Garde* (written in German in 1974 and translated into English a decade later), was the first to differentiate an early- to mid-twentieth-century "historical avant-garde" from a postwar "neo-avant-garde." Exemplified by dada and surrealism, the historical avant-garde's project, in breaking with the "historical succession of techniques and styles," was to attack art as an institution "such as it has developed in bourgeois society" (63). Avant-garde artists rejected stylistic and technical compliance for more general tactics of shock and defamiliarization, transforming art into "a simultaneity of the radically disparate" (63). However, Bürger tells of the failure of the avant-gardes to reintegrate art into the praxis of life, further claiming that "art as an institution neutralizes the political content of the individual work" (90). With the institutionalization of the avant-garde (the commencement of a neo-avant-garde), once-radical artistic strategies (such as montage) are rendered futile in criticizing cultural conventions. According to Bürger, this zombie form of the avant-garde is exemplified by artists such as Andy Warhol, who, allured by "the new" rather than by dialectical shock, manifested an art of anything goes, an art "void of sense and that permits the positing of any meaning whatever" (61).

Bürger ultimately surveyed the purportedly radical, progressive, and "hip" art practices of the 1950s and 1960s and found them to be institutionally endorsed, politically contained, and historically predictable. His polemical framing of the avant-garde's legacy, as either resistant or permissive, anticipated the vocabulary of much postmodern art discourse to come, involving theorists, critics, and art historians questioning whether, or to what degree, an artist's supposed selling out—their claim to institutional and/or market authority—invalidated the progressive resonance of their work.

The avant-garde obviously played a fundamental role in the history of modernism, disturbing any sense of continuity through its radical surges, retrievals and repressions. How to interpret this; how to locate Charles

Baudelaire's "eternal and immutable" (23) elements of culture in the midst of these radical disruptions became a serious consideration in Western art, especially after World War II. Doubts about the stability and effectiveness of Enlightenment doctrines of equality, liberty, faith in human intelligence, and universal reason led to twentieth-century conceptions of the self that internalized the avant-garde's radical disposition. Hand in hand with the development of structuralist and post-structuralist discourse was a belief that the self could be remade in the most radical of ways, incompatible with the moral basis of a purposive, rational way of life. After Michel Foucault's impact, a new politics of identity in the seventies conceived of theoretical formulations not as truth statements but as "practices" that could be analyzed through the fields of institutionalized power and the systems of legitimation that form and regulate subjectivity. As Nigel Blake points out, an important principle of this shift from modern to postmodern identity is the rejection of the idea of the transcendental self: a loss of faith in "the sovereign subject of knowledge and of rights, in whose terms the differences of a plural society could be conceived as 'mere contingencies,' and as such secondary and negotiable" (58).

In the blurring of essential and contingent realities in postmodern discourse, the separation of mass culture on the one hand and advanced culture on the other (the latter supposedly informed by rigorous, diagnostic assessments of history) appeared unsustainable, especially in art. This shift was ushered in by a swelling cultural class (the fading of bohemian marginalization), the decline of a distinct bourgeois culture (no longer providing the avant-garde with an adversary), increased institutional representations of "alternative" cultural interests, and the lucidity of sociological studies such as Pierre Bourdieu's, which argued that modern art was underwritten by elitism; its institutions were politically contrived and the aesthetic attitude of disinterestedness covertly expressed a class ethos.

Writing on the state of the art museum in 1984, Bourdieu asserts,

> Everything in these civic temples, ... in these holy places of art, in which the chosen few come to nurture a faith of virtuosi while conformists and bogus devotees come and perform a class ritual, ... everything combines to indicate that the world of art is as contrary to the world of everyday life as the sacred is to the profane. (236)

The constitutions of pure, advanced, and adversary gazes in art, Bourdieu argued, were the outcome of deliberate institutional manipulations—the galleries, museums and professional bodies that support and persuade viewers about art's supposedly higher levels of meaning. Bourdieu and Bürger thought that because art objects, like all valuable creations, get separated from the contexts in which they are created, this separation has important consequences for how they are appreciated. After Warhol's emergence in particular, the post-sixties period was a time when the art world needed to confront how they could still lay claim to "advanced" or even "hip" status when art's once-discrete institutional structures of legitimization were regularly being challenged.

Pastiche Postmodernism and a Resistant Neo-Avant-Garde

The American art historian Hal Foster, in his introduction to *The Anti-Aesthetic* (1983)—a collection of writings on the then-emergent theme of postmodern art—referenced Bürger's earlier publication to reflect on the dwindling of avant-garde resistance in the 1980s and the impact of what would later be called the US "culture wars." The legacy of the avant-garde, which fused artistic expression with social change, was, according to Foster, confronted in America by neoconservative attempts to sever the cultural from the social: by those who welcomed the "process of societal modernization on the one hand" but lamented its "cultural development" on the other (7). This was exemplified by Republican supporters of then President Ronald Reagan who, citing the deleterious cultural effects of societal modernization, strove to reclaim "lost" traditional values, particularly those entwined with religious faith. Foster opposed such conservative trends, taking aim at their manifestation in the art world by denouncing aesthetics itself—as a paradigm that privileges painting and presence at the expense of politics.

Against the aesthetic, Foster named as "anti-aesthetic" those cross-disciplinary post-conceptual artists who produce "cultural forms engaged in a politic" (xv). As well as targeting the neoconservative right-wing Republican voice in American society, the nomination of a resistant, post-structuralist strain of eighties art also sought to ameliorate the effects of neoconservatism internal to the art world. Foster challenged artists who, representing a "false normativity," rejected the oppositional tendencies of the prior decade and instead sought traction in the expanding commercial art market, where pastiche became a "ubiquitous mode" (xiv).

The neoliberal hipster *avant la lettre* can be glimpsed here in Foster's portrayal of the pastiche postmodern painter who collects and rearranges elements blankly. Pastiche art resembled the practice of fashion, taking from the past in order to emulate it as style, albeit with different, seemingly incidental, implications. Following Fredric Jameson, who contributed to *The Anti-Aesthetic*, Foster defines pastiche as a parody of existing styles performed in a postmodern context where no common ground can be assumed. For Jameson, pastiche was "blank parody ... without that still latent feeling that there exists something normal compared to which what is being imitated is rather comic" (114). Characterizing the split between neo-expressionism and post-conceptualist art as a battle between "complicit" and "resistant" forms of cultural postmodernism, pastiche attested to a new neoconservatism, where artists exploited cultural codes and concealed their political affiliations, rather than questioning and critically examining them. Calling pastiche a "pseudo-historical" form (xii), Foster argued that so much art in this period failed to meaningfully engage with history. Pastiche exemplified a postmodern society "awash in a sea of private languages," one "recalled to times less problematic than our own" (xiv).

In a subsequent publication, *Recodings* (1985), Foster continued to rail against the easy embrace of quotation-oriented postmodern art, warning of its ahistorical underpinnings. He states,

> This "return to history" is ahistorical for three reasons: the context of history is disregarded, its continuum is disavowed, and conflictual forms of art and modes of production are falsely resolved in pastiche. Neither the specificity of the past nor the necessity of the present is heeded. Such a disregard makes the return to history also seem to be a liberation from history. (16)

The work of the American artist Julian Schnabel epitomized pastiche's exhausted and empty iconography, combining recycled historical motifs with slap-dash, regurgitated modernist expressive brushstrokes. According to Foster, these "mucho painterly confections" promulgated "art that is made popular by clichés," coming off as "historical to the naive and campy to the hip" (28). Schnabel's neo-expressionism achieved significant commercial success at a time when critics such as Douglas Crimp (Foster's colleague at the academic art journal *October*, and a prominent supporter of post-conceptual "Pictures" artists) were declaring the end of painting. Neo-expressionism contrasted with the largely photographic- and sign-based art of Sherrie Levine and Cindy Sherman, who exposed clichés in a manner fit to be compared with post-structuralist deconstruction, of which Roland Barthes and Jacques Derrida were exemplars (166).

The extreme exaggerations of neo-expressionism—in Schnabel's work but also in works by artists such as Sandro Chia and Anselm Kiefer—pointed to a loss of faith in style itself. This is comparable to the first wave of punk's use of anti-establishment and nihilistic iconography (Nazi symbols and associated paraphernalia) which served to distance such fashionable stances from any prevalent, hegemonic, "received" codes of meaning, in spite of being historical sources themselves. As a mode of postmodern iconoclasm, pastiche in art succumbed to, rather than reflected on, the fluid and unstable nature of meaning itself. In painting, pastiche untethered the medium from authenticity as if absorbed in the simulacra, conforming to Jean Baudrillard's 1976 diagnosis of the "loss of referentials" (130). Like a form of retro bricolage, pastiche fetishized history, employing it for aesthetic value—or, even worse, to denote contrarian anti-value, emblematic of the postmodern artist's desire to say nothing, loudly, by reducing historical references to market strategy. For critics like Foster who saw the need to leverage critical and historical engagement, to aestheticize in this way was to produce a naïve and apolitical form of iconoclasm. In *Recodings*, he states, "To see other periods as mirrors of our own is to turn history into narcissism; to see other styles as open to our own is to turn history into a dream. But such is the dream of the pluralist: he seems to sleepwalk in the museum" (17). As "an auratic disguise for the commodity," pastiche's pseudo-historical gesture became "an avant-gardist alibi for turning the historical into a consumable" (*Recodings* 227).

Craig Owens, another editor of *October*, similarly assisted this polemic in US art criticism between resistant ("anti-aesthetic") and complicit ("aesthetic pleasure as false consciousness") modes of historical representation. In *The Allegorical Impulse: Toward a Theory of Postmodernism* (1980), published in two separate issues of *October*, Owens asserted, in reference to Walter Benjamin, that the most interesting artists in this transitional postmodern period adopted a fragmentary allegorical aesthetic. With the decline of the avant-garde, postmodern art's resistance, for Owens, came in the form of artists who portrayed history allegorically, who "doubled" (68) or multiplied the texts within which their subject matter could be read. Although the use of allegory in art did not first emerge under postmodernity, Owens claims that it took a definitive postmodern form when art began allegorizing its own function, when art foregrounded its own textuality as an allegory of its emergence.

Owens highlights the ironic, rhetorical, and ambiguous aspects of allegory in opposition to earlier "symbolic" approaches—against the modernist impulse to provide an "indissoluble unity of form and substance" (81). Whereas to symbolize is to direct and motivate meaning, to allegorize is to position multiple relations of meaning in more unmotivated and arbitrary ways (83). Postmodern allegory follows the logic of the supplement, the act of adding to and obscuring another expression not as a return to an original source but as a pluralist extension of it—a framing of the framing. If the modernists tended to symbolize (commensurate with the assertion of an artwork's presence), postmodernist allegory exploited the gaps between signifiers and signifieds, aiming to simultaneously "proffer and defer a promise of meaning"—to both proliferate and withdraw meaning as a critically conscious act (70).

According to Owens, allegorical postmodern art tends toward openness by conveying its significance in nonlinear, accumulative ways. However, his nominated artists are assumed to achieve this openness self-consciously, making them immune from the same accusations leveled at makers of pastiche art—of being so open to interpretation that their works are devoid of depth. In postmodern allegory, the past is not revisited, emulated, or parodied so much as usurped by a surplus of significance. At the same time, this surplus has a self-conscious "deconstructive thrust" aimed "not only against the contemporary myths that furnish its subject matter, but also against the symbolic, totalizing impulse which characterizes modern art" (Owens 80). To this end, like Foster, Owens affirms allegiances between post-conceptual art and de-disciplinary, deconstructive critical practice, suggesting that, by favoring the mechanically reproduced image over the singularity of the hand-produced painting, allegorical art resists the contemporaneous, largely market-based revivals of aesthetic pleasure, intuitive feeling and originality.

Pluralism with a Critical Gaze

From "empty quotations" to the "framing of the frame," pastiche art and the allegorical impulse represent two significant characterizations of the artist as hipster: one as empty-headed capitalist, the other as pretentious, historically conscious ironist. What these *October* writers were essentially railing against was a newly defined pluralist culture, which had become "an arena not of dialectical dialogue but of vested interests, of licensed sects: in lieu of culture we have cults. The result is an eccentricity that leads, in art as in politics, to a new conformity: pluralism as an institution" (Foster, *Recodings* 15). Here, Foster puts his finger on the "problem" of the hipster, whose pluralism equates to a lack of antagonism, who favors, instead, consumerism, nostalgia, and mainstream recognition.

Proponents of what Foster calls the "art-critical version of postmodernism" ("Postmodernism in Parallax" 4) thought they were witnessing not a gradual collapse of high and low culture so much as the neutralization of art's critical capacity by the spread of capitalist myths and neoconservative values, now filling the recently vacated spaces of the avant-gardes. Foster underlined the impossibility of accounting for the ubiquity of "minor deviations" and "isolated gestures" that pluralist societies, by definition, produce (*Recodings* 31). Like Bürger, the *October* writers portrayed post-sixties art as in danger of losing the "critical edge" it had inherited from the avant-garde. But, unlike Bürger, they employed their at times overwrought hermeneutics to advocate for artists who stood for left-wing progression; whose works represented not the flattening of value but the survival of something they could categorically define as "discerning," "intelligent," or "historically cognizant".

Because pluralism is without criteria of its own, old values in art tend to be revived in its name, "ones necessary to a market based on taste and connoisseurship, such as the unique, the visionary, the genius, the masterpiece" (Foster, *Recodings* 17). However, the impulse to critically counter such old values—to react against nostalgia, market hype, and revivalist myths—may not be so far removed from the impulse that drives the purported non-hipster to exclaim "hipster!" It is concern at the fact that this pluralist state of affairs has reduced criticism to "the homogeneity of local advocacy" (Foster, *Recodings* 31). Ultimately, the leveraging of "critical" over "complicit" art was informed by the reality of an adversarial left-wing art scene being transformed into a massified, hybridized one. Here, the radical left was no longer forced to battle with modernist (Greenbergian) snobs but now with their apparently dim-witted, pro-capitalist peers.

Some artists in the 1980s (Mark Dion being one) would have seen their new neo-avant-garde roles in terms of creating what Boris Groys calls the "new, interesting differences that further drive the condition of pluralism"—a pluralism that the historical avant-garde actually helped to create (114). However, what if the hegemony of multinational capitalism was elevating historical indifference to the status of a false democracy? This was how Foster saw the rise of pastiche, as constituting the "disavowal not only of radical art but also of radicality *through* art" (*Recodings* 30). In warning against empty postmodern openness, a declaratively critical version of postmodernism called for artists to, instead, "reinvent old truths radically" (Foster, *Recodings* 31).

As probably any middle-aged art critic knows, clearly distinguishing between art that reinvents and art that rehearses the past is not easy, often requiring access to the artist's intentions, deduced through exegetical sources. How do we definitively gauge whether an artwork has satirical or sincere intentions behind it? What value should we even put on intention? How do we go about determining whether a work "questions" rather than "exploits" its cultural codes, "explores" rather than "perpetuates" its artistic myths and/or political affiliations? The open-endedness of such questions is antithetical to the concept of the hipster, which, as an accusation, is a distancing device for those who think they can clearly cut through the ambiguities; who know which side of "critical" and "uncritical" their subject sits. In more recent years, Foster has admitted that at times he and his *October* colleagues "inverted the aesthetic and the modernist more than we deconstructed them," continuing, "the rigidity of a modernist notion of medium-specificity did prompt the laxity of a postmodernist medium-hybridity, and often that was simply a banal reversal, a mirror image" (Elkins and Montgomery 32).

Through the neo-avant-garde, postmodern critics perpetuated the notion that there are critical and uncritical ways to portray history in art, internalizing the broader cultural wars to rail against art's new populist frontier. As Michael Newman argues, in the post-conceptual phase of innovative art from the late-seventies to the mid-eighties, successful commodification depended, paradoxically, on artworks conveying a criticality that would distinguish them from mass culture. The critic in this context, who writes in support of an advanced art, "finds him/herself in a contradictory position, since the attribution of criticality may serve to legitimate the work in the market," thereby reducing the "critical" codes of the work to the codes of market differentiation, and the critic to a willing, public-relations-type accomplice (33). "Hipster," as an utterance, obfuscates precisely such a dilemma, obscuring the fact that all opinions in this pluralist "creative industry" context are vulnerable to being read in terms of market advocacy, as one niche competing with another.

Toward a Post-Critical Ethics

At their best, declarations of pluralism in art promise an eclecticism that could potentially give overlooked forms a chance at gaining greater legitimacy, challenging the prejudices of academic, white, male, and leftist-elite gatekeepers. But, at their worst, they represent what Herbert Marcuse, in 1965, called "repressive tolerance" (81). This is an anything-goes relativism generated by the liberal toleration of dissent, which can neutralize undesirable ideas by granting them a specific social space, at a safe distance from mainstream, populist, or consumerist values. Reflecting on the relation between pluralism and ideology, WJT Mitchell notes in a 1982 essay,

> There seems to be some sort of fundamental contradiction involved in even bringing terms like "ideology" and "pluralism" together, for pluralism is so often regarded as a sort of nonposition, beyond ideology, a stance which is regarded as smug self-deception by the ideologue and as a commitment to free inquiry and intellectual liberation by the pluralist. The notion of an "ideology of pluralism" seems self-contradictory, for the ideologue must deny the possibility of pure pluralism, and the pluralist must affirm the possibility of transcending ideology. (613)

In applying this to the hipster, the pejorative subject manifests in the labeling of the arty pluralist by the critical ideologue, who registers the arty pluralist's stance as one of "smug self-deception." But both positions—the hipster and their accuser—are ideological. Žižek has argued that whenever some procedure is denounced as ideological, its inversion should never be equated with ideological neutrality. He states,

> "Ideology" can designate anything from a contemplative attitude that misrecognizes its dependence on social reality to an action-orientated set of beliefs, from the indispensable medium in which individuals live out their relations to a social structure to false ideas which legitimate a dominant political power. It [ideology] seems to pop up precisely when we attempt to avoid it, while it fails to appear where one would clearly expect it to dwell (Žižek, *Mapping Ideology* 4).

As passive embodiments of pretentious ideology, hipsters typically represent non-antagonistic, non-hegemonic fragmentations of the social, where absolute difference is foregrounded over more relational identities. Meanwhile, their hipster-accusers are more outwardly antagonistic, pointing out their subject's failings in the name of critique and taking enormous pleasure from doing so.

This pleasurable discursive drive of hipster hate echoes what Jacques Lacan calls the "sinthome": an irreducible *jouissance* in which enjoyment is bound to a certain signifying formation, assuring a level of consistency to one's being in the world (*The Seminar* 5). The fundamental incurability of the symptom—our inability to truly demystify every effect so as to name and overcome every cause—is connected by Lacan to this drive, derived from the ancient word for "symptom" and a Joycean pun on both "saint homme" (holy man) and "Saint Thomas" (Doubting Thom, or "the one who probes the Real Thing with his Finger" (Watts 223)). Following the logic of "nothing says 'hipster' like a sign that says 'no hipsters,'" when threatened by our uncritical, superficial doubling, we (the critically conscious aesthetes) deploy the master-signifier "hipster" as if probing the Real. Our oppositional discourse takes pleasure in itself, acting out a kind of ideological immunity at the core of our identity, a fantasmatic exception to the pluralist terrain of taste. Examined in one of Lacan's last seminars, the *sinthome* is the fourth, interlocking ring of his Borromean knot that keeps the knot of the Real, the Symbolic and the Imaginary from breaking, manifesting when what I unconsciously require, through my signifying activity, is the preserving of a unique sense of me (Lacan 77).

Pondering the "me/not me" defense integral to the concept of the hipster, Rob Horning questions whether the twenty-first-century hipster should be understood as an embodiment of postmodernism as "a spent force, revealing what happens when pastiche and irony exhaust themselves as aesthetics" (83–4). In response, we can say that it is the very nomination of a "spent force" that is also exhausted—the impotence of historical end points, the impotence of treating cultural expressions as symptoms waiting to be cured.

"Hipster," as a remnant of postmodern criticality, extends the neo-avant-garde tendency to portray critically inferior peers as contrary, superficial, and excessive narcissists. Signed and cosigned by the likes of Jean-François Lyotard and Fredric Jameson, postmodern discourse was supposed to be able to reveal the image's supplanting of reality and, paradoxically, the impossibility of telling true and timeless stories about society. In other words, postmodernism stands for the "confused multiplicity of historical experience" which is brought to our attention by the theorist's singular and authentic act of nomination (Žižek, *First as Tragedy* 52). In this way, "postmodern", like "hipster," wishes an order of intelligibility into the confused pluralist scene that constitutes it. Postmodern art criticism portrays a world in which critical perspective can be retained even when accounting for its loss, its dwindling blamed on the fact that cultural pluralism is dysfunctionally pluralistic; there are too many individuals in too many contexts capable of appropriating all manner of words, images, intentions, and forms of lived experience.

This is why "the contemporary" post-postmodern era in art functions primarily as an art-historical placeholder, involving commentators who reflect on what a pluralist "contemporaneity of differences" might look like even as they reject the idea that a world-picture of this scenario could ever do the paradigm any justice (Smith, "Rethinking Modernism" 274). Following the notion that art "can no longer be adequately characterized by terms such as 'modernity' and 'postmodernity'" ("Questionnaire on Contemporary" 48), Terry Smith claims that contemporary currents in art are not symptoms of the conditions of our time, but are, rather, "the actual kinds of art that these conditions have generated", whose "friction in relation to each other is of their essence" (*Contemporary Art* 269). If we look closely, the demystification imperatives of postmodern art criticism are abandoned here in favor of encountering and generating irreconcilable differences, experiencing them as embodiments rather than signs. Smith writes,

> [C]ontemporaneity consists precisely in the acceleration, ubiquity, and constancy of radical disjunctures of perception, of mismatching ways of seeing and valuing the same world, in the actual coincidence of asynchronous temporalities, in the jostling contingency of various cultural and social multiplicities, all thrown together in ways that highlight the fast-growing inequalities within and between them. ("Contemporary Art and Contemporaneity" 703)

The art worlds of the twenty-first century still grapple with how to represent a pluralism that is both liberating and "antagonistic," in Ernesto Laclau and Chantal Mouffe's sense of the term, for whom democratic societies are those in which relations of conflict are sustained, not erased (*Hegemony* 125). This model of antagonistic pluralism rejects "any kind of essentialism—either of the totality or of the elements—and affirms that neither the totality nor the fragments possess any kind of fixed identity, prior to the contingent and pragmatic form of their articulation" (Mouffe, *The Return* 7).

The late Nigerian curator Okwui Enwezor's curatorially driven notion of the "postcolonial constellation" of twenty-first-century art is derived, in part, from Mouffe and Laclau's work. He supported a radicalized understanding of democracy that tried to counter Fukuyama-style triumphalism by being "a fundamentally unrealizable project," one that constantly challenges distinctions between local and cosmopolitan culture and the points at which colonialist, nationalist, and creole histories are blurred (Enwezor, "The Black Box" 51). Enwezor defines the permanent transitional state of contemporary art's postcolonial constellation "as a set of arrangements of deeply entangled relations and forces that are founded by discourses of power" ("The Postcolonial Constellation" 58). Postcolonial art theory, particularly since the early 2000s, has adopted curatorial and practice-based models over postmodernism's emphasis on (critical) diagnostics. The twenty-first-century state of art is conceived by Enwezor not in terms of postmodernism but as a modernist laboratory that never ends, a paradigm that may be constantly reinvented and de-Westernized rather than overcome: as having "many streams that do not all empty into the same basin," and as underlining "the utter disability of the one true judgment of art" ("The Postcolonial Constellation" 68).

Conclusion

Whereas debate about the neo-avant-gardes and their counterparts stemmed from a crisis of critical perspective in the 1980s, ethical considerations of marginalized voices dominate art criticism and art-historical writing today, especially over the last decade. The shortage of authoritatively critical voices in contemporary art is justified by these moral gains. Ethical attentiveness augments the historical uncertainties of global art. This shift has turned neo-avant-garde debates about "post-conceptual" versus "neo-expressionist" aesthetics into dated, provincialist affairs, more reflective of Freud's "narcissism of minor differences" than a genuine attempt to address globalization's altering of the temporal and spatial distances that once definitively separated cultures and practices.

Art in the contemporary era is constituted by the specific rather than the general encounter. The inability to identify and defend a paradigmatic "contemporary scene" goes hand in hand with the idea that anything one can do to multiply and diversify the voices surmising art's many pasts and futures is a good thing. Although every individual has their own contemporaneity, again, according to Terry Smith, "at any given time and place there will be a limited number of contemporalities in play with each other. The ones that make sense are the ones that cluster and shape relationships and move forward and change things, and there are usually only a few of those at any given time and any given place" (qtd. in Williams 385). Therefore, in twenty-first-century art the logic of sociohistorical continuity has diminished along with any stable notion of critical perspective, with Smith rhetorically asking, in paraphrase of Tim Griffin, what happens to "art-critical discourse" when "the critical models of previous eras do not, and cannot, be asked to function as they once did?" (Smith, *Contemporary Art* 49). Hipster hate reveals itself as a refutation of this inquiry. Instead, it promotes the productive incapacity of the neo-avant-garde: a neo-avant-garde that services, above all, the progressive identities of those who weaponize critical perspective.

The demise of the liberal citizen-state and the development of the neoliberal consumer-state in its place has seen the property-based logic inherent in liberal democracies converge with the trade in identity as commodity. In *Ethnicity, Inc.*, Jean and John Comaroff have dubbed this phenomenon "the identity industry" (15) echoing Jacques Rancière's (2009) claims, via the concept of the post-political, of how advocates of identity politics foster an *a priori* ethical consensus that sets social groups apart from one another, depoliticizing subjects and protecting neoliberal capitalism and its allied structures from threats of revolt. In this climate, the image of the hipster as a sign of generic individualism looks positively quaint by comparison.

Today one is faced with a new challenge: for art to do more than just provide fuel for the in-fighting of the left: to do more than just will one's critique from a position outside the market, or from some place where it cannot be incorrectly (uncritically) construed. What does the remnant critical-postmodern accusation of "hipster!" tell us about art's oppositional agency today? As a rhetorical mode of one-upmanship that actually weakens one's self-positioning, it might be of little use in light of current demands that we contend with the ethical consequences of our differences.

Works Cited

Baudelaire, Charles. "The Painter of Modern Life." *Modern Art and Modernism*, edited by Francis Frascina and Charles Harrison. Harper & Row, 1987, pp. 23–7.

Baudrillard, Jean. "Symbolic Exchange and Death." *Jean Baudrillard: Selected Writings*. 1976, edited by Mark Poster. Stanford University Press, 1988, pp. 119–48.

Bhabha, Homi K. *The Location of Culture*. Routledge, 1994.

Blake, Nigel. "Between Postmodernism and Anti-Modernism: The Predicament of Educational Studies." *British Journal of Educational Studies*, vol. 44, no. 1, 1996, pp. 42–65.

Bourdieu, Pierre. *The Field of Cultural Production*, edited by R. Johnson. Polity Press, 1993.

Bürger, Peter. *Theory of the Avant-Garde*. 1974, translated by Michael Shaw. University of Minnesota Press, 1984.

Comaroff, Jean, and John Comaroff. *Ethnicity, Inc.* University of Chicago Press, 2009.

Dion, Mark. "80s Again." *Artforum*, April 2003, pp. 192–3.

Elkins, James, and Harper Montgomery. *Beyond the Aesthetic and Anti-Aesthetic*. Penn Press, 2013.

Enwezor, Okwui. "The Black Box." *Documenta 11 Platform 5: Exhibition, Catalogue*. Hatje Cantz, 2002, pp. 42–55.

Enwezor, Okwui. "The Postcolonial Constellation: Contemporary Art in a State of Permanent Transition." *Research in African Literatures*, vol. 34, no. 4, 2003, pp. 57–82.

Foster, Hal. *The Anti-Aesthetic: Essays on Postmodern Culture*. Bay Press, 1983.

Foster, Hal. "Postmodernism in Parallax." *October*, vol. 63, 1993, pp. 3–20.

Foster, Hal. *Recodings: Art, Spectacle, Cultural Politics*. Bay Press, 1985.

Freud, Sigmund. *Civilization and Its Discontents*. 1930. W. W. Norton, 1962.
Greif, Mark. "Positions." *What Was the Hipster? A Sociological Investigation*, edited by Mark Greif, Kathleen Ross, and Dayna Tortorici. n+1 Foundation, 2010, pp. 4–13.
Groys, Boris. *Art Power*. MIT Press, 2008.
Horning, Rob. "The Death of the Hipster." *What Was the Hipster? A Sociological Investigation*, edited by Mark Greif, Kathleen Ross, and Dayna Tortorici. n+1 Foundation, 2010, pp. 78–84.
Jameson, Fredric. "Postmodernism and Consumer Society." *The Anti-Aesthetic: Essays on Postmodern Culture*, edited by Hal Foster. Bay Press, 1983, pp. 111–25.
Lacan, Jacques. *The Seminar of Jacques Lacan Book XXIII: The Sinthome*, edited by Jacques-Alain Miller. Polity Press, 2016.
Laclau, Ernesto, and Chantal Mouffe. *Hegemony and Socialist Strategy*. Verso, 1985.
Marcuse, Herbert. "Repressive Tolerance." *A Critique of Pure Tolerance*. Beacon Press, 1965, pp. 81–118.
Mitchell, W. J. T. "Critical Inquiry and the Ideology of Pluralism." *Critical Inquiry*, vol. 8, no. 4, 1982, pp. 609–18.
Mouffe, Chantal. *The Return of the Political*. Verso, 1993.
Newman, Michael. "The Specificity of Criticism and Its Need for Philosophy." *The State of Art Criticism*, edited by James Elkins. Routledge, 2008, pp. 29–60.
Owens, Craig. "The Allegorical Impulse: Toward a Theory of Postmodernism." *October*, vol. 12, 1980, pp. 67–86.
Rancière, Jacques. "The Aesthetic Dimension: Aesthetics, Politics, Knowledge." *Critical Inquiry*, vol. 36, no. 1, 2009, pp. 1–19.
Rosenblatt, Daniel. "Stuff the Professional-Managerial Class Likes: 'Distinction' for an Egalitarian Elite." *Anthropological Quarterly*, vol. 86, no. 2, 2013, pp. 589–623.
Smith, Terry. "Contemporary Art and Contemporaneity." *Critical Inquiry*, vol. 32, no. 4, 2006, pp. 681–707.
Smith, Terry. "Questionnaire on the Contemporary." *October*, vol. 130, 2009, pp. 3–124.
Smith, Terry. "Rethinking Modernism and Modernity Now." *Filozofski vestnik*, vol. 35, no. 2, 2014, pp. 271–319.
Smith, Terry. *What is Contemporary Art?* University of Chicago Press, 2009.
Watts, Oliver. "Contemporary Indigenous Art, Resistance and Imaging the Processes of Legal Subjection." *International Journal for the Semiotics of Law*, vol. 29, 2016, pp. 213–35.
Williams, Jeffrey. "The Contemporist: An Interview with Terry Smith." *Symploke*, vol. 22, 2014, pp. 381–405.
Žižek, Slavoj. *First as Tragedy Then as Farce*. Verso, 2009.
Žižek, Slavoj. "L'etat d'hipster." *Rhinocerotique*, translated by Henry Brulard, 2009, pp. 3–10.
Žižek, Slavoj. ed. *Mapping Ideology*. Verso, 1994.

16

Hipster Post-Communities and Digital Nostalgia Design

Marek Jeziński and Łukasz Wojtkowski

In this chapter we examine nostalgia as a central element of hipster design in the social media. Our theoretical approach is built up inductively and combines the netnographic observation of hipster digital post-communities with a content analysis of visual data collected from Tumblr, Instagram, Facebook accounts and websites. We define hipsters as a discursive formation that epitomizes the features of a post-community, that is, a community whose identity formation is discursively framed in the process of technology-based media practices and thus is characterized by weak group ties, dynamic identity transformations, and an emphasis on style and aesthetics (Jeziński and Wojtkowski, "Hipsterzy"; Jeziński and Wojtkowski, "Narcyzm hipsterski"). Media practices are directly connected to discourse, which we conceptualize as a form of communicative social practice. Discursive practices are forms of social practices (Bennett 6) and discourse is "a two-way relationship between a particular discursive event and the situation(s), institution(s) and social structure(s), which frame it: the discursive event is shaped by them, but it also shapes them" (Unger, Wodak, and Khosravink 1175). Digital post-communities operate as discursive cultural formations created and sustained mostly through the use of digital media technologies. As such, they cannot be perceived as a coherent, identity-based social or cultural group.

Hipsters, on the one hand, take inspirations from other cultural trends prevailing in digital post-communities, and on the other hand, they themselves have strong trendsetting potential. Hipsterism's strong potential to redefine cultural codes makes it one of the most visible cultural trends of the last decade. Its dynamics, however, cause difficulties in studying hipsterism as a limited set of distinctive elements. Moreover, mediatization and commodification processes have affected both the actual functioning of hipsterism and its studies (Jeziński and Wojtkowski, *Nostalgia Commodified*). We study how specific digital cultures use a certain form of design described as "hipster" as their social practice of nostalgia recirculation in culture. These hipster groups reestablish "traditional" values through nostalgic practices. "Hipster design", for instance, refers to the past by restoring old commodities (e.g., bikes, cameras, cassette-tape recorders, record players, vinyl records, old-fashioned newspapers, books, furniture, musical instruments, ceramic, fashion, mugs, cups, or objects used in everyday routines) and lifestyles perceived as traditional (reverting back to one's roots or back to nature-oriented practices). In the digital media sphere, nostalgia functions as a sphere of cultural commodity of emotions and is manifested in internet blogs, shops, and "memory" sites that are intended to foreground recollections of the past (Jeziński and Wojtkowski, "Hipsterzy").

Post-Communities and Digital Nostalgia

Hipster culture is a post-community especially visible in the digital sphere, which, in turn, determines key features of hipster culture and allows for the manifestation of its constitutive values. Communities of this kind, labeled in sociological theory as post-subcultures, differ significantly from traditionally understood subcultural groups in terms of their actors, collective activities, and cultural manifestations. Dick Hebdige in *Subculture: The Meaning of Style* states that modernist cultural communities were based on their tendencies to differentiate themselves from other subcultures. At the center of their style were originality and the maintenance of signs, and these elements were the factors that distinguished a particular group from other subcultures. As Hebdige wrote in 1979, "[t]he communication of a significant *difference*, then (and the parallel communication of a group *identity*), is the 'point' behind the style of all spectacular subcultures" (102). Traditional subcultures were characterized by quantifiable attributes of their actors' identities, that is, the ones which could be observed, processed, and presented in measurable categories, such as dressing style, culinary taste, artistic preferences (i.e., favorite movies, theatre companies), entertainment, or revealing preferences for particular musicians and bands, including the processes of music reception, namely, listening to records or taking part in concerts and festivals.

With the technological developments that have occurred in Western societies in the first decades of the twenty-first century, the landscape of group cultures, the nature of their activities, and the forms of their activity have also been changing. As David Muggleton puts it,

> for the peculiarity of postmodern time has now and for evermore precluded any possibility of subcultural "originality." The concept of "authenticity" must likewise be expunged from the postmodern vocabulary. The all-encompassing power of the contemporary mass media has ensured that there can no longer be a sanctuary for the original, "pure," creative moment of subcultural innovation that preceded the onset of the contaminating processes of commercialization, commodification and diffusion. (54)

The hybrid and syncretic character of post-subcultural communities is composed of fragmentation, borrowing from other group cultures, or scattering. Their diffusional essence is a derivative of the character of late-modern culture as a whole, with its syncretism, hybridity, and the usage of cultural "ready-made" borrowings. The members of the post-subcultures choose diverse cultural elements that seem convincing and legitimate from their perspective. As we show in the context of hipster social media blogs, visual content forms a specific bricolage posted from and shared with the other members of the respective post-community. Thus, the meaning that particular social media feeds communicate sustains the cultural inner-community cohesion developed by hipsters.

An important aspect of hipster post-subculture is the combination of activities undertaken by the participants in both virtual and real spaces. For the participants the activities in the virtual new media environment have the same quality and value as off-network relationships. Interactions undertaken in the real world are sanctioned by documenting them in a network environment, framing them in form of a digital discursive ritual. This functions in accordance with Edmund Leach's idea of a "communication event" where every communication act has two elements: The first is the actual communication between the "sender," who sends the message and the "receiver," who decodes it (11). The second is an expressive action where the sender chooses and communicates the message and the receiver firstly interprets and then circulates it further (or stops the action). This means that every online communication—in the case of our study, mainly visual—is not only a transmission of information as such, but also an actual symbolic social practice focused on the creation and circulation of important meanings defined by the community as acceptable means by which a particular group is integrated and maintained.

In the case of the hipster post-community we have analyzed, such ritualized communication follows a nostalgia pattern, where the codes known from the past are once again recirculated in a new cultural space, with transformed and recontextualized meanings. We do not claim that all hipster communicative patterns are nostalgic, but our qualitative study indicates their dominance. Moreover, these patterns are not limited to the studied post-community. Due to incorporation/excorporation processes the nostalgia-driven codes are widespread also among other social groups and tend to characterize larger cultural trends. Such trendsetting and discursive potential combined with a commodification of hipsterism make both hipsters and nostalgia constant elements of contemporary culture. Yet to capture how hipster digital nostalgia patterns work, attention needs to be paid to nostalgia discourses as a driving force of hipster post-communities.

Nostalgia in general, as defined by Svetlana Boym, can be understood as "a longing for a place, but actually it is a yearning for a different time—the time of our childhood, the slower rhythms of our dreams. In a broader sense, nostalgia is rebellion against the modern idea of time, the time of history and progress" (Boym, *Future of Nostalgia* 12). This notion, according to Bryan S. Turner, is based on a hankering for bygone times, both in individual and group experience, seeking for straight and authentic social relations with trustworthy people, in a contemporary context of perceived diminishing and weakening emotional bonds and in light of the present social position of an individual. Thus, nostalgia implies that people glorify the past as the root of positive experiences, spontaneous behavior, natural activities, and simple attitudes toward life. As summed up by Elizabeth Guffey, "obviously the past is simpler and less painful than the present. It has been lived through. In a world with very few standards left, the past offers those standards whether you live by them or not" (122). In the context of the hipster post-community, the constant reference to the past functions to construct particular notions of cultural authenticity. This is based on the assumption that in bygone times everything was better, tasted differently, life as such was slower and people could be trusted. Since the past was "a better and a safer place," the orientation toward tradition and cultural heritage affects the political dimension of hipsters' discursive formation. On the one hand, hipsterism is often perceived as left-wing culture. On the other hand, it has strong conservative discursive frames. Nostalgia can be considered as a glorification of the *Gemeinschaft* sphere of human interactions, in which the essence of human contacts is determined not by the individual's position in the social hierarchy but by the inner characteristics of a human being as such. Nostalgia, as a form of attitude toward the past, denotes the presence of a coherent cultural framework embedded in bygone undertakings or deeds and accomplishments that are valuated positively, and therefore, they create a sphere of positive emotions and meanings (Boym, *Future of Nostalgia*; Wilson; Atia and Davies; Halbwachs; Todorova; Boyer; Angé and Berliner).

According to Bjørn Schiermer, contemporary hipsterism has three dominant designates: individualism, irony, and nostalgia (167–81). Starting with individualism, hipsterism constantly needs to accentuate its originality and seeming authenticity. Hipsters do so by creating a sort of the authentic patchwork composed of other cultural conventions and past trends. Irony is perceived as a specific rule of belonging and serves to build social interactions and ties. Moreover, it functions as the exclusive mechanism used to reinforce the hipsters' authenticity and preventing the imitation of hipsterism. As Schiermer notices, "[t]he successful understanding of an ironic remark creates instant social bonds, whereas mistaken irony often creates embarrassing and awkward situations" (171). Finally, nostalgia allows for understanding hipsterism as a conservative post-community rather than as a countercultural one. Hipsters restore old commodities and lifestyles. In a sense, hipsters incorporate them from the past, use them as their own cultural practices, and then communicate them to the dominant culture. In contrast to Schiermer's definition, in our study we have found no significant role of irony in the communication of post-community members. Instead, the analyzed post-community was mostly framed discursively in terms of nostalgia and individualism.

Research Method and Data

The study concerns visual data collected during structured and everyday participant netnographic observation. It combines qualitative and quantitative content analysis of, firstly, forty-eight blogs on Tumblr, Instagram, and Facebook (observed during the period December 2012–April 2016); and secondly, websites and social media accounts of twelve design brands (December 2015–July 2020).[1] Particular users and brands were chosen based on the following: (a) cross-media practices (namely, Tumblr account handled with a Facebook and/or Instagram one); (b) the status of the user, that is, whether the user was/is running a blog, business and/or online store connected with the content of the social media platform account; (c) data accessibility (i.e., during the process of collecting the data, some users deleted their accounts or stopped their blog activity). Methodologically, we analyzed not a particular group of a coherent community, but rather the discursive (in this paper: visual) construction of a post-community.

The research process was divided into three phases. The first was an outside netnographic observation of fourteen blogs on Tumblr that helped to build a skeleton of media practices and discursive cultural codes deployed by users. Findings of this stage indicate that the main discursive denominator used by these accounts was nostalgia. However, we did not follow exclusively nostalgia as a main discursive category. More important was to capture the actual social/cultural relations between particular users. Thus, in stage

[1]The brands chosen for the analysis were mostly either observed on the Tumblr accounts or in some way related to the content posted online by the Tumblr users. For instance, one of the users developed an interior design brand which was directly based on the user's www. account. Another one works in a wood shop: he restores old furniture and makes new one from the pieces of old wood, while yet others run clothing brands designing vintage fashion and nostalgic imprints.

two we started in-depth observation of forty-eight Tumblr users that were connected to one another and run cross-media practices framing the specific hipster discourse. The third phase included the observation of discursive codes used by twelve design brands. These brands mostly evolved from the Tumblr accounts or were in some way connected with the content that users posted online.

Since the analysis concerned the discursive, mostly visual, construction of a post-community, our observation was quite limited in terms of the demographic factors, and it was not always possible to tell the race/ethnicity, class, nationality, or gender of a particular user. But the data we have indicate more or less equal distribution in terms of gender. In terms of the nationality and ethnicity, users were mostly white American, Canadian, British, and French. As regards social class, we did not gather relevant information. The visual content was dominated by photos, GIF files, and graphic design with some music embedded into the posts. Also, we have never excluded the circulated content that was owned and created by the corporations (e.g., clothes, bikes, motorbikes) during professional brand sessions.

Hipster Nostalgia Discourses

"Hipster nostalgia" in this chapter is defined as a specific media practice of a discursively framed post-community and aimed toward everyday objects, clothing, and gadgets which are characterized by vintage style. This includes clothes, physical appearance (e.g., old-fashioned beards, monocles and binoculars instead of glasses), everyday items (gadgets such as old-model mobile phones, old-fashioned bicycles, fixed-gear bikes, old-fashioned book covers, or timeworn photographs), residential design, and choices in the domain of art and popular culture (listening to specific music both in private spaces and in shared hipster spaces such as forums and tribal meetings), the cultivation of vintage fashion (vinyl records, cassette tape-recorders), dress code, styling, being seen in appropriate places (galleries, clubs, restaurants, and bars), and attitude to the environment and other global issues.[2] The representation and consistent ritualization of hipster values are the essential elements of hipster nostalgia manifested on social media (e.g., Facebook and Twitter) and in the new media in general (including the blogosphere). This means that videos, photos, and entries published in social media space usually contain substantial elements of nostalgic styling, with regard to places, people, and activities, and they take the form of ritualistic discourse. Thus, nostalgic cultural products and objects become a kind of guarantee

[2]For the discussion on hipsterism and the hipster movement see Maly and Varis; McArthur; Michael; Schiermer; Scott.

of the authenticity of the hipster post-community: a form of the "true" experience shared in social media through the visual discursive categories ritually composed of selected symbols or icons arranged in schematic and predictable ways. These categories cover a variety of human activities as well as individuals' relationships with nature. Our netnographic study showed visual content used by members of hipster post-communities were commented on and shared more often if they contained the same sets of cultural codes. In-depth analysis in the second phase of the netnographic observation proved that posts that differed from the ones that shared codes common for the group were circulated and commented on less frequently. Firstly, in regard to formal arrangements, posts with no filters and more chaotic composition had a lower share ration. Secondly, in regard to objects, posts with personal photos, for example selfies, were shared less. By posting photos and videos, the blog users evaluate the work and posts of others, express their views and opinions, and, more importantly, they use the posts as a means to maintain their status within the hipsters' group. In other words, hipsters publishing their messages try not only to convince others of their point of view but also to confirm their participation in the group to which they belong or aspire. An entry is expected to be published in a form that follows the group convention, and the entry style maintained by the group is usually expected for those who exchange messages and comments. Therefore, by reading digital forms of network activities, both researcher and user have to deal with a set of fixed, ritually appearing elements that are present on web pages, blogs, or Twitter accounts in a defined form.

The nostalgic narrative of hipster blogs is an expression of post-community values and of creating a particular world based on the ritualized use of visual codes and, at the same time, the way to organize an amorphous reality based on codes accepted by the post-community members and considered relevant to their social milieu. Narrativity in which "an agent relates ('tells') a story in a particular medium, such as language, imagery, sound, buildings, or a combination thereof" (Bal 5) organizes the process of storytelling (Gubrium and Holstein; Maynes, Pierce and Laslett; Somers). Hipsters' narrative by using codes and symbols typical for a given post-community frames their personal emotions and practices into more general experiences coined with the nostalgia discourse.

The Main Discursive Categories of Hipster Nostalgia Design

In the following part, we will examine how digital nostalgia functions as one of the constituent elements for hipsters as a group and for within-group communication. The communication codes that make up the nostalgic reference system are manifested as visual representations on hipster blogs: photographs, text layout, the content, and the world represented in the images are designed to create a post-subculture community that, in essence, manifests its activity in the web domain. Thus, the study examines how hipster media practices form institutions of mediatized post-communities. Although institutionalization may seem paradoxical in the context of hipster subculture with its anti-institutional character, it accompanies every human activity that turns ritualistic in time.

The visual and verbal content published on social media accounts by hipsters serve as a means to amplify the distinctiveness of the blogger's personality and position in a particular post-community. This means that the blogger's online presentation is defined by the usage of discursive frames, such as photo filters, lights, colors, or postproduction. However, the number of topics presented in the photographs in the hipster blogosphere does not create any coherent thematic class but rather highly differentiated visual clusters. The blog reader can see the pictures of landscapes and wildlife often placed next to representations of cities: objects that accompany people in the public space or people at home (in a private sphere). Although hipster post-communities are predominantly an urban phenomenon, the discursive codes present on the blogs mix urbanism and post-industrial elements with the one of nature. In general, hipsters seem to consider nature, countryside, and traditional lifestyles as forms of a nostalgic escape that guarantees a sort of stability in times of social and economic uncertainty. Significantly, there was no discursive evidence that the analyzed post-communities have personally experienced those lifestyles, but they develop those lifestyles as a cultural reconstruction based on movies, books, family stories, etcetera. Thus, we perceive the visual data collected during the first step of a netnographic observation as saturated with particular discursive categories that are manifested as several opposite categories such as the following: living beings–inanimate entities, nature landscape–cityscape, human–other living beings (especially animals), city–village, city–landscape of nature, home/private sphere–public sphere, places marked by humanity–places untouched by humanity. These oppositions are deeply rooted in Western culture and as such are the bases on which hipsters build their group mythology.

However, such binary discursive structure was only the general narrative frame of the analyzed post-community. The dynamics of discursive shifts through the entire period of analysis allowed for filling the initial structure with other dominant visual codes grouped in these categories: living beings, places, cultural activities, objects, spaces, subjects and the contents of photographs, action themes, and motifs. Categories of persons and other beings (who?, what?), places (where?), objects (what?), and activities (what they do?) were coded based on symbols and narrative elements that dominated the sample. They are presented in Table 16.1.

TABLE 16.1. *Features of Hipster Digital Nostalgia Design.*

LIVING BEINGS	people	predominantly young, white persons (mainly longhaired women and bearded men wearing casual clothes)	
	animals	mammals, wild animals, pets	
	plants	food, bouquets, herbaria; home ecologic plant gardens; growing in the state of nature	
PLACES / INANIMATE ENTITIES	not developed by people	lakes, mountains, forests, wild nature, wilderness, space	
	partially developed	hiking, a hut in the forest, tent at a lake (periodically settled)	
	entirely developed by people	places in cities: tenement houses, bridges, stairs, old buildings	
	a city	panoramic views	roofs, streets, cityscape, public communication, places, non-spaces
		detailed views	a particular street, a monument, special places, houses
	a village	vintage stylizations	huts, streets, rusticity, wooden houses, wells, animal shelters, old-fashioned home appliances in their natural surroundings
	houses	house from outside	a cottage, a single house, tenement house
		house interiors	bricolage of rustic, scandinavian, hampton, boho interior design
OBJECTS	the private sphere	spaces filled with clothes, gadgets for daily use or luxury objects, and musical instruments	
	outdoor area	a bicycle stand, a boat, bike, motorbike, tent, axe, wood (logs), shoes, map, hat, backpack, woodworking tools	
HUMAN ACTIVITIES	coffee drinking, walking, waiting, enjoying lazy time, expedition, adventure, traveling / travel plans, swimming, playing the guitar, playing the piano, listening to vinyl records, preparing food, body care		

The discursive categories listed in the table are not, and by definition cannot, be separated from one another. The individual elements of these classifications form a grid of overlapping representations rather than linearly defined intervals containing the types and their manifestations. Moreover, a specific element can appear in the same form in different places and environments, for instance, a cup of coffee or a bicycle can successfully identify a particular user in the private sphere (in the kitchen or at a house corridor) as well as in public spaces (cycling on the street, parking a bike in front of the store, drinking coffee on the subway, in the hallway of a college, or walking with a mug/cup on the street). Additionally, within one screen one can see photographs containing elements from different categories, seamlessly integrated into the common universe created on a particular blog. The qualitative analysis shows how such discursive bricolage structure of the entire social media blog works in terms of nostalgia. For instance, users often deployed the narrative frame composed of the landscapes related to traveling and seasons. The moments of transition from one season to another and the waiting for them were especially popular. Interestingly, the most popular narrative categories were connected with a nostalgic-romantic view of autumn, winter, and spring. Therefore, we are dealing here with a kind of waiting for a change, the result of which is a metamorphosis of the style of dressing, decorating space, a new direction of travel/life transformation. Moreover, the second crucial narrative frame derivates from the first, as it includes visual representations of escapism into nature, to the forest, spending time in houses by the lake, by the sea, in the mountains. Importantly, such escapist narratives were nostalgic in terms of imitating old travel practices, the attributes of which were traditional maps, compasses, axes, boats, watches, vintage thermoses. Thus, this narrative frame was based on an alternative view of resourcefulness and the ability to cope with difficult conditions and tame nature, for example, by building a cabin in the forest. Such narrative was connected to the specificity of the particular cultural connotations related to the places where the hipsters were from. Thus, in case of the US and Canadian users, the myth of the Western frontier was pictured in the visual representations. Although the mountains (mostly Rocky Mountains and Appalachians), forests, and woods dominated this narrative as the places to master/conquer, male users were posting pictures of the Western deserts as well. Female users were often posting visual representations that connoted the human–nature relation rather in terms of solitude/escape to the woods. In such terms, we are dealing with a post-community discourse focused on the past, which, after all, hipsters have not experienced themselves. Even activities undertaken within cities, such as strolling in the streets or parks referred to nature as an inherent part of the city space, an impression amplified by vintage-alike filtering of the image. By deploying such a specific narrative frame, hipsters preserve these tradition-based social practices, make them visible through their media practices, and eventually trending. Finally, narrative frames of everyday cultural practices were saturated with codes, which can be described as a topoi of carefully arranged visually and compositionally small pleasures. There were frequent depictions of drinking coffee, cooking, baking in form of stylized photos of food, drinks, dinner eaten with friends who, like the presented meals and tables, fit the narrative frame of hipsterism with both clothing and other distinctive elements, for example, tattoos, hairstyles, or headgear (hat, beanie, flat cap). Even listening to records referred to the bygone, but reviving, tradition of using turntables. The way of performing these activities can be described as unhurried life and everyday rituals: listening to vinyl records, sipping coffee, celebrating meals.

Although the dual mode causes difficulties in studying hipster design, the empirical study undertaken for this article does indicate some specific elements that are characteristic of hipster nostalgia design framed as specific narrative categories. Hence, hipster nostalgia design is based on the restoration of past commodities and styles, and it operates via well-known cultural narrative codes incorporated from the past with a specific meaning. The first meaning operates on the nostalgia level, so the hipster commodity is not only about the present but also recontextualizes positive emotions and memories about the (illusion of the) past. The second links to contemporary post-community formation where the new meaning of design serves as a common discursive frame. It is difficult to name only a few distinctive features of hipster nostalgia since the culture operates always in the dual mode of incorporation (when a culture draws on other codes) and operational closure (when the codes circulate inside the formation and obtain new meaning).

The discursive category of an axe is an interesting case of how the meanings from the past are adopted/transformed by hipsters. In the digital discourses analyzed, the axe, usually a tool used for chopping wood, was transformed into a symbol of belonging to the specific post-community. The axe, as a symbol, appears in relationship to other symbols, for example, travel or interior design. In the case of travel, an axe becomes a piece of equipment. In the case of interior design, an axe is placed on the walls as a decoration. However, it is not just a regular axe but the traditional/vintage hickory wooden handled axe. Thus, the hipster axe becomes a metaphor of the adventurous lifestyle. By posting photos of axes of specific brands or made by themselves, hipsters transform the meaning of the category as an element by putting it into a new narrative frame. Thus, the axe (but also other similarly transformed symbols and objects) becomes an iconic representation of their lifestyle and discourse. At the same time, the commodification process is catching up with the new meaning of the axe as mass producers of this tool create new lines of vintage axes designed by new craftsmanship brands such as Best Made Co., bushcraft tool producers as wilderness axes by Ray Mears, or top mass produces as axes and hatchets vintage lines of Husqvarna and Hultafors.

Conclusion

Hipster nostalgia design as discursive formation framed in specific narratives is formed as a result of three overlapping processes. Firstly, as we stated in the initial paragraphs, the analyzed post-community was shaped in the process of mediatization, where digital media practices of hipsters or hipster-alike formations increased their social visibility. Thus, secondly, it enabled the construction of the specific discursive frame of nostalgia design that was a core visual narrative *modus operandi* used by the analyzed post-community. Finally, the hipster post-community operates in a dual mode based on the process of incorporation and excorporation. It was characterized by operational closure and even *autopoiesis* at some stage of its development. During the span of the initial stages of research, we observed that hipsters have been communicating with a limited set of discursive categories. It allowed us to indicate the basic elements differentiating this particular post-community. However, the *autopoiesis* phase was the exact time when hipsters transformed the meaning of the discursive categories. Eventually, excorporation of transformed meaning affected not just the nostalgia-based discursive formation of hipsterism but also the contemporary culture making hipsters and nostalgia design one of its substantial phenomena.

Works Cited

Angé, Olivia, and David Berliner. "Introduction: Anthropology of Nostalgia—Anthropology as Nostalgia." *Anthropology and Nostalgia*, edited by Olivia Angé and David Berliner. Berghahn Books, 2016, pp. 1–15.

Atia, Nadia, and Jeremy Davies. "Nostalgia and the Shapes of History." *Memory Studies*, vol. 3, no. 3, 2010, pp. 181–6.

Bal, Mieke. *Narratology: Introduction to the Theory of Narrative*. University of Toronto Press, 2009.

Bennet, Sam. *Constructions of Migrant Integration in British Public Discourse: Becoming British*. Bloomsbury Academic, 2018.

Bennett, Andy. "The Post-Subcultural Turn: Some Reflections 10 Years On." *Journal of Youth Studies*, vol. 14, no. 5, 2011, pp. 493–506.

Boyer, Dominic. "From Algs to Autonomos: Nostalgic Eastern Europe as Postimperial Mania." *Post-Communist Nostalgia*, edited by Maria Todorova and Zsuzsa Gille. Berghahn Books, 2010, pp. 17–28.

Boym, Svetlana. *The Future of Nostalgia*. Basic Books, 2001.

Boym, Svetlana. "Nostalgia and Its Discontents." *Hedgehog Review*, vol. 7, 2007, pp. 7–18.

Gubrium, Jaber F., and James A. Holstein. *Analysing Narrative Reality*. Sage, 2009.

Guffey, Elizabeth E. *Retro: The Culture of Revival*. Reaktion Books, 2006.

Halbwachs, Maurice. *On Collective Memory*. University of Chicago Press, 1992.

Hebdige, Dick. *Subculture: The Meaning of Style*. Routledge, 1979.

Jeziński, Marek, and Łukasz Wojtkowski. "Hipsterzy jako postwspólnota cyfrowa: Uwagi o post-subkulturowym internetowym folklorze" [Hipsters as a Digital Post-Community: Remarks on Post-Subcultural Internet Folklore]. *Przegląd Kulturoznawczy*, vol. 2, no. 32, 2017, pp. 176–90.

Jeziński, Marek, and Łukasz Wojtkowski. "Narcyzm hipsterski" [Hipster Narcissism]. *Kultura Współczesna*, vol. 1, 2020, pp. 29–42.

Jeziński, Marek, and Łukasz Wojtkowski. "Nostalgia Commodified: Towards the Marketization of the Post-Communist Past Through the New Media." *Medien und Zeit*, vol. 4, 2016, pp. 96–104.

Leach, Edmund. *Culture and Communication: The Logic by Which Symbols Are Connected*. Cambridge University Press, 1976.

Maly, Ico, and Piia Varis. "The 21st-Century Hipster: On Micro-Populations in Times of Superdiversity." *European Journal of Cultural Studies*, vol. 19, no. 6, 2016, pp. 637–53.

Maynes, Mary J., Jennifer Pierce, and Barbara Laslett. *Telling Stories: The Use of Personal Narratives in the Social Sciences and History*. Cornell University Press, 2008.

McArthur, John A. "Digital Subculture: A Geek Meaning of Style." *Journal of Communication Inquiry*, vol. 33, no. 1, 2009, pp. 58–70.

Michael, Janna. "It's Really Not Hip to Be a Hipster: Negotiating Trends and Authenticity in the Cultural Field." *Journal of Consumer Culture*, vol. 15, no. 2, 2015, pp. 163–82.

Muggleton, David. *Inside Subculture: The Postmodern Meaning of Style*. Berg, 2002.

Schiermer, Bjørn. "Late-Modern Hipsters: New Tendencies in Popular Culture." *Acta Sociologica*, vol. 57, no. 2, 2014, pp. 167–81.

Scott, Michael. "'Hipster Capitalism' in the Age of Austerity? Polanyi Meets Bourdieu's New Petite Bourgeoisie." *Cultural Sociology*, vol. 11, no. 1, 2017, pp. 60–76.

Somers, Margaret. "The Narrative Construction of Identity: A Relational and Network Approach." *Theory and Society*, vol. 23, 1994, 605–49.

Todorova, Maria. "Introduction: From Utopia to Propaganda and Back." *Post-Communist Nostalgia*, edited by Maria Todorova and Zsuzsa Gille. Berghahn Books, 2010, pp. 1–14.

Todorova, Maria, and Zsuzsa Gille, eds. *Post-Communist Nostalgia*. Berghahn Books, 2010.

Turner, Bryan S. "A Note on Nostalgia." *Theory of Culture and Society*, vol. 4, no. 1, 1987, pp. 147–56.

Unger, Johann, Ruth Wodak, and Majid Khosravink. "Critical Discourse Studies and Social Media." *Qualitative Research*, edited by David Silverman. SAGE, 2016, pp. 1170–241.

Wilson, Janelle L. *Nostalgia: Sanctuary of Meaning*. Bucknell University Press, 2005.

Hipster Foodways and Cultural Politics

17

The Pursuit of Culinary Capital in *Portlandia* and *Master of None*

Justine Gieni

In their descriptions of hipsters, Robert Lanham (2003) and Brett McCracken (2010) include lists of food related practices as part of their definitions of the hipster collective identity. Indeed, as Lanham states in the satirical anthropological study of the hipster, *The Hipster Handbook*, there is a close connection between a hipster identity and rarefied food practices: hipsters are "always more culturally aware than most … enjoy[ing] Tibetan, Vietnamese, Moroccan and American food with equal zest" and they "know the difference between pinot noir and cabernet sauvignon" (10). While parodic, Lanham's representation illustrates how specific foodways are one of many status-driven activities, like taste in music or fashion, that confer cultural capital and delimit the group identity of a hipster; notably, the emphasis on ethnic foods is one signifier that differentiates hipster foodways from mainstream culture. The more remote or norm-breaking the food, the more likely it seems that a food is delineated as hipster. Likewise, in *Hipster Christianity*, McCracken provides a list of hipsters' eating patterns: "Hipsters … like to eat at greasy downtown diners and seedy dive restaurants off major highways. They like Vietnamese food, Viennese coffee, and farmer's markets, particularly if the farmer's market is not a touristy one" (63). McCracken's description of hipster foodways emphasizes the distinction of hipster food choices and suggests there is a stylization of taste that purposefully differentiates itself from mainstream culture by approaching food as a means of separation and resistance.

As they depart from mainstream culture, hipster food trends also provoke both ridicule and derision, exemplified by internet headlines such as "24 of the Worst Things Hipsters Did to Food in 2016" (Barrett), or "15 Hipster Food Trends That Need to Die in 2017" (No). It is clear that some hipster food trends are culturally divisive.[1] In general, hipster culture is often ridiculed and maligned in media, and food trends are often part of this attack. Indeed, one can see hipster food trends as an intentional pursuit to challenge and subvert mainstream culinary norms through foods that purposely challenge the status quo. For example, by serving a latte out of a halved avocado shell that would normally be considered rubbish or by serving a black charcoal flavored ice cream, one can see an intention to upset or undermine established culinary norms. In this way, hipster foodways are both status-seeking actions that confer cultural capital and a means to deviate from norms of mainstream culture, even while still participating in consumerism. As such, hipsters can be seen as occupying a contentious position in society: at once, exalted for upholding idealistic values about food artistry and a return to quality, yet ridiculed for absurd expressions of the culinary avant-garde.

One way that hipster foodways are most clearly evidenced in contemporary culture is through media representations—in particular, the fictional portrayals of hipsters in film and television. Such is the case with popular television programs like IFC's *Portlandia* (2011–18) and the Netflix series *Master of None* (2015–), where hipsters are represented through specific foodways that demarcate difference and distinction from traditional or mainstream food practices, including how food is produced, procured, and consumed. *Portlandia*, a sketch-comedy television series by creators Fred Armisen, Carrie Brownstein, and Jonathan Krisel, portrays hipster characters in a fictionalized version of Portland, Oregon, where Armisen and Brownstein play characters who embody hipster culture and practice hip or trendy foodways. Brownstein and Armisen portray hipster characters in ironic and self-reflective ways, incorporating cultural trends that they see and participate in both on and off screen. To represent hipster culture, Armisen and Brownstein draw from real food trends associated with hipsters, including locovorism, veganism, artisanal producers, foraging, and raw food diets. By drawing from real Portland food trends, *Portlandia* has helped define the collective hipster identity in mainstream culture, particularly in its representation of hipsters as those who gain status and define group identity through the pursuit of food authenticity, artisanship, and distinction from mainstream culinary norms. *Portlandia* uses food themes to capture the

[1]In an example of this, when a photo of a deconstructed coffee served at a hipster café was shared on social media by writer Jamila Rizvi, who asserted her disappointment and irritation when her coffee was served in three separate beakers, her post went viral with over twenty-five thousand likes on Facebook (Crane). The coffee was derided, so much so that it was even mockingly deemed "a signal for the irreversible decline of our once productive and healthy societies" (Lieu).

absurdities of hipsters in their pursuit of coolness and distinction. However, at the same time, Brownstein, Armisen, and Krisel create characters who are likeable, kind, sensitive, and largely relatable for the intended audience of *Portlandia* who are in on the joke, because they too participate in hipster foodways in their everyday life.

Likewise, the televisual series *Master of None* by creators Aziz Ansari and Alan Yang also draws much humor from hipster foodways, particularly in the intersections of food and technology, where food photographs are shared all over social media and characters will engage in intensive internet research before going out to eat. At the same time, for the protagonist Dev Shah, a 30-something Indian-American man in New York City, foodways are also metaphorical, representing Dev's pursuit of an authentic self, distinction from orthodox traditions of his family, and a celebration of diversity and social connections. Through parody and ironic self-reflection, *Portlandia* and *Master of None* represent hipsters as deriving both status and meaning from food. While both series find humor in parodying the hipster's search for culinary capital, there are differences in how each series constructs meaning of hipster foodways. *Portlandia* focuses primarily on the moral impetus and countercultural motivations behind hipster food choices that disrupt norms of mainstream industrial food production and consumption, while *Master of None* addresses some of the larger systemic problems associated with hipsters and cultural capital, namely the barriers of access for racialized individuals to gain both cultural and culinary capital in America. Each example shows that hipster foodways are not solely an empty affectation, but as demonstrated in both *Portlandia* and *Master of None*, hipster food and foodways are meaningful signifiers of the ideals and identities of a generation of young people who are challenging mainstream cultural norms.

Hipster Foodways as Culinary Capital

In North America and other wealthy countries around the world, there has been a shift around foodways. This shift occurs, as Mark Greif identifies in his essay "On Food," in countries where "the reason to eat food is no longer hunger" and where transformations in food accessibility have made "eating a 'hobby.'" For those who have access to the super-abundance of food choices associated with First World countries, this has resulted in a shifting relationship to food. In countries and communities with food abundance, food and food related practices have become a spectacle and an expression of one's identity, rather than merely a perfunctory act to satiate hunger or meet nutritional needs. No longer is the pursuit to eat just to satisfy one's hunger, but rather one eats and shares one's meals, often strategically, as means to define one's individual and group identity through the social construction of self.

For many, food has become part of the pursuit of status and power associated with the cultivation of taste. In *Culinary Capital*, Naccarato and LeBesco elaborate upon Bourdieu's concept of cultural capital to discuss how "certain food practices give people a sense of distinction within their communities" and confer "power and status" (7). What Naccarato and LeBesco call "culinary capital" refers to how food and food practices "play a unique role as markers of social status" (2) by conferring "status and power on those who know about and enjoy" certain food-related practices (3). Indeed, as Naccarato and LeBesco discuss, both food people ("foodies") and hipsters "seek to acquire culinary capital" by participating in the food-related practices of hipster neighborhoods, whether its shopping at locally sourced food markets or supporting artisanal producers ("Distinction" 122). However, as Naccarato and LeBesco point out, the cultural capital associated with hipsters and foodies also confers distinction between these group identities, as hipsters are more likely localized in the same enclaves where they produce and consume food, which, in turn, gives hipsters a means to claim their authenticity and distinction ("Distinction" 122). Indeed, it becomes clear that where the foodie mainly enjoys food, hipsters revere food and foodways as a source of meaningful expression, as food becomes a politicized statement of one's (countercultural) beliefs.

Hipsters gain a part of their social status and identity from their distinct knowledge and enjoyment of gustatory choices and stylized performances of eating and cooking, but also from the hands-on participation in food production. The terms "artisanal" or "artisanship," which are often used as descriptors for hipster food, signify an elevation of food as an object of sublimity or reverence as well as an elevation of social status for the person or "artist" who creates the food. In many ways, hipster food producers have restored and reinvigorated certain professions that were out of fashion or deemed inefficient in the advent of industrial food factories. As such, the hipster's embrace of preindustrial techniques of food production speaks for a distinct move away from overly processed or mass-produced foods in pursuit of authenticity. As noted by David Inglis (2016), authenticity is of particular importance for urban hipsters, where there is much uncertainty and instability in navigating the shifting ground of coolness from one minute to the next. Indeed, while there is irony in a lot that the hipster says or does, when it comes to food there seems to be a sincere appreciation of how food is produced and consumed. At its core, this careful consideration of food is not merely a status-seeking hipster affectation like over-sized glasses, but rather it speaks for an underlying desire for meaning and purpose. As Johnston and Baumann identify, "there are real, democratic social benefits that result from a focus on authenticity. The democratic element of authenticity involves a reconnection with food knowledge, reclamation of lost culinary skills, and sincere investigation into the troubled origins and implications of industrial food production" (84). In this way, the emphasis on food stuffs that are homemade or homegrown, gourmet or organic, and ingredients that are rare and exotic, can speak of the hipsters' pursuit of authenticity and, in turn, their desire for countercultural resistance against mass market industrial forms of consumption.

However, as food scholars Johnston and Baumann argue, notions of authenticity in relation to food are problematic as such claims to products being "artisan" quality and "authentic" are not intrinsic, but socially constructed (65). As Johnston and Baumann explain, "authenticity is generated through perceptions of how a cultural object negotiates a set of standards and values, instead of emerging from a cultural object's qualities" (63). In other words, authenticity is more perceived than real. It is evident within the cultural realm of hipsters that certain qualities of food products and preparations are agreed upon to signify authenticity: "foods are deemed authentic when they can be framed as geographically specific, 'simple,' have a personal connection, are historically grounded, and have ethnic connection" (Johnson and Baumann 84). In this way, hipsters confirm their identity and gain cultural capital by engaging in the foodways that are collectively affirmed to signify authenticity.

"Is It Local?": The Pursuit of Authenticity in *Portlandia*

The admirable and absurd qualities of hipsters' food choices are prominently celebrated and satirized on the television series *Portlandia* through skits such as "We can pickle that," "Is the chicken local?" and "Brunch village." While *Portlandia* has parodied other hipster tropes such as being a disc jockey, living in a microhouse, and riding a fixed gear bicycle, food remains one of the show's most consistent comedic motifs used to characterize hipster culture, so much so that there was even a *Portlandia* cookbook published in 2014. In *Portlandia*, foodways of hipsters are exaggerated to a hyperbolic level to illustrate how food has become a status driven means to define group identity through the pursuit of authenticity, artisanship, and distinction from mainstream culinary norms.

At its core, *Portlandia* is a show about group identity. As Jonathan Nathan suggests, "this is not a show that speaks to everyone," because it is a show made by and for hipsters. As Fred Armisen, creator and performer of *Portlandia* explains, "[t]he characters on *Portlandia* are very much like us, right down to the way they talk. They pretty much sound just like we do. And their personality traits are very much like us. If we're skewering anyone, it's ourselves" (qtd. in Spitznagel). In this way, the particular behaviors, values, and stylizations of hipsters are a main source of humor in the show, but only if the viewers are in on the joke. In interviews, Brownstein and Armisen both reject the "hipster" label of the show, in true hipster-fashion,[2] and yet the show portrays many of the defining attributes of what is considered hipster in popular culture by representing trends in music, fashion, and food. Simultaneously, the show also expands the mainstream notion of hipster by delving into adjacent countercultures that overlap with the hipster identity: from gutter punks to dumpster-diving freegans, bike messengers to coffee baristas, there are countless iterations of individual and collective identities that coexist within the catch-all category of hipster. As evidenced in the sketch "Dream of the '90s" (season 1, episode 1)[3] and the subsequent sketch "Dream of the 1890s" (2.5), which Nathan refers to as "the show's mission statement," there is a collective identity defined for the "cool, plugged-in, young, urban progressives" who live in Portland and, indeed, in the Portland-like locations around the world. Along with cool girls who wear glasses, and men who have waxed handlebar mustaches, the songs also characterize the particular foodways of this hipster demographic who "pickl[e] their own vegetables," "bre[w] their own beer," "gr[ow] up to be artisan bakers," "carve their own ice cubes," "raise their own chickens and cure their own meats" (2.5). In this way, foodways are conveyed as an integral characteristic of hipsters' collective identity in Portland and beyond, as Portland transforms from a real location to a utopian mecca, the fictional Portlandia, where individuals can pursue passions without the normal constraints of time or worries of economic compensation (Nathan).

Indeed, in sketches like "We Can Pickle That" (2.1), the hipster's pursuit of artisanal food production as a source of distinction from mainstream culture is satirized for its impracticality and divergence from culinary norms. In "We Can Pickle That," Brownstein and Armisen play Bryce and Lisa, two artisans who proudly turn waste into a consumable commodity through pickling. As Lisa says, "[i]t's hard work" but also a point of pride as Bryce and Lisa are seemingly able to pickle anything—edible and non-edible products alike. Whether it is the excess cucumbers that are left unsold from a farmer's market stall or a viable solution to a neighbor's prolific egg-laying chicken, Bryce and Lisa have a solution by pickling items that would otherwise be thrown away. In this regard, Bryce and Lisa exemplify the hipster's attempt to be distinct from mainstream culture in their rejection of the food waste associated with Western capitalism. By rescuing and reusing waste, they can also be seen as participating in a larger

---

[2]In an interview with Nolan Feeney, Carrie Brownstein discusses the "hipster" label as a term used often in a derogatory way by people who are insecure about their own hipness. Likewise, in an article by Eric Spitznagel, Fred Armisen rejects the "hipster" label, noting that nobody refers to oneself as a hipster.

[3]Henceforth, season and episode numbers will be abbreviated in the following format: (1.1).

movement of freeganism, one of many countercultural practices associated with hipster identities (Greif, "What Was the Hipster?" 220). As defined by Barnard, a "freegan" is "a combination of the words 'free' and 'vegan'" and refers to a group of individuals who hold a philosophical opposition to "the entire capitalist economy" and particularly food waste associated with overconsumption (12). While the pickle-making of Bryce and Lisa at first illustrates the practicality and virtue of artisanal production by ascribing value to disposed-of objects, the premise of the sketch takes on a satirical tone once Bryce and Lisa begin to make pickles from inedible items: a dead bird, a band-aid, a broken high heel, a parking ticket, and empty CD cases, rendering them (somewhat?) edible in the process, as evidenced by Lisa's labored chewing and swallowing. In this way, the show exaggerates the behaviors of those groups—like freegans or hipster artisans—who reclaim or ascribe new value on so-called waste products. As this sketch exemplifies, foodways of hipster culture—including artisanal food production and countercultural patterns of freeganism—are a means to differentiate and construct hipster identity as distinct from the mainstream—in this case, as distinct from wasteful capitalist market economies. Through hyperbolic examples of hipster culinary trends, *Portlandia*'s creators reflect through ironic distance the values and artisanship of hipster producers in their pursuit of culinary alternatives to mass market production.

While *Portlandia*'s hipster characters like Bryce and Lisa engage in the foodways that derive cultural capital through DIY and artisanal approaches to food production that opposes mainstream capitalist culture, the reoccurring characters of Peter and Nance (played by Armisen and Brownstein), a middle-aged bohemian couple who are trying to remain plugged into all that is hip and socially responsible in Portland, partake in hipster food trends through what Ulver-Sneistrup, Askegaard, and Kristensen (2011) call "moralizing consumer resistance" (qtd. in Cronin et al. 4). Specifically, while Peter and Nance do not oppose capitalism and actively engage in consumerism, they do so only with moral consideration. In regard to the food products they choose to purchase and consume, there is an emphasis on the morality and authenticity of these choices. As Cronin explains, the moralizing consumer "engages in moral considerations in separating 'good' brand choices from 'bad' brand choices so as not to be 'polluted' by the products of 'a capitalist marketplace'" (4). In this configuration of socially conscious eating, there is a moral division between "authentic" foods, that is foods that are produced on a small-scale through local channels, with an emphasis on organic, artisanal products, and "inauthentic" foods that are mass-produced by multinational corporations, using highly processed, non-organic ingredients.

The couple's morally conscious eating is clearly evident in the sketch "Is the Chicken Local?" (1.1), where Peter and Nance insist on visiting the farm where the chicken they ordered in a restaurant was raised. The dialogue between Peter, Nance, and the waiter satirizes hipster eating habits in their insistence on moral consumerism:

Nance: [A]bout the chicken if you could just tell us a little more about it.
Server: Uh, the chicken is a heritage breed, a woodland raised chicken, that's been fed a diet of sheep's milk, soy, and hazelnuts.
Peter: I guess this is, this is local?
Server: Yes, absolutely.
Peter: I'm going to ask you one more time. It's local?

Nance and Peter's incessant questioning of the waiter seeks to determine whether the food they will consume is indeed authentic as farm-raised, local, and organic, all qualities that will determine if their dinner is a moral choice. In the end, Armisen and Brownstein satirize this moral consumerism of hipsters by having Peter and Nance decide not to eat the chicken at all, but rather defer eating until they can authenticate for themselves the conditions in which "Colin" the chicken was raised. By exaggerating the ethically conscious consumption of hipsters, *Portlandia*'s portrayal not only mocks the vigorous scrutinizing of the couple's eating habits but also addresses the strategic ways that hipsters are resisting and navigating the capitalist marketplace in moralistic ways.

The cultural value of authentic artisanal food is also satirized in the sketch "Brunch Village" (2.10), where Peter and Nance, along with a large number of Portland's hipsters, have decided to try Fisherman's Porch, Portland's newest brunch spot. With a line that seems to go on forever, and an hour and a half wait for a seat, the cultural capital of this brunch spot is clear. Peter and Nance are just one of the couples waiting in line, along with others who are also seeking to affirm their status by participating in what Sonia Saraiya calls "the urban yuppie brunch ecosystem." The crowd includes the stereotypical hipster, a guy who laments that he liked the Fisherman's Porch before it was cool, as well as other characters like a girl who faints in the line-up for brunch after not eating for ten days while on the trendy "master cleanse" diet. The quest for brunch becomes increasingly absurd when Nance is captured by a vigilante overlord (played by Tim Robbins) who wants to punish her by force-feeding her a pop tart: "You want your brunch before everyone else. Little piggy, piggy! Well, here it is. Your brunch, and there's corn oils and some kind of preservatives all mixed together in some kind of chemical stew." As a punishment, the pop tart symbolizes the "bad" or "inauthentic" foods of overprocessed, mass-marketed junk food that goes against everything that Nance (and Portland) holds as morally and corporally right. The pop tart threatens to pollute her body and corrupt Nance's moral and social status as a hipster. Before she is force-fed, Nance is rescued by Peter and they are able to eat at Fisherman's Porch. In this way, the satire of "Brunch Village," like the comedy of other food-related sketches on *Portlandia*, demonstrates what is at stake for hipsters in their pursuit of culinary capital. Indeed, as characters like Bryce, Lisa, Peter, and Nance illustrate, the construction of hipsters' culinary capital is not purely a stylization, but rather confirms one's ethical resistance to the toxicities of mainstream mass-market food production. In this way, *Portlandia*'s portrayal of hipster food culture highlights the small victories of individuals who oppose or resist mainstream food culture through artisanship (Bryce and Lisa) or moral consumption (Peter and Nance).

Hipster Tastemakers in *Master of None*

In the pattern of televisual representations like *Portlandia* which represent hipster foodways like locovorism, freeganism, and a penchant for brunch, the character of Dev Shah in the Netflix series *Master of None* embodies the hipsters' cultural obsession with food as a defining quality of identity and social status. Dev is a thirtysomething, food obsessed, working actor of Indian ancestry who lives in New York City. In many ways, Dev is a tastemaker, as someone who occupies a position of economic privilege and partakes in a highly curated display of culinary consumption. Like their character, the show's creators Aziz Ansari and Alan Yang are also tastemakers, as foodie fans of the show now flock to the restaurants and bars featured on the series.[4] As the title of the show implies, Dev is a "jack of all trades, master of none" who is in search for something in life that is authentic and deeply satisfying, which applies to both his search for love and food. However, while Dev's love life often falters, his food experiences rarely disappoint. Food and food practices (whether he is studying and cooking authentic Italian food in Modena, flaunting his food experiences on social media, or hosting a prominent culinary television program) empower Dev as markers of his elevated social status as a hipster. However, unlike the hipster archetype popularized in mainstream culture that is predominantly white, Dev's identity is defined in large part by his ethnic heritage as an Indian-American man from a traditional Muslim family. Dev occupies a dual subject position that is characterized by being both Othered as a person of color in mainstream American culture as well as awarded privileges as a young, urban hipster with economic and cultural capital. Food and food practices become one means by which Dev challenges the boundaries of mainstream identity categories like hipster, Indian, Muslim, and American, as food becomes a means to celebrate diversity and bridge connections between different people through shared culinary experiences.

[4]Websites including Eater, *The New York Times*, Vulture, and Gothamist have all featured dining guides based on the locations included in the series.

Like *Portlandia*, Aziz and Yang satirize the hipster's fetishizing of food as a lifestyle aspiration and defining quality of identity, but even more than the former, they present hipster foodways as an aspirational model of cultural diversity through a diverse palate.

Television series that portray hipsters like HBO's *Girls*, Netflix's *Love*, and IFC's *Portlandia* have been criticized for their lack of diversity and ironic or "hipster racism."[5] In her article, "The Truth About Being a Black Woman in a Liberal City," Lakeya Omogun discusses the intersections of race in her experience of hipster culture in Austin, Texas: "Our shared experience contrasts with that of the white millennials who navigate the city with ease and nonchalance ... they grab drinks at the local bar, listen to live music, and enjoy Austin to the fullest. When Blacks enter the same spaces, we often endure stares that silently question our existence." In this description, Omogun captures the marginalization and exclusion present in mainstream hipster communities that relegate people of color to the position of Other. Given the systemic barriers for people of color in mainstream Western culture, the diversity in the cast of *Master of None* stands out. All of Dev's friends, excluding Arnold (played by Eric Wareheim) and Jeff Pastore known as "Chef Jeff" (played by Bobby Cannavale), are persons of color, including Denise, who is African American, female, and lesbian (played by Lena Waithe). Notably, Waithe was recently awarded an Emmy, making her the first Black woman to win an Emmy in comedy writing (Littleton). She was awarded the Emmy for the Thanksgiving episode (2.8) where her character comes out as a lesbian to her family at Thanksgiving dinner, which is just one of the many instances in the series where food is used to bridge connection between people, despite their differences.

The series has been lauded by critics for capturing the voice and experiences of young people in the twenty-first century (Talmadge; Kadakia; Rivera). Indeed, there is much to relate to with Dev's character and experiences, particularly the cultural value he places on his hip, foodie lifestyle, and his reliance on technology, but also in the generational conflicts that emerge in Dev's relation to the familial and cultural traditions of his parents. As a hipster, Dev relies on technology as a means of supporting interpersonal connections and also as a means to gain cultural capital by sharing his food experiences. For example, Dev's go-to pick-up line when using a dating app like Tinder or OkCupid is to write, "I'm going to Whole Foods. Need me to pick you up anything?" (2.4). The line perfectly captures a central theme of the series: the pursuit of meaningful connection. And it is Dev's connection with food whereby those meaningful connections are created and supported.

---

[5]When HBO's *Girls* was criticized for not including any non-white main characters, one of the writers from the show, Lesley Arfin, responded to this by tweeting, "What really bothered me most about *Precious* was that there was no representation of ME." Her response has been taken as an example of ironic or "hipster racism" (Reeve).

Dev uses technology as a means to share his culinary knowledge and experiences to gain what Eve Turow calls the "badge of hipness" (50). What Turow identifies in her description of the technological foodways of hipster culture is a paradoxical desire for social validation and connection, albeit through the alienating distance of online communication. In a similar way, Ansari and Yang satirize the hipster's use of social media as a signifier of social status. For example, in the episode titled "Le Nozze" (2.2), which takes place during Dev's extended stay in Italy where he is apprenticing in the craft of authentic pasta making, both Dev and his friend Arnold record themselves kissing a sandwich and waving to the camera; Arnold sends his video to the different women that he has contacted on dating apps, and Dev sends the video to his former girlfriend. Arnold explains how the food-themed video communicates a message about his identity:

Dev: Does that really work?
Arnold: Dude, who wouldn't want to date this guy? [referring to himself] He loves food. He loves travel. He's devilishly handsome, and he knows how to do a classic wave and kiss.

In this way, Arnold's strategic and performative use of foodways on the dating app helps him confer his status as a worldly, adventurous, and desirable person. For Dev and his friends, the culinary experience takes on a symbolic quality of interpersonal connection that transcends the often impersonal barriers of twenty-first-century technology and also confers status as a worldly hipster. Yet Ansari and Yang also undermine this social media persona later in the episode by showing Arnold's emotional insecurity as he breaks down at his ex's wedding and expresses his longing for a meaningful connection.

Dev's search for meaningful connection through technology is also problematized by the bombardment of options. As expressed by Stephanie Talmadge in her discussion of the series, there is a "bizarre paradox" exemplified by Dev and this hip, young socially connected generation. Drawing from the work of psychologist Barry Schwartz in *The Paradox of Choice* (2004), Talmadge explains how this young generation is not empowered by the unlimited options presented to them through the accessibility of technology but how instead these unlimited choices have rather rendered them anxious, depressed, and dissatisfied. While this anxiety and disappointment is clearly evident in Dev's failed online dating experiences through the first and second seasons of the series, it is also conveyed in his culinary experiences. For example, when Dev and Arnold are deciding where to eat (1.1), the indecision results in forty-five minutes of internet research trying to find "the best tacos in New York City." Dev's frantic search through Yelp reviews, articles, lists, and rankings represents his anxiety-induced panic to confirm his culinary capital, even in making seemingly insignificant decisions like where to eat. In an ironic twist, the taco spot that Dev has painstakingly researched is closed once they arrive. In this way, creators Ansari and Yang satirize the use of technology and represent the futility of a hipster's never-ending search for the next food trend or restaurant. In an interview, Ansari explains the meaning of Dev's culinary research: "That whole research process—[it's] obviously something Alan and I have done so many times. I really did that research and they filmed it. It's very true to life. I do that pretty much every time I go to eat lunch. That's the big theme of the show: the paradox of choice" (Ansari qtd. in Safronova). Dev's "paradox of choice" captures the underlying anxiety of hipster culture in regard to the search for meaningful connections and experiences beyond superficial or ironic enjoyments. As Christy Wampole explains, a combination of hipster irony and technological savvy has resulted in a sense of anxiety and emptiness: "The ironic life is certainly a provisional answer to the problems of too much comfort, too much history and too many choices, but it is my firm conviction that this mode of living is not viable and conceals within it many social and political risks." What Wampole articulates is an "emptiness and existential malaise" that results from a life that lacks serious and sincere engagement with others.

One way that Dev copes with the anxiety-inducing choice in his hipster lifestyle is to pursue authenticity. When Dev's long-term relationship with Rachel ends at the end of season one, Dev decides to pursue the one thing that he feels sincere about: his love for making pasta. Therefore, Dev travels to Modena, Italy, to learn authentic pasta making techniques. Through this experience, Dev cultivates the knowledge and cultural capital that confirm his identity as a culinary tastemaker.[6] However, Dev's pursuit of authenticity through pasta, a classic comfort food, suggests that he is pursuing more than just culinary knowledge. For Dev, pasta represents a desire for authenticity in a world where other pleasures, such as human connections, are fleeting and uncertain. Thus, when Dev is caught in the flux of broken relationships and endless options of online dating, he finds himself drawn to the comfort and authenticity of pasta. By traveling to the culinary home of pasta-making, Dev pursues the qualities of authenticity outlined by Johnston and Baumann: namely, geographic specificity, "simplicity," personal connection, history and tradition, and ethnic connection (65). By pursuing authenticity, Dev attempts to find meaning and purpose as a solution to the hipster's existential malaise.

---

[6]According to Pierre Bourdieu, one's gustatory tastes are an essential marker of one's class tastes: "Taste, a class culture turned into nature, that is, embodied, helps to shape the class body. It is an incorporated principle of classification which governs all forms of incorporation, choosing and modifying everything that the body ingests and digests and assimilates, physiologically and psychologically. It follows that the body is the most indisputable materialization of class taste" (190).

Dev's passion for pasta also speaks for a larger theme of cultural diversity that is represented through the series. Aziz and Yang portray this convergence of cultural differences and identities through the sharing of culinary experiences across borders—transnationally between America and Italy but also figuratively as food experiences in the series bridge differences of race, religion, sexuality, and ethnicity. For Dev, food is revered like a religion and, indeed, surpasses his devotion to the orthodox religious practices of his family; this difference marks a generational and cultural conflict between Dev and his parents that is eventually resolved through the sharing of culinary experiences. In the episode "Religion," (2.3) Dev defies the identity ascribed to him through his family's religious practices as he chooses to eat bacon, skip Eid prayer to go to a barbecue festival, and chooses not to fast for Ramadan despite the fact that he was raised with Islamic values. In defiance of tradition, he places more cultural value on his food choices than he does on his family's orthodox religion. As a result, Dev's food choices cause generational and cultural conflict for his parents as Dev's eating habits have been clearly influenced by secular Western values. As he explains to his family, "I'm not that religious ... And I eat pork. But it's OK because I'm a good person and I'm 33 years old and I can make those decisions. I eat what I want. And I want to eat the crispy pork with broccoli ... For you guys, religion has its cultural value. It's not like that for me" (2.3). As Dev identifies to his parents, it is food that carries "cultural value" for him, not religion; thereby, it is food that is the most authentic marker of his identity and social status. Despite this initial clash of ideologies between Indian and American cultural values, Dev is able to make peace with his parents when he quotes the Qu'ran: "To you be your religion, and to me, my religion." He is thus able to justify his defiance of tradition, as he pursues his own profound experiences through food and friendship. The final scenes of the episode cut between Dev's father praying and socializing at the mosque and Dev meeting his friends for brunch; in this way, Ansari and Yang emphasize the similarities as both activities, while different, are sources of connection, community, and nourishment.

Dev's food choices not only help to define his identity as distinct and separate from his more traditional, first-generation immigrant parents but also allow him to participate in and achieve success in predominately white industries and culinary settings despite his racialized identity. Dev's hipster foodways allow him to challenge the status quo on multiple levels—including breaking racial barriers in American culture when he becomes a successful food television host of *Clash of the Cupcakes* and to successfully pitch his own passion project: a food and travel series *BFFs: Best Food Friends* with his friend and colleague Chef Jeff, a prominent celebrity chef. In an ironic twist, Dev's dream job is canceled and his culinary aspirations are sidelined when Chef Jeff is accused of sexual harassment by fourteen women, including Dev's makeup artist (played by Ilfenesh Hadera), a woman of color. Although Dev was not aware of Jeff's behavior when he signed on to star alongside him for their culinary television show, he is not completely innocent either. As Marissa Martinelli argues, "Dev didn't knowingly enable Jeff's behavior, but as Jeff's protégé, he benefitted from the same power that let Jeff take advantage of women who were less powerful than he was." Season two of *Master of None* ends with Dev struggling to come to terms with his complicity in his association with Chef Jeff, and as part of an industry plagued by the continued marginalization and exclusion of women and people of color. These problems are also present in mainstream hipster communities. In this way, the series problematizes Dev's position as a hipster tastemaker as precarious, illustrating how power and status associated with culinary capital continue to be predicated on white, male privilege.

Conclusion

As discussed, the collective identity of hipsters is represented in large part by the cultural value placed on foodways as a source and expression of distinction from the mainstream and as a means to depart from traditional systems that limit personal expression and freedoms. The hipster demographic is often maligned or misunderstood in mainstream culture. However, as both *Portlandia* and *Master of None* convey, to dismiss the hipster as purely an aesthetic or affection is to ignore the differing values and priorities of a young generation who are clearly leaving their mark in the world. In *Portlandia*, Brownstein, Armisen, and Krisel create relatable characters for its audience in their representation of individuals who seek culinary capital through artisanship and authenticity for both moral and social reasons. In *Master of None*, Aziz and Yang add much needed cultural diversity to televisual representations of hipsters, and in a way address the barriers that continue to marginalize or exclude certain voices from accessing the status and power associated with the cultivation of taste. While both series find humor in satirizing the aesthetic choices and affectations associated with hipster culture, they also represent the underlying meaning and purpose of culinary consumption beyond layers of hipness and irony. For a young generation, food is no longer valued solely for its nutrition or to satisfy hunger but, like an art form or religion, is imbued with meaning and purpose as an expression of group and individual identity.

Works Cited

Barnard, Alex V. *Waving the Banana at Capitalism: Freegans and the Politics of Waste in New York City*. University of Berkeley California, 2018, Wordpress, oxthepunx.files.wordpress.com/2010/11/barnard-waving-the-banana-at-capitalism.pdf. Accessed October 21, 2020.

Barrett, Gena-mour. "24 of the Worst Things Hipsters Did to Food in 2016." *Buzzfeed*, December 13, 2016, www.buzzfeed.com/genamourbarrett/the-worst-things-hipsters-did-to-food-in-2016. Accessed October 21, 2017.

Bourdieu, Pierre. *Distinction: A Social Critique on the Judgement of Taste*, translated by Richard Nice. Harvard University Press, 1984.

Carlson, Jen. "Here Are the NYC Bars & Restaurants in 'Master of None' Season Two." *Gothamist*, May 10, 2017, gothamist.com/food/here-are-the-nyc-bars-restaurants-featured-in-master-of-none-season-two. Accessed October 22, 2020.

Chopra, Sonia. "Master of None's Season Two Restaurants and Bars, Mapped." *Eater*, May 12, 2017, ny.eater.com/maps/master-of-nones-season-two-restaurants-and-bars-map. Accessed October 22, 2020.

Crane, Emily. "Have We Reached Peak Hipster? Trendy Café Serves Up 'Deconstructed' Coffee with Water, Milk and Espresso in Three Different Beakers." *Daily Mail Australia*, June 1, 2016, www.dailymail.co.uk/news/article-3618960/Woman-hits-Melbourne-hipster-cafe-coffee-served-deconstructed-beakers.html. Accessed October 21, 2017.

Cronin, James M., Mary B. McCarthy, and Alan M. Collins. "Covert Distinction: How Hipsters Practice Food-Based Resistance Strategies in the Production of Identity." *Consumption, Markets and Culture*, vol. 17, no. 1, 2014, pp. 2–28.

Feeney, Nolan. "*Portlandia*'s Carrie Brownstein: The Word 'Hipster' Doesn't Mean Anything Anymore." *Time Magazine*, January 8, 2015, time.com/3658544/carrie-brownstein-portlandia-sleater-kinney/. Accessed October 22, 2020.

Felton, Sean. "73 Questions with Aziz Ansari." *Vogue Magazine*, April 30, 2017, www.vogue.com/article/aziz-ansari-73-questions. Accessed June 1, 2017.

Fernandez, Maria Elena. "'Master of None': Here's Where They Ate in Italy." *Vulture*, May 15, 2017, www.vulture.com/2017/05/master-of-none-italy-where-they-ate.html. Accessed October 22, 2020.

Greif, Mark. "On Food." *n+1 magazine*, no. 7, 2008, nplusonemag.com/issue-7/essays/onfood/. Accessed October 22, 2020.

Greif, Mark. "What Was the Hipster?" *Against Everything: Essays*. Pantheon Books, 2016, pp. 211–24.

Inglis, David. "Globalization and Food: The Dialectics of Globality and Locality." *The Routledge International Handbook of Globalization Studies*. 2nd ed., edited by Bryan S. Turner and Robert J. Holton. Routledge, 2016, pp. 469–89.

Johnston, Josee, and Shyon Baumann. *Foodies*. 2nd ed., Routledge, 2015.

Kadakia, Crystal. "Why Watching Aziz Ansari's 'Master of None' Will Teach You More about Millennials than a Thousand Whitepapers." *Huffpost*, December 17, 2015, www.huffpost.com/entry/why-watching-aziz-ansaris_b_8839286. Accessed October 21, 2017.

Lanham, Robert. *The Hipster Handbook*. Anchor, 2003.

Lieu, Johnny. "This Deconstructed Coffee Is Peak Hipsterdom and How the World Ends." *Mashable*, June 1, 2016, mashable.com/2016/05/31/deconstructed-coffee/?europe=true. Accessed October 21, 2017.

Littleton, Cynthia. "Lena Waithe Makes Emmy History as First Black Woman to Win for Comedy Writing." *Variety*, September 17, 2017, variety.com/2017/tv/news/lena-waithe-wins-emmy-black-woman-comedy-writing-1202562040/. Accessed October 21, 2017.

Martinelli, Marissa. "*Master of None*'s Sexual Harassment Episode Now Feels Weirdly Prophetic." *The Slate*, November 16, 2017, slate.com/culture/2017/11/revisiting-master-of-nones-harassment-episode-after-the-louis-c-k-revelations.html. Accessed July 16, 2020.

Master of None. Created by Aziz Ansari and Alan Yang, performance by Aziz Ansari. *Netflix*, 2017–, www.netflix.com/search?q=master%20of%20none&jbv=80049714. Accessed October 21, 2017.

McCracken, Brett. *Hipster Christianity: When Church and Cool Collide*. Baker Books, 2010.

Naccarato, Peter, and Kathleen LeBesco. *Culinary Capital*. Berg, 2012.

Naccarato, Peter, and Kathleen LeBesco. "Distinction, Disdain, and Gentrification: Hipsters, Food People, and the Ethnic Other in Brooklyn, New York." *A Place-Based Perspective on Food in Society*, edited by K. M. Fitzpatrick and D. Willis. Palgrave Macmillan, 2015, pp. 121–39.

Nathan, Jonathan. "Quicklet on Portlandia Season 2." *Apple Books*, July 2012, books.apple.com/ca/book/quicklet-on-portlandia-season-2-tv-show/id652844104?ign-gact=1. Accessed October 21, 2017.

No, Michelle. "15 Hipster Food Trends That Need to Die in 2017." *Buzzfeed*, November 28, 2016, www.buzzfeed.com/michelleno/foods-that-hipsters-ruined-in-2016?utm_term=.koaYLV8O7x#.vidrvLaoyP. Accessed October 21, 2017.

Portlandia. Written by Jonathan Krisel, directed by Fred Armisen et al., performance by Fred Armisen, Carrie Brownstein. IFC, 2011–18.

Reeve, Elspeth. "'Girls' Writer Is Learning There's No Such Thing as Ironic Racism." *The Atlantic*, April 19, 2012, www.theatlantic.com/culture/archive/2012/04/girls-writer-learning-theres-no-such-thing-ironic-racism/329126/. Accessed October 23, 2020.

Rivera, Joshua. "*Master of None* Is Back to Ask You Some Questions, Millenials." *GQ*, May 12, 2017, www.gq.com/story/master-of-none-season-2-review. Accessed October 23, 2020.

Safronova, Valeriya. "Aziz Ansari Walks Us Through 10 'Master of None' Dining Spots." *New York Times*, December 2, 2015, www.nytimes.com/interactive/2015/12/02/style/aziz-ansari-master-of-none-10-locations.html. Accessed October 21, 2017.

Spitznagel, Eric. "Fred Armisen Explains Why There's No Such Thing as Hipsters." *MTV News*, April 1, 2012, www.mtv.com/news/2695206/fred-armisen-interview/. Accessed October 22, 2017.

Talmadge, Stephanie. "*Master of None*: How Aziz Ansari Captures the Bizarre Paradox of Being a Millennial." *The Week*, November 11, 2015, theweek.com/articles/587803/master-none-how-aziz-ansari-captures-bizarre-paradox-being-millennial. Accessed October 22, 2017.

Turow, Eve. *A Taste of Generation Yum: How the Millenial Generation's Love for Organic Fare, Celebrity Chefs and Microbrews Will Make or Break the Future of Food*. Pronoun, 2015.

Wampole, Christy. "How to Live without Irony." *New York Times*, November 17, 2012, opinionator.blogs.nytimes.com/2012/11/17/how-to-live-without-irony/. Accessed October 22, 2020.

18

Pabst Blue Ribbon: The Hipster Experiment with Critical Anti-Consumerism in Beer and Beyond

Daniella Gáti

What beer should a hipster drink? While there are many definitions of the hipster, hipsters around the world seem to converge on a preference for craft beers, which are as varied in taste as their ethos and aesthetics are unified. Apart from and against this slew of sophisticated beers, hipsters in the United States have also espoused a single, simple, non-craft lager—Pabst Blue Ribbon (PBR), one of America's oldest and simplest lager-style beers.[1] Indeed, PBR, a beer that faced near extinction at the turn of the millennium, has become associated with American hipsters to such a degree that many colloquial sources on hipsterdom bring up PBR as one of the primary definitional aspects of hipsters per se. How has PBR become so foundational for the concept of the hipster, and what does the centrality of this simple lager signify for American hipsterdom and society at large?

This chapter reads the hipster love affair with PBR as a sign of the response of hipsters to an understanding of their own failed attempt to

[1]For purposes of clarity, I will refer to the beer as PBR, whereas I reserve Pabst for Pabst Brewing, the company that produces PBR.

reject consumerism and as a response to changing affective attachments within the hipster group itself. In particular, I contribute a more generous critical perspective by examining a self-critical affective strand among hipsters. Taking seriously hipsters' critical awareness of their own consumerist tendencies, I link PBR to an attempt to reject those tendencies. This perspective offers an important complement to existing scholarship in attempting to assess the critical, anti-capitalist impulses in hipsterdom rather than its more thoroughly studied gentrifying and more comfortably consumerist aspects.

Popular opinion and scholarship alike decry hipsters' colonization of spaces, objects, aesthetics, and practices associated with marginalized populations (Greif, Ross, and Tortorici 10; Maly and Varis 650). In such a view, PBR, as an artifact of working-class culture, is merely an extension of the larger hipster tendency to co-opt already existing subcultural ways of life and turn them into fashionable "lifestyles." I argue that it is important to grasp hipster consumption's more genuinely critical impulses, a perspective that also enables a more thorough understanding of how and why such impulses ultimately fail. Thus, in reading the choice of PBR as the expression of a primarily critical and anti-consumerist rather than appropriative stance, this essay provides analysis of the affective process mobilized by the dynamics of neoliberalism, in which such critical possibilities are stifled and converted into a masculinist ideology of exclusion. The story of PBR's popularity among hipsters, then, offers important insights into the dynamics through which critical anti-capitalist impulses themselves fall prey to the logics of consumption and how, in the process, these impulses become corrupted into pernicious ideologies of purity and chauvinism.

Which Hipsters? Which Affects?

Few people who attempt to pinpoint what a hipster is would neglect to mention the hipster's adversarial relationship to consumption. The popular imagination, as exemplified by Urban Dictionary and Wikipedia, clearly associates the hipster with an attempt to resist mainstream consumption patterns. The most popular definition out of a full 549 definitions in the Urban Dictionary states that "[h]ipsters are a subculture of men and women typically in their 20's and 30's that value independent thinking, counter-culture, progressive politics, an appreciation of art and indie-rock, creativity, intelligence, and witty banter" ("Hipster, def. 5"). The Wikipedia entry claims that hipsters "also frequently flaunt a varied non-mainstream fashion sensibility, vintage and thrift store-bought clothing, generally pacifist progressive and green political views, veganism, organic and artisanal foods, alternative lifestyles and snobbery" ("Hipster (Contemporary Subculture))." Both sources acknowledge that hipsters are constituted by a resistance to the mainstream, and Wikipedia ties that resistance specifically to consumption ("fashion" and "foods"). Resisting "being like everybody else" thus means resisting the primacy of consumption. Many elements in the hipster's typical characteristics, such as "vintage and thrift store-bought clothing" or the hipster's much-reviled irony, can be read as attempts to counter the centrality that consumption has come to occupy in the individual's construction of their identity. The crux of the hipster's identity, then, is the question of how he or she should relate to consumption.

Scholars too hold consumption as central to hipster identity, but they also simultaneously tend to reinforce the notion that any anti-consumerist potential is predominantly a question of posturing rather than an authentic commitment. For example, Louise Thody, in observing the hipster attempt to "shun commercialism" (182) ultimately accepts R. Jay Magill's notion that hipsters are only "aping a lower social class status" in order to "camouflage or escape humdrum bourgeois life" (Magill 209–10). Similarly, Mark Greif rejects the possibility of hipsters' genuine anti-consumerism when he writes that the hipster "aligns himself [*sic*] *both* with rebel subculture *and* with the dominant class" (Greif, Ross, and Tortorici 9). Ico Maly and Piia Varis are even more unapologetic in their insistence that hipsters "are not *anti*-consumption, but constitute a specific niche consumption market" (646); in fact, for Maly and Varis, hipster "culture ... does not question neoliberalism and the consumption-driven society" (650). These scholars point to the complex and simultaneous imbrication of hipsters in questions of consumption and resistance; however, they tend to reinforce a perhaps too uniform notion of hipsters' culturally negative impacts. Instead, following a productive attempt by Bjørn Schiermer to grasp the positive contributions of hipsterdom to the cultural field (168), I argue that not only do hipsters at times embody genuine feelings of unease about mainstream or inauthentic modes of life, but also that some of those attitudes—specifically what I will call the PBR affect—come from the politically progressive impulse to reject mainstream consumerism. In reading hipsterdom as a series of shifting attempts to opt out of consumption patterns associated with the dominant class, this essay recuperates a genuine political commitment within hipster culture and demonstrates how such a commitment ultimately degenerates under the pressures of capitalism into a deleterious chauvinist ideology that envisions exclusionary nationalism as the alternative to flamboyant consumption.

In American beer culture, the question of how to avoid mainstream consumption has tended to produce two potential answers: craft beer and PBR. Yet, PBR seems cemented in the cultural imaginary around hipsterdom unlike any other single beer, even any single craft beer. While it is difficult to verify quantitatively what beers hipsters actually drink since this would require people to self-identify as hipsters, which, as Maly and Varis discuss, tends to be rare (638), the journalist Rob Walker reports a hipster

PBR-drinking culture in early 2000s Seattle, which he presents as one of many local hipster scenes saving Pabst from near extinction. Although ultimately it cannot be claimed with certainty that hipsters are the only or even primary drivers of PBR's resurrection, countless pop cultural sites and objects link PBR to the hipster. In film, PBR frequently appears as a prominent object in movies that can be considered part of the hipster canon. For example, Dennis Hopper's redneck villain in David Lynch's cult classic, *Blue Velvet* (1986), insists on PBR as the standard beer for suburban blue-collar people, and Clint Eastwood's reluctant benefactor in *Gran Torino* (2008) extends this association explicitly to the rural Midwest. Other proliferating pop cultural artifacts make the association more explicit. For example, when I asked students for their ideas of a hipster, their responses of various internet-found depictions of hipsters inevitably included PBR as the hipster's accessory. One such depiction was a caricature image from a hipster-critical blog of a male hipster complete with plaid shirt, skinny jeans, a cigarette, and a six-pack of PBR (Faust).[2] Notably, neither pop cultural websites nor the students brought up craft beer as a foundational attribute of hipsters.

If PBR is a definitional characteristic of the hipster, the reverse is also true: out of the various and fluctuating definitions of PBR on Urban Dictionary, one or more have consistently relied on hipsterdom to define the beer. This paradigmatic status of hipsterdom in the image of PBR has repeatedly sparked lengthy online discussion across sites such as the news aggregation and discussion site Reddit, the reviewer site Yelp, and miscellaneous personal blogs (u/unused-username; "Hipsters and PBR"; "Pabst Blue Ribbon"). The contributors to the n+1 publication *What Was the Hipster?* thus respond to a fait accompli when they treat the link between hipster and PBR as self-evident (Greif, Ross, and Tortorici 9, 45, 154). Furthermore, this link has shown itself fairly stable across time: Greif observes it in 1999 (9), while the sources above are dated 2007, 2009, 2014, and 2015, respectively. Thus, the question of why hipsters drink PBR continued to preoccupy the popular imagination with relative regularity half a decade after the hipster's supposed death in 2010 (Greif, Ross, and Tortorici vii).

Thus, the PBR affect, which has accompanied hipsterdom since at least 1999, provides a good way of understanding disparities among hipster populations' roles in consumption and gentrification. Hipsters are often regarded as drivers of gentrification and motors of the increasing prevalence of unaffordable luxury goods, but did or do all hipsters contribute in

---

[2]Thanks go to my students Ally, Kate, Ben, Renée, Greer, Gabriella, Sebastean, Elaine, Ryan, Julia, Sarah, and Nic for drawing my attention to this and other examples of the online representation of hipsters.

equal measure to the commodification of subculture? Regarding PBR as an affective attachment to a different model of consumption—one that remains resistant to exorbitant price tags—allows us to surmise that even as the commodifying developments were taking place, some hipsters were registering them with discomfort and attempting to find different behaviors. PBR indexes this discomfort and these attempts.

Although no data quantifying hipster PBR drinking exists to my knowledge, PBR's continued low-cost and unsophisticated taste come to signify an alternative hipster vision that remains wary of costly consumption goods such as the American Apparel, Obey, and Urban Outfitters clothing brands and barista coffee that Maly and Varis consider so "necessary" to hipster style (643, 649). It is these synchronous and overlapping movements that can be theorized as different affective registers within hipsterdom—different, though not fully distinct, and coexisting perhaps at times even within single individuals. Lacking data on hipster drinking patterns renders this endeavor a necessarily theoretical one, but following the work of affect theorists Lauren Berlant and Sianne Ngai, and relying on Raymond Williams's influential notion of "structures of feeling," I articulate the PBR affect as an emotional register and feeling-based identity structure that animates cultural expression and a way of life as well as a politics. The PBR affect is tied to those hipsters who continuously and critically observe themselves with respect to their own consumer behavior, and who view rapprochements to consumerism with suspicion and attempt to correct it.

Thus, if the two predominant hipster beer choices, craft and PBR, both stem from a discomfort with late capitalist consumption and production practices, they provide different answers to that discomfort. Indeed, these two affective strands are partially overlapping movements within hipsterdom that continuously reflect on each other in order to assess their success on a shared goal: the elision of capitalist mass production and consumption. For hipsters, then, choosing between craft beer and PBR is a paramount decision with ideological ramifications—even if at first glance, the question seems to be just a question of taste.

Craft or PBR? A Brief Beer History

What beer should a hipster drink? A brief look at American beer history reveals that, conditioned by their different market trajectories, PBR and craft beer were uniquely positioned to provide two distinct possibilities for beer drinkers who had grown weary of the multinational corporations' stranglehold on the beer market. Although possessing strikingly different histories, PBR and craft beer could both appear as outsiders on the beer scene, challenging the dominance of the big players but, at least ostensibly, without aspiring to the same hegemonic status.

PBR's history endows it with a connection to tradition and simplicity, making the beer a potential object of nostalgia. As one of America's few beers dating back to the nineteenth century, PBR is part of the early tradition of simple, European-style lagers. In the post-Prohibition period, such lagers produced by larger breweries became dominant in the US beer market due to the near total extinction of smaller breweries during Prohibition. PBR and other simple, light lagers such as Budweiser, Schlitz, Miller, and Coors became the predominant beers of American households (Vinton). In addition, as Lisa M. George shows in her study of the effects of television advertising on the beer market, when television became a household staple, TV commercials allowed these national brands to reach all parts of American society, making the big names essentially synonymous with beer (86). In this pre-craft era of American beer consumption, PBR pursued an aggressive marketing strategy, infiltrating the imaginaries of beer consumers with the image of the white, blue, and red bottle as the sine qua non of everyday beer—so much so that William Coors of Coors Brewing, itself a large brewery with wide reach, complained that Pabst had virtually displaced "all the little guys" with its large presence on the TV screen (George 85).

This strategy, which successfully secured a prominent place for PBR in people's minds as well as in their refrigerators, paradoxically exhausted itself toward the end of the century. As reported by Walker in the *New York Times* in 2003, PBR sales had been on the decline since the 1970s, forcing Pabst to cut down on its marketing and ultimately to virtually eliminate it by the 1990s. Thus, unlike a similarly traditional beer in the UK context, the Newcastle Brown Ale, whose connection to a working-class industrial past was a major objective of an aggressive, if ironic, marketing campaign in the early 2000s (Thody 177–9), PBR was never marketed to establish such a historical image: Pabst simply did not possess the means to pursue such marketing. Indeed, the beer that had overwhelmed smaller breweries in the 1950s and 1960s was, by the turn of the century, teetering on the edge of complete financial collapse. Meanwhile, the beer market at large experienced a steady increase in concentration between 1950 and 2000, meaning that larger brands commanded larger market shares while the number of breweries went down (George 89–90). The breweries familiar for their size today—Budweiser, Miller, and Coors—established and stabilized their dominance in this period. Thus, for hipsters in the early 2000s, PBR could simultaneously signify the staple household beer from the age of classical Americana and yet avoid the aggressive corporate image of other beers in its category such as Budweiser or Miller.

When hipsters at the turn of the century were deciding what beer to drink, then, this choice had to be made in an environment dominated by the large brands, as well as by imports of similarly large brands such as Corona or Heineken. These brands, both foreign and domestic, were the products of multinational corporations operating on the scale that Fredric Jameson has famously described as the "new space of late or multinational capital" (6). Consequently, and in spite of their commercial success, such brands had the potential to give rise to a feeling of resentment and alienation, since the beers' tastes and their production allowed them to be tied to anywhere and nowhere in particular. Shorn of any individualizing feature, such beers came to seem like nothing more than an image of production itself: an alienated image of beer "in the age of mechanical reproduction" (217), to borrow Walter Benjamin's phrase. People desiring to "disidentify" (Muñoz 4–5) with such anonymous and global production mechanisms while still drinking beer had to seek other, less prominently visible kinds of beer.

In a reaction against the delocalized and departicularized beers and production practices of these so-called macro-breweries, the 1980s saw the appearance of breweries that emphasized the particularity of their different beers and which limited their distribution, at least initially, to the near vicinity of production: craft brewing was born. Boston's Samuel Adams and the Californian Sierra Nevada, both brands that now have a nationwide appeal, were founded at this time, in 1984 and 1979, respectively, and both started with a strictly local and particular focus. Not only were the beers of such brewers radically different—preferring beer types other than the traditional lager, such as India Pale Ales (IPAs), and oriented towards experimentation with hops and spices—but also their marketing strategies tended to preclude the kinds of aggressive television marketing and sports events sponsorship that made the likes of Budweiser repulsive to many beer drinkers. These emerging breweries therefore presented promising alternatives to the mechanical-corporate ones of macro-breweries.

What in the early 2000s seemed like a significant, though small, change in the US beer market solidified as a new and permanent market arrangement in the second decade of the new millennium. Both Samuel Adams and Sierra Nevada are now available in liquor stores across the country, and craft beer sales seem to have reached a more or less stable market share at around 14 percent; this share was 13.6% percent in 2019 ("National Beer Sales"). Furthermore, the craft movement has continued to expand in other ways: most importantly through a veritable mushrooming in the numbers of extremely small breweries, so-called microbreweries.[3] The latest available

[3]The Brewers Association defines microbreweries as breweries that produce less than fifteen thousand barrels of beer per year ("Craft Beer Industry") and considers microbreweries as just one out of many types of craft brewing; the others include categories such as brewpubs and taprooms. In the remainder of this article, the term craft will refer to all small breweries, without differentiating between these subcategories. Brands with craft origins but which now have more or less nationwide appeal (such as Samuel Adams, Sierra Nevada, Lagunitas, Brooklyn Brewing, or Dogfishhead), and so-called zombie brands (brands that may have a craft origin, but which have been bought up by the traditional large companies, e.g., Shocktop, Blue Moon, and Goose Island) will not be considered craft. The reason is that the minuscule size as well as the remarkable increase in number of small breweries is central to the changing

data provided by the Alcohol and Tobacco Tax and Trade Bureau and the Brewers Association, collected in 2019, suggests that while the total volume of beer production has remained more or less constant over the last decade, craft brewing continues to blossom in terms of ever more microbreweries. This growth accounts for most of the growth in the total number of breweries between 2007 and 2019 (from 1619 to 6400). The number of breweries in the largest category (producing over 6 million barrels) declined slightly from 17 to 15 in this period, while the category of microbreweries (with less than 15000 barrels) grew from 1485 to 6121 breweries ("Beer Statistics"). In terms of retail dollar sales, craft beer actually accounts "for more than 25% of the $116.0 billion U.S. beer market," according to the Brewers Association's data for 2019. The trend, then, is toward an ever-larger set of increasingly small and particularized breweries, which make up a stable and significant portion of retail income. Notably, this trend is already well in place in 2007, when microbreweries make up 1485 out of the total 1619 breweries, which is almost 92 percent of the total number of breweries.

The beginning of this process, then, sometime during the 1980s, imbued the decision of what beer to drink with the significance of choosing between two competing models of capitalist production. Or, more adequately, the choice of beer translated into the choice of a model of consumption that endorsed a specific type of production. Choose one of the large brands, and you would opt into familiar grounds in terms of the beers you drank, as well as financially support a multinational corporate model of beer production and sale. Choose a craft beer, and you would withhold your money from the large corporations in favor of smaller, local enterprises and at the same time commit to experimental, new flavors in your beer.

The emergence of craft beer, then, which roughly coincides with the emergence of the contemporary hipster, provided a viable alternative for those beer drinkers who were skeptics of corporate capitalism and, at the same time, had a penchant for aesthetic experimentation. Craft beers therefore seem like the perfect fit for hipsters who evince anti-capitalist sentiments and who embrace an aesthetics of the vanguard of the next "cool." Indeed, craft beer—which has certainly become what Maly and Varis call "indexicals" of hipster culture on "a global scale" (650)—provides a space outside of Jameson's "space of ... multinational capital" by opting for a much more localized circuit of production and consumption. Ingredient sourcing, marketing reach, and distribution are all centered around a smaller scale in craft brewing. For many hipsters, this type of consumption then

---

attitudes of hipsters toward craft beer consumption, and to how that consumption relates to mainstream consumption. The larger, more eclectic craft-like brands do not play an important role in these developments.

represents one attempt to escape mainstream consumption. This sensibility constitutes the craft affect.

However, ideal as craft may seem to hipsters, the high cultural visibility of PBR suggests that there has also been suspicion among hipsters regarding these developments. That suspicion has to do with the tendency of spaces outside of multinational circuits to develop into market niches and themselves become commodities in circulation—the capitalist trap described by Herbert Marcuse in *One-Dimensional Man* (11–2) and alluded to by Maly and Varis when they describe hipsters as "constitut[ing] a specific niche consumption market" (646). The beer market has simply accommodated craft beers by allotting them their own space: that of the luxury good. Most bars carry craft beers on tap, and while macro brands like Budweiser and Miller usually cost around 2–4 dollars, craft beers tend to be priced at 6–10 dollars, and often come in smaller pours. Thus, the skeptical hipster will observe that craft beer is no longer defiantly on the margins of mainstream consumption, but rather dead at the center, or at the top, of consumption hierarchies.

The hipster rejecting craft consumption will have observed PBR as a visible alternative already in 1999, but Walker dates its rise to prominence in hipster circles to the early 2000s, and this prominence is salient in the popular imagination to this day. Therefore, favorable hipster attitudes towards PBR are coeval with, and responsive to, craft beer and the craft affect. This attitude is the PBR affect: the critical desire shared with the craft affect to elide mass consumption and production, while at the same time critiquing craft and its emerging role as luxury good. When twenty-first-century hipsters turn to PBR, they evince an awareness of the upper-class tendencies of their own group; thus, PBR becomes one important piece in a more complex struggle to reject cultural snobbery and elaboration.

The expansion of hipsterdom into different cities across the globe tends to introduce a uniform aesthetic to these areas, if with some local variation (cf. e.g., Melissa Tandiwe Myambo and George Alexandru Condrache in this volume). This global aesthetic is aligned with craft, and its colonialist whitewashing and appropriative tendencies are key reasons why hipsters might reject craft beers and espouse PBR instead. Craft's imposition of an ever more unified aesthetic and taste schema over a diverse global landscape, resulting in gentrification and the erasure of local particularities, renders it ever more difficult to embrace as countercultural and anti-consumerist stance—and this in spite of craft ideology's original commitment to locality and its rejection of multinational corporate production. Thus, when hipsters turn to PBR in the first decade of the twenty-first century, this act should be read as possessing at least an initial impetus of self-critique: the recognition that luxury consumption, no matter how sophisticated, remains committed to consumerism in the name of global, imperialist capitalism.

The Craft Aesthetic

The following example of the craft aesthetic is a brewery probably unfamiliar to most readers, which is itself an important part of the craft sensibility. Aeronaut Brewing is a small brewery located in Somerville, Massachusetts, the United States, a rapidly gentrifying former blue-collar neighborhood of the Boston area. Aeronaut, founded in 2014, is well known to the locals; yet, although it distributes its beers to liquor stores across Massachusetts, it seems safe to say that it is predominantly consumed by a specific demographic within the Boston area, namely young professionals in the area's IT, biotech, or other similar sectors, many of whom also contribute to the gentrification processes of Somerville and the metropolitan area in general. The brewery occupies a former factory space and understands itself as fulfilling a mission for the local community, as evidenced by their concise and remarkably telling mission statement: "We are a BREWERY and COMMUNITY SPACE in Somerville, MA. We push the boundaries of beer through fearless recipe design, creative ingredient-sourcing, and house-cultured fermentations. Our mission is to brew world-class beer, amplify the voice of our community and support arts and culture" (Aeronaut Brewing Co.). In this statement, Aeronaut links craft beer brewing to a social justice project whose "fearless" choice of hops and flavors somehow translates into the amplification of "the voice of our community." The space is regularly used for various kinds of community events such as concerts, talks on local history, film screenings, or yoga classes. Indeed, both in words and programming, the brewery connects craft brewing with cultural and artistic leisure activities.

The beers themselves, the package and logo design, as well as the decoration of the space serve to delineate the craft aesthetic. In terms of flavor, Aeronaut's aesthetic favors all kinds of different IPAs, as well as specialty styles such as saison or gose, which were virtually unknown by the average American beer-drinker some twenty or thirty years ago. Indeed, the beer list is constantly changing as the brewery experiments with new beer, focusing on novel and often unexpected flavors. Additionally, the creative, often punning names of beers ("A Year with Dr. Nandu," "Hop Hop and Away") do not aid the thirsty visitor in making a choice of beverage. Finally, in terms of visual aesthetics, the cans and logo evince a clean, urban style with sans serif fonts and drawings by hand, while the interior is decorated with an eye for industrial chic. In sum, Aeronaut—building, beers, cans, names, and activities—represents the brewery version of a hipster urban chic.

More than just embodying the ideal aesthetic of craft beers, Aeronaut also exemplifies how the craft sensibility tends to transcend focusing on just the beer itself. Although beer brewing is Aeronaut's main occupation, the brewery places so much emphasis on surrounding activities and general design that the visitor may have the impression that beer is actually but one aspect out of many. The many programmed activities—food pop-ups, board game nights, concerts—link the consumption of Aeronaut beer with the social life of the local community. Additionally, the small distributional range limits the presence of Aeronaut's beer to the immediate vicinity of the brewery, further tying the beer explicitly to the space of the brewery in the imagination—an attempt to remove Aeronaut from Jameson's space of multinational capital and anchor it firmly in the local. This imaginary is the exact opposite of that which Pabst had achieved in the 1960s, an imaginary in which PBR beer had become disconnected from any particular physical space and referred only to itself. While PBR was meant to be simply a bottle of beer, Aeronaut is a space—a space filled with many different beers, to be sure, but also a space for a specific aesthetic experience constituted by a wide range of social activities. Thus, Aeronaut exemplifies the set of aesthetic stipulations of the craft aesthetic. A relatively late arrival on the beer scene, Aeronaut can be seen as reflecting the solidification of the formal features of craft, features which had established themselves during the explosion of microbreweries in the preceding decade.

For hipsters concerned with the alienation of the large corporations from the actual beer drinkers, craft's aesthetic awareness, community involvement, and experimental flavors must initially have been appealing. But the fast expansion of microbreweries worked against this appeal on at least two accounts. First, if hipsters' resistance to mainstream consumption patterns was conducive to craft beer consumption initially, the development of the craft movement quickly began to violate the injunctions against both *mainstream* and consumption *patterns*. With 1485 microbreweries already in 2007, craft beer consumption had moved very quickly from being an alternative, marginal form of consumption to being mainstream. More damning, however, was the pattern in which this type of consumption seemed inevitably implicated. If hipsters were drawn to the locally conscious but also aesthetically experimental brewery spaces, such spaces became increasingly formalized, growing ever more conscious of which parts of their aesthetic possessed the highest appeal and crystallizing those into an increasingly uniform style. Thus, the aesthetic exemplified by Aeronaut—beer and brewery alike—is difficult to distinguish from such nationally known craft brands as Stone, or from Aeronaut's close neighbors Remnant, Lamplighter, or Lord Hobo. For these breweries, design gradually took the upper hand, assuming larger significance vis-à-vis the beer itself. In particular, similar styles became formalized into aesthetic patterns that people came to recognize as the stamps of a hipster aesthetic. That is, not only had craft beer consumption become mainstream, but it had also become formalized into the perfect embodiment of luxury consumption, expanding seemingly unstoppably into the spaces formerly occupied by marginalized communities and diverse beer drinking practices. Loudly proclaiming experimentation and local consciousness, craft beer had come to impose the same—white and consumerist—standards on beer drinking. Indeed, beer consumption had moved from being the consumption of a beverage to the consumption of a lifestyle, and one with a high price tag at that—and one in which people of color remain drastically underrepresented (Watson). From having been an alternative to consumerism, then, drinking craft beer had become a luxury good of a quintessentially American kind: the veritable embodiment of consumerism.

Drinking Back the Real: The Promise and Failure of PBR

If some hipsters were already turning to PBR as an alternative to craft in the early 2000s, later, as craft beer's transformation into a luxury good became increasingly visible, drinking PBR became codable as an act of active rejection. Indeed, for hipsters seeking alternatives to capitalist consumerism, the insight that craft beer had become a luxury good constitutes a fundamental traumatic moment. Like the Lacanian moment of self-recognition in the mirror, where the child realizes its own identity as constituted by the split from the mother and from the outside world (Lacan 78–9), the epiphany for capitalist-critical hipsters is the recognition of the self as constituted by a rupture from what was thought to be central to that self: anti-consumerism. This recognition amounts to the insight that, in Jameson's terms, the space supposedly outside of multinational capital's circuits actually turned out to be the niche of the luxury good. The impulse to break out of the one-dimensionality of consumption-production has ironically produced a self who engages in luxury consumption.

If hipsters recognize a split between their intent to opt out of consumerism and the fact that they have become luxury consumers, then the turn to PBR can be understood as an attempt to restore wholeness or the hipster's identity with oneself. This attempt has two debilitating implications. The first comes from the concept of wholeness, as opposed to fragmentation—the attempt to return to a sense of unified identity against what appears to be a newer, depraved state of fracture. This project amounts to hipsters' attempts to return themselves to a perceived earlier state as consumers on the margins. Thus, instead of participating in the mainstream and luxury consumption of craft beers, the hipster would choose PBR, a beer whose consumption cannot be considered luxury. Drinking PBR approximates the supposed consumption behavior of those who do not drink beer for its luxury value, but merely for its qualities as beer. In this sense, the demand for PBR signifies the type of need that is arguably as close as it is possible to get to what Marcuse calls a vital need as opposed to a false one (6). Thus, PBR becomes a sign of the real: it represents only its "beerness" and not the entire package of community spaces, yoga classes, and conscious design, which become coded as luxury—excessive and therefore "fake." In this manner, the consumer who rejects luxury consumption as unnecessary and superfluous, indeed superficial, becomes associated with realness and groundedness.

What this association ignores is that those consumers who do not partake in luxury consumption tend to do so not out of choice but due to material conditions. For example, as analysis by Brewers Association chief economist Bart Watson demonstrates, the percentage of craft drinkers coming from minority (nonwhite) backgrounds has stagnated at around 15 percent, as opposed to their share in the general population at around 30 percent. Further, data presented by chief economist of the National Beer Wholesalers Association, Lester Jones, show that craft beer is the least popular form of *any* type of alcoholic beverage among Latinx Americans (slide 10). Although neither economist addresses the reasons for this disparity in beer drinking habits across ethnicities, it is likely owing to the continued rift in wealth between white and nonwhite US residents (Hannah-Jones). Thus, the desire to align oneself with marginalized, "real" consumption practices results in an idealization of specific notions of what it means to be real. Importantly, such notions fail to account for the actually existing economic conditions that undergird those notions of realness, in particular overlooking systemic and racialized poverty. In an ironic repetition of the American tradition to co-opt the counterhegemonic status of people of color and marginalized communities, the PBR affect ends up idealizing figures from lower socioeconomic classes as cachets of authenticity and resistance, but without an articulation of the material structures of marginalization that these communities actually face.

While many have pointed to this troubling characteristic of hipster populations (see, for example, Thody 183–4; Greif, Ross, and Tortorici 10; Michael 164–5), the insight that the problem's origins might reside in a genuine critical impulse is less firmly established. Yet, it is paramount to recognize the possibility that the route by which hipsters arrive to the co-optation and exploitation of marginalized communities is not one of avowed consumerism or capitalist colonization, but rather of a continued unease with consumerism and of an ongoing attempt to evade it. What is at stake in affording such a possibility is a nuanced understanding of how the genuine effort to avoid the hipster's own imbrication in exploitative consumption paradoxically ends up reproducing exploitation, co-optation, and marginalization on its own terms.

The failure of this critical effort is fully accomplished by another line of troubling implications that the PBR affect ultimately generates. To view the consumption of craft beers as somehow impure is not only to reject luxury consumption but also to reject sophistication, experimentation, and elaboration. There is little that separates this rejection from the rejection of all those notions that have tended in the Western tradition to be associated with the fine and the sophisticated: femininity, gayness, or even the intellect as such. In this line of thought, craft beer becomes decadent and depraved because it represents a sophistication—a kind of dandyism—that is dangerously nonnormative, at least for standard notions of masculinity. Floral, fruity beers do not lend themselves easily to traditional ideas of manhood; in fact, the often aggressively masculine marketing strategies of craft beers arguably serve precisely to counteract the potentially gay associations of flowers and fruit. Similarly, marketing efforts that emphasize the scientific knowledge and expertise required to produce, perhaps even to enjoy, craft beer likewise attempt to situate craft in the domain of men, who have traditionally had exclusive access to such specialized knowledge. PBR stands on the opposite end of the spectrum as a beer that is only that: beer. Simple, crude, and plain, it is the beer for real men.

What are real men like—and in particular, what are real men who reject late capitalism like? The imaginary surrounding PBR gives some tentative answers. First, the real man's beer is simple in taste, disallowing experimentation. It rejects newness and harkens back to earlier ages in American brewing. In its presentation, it is similarly plain, rejecting the craft aesthetic and emphasizing the colors of the American flag. In terms of marketing, it is virtually absent, a fact that reinforces its image as standing on its own: people who drink this beer supposedly do so out of a plain, "authentic" desire to drink beer, not because they were convinced by marketing. The kinds of men that are implied by this set of characteristics would have to be simple, reject novelty and change, drink beer for its plain "beerness," and resent the idea of being treated as objects of marketing ploys. To articulate this another way, real men would embody stereotypical notions of working-class laborers, in touch with their roots in the American heartland, and not forced to confront the speed, interconnection, virtuality, and supposed "fakeness" of the contemporary global world. Drinking PBR, then, can arguably amount to an attempt to shore up one's image of oneself as this kind of authentic, lower-class white man. In this vision, materiality is both paramount and disavowed. The desired experience of authentic life outside of capitalism is one where postmodern flux is arrested, where signification is stable and obvious, where things are "simply what they are": beer is just beer and men are just men.

It is not hard to see how such a vision quickly becomes hostile to ideas of difference and novelty, and how hipsters of the PBR affect might reject change altogether. It is the tragedy of this affective stance that the protest against luxury consumption and gentrification thus devolves into a fundamentally conservative, even chauvinistic, attitude. Although hipsters typically do not return to the material conditions of the working class, from whose ranks they may never have come in the first place, the ostensible origins in working classness continue to remain the objects of yearning. This yearning manifests in expressions of the qualities that supposedly make up the working class: straightness, masculinity, simplicity, physicality, rurality. In the end, it is not enough to arrest change; change must be reversed in order to restore an America that was somehow, ostensibly, still straightforwardly American. Of course, this illusory but idealized image is of an America that tolerates no heterogeneity: it is white, male, blue-collar, simple, and straight.

Ultimately then, the PBR affect points to a social problem that is much larger than the question of beer drinking: it highlights the perhaps inevitable dangers in white anti-consumerist thinking in the twenty-first-century United States. What happens when a group of mostly well-educated people belonging to the (upper) middle class take as their model the illusory image of a homogenous, authentic, and simple American working class? How is society affected when a young elite demographic turns its gaze back to an imagined past in order to conceive of a future? Such an affective stance does not merely dally with the appeal of an exclusionary, nationalist, and white supremacist notion of twenty-first-century America; nor can it easily be dismissed as simply the obsession of naïve and uninformed people, hearkening back to an earlier golden age. Rather, it is for a critically minded population that working classness becomes an appealing, mythicized emblem of unproblematic realness, disconnected from actual material conditions. Thus, the very people who recognize that craft consumption has become just another means by which late capitalism folds dissent back into itself are not invulnerable to ignorance about their own imbrication in such ideologies. In seeking to avoid the bourgeois dead end of craft consumption, PBR and its affective attachments deteriorate to a chauvinist politics yearning for a white, homogeneous, and anti-intellectual America. Thus, PBR as a critically minded consumer choice demonstrates how what started out as a genuine critical impulse against capitalist consumerism slips, seemingly inevitably, into a deleterious ideology and a masculinist, racially purified vision of social life.

Works Cited

Aeronaut Brewing Co. www.aeronautbrewing.com/. Accessed July 17, 2020.

"Beer Statistics." *Alcohol and Tobacco Tax and Trade Bureau*, www.ttb.gov/beer/beer-stats.shtml. Accessed October 13, 2017.

Benjamin, Walter. "The Work of Art in the Age of Mechanical Reproduction." *Illuminations: Essays and Reflections*, translated by Harry Zohn, edited by Hannah Arendt. Schocken, 1968, pp. 217–51.

Berlant, Lauren. *Cruel Optimism*. Duke University Press, 2011.

Blue Velvet. Directed by David Lynch, De Laurentiis Entertainment Group, 1986.

"Craft Beer Industry Market Segments." *Brewers Association*, www.brewersassociation.org/statistics/market-segments/. Accessed October 14, 2017.

Faust, Coronare Modestus. "I Am Not a Hipster—Has the Peak of Hipster Arrived?" *Faustian UrGe*, January 8, 2015, Wordpress, spfaust.wordpress.com/2015/01/08/i-am-not-a-hipster-has-the-peak-of-hipster-arrived/. Accessed October 19, 2017.

George, Lisa M. "National Television and the Market for Local Products: The Case of Beer." *Journal of Industrial Economics*, vol. 57, no. 1, 2009, pp. 85–111.

Gran Torino. Directed by Clint Eastwood, Warner Bros. Pictures, 2008.

Greif, Mark, Kathleen Ross, and Dana Tortorici, eds. *What Was the Hipster? A Sociological Investigation*. n+1 Foundation, 2010.

Hannah-Jones, Nikole. "From the Magazine: 'It Is Time for Reparations.' " *New York Times*, June 24, 2020, www.nytimes.com/interactive/2020/06/24/magazine/reparations-slavery.html. Accessed July 17, 2020.

"Hipster, def. 5." *Urban Dictionary*, November 22, 2007, www.urbandictionary.com/define.php?term=hipster. Accessed October 13, 2017.

"Hipster (Contemporary Subculture)." *Wikipedia*, September 26, 2017, en.wikipedia.org/w/index.php?title=Hipster_(contemporary_subculture)&oldid=802467070. Accessed October 13, 2017.

"Hipsters and PBR ... What the F*ck? San Francisco." *Yelp*, www.yelp.com/topic/san-francisco-hipsters-and-pbr-what-the-f-ck. Accessed October 8, 2017.

Jameson, Fredric. *Postmodernism, or, the Cultural Logic of Late Capitalism*. Duke University Press, 1992.

Jones, Lester. *The Economics and Demographics That Drive the US Beer Industry*. 2019, www.bevindustry.com/ext/resources/bofs/presentations/Lester-Jone-NBWA---Wide-Screen.pdf. Accessed July 17, 2020.

Lacan, Jacques. "The Mirror Stage as Formative of I Function as Revealed in Psychoanalytic Experience." *É crits*, translated by Bruce Fink et al., Norton, 2006, pp. 75–81.

Magill, R. Jay. *Sincerity: How a Moral Ideal Born Five Hundred Years Ago Inspired Religious Wars, Modern Art, Hipster Chic, and the Curious Notion that We All Have Something to Say (No Matter How Dull)*. Norton, 2013.

Maly, Ico, and Piia Varis. "The 21st-Century Hipster: On Micro-Populations in Times of Superdiversity." *European Journal of Cultural Studies*, vol. 19, no. 6, 2016, pp. 637–53, doi:10.1177/1367549415597920. Accessed July 18, 2020.

Marcuse, Herbert. *One-Dimensional Man: Studies in the Ideology of Advanced Industrial Society*. 2nd ed., Beacon Press, 1991.

Michael, Janna. "It's Really Not Hip to Be a Hipster: Negotiating Trends and Authenticity in the Cultural Field." *Journal of Consumer Culture*, 2013, pp. 163–82, *Sage Journals*, doi:10.1177/1469540513493206. Accessed July 18, 2020.

Muñoz, José Esteban. *Disidentifications: Queers of Color and the Performance of Politics*. University of Minnesota Press, 1999.

"National Beer Sales and Production Data." *Brewers Association*, www.brewersassociation.org/statistics/national-beer-sales-production-data/. Accessed July 17, 2020.

Ngai, Sianne. *Our Aesthetic Categories: Zany, Cute, Interesting*. Harvard University Press, 2015.

"Pabst Blue Ribbon." *Urban Dictionary*, www.urbandictionary.com/define.php?term=pabst%20blue%20ribbon&page=2. Accessed December 8, 2020.

"Pabst Blue Ribbon: There Is No Good Reason to Drink This Beer." *No Pun Intended*, November 4, 2009, npinopunintended.wordpress.com/2009/11/04/pabst-blue-ribbon-there-is-no-good-reason-to-drink-this-beer/. Accessed October 13, 2017.

Schiermer, Bjørn. "Late-Modern Hipsters: New Tendencies in Popular Culture." *Acta Sociologica*, vol. 57, no. 2, 2014, pp. 167–81.

Thody, Louise. "From Working Class to Hipster Flash: Locating Newcastle City in Newcastle Brown Ale." *Visual Culture in Britain*, vol. 15, no. 2, 2014, pp. 173–91.

u/unused-username. "Why Is PBR Considered a Hipster Beer? I Notice It in Person As Well, So What Made That Their Drink of Choice?" *Reddit*, 2015, www.reddit.com/r/OutOfTheLoop/comments/3139w3/why_is_pbr_considered_a_hipster_beer_i_notice_it/. Accessed October 9, 2017.

Vinton, Kate. "How Breweries Like Coors, Yuengling and Anheuser-Busch Survived Prohibition." *Forbes*, November 4, 2015, www.forbes.com/sites/katevinton/2015/11/04/how-breweries-like-coors-yuengling-and-anheuser-busch-survived-prohibition/#595c3e44fabd. Accessed June 16, 2018.

Walker, Rob. "The Marketing of No Marketing." *New York Times*, June 22, 2003, www.nytimes.com/2003/06/22/magazine/the-marketing-of-no-marketing.html. Accessed December 8, 2020.

Watson, Bart. "Shifting Demographics Among Craft Drinkers." *Brewers Association*, June 12, 2018, www.brewersassociation.org/insights/shifting-demographics-among-craft-drinkers/. Accessed December 8, 2020.

Williams, Raymond. "Structures of Feeling." *Marxism and Literature*. Oxford University Press, 1977, pp. 128–35.

19

The Paradox of the Hungry Hipster: The Representation and Cultural Politics of Hipster Foodways

Kathleen LeBesco and Peter Naccarato

Search the internet for articles about hipsters and their foodways and you are likely to come up with titles like "10 Hipster Food Trends We Hate" or "Why Is My Food So Expensive? Blame Hipsters." Although the figure of the hipster may be enigmatic, one thing seems clear when it comes to representation of hipsters' influence on contemporary food culture, namely that it has not been particularly positive. But while many recent mainstream assessments of so-called "hipster foodways" are critical, they also reveal a more ambiguous relationship with the food trends they critique. In fact, while popular representations of hipsters typically identify them as apolitical and outside of mainstream culture, many of the food practices they are said to have adopted undermine these assumptions. Are hipster food practices really that different from culinary trends that have become popular across mainstream culture or been embraced by self-proclaimed "foodies," those who think about food "not just as biological sustenance, but also as a key part of their identity, as a kind of lifestyle" (Johnston and Baumann 1)? Or are those non-hipsters who direct their criticisms of these trends toward hipsters attempting to deflect their own culpability for things like rising food costs, cultural appropriation, gentrification, and other consequences of a shifting economic and social landscape?

In this chapter, we aim to answer these questions by examining representations of hipster food practices in recent news articles and blog posts.[1] Rather than taking them at face value, we consider what popular representations of hipster foodways reveal about how mainstream culture imagines the hipster figure. Broadly speaking, we recognize several character traits often used to identify hipsters: their left-leaning social views, their artistic sensibilities, their heightened sense of their own cultural awareness, their generally ironic worldview, their disdain for labels, including hipster (Lanham). More specifically, we focus on what is increasingly identified as a unique hipster food culture, with defining attributes like claiming refined tastes that shun popular, establishment eateries and preferring restaurants that "write their menus on chalkboards, have low ceilings, use soft light, and have waiters with body odor" (Lanham 29). But rather than uncritically accepting such representations, we ask how those who would identify as non-hipsters use such representations to deflect their own privilege and role in the commodification of marginalized cultures. As we found in our previous work on the spread of hipster culture in Brooklyn, New York (LeBesco and Naccarato), hipster food practices are often associated with gentrification processes that implicate the hipster in the marginalization of communities of color; however, we argue that such representations of hipster food culture serve to redirect such accusations away from non-hipsters who may also be implicated in such processes. In fact, we find that many social media outlets utilize this tactic of constructing a distinct hipster food culture only to express exhaustion with it and blame it for rising food costs and gentrification of lower-income neighborhoods. Thus, our analysis exposes the ways in which the seemingly apolitical figure of the hipster serves a deeply political purpose, particularly as a scapegoat for those whose foodways contribute to structural inequalities.

The overall goal of this project is to understand how the hipster figure, in general, and hipster food culture, in particular, have been and continue to be constructed in soft news stories—often associated with "infotainment" (Tewksbury and Rittenberg)—and across social media. A Google search for the term "hipster food" in the summer of 2017 produced thousands of hits for results written in English, many of which were blog posts or image-heavy, listicle-style articles with enticing headlines. A careful analysis

[1]The ease with which everyday citizens can share their views using new media and the perceived lack of consequence for doing so differentiate them from older forms of publication, like books, that explicitly appropriate hipster aesthetics but tend to lack such outspoken critiques.

of twenty articles and their comments section published primarily on US, UK, and Australian-based websites between 2012 and 2017 paints a curious picture of the hipster, from a lighthearted and often playful mockery of this enigmatic figure to a downright hostile attitude toward it. We have organized our analysis of this material around five thematic frames: The Hipster as "Clickbait"; Hipster Foods as Frivolous Presentation and Photo-Ops; Hipsters to Blame for Rising Food Costs; Hipsters Blamed for Cultural and Culinary Appropriation; and Defending the Hipster: "A Straw Man in Skinny Jeans." What this analysis reveals is that contemporary representations of hipsters and their food culture are generally negative, perhaps revealing mainstream culture's ambivalence about the economic and cultural impact of its own food trends.

In media studies, framing means directing attention to certain aspects of a thing—but colloquially, people who are "framed" are made to look like they are responsible for something when they are not. Our survey of popular culture discourse about hipsters reveals an evolution toward this kind of dual meaning of "framing" at work for the hipster. From a sociological perspective, framing is often used by specific groups to define issues in ways that, "mobilize potential adherents and constituents, to garner bystander support, and demobilize antagonists" (Snow and Benford 198). For us, examining how news sites and social media frame hipsters and their foodways is essential for revealing the interests and anxieties of the content creators and their readers. We assert that by framing concerns about gentrification, rising food costs, and cultural appropriation as consequences of the spread of hipster food trends, these writers have tended to literally "frame" hipsters for offenses for which non-hipsters are likely culpable.

The Hipster as "Clickbait"

An initial indicator of attitude toward the hipster figure comes in the number of recent articles that use the term "hipster" in their titles as an enticement to readers without mentioning, let alone analyzing, the concept of the "hipster" within the body of the article. Because these articles tend to have a negative attitude toward hipsters, often expressing disdain for their food practices or blaming them for what the authors dismiss as annoying trends, such "clickbait" is geared mostly to readers who are similarly critical of hipsters. But rather than actually reinforcing such negative assessments through the content of their articles, these authors or editors presumably put "hipster" in the titles as enticement for readers to click on these stories even though they contain very little, if any, content that focus on hipsters.

In Tony Naylor's March 2017 article, "It's Poké, Man: The Ultimate Hipster-Food Glossary," on TheGuardian.com, there is very little mention of hipsters outside of the headline. Naylor notes,

> Where once, influences from star chefs would disseminate slowly and new products could take years to establish themselves, today rare ingredients and new dishes can proliferate online, globally, almost instantly. On Instagram, a coalition of food nerds—not just chefs, but (amateur) bakers, baristas, brewers and artisan producers—are generating a creative frenzy of new ideas and potential break-out trends.

This claim that star chefs exert dramatic influence on everyday food trends is unsubstantiated—but Naylor's naming of "food nerds" seems not as damning as "hipsters," a label he saves for his "ultimate hipster food glossary," which is composed of a hodgepodge of specific foods (including jackfruit, calçots, kalettes, and cacao nibs) and food practices (including unicorning, #icemanpouring, and root-to-shoot cooking) that Naylor disparages. While he uses "hipster" in the title of his glossary, the term only appears once in the list of sixteen items, when he tells his readers that they can "freak out [their] hipster friends" by mentioning khachapuri ("imagine a pizza-like dough-boat filled with cheese, eggs and butter"). "Hipster" is used to attract readers to an article that offers no engagement with the term, only employing it in a cursory way in its rant about contemporary food culture.

A similar tactic is utilized by Lucy McGuire, writing for the *Huffington Post UK*, in an April 2015 article titled "Hipster Food Trends: Love or Loathe?" McGuire begins with the premise that how we eat and drink outside the home is "getting wackier ... some would say a bit ridiculous." She suggests that restaurants that "do something unique ... create a concept, a talking point or do something down right [*sic*] weird or unexpected" are the ones that "reach hipster status." Beyond this, she barely mentions hipsters, seemingly equating "hipster" with food trends that she deems wacky or ridiculous, including "dressing up" fast food or very ordinary fare, "hybrid hysteria," creating new "fusion" food or just "combin[ing] food that shouldn't go together," or making customers prepare their own food, thereby piling on to the negative characterization of hipsters and their foodways.

Some better-written pop culture sources use the hipster bait and switch as well. A thoughtful article by Stephen Tucker Paulsen in January/February 2017 about "hipster food towns" on MotherJones.com offers a thoughtful analysis of "food mirages" but never mentions the word "hipster" anywhere beyond its headline. Such deceptive titling decisions frame frustrations with current food trends as caused by hipsters, inviting those who want to participate in "hipster bashing" to click on the headlines and join in the fun. But as the next sections demonstrate, other articles delve more deeply into their critique of hipsters and their food culture, either dismissing them as frivolous or blaming them for various social, political, and economic problems. As these articles transition from playful mockery to full-throated critique of hipsters and their influence on contemporary (food) culture, we become increasingly interested in understanding the motivations of authors and readers alike.

Hipster Foods as Frivolous Presentations and Photo-Ops

A substantial amount of internet content frames hipsters as preoccupied with how food is presented with the singular goal of snapping attention-grabbing pictures that make for trending social media posts. Such critiques characterize hipsters as frivolous, dismissing their foodways as focused on gimmicky presentations, superficial appearances, or "Instagrammability" over other considerations. Although these articles often suggest that hipsters have great sway over contemporary food trends, they simultaneously dismiss such influence as less about any culinary knowledge or expertise and more about the pointless photographing of food.

Many of the articles contain criticism of gimmicky presentations of hipster foods served at restaurants. For instance, Mel Buttigieg's August 2017 Yahoo News article, "'What Did Plates Ever Do to You?': Outrage over Café's Hipster Spin on Traditional English Breakfast," reports fury over a Cardiff, UK, café's decision to serve traditional English breakfast jumbled together in a mason jar, an object fraught with hipster ethos and caught squarely in the center of debates about contemporary hipster food trends (Kelly). One Instagram user derides the move as "some sort of sh** hipster wanker joke" (Buttigieg). The article also mentions a Melbourne, Australia, pop-up café slammed for serving $5 spoons of Nutella, and the author questions food presentation gimmicks like "the Jafflechute," a grilled cheese sandwich attached to a parachute and dropped from a building (Buttigieg). In a similar vein, a slideshow accompanying Daniel Jones's *The Sun*, UK, article on hipster food fads depicts salad on a shovel, French fries in a tiny shopping cart, and a variety of things in mason jars (Jones). A video presented alongside the Jones article shows a MasterChef winner's restaurant that serves food on the backs of diners' hands, presumably illustrating the ludicrous nature of hipster food presentation. In these articles, the critiques center on how food is served, rather than what is being served. There seems to be little complaint about grilled cheese sandwiches, salad, or French fries in and of themselves; rather, disdain is focused on ludicrous presentations promoted by the hipster owners and patrons of such eateries. Such frivolous displays are dismissed as publicity stunts for otherwise "ordinary" eateries and as an avenue toward hipster status for the "wannabe-hipsters" who snap photos and post them on their social media.

The epitome of all "hipster food as frivolous" content is found at WeWantPlates.com, an "online crusade against serving food on bits of wood or roof slates, chips in mugs and drinks in jam jars" (Di Nuzzo). The site does not explicitly mention hipsters but takes humorous aim at food served in unusual, and sometimes unappealing, ways. Ross McGinnes, the site's curator, collects dozens of photos from contributors, adding his own funny captions. We reached out to him to find out if he thought the kinds of foods his site depicts are associated with hipsters. He responded, "I do play on the Hipster notion because any tweets with 'Hipster' in [them] tend to do well. If I'm honest I find it a bit of a lazy, broad brush. A funny one, though." At the same time, he notes the success of this strategy as the site continues to grow, with approximately three hundred thousand users across all social media (McGinnes, personal correspondence). Of course, this begs the question that if We Want Plates is a website for people who are ostensibly tired of these oddball presentations, why would they order and then photograph food that they find ridiculous? It seems possible that the actual critiques found on social media are overblown and that people find these wacky presentations at least as amusing as annoying.

Another subtheme under the category of frivolity is the claim that hipster food is superficial, existing primarily to be photographed and posted to social media sites like Instagram in a bid for status and coolness, rather than to nourish, sustain, and give pleasure to the eater. Signe Rousseau has written about the ways in which social media provide "endless opportunities to look at and fantasize about everything we are told is 'bad' for us" (xv), pointing out the tensions that exist between food and its representations. Leer and Povlsen note renewed interest in "media as both relays for individual and societal food practices, focused on 'normal' and routinized media practices embedded in the context of everyday life" (4). Pop culture attention to the mediation of certain foodways via image-focused social media like Instagram is apparent in many of the sources we examined, which link the superficiality of food imagery explicitly to hipster culture.

For instance, Michelle No, writing for BuzzFeed, depicts colorful carbs in a listicle of "Hipster Food Trends That Need to Die in 2017" as such: "A rainbow-dyed bagel might make for a great 'gram, but I'd rather wait an hour in line for a food that's objectively superior in taste and not just different in appearance." A 2017 article on ABC News Australia similarly identifies social media as at least partly responsible for current food trends. In it, Patrick Wood maintains that "the ability to take a quick photo of your food and share it before tucking in has driven chefs to create ever-more elaborate designs." Wood cites food writer Dani Valent, who explains, "We haven't yet learnt how to share aroma or taste via social media, so presentation is privileged." Arguably, this is a problem for almost anyone who is digitally connected, not just those identified as hipsters; thus, we are intrigued by the heavy lifting being done by the figure of the hipster, even in articles that ostensibly begin by rescuing the hipster figure from black-hat status but then waver, as in this example from Thrillist.com. Wil Fulton laments the use of the term "hipster," but gives in anyway, linking image obsession with frivolous presentation: "Though the word 'hipster' is basically a final fart from the dying corpse of '00s culture, it's frankly the best adjective to describe foods like locally sourced Sriracha-soaked kale in artisanal Mason jars served on reclaimed-wood plates with post-ironic sporks." He labels Instagram as "the preferred communication method of hipsters everywhere," suggesting that Instagram posters use "new," "trendy," and "hipster" interchangeably.

One thing worth noting is how these blog posts and articles rely on the very frivolous images that they critique to illustrate their articles. Most of the content available on "hipster food" is poorly written and sometimes pieces are downright incoherent, with no through-line from one paragraph or bullet-point to the next; moreover, listicles prevail over articles and hipster aesthetics dominate. Popular "literature" on hipster food is thus guilty of the very same image obsession and gimmicky-yet-hackneyed presentation for which it places blame onto hipsters.

Hipsters to Blame for Rising Food Costs

Another prominent theme in popular discourse about hipster food is that hipsters are willing to overpay for food, thus driving up food costs for everyone. Such critiques serve to reinforce the stereotype that hipsters are mostly recent college graduates who enjoy continued financial support from their middle- and upper-class parents, thus shielding them from various financial concerns, including rising food prices. Salon.com summarizes the problem: "Somehow, basic foods like coffee, guacamole, hummus and smoothies have become attached to the hipster, who is willing to overpay for 'artisanal' products, which have become little more than a flashy outfit made from cool packaging and slick branding" (Perry). The author expresses confusion about how this association has come to be ("somehow,") but does not question the basic premise that hipsters are willing to pay too much for artisanal things. The listicle includes eight items, from sprouted beans to artisanal doughnuts, that Perry says can easily be made at home, although no recipes or instructions are included, suggesting that Perry imagines his readers to be more interested in critiquing hipsters and feeling superior to them than doing any of the things he suggests.

Simpler listicles that lack analytical power also emphasize hipsters' willingness to overpay for food. Sophie Gadd's 2016 BuzzFeed listicle "24 Things You'll Find in Every Hipster Restaurant" includes a few noteworthy items that indicate hipsters' disregard for price: "Menus printed on 'distressed' paper, and then stuck to a clipboard. Without the currency in the price, to trick you into not realising how expensive it is" and "[r]eally fucking expensive versions of food you ate as a child." Once again, hipsters are characterized as enjoying a class privilege that allows them to make food choices based on aesthetics or nostalgia with less concern for price.

Julie Verhage, writing for Bloomberg.com, links rising food prices to hipster demand: "Hipsters have been blamed for polarizing trends from jeans to facial hair. Now they're making it more expensive to enjoy breakfast." She points specifically to a 31 percent increase in cream cheese costs and suggests that hipster obsession with Instagramming "unicorn toast" (bread topped with a rainbow of cream cheese colors) is to blame. Likewise, peaking costs for avocado and cauliflower are attributed to their surge in popularity due to hipster promotion. Hipsters are only absolved partially for the rise in the price of vanilla, which Verhage says, "might be better laid at the feet of corporate America, but hipsters can't be absolved entirely," although she fails to explain why. Hipster blame for rising food prices is not only found in popular sources. An article from NPR.org about bone broth also employs the bait-and-switch maneuver described earlier. Tove Danovich's 2017 article "Broth-Loving Hipsters Are Pushing Up the Price of Bones" stands out within the "hipster blame lit" field for the quality of its writing, but it too falls prey to specious titling. The article itself never mentions hipsters; instead, it simply describes "people's" increasing demand for bones since bone broth, a "well-marketed take on an ancient beverage, started sweeping hip enclaves like New York, Austin and Los Angeles a few years ago." The article's bait-and-switch maneuver pulls in readers who have an axe to grind with hipsters and fuels their irritation, even going so far as to apologize to the dogs of America who will surely be shortchanged by the rising price of bones due to pent-up human demand.

Another well-written piece on MotherJones.com, Stephen Paulsen's "The Depressing Truth About Hipster Food Towns," describes not food deserts, but "food mirages": places where there are a lot of overpriced markets that fail to sell cheap staples, keeping low-income people from eating well. Paulsen links this to urban gentrification and changing neighborhoods, where "specialty stores flock to newly hip districts while cheap supermarkets are pushed out." Absent is any discussion of "hipster" beyond the article's title, but front and center is the blame on hipsters for creating food mirages that have dire consequences for poor people. The blog Highsnobiety.com also focuses on the economic impact of hipster taste, in an apocalyptically titled article "How Hipster Food Trends Are Literally Ruining the World." Eror writes that while a love for trendy foods

> is often held up as a signifier of cosmopolitan sophistication, there's a dark side to them that's seldom talked about. For all the supposed liberal values that these foods represent, their rising trendiness often has a terrible effect on the lives of poor people that traditionally rely on them.

> The concept of hip food might sound absurd, but it's real, as is food gentrification.

He uses the example of quinoa and the impact its popularity in the Global North has had on the pocketbooks and diets of Peruvians, from causing its price to triple in the years between 2006 and 2013 to "forcing the local populace into spending their money on cheaper imported Western junk food because they can afford little else." Eror's arguments are countered elsewhere by better-researched articles that maintain that the "global price rise for quinoa was a good thing for people in Peru, especially quinoa farmers, and had no bad effects on nutrition" (Cherfas). But Eror's factual error is less important than is his framing of hipsters as responsible for the rising cost of quinoa, when consumption in the United States and Europe increased dramatically only after years of promotion from the likes of NASA, the United Nations, and Oprah Winfrey ("Quinoa"). It is telling that hipsters are singled out to blame for something that may not even be blameworthy. Hipster-blaming is also at the heart of Tyler Amato's posted response to the BuzzFeed article "32 Photos That Show the Difference Between Normal Food and Hipster Food":

> Hipster fad foods make eating healthy so unnecessarily difficult for the rest of us ... Quinoa and kale used to be dirt cheap (they used to use kale to *decorate* the salad bars at pizza hut) but now its [*sic*] trendy and making the lives of farmers in other countries harder. You want your sandwich separated into individual molecules and served on a toilet seat, go right ahead, but stop making basic nutrition and health a popularity contest so you can look cool on instagram while people starve.

While willing to tolerate hipsters' penchant for ridiculous food displays, Amato calls them out for the consequences of their trendy foodways, namely price inflation and misery for struggling food producers in other countries. Surely, responsibility for such matters cannot rest solely on the shoulders of hipsters, but they make a convenient scapegoat for everyone else whose food choices have local and global consequences. Placing the blame at the feet of hipsters allows others to avoid critical reflection about how their foodways contribute to serious problems.

Hipsters Blamed for Cultural and Culinary Appropriation

The focus on rising food prices is often linked to critiques of hipsters for their appropriation of ethnic cultures. In the Highsnobiety.com blog discussed above, which focuses on the economic consequences of hipster food trends, the author also critiques the international consequences of these trends and their impact on the "ethnic other." Eror discusses the consequences of the rising popularity of avocados on farmers in Mexico and New Zealand and concludes with a sharply worded critique:

> The middle-class liberals who brunch at vegan cafes and upload snaps of their quinoa salads or avocado toast onto Instagram probably view their dietary choices as a mark of their intrinsic open-mindedness, but it's arguably a very modern form of colonialism. Just as the British plundered India for its tea and spices with force, this modern arrangement leverages the financial muscle of developed nations against the poverty and desperation of lesser powers. Sure, there's an economic exchange, it's not comparable to the horrors of slavery, but it's still pure exploitation. Money just coats it in a civilized veneer and gives us something to scrub our conscience with.

Many of the comments associated with this post echo the author's perspective. Atirem, for instance, blames "this subculture of self-righteous, vegan, social activist, ecological people who buy their products in specialised bio shops with beautiful interiour that screams 'fair trade,' 'organic' " for failing to recognize the inherent inequalities in the global food market, ignoring the fact that the "exotic" foods on their plates in London came from a poor Mexican village. Jackie Outlaaw, in the comment section to the BuzzFeed listicle described above (No), writes of hipsters that "[t]hey are hated for mainly gentrification and appropriation" and later connects the high price of hipster food with its appropriation of "authentic" cooking: "I do feel frustrated that they can sell something that didn't cost that much to create with a price about ten times more than it's [*sic*] actual value and get ridiculously rich. Meanwhile there are so many great chefs who make great authentic dishes from their home country and are not getting enough credit for their craft."

Noiseformind, commenting on Naylor's article described earlier, concludes that "being hipster is really a vulgar affair" insofar as it involves "drop-naming something perfectly pedestrian somewhere in the world in a completely different region where it will sound that the person referring to the term or craving given item is knowledgeable about that country/region the item is coming from." From this perspective, the cultural cachet of the would-be hipster comes at the expense of those whose culinary and cultural practices are being appropriated for the sake of social status. Likewise, DaveWhelanIsMyHero writes that "when it's appropriated, price-inflated, and repackaged as 'new,' it's the epitome of hipster" (Naylor). Once again, while hipsters alone cannot be held responsible for cultural appropriation and price inflation, they serve as convenient scapegoats for those whose own food practices likely contribute to these problems. But while many readers reinforce the hipster bashing through their comments, others push back, placing the blame more broadly on Western consumers who seem oblivious to the global impact of their foodways. For example, although Wil Fulton identifies the Hawaiian staple poke as a "hipster trend," noting "slight levels of cultural appropriation, which is always a sign of a big food trend," in the comments section, Julia Rine counters Fulton's critique, stating "[I]t seems culturally insensitive to label spam and poke 'hipster food trends' when they are things Pacific Islanders have been eating for years and are important to Islander culture and families. It's not a 'trend' people will get bored with, but something mainland individuals just happened to discover recently." For Rine, the critique is not of hipsters, per se, but of Western consumers—including Fulton and his readers—who are themselves culpable for the cultural and culinary appropriation that he blames on hipsters.

This idea is also explored in Mayukh Sen's 2017 Food52.com article, "What We Lose When We Call Foods 'Hipster,'" which critiques fellow writers for including what "a publication would've regressively referred to as 'ethnic foods' in a bygone era"—horchata, jackfruit, khachapuri, and poke. Sen is irritated that international foods are slapped with the noxious hipster label, and he urges fellow writers to focus on "what foods, especially those consumed primarily by immigrant groups in the West, gain sudden popularity among a certain crowd of moneyed, coffee-guzzling urbanites." He wants to see less glib labeling of international foods as "hipster" and more thoughtful efforts to "situate these foods within the knotty dynamic of who co-opts these dishes, and how they're packaged, framed, and re-sold to consumers at large." Much scholarly literature (Peterson and Kern; Peterson; Johnston and Baumann; Naccarato and LeBesco) suggests that foodie omnivorousness is associated with a taste for truly authentic international foods, and "foodie" is a broad category (LeBesco and Naccarato)—so why is the narrow subcategory of hipsters taking the fall here? If the international foods had been labeled with the more neutral "foodie" rather than "hipster," would Sen be as concerned? Is it the damning power of the "hipster" label that has him riled up? Sen raises questions about who appropriates what kinds of foods, and the kind of nuanced analysis he is calling for is both completely needed *and* likely to implicate actual foodies, not just hipsters.

Defending the Hipster: A "Straw Man in Skinny Jeans"?

Although dominant voices in mainstream internet culture regard the hipster as a problem in the ways we have just described—as frivolous and image-obsessed, responsible for rising food costs, and participating in cultural appropriation—another picture emerges in the comments sections of several of these same media sources, suggesting that popular culture messaging about hipster foodways is not monolithic. Jace Clayton has noted that the hipster figure serves as a "straw man in skinny jeans" (30)—a figure onto which all sorts of anxieties can be displaced, and we see this dynamic recognized for what it is in several of the sources we examined. This tension is rarely voiced in the articles themselves, but rather is animated in the comments sections, where readers often challenge negative characterizations of the hipster or engage in debate about this much-maligned figure.

Following its critique of the economic impact of hipster taste, one commenter on the Eror Highsnobiety.com article discussed earlier pushes back, shifting focus from the individual responsibility of the hipster to structural causes for rising food prices and global inequalities. Ethical Capitalism Now writes, "Yes, hip food marketing is partly a major contributor to the persistence of this issue in 2016/17, but it's a symptom of a much larger cancer: Laws, (like NAFTA) that protect major corporations that benefit from the laissez-faire economic polices [*sic*] and fractured infrastructure present in nearly EVERY 3rd world (and 2nd world) country" (Eror). In addition, although Michelle No's article discussed previously offers a rather lighthearted list of food trends accompanied by snarky one-liners, it generated a lengthy set of comments. Although some commenters pile on with hipster bashing, Deanna Starnes offers a positive defense of hipsters, commenting, "I like hipsters, I love that they can take something and deconstruct it, or put it together in a new way, or combine it with something no one has done before. Instead of just consuming, they are thinking and engaging—they are making an event out of it. I think that is really awesome." Other articles generate debate among commenters as to the status of the hipster. For example, Sen's article on the mislabeling of international foods invites commenters to share their thoughts about hipsters with the following prompt: "Does the 'hipster' label also make you bristle? Let us know in the comments." Many commenters share Sen's annoyance that international foods have been tainted with the label of hipster, but some dig more deeply. Kartoffellöffel asks, "Perhaps you would have preferred the more old-fashioned terms used in years past, such as 'trendy' or 'faddish,'" claiming these terms are used interchangeably with "hipster" to describe "foods that briefly become fashionable then fade as the next 'new' (whether it's new or not) trend arrives." Caninechef defends hipsters from being associated with certain food trends, writing, "I can't imagine any self-respecting hipster being taken with unicorn cakes or rainbow bagels. But what do I know, I had to look up both terms." This is interesting as it seems like s/he identifies with the hipster, as opposed to reviling them. Heather Delicious Not Gorgeous makes it plain:

> [I]f anything, the thing that stands out to me most is the misuse of the label "hipster," and I think "trendy" would be more appropriate.

> [H]ipster is the opposite of mainstream (in my eyes), which immediately rules out the rainbow/unicorn trend (which is splashed everywhere) and the prevalence of poke (though, admittedly, I lived/live in Asian dominant communities, where everyone and their grandma eats poke).

It should be noted that these attempts to rehabilitate the hipster are on a thoughtful, critical food blog, rather than the less nuanced mainstream/ commercial sources cited above.

Defense of the hipster comes in other forms as well. In the comments section of Naylor's article ("It's Poké, Man: The Ultimate Hipster-Food Glossary"), Pavanne pushes back against criticism of hipsters, writing, "The hipsters I know are much less irritating than the anti-hipster lot. Basically, hipster is a word for a generation that prefers to spend time and money looking for experiences than stuff. This makes them seem pretentious to previous generations who spent their whole lives properly paying the mortgage and scrupulously avoiding being different from anyone else." Similarly, Tiffany Hart, responding to No's BuzzFeed listicle, comes to the hipster's defense: "So we should all just eat fast food and drink Bud, right? Because fuck those 'hipster' trends with wholesome food and local brews and give me my homogenized frozen patty and shitty beer." Such outright defense of quality hipster foodways is relatively unusual among top internet hits; most defenses invoke reasons ranging from bullying to ageism to snobbery. Hipster defenses, which are more likely to be found in the comments sections of articles or blog posts rather than in their headlines or content, point to the creativity of hipsters, their emphasis on experiences over things, and the hypocrisy of snobbish writers who criticize hipster snobbery. But few defenses address the charges of rising food costs or cultural/culinary appropriation that we discussed earlier.

Conclusion

Hipsters have been at least the nominal focus of a great deal of internet content in recent years. As we have shown, much content lures readers with promises of hipster bashing in the title but then does not mention hipsters at all. In internet content that does frame hipsters, the picture is not pretty; whether they are derided as frivolous and image-obsessed, castigated as driving up food costs, or reproached for culinary and cultural appropriation, in recent years, hipsters are touted as powerful culprits for any number of contemporary social, political, and economic problems. We hope to have made the case for how these frames allow foodies—generally, the type of people interested in creating and reading internet content about food trend—to use the hipster figure to deflect criticism while still staking their own claim to the food practices (local, farm-to-table, artisanal, omnivorous, etc.), through the same mechanisms (cultural and culinary appropriation), with the same consequences (gentrification, rising food prices) that are attributed solely to hipsters. We see, in the hundreds of articles and blog posts we examined for this chapter, that "criticizing the hipster is a way of discussing gentrification and neighborhood change while exempting oneself from the process" (Clayton 29). We wonder how food discourse would change if lazy censure were no longer directed at hipsters, and instead foodies were hailed to recognize and reform their own complicated relationships to the consequences of their foodways.

Works Cited

Amato, Tyler. Comment on "32 Photos That Show the Difference Between Normal Food and Hipster Food." *BuzzFeed*, April 19, 2016, www.buzzfeed.com/jemimaskelley/hipster-food?utm_term=.ai7B1PdML3#.knGe0Rodzm. Accessed August 13, 2017.

Buttigieg, Mel. "'What Did Plates Ever Do to You?' Outrage Over Cafe's Hipster Spin on Traditional English Breakfast." *Yahoo7 News*, August 13, 2017, au.news.yahoo.com/world/a/36700826/cadriff-uk-cafe-serves-english-breakfast-in-a-jar/. Accessed August 20, 2017.

Cherfas, Jeremy. "Your Quinoa Habit Really Did Help Peru's Poor. But There's Trouble Ahead." *NPR*, March 31, 2016, www.npr.org/sections/thesalt/2016/03/31/472453674/your-quinoa-habit-really-did-help-perus-poor-but-theres-trouble-ahead. Accessed October 9, 2017.

Clayton, Jace. "Vampires of Lima." *What Was the Hipster? A Sociological Investigation*, edited by Mark Greif, Kathleen Ross, and Dayna Tortorici. n+1 Foundation, 2010, pp. 24–30.

Danovich, Tove. "Broth-Loving Hipsters Are Pushing Up the Price of Bones." *NPR*, April 4, 2017, www.npr.org/sections/thesalt/2017/04/04/522190305/broth-loving-hipsters-are-pushing-up-the-price-of-bones?utm_source=twitter.com&utm_campaign=food&utm_medium=social&utm_term=nprnews. Accessed August 20, 2017.

Di Nuzzo, Rebecca. "Melbourne Cafes—You've Had Your Fun, Now Stop It." *Herald Sun*, January 13, 2017, www.heraldsun.com.au/leader/inner-south/melbourne-cafes-youve-had-your-fun-now-stop-it/news-story/765f19f1edca4924a8867ce082e4cb41. Accessed August 13, 2017.

Eror, Aleks. "How Hipster Food Trends Are Literally Ruining the World." *Highsnobiety*, October 27, 2016, www.highsnobiety.com/2016/10/27/hipster-food-trends-ruining-world/. Accessed August 20, 2017.

Fulton, Wil. "The Next Big Hipster Food Trends You'll Be Over in a Year." *Thrillist*, April 19, 2016, www.thrillist.com/eat/nation/the-next-big-hipster-food-trends-to-eat-before-theyre-cool. Accessed August 20, 2017.

Gadd, Sophie. "24 Things You'll Find in Every Hipster Restaurant." *BuzzFeed*, February 3, 2016, www.buzzfeed.com/sophiegadd/

things-youll-find-in-every-hipster-restaurant?utm_term=.vxnW1BJ2xY#.yhZmp13RgL. Accessed August 20, 2017.

Johnston, Josée, and Shyon Baumann. *Foodies: Democracy and Distinction in the Gourmet Foodscape*. Routledge, 2010.

Jones, Daniel. "Hipster Food Fads Such as Meat Ice Lollies and Drinks Served in Mason Jars Are Off the Menu as Diners Ditch Trends for Taste." *The Sun*, June 29, 2017, www.thesun.co.uk/living/3906959/hipster-food-fads-such-as-meat-ice-lollies-and-drinks-served-in-mason-jars-are-off-the-menu-as-diners-ditch-trends-for-taste/. Accessed August 13, 2017.

Kelly, Ariana. "The Mason Jar, Reborn." *The Atlantic*, September 24, 2015, www.theatlantic.com/technology/archive/2015/09/mason-jar-history/403762/. Accessed December 28, 2017.

Lanham, Robert. *The Hipster Handbook*. Anchor, 2003.

LeBesco, Kathleen, and Peter Naccarato. "Distinction, Disdain, and Gentrification: Hipsters, Food People, and the Ethnic Other in Brooklyn, New York." *A Place-Based Perspective of Food in Society*, edited by Kevin M. Fitzpatrick and Don Willis. Palgrave Macmillan, 2015, pp. 121–39.

Leer, Jonatan, and Karen Klitgaard Povlsen, eds. "Introduction." *Food and Media: Practices, Distinctions and Heterotopias*. Routledge, 2016, pp. 1–17.

McGinnes, Ross. "Re: Question re. We Want Plates." Received by Katie LeBesco, August 20, 2017. Email Interview.

McGuire, Lucy. "Hipster Food Trends: Love or Loathe?" *Huffington Post*, April 15, 2015, www.huffingtonpost.co.uk/lucy-mcguire/hipster-food-trends_b_6660690.html. Accessed August 13, 2017.

Naccarato, Peter, and Kathleen LeBesco. *Culinary Capital*. Berg, 2012.

Naylor, Tony. "It's Poké, Man: The Ultimate Hipster-Food Glossary." *Guardian*, March 1, 2017, www.theguardian.com/lifeandstyle/2017/mar/01/ultimate-hipster-food-glossary-coolest-trends. Accessed August 13, 2017.

No, Michelle. "Hipster Food Trends That Need to Die in 2017." *BuzzFeed*, November 28, 2016, www.buzzfeed.com/michelleno/foods-that-hipsters-ruined-in-2016?utm_term=.koaYLV8O7x#.vidrvLaoyP. Accessed August 13, 2017.

Paulsen, Stephen Tucker. "The Depressing Truth About Hipster Food Towns." *Mother Jones*, January/February 2017, www.motherjones.com/politics/2017/04/food-desert-mirage-gentrify-brooklyn-portland-groceries-snap/. Accessed August 20, 2017.

Perry, Julien. "8 Ways to Eat Like a Hipster Without Going Broke." *Salon*, May 7, 2017, www.salon.com/2017/05/07/8-ways-to-eat-like-a-hipster-without-going-broke_partner/. Accessed August 13, 2017.

Peterson, Richard A. "The Rise and Fall of Highbrow Snobbery as a Status Marker." *Poetics*, vol. 25, 1997, pp. 75–92.

Peterson, Richard A., and Roger M. Kern. "Changing Highbrow Taste: From Snob to Omnivore." *American Sociological Review*, vol. 61, 1996, pp. 900–7.

"Quinoa: Against the Grain." *The Economist*, May 1, 2016, www.economist.com/news/finance-and-economics/21699087-fad-andean-staple-has-not-hurt-pooryet-against-grain. Accessed October 9, 2017.

Rousseau, Signe. *Food and Social Media: You Are What You Tweet*. Rowman Altamira, 2012.

Sen, Mayukh. "What We Lose When We Call Foods 'Hipster.' " *Food52*, March 8, 2017, food52.com/blog/19233-what-we-lose-when-we-call-foods-hipster. Accessed August 20, 2017.

Snow, David, and Robert D. Benford. "Ideology, Frame Resonance and Participant Mobilization." *International Social Movement Research*, vol. 1, 1988, pp. 197–217.

Tewksbury, David, and Jason Rittenberg. *News on the Internet: Information and Citizenship in the 21st Century*. Oxford University Press, 2012.

Verhage, Julie. "From Unicorns to Avocado Toas: Hipster Fads Jack Up Food Prices." *Bloomberg*, May 3, 2017, www.bloomberg.com/news/articles/2017-05-03/from-unicorns-to-avocado-toast-hipster-fads-jack-up-food-prices. Accessed August 20, 2017.

Wood, Patrick. "Why Hipster Food Has Gone Viral—and When It Will End." *ABC News Australia*, October 10, 2016, www.abc.net.au/news/2016-10-10/why-hipster-food-has-gone-viral-and-when-it-will-end/7917284. Accessed August 13, 2017.

Hipsters as Intersectional Identities

20

Mipsterz: Cultural Capital, Racialization, and the Emergence of Muslim Cool

Anwar Ouassini and Mostafa Amini

The emergence of the "mipsterz" label to describe a large segment of the American Muslim youth subculture has garnered the attention of religious leaders, academics, and media corporations alike (Shaikley). The release of the music video "Somewhere in America," in which American Muslim women in hijab were juxtaposed with untraditional, pop-cultural symbols in the urban landscape is seen as the moment of inception for the #Mipsterz scene in November 2013. The music video facilitated discussion among American Muslims on exactly what it means to be a Muslim hipster, or a so-called "mipster" (Rumbelow). While the mipster phenomena highlights the "Muslimization" of the hipster trend, the reality reflects a larger attempt by American Muslim youth to articulate a sense of self, while internalizing what is perceived as nonthreatening, friendly forms of cultural "whiteness."

The attachment and internalization of the white, middle- to upper-class values that have constituted the hipster trend (e.g., contrarianism, liberal politics, new-age belief systems, creativity, free thinking, etc.) have become a defining characteristic of the mipster cultural identity framework. This has shaped their perceptions of culture, religious practice, and relations with society. In this fashion, the application of the "hipster" label to American

Muslim youth has facilitated integration into the larger American cultural fabric, while simultaneously giving the impression of authentic creators of a new American subcultural form that is unique to being both American and Muslim. The fluid mipster label, thus, becomes a vehicle for ideological and cultural expression that situates American Muslims with the power to authoritatively define Muslim youth culture and its variegated forms.

The current discussion explores issues related to the mipster subculture by utilizing content and thematic analysis of mipster oriented websites, social media, music videos, videos, magazines, and fashion trends. First, the contours of mipsterz identity in reference to hipster cultural forms will be defined. We argue that the differentiating link between the mipster and the hipster is one that is highly gendered and constructed around the use of the hijab as a symbolic cultural trope that circumscribes difference but also reinforces ideological affinities with the non-Muslim majority. Second, we contend that the identity of a mipster embodies a form of self-racialization (Gans), or the intentional internalization of ethnic and racial symbolic markers, toward a "hipster" strain of white cultural identity. Consequently, a central component of the mipster identity is self-identification; to be a mipster is to self-identify with the larger hipster subculture. The formation of this identity is in contrast to most subcultural identity forms, where certain criteria or parameters are first met to initiate or qualify individuals. The fetishism with the hipster identity legitimates their presence in the American context, all the while situating themselves as interlocutors of Muslim youth identity. Finally, we illustrate how the mipster subculture has facilitated the creation of new Muslim consumer markets and their profound effect in shaping a new Muslim "cool."

Given attempts at evading definition, the literature is justifiably unclear on what comprises a mipster identity. Therefore, we propose a framework that can be referenced when trying to conceptualize a coherent understanding of this subculture. Moreover, popular definitions provided by authoritative sources on mipster self-perception, including the Mipsterz Facebook group (Mipsterz - Muslim Hipsters), lack structure and boundaries, thus granting Muslim youth the agency to come and go as they please. The variegated claims to authenticity allow us to conclude that mipsterz celebrate the ambiguous nature of their claims that they "come in all colors, shapes, sizes and nationalities" (Lanham 1).

What exactly is the origin of the mipsterz movement? The term mipster first emerged in 2013 to describe a subcultural movement of American Muslim youth who linked their Muslim identities with hipster values by stating,

> [t]he "Mipsterz" first began as a satirical, thought-generating jab at corporate culture (e.g., Muppies) and evolved into a limitless collective that empowers individuals to find coolness in themselves and share their

> God given gifts with all. You see, hipster rule number 1: never self-identify as a hipster—namely, because these labels are a social constructed means of typecasting limitless beings. But let's be honest, (and this [*sic*] where the tongue-in-cheek ethos of Mipsterz enters) you are a hipster. (Mipsterz - Muslim Hipsters)

For the mipster, the values of the hipster are not only a reflection of their own areligious worldviews but also converge with their Islamic ones. As the Mipsterz Facebook page states,

> A Mipster is someone at the forefront of the latest music, fashion, art, critical thought, food, imagination, creativity, and all forms of obscure everything. A Mipster is someone who seeks inspiration from the Islamic tradition of divine scriptures, volumes of knowledge, mystical poets, bold prophets, inspirational politicians, esoteric Imams, and our fellow human beings searching for transcendental states of consciousness. (Mipsterz - Muslim Hipsters)

At its foundation, the goal of the mipster is to create an identity that bridges between what appears to be an identity negotiation between ostensibly disparate perceptions of the "self." The interconnectedness between Muslim youth, Islamic values, and hipster culture coalesce in the context of vulgar Islamophobia in the media, politics, and society. This consequently superimposed a temporal dualism of "us" and "them" for many American Muslim youth. Thus, the creation of the mipsterz movement was an attempt by American Muslim youth to connect with a far-reaching hipster subculture: a subculture that has historically internalized white cultural sensibilities while also generally accepting the Other (Maly and Varis). The integration of the hipster cultural collectivity within the mipsterz identity discourses was an attempt to reconstruct the trajectory of their image and faith in the American public sphere. The claim to authenticity is a declarative attempt to reframe a Muslim cool as a counter-hegemonic movement that connects with the transcendent styles of middle- to upper-class, white culture.

Markers of Identity

The hipsters, unlike the mipsterz, have positioned their identities as rebel consumers (Frank), a cultural type that achieves distinction through shunning brands and acts common through consumerist practices (Cronin et al.)—usually in opposition to mainstream consumerism and the larger culture of consumption. Although hipsters are often said to be defined by their taste and the lack of self-definition of their cultural boundaries, to be a mipster is to self-identify as a mipster. The hybridized cultural collectivities of the mipsterz facilitates self-identification because of visible racial and religious markers. The markers of identity that demarcate between hipster culture and the mainstream are often blurred, which enables meaningful participation and greater social inclusiveness. Motivated by the desire to articulate an independent identity, a mipster is "made visible through performative consumption, where expressions of taste via clothing, music, activities, evince aspirational categories of identity" (Alfrey 34–6).

Why self-identify as mipsterz if their religious and racial orientations were not accepted and considered faithful to the hipster cultural framework? The reasoning behind the construction of the mipster movement lies primarily in the fluid definitions oriented around the hipster label that links the subcultural group with progressive values, counterculture, and white forms of social and cultural capital (Schiermer 179). The permanent mobilization around the hipster movement is a strategic move to connect with a predominantly white subcultural collectivity that is perceived to be allies in the context of political and social Islamophobia, while also reflecting the class interests of the middle to upper class positions of the majority of American Muslim youth.

To understand the paradox of the mipster-hipster orientation we build off Schiermer's notion of imitation and authenticity in exploring the components of hipster identity and community (169–71). While Schiermer's conception of imitation is one that is seen as "unconscious participation in forms of collective imitation" (169), we find that the mipsterz movement is one that is actively imitating and selecting cultural forms as their own. This allows tremendous agency in the process of defining the ideational boundaries around the mipsterz' articulation of self. Moreover, a closer look at the mipster phenomena reveals that imitation is profoundly realized when related to the identity discourse surrounding gender. The mipsterz fixation on the presentations of American Muslim women in headscarves reveals an articulation of difference from the mainstream. However, the underlying "action" of each image circumscribes a message of likeness to the broader American cultural context.

The quest for authenticity is another important component of the mipster movement. The self-reflective narrative presented by the mipsterz is one that reinforces American Muslims to live their authentic selves as both Americans and Muslims. The quest for authenticity allows for a partial rejection of the hipster subculture—or at least a rejection of aspects that are ostensibly contrary to Islamic values—while also maintaining meaningful links with hipsterism by internalizing pop-cultural trends that challenge conservative Islamic norms. The decision to imitate and authentically employ the mipster label primarily lies in the subjective and fluid hipster category that "has no cause; hipster culture possess no manifestos; it has no instituted leaders; it has no clear borders; it is more inclusive and less uniform than the traditional subculture; it does not promote drug use; it does not battle the police or the authorities; (and) it does not market itself discursively as a distinct alternative or rebellious lifestyle" (Schiermer 170). American Muslim youth are able to engage and attach their identities to the hipster subcultural movement which superimposes the freedom for individuals to construct and define their own form of hipsterism as they see fit. For the mipsterz, their intrinsic structure and ideational boundaries are not only perceived by the larger public as an authentic expression of their movement collectivity but also linked to an American cultural form that is nonthreatening to the political and social structure that has been largely defined by Islamophobia.

Mipsterz, Gender, and Islam

When the video "Somewhere in America #Mipsterz" was released in 2013, it caused a tremendous stir in the Muslim community and media circles (Beusman). Major news outlets reported on the emergence of this new subculture that epitomized hipster culture, trendy music, and fashionable American Muslim women in their headscarves participating in what is perceived to be "traditionally" "un-Islamic" activities including skateboarding, dancing, and posing, in the backdrop to Jay-Z's "Somewhere in America" (Rattani and Yazdi). The video garnered a lot of attention and debate regarding the far-reaching impact the mipster movement would superimpose on the American Muslim community and also upon American pop culture. The point of contention in nearly every debate was the role of women in the mipster trend. Competing narratives within the Islamic community arose regarding the religious permissibility of participating in the mipster movement. Were the hijabi women violating Islamic law? Are the mipsterz commodifying the hijab? Are they differentiating the hijab from its religious underpinnings? This dynamic was a source of conflict in the Muslim community but also revealed the centrality of Muslim women in the mipster movement's identity and the overall cultural landscape. The complexity of the presentation of Muslim women as hip, fashionable, and also symbolically Islamic becomes the primary medium shaping contemporary mipster narratives. With this analysis, mipsterz identify with what is perceived to be the fragmentation of hipster identities or trends which crystalizes in the perfect concoction of a "media gaze" over Muslim women's bodies but also simultaneously and unintentionally mobilizes what Gökarıksel and McLarney called an "Islamic culture industry," a "series of images, practices, knowledges, and commodities [that] are marketed specifically to Muslim women" (2).

The #Mipsterz video lay the visual framework for what the mipster counterculture represents (Rattani and Yazdi). The clothing in the video follows the "blue-collar chic," urban wear that is typically viewed in pop-cultural circles as hipster wear, following in the spirit of middle- to upper-class whites (Rattani and Yazdi). The hijab worn by the women confer difference in the spectrum of perceived religiosity. In fact, the hijab becomes just another accessory, similar to the matching necklace or watch in the overall presentation of self. The decentering of the hijab is intentional as the producers of the video want the audience to focus on the images of authenticity which include but are not solely defined by the hijab.

Another crucial voice to the mipster movement, and one who had direct involvement in the making of the music video "Somewhere in America," is Layla Shaikley. Entrepreneur, artist, and self-proclaimed mipster, Shaikley's coproduction of the music video sought to redefine the image of Muslim women within the American lens and present it in the context of mipster symbolism. While Shaikley's Twitter discourse is almost completely lacking any active references to mipster identity in the form of tweets, her Twitter description imposes her self-definition to the public as "actually just a #mipster" (@Laylool). This characterizes the boundaries of the identity as being structured around her self-identification with the subcultural movement. In her article, "The Surprising Lessons of the 'Muslim Hipsters' [*sic*] Backlash," Shaikley states, "The video is a celebration of our daily lives. No burqas, bombs, or other symbols ignorantly associated with the hijab on our heads ... We made the video as a self-portrait." Once more, the self-definition process, whereby the hijab is transformed from simply a religious head garb to an icon of fashion, liberation, and coolness is highlighted.

This utilization of the "hijabed" female as a symbolic representation of the mipster subculture can be seen quite clearly in the various forms of communication and discourse amongst mipsterz. The Facebook group "Mipsterz - Muslim Hipsters" serves as perhaps the most central voice for mipsterz online. The topic of the hijab, both in its physical manifestation and its emblematic significance amongst mipsterz is apparent and at the forefront of their identity discourse. The word "hijab" is referenced over 180 times throughout the various posts and links by the Mipsterz Facebook groups, with topics ranging from a "Photo of the Day" where an image of a sophisticatedly dressed bearded man and a woman wearing hijab is captioned with the comment that stresses how the hijab doesn't necessitate the prevention of "fancy and elegant designs" (Revista Hogar). It also includes the promotion of an article that highlights H&M featuring a Muslim model wearing hijab (Sarkar). Out of the top twenty group posts that have more than two hundred "likes," nine of them are links and/or statements that somehow reference Muslim women who wear a hijab.

The main theme that seems to guide the emphasis upon the hijab as a powerful and centralizing form for the mipsterz' frames is that of empowerment and a sense of resilience. Whereas the hijab has been symbolized as a restrictive cultural practice in the modern context, the mipster narrative seeks to redefine the usage of the hijab as an expression of feminism and liberation. But, to take the argument even further, the hijab is of ancillary concern compared to perhaps the most significant aspect of mipster culture: the usage of the female form as the basis for the mipster framework. Many examples can be found in the Mipsterz Facebook group, where lists of "Muslim Women in Media," "Muslim Women Fashionistas," and "10 American Muslim Women You Should Know" populate the numerous posts on their page, including occasionally making the designation of the "Mipsterz of the Day." Of the top sixty posts based on the number of "likes," thirty posts, or 50 percent were explicitly for the purpose of highlighting a remarkable profile or great feat that was achieved by a Muslim woman. The remaining 50 percent were either posts that contained general information with no emphasis on individuals, with the exception of a handful, which focused specifically on the achievements of Muslim men. Such a stark discrepancy, once more, shows the emphasis upon Muslim women as the front-end focus of the mipster cultural framework.

The same relative trend can also be seen in the social media platform Twitter. A simple search for "#Mipsterz" provides an output where of the first fifty results, sorted by "top" results, roughly twenty-three contain tweets that are exclusively regarding Muslim women and their various issues and/or achievements. One such prominent female activist voice is Mona Haydar (@Mona_Haydar) whose popularity initially stemmed from two music videos, "Hijabi" and "Dog," which have struck a chord with counter-narrative Muslim activists. As one online magazine puts it, she has "smashed the patriarchy" (Mohammed). The former music video, "Hijabi," attacks the fetishization of the hijab and the objectification of the Muslim female, where a pregnant Haydar makes explicit references to "swag," "feminism," "yoga," and the "mipsterz." The latter video, "Dog," is a direct attack by Haydar on the abuse of religious authority, where she leads a resistance against the prevailing "structures within our culture" that legitimize abuse against women. Both videos embody the spirit of the gendered, mipster cultural framework, which reinforces a counter narrative where the Muslim female body is utilized as the site of cool, and the hijab is its vehicle. In a video response created by Haydar on Twitter to a Muslim male who questioned the style of her hijab, she states, "I'm done with the days of letting men think Hijab has anything to do with them. It's not about men. It's about spiritual practice and a woman's elevation of consciousness." Such a statement of "taking back" the hijab is a form of rebellion against the common and popular display of women being submissive or oppressed and, thus, is articulating her own narrative on her own terms.

The Mipsterz and Whiteness

While the images reinforced by the mipsterz are claimed to reflect the multicultural diversity of the American Muslim community, one of the underlying questions is, why model one's identity on hipsters, a subcultural group that represents primarily middle- to upper-class white individuals? The conscious decision to associate Muslim youth culture with hipsters is certainly not by accident. This identity formation reflects the overall attitude and socioeconomic position of second and third generation Muslim immigrants. The process of self-racialization (Gans) toward whiteness is seen as an attempt to mainstream American Muslims while simultaneously packaging Muslim identity in nonthreatening forms. The process of white self-racialization can be captured in three themes: the first being the utilization of progressive forms of Islam; secondly, the representation of mipster fashion in the form of "blue-collar chic" clothing; and last, the opposition to "white privilege" as an embodiment of white self-racialization.

Inherent to the mipster ethos is the manifestation of an Islamic identity that is ingrained in a progressive spirituality, which is in and of itself a religious trend that is tied to white progressive movements in the Western context. Islamic spirituality in the American context is popularly associated with a white and leftist Islamic trend, utilizing symbols that are a fusion of both traditional Islamic spirituality and "Americanness" in the form of middle- to upper-class whiteness (Suliman). Whereas non-spiritual, normative manifestations of Islam are perceived as radical and violent, Islamic philosophy that is focused on spirituality is seen as a tolerant alternative where "themes of love, spirituality, and journey" are its trademark characteristics (Feuer, "Sufism"). The identity of "whiteness" is even more clear in its usage by American political institutions and administrations as an "alternative to extremism," where policy initiatives are built upon using a focus on Islamic spirituality as a rival to normative Islamic expressions (Feuer, "Sufism"). Guided by contemporary and "new age" views on the role of religion in modern society, Islamic spirituality and its multiple forms provide the cultural and religious legitimation of the mipsterz' views on culture in relation to gender relations, sexuality, and the self. In fact, a part of their own definition of "what is a mipster" includes a very spiritual understanding of a mipsterz' Islamic faith and identity that moves beyond the confines of traditional Islamic law and a focus on contemporary manifestations of social and economic justice, as they state:

> A Mipster has a social mind, and yearning for a more just order, a more inclusive community unbounded by stale categories, unwilling to plod blindly along in a world as obsessed with class as it is unmindful of its consequences. The Mipster is a bold, yet humble mind, open to disparate

> ideas and firm enough in conviction to act, speak out and drop the hammer when the time is right. (Mipsterz - Muslim Hipsters)

The emphasis on contemporary forms of justice is reinforced in another quote on the Mipsterz Facebook page where the thirteenth-century scholar and poet Jalal Al-Din Al-Rumi is referenced. Rumi is one of the most recognized Muslim poets in the world and is a common trope associated with middle- to upper-class clichés, including yoga, poetry, and popular obsession over the performance and routines of elites (Ferriss). The quote utilized from Rumi's poetry states, "Beyond Islam and unbelief there is a 'desert plain.' For us, there is a 'yearning' in the midst of that expanse. The knower of God who reaches that plain will prostrate in prayer, for here is neither Islam nor unbelief, nor any 'where' in that place" (Ferriss). Echoing the general intent of the mipster movement, Rumi's poetry embodies a sense of "otherworldliness" and a straying from the material world, where a deeper state of being is adventured upon, without clearly designated or delineating social constructs. In essence, the mipster is in interstitial space, stuck between the nostalgic past and contemporary ideals of cool. Rumi becomes a transcendent figure in symbolizing a cultural frame that reinforced a positive, nonconfrontational, hermeneutically open Islamic tradition. One example is Humaira Mubeen, cofounder of *Hipster Shaadi* (renamed to *Ishqr*), a Muslim matchmaking website sought to help mipsterz find love. The tag line she created for the website is "if you're a feminist looking for your bold, humble, feminist brother or a Rumi-and-granola-loving-Muslim, Ishqr is the place for you" (Taylor).

Another example can be seen in the different forms of artistic expressions that communicate mipster culture. The music video, "Somewhere in America" (Rattani and Yazdi) represented a clear alignment with whiteness manifested in the representation of clothing, demeanor, and sport. The usage of skateboards, motorcycles, hipster clothing, and the vogue-inspired posing in the streets of New York are powerful indications of a self-racializing movement that seeks to insert themselves into whiteness. Fashion statements, including the usage of the Hijab, are another element by which the self-racialization is taking place. In particular, using blue-collar chic representations of a "mipster" (flannel shirts, bucket hats, oversized glasses, suspenders, and backpacks), fused with the donning of the hijab, is precisely aligned with traditional notions of being a hipster with an Islamic "twist." For example, when looking at #Mipsterz within the social media platform of Instagram, 66 percent, or thirty-three out of fifty most recent posts, deal with mipster female fashion, almost all of whom are light-skinned women in vogue-inspired poses. The reinforcement of whiteness through popular culture is done through consolidating links with and ties to the fashion industry which is primarily driven by the dominant white culture industry.

The final element that serves as a critical component of the embodiment of whiteness is the insistence of social awareness and activism as a mechanism to break racially oppressive patterns that have been perpetuated by the very same whiteness they simultaneously embody and oppose. With the insistence on concepts like white privilege, the mipster takes a stab at negotiating their own privilege and justifying their own affluent socioeconomic status. The fact that mipsterz tend to embody dimensions of middle- to upper-class privilege creates a unique situation where the messenger must self-negotiate the validity of the message. The identity negotiation is further convoluted by the fact that the same privileged individuals that the mipsterz seek to denounce happen to be within their own social networks. In essence, the mipsterz' resistance is an act of self-critique. In other words, a hallmark of mipsterism is the alignment with progressive, socially conscious white trends and movements—a goal that in and of itself should be lauded, yet brings a multifaceted dimension in the identity negotiation by the mipster. Such phenomenon can once more be seen in the use of posts in the Mipsterz Facebook group, where daily posts are more likely than not centered around articles, events, or opinions related to social justice issues which reflect the larger hipster trend (Mipsterz - Muslim Hipsters).

The articulation of the self in relation to whiteness for many mipsterz is a double-edged sword. On one end, as mostly second and third generation Muslims from the Indian subcontinent and the Middle East, they are publicly seen as a racial and religious minority especially in the post-9/11 context. However, in the United States the majority of Muslims from the Middle East and North Africa are racially categorized as Caucasian. While many mipsterz are conscious of the contradictions beset in these categorizations, it still shapes their opportunities, cultural experiences, and over all habitus. Thus, activists like Linda Sarsour, a self-identified mipster who is also one of the lead organizers of the 2017 Women's March, is an individual whose track record on activism relating to minority issues is unrivaled. Yet, similar to other Muslim activists who adhere to a mipster identity, her ambiguous self-identification is embedded in the frameworks of white privilege (Feuer, "Linda Sarsour"). It is precisely because of this manifestation of whiteness that prominent mipster activists are able to reflexively denounce white privilege while also claiming a mipster identity that facilitates this very same whiteness.

Anything Muslim and Anything Cool Is Mipsterz Cool

It is important to remember how American Muslims via the mipster label are now beginning to impact the global Muslim youth market. With social media as their primary networking tool, American Muslims are defining the contours of a global Muslim cool. The transformation of the interactive landscape has shifted onto the virtual sphere where Muslim youth are creating and sustaining transnational networks and ties beyond the traditional affinities. The American Muslim mipster movement becomes a unifying cultural trend across transnational boundaries where aspiring mipsterz in Europe, the Middle East, and South-East Asia all seek to embody a unified vision, fashion, and sense of cool. The cultural content along with the corresponding values of the mipsterz allow for the Islamic cultural industry (Gökarıksel and McLarney) to be dominated by the synthesis of Islamic symbols like the hijab and pop-cultural trends and values of middle- to upper-class white Americans. The paradox of the emerging Islamic cultural industry, as it is defined by the mipsterz, is the homogenization of a previous diversified Muslim cultural context. Therefore, in the process of constructing mipster culture they are also simultaneously deconstructing traditional Muslim cultural identities. Mipster cultural identity then facilitates assimilation while challenging the Islamophobic narratives of Otherness, especially in the post-9/11 context.

Furthermore, it allows American Muslims who come from variegated cultural backgrounds to link up with and internalize an acceptable American cultural frame, that is, the hipster. This, for the American Muslim community, allows for the creation of an American Muslim subculture that links their differences to reflect their American cultural experience. This is indicative of a maturing second and third generation public that is self-expressive in performing rebellion via their hybridized realities which ultimately produces a succinctly new cultural form. As Layla Shaikley states in a CNN interview regarding the rise of the mipsterz, "a young Muslim American [is] just trying to find a space for themselves unapologetically ... reconciling multiple identities and doing it like a rock star" (Assefa). This creates a form of cultural solidarity, a shared habitus that the mipsterz would insist is authentic and transcends the traditional boundaries of both the hipster and their traditional Islamic identities. In her interview with *The Daily Beast*, Yasmin Chebbi states, "[T]he stereotypes of being meek, submissive, backward, and bland have been projected onto me far too many times. Growing up wearing the hijab and living in America, I never felt I belonged to a particular group. I felt that to others, being devoted to my faith and adopting interests such as music, art, and fashion were in conflict" (Cunningham).

Consequently, the external markers of cool alongside their Islamic identities automatically reinforces the unconventionality (Warren and Campbell) of their positions in both the Western and Islamic world contexts but also creates new consumer markets. The mipster movement has allowed Muslim youth to navigate the market around Muslim youth identity and culture that is worth nearly 170 billion dollars (Ogilvy

Noor). In line with contrarian movements of the past, where female Muslim clothing was utilized as "anti-fashion, anti-consumerist and anti-capitalist statement" (Ulmi), today's mipster clothing, while being an attempt at manifesting a counter narrative, is inherently subservient to consumerist overlords and the objectification of female bodies. The mipster subculture becomes a consumer tribe (Cova, Kozinets, and Shankar) seeking meaning, identity, and social relationships through the "consumption of cultural resources circulated through markets" (Cova, Kozinets, and Shankar 5). An example can be found in the marketing of the hijab: mass markets are now taking advantage of the religious garb's centrality in the Islamic tradition, and in turn marketing it as a fashion product that the consumer devours in similar style to any other popular attire. Consequently, the hijab is no longer only defined by religious legal frameworks but instead characterized by the brand, texture, color, and style. As one critic of "Somewhere in America" stated, "[a] body clad in a headscarf is not a body liberated from social expectations and demands. From both within the Muslim community and from outside of it, women remain encumbered with pedestals for their looks, their personalities and their bodies. This isn't a problem of religion; it is a problem of cultures and communities—often clashing." (Saeed)

Hijab, Mipsterz, and the High Street

The mipsterz' success in challenging and transforming societal perceptions of the hijab while linking their identity to successive white cultural fads (hippie, blue collar chic, American punk, minimalist gothic) has allowed multinational corporations to latch onto the growing trends. Mipsterz online media presence generates the standards and boundaries of Muslim cool identity through images representing the latest Islamic fashions and music trends, alongside ideological sentiments that reflect progressive, leftist values. This cultural framework essentially becomes the globally constituted script that multinationals employ. Thus, when the world's second largest retailer H&M decided to include a Muslim hijabi along with a "man in drag, a plus-size model and a boxer with a prosthetic leg" (Elliot), they were announcing to the world that they are the "Muslim Cool." The cultural appropriation is even seen at the most micro level, with beverages, like *chai* that are being co-opted by the mipster subculture, where the Mipsterz Facebook page states,

> Probably the single best excuse to bring Mipsterz together, an authentic cup of Chai. Chai, as in tea, not the Hebrew word for "life" (though there is something ironic to be said). Many American coffee shops have tried to capitalize on the Chai market by offering a bullshit version of this

great drink and calling it "Chai Latte." WTF? A true Mipster can spot the counterfeit easily. (Mipsterz - Muslim Hipsters)

This allows corporations to establish links with new markets while disseminating a cultural ideal type vis-à-vis the mipster that is easily packaged, geographically dispersed, and then sold to the masses. This mipster ideal type becomes a framework from which the culture industry now targets a new Muslim consumer base to sell brands and more importantly couture and chic lifestyles. When analyzing the recent marketing campaigns of Coca Cola, Apple, Jeep, GAP, Cover Girl, Uniqlo, and Dolce & Gabbana, we find that the constructed link to the brand name and identity of the product is through the image of the identifiable Muslim hijabi who is dressed in fashionable clothing and is in tune with pop culture, while also seemingly reflecting the progressive values of the company. For example, the recent campaign by Cover Girl to include a hijabi fashion blogger in their lash-equality campaign reflects the overall company's goal to reinforce a positive-inclusive message while reinforcing the now popular and cool image of the hijabi in an ad campaign. While there were no specific cultural markers that differentiated the Muslim women in the ad from the others in terms of dress and style, the only major difference was the hijab, therefore acting as an external marker of her religious affiliation (Jha). Thus, the use of the image of the hijabista, or any "muslim [*sic*] women who dresses stylishly" (Waninger 2), is automatically seen by the larger public and more importantly the multinationals as the vehicle of the new Muslim cool and a way to reach out to Muslims, that is, mipsterz who have been seeking their attention.

Conclusion

The study of mipsterz illustrates how American Muslim youths are seeking to construct and define their identities in the post-9/11 context where the sociopolitical environment viewed the American Muslims as outsiders. Mipsterz are able to construct a cohesive identity through the virtual spaces they occupy. It is through social media platforms like Facebook and Twitter where the mipsterz come together as a bounded community. When analyzing the subcultural spaces they occupy online, we found that the demarcating factors that shape the overall identity of the mipster movement are gender identity and the presentation of Muslim female bodies. Thus, in this example, the mipster is distinguished as a mipster because of the appearance of the female Muslim headscarf and its various cultural manifestations (whether partially or fully covered), which remains the constant in the ever-changing culture industry.

This mipster identity also seeks to achieve whiteness through cultural affiliation and distinction. The process of self-racialization toward whiteness is expressed in the cultural identities that mipsterz internalize and identify with. The mipster identity becomes a vehicle to attain acceptance into middle- to white upper-class cultural forms from which their own class position reflects. Moreover, the social logic behind the attachment to whiteness in the post-9/11 context reflects a larger external posturing by mipsterz to associate with members of the hipster subcultural group that generally values and accepts their presence as American Muslims. This is illustrated in their outward manifestation of clothing, hobbies, and topics of concern as displayed in social media. This imitation of whiteness through self-identifying as mipsterz is not only inherently anti-hipster in method and in spirit, but it also creates a problematic distinction between the first and second generation of Muslims in the United States who were debating nationally about the merits of the "Somewhere in America" video. Granted, the mipster subculture has been consistently addressing racial politics in America, white supremacy, and supporting feminist causes; the reality is that some have taken on the ideological sentiments from within the perspective of white progressive activists and thus culturally are reflecting their tastes, sentiments, and ideological frameworks.

The study presented here is not meant to be a definitive guide on the mipster cultural framework nor is it meant to give a comprehensive introspection into the relatively new phenomenon of the Muslim hipster. Instead, we attempted to situate the mipsterz' experience in the American context, where on the one hand, faithful mipsterz seek to construct an alternative narrative that challenges prevailing perceptions of Islam and Muslim women, while also succumbing to the aforementioned social forces that reveal a deeper cultural struggle taking place.

Works Cited

Alfrey, L. *The Search for Authenticity: How Hipsters Transformed from a Local Subculture to a Global Consumption Collective*. 2010. Georgetown University, MA thesis, repository.library.georgetown.edu/handle/10822/552895. Accessed October 11, 2017.

Assefa, Haimy. "Mipsterz: A Space for Muslim Hipsters." *CNN*, June 3, 2015, edition.cnn.com/2015/06/03/living/mipsterz-muslim-hipsters/index.html. Accessed October 11, 2017.

Beusman, Callie. "'Muslim Hipsters' Music Video Ignites Debate." *Jezebel*, December 3, 2013, jezebel.com/muslim-hipsters-music-video-ignites-debate-1475885148. Accessed October 10, 2017.

Cova, Bernard, Robert Kozinets, and Avi Shankar, eds. *Consumer Tribes*. Elsevier, 2007.

Cronin, James M., et al. "Covert Distinction: How Hipsters Practice Food-Based Resistance Strategies in the Production of Identity." *Consumption Markets and*

Culture, vol. 17, no. 1, 2012, pp. 2–28., doi:10.1080/10253866.2012.678785. Accessed October 10, 2017.

Cunningham, Erin. "Meet the Mipsterz." *Daily Beast*, January 15, 2014, www.thedailybeast.com/meet-the-mipsterz. Accessed October 11, 2017.

Elliot, Annabel. "H&M Features Its First Muslim Model in a Hijab as She Claims Women Who Cover Their Heads Are Usually 'Ignored' in Fashion World." *Daily Mail Online*, September 28, 2015, www.dailymail.co.uk/femail/article-3250863/H-M-features-Muslim-model-hijab-claims-women-cover-heads-usually-ignored-fashion-world.html. Accessed October 11, 2017.

Ferriss, Tim. "Becoming the Best Version of You." *Tim Ferriss Blog*, September 25, 2017, tim.blog/2016/12/20/becoming-the-best-version-of-you/. Accessed October 9, 2017.

Feuer, Alan. "Linda Sarsour Is a Brooklyn Homegirl in a Hijab." *New York Times*, August 7, 2015, www.nytimes.com/2015/08/09/nyregion/linda-sarsour-is-a-brooklyn-homegirl-in-a-hijab.html#story-continues-1. Accessed October 5, 2017.

Feuer, Sarah. "Sufism: An Alternative to Extremism?" *The Washington Institute for Near East Policy*, March 11, 2015, www.washingtoninstitute.org/policy-analysis/view/sufism-an-alternative-to-extremism. Accessed October 1, 2017.

Frank, Thomas C. *The Conquest of Cool: Business Culture, Counterculture, and the Rise of Hip Consumerism*. University of Chicago Press, 1997.

Gans, Herbert J. "Racialization and Racialization Research." *Ethnic and Racial Studies*, vol. 40, no. 3, 2016, pp. 341–52.

Gökarıksel, Banu, and Ellen McLarney. "Introduction: Muslim Women, Consumer Capitalism, and the Islamic Culture Industry." *Journal of Middle East Women's Studies*, vol. 6, 2010, pp. 1–18.

Jha, Rega. "Can a Veiled Muslim Woman Also Be an American Hipster?" *BuzzFeed*, December 2, 2013, www.buzzfeed.com/regajha/a-group-of-muslim-hipsters-made-a-video-thats-really-really?utm_term=.jn5RRGqvwJ#.ffoNNPZrwJ. Accessed October 8, 2017.

Lanham, Robert, et al. *The Hipster Handbook*. Anchor Books, 2002.

@Laylool (Layla Shaikley). "Wise Systems cofounder, @MIT + @NASA alum but actually just a #mipster." *Twitter*, twitter.com/laylool?lang=en&lang=en. Accessed October 1, 2017.

Maly, Ico, and Piia Varis. "The 21st-Century Hipster: On Micro-Populations in Times of Superdiversity." *European Journal of Cultural Studies*, vol. 19, no. 6, 2016, pp. 637–53.

Mipsterz - Muslim Hipsters. *Facebook*. www.facebook.com/Mipsterz/. Accessed October 8, 2017.

"Mipsterz | Muslim Hipsters." *Tumblr*, muslimhipsters.tumblr.com/about. Accessed September 14, 2020.

Mohammed, Saffiyya. "Mona Haydar Speaks Out on Her Newest Hit 'Dog,' Smashing the Patriarchy, and Hip-Hop." *The Tempest*, July 27, 2017, thetempest.co/2017/07/27/interviews/mona-haydar-smashing-patriarchy-hip-hop/. Accessed October 11, 2017.

@Mona_Haydar (Mona Haydar). *Twitter*, twitter.com/mona_haydar?lang=en. Accessed October 10, 2017.

Ogilvy Noor. "Islamic Branding." *Ogilvy*, ogilvy.co.uk/agency/islamic-branding. Accessed October 9, 2017.

Rattani, Abbas, and Habib Yazdi. "Somewhere in America #Mipsterz." *YouTube*, uploaded by Sheikh Bake, November 20, 2013, www.youtube.com/watch?v=68sMkDKMias. Accessed October 1, 2017.

Revista Hogar. "A Hijab Does Not Prevent Women from Wearing Fancy and Elegant Designs." *Facebook*, July 9, 2015, 10:25 p.m., www.facebook.com/RevistaHogar/photos/a.231938506903579.49130.207068909390539/798645320232892/?type=3&theater. Accessed October 1, 2017.

Rumbelow, Helen. "Meet the Mipsterz: Hipsters in Hijabs." *The Times*, January 27, 2014, www.thetimes.co.uk/article/meet-the-mipsterz-hipsters-in-hijabs-bpk50fthzw0. Accessed October 11, 2017.

Saeed, Sana. "Somewhere in America, Muslim Women Are 'Cool.'" *The Islamic Monthly*, December 2, 2013, www.theislamicmonthly.com/somewhere-in-america-muslim-women-are-cool/. Accessed October 11, 2017.

Sarkar, Monica. "H&M's Latest Look: Hijab-Wearing Muslim Model Stirs Debate." *CNN*, August 26, 2016, www.cnn.com/style/article/hm-hijab-model/index.html. Accessed October 10, 2017.

Schiermer, Bjørn. "Late-Modern Hipsters: New Tendencies in Popular Culture." *Acta Sociologica*, vol. 57, no. 2, 2014, pp. 167–81.

Shaikley, Layla. "The Surprising Lessons of the 'Muslim Hipsters' Backlash." *The Atlantic*, March 13, 2014, www.theatlantic.com/entertainment/archive/2014/03/the-surprising-lessons-of-the-muslim-hipsters-backlash/284298/. Accessed October 11, 2017.

Suliman, Adela. "Sufi Sect of Islam Draws 'Spiritual Vagabonds' in New York." *New York Times*, September 23, 2016, www.nytimes.com/2016/09/25/nyregion/sufi-islam-new-york-converts.html. Accessed October 9, 2017.

Taylor, Lin. "Muslim Tinder: Seeking Love with a Young Muslim Hipster? There's an App for That." *SBS News*, February 10, 2015, www.sbs.com.au/news/muslim-tinder-seeking-love-with-a-young-muslim-hipster-there-s-an-app-for-that. Accessed October 11, 2017.

Ulmi, Nic. "Muslim and Hipster, Why 'Mipster' Fashion Is Trending." *Worldcrunch*, December 14, 2016, www.worldcrunch.com/culture-society/muslim-and-hipster-why-mipster-fashion-is-trending. Accessed October 9, 2017.

Waninger, K. *The Veiled Identity: Hijabistas, Instagram and Branding in the Online Islamic Fashion Industry*. 2015. Georgia State University, MA thesis.

Warren, Caleb, and Margaret Campbell. "What Makes Things Cool? How Autonomy Influences Perceived Coolness." *Journal of Consumer Research*, vol. 41, no. 2, 2014, pp. 543–63.

21

Skinny Jeans in the Sanctuary: The Hipster Christian Subculture

Caroline Barnett

As the ideology of hipsters, characterized by a strong sense of individuality, anti-intuitionalism, and a love of things outside mainstream culture, has become a prominent subculture of millennials in the United States, it has found its way into seemingly antithetical subcultures, namely conservative evangelical Christianity in the United States. A populist form of Protestant Christianity, characterized by religious experience of conversion and having a personal relationship with Jesus Christ, American evangelical Christianity has an ambivalent relationship with popular secular culture—at once viewing it as anti-Christian and adopting its aesthetics to appeal to younger people. Hipster Christianity—a term that, like hipster, is more often used to describe others than as a self-identifier—interweaves traits and values associated with both evangelical Christianity and hipsters. While neither hipsters nor evangelical Christianity are groups with formally defined boundaries, and few people explicitly self- identify as hipster Christians, the incorporation of aesthetics and norms associated with hipsters into evangelical Christianity creates a way for millennial evangelical Christians to articulate their own understanding of the secular/religious boundary.

American evangelical Christianity, the "parent" to hipster Christianity, emerged from the eighteenth century First Great Awakening, a religious revival throughout the United States which emphasized personal piety and religious devotion for individuals. Evangelical Christianity is not a formal denomination—one can be evangelical and a part of a denomination or nondenominational—but it is often characterized by three core beliefs: an experience of salvation, the inerrant authority of the Bible, and the saving power of Jesus Christ. The specific combination of these three tenets creates a religious experience regulated by conversion and entering a personal relationship with Jesus Christ (Reimer 153). It is an understanding of faith that is marked by personal piety and an individualized experience of faith.

Hipster Christianity, as an outgrowth of evangelical Christianity, is formed in this understanding of religion, but also inherits and reinterprets a specific relationship to a secular sphere. The theoretical idea of an inflexible religious-secular binary, reminiscent of Emile Durkheim's division of the world into the sacred and profane (37), is a powerful way of organizing the world for many, yet the reality is far more porous (Taylor 491). For much of the twentieth and twenty-first centuries, the conservative evangelical culture of the United States has articulated a chasm between secular and religious culture, while never fully abandoning the relationship. For many evangelical Christians, the mandate to "share the Good News" with non-Christians requires participating in spaces that are not explicitly Christian. Therefore, unlike more fundamentalist religious groups, evangelical Christians continue to grapple with secular culture, and in influencing secular culture, they are changed as well.

Evangelical Christianity has manifested this tension between religion and secular spaces in their treatment of young people. As early as the 1930s, evangelical Christian youth culture has been framed in contrast to a corrupting non-Christian force: Nazism, communism, sex, drugs, and rock and roll, depending on the decade (Bergler 4). To keep adolescents safe from such influences, evangelical Christianity developed an alternate youth culture and youth groups that kept young people from engaging in risky behavior by utilizing secular culture aesthetics. Evangelical youth culture in the 1990s and early 2000s, formative years for many who now fall in the age range of hipster Christianity, attempted to identify Christianity "as just as cool as anything on MTV" (McCracken 87) and created youth group programming that actively appropriated secular culture to create a fun and cool Christianity (85). Notably, the Contemporary Christian Music (CCM) industry is built on music that sounds similar to secular music and yet includes explicitly Christian messages in its lyrics (Luhr 123). Fearful that secular music could corrupt youth and turn young people away from Christianity, these alternatives hoped to capture the attractive features of secular music while still promoting evangelical Christian values.

The hipster Christian subculture, then, exists in a worldview in which a binary is articulated, and yet practice tells a different subtext. Hipster Christianity, though discussed as a unique or surprising phenomenon, particularly in their integration of secular things, such as music and clothing, into their spiritual lives is not unheard of in evangelical Christianity's recent history. However, a key identifying difference in hipster Christianity's relationship to secular culture is their affirmation of it as a source of spirituality. Hipster Christianity does not shy away from discussing the aspects of secular culture they enjoy even if they are not condoned in evangelical Christian circles. Hipster Christians, while never abandoning their faith, subvert their parents' articulation of the secular/religious boundary and embody the rebellious and anti-institutional aura associated with hipsters.

While hipster Christianity openly embraces aspects of secular culture, particularly things associated with hipsters, and appears to break down the secular/religious binary, it does maintain other boundaries it inherits. Namely, as a product of a largely white, middle-class culture, hipster Christianity does little to confront the racial segregation and classist structures in the evangelical church. Likewise, hipster Christianity still maintains fairly conservative and traditional views when it comes to gender and sexuality. Though the hipster Christian rhetoric is one of boundary breaking, the subculture does maintain certain power structures. When analyzing the binaries hipster Christianity subverts, it is crucial to see the boundaries that are upheld.

Foundational to my understanding of hipster Christianity is Brett McCracken's 2010 book: *Hipster Christianity: When Church and Cool Collide*. McCracken, who self-identifies as a hipster Christian (14), perhaps to position himself as a knowledgeable insider, traces the history of "coolness" and the foundations of hipster Christianity as well as specific identifiers of hipster Christians in both appearance and theology.[1] A book written by an evangelical Christian for an evangelical Christian audience, made apparent by McCracken's decision to write from the first-person plural pronoun, *Hipster Christianity* contains elements of ethnography, history, theology, and tongue-in-cheek satire. His purpose, he writes, is not to create a definitive picture of hipster Christianity but rather to offer the broader evangelical church insight into the issues surrounding hipster Christianity, and in doing so, provides an insider's perspective into the subculture. Additionally, the media company *Relevant* magazine, pastors and churches famous for their ability to be Christian and cool at the same time embody the ways in which hipster Christianity negotiates its boundaries that, while rarely explicitly stated, are ever-present. Finally, the sociological study *What Was the Hipster?* edited by Mark Greif, Kathleen Ross, and Dayna Tortorici, Bjørn Schiermer's article "Late-Modern Hipsters: New tendencies

[1]McCracken devotes a short section of his book *Hipster Christianity* to discuss if he is a hipster Christian (14). By his own classifications, he admits he would be one but is hesitant to spend too much time definitively classifying himself or others as hipsters (though later, he names other individuals as hipster Christians). I suspect McCracken self-identifies as a hipster Christian as a way to name his authority as someone who understands the culture of which he speaks. Even still, he does not fully embrace the label.

in popular culture," and John Leland's *Hip: The History* all provide analyses of secular hipsters to which hipster Christianity can be compared.

What Exactly Is a Hipster Christian?

Both the terms "hipster" and "Christian" can have many meanings and are not readily defined when used in passing conversation. Combined, the two words form an intriguing phrase, but the meaning is still obfuscated. Hipsters are a subculture resistant to explicit classification and yet can be defined as a subset of young adults with tastes that run contrary to mainstream culture. According to McCracken, "the only real requisite for being a hipster is a commitment to total freedom from labels, norms, and imposed constraints" (52). However, aesthetically, the hipster identity is constrained and understood in a certain image. Hipsters wear on-trend clothing that appears effortless, such as the "right vintage T-shirt" and the "right jeans" (Greif 12). Flannel, leather jackets, and skinny jeans are common wear for hipster churchgoers (Harlow). They are, according to McCracken, invested in the arts culture; they love indie music and film (53), and they typically reside in "cool" urban centers (62). Hipster taste appears to distinguish itself by eschewing mass-produced mainstream products, yet is just as defined by its own consumerist tendencies (Greif 12). Underneath their aesthetic choices, hipster Christians are attracted to things that break "the taboos that used to be taboo for Christians" (McCracken 98). They are vocal about their love of secular music, clothing styles, and celebrities; a far cry from previous generations' fear that rock 'n' roll music would corrupt their children. According to McCracken, while these traits have common ground with secular hipsters, hipster Christians maintain "their belief in Jesus Christ as the Son of God" (96) and seek ways to integrate their aesthetic tastes with their spiritual convictions.

Emerging from a big-budget, exuberant form of youth-focused evangelical Christianity, hipster Christianity rebels against what it knows. Jaded and wary of the Christian market, such as Contemporary Christian Music used to keep them separated from secular culture, young Christians began to question the need for explicitly Christian pop culture, and in 2003, the year McCracken places the birth of hipster Christianity, *Relevant* magazine was formed to speak to the desires of this group of Christians (88).[2] The magazine, and now online platform, reports and reviews secular music and media and satirizes the evangelical Christian culture and market from which hipster Christianity emerged (88). With a sleek design and tongue-in-cheek humor, *Relevant* magazine draws on both secular and religious culture,

[2]McCracken is a former contributor to *Relevant* magazine.

noting that they "publish ideas that break stereotypes, challenge the status quo, and spur a generation to know God more" ("The Relevant Story"). As hipster Christians no longer felt the need for an exclusively Christian environment, they were free to adopt and adapt the burgeoning styles of hipsters—a sense of irony, similar tastes in music, clothing, etc.—that were forming concurrently with a similar history of emerging out of previous youth movements (Greif 5).

Other than McCracken's *Hipster Christianity*, relatively little has been written on the norms and values of hipster Christianity, further creating an aura of indefinability of the subculture. However, despite the lack of discussion, hipster Christianity does have a set of ideals that function beneath the aesthetic sensibilities. Hipster Christians may have varying styles and preferences but ultimately are concerned with issues of individuality, rebellion against the mainstream, and youthfulness. These core traits, which will be expanded upon later in this chapter, unify the subculture despite it appearing disparate. For example, in a list of famous hipster Christian churches, McCracken describes congregations worshipping in traditional church spaces with little technology, multicampus churches set in warehouses, and churches in non-church spaces with a strong emphasis on technology, such as advanced audio-visual set up and congregational participation through texting (118–32). All of these things, while vastly different in aesthetics, are considered attractive to hipster Christians in the right context, according to McCracken. These different types of churches speak to primarily young people seeking an individualized experience that subverts the expected norms of the greater evangelical culture.

Though hipster Christianity manifests in a variety of church contexts, certain churches and their pastors have gained celebrity as embodying hipster Christianity. Two such pastors, Carl Lentz of Hillsong Church in New York City and Rich Wilkerson Jr. of VOUS Church in Miami, Florida, have made headlines, in secular and Christian media alike, for their hipster tastes and extremely fashionable churches. Articles such as "Inside Manhattan's Most Hipster-y Megachurch" (Harlow) and "Rich Wilkerson Jr., Kanye's Miami-Based Hipster Pastor, Preaches Controversial Brand of Christianity" (Swenson) attach Lentz and Wilkerson Jr. to the hipster subculture, even if, like most hipsters, they are reticent to identify themselves as such (Harlow). Additionally, Wilkerson Jr. is the subject of a 2015 reality TV show, *Rich in Faith*, which chronicles his and his wife DawnCheré's journey to start VOUS Church ("The Calling"). Both Lentz and Wilkerson Jr. are noted by media outlets as hipsters because they appear to buck taboos in American evangelical culture and offer a version of Christianity that seems cooler than the one that precedes it.

Not only do hipster Christians enjoy secular music for its entertainment value, but they find spiritual resonance in it. Liz Riggs, freelance writer for *Relevant* magazine, discusses the need to see secular music as a legitimate source of Christian inspiration. For her, artists such as British folk band Mumford and Sons perform songs that are not explicitly Christian but provide spiritual content. Lyrics such as "in these bodies we will live/in these bodies we will die/where you invest your love/you invest your life" (Mumford and Sons) are ambiguous enough that they could be interpreted through a Christian lens. Likewise, McCracken includes theological reflection about secular music and art holding spiritual relevance and finds this a welcome change from the broader evangelical culture (166). Thus, hipster Christianity not only challenges the evangelical assumption that listening to secular music is unchristian, but it asserts that secular music has the capacity to positively affect spirituality. In finding spiritual and aesthetic meaning that would not be valued by the mainstream culture of evangelical Christianity, hipster Christianity rebels against previous conceptions of what can hold sacred meaning.

Looking at these examples of hipster pastors, churches, and media, one finds, that like their secular siblings, discourse around hipster Christianity relies on material objects for definition. They are known for their trendy clothing, their indie music, their edgy worship spaces. While these seem like superficial markings of the subculture, their integration into the religious and spiritual lives of evangelical Christians indicates a change in how they view the secular/sacred divide from their predecessors. Raised in a culture that views the boundary as resolute, hipster Christians not only cross the divide but also integrate the two spheres they were taught were incompatible. In traversing this boundary, certain characteristics of hipster Christianity emerge, giving greater understanding of the norms that, while never explicitly articulated, guide the way the subculture manifests. Less obvious than their material culture, an emphasis on their youngness, the desire for uniqueness and individuality, and a rebellious, anti-institutional mindset nonetheless underpin hipster Christianity.

Youth and Youngness

It is not surprising that hipster Christianity is partially defined by its youthfulness. Stemming from an evangelical culture that emphasizes specific programming and groups for youth (Bergler 22–3), those who fall into the hipster Christian category are accustomed to age-specific rather than intergenerational programming as a definitive part of their religious experience (153). For millennials who grew up in youth group programs such as Young Life and Youth for Christ (148), a religious experience that is specific to their age group is not unexpected. Therefore, hipster Christianity, in which hipsters are already associated with the millennial generation, is uniquely bound to this group of young adults and becomes an important point of note for those who discuss hipster Christianity.

For *Relevant* magazine, the desire to engage young adults is explicit. They are known for their ability to communicate with young adults and refer to themselves as the "the leading platform reaching Christian twenty- and thirty-somethings" ("The Relevant Story"). Their content often addresses issues faced by young people. Articles like "8 Things I Wish I'd Known as a Newlywed" (Ward), "9 Things to do While Single" (Jasinski), and "Three Reasons Christians Should Consider a Non-Christian College" (Unseth) have all graced the web pages of *Relevant* magazine and signify their readership's young adult age range. In the "about" section, *Relevant* writes that they look at issues "relevant to our lives and world and give voice to what God is doing in and through our generation" ("The Relevant story"). *Relevant*, as a site of hipster Christianity, develops content that bridges the secular/religious gap and advocates for integrating the two spheres. By emphasizing their audience as twenty- and thirtysomethings, they tag their mission as specific to millennials.

Likewise, churches that are branded as hipster churches are filled with young people, and leadership is similarly young. Carl Lentz, pastor of Hillsong Church NYC, who is called a hipster pastor (Harlow), is a millennial and works to make his church desirable for young people (Couric). In his reality TV show for the Oxygen Network, Rich Wilkerson Jr.'s age and his engagement with young people are emphasized ("Get Connected"). The age of hipster pastors as well as the age of their congregants is a prominent feature in discussions about hipster Christianity. The emphasis on young adults who are taking part in hipster Christianity is striking as narratives emerge about young adults disengaging from religion in the United States ("Religion Among Millennials"). The youthfulness of these churches is seemingly countercultural to current trends around religion and young adults, making it a feature many highlight as they discuss hipster Christianity.

Anti-Institutionalism

As a subculture for young people, hipster Christianity defines itself against the older, establishment generation of evangelicalism, and builds on a mentality of rebellion and anti-institutionalism. Though younger Americans are less likely to be affiliated with an organized religion ("Religion Among Millennials"), hipster Christians have not abandoned their religious affiliation but are still wary of the institutions that raised them. This is not a new phenomenon: American evangelicalism, as a part of the Protestant tradition, is a result of repeated splits of Christian identities forming new denominations and other groups navigating the balance of unity and doctrinal purity (Gunther Brown 8). For hipster Christianity, this is apparent in its move away from the established evangelical Christian norms, such as only listening to explicitly Christian music, here representing mainstream culture for hipster Christianity to react against. The previously articulated boundary between the secular and religious spheres is rebelled against through the integration of secular music in worship—even if the music is more mainstream in secular culture than typical hipster tastes—such as hip-hop lyrics in a sermon (Tietjen) or rejecting more conservative ideas about clothing, alcohol, and tattoos (McCracken 96).

Relevant magazine is upfront with their anti-institutionalism—further bolstering its prominence in the hipster Christian identity. Embedded in its mission, *Relevant* pushes against values they associate with institutional evangelical Christianity. They write, "[W]e don't think believers should be known primarily for legalism and bigotry. We believe in dialogue—about Truth, about faith, about freedom in Christ" ("The Relevant Story"). Headlines such as "What the Church Gets Wrong about Singleness and Marriage" (Sprinkle) and "What Churches Get Wrong about the Holy Spirit" (Morris) suggest that previous iterations of Christianity have made mistakes, and younger, newer Christian subcultures are closer to the truth. By setting up a dichotomy of Christians who are legalist and bigoted, and what *Relevant* is about—Truth, faith, and Christ—the publication distances itself from past iterations of American Christianity and their perception of it.

Hipster Christianity's rebellion over what is acceptable culture for Christians is in many ways a tension felt between two generations of Christians and reflective of a broader understanding of coolness outside of Christian culture. John Leland defines the term "hip" as "a subversive intelligence outsiders developed under the eye of insiders" (6). Though hipster Christianity may not be an "outsider" to evangelical Christianity's "insider," per Leland's definition of secular hipness, it does contain an element of subversion. Rich Wilkerson Jr., a Miami pastor frequently touted as hipster or cool, epitomizes this hipster ideal in his quest to start a worship service in a bar. In the second episode of his reality TV show, *Rich in Faith*, Wilkerson Jr. approaches his parents Robyn and Rich Wilkerson Sr., who is an evangelical megachurch pastor, about his idea for worship service held in a place that serves alcohol ("Bar Service"). The older generation expresses reservations about this idea and appeals to evangelical Christianity's abstention from alcohol for support. But Wilkerson Jr. sees his parents' views as antiquated and unnecessary. Wilkerson Jr. also quarrels with his parents over advertising methods: his parents are dismissive of a social media marketing strategy. In this episode, Wilkerson Jr. acts as an archetype for hipster Christianity as he pushes against previously held beliefs about what spaces are appropriate for Christians to utilize for spiritual and religious practices.

Above all else, hipster Christianity wants to be authentic. McCracken devotes an entire chapter to the discussion of "wannabe hip churches" who misuse coolness as a way to shallowly attract young people to their churches (179–90). However, many of his indicators of wannabe hip congregations—leveraging pop culture, looking cool, and being technologically savvy are among his examples—are also found among churches he calls representations of hipster Christianity. He writes of hipster churches, "[T]hey all tend to be media savvy, fashionably designed, and friend to art and culture" (118). For McCracken, authenticity is elusive: a strong technological presence or focus on popular culture is only cool rather than gimmicky if the church is "striving to be an authentic, loving, holy community of Christ follower" (206). By claiming authenticity as a hallmark of hipster Christianity, hipster Christianity can move away from anything that becomes too mainstream or "wannabe hip."

This anti-institutionalism of hipster Christianity is a striking trait as those associated with it push against previously conceived notions of boundaries in Christian culture. Previously considered taboo, secular music is not only reviewed in *Relevant* magazine but also considered to have positive spiritual implications (Riggs). Church services are held in bars, as is the case for Wilkerson's church VOUS and in nightclubs for Hillsong Church NYC. Hipster Christianity does not share evangelical Christianity's disapproval of alcohol or songs that do not have explicit Christian themes. What was once considered inappropriate is now cutting edge. For hipster Christians, one's authentic experiences of Christianity trumps out-of-touch traditions, and though they maintain their Christian spirituality, they do so in a way that seems at odds with the evangelical Christianity in which they were raised.

Individuality

In part, hipster Christianity's sense of anti-institutionalism stems from a strong emphasis on the individual. In both secular American culture and evangelicalism, individual identity is of utmost importance. In the evangelical world, the defining moment of faith is characterized by a personal decision to enter into a relationship with Jesus Christ. In describing evangelicals, Reimer notes that this conversion experience endows the evangelical faith with meaning as real on a deeply personal and individual level (70). Religious faith is not something that can be inherited from one's parents but must be chosen for oneself (70). Since the 1960s, many evangelical churches, in an effort to draw wandering young people back to the church, emphasized this stance that lifted up personal fulfillment over duty. Today, Thomas Bergler notes that a youth-centric Christianity that has emphasized personal fulfillment and an individual's decision "for himself or herself what to believe" is now the norm for adults as well (220, 222). In interviews, Lentz continually calls faith a relationship rather than a religion. Reacting against the term "religion," Lentz says, "You can be religious about being a car thief, you can be a religious criminal, but we have a relationship with God" (Harlow). Just as hipster Christianity has inherited ideals of anti-institutionalism and youthfulness from the evangelical church, it conceptualizes spirituality as an individualized relationship where personal choices are the cornerstone of that relationship.

Likewise, secular hipster culture valorizes individuality and the commodification of the individual. Leland writes that coolness mirrors the story of America in that both are identified as "coarse, robust, resourceful, independent," and within the twenty-first century, this rebellious, independent sense of cool is disseminated through the mainstream market so that any person can attempt to be "hip" (13–14). Additionally, middle-class adolescents and young adults, free from financial obligation to their family, have buying power as individuals in markets geared toward them (Bergler 13–4). Individualism, linked with choice, allows hipsters to distinguish themselves in their consumerism (Greif 12). According to Bjørn Schiermer, hipster culture relies on the image of nerds and loners as models of individuality as they do not fit into mainstream culture nor do they want to (171). Even though hipsters and hipster Christianity are collectives of likeminded people, hipster Christianity is settled at the crux of interlocking ideologies of spirituality and consumerism, both of which promote an individualized self.

Whiteness in Hipster Christianity

While hipster Christianity pushes against evangelical understanding of the boundary of religious and secular, other boundaries and norms remain unexamined. One such norm is the preeminence of whiteness, as people associated with hipster Christianity—both as de facto leaders and common stereotypes of hipster Christians—are almost always white. According to Mark Greif, secular hipsters "represent what can happen to middle class whites, particularly, and to all elites, generally, when they focus on the struggles for their own pleasures and luxuries" (Greif, Preface) and says that hipsters are "coded 'suburban white'" (146). Whiteness, in his estimation, is a touchstone of hipster subculture. The same whiteness can be found in the hipster Christian subculture. In McCracken's *Hipster Christianity*, his portraits of common hipster stereotypes are not explicitly labeled as any race, but like Greif's analysis of secular hipsters, many are coded as white with their choices in clothing and musical taste (54–62). McCracken also identifies seven public figures as hipster Christian icons, all of whom are white (98–106). Likewise, the majority of *Relevant*'s staff and high-profile pastors labeled as hipster Christians, such as Lentz and Wilkerson Jr., are white. It appears that those who are considered the leaders and figureheads of this subculture reflect the dominant culture of white American evangelicalism from which hipster Christianity emerged.

For much of Christian America, evangelical or otherwise, church is a segregated space. Furthermore, the evangelical emphasis on individual relationships limits the subculture's ability to discuss racism as a systemic issue, preferring to understand it as a problem between two individuals. The language of a "personal relationship with Jesus Christ" is translated into a pervasive ideology that limits how white evangelical Christians discuss racism. Michael Emerson and Christian Smith's analysis of this ideology is outlined thoroughly in *Divided by Race: Evangelical Religion and the Problem of Race in America*. Interviewing evangelical individuals of many races, Smith and Emerson find the relational worldview of religion seeping into white evangelicals' understanding of racial tension. White interviewees responded negatively to any discussion of race, often calling those who bring up racial difference as racist (70). Reconciliation between individuals is stressed over collective and systemic change by white evangelicals. White interviewees maintained that conflicts between two people (whatever their racial identities) are simply arguments, but society is quick to call it a race issue when it is between two people of different races (70). The evangelical Christian narrative of personal relationships is not simply a theological tenet but becomes an ideological one when it pertains to systemic issues. Because hipster Christianity is an outgrowth of evangelical Christianity, particularly of white evangelical Christianity, this mindset affects how hipster Christians understand race.

However, discussions of race are not absent in hipster Christianity and, at times, they push against the narrative that racism is an individual issue rather than systemic. *Relevant* magazine publishes not only content that reports on current events related to race ("Apple pledges $2 million") but also opinion pieces about the need for a Christian understanding of systemic racism (Henry, "If You Think"). Likewise, in 2016, the *Washington Post* reported that, following multiple police shootings of Black men in the United States, Carl Lentz preached that his church says "Black lives matter" rather than "all lives matter" explaining that there are significant risks that Black people face that others do not (Bever). That Lentz and *Relevant* will publicly address racism as issues larger than individual conflict points to possible new developments in how white evangelical Christians discuss race.

Though Lentz and *Relevant* appear to understand the systemic nature of racism, hipster Christianity does not address the ways in which the subculture itself implicitly equals whiteness. Hipster Christianity will occasionally discuss racism, but there is little discussion around the implicit whiteness of the subculture and its ramifications. In 2019, Andre Henry, a Black former managing editor for *Relevant*, published an article in which he criticized *Relevant* for positioning itself as a leader in discussions of racism and the evangelical church without confronting its own racial biases and treatment of its nonwhite staff (Henry, "Black Christians"). He writes that members of the staff dismissed his ideas for content addressing race as the media company was more concerned with retaining their white audience rather than reaching out to nonwhite audiences. His words and experiences were amplified by other former employees of color who also claimed the *Relevant* work environment was toxic (Graham).[3] Hipster Christianity may advocate for the transgression of the secular/religious binary, but their ambivalence around race reinforces previous evangelical power structures. In doing so, it holds onto the power whiteness brings and undercuts its own ethos of rebelling against the norm.

Working-Class Aesthetics, Middle-Class Dollars

Just as hipster Christianity is unable to address its racial boundaries, it reinforces class fault lines. What is considered cool in hipster culture stems from a working-class aesthetic, thrift store clothing, and urban environments, but hipster Christians are largely from upper- or middle-class backgrounds. Hipsters give off the appearance of a working-class aesthetic while maintaining its power as a part of the middle-class dominant culture (Greif 8). For white, middle-class communities, what constitutes coolness is contrasted against what is normal and, therefore, boring and is present in many youth subcultures (Wilkins 3). Sociologist Amy Wilkins notes that young evangelical Christians, goths, and wannabes[4] all rebel against the white, and typically middle-class values of their upbringing (248). They reject "normalness" and turn to alternate tastes and styles. "Normalness" in middle-class evangelical Christianity is positioned against the fear of younger generations engaging in working-class activities. According to Bergler, the rise of youth groups in the evangelical church flourished in communities that could afford to fund expensive youth programs and were worried "that their children will 'fall' into lower economic classes through 'poor life choices'" (14). Middle-class adults are more willing and able to pay for youth groups that provide appealing Christian alternatives to more "risky, lower-class ways of having fun" (14). Hipster Christianity, a generation raised in these youth groups, takes up these risky, working-class markers of rebellion.

While hipster Christians take on working-class aesthetics, they do not completely abandon their middle-classness. Their consumption of art and culture needs money. Even McCracken notes the class implications of hipster Christianity as he acknowledges it "tends toward middle- and upper-class white kids who have the money to go to college and learn the lingo of

[3]Following the publication of these articles, Cameron Strang, CEO of *Relevant* Media Company took a leave of absence to "engage in a process of healing, growth, and learning" (Graham).

[4]Wilkins defines the wannabe subculture as "young white women from various class backgrounds who identify with local Black and Puerto Rican hip-hop communities" (5).

counter-cultural subversion, and who can afford to take material goods for granted and still buy all the fashionable bric-a-brac that the maintenance of a hipster lifestyle requires" (109). A famous hipster Church, Mars Hill Bible Church in Grandville, Michigan, offers trips to music and film festivals, such as the Sundance Movie Festival through a program called Into the Noise. Their goal: "We engage with culture, spirituality, and each other at today's most eminent events, ready to be mystified, stirred, and changed for the better" ("Into the Noise"). Though previous iterations of evangelical Christianity might have created their own Christian film festivals, producing a similar but explicitly Christian environment, hipster Christianity finds spiritual engagement in secular and hipster, such as in independent films. This trip, rebelling against the evangelical ideology of the separation secular and religious spheres, also has a price tag around $1,000 ("Sundance 2017 Deposit"). Hipster Christianity, pushing against some norms of their predecessors, still maintains their class status.

In some cases, hipster Christianity appears to embrace its classed nature rather than masquerading as working class. Wilkerson Jr., who gained secular fame for his friendships with celebrities such as Kanye West and Justin Bieber (who admittedly is not a name typically associated with hipsters), rejects the evangelical disassociation with secular culture but not the prosperity gospel of middle-class evangelicalism. Wilkerson Jr. lives in a penthouse apartment, drives expensive cars, dresses in expensive clothing, and advocates for a stylized and consumable Christianity (Sharlet). Here Wilkerson Jr. diverges from the hipster working-class aesthetic for a style that seemingly embraces upper-class showmanship. This version of hipster Christianity, still defined by a rebellion against a secular-religious dichotomy, does not appear to abandon its classed status; it embraces this boundary.

Gender and Sexuality

Hipster Christianity also fails to address the gender essentialism present in evangelical Christianity. In McCracken's book, he writes of hipster Christian activism and "pushing against those in power" (148), but there is no mention of patriarchy or issues surrounding gender roles and norms. The silence surrounding gender issues, as well as the lack of female leaders, indicate a cultural attitude in which maleness is seen as the norm. Among McCracken's list of figureheads, only one is a woman (101), men write all the books he recommends (140), and all of the famous hipster churches he lists have male heads of staff (118–32). For hipster Christian celebrities such as Lentz and Wilkerson Jr., their wives Laura Lentz and DawnCheré Wilkerson are also listed as lead pastors on their websites, and they do lead worship, but never quite seem like equal partners in interviews. They do not appear in as many interviews as their husbands and their relationship to their husband is often the focus of their appearances. When secular articles discuss hip pastors, they profile men. Women are not necessarily forbidden from preaching or leading in evangelical churches, but their presence in leadership positions is rare, and the assumption of male leadership goes unexamined.

Hipster Christians attempt to take a softer, less judgmental approach to controversial issues than their predecessors, but they do not reject evangelical Christianity's position on many issues surrounding sexuality. In an interview, Carl and Laura Lentz say gay men and women are welcome in their church but decline to make an official statement about same-sex marriage, citing that Jesus never discussed homosexuality (Harlow). In other interviews, though, Carl Lentz understands homosexuality as a sin, as well as abortion. However, he maintains that these stances do not make his congregation unwelcoming (Brodesser-Akner). *Relevant* magazine does not appear to state an opinion on sexuality, but in their numerous articles that discuss relationships, heterosexuality is assumed. Searching for content explicitly related to homosexuality reveals reported news articles, but very few op-eds or commentaries ("Search Results: Gay"). Hipster Christians talk frankly about sex, a far cry from traditional evangelical sensibilities, but do so in the context of heterosexual marriage (McCracken 96). Hipster Christians, though softening their language around issues of sexuality, do not fundamentally differ from mainstream evangelical Christianity in their views.

Conclusion

In conversations about the American religious landscape, hipster Christians are treated as if they are an anomaly. Secular news publications publish articles about famous hipster Christians expressing surprise at the integration of popular culture with religion (Brodessor-Akner; Harlow; Harwood; Swenson). Hipster Christians are millennials who are actively involved in a religious group, a concept at odds with recent conjectures about young people and religion. They do not appear to be mired in the culture wars of their predecessors, but instead seem … fun. They are funny, irreverent, and a part of a subculture that is amorphous and organic in nature. As such, hipster Christianity is viewed as a fad rather than a legitimate manifestation of American evangelical Christianity.

This tendency to trivialize the subculture ignores the significant ways hipster Christianity interacts with culture at large. In the integration of secular culture into its material and spiritual culture, hipster Christianity muddies the evangelical understanding of the secular-religious divide, challenging the idea that they exist independent of one another. However, evangelical Christianity is not only influenced by secular culture (or fearful of that influence) but it also influences the broader American landscape through politics, economics, and cultural norms. Hipster Christianity inherits that power and privilege. Despite the language of living counterculturally and in the aura of rebellion, hipster Christianity is by and large much of the same when it comes to systemic issues. Thus, hipster Christianity is a snapshot of evangelical Christianity's long-standing negotiation of fluctuating boundaries: in reorienting boundaries of secular and religious culture, hipster Christianity seeks uniqueness and rebellion, all the while grounding itself in white evangelical history and social location.

Works Cited

"Apple Pledges $2 Million Donation to Anti-Racism Organizations." *Relevant Magazine*, August 17, 2017, www.relevantmagazine.com/current/apple-pledges-2-million-donation-to-anti-racism-organizations/. Accessed May 1, 2018.

"Bar Service." *Rich in Faith*, season 1, episode 2, Oxygen Media Productions, December 9, 2015.

Bergler, Thomas E. *The Juvenilization of American Christianity*. William B. Eerdmans, 2012.

Bever, Lindsey. "Why This White Pastor Is Not Saying 'All Lives Matter.'" *Washington Post*, October 6, 2016, www.washingtonpost.com/news/acts-of-faith/wp/2016/10/06/why-this-white-pastor-is-not-saying-all-lives-matter/. Accessed July 28, 2020.

Brodesser-Akner, Taffy. "Inside Hillsong, the Church of Choice for Justin Bieber and Kevin Durant." *GQ*, December 17, 2015, www.gq.com/story/inside-hillsong-church-of-justin-bieber-kevin-durant. Accessed October 1, 2017.

"The Calling." *Rich in Faith*, season 1, episode 1, Oxygen Media Productions, December 9, 2015.

Couric, Katie. "Carl Lentz with Katie Couric 12:14." *YouTube*, uploaded by Tom Manning, June 4, 2014, www.youtube.com/watch?v=_3wLm6pPvRY. Accessed September 24, 2014.

Durkheim, Emile. *The Elementary Forms of the Religious Life: A Study in Religious Sociology*, translated by Joseph Ward Swain. George Allen & Unwin, 1915.

Emerson, Michael O., and Christian Smith. *Divided by Faith: Evangelical Religion and the Problem of Race in America*. Oxford University Press, 2000.

"Get Connected with Faith and Be Inspired by Love with Oxygen's 'Rich in Faith.'" *Oxygen*, 2017, www.oxygen.com/rich-in-faith/season-1/blogs/get-connected-with-faith-and-be-inspired-by-love-with-oxygens-rich-in. Accessed September 23, 2017.

Graham, Ruth. "'They're Using Us as Props for the Show': Former Employees at Relevant, a Hip Evangelical Culture Magazine, Have Sparked a Sprawling Conversation about Race and Christian Office Politics." *Slate*, September 27, 2019, slate.com/human-interest/2019/09/relevant-evangelical-magazine-strang-racist-controversy.html. Accessed July 28, 2020.

Greif, Mark, Kathleen Ross, and Dayna Tortorici, eds. *What Was the Hipster? A Sociological Investigation*, Kindle ed. HarperCollins, 2010.

Gunther Brown, Candy, and Mark Silk, eds. *The Future of Evangelicalism in America*. Columbia University Press, 2016.

Harlow, Poppy. "Inside Hillsong's 'Hipster' Church." *Anderson Cooper 360*, uploaded by AC360, June 3, 2014, ac360.blogs.cnn.com/2014/06/03/inside-hillsongs-hipster-church/?hpt=ac_bn1. Accessed September 24, 2014.

Harwood, Erika. "A Guide to Justin Bieber's Renewed Bromance with Pastor Carl Lentz." *Vanity Fair*, August 2, 2017, www.vanityfair.com/style/2017/08/justin-bieber-pastor-carl-lentz-bromance. Accessed October 1, 2017.

Henry, Andre. "Black Christians Deserve Better than Companies (and Churches) like Relevant Media Group." *Medium*, September 18, 2019, medium.com/@andrehenry/black-christians-deserve-better-than-companies-like-relevant-media-group-42aed44528c9. Accessed July 28, 2020.

Henry, Andre. "If You Think Only Jesus Can Do Something about Racism, You're Wrong." *Relevant Magazine*, January 25, 2018, relevantmagazine.com/culture/think-jesus-can-something-racism-youre-wrong/. Accessed May 1, 2018.

"Into the Noise." *Facebook*, 2017, www.facebook.com/pg/intothenoise/about/?ref=page_internal. Accessed October 27, 2017.

Jasinski, Molly. "9 Things to Do while Single." *Relevant Magazine*, July 22, 2014, relevantmagazine.com/life5/relationships/9-things-do-while-youre-still-single/. Accessed October 2, 2014.

Leland, John. *Hip: The History*. HarperCollins, 2004.

Luhr, Eileen. *Witnessing Suburbia: Conservatives and Christian Youth Culture*. University of California Press, 2009.

McCracken, Brett. *Hipster Christianity*. Baker Books, 2010.

Morris, Jessica. "What Churches Get Wrong about the Holy Spirit." *Relevant Magazine*, August 15, 2014, relevantmagazine.com/faith/what-churches-get-wrong-about-holy-spirit/. Accessed September 5, 2020.

Mumford and Sons. "Awake My Soul." *Sigh No More*. Glassnote Entertainment Group, 2010.

Reimer, Sam. *Evangelicals and the Continental Divide: The Conservative Protestant Subculture in Canada and the United States*. McGill-Queen's University Press, 2003.

"The Relevant Story." *Relevant Magazine*, 2017, relevantmagazine.com/about/. Accessed September 23, 2017.

"Religion among the Millennials." *Pew Research Center*, February 2010, www.pewforum.org/files/2010/02/millennials-report.pdf. Accessed May 1, 2018.

Riggs, Liz. "When the Secular Is Sacred." *Relevant Magazine*, July 27, 2010, relevantmagazine.com/god/when-secular-sacred/. Accessed October 2, 2014.

Schiermer, Bjørn. "Late-Modern Hipsters: New Tendencies in Popular Culture." *Acta Sociologica*, vol. 57, no. 2, 2014, pp. 167–81.

"Search Results: Gay." *Relevant Magazine*, 2017, relevantmagazine.com/?s=gay. Accessed October 7, 2017.

Sharlet, Jeff. "The Ministry of Fun: The Feel-Good Gospel of the Pastor Made Famous by Kimye and Bieber." *Esquire*, August 26, 2016, www.esquire.com/news-politics/a48039/rich-wilkerson-pastor-kanye-west-kim-kardashian/. Accessed May 1, 2018.

Sprinkle, Preston. "What the Church Gets Wrong about Singleness and Marriage." *Relevant Magazine*, May 30, 2017, relevantmagazine.com/love-and-money/what-the-church-gets-wrong-about-singleness-and-marriage/. Accessed May 1, 2018.

"Sundance 2017 Deposit." *Into the Noise*, 2017, www.intothenoise.org/register/sundance-2017-deposit. Accessed October 11, 2017.

Swenson, Kyle. "Rich Wilkerson Jr., Kanye's Miami-Based Hipster Pastor, Preaches Controversial Brand of Christianity." *Miami New Times*, September 30, 2014, www.miaminewtimes.com/news/rich-wilkerson-jr-kanyes-miami-based-hipster-pastor-preaches-controversial-brand-of-christianity-6531078. Accessed May 1, 2018.

Taylor, Charles. *A Secular Age*. Belknap Press of Harvard University Press, 2007.

Tietjen, Alexa. "Pastor Carl Lentz Talks Preaching in Ripped Jeans, Bonding with Bieber." *WWD*, November 1, 2017, wwd.com/eye/people/carl-lentz-talks-preaching-in-jeans-bonding-with-bieber-11037192/. Accessed May 1, 2018.

Unseth, Christopher. "3 Reasons Christians Should Consider a Non-Christian College." *Relevant Magazine*, November 30, 2012, www.relevantmagazine.com/relevant-u/undergrad/3-reasons-christians-should-attend-non-christian-college. Accessed October 2, 2014.

Ward, Tyler. "8 Things I Wish I'd Known as a Newlywed." *Relevant Magazine*, July 3, 2014, www.relevantmagazine.com/life/relationships/8-things-i-wish-id-known-newlywed. Accessed October 2, 2014.

Wilkins, Amy. *Christians, Goths, and Wannabes: The Boundaries of Sex, Style, and Status*. University of Chicago Press, 2008.

22

The Hipster Animal: Human–Animal Interactions in Hipsterdom

Jayson Scott Grimes

As Clinton R. Sanders States in *The Animal "Other": Self Definition, Social Identity and Companion Animals*, "Human participants in relationships with companion animals are engaged in the 'social construction of humanness' in orienting their interactions vis-à-vis their pets" (662). Humanness, with its broad interpretations, is highly individual and cultural and therefore particular in its expression, that is to say, the means by which it is evident in the subject are variant. Indeed, the very notion that a nonhuman animal might be able, through perhaps no cognitive volition of its own, to factor somehow into the complex processes that create that particular mix of attributes, that is, humanness, is already a tacit acceptance of an agency that animals are afforded. This occurs within the definition of what constitutes the properties of the human animal as well as the nonhuman animal. In the case of hipster identity, while nonhuman animals may not be empowered with the ability to explicitly embody hipster humanness, they are used as a means whereby the hipster identity, itself an intersectional identity highly based upon subjective and cultural demarcation, is reinforced. But what might the relation of the use of mostly domestic animals be in the identity building of self-professed hipsters, or perhaps by those who are labeled as hipsters by others? Why are some nonhuman animals evidently preferred and agented with this role of identity reinforcement and for what purposes: parody, companionship, household economy, etc.? What are the observable modes of interaction between the hipster identity and the positioning of animals within the makeup of the hipster demonym or hipsterdom at large? In order to address belonging to something which could be called hipsterdom, the hipster label will be defined as those who either self-identify as such or who are marked as such by the "mainstream" society in which their identity building takes place.

Kinzey argues that the hipster "was born in the era of globalization driven by free-market fanaticism; they represent the socio-economic realities around them" (3). He goes on to insist that, "[i]n their attempt to achieve absolute individuality, hipsters somehow overlook the fact that they are doing the exact same thing in the exact same ways as everyone around them" (3). This was echoed in an article in *The Independent* titled "Meet the Global Scenester: He's Hip. He's Cool. He's Everywhere" in 2013 in which the ubiquitous consumerism of the hipster was compared around the world and concluded to be consistently related to some identifiable consumer behaviors and attitudes (Walker). The extent to which this conformity of nonconformity involves the nonhuman animal has also been reported on in the media with examples appearing in *New Phoenix Times* in 2012 and the *Atlantic* in 2013 which explicitly mention the keeping and subsequent abandoning of farm chickens which had become trendy among hipsters for presumably sustainability-related reasons (Lawton; Levenson).

Positioned within the first half of the twenty-first century, hipster identity, at least as a recognizable cultural phenomenon, is present across multiple media platforms. These platforms are themselves well positioned within the contemporary discourse surrounding media and identity building. By assessing online platforms such as blogs and social media, as well as more traditional forms of media (magazines, journals, etc.), we can get a better picture of just how nonhuman animals are appropriated within the hipster discourse. These sources are also useful in establishing the presence of concretizations concerning or including the nonhuman animal as they relate to hipsters. These concretizations can be viewed as a kind of discursive formation which is less susceptible to influences and transferences than might be immediately recognizable. For example, "human" and "humanness" might very well be considered prerequisites for a hipster identification. While such terms could be initially evident, are they really? Their basis as a given starting point for identity building is, in most instances, self-evident and therefore less likely to be transformed by competing and intersectional strains of discourse. Additionally, in reviewing the discourse surrounding the incorporation of pets and other domestic animals which solidifies into concretizations, we can draw a fuller picture of how integral the nonhuman animal, agented with a kind of mirroring function, can truly be in the identity of hipsters, without them necessarily being consciously aware of this identity-building process themselves. What may be perceived as a trend, or just a shared common interest, through even an elementary discourse analysis can be determined as a factor in the gathering of certain formations, what Foucault referred to as discursive formations: "a discursive formation is defined (as far as its objects are concerned, at least) if one can establish [such] a group; if one can show how any particular object of discourse finds in it its place and law of emergence; if one can show that it may give birth simultaneously or successively to mutually exclusive objects, without having to modify itself" (44).

Only from within a context whereby concretizations are established and taken as given platforms from which questions can be posed that review, reinforce, reposition, and reestablish their legitimacy, can we begin to accept as valid notions of what might constitute hipster identity (insofar as their self-identification concerning animals is under examination). In this way, it is possible to systematically eliminate the occasional and more intermittent aspects of the hipster/nonhuman animal relationship and focus on what modes within that interaction are consistently observable, well established, and therefore, in the terms used here, concretized. It is impossible to view these concretizations outside of their unique composition as a more generalized occurrence or trend. Concretization is not merely synonymous with a discursive formation. Therefore, every hipster who keeps a dog as a pet may not be keeping that dog for any purposes of identity-reinforcement. Yet, a hipster could be keeping the pet as a form of identity-reinforcement depending on what kind of dog is kept, why the dog is kept, if there is something of an observable trend of keeping this breed of dog among other hipsters, and whether or not there are some discursive elements which suggest that keeping a given breed of dog is indicative of hipster aesthetics, trends, lifestyle, etcetera. This does not imply that someone who does not keep a particularly trendy breed of dog is not involved in the complexity of identity-reinforcement via the agency granted to the pet, but only that there is no intersection of that act and the act of self-identification as a hipster. Yet here it is posited that indeed there is some relation between hipster identity reinforcement and their relationships to nonhuman animals.

Although this could lead to more abstract notions of what might, or might not, be considered integral to this particular interspecies relationship inasmuch as identity building is concerned, it helps to realize the constant state of flux in which the act of identity building occurs. In order for the human animal to imbue the nonhuman animal with any agency whereby they would ever be able to underpin the construction of a human animal identity, there must first be an acceptance of the human animal status. So then, we can see that the identity of the human animal is one which unfolds as a state of becoming. Only once the human animal has fully "become" human can they then begin to incorporate other modes of human identity expression. Just as it has been posited that one becomes a woman and that womanhood is not innate (De Beauvoir 301), it could be that it is at least possible that one is not born a human but becomes a human through performing humanness. De Beauvoir famously claimed that one becomes a woman partly via what one is subjected to and partly through identification with a given gender, and partially by factors of time, place, culture, and existing regimes of authority and normativity. This defines what a woman might be, and how that being is defined by the changes that the flesh undergo, and how those changes, that new identity, is observed and made use of by others (Joseph). Likewise, Butler elucidates upon the idea that gender is largely performative and that those performances are subject to the same evolving notions of what constitutes identity, both individually and socially. Within the modes of intersection, the media of being (or at least becoming) are observably other than those that are assumed. In Butler's estimation, this might lead to the recognition of a gender that is other than the one with which the observer identifies: "The binary relation between culture and nature promotes a relationship or hierarchy in which culture freely 'imposes' meaning on nature, and, hence, renders it into an 'Other' to be appropriated to its own limitless uses, safeguarding the ideality of the signifier and the structure of signification on the model of domination" (50).

The hipster subculture adds yet an extra layer to the identity building process. An examination of some of the ways that hipsters interact with nonhuman animals sheds light on that process of becoming an "Other" in order to establish a particular hipster identity. By thoroughly delineating what is hipster and what is not, the process of becoming is simplified and othering happens not necessarily only with other humans who are excluded from the hipster world because they are either not interested or do not participate in the modes of interaction with other hipsters but also with the animals that are kept, or with whom relationships are built.

The hipster aesthetic concerning fashion or grooming trends is observable in many hipsters and this is of importance not only as an act of identity assertion but also as a communicative means whereby mutual recognition is the goal. Hipsters, in that respect, may self-identify with a certain kind of animal to take care of, implying that part of the identity-building concept rests in the hipster's realization that the companion animal is there not only to be cared for but also simultaneously functions as a means whereby identity is validated in relationship to the animal other. In essence the hipster's kept animals simultaneously build and deconstruct hipster identity through a process of ongoing reinforcement. To define this process, we can say that building occurs through a set of assumed characteristics (including style and lifestyle) and is extended to the animal via the human. Entailed in the extending of certain values is a constant reevaluation of identity and levels of willingness to extend. In essence, extension leads to the giving away of certain characteristic aspects on the human's part.

Nonhuman Animals and Hipster Identity: Functions and Purposes

Even when nonhuman animals are not directly subjected to the purposes and functions of underpinning a hipster identity, their images are still considered fair game for mass media as was evident in the New Zealander shaver brand Schick's Free Your Skin campaign which depicted bearded men (fitting the hipster aesthetic) with nonhuman animal imageries shaved into or superimposed into their facial hair (Schick). All of the animals appropriated are rodents including a bunny and other woodland rodents. By drawing attention to the connotations of the wild beard, Schick draws our attention to the notions that a beard might be able to communicate specific identifying markers to certain people who can recognize them. A big, bushy beard is an aesthetic grooming choice popular among hipsters, and there are myriad search engine results regarding the best methods to grow, promote, keep, care for, shape, style, perfume, and ultimately shave off the beards. The beard is also one of the most common stereotypes associated with the hipster figure in terms of personal appearance. In constructions of hipster masculinity, the beard holds a particularly prominent place:

> The beard has returned ... to its Romantic roots as evidence of its wearer's proximity to nature. It connects the contemporary Romantic to his inner animalism, his hormonal tether to the wild and biological self, his opposition to civilized, bourgeois society: no tricks, no cunning, no fake, polite crap. Just mano a mano. The beard thus resolutely evidences its opposition to the white-collar world's prohibition of it, conveying a sense of trendy insubordination. (Magill)

It seems fair to suggest that by craftily shaving or superimposing images of nonhuman, woodland animals into the models' beards, the brand sought to further underscore the animalistic and raw masculinity of those who buy their shavers or to inversely suggest shaving off their beards to those men who definitely do not want to be associated with hipsters in order to underline their civilized status: nonthreatening and fully within the easily recognizable categories of humanness. In this case, nonhuman animal imagery has been used to identify the hipster male not only as opposed to civilization and bourgeois society but also as someone who is himself more authentically male, more nonhuman animal and therefore, one might assume, more wild, virile, and untamed: *ergo* cool. While this is but one example whereby nonhuman animal imagery has been used in order to underscore a sense of identity, an extrapolation can be made regarding the different identity interplays that, in this case, establish hipster maleness but in other examples might function to intensify, exaggerate, reinforce, juxtapose, or counter one of the various identities which intersect within the realm of hipsterdom to create the hipster identity.

Yet, it is relevant to the discourse surrounding the formation of something that might be labeled hipster not only to establish functions of nonhuman animal modes of interaction, such as in the previous example in which animalistic imagery is used in order to express intangible attributes, but also to acknowledge the symbolic outcomes of what this process of incorporation of the nonhuman animal as an object of othering has led to. That means going beyond the functions, the *how* of modes of identification and their interplay with humanness and non-humanness, and considering the purposes, the *why* elements of participation in such intersectional modalities. Enhancing the perception of what constitutes cool, or rather what a subject involved in a performative act believes constitutes cool (once the formative elements with which the dominant cultural surrounding, or in this case subcultural or post-subcultural surrounding have been assumed, accepted, and deemed attractive to the subject for their own ends of identity building), must mean something (at least to the observed). Finding that representational meaning, the intangible reason *why*, must be given just as much priority as the functions themselves: "the representational, symbolic and rhetorical uses of the animal must be understood to carry as much conceptual weight as any idea we may have of the 'real' animal, and must be taken just as seriously" (Baker 10).

Concretizations of the Nonhuman Animal in Hipsterdom

Beyond the functions and purposes of the intertwining of nonhuman animals into the human animal's subjective identity-building process and the human animal's benefit of relationships with them, observable patterns emerge. These repeating elements (whether material or otherwise) may serve multiple functions, including modes of mutual recognition, exclusion, and even parody. Here, this is referred to as concretization and encompasses both process and result. Additionally, some nonhuman animals may have a functional utility to their nonanimal human counterparts, through no agency of their own other than that of which they are seemingly unaware of and which is constructed by human animals and then imbued to the nonhuman animal so that they can in turn underline the hipster's self-identification. Although, this process is somewhat observable, that is not to insinuate that the discursive field from which concretizations arise is static. On the contrary, it is constantly in flux: always changing.

Foucault mentions that through the act of agenting the object does not decide on any formative potential, or create spontaneous concretizations based on singular events, because while these aspects are formative, meaning that they are the action of the coming together of various modes of being into one conglomerate, they must come into existence as words and things, as symbols, and get ordered and taxonomized (if they are to be communicated). This entails that they are born on a field of potential for meaning for groups of signs or signifying elements and that the task in analyzing them as formations lies in also identifying the field upon which they arise and which is itself highly subject to forces of change (Foucault 46). It is a task, he posits,

> [t]hat consists of not—of no longer—treating discourses as group of signs ... but as practices that systematically form the objects of which they speak. Of course, discourses are composed of signs; but what they do is more than use these signs to designate things. It is this *more* that renders them irreducible to the language (*langue*) and to speech. It is this *more* that we must reveal and describe. (Foucault 49)

Only by revealing and describing these subjective one-sided agenting and identity building modes can we begin to find any areas in which there are intersections with other identities that hipsters might take on, identities that were already expressed prior to the hipster label, for surely one is not born a hipster. In so doing, it is helpful to review uses of non-human animals for their roles in forming other identities or aspects of identities adjacent to, but not necessarily fully disconnected from, the hipster identity.

With search results such as BuzzFeed's "The Best of Hipster Dog" (Laessig) and Pet Central's slideshow of "The 8 Most Hipster Dog Breeds" (Pajer), a clear bias toward certain dog breeds among hipsters is evidenced. Not only can these search results be found on readily accessible mass media, but they are only three examples of many in which the hipster relationship to dogs is explored for the purposes of entertainment, and not just any type of entertainment but often humorous or satirical entertainment for the purposes of parody and sometimes social commentary. Taking the BuzzFeed example into account, the agency granted to the dog by the human animals who must have had the idea in the first place to even create such a platform is both tangible (as there is real labor and creativity involved) and simultaneously theoretical (as ideas are being expressed, power implications drawn out, and identity building and deconstructing is occurring). Both of these seemingly one-sided processes can be reconciled in that, once again, the animal itself is not the object upon which identity is built. It is rather the act of recognizing hipsterdom in the dog in the meme through the use of hipster aesthetics that would be readily comprehended by those familiar with the contemporaneous scopic regime, that is noteworthy and which evidences a visual constant, an awareness of hipster characteristics, and a concretized discourse.

Hipster Dog wears glasses and a scarf and not much else. Additionally, all of the memes possess characteristically large, white font with phrases written across them (usually along the top and bottom of the meme), and these phrases are written either in the spirit of irony or in parody, and the viewer/reader of such a meme must then have enough familiarity with the prevalent scopic regime that they are able to correctly respond to the image by actively and cognitively connecting the image and language they are perceiving with stereotypical discursive elements they associate with hipsterdom. Hipster Dog is not just a dog with oversized rim glasses and a chunky knit scarf but is a greatly altered mirror used by hipsters as a means to self-reflect, self-identify with others, and possibly to laugh at themselves. Thereby, individual aesthetic choices made consciously by hipsters are transferred onto a nonhuman animal, reflected back at them as a concretized version of their intersectional identities as expressed through material goods associated with hipsterdom, and ultimately estimated to be of entertainment value. It is certainly not only hipsters who have access to these particular memes, and others who do not self-identify as hipsters would likely also find this content humorous, they would however only be able to do so within given parameters (taxonomies) of explanation (characterization) because there is an already established zoomorphological concretization in regards to hipsters that is immediately recognizable to both hipsters (whose identities are reinforced by such imageries through recognition of elements of expression which are closely related to, or identical to, their own) and those who do not self-identify as hipsters for whom these images represent an objective other. For both hipster and non-hipster alike, there is a relational quality based on a referent, an actual object upon which the signs of hipsterdom are based and from which they can be understood to be indicative of a particularized intersectional identity that is somehow conventional.

In this case, nonhuman animals are used as beings of signification; they are signified. As Gillian Dyer points out in *Advertising as Communication*, various adverts require viewers to understand certain signs which are understandable in relation to a dominant scopic regime whereby particular qualities are conveyed through transfer of those qualities from the human viewer to the product even when there are people depicted in the advert. Dyer then goes on to offer a checklist of what different elements of the human signs present in the advert might imply about the product (the object) (96–104). In order for this same process to occur within the context of the hipster identity and the nonhuman animals visually present within their discursive corpus online, there is a process of concretization of those signs into an understandable composite whereby nonhuman animals, who could never self-identify as hipsters, have that identity projected onto them and whereby they imply meaning to those who are hipsters, or who are not hipsters but have a concretized idea of what a hipster is and how it can be represented void of explicit human animal imageries.

In summation, the concretizations must be present within the human animal–nonhuman animal relationship, especially within the discourse about hipsters, because without such concretized intersections of identity whereby the obvious projection of a desired identity is sought after, recognition of the signs which lay the groundwork for the implication would be unrecognizable, and the signifier could not be certain that the signified would be understood. Here, visual examples have been used from sources that are open, freely accessible, and widely disseminated, and while it has not been within the focus of this work to do so, examples outside of merely visual representations should be explored including the language surrounding these concretizations, as well as wider discourses on the individual aesthetics used in demarking these non-human animal objects as agents of identity signification. These might be merely textual in nature (narratives by and about hipsters), or multimedia (film, audio, mixed media).

Modes of Interaction

The major question to be addressed when speaking of modalities within the relationships between the human animal and the non-human animal concerning the framework of hipster identity is why some animals are preferred over others in the process of identity reinforcement, or which modes of selection are used, and which modes of interaction are observable, meaning which modes exist in an explicit manner wherein observation is possible outside of the simple subject–object, signifier–signified structure.

Overwhelmingly, representations of dogs fill the discourse surrounding and encompassing hipsterdom. While other species of domestic or semidomestic nonhuman animals also enter into the hipster composite from time to time, it is undeniable that the majority are household pets, and more narrowly dogs. The human animal relationship to dogs is approximately thirty thousand to forty thousand years old, much older than that between humans and most other domesticated nonhuman animals (Ostrander and Wayne). This provides for a long history in which the two species have been able to learn each other's ways, and yet, it seems to be solely the human animal which uses this relationship for purposes outside of mutually beneficial survival. This suggests that hipsters are not different from other human animals in selecting dogs as a bonded species, and it suggests something of a Hegelian identity dialectic, in that there is no evidence which proves that the nonhuman animal, who is agented with whichever properties instilled upon it, is able to ever fulfill the potential of that agency, and this is where the viewer, the one who recognizes both the hipster and the nonhuman animal, functions as an interlocutor between the two. The synthesis of the hipster and the nonhuman animal into the hipster animal is only completed with the introduction of an outsider, a viewer, who can pair these two identities (the hipster's and the one the hipster has agented the nonhuman animal with).

Finally, the reason that some animals are chosen to be agented in the hipster identity building process is the same that any other group of people has for keeping, bonding with, or assigning certain animals' roles in their lives, namely that they are the animals that we have most grown accustomed to due to a long, shared history. Hipsters are not exceptional in this respect as human animals have been incorporating nonhuman, domesticated animals into their emotional, psychological, and social lives for a very long time. The integration of nonhuman animals, and the discourse, visuality, and power structures surrounding how they are appropriated for human animal purposes suggest that by affording the nonhuman animals participatory agency in the construction of abstractions such as humor, a sense of companionship, kinship, etc., is realized on the part of the nonhuman animal (Walsh).

Ultimately, the hipster animal is a kind of composite of the human animal to nonhuman animal relationship as engineered by the human animal and applied specifically within hipsterdom. While the nonhuman animal is an unknowing participant, an intricate mechanism of identity reinforcement unfolds via the voluntary agency handed over to the nonhuman animal through which reflection takes place. The non-human animal, though unaware of this act of reflection, serves as a kind of mirror through which hipsterdom is both reflected and made widely identifiable. There is also a simultaneous process of recognition/labeling taking place by viewers who may be outside of hipsterdom but who are nonetheless able to recognize intersections involving hipster animals within the context of the hipsters' very human identity. The hipster animal is, therefore, the synthesis of what the hipster wants to perform in the world but cannot alone; the hipster animal is effortlessly cool.

Works Cited

Baker, Steve, and Carol J. Adams. *Picturing the Beast: Animals, Identity and Representation*. University of Illinois Press, 2006.

Butler, Judith. *Gender Trouble: Feminism and the Subversion of Identity*. 1990. Routledge, Taylor and Francis, 2015.

De Beauvoir, Simone. *The Second Sex*. 1949. Alfred A. Knopf, 2009.

Dyer, Gillian. *Advertising as Communication*. Routledge, 1982.

Foucault, Michel. *The Archaeology of Knowledge and the Discourse on Language*. 1969. Vintage Books, 2010.

Joseph, Felicity. "Becoming a Woman: Simone de Beauvoir on Female Embodiment." *Philosophy Now*, 2008, philosophynow.org/issues/69/Becoming_A_Woman_Simone_de_Beauvoir_on_Female_Embodiment. Accessed July 17, 2017.

Kinzey, Jake. *The Sacred and the Profane: An Investigation of Hipsters*. Zero Books, 2012.

Laessig, Gavon. "The Best of Hipster Dog." *BuzzFeed*, May 13, 2011, www.buzzfeed.com/gavon/the-best-of-hipster-dog?utm_te.qi05eXkeq#.kfnyOXKOA. Accessed June 30, 2017.

Lawton, Claire. "A Hipster's Guide to Farm Animals." *Pheonix New Times*, May 15, 2012, www.phoenixnewtimes.com/restaurants/a-hipsters-guide-to-farm-animals-6514949. Accessed July 23, 2017.

Levenson, Eric. "Hipsters Are Ditching Their Pet Chickens." *The Atlantic*, July 9, 2013, www.theatlantic.com/national/archive/2013/07/chickens-are-taking-over-animal-shelters-because-hipster-farmers-are-irresponsible/313500/. Accessed July 20, 2017.

Magill, R. Jay. *Sincerity: How a Moral Ideal Born Five Hundred Years Ago Inspired Religious Wars, Modern Art, Hipster Chic, and the Curious Notion That We All Have Something to Say (No Matter How Dull)*. Google Books. W. W. Norton, 2012. www.google.de/books/edition/Sincerity_How_a_Moral_Ideal_Born_Five_Hu/FL-yXCDJl1YC?hl=de. Accessed July 12, 2017.

Ostrander, E., and R. K. Wayne. "The Canine Genome." *Genome Research*, vol. 15, 2005, pp. 1706–16, m.genome.cshlp.org/content/15/12/1706. Accessed July 23, 2017.

Pajer, Nicole. "The 8 Most Hipster Dog Breeds." *Pet Central*, December 21, 2016, petcentral.chewy.com/behavior-breeds-the-8-most-hipster-dog-breeds/. Accessed June 30, 2017.

Sanders, Clinton R. "The Animal 'Other': Self Definition, Social Identity and Companion Animals." *Advances in Consumer Research*, vol. 17, 1990, pp. 662–8, www.acrwebsite.org/search/view-conference-proceedings.aspx?Id=7082. Accessed July 12, 2017.

Schick Men's: Free Your Skin. schickfreeyourskin.co.nz/men. Accessed October 10, 2017.

Walker, Tim. "Meet the Global Scenester: He's Hip. He's Cool. He's Everywhere." *The Independent*, August 13, 2008, www.independent.co.uk/life-style/fashion/features/meet-the-global-scenester-hes-hip-hes-cool-hes-everywhere-894199.html. Accessed June 30, 2017.

Walsh, Froma. "Human-Animal Bonds II: The Role of Pets in Family Systems and Family Therapy." *Family Process*, vol. 48, no. 4, 2009, pp. 481–99.

CONTRIBUTORS

Mostafa Amini is currently a Data Scientist at the Harvard Medical School, Office for Diversity Inclusion and Community Partnership. His research interests lie at the intersection of computational analysis and social sciences, utilizing machine learning and information-extraction techniques to parse through various domains of knowledge, including religion, law, and culture.

Katje Armentrout holds a PhD in American studies from Purdue University. She received her BFA in fiber arts and sculpture, as well as an MA in humanities from Central Michigan University. Most currently, her research interests include rural culture, farming, and food studies, and she is editing her dissertation titled "Notes on the State of American Agriculture: Young Farmers and 'The Farm' After the 1980s Farm Crisis" for publication.

Caroline Barnett is the associate pastor/campus minister for First Presbyterian Church of Auburn, Alabama. She has written on the intersection of evangelical Christianity, politics, and American culture for religious publications, including *Sojourners* magazine.

George Alexandru Condrache is a fourth-year doctoral student in comparative literature at the University of Western Ontario. He earned a doctoral degree in philological sciences from the West University of Timisoara, Romania. His thesis analyzed the use of scatology in postwar Central European literature. He recently submitted a doctoral thesis on post-socialist nostalgia. He has published articles on communist food brands and contemporary Central European literature.

Annabel Friedrichs is a PhD candidate of American studies at Leibniz University Hannover, Germany, where she also studied urban and landscape architecture. She has presented and published on green gentrification and critical approaches to urban planning, urban DIY movements, the entanglements of New York City's parks and class, and the creative city. Expanding on her research interest in the visual arts, feminism, and creativity, she is currently finishing her PhD thesis on female illustrators' visual and textual representations of femininity in mass and avant-garde magazines, 1880–1920.

Daniella Gáti is a PhD candidate in English at Brandeis University who specializes in twentieth- and twenty-first-century American literature, queer theory, digital media and culture, digital humanities, and popular culture. Her dissertation examines contemporary forms of social critique fiction modeled after social media activisms. Her publications appear in *The Faulkner Journal* and *ASAP/J*.

Justine Gieni is currently an instructor for the University of Regina and holds a PhD in English language and literature from the University of Saskatchewan. Her current research interests include food studies, gender, and illness. Her writing has been published in *MP: Online Feminist Journal*, *Journal of Monsters & the Monstrous*, *Forum: Postgraduate Journal*, as well as the anthologies *Reading in the Dark: Horror in Children's Literature and Culture* and *Incest in Contemporary Literature*.

Lena Gotteswinter is a research associate and PhD candidate at the University of Regensburg, Germany. Her research examines contemporary manifestations of hipness, focusing on the Black hipster. She received her MA in North American Studies: Culture and Literature at Friedrich-Alexander-University Erlangen-Nuremberg (FAU) in 2016 and her BA in English and American Studies and Book Studies in 2014, also at FAU. Her research interests include performance studies, popular music studies, and fashion studies, as well as their confluence in the figure of the contemporary hipster.

Jayson Scott Grimes received a PhD in English literature from Jacobs University Bremen, Germany, in 2015, culminating in a dissertation titled "Migrating Imageries: Zoomorphic Depictions of Immigrants in American Illustrations." He holds a BA from the University of Illinois, USA, and a MA from Maastricht University, the Netherlands. His primary research interests revolve around immigrant narratives as collective imageries, immigrant pictorial representations, and human-animal studies. He has taught at universities in the United States and Germany.

Florian Groß teaches American studies at Leibniz University Hannover, Germany, where he is currently finishing his PhD thesis on "Cool Creativity in Post-Network Television Series." He is coeditor of the *Aesthetics of Authenticity: Medial Constructions of the Real* (transcript, 2012) and has published articles on the television series *30 Rock*, Michael Chabon's novel *The Amazing Adventures of Kavalier & Clay*, and the High Line Park as well as world's fairs in New York City. His research interests include questions of seriality (especially with respect to American television culture, podcasting, and world's fairs), questions of authenticity in relation to contemporary notions of creativity, and the cultural history of New York City.

Alexandra Hauke is a lecturer in American studies at the University of Passau, Germany, where her research and teaching focus on North American literatures, indigenous studies, detective fiction, American folk horror, ecofeminism, digital cultures, and American popular culture. She has written on law and legal cultures in Native American detective fiction, American ecofeminist gothic fiction, Blackness in horror film, utopian idealism in dystopian literature, and self-branding on YouTube and has coedited essay collections on Native American survivance, twenty-first-century Canadian literatures and politics as well as the post-truth era in the United States.

Wes Hill is a senior lecturer in art history and visual culture at Southern Cross University, Australia. His publications include *Emily Floyd: The Dawn* (2014), *How Folklore Shaped Modern Art* (2016) and *Art after the Hipster: Identity Politics, Ethics and Aesthetics* (2017). He regularly writes on art for *Artforum*, *Frieze*, *Eyeline*, *Artlink*, and *Art Monthly Australasia*.

Philip Jacobi is a lecturer at the University of Passau, Germany. He studied American and Japanese studies at LMU in Munich, Germany, and English literature, British cultural studies, and psychology at the University of Passau. He is the author of *Postmillennial Speculative Fiction and the Culture of Longing* (2016) and has published articles on British TV comedies, crime television, contemporary fiction, and pornography. His research interests include nostalgia culture, seventeenth- and eighteenth-century food and health discourse, speculative fiction, and contemporary theory.

Marek Jeziński is the head of the Department of Journalism and Social Communication at the Nicolaus Copernicus University in Toruń, Poland. His main academic interests include social anthropology and contemporary popular culture. He has published widely on political science, sociology, popular culture, and contemporary theatre and music. He published five books, including *The Quest for Political Myth and Symbol in the Political Language of Akcja Wyborcza Solidarność and Sojusz Lewicy Demokratycznej between 1997 and 2001* (2003), *Muzyka popularna jako wehikuł ideologiczny* (2011), and *Mitologie muzyki popularnej* (2014). He has also published a number of edited books and is the head editor of the academic journal *New Media*.

Kathleen LeBesco is Associate Vice President for Strategic Initiatives and Professor of Communication and Media Arts at Marymount Manhattan College in New York City. She is author of *Revolting Bodies: The Struggle to Redefine Fat Identity*, coauthor of *Culinary Capital*, and coeditor of *The Bloomsbury Handbook of Food and Popular Culture*, as well as *Bodies Out of Bounds: Fatness and Transgression, Edible Ideologies: Representing Food* *and Meaning*, *The Drag King Anthology*, and several journal special issues. Her work concerns food and popular culture, fat activism, disability and representation, working-class identity, and queer politics.

Stephanie Li is the Lynne Cooper Harvey Distinguished Professor of English at Washington University in St. Louis. She is the author of six books including the award winning *Something Akin to Freedom: The Choice of Bondage in Narratives by African American Women* (2010) and *Playing in the White: Black Writers, White Subjects* (2015). Her work has also appeared in *Callaloo*, *American Literature*, *SAIL*, *Legacy*, and *SAQ*.

Heidi Lucja Liedke is Assistant Professor of English Literature at the University of Koblenz-Landau, Germany. In her postdoctoral project, she examines the aesthetics of live theatre broadcasting and how it oscillates between the poles of spectacle, materiality, and engagement. She completed her PhD in 2016 at the University of Freiburg and published a monograph based on it as *The Experience of Idling in Victorian Travel Texts, 1850–1901*. Heidi was a Postdoctoral Humboldt Fellow at Queen Mary, University of London from 2018–20. Recent articles have dealt with quasi-experts in the context of contemporary British theater, live broadcast spectators, and Polish decadent poetry.

Brandon McFarlane is a Professor of Creativity and Creative Thinking at Sheridan College. He authors the annual omnibus review of emergent Canadian fiction for the *University of Toronto Quarterly* and founded the creative humanities research hub which mobilizes scholarly knowledge to create innovations for Canadian communities. He has won numerous awards for excellence in experiential learning, accessibility and inclusivity, and applied research.

Melissa Tandiwe Myambo is the editor of *Reversing Urban Inequality in Johannesburg*. She is a Research Associate at the University of the Witwatersrand, South Africa. After receiving her PhD from New York University, she held postdoctoral fellowships at University of California, Los Angeles, and the University of Cape Town. She has also been a Johannesburg Institute for Advanced Study Writing Fellow and the recipient of a Fulbright-Nehru Academic and Professional Excellence Award to conduct research in India where she was affiliated with the Centre for the Study of Developing Societies in Delhi. Her research focuses on globalization, migration, inequality, diasporas, political economy, borders, race/ethnicity, the global middle classes—especially hipsters—and urban studies. She has published in *Writers and Social Thought in Africa*, edited by Wale Adebanwi (2016), *Diaspora* (2007), and *Comparative Literature* (2011).

Peter Naccarato is Interim Vice President for Academic Affairs/Dean of the Faculty and Professor of English and World Literatures at Marymount Manhattan College. He is coauthor of *Culinary Capital* and coeditor of *The Bloomsbury Handbook of Food and Popular Culture* as well as *Representing Italy through Food* and *Edible Ideologies: Representing Food and Meaning*. His work is in the area of food studies, focusing on the role of food and food practices in circulating ideologies and sustaining individual and group identities.

Christopher Oldstone-Moore is Senior Lecturer of History at Wright State University in Dayton, Ohio. He holds a doctorate from the University of Chicago and specializes in the history of masculinity. His most recent book is *Of Beards and Men: The Revealing History of Facial Hair* (2016). His current project is a history of adventure.

Anwar Ouassini is currently an Associate Professor of Sociology and Criminal Justice at Delaware State University. His research/teaching interests lie at the intersection of race, religion, crime, and culture in the Muslim world.

Ben Robbins is an assistant professor in the Department of American Studies at the University of Innsbruck. His work on modernist literature, Hollywood cinema, and gender and queer studies has appeared in *Genre*, *The Faulkner Journal*, *Faulkner and the Black Literatures of the Americas*, and the *Journal of Screenwriting*. His current research focuses on twentieth-century queer exile literature.

Catharina Rüß is a scholar for Fashion and Textile Studies at the TU Dortmund, Germany. She studied cultural anthropologies, German literature and museum management with a focus on garments and youth cultures at the University of Hamburg. From 2008 till 2018 she was a scholar for fashion studies in Hannover and Berlin, from 2018 till 2019 she also worked as a research assistant at the University of Paderborn and was a lecturer for fashion and design theory at the HFK in Bremen and at the AMD in Hamburg. Her research interests include (anti-)fashion, literature, postcolonial studies, and pop/sound cultures.

Katharina Scholz graduated with an MA in creative writing from the University College Dublin. She is a writer, critic, and journalist dividing her time between Dublin and Berlin.

Heike Steinhoff is Junior Professor of American studies at Ruhr-University Bochum, Germany. She is the author of *Transforming Bodies: Makeovers and Monstrosities in American Culture* (2015) and *Queer Buccaneers: (De) Constructing Boundaries in the Pirates of the Caribbean Film Series* (2011).

Her research focuses on gender studies, body studies, urban studies, and the study of American popular culture from the nineteenth to the twenty-first century. She has published on beauty culture, city mystery novels, urban masculinities, Hollywood pirate films, and animated children's movies.

Łukasz Wojtkowski is Assistant Professor in the Department of Journalism and Social Communication at the Nicolaus Copernicus University in Toruń, Poland, and manager at the NCU Media Lab. He is the author of two books on the mediatization of politics and culture and of a number of peer-reviewed articles and book chapters. His research interests focus on mediatization of culture and society, digital culture, critical theory, and social movements.

INDEX

Acres U.S.A. 85, 86, 99
activism/activist(s) 27, 29, 31, 34–7, 40–3, 59, 68, 78, 79, 149, 179, 216, 255–6, 265, 348, 363, 366, 370, 385
African American(s) 3–4, 108, 201, 219, 221, 258–60, 264–6, 314
agriculture (American) 85–100
Alejandro, Noel 19, 147, 148–53, 155, 159
alt-right (*See also*: nipster/Neo-Nazi hipster) 15, 19, 117
America/American 1–7, 11–15, 18–21, 29, 34, 47, 52, 57, 58–61, 69, 72, 85–100, 106–12, 114, 117, 131, 134–6, 147, 148, 153–4, 157–8, 183, 186, 187–9, 191–2, 194, 204, 207, 211–12, 213, 217–18, 219–20, 221, 230, 235–6, 254, 256–60, 261, 264, 265–7, 275, 278–9, 294, 305, 307, 313–14, 317, 321, 323, 325, 326, 330, 332, 333–5, 346, 357–70, 373, 377, 379–82, 386–7
American hipster (*See also*: hipster) 1, 3, 6, 11, 217, 218, 219, 220, 230, 260
American Muslim(s) (*See*: American Muslim youth, Muslim hipster/Mipsterz)
American Muslim youth (*See also*: Muslim hipster/Mipsterz, youth(s)) 13, 357–70
animal(s): 5, 17, 21, 87, 95, 96, 247, 296, 297, 391–400
anti-fashion (*See also*: fashion) 19, 105–21, 141, 368
apriorism/a priori knowledge (*See also*: Boryard, Anatole) 3, 17, 209, 221, 257, 262, 263, 265, 266
appropriation/appropriate/appropriators 1, 3–5, 7, 12–13, 15, 34, 40, 42, 62, 86, 88, 91, 93, 94, 110, 113, 117, 121, 130, 139–41, 167, 171, 189–90, 193, 195, 196, 201, 215–30, 257, 260, 264, 285, 322, 329, 340, 341, 347–9, 350, 351–2, 368, 374, 392, 394, 400
art hipster (*See also*: hipster) 20, 273–87
artisanal 10, 13, 31, 50, 53, 55, 86, 88, 92, 95, 95–9, 129, 130, 274, 306, 308, 310–2, 322, 345, 351
Art Nouveau 110
Artforum 275
Arts and Crafts Movement 117
Asian American 20, 254, 258, 261, 267
authenticity/authentic 1, 4, 9–11, 12, 19, 28–9, 30, 32, 42, 43, 53, 55–6, 70, 73, 74, 89, 92, 93, 94–5, 98, 99, 113, 130–1, 132–3, 134, 136, 137, 138, 139–41, 151, 167, 200, 201, 204, 205, 206, 208–12, 216, 220, 236, 245, 257, 263, 265, 274, 279, 291, 292, 295, 306, 307, 308–9, 309–18, 323, 333, 334, 335, 348, 349, 358, 359, 360–1, 362, 367, 368, 380–1, 395
  inauthenticity/inauthentic: 107, 114, 116, 140, 216, 245, 323
avant-garde (*See also*: neo-avant-garde) 4, 18, 75, 112, 117, 168, 169, 236, 254, 273, 275–8, 280, 281–2, 306

Baby Boomers/baby boom generation 169, 170, 176, 177, 192
bars 48, 60, 68–9, 71–4, 75, 79, 80, 167, 203, 294, 313, 314, 380–1
baristas 57, 116, 310, 325, 342
Bartz, Andrea (*See also*: Ehrlich, Brenna) 16–17
beard(s) 1, 5, 6, 11, 14, 19, 33, 51, 72, 87, 88, 95, 115, 117–18, 120, 129–41, 152, 203, 220, 222, 236, 294, 297, 362, 395
Beat Generation/Beatniks 3, 19, 69, 105–14, 118, 215, 219, 226, 227, 228
Benjamin, Walter 106, 115, 238, 280, 327
Berlin 6, 114, 203, 222
Black feminism (*See under*: feminism/feminist)
Black hipster/Blipster 13, 20, 254, 258–60, 263–7
bohemia/bohemian (*See* also neo-bohemia/neo-bohemian) 4, 5–6, 87, 108, 109, 110, 112, 117–18, 167, 168, 171, 172, 176, 242, 277, 311
boho 1, 109–10, 113, 246, 297
Bourdieu, Pierre (*See also*: cultural capital, distinction, habitus) 3, 49, 55, 58, 62, 110, 277, 308
bourgeois 5, 108, 111, 113, 115, 130, 134, 139, 179, 208, 276, 277, 323, 335, 395
Breaking Bad 136
Bricolage/bricoleur 7, 11, 17, 18, 108, 151, 179, 279, 291, 297, 298
Brooklyn (*See also*: New York/ New York City (NYC)) 3, 11–12, 15, 28, 34, 48, 50, 54, 55–6, 57, 58, 93, 133, 184, 211, 240, 246, 249, 340
Broyard, Anatole 3–4, 18, 106, 108–9, 219, 221, 257
Butler, Judith 16, 225, 394

Canada/Canadian 19, 167–81
capital
 culinary capital 305–18
 cultural capital 3, 49–51, 56–7, 59, 60, 107, 110, 247, 305–18, 357–70
 social capital 58
 subcultural capital 3, 218, 224–30, 254, 264
Capitalism/capitalist 8, 9, 11, 21, 30, 31, 37–8, 42, 51, 57, 58, 62–3, 72, 74, 89, 95, 111, 116, 118, 158, 167–8, 216, 219, 235, 242, 274, 281–2, 310, 323, 327, 328–9, 331, 332–5, 350
 global capitalism:11, 89, 158, 167, 273, 329
 late capitalism (*See also*: Jameson, Fredric) 7, 9, 16, 89, 325, 334, 335
 neoliberal capitalism/capital (*See also*: neoliberalism) 91, 180, 273, 287
celebrity 215, 216, 221, 222, 317, 377
Cheadle, Harry 131–3, 137
childhood 9, 11, 12, 73, 75, 139–40, 183, 209, 246, 292
 childish/childishness 13, 96, 140, 194
Christianity (*See*: Evangelicalism/ Evangelical Christianity, hipster Christianity/hipster Christian)
Christie, Michael 173, 175–81
class (*See*: creative class, middle-class, working-class)
Clover Mead Farm 96–7
comedy 5, 138–9, 168, 170, 216, 246, 306, 312, 314
commodification/commodified 1, 3, 10, 11, 12–13, 28, 40, 48, 51, 62, 85–100, 147, 149, 153, 210, 257, 282, 290, 291, 292, 299, 324, 340, 361, 382
communism/communist 19, 68–9, 72–5, 109, 374
consumerism/consumer culture 7, 8, 21, 30, 41, 42, 55, 62, 67, 79, 89, 92, 96, 107, 146, 148, 157, 235, 242, 273, 281, 283, 306, 311–12, 321–35, 359, 367–8, 382, 392
 anti-consumerism 106, 321–35

hip consumerism (*See also*: Frank, Thomas C.) 7, 30, 42
consumer(s) 7, 8, 10, 30, 62, 63, 72, 73, 86, 87, 89, 97–9, 107, 116, 130, 131, 139, 146, 147, 149, 156, 160, 173, 177, 206, 210–2, 237, 246, 311–12, 349, 358, 359, 368, 369, 392
rebel consumer 1, 146, 359
cool/coolness 4, 31, 40–1, 55, 61, 62, 69, 87, 93, 95, 105, 106, 107, 109, 111–12, 114, 116, 117, 138, 145, 154, 167, 170, 186, 225, 226, 228, 236, 246, 256, 258, 263, 265, 274, 307, 308, 310, 312, 328, 344, 345, 347, 357–70, 374, 375, 376, 377, 380–1, 382, 384, 392, 395, 396, 400
cosmopolitan/cosmopolitanism 57, 58, 59, 72, 176, 235, 259, 285, 346
counterculture/countercultural 3–4, 8–9, 14, 51, 69, 87, 89, 106–7, 114, 120, 131, 138, 141, 146, 147, 148–53, 157, 160, 171, 178–9, 188, 204, 219, 221, 293, 307–11, 322, 329, 360, 362, 379, 387
craft(s)/craftmanship 2, 13, 14, 28, 29, 34–6, 40–1, 55, 63, 95, 117, 210, 299, 315
craft beer 203, 321, 323–35
craftivism 34
creativity/creative 7, 8, 12, 27–43, 47–8, 58, 59, 60, 61, 87, 94, 95, 112, 114, 116, 146, 147, 149, 154, 167, 169, 170, 171, 173, 179, 199, 201–2, 207, 210, 211, 212, 219, 221, 222, 240, 243, 273, 274, 291, 322, 330, 342, 351, 357, 359, 397
creative cities (*See also*: Florida, Richard) 8, 167
creative class (*See also*: Florida, Richard) 8, 32, 47, 167, 210, 243
creative culture 18, 27–43
creative economies/creative industries 8, 14, 18, 107, 167, 171, 283
culinary capital (*See under*: capital)
cultural capital (*See under*: capital)
Cultural Time Zones (CTZs) 47–63
Czech Republic 69, 71

Dadaism/dadaist 19, 168, 171–2, 173–5, 177
dandy 5–6, 11, 111, 263–4, 334
David Thoreau, Henry 93, 117
Deschanel, Zooey 258
design 1, 18, 48, 52, 53, 55–6, 62, 70, 91, 92, 94, 95–6, 98, 120–1, 167, 173, 243, 330, 331, 333, 344, 362, 376, 381
design aesthetic(s) 49, 50, 52, 53, 55, 62
Design Districts 48
designers 42, 58, 112, 116, 178
(digital) nostalgia design (*See under*: nostalgia)
Dickens, Charles 135
distinction (*See also*: Bourdieu, Pierre) 3, 9, 10, 16, 20, 62, 116, 121, 306–7, 308, 309, 310, 318, 359, 369
dot.hipster 106–7, 110–5, 121
Du Bois, W. E. B. 260

Eggers, Dave 20, 183–96
Ehrlich, Brenna (*See also*: Bartz, Andrea) 16–17
elitism /elite/elitist 59, 79, 80, 116, 139, 168, 210, 221, 235, 276, 277, 283, 335, 365, 382
emancipated spectator(ship) 235–50
Esquire magazine 203
ethnicity/ethnic 2, 3, 4, 5, 6, 12–13, 15, 17, 32, 33, 38, 41, 43, 57, 59, 72, 80, 130, 140, 176, 180, 188, 253, 255–6, 258, 261, 267, 287, 294, 305, 309, 313, 316, 317, 333, 347–9, 358
ethics/ethical 21, 62, 149, 195, 216, 283–7, 312, 313
Europe/European 5–6, 15, 19, 56, 61, 67–80, 109, 117, 118, 134, 135, 157, 188, 191, 200, 326, 347, 367

Evangelicalism/evangelical Christianity 21, 374–87

farm(er)/farming 6, 19, 53, 85–100, 311–12, 347, 348, 392
family farm/farmer 85–6, 88, 90, 92, 93, 96, 98, 99
farmer's market 95, 97, 310
farm-to-table restaurants/movement 86, 96, 98–9, 351
hipster farmer 6, 19, 85–100
Farm Aid 90
fashion (*See also*: anti-fashion) 2, 6, 8, 12–13, 14, 19, 40, 42, 49, 58, 70, 78, 79, 87, 88, 105–21, 132–3, 135, 137, 138, 140, 141
female hipster/female hipsterism 5, 13–14, 20, 34, 88, 114, 116, 235–50, 253, 255, 257–8, 260, 261, 267
femininity 13, 29, 106, 111, 115–6, 237, 241, 244, 249, 257–8, 261, 334
feminism/feminist 14, 34, 149, 152, 153, 223, 242, 254, 255, 258, 261, 263–5, 267, 363, 365, 370
black feminism 256, 264–6
fourth wave feminism 14
popular feminism 255–6, 262
postfeminism 14, 235, 237, 239, 241, 243, 245, 247, 249, 255, 257, 261–2
second wave feminism 256
third wave feminism 14, 255–6
Florida, Richard 8, 32, 167, 243
folk 68, 77, 91, 110, 150, 263, 378
food(ways) 1, 3, 10, 11–12, 20–1, 31, 48, 55, 58, 61, 67, 70, 85, 86, 88, 89, 91–2, 97–9, 156, 176–8, 195, 236, 297, 299, 305–18, 339–52
foodie 55, 178, 308, 313, 314, 339, 349, 351–2
Foucault, Michel 159, 277, 393, 396–7
fourth wave feminism (*See under*: feminism)
Frances Ha 20, 235, 237–42, 246–50
Franco, James 20, 215–30
Frank, Thomas C. 8, 30, 146, 359
Freud, Sigmund 274, 286
Frye, Northrop 168, 171, 179

Game of Thrones 136–7
Gast, John 93
gay 14–15, 108, 146, 148–53, 176, 217–18, 220–2, 225–8, 334, 386
gaze 237–8, 239, 240–1, 277, 281, 361
male gaze 240–1, 246, 249
gender 3, 5, 13–15, 16, 18, 20, 21, 29, 33–4, 59, 79, 106, 116, 132, 141, 146, 156, 176, 180, 189, 207, 220, 223, 228, 236, 238, 239–40, 242, 245, 247, 249, 253–8, 260–7, 276, 294, 358, 360, 361–3, 364, 369, 375, 385–6, 394
gender-bending 88, 236, 263
gender politics 15, 223, 256–8, 266
Generation X 183
Generation Y (Gen Y) (*See also*: millennials) 7
gentrification/gentrified 1, 6, 8–9, 15, 16, 17, 18–19, 27–43, 47–63, 77, 97, 99, 146, 167–8, 170, 173, 175, 178–9, 236, 246, 322, 324–5, 329, 330, 334, 340–1, 346–7, 348, 352
anti-gentrification 28, 31, 179
Germany/German (*See also*: Berlin) 6, 117
Ginsberg, Allen 107, 118–20, 202, 217, 219, 227
Girls 14, 20, 184–5, 235–50, 314
global/global culture 2, 6, 8, 11, 15, 16, 19, 31–2, 47–63, 168, 171, 173, 177, 200, 286, 294, 327, 328, 329, 334, 342, 347, 348–9, 350, 366–7, 368
global capitalism (*See under*: capitalism)
globalization 3, 6, 47–63, 89, 167, 177, 273, 286
glocal 6, 47–63
Gold Cash Gold 86, 98–9
graffiti 28, 34, 41, 53, 155, 158, 176, 178, 227

"green hipster" 5–6
Greer, Betsy 34
Greif, Mark (*See also*: Ross, Kathleen, Tortorici, Dayna) 1–2, 3, 5, 18, 41, 87–8, 88–9, 130, 138, 139–40, 146, 148, 157, 200, 205, 209, 210, 222, 223, 237, 257, 274, 307, 323, 324, 382

habitus (*See also*: Bourdieu, Pierre) 50–1, 55, 58–63, 254, 256, 366, 367
Hasidim/Hasidic beards 133–4
Hebdige, Dick (*See also*: subculture) 7, 108–9, 290
Hemingway, Ernest Miller 199, 202–6, 207, 209, 210
heteronormativity/heteronormativite 14–15, 132, 149, 156, 236, 237, 265
heterosexuality/heterosexual 12, 13, 132, 180–1, 184, 221, 226, 229, 243, 386
hijab/hijabi 357–70
hijabista 13, 369
hip 1, 4, 8, 12, 28–36, 40–3, 85, 106, 109, 111, 112, 115, 117, 167, 168, 172, 173, 202, 208, 240, 246, 255, 256, 261, 267, 273, 276, 278, 279, 306, 311, 314, 315, 346, 347, 350, 361, 380–1, 382, 386
hip consumerism (*See under*: consumerism)
hippies/hippie culture 10, 107, 110, 118, 368
hipster (*See*: American hipster, art hipster, Black hipster/Blipster, dot.hipster, female hipster/female hipsterism, "green hipster", hipster Christian, hipster farmer, "hipster primitive", male hipster, Muslim hipster/Mipsterz, proto-hipster, white hipster)
hipster animal (*See also*: animal(s)) 17, 391–400
hipster bars (*See*: bars)
hipster bashing 17, 116, 342, 349, 350, 351
hipster beard (*See*: beard(s))
hipster café 48, 50, 52–63
hipster Christianity/hipster Christian 21, 373–87
hipster culture (definition of) (*See also*: subculture, post-subculture) 1–21
hipster dog 397–8
hipster farmer (*See under*: farm(er)/farming)
hipster fiction (*See also*: hipster literature) 19, 167–81
hipster food(ways) (*See*: food(ways))
hipster identity 5, 7, 9, 11, 13, 16, 20, 21, 86, 215, 243, 263, 305, 306, 310, 311, 323, 358, 360, 376, 391–400
hipster literature (*See also*: hipster fiction) 9–10, 11, 19–20, 186, 196
hipster music (*See under*: indie, *See also*: music)
hipster movies/film (*See under*: indie, *See also*: movies/film)
hipster nostalgia (*See*: nostalgia, design)
hipster porn/ography 19, 145–60
"hipster primitive" 5, 87–8
hipster racism (*See also*: racism/racist) 14, 314
hipster self-fashioning (*See also*: self-fashioning) 3, 15–18, 19
hipster sexism (*See also*: sexism/sexist) 14
hipster style 8, 13, 15, 18, 70, 112, 114–15, 121, 129, 130, 140–1, 254, 325
hipsterism (*See also*: hipster culture, subculture, post-subculture) 10, 13–14, 15, 18, 20, 87, 116, 129, 138, 139, 191, 196, 235, 237, 238, 240–50, 275, 289–90, 292–3, 299–300, 360–1
hooks, bell 12, 258, 266

Horning, Rob 18, 140, 216, 273, 284
Hummel, Carol 29, 34, 37–40, 43
Hungary 68–69, 71, 79

identity politics 12–13, 18, 20, 158, 260, 275, 287
India/Indian (*See also*: New Delhi) 57–63, 313, 317, 366
Indian American 307, 313–18
indie 53, 105, 107, 112
  indie (youth) culture/generation 3, 146, 148, 253
  indie cinema/movies/film 70, 216, 235, 240, 376
  indie music/bands 17, 70, 87, 109, 110, 175, 180, 222, 253–67, 322, 376, 378
individualism/individuality/ individualist 8–9, 11, 31, 32, 35, 38, 110, 130, 136, 137, 139, 141, 146, 201, 211, 237, 239, 240, 241, 254, 255, 257, 261–3, 264, 265, 267, 287, 292–3, 327, 373–4, 377–8, 381–2, 392
industrial aesthetics/spaces/processes 1, 8, 27, 53, 72, 73, 86, 91, 92, 95, 98, 130, 308–9, 326, 330
industrialization/deindustrialization 90, 117, 135, 176–7, 180
intersectionality/intersectional 3, 15, 21, 147, 176, 200, 256, 264–6, 391
irony/ironic 3, 7, 9–11, 14, 17, 19, 53, 55, 61, 69, 70–77, 79, 107, 129–34, 139–41, 150–1, 168–70, 183, 184, 181, 196, 208, 209, 212, 218, 223–4, 226–9, 236, 245, 253, 258, 259, 262–3, 267, 273, 280, 281, 284, 292–3, 306–7, 308, 311, 314, 316, 318, 323, 340, 345, 377, 398
Islam 317, 357–70

Jameson, Fredric 71, 89, 278–9, 284, 326–7, 328, 331, 332
Janelle Monáe 20, 254, 260, 263–5
jazz 3–4, 60, 77, 201, 219
Jewish 118–20, 134, 228
Johannesburg 6, 18, 47–63
journalism 200, 204–5
July, Miranda 9–10, 12–13, 186

Karen O 20, 254–6, 261–3
Kaye O'Donnell, London 27–9, 32–6, 38, 40, 42–3

Lacan, Jacques 284, 332
Lanham, Robert 5, 16–18, 305
Latina/o/x 57, 28, 258, 333
Lefebvre, Henri 49, 52, 172
Leland, John 4, 204, 256, 258, 376, 380, 382
lesbian 51, 174, 187–8, 228, 314
LGBT/LGBTQIA+ 15, 51, 60, 175–6, 264
lifestyle 2, 6–12, 28, 49, 59–60, 86–91, 93–96, 98, 116, 118, 146, 170, 174, 211, 237, 240, 243, 264, 290, 293, 296, 299, 314–16, 322, 332, 339, 361, 369, 385, 393–4
liminality/liminal 2, 9, 188, 228, 267
Lloyd, Richard 8, 167, 169, 171
local/locally 6, 10, 19, 27, 29, 31–2, 35, 40, 48, 50–2, 55–6, 56–8, 59–63, 67, 69, 72, 80, 95–6, 97–9, 170–2, 173, 177–8, 206, 282, 285, 308, 309–13, 314, 324, 327–9, 330–1, 345, 347, 351
lumberjack 5, 6, 33, 51, 87, 109, 115, 117, 130, 132, 133–4
lumbersexual 5, 6, 14, 132, 253

Magill, R. Jay 9, 130, 139–40, 323
Mailer, Norman 4–5, 18, 30, 106, 108, 168, 200–1, 207, 209, 219–20, 257
mainstream 1, 3–4, 6, 7–8, 10–11, 12–13, 18, 21, 30–1, 32, 42, 47–9, 51–3, 57, 59, 62, 70, 74–8, 79, 80, 87–8, 99, 110, 111, 114–15, 130, 134, 138, 141, 146, 148–53, 154, 157, 159–60, 168, 176, 185–7, 202–3, 212, 216–18, 219, 221, 228–9, 237, 242, 246, 253–5,

258, 263, 265, 274, 281, 283, 305–7, 309–11, 313–14, 318, 322–3, 329, 331–2, 339–41, 349, 351, 359–60, 364, 373, 376–8, 379–81, 382, 386, 392
male hipster 14, 19–20, 88, 114, 129, 141, 208, 217–18, 219–20, 221, 223, 237, 240, 242, 257, 324
Maly, Ico (*See also*: Varis, Piia) 2, 323, 325, 328–9
manele (*See under*: music)
marginalization/marginalized 1, 3–4, 7–9, 19–20, 35, 43, 60, 68–9, 76–7, 80, 88–9, 109, 172, 175, 187, 189–90, 193, 200, 216, 218, 219–20, 227, 230, 254, 255, 258, 260, 266, 277, 286, 314, 318, 322, 331, 333, 340
masculinity/masculinities 14, 19, 51, 106, 111–14, 114–16, 118, 121, 130, 132–3, 136–7, 139, 149, 189, 200–1, 202, 207, 209, 212, 215–18, 219–20, 226, 229–30, 334–5, 395
Master of None 305–18
McCracken, Brett 130, 140, 305, 375, 376–8, 380–1, 382, 384, 385
McGinley, Ryan 19, 145–8, 153–9
McInnes, Gavin (*See also*: Proud Boys, *VICE* Media) 119–20, 205, 207, 254, 261
metamodernism/metamodern (*See also*: post-postmodernism/post-postmodern) 10–11
metropolitan 86, 89, 94, 97, 99, 330
metrosexual 14, 132
middle-class 1, 3, 4–6, 11–13, 30, 49, 51, 52, 57, 59–60, 67, 71, 77, 85, 89, 92, 94, 111, 113, 133, 139, 168, 170, 184–5, 188–9, 199, 201, 208, 238, 243, 249, 253, 265, 335, 348, 375, 382, 384–5
millennials (*See also*: Generation Y) 7, 28, 49, 55, 58, 85, 95, 97, 105, 115, 235–6, 239, 342–4, 247, 249, 314, 373, 378–9, 386
Modern Farmer 86, 92–3, 99
modernism/modernity/modernist/modernization 57, 58, 106, 111, 117, 130, 134, 276, 278–9, 280, 282, 285–6, 290
movies/film 2, 3, 7, 9–10, 20, 70, 209, 216–17, 222, 228, 235, 237, 239–40, 246–9, 259, 290, 296, 324, 385
multicultural/multiculturalism 176, 178, 184, 261, 364
multinational 282, 311, 325–9, 331, 332, 368–9
music 3, 14, 17, 20, 48, 53, 60, 68–9, 74–8, 79, 80, 87, 110, 112, 176, 219, 237, 253–67, 275, 290, 294, 297, 305, 310, 314, 357, 358, 359, 362–3, 365, 367, 368, 374, 376–8, 379–80, 381, 382, 385
  folk music (*See*: folk)
  indie music (*See under*: indie)
  manele 67–80
  muzică ușoară 68–9, 74–8
  popular music/pop music 68, 75, 253–67
  rock 68, 75, 87, 180, 254–5, 257–8, 261–2, 263, 322, 367, 374, 376
Muslim hipster/Mipsterz (*See also*: American Muslim youth) 13, 21, 357–70
muzică ușoară (*See under*: music)

narcissism/narcissistic/narcissists 7, 114, 157, 194, 196, 201, 210, 211, 241, 243, 274, 280, 284, 286
National Young Farmers Coalition 86, 96–7, 99
nationalism/nationalist 21, 118, 120, 207, 285, 323, 335
Native American 5, 87–8
nature 6, 11, 70, 91, 117–18, 130, 133, 135, 139, 141, 171, 290, 295, 296–8, 394, 395
Nature Boys 117–21
neo-avant-garde 20, 275–6, 278–81, 282, 284 286

neo-bohemia/neo-bohemian 8, 168, 169–70, 180
neoliberalism/neoliberal (*See also under*: capitalism) 10, 11, 16, 34, 50, 63, 89, 91, 92, 107, 146, 167–8, 170–2, 173–5, 177, 180, 242, 273, 278, 286–7, 322, 323
New Delhi 6, 18, 47–63
New York/New York City (NYC) (*See also*: Brooklyn) 3, 6, 11, 15, 18, 27–43, 47–63, 94, 96, 109, 118, 129, 133–4, 138, 145, 158, 212, 217, 240, 249, 253, 261, 266, 307, 313, 315, 340, 346, 365, 377, 379, 381
nipster/neo-Nazi hipster 19, 117–21
nonconformism/nonconformist (*See also*: nonconformity) 33, 70, 79, 108, 112, 116, 118, 121, 134, 139, 203
nonconformity 130, 131–2, 136, 392
North America (*See also*: America/American) 15, 69, 117, 173, 235, 307
nostalgia/nostalgic/nostalgically 1, 7, 9, 11, 19–21, 38, 51, 52, 67–80, 86, 89, 90, 93, 99, 157, 159, 183, 193–4, 199, 200, 204, 208–9, 210–11, 212, 228, 236, 240, 281, 289–300, 326, 346, 365
  digital nostalgia 7, 20, 289–300

O'Neil, Luke 131–3, 137
October 279–80, 281–2
organic 1, 10, 31, 35, 70, 97, 151, 259, 309, 311–12, 322, 348, 386
Other 5, 12, 16–17, 107, 188–9, 192, 207, 220, 225, 237, 264, 313–14, 359, 391, 394
Otherness 12, 109, 185–6, 189, 367

Pabst Blue Ribbon beer (PBR) 5, 21, 88, 321–35
parody/parodic 5, 7, 105, 211–12, 223, 278, 280, 305, 307, 309, 391, 396–8
pastiche/pastiching 7, 9, 11, 17, 53, 85–100, 218, 222–3, 227, 263, 264, 278–81, 282, 284
pastoralism/pastoral 11, 85–100, 171, 179–80
  pastoral sentimentalism 86, 89–91, 97, 99
people of color 94, 97, 170, 176, 187, 314, 318, 332, 333
performativity/performative 14, 16, 106, 148, 151, 169, 202–3, 207, 211, 218, 257, 261, 315, 360, 394, 396
Plotsky, Andrew 94–6
  Farmrun 86, 94–6, 99
Polaroid 5, 7, 154–7, 159, 215
popular culture/pop culture 1–2, 4, 7, 30–1, 76, 77, 111, 129, 132, 136, 154, 170, 208, 212, 255, 294, 310, 341, 342, 344, 350, 361, 365, 369, 376, 380, 381, 386
porn/pornography (*See also*: hipster porn/ography) 5, 19, 87, 145–60, 207–8, 217
Portland 6, 96, 184, 306, 310–2
Portlandia 5, 20, 138, 305–18
postindustrial 28, 30, 32, 52, 167–81
postmodernism/postmodern/postmodernist/postmodernity (*See also*: post-postmodernism) 1, 3, 7–11, 16, 19–20, 70, 74, 89, 168–9, 183, 204, 223, 235, 247, 273–87, 291, 334
post-postmodernism/post-postmodern (*See also*: metamodernism/metamodern) 1, 3, 7–11, 16, 285
post-subculture/post-subcultural 2, 7–11, 290–1, 296, 396
proto-hipster 19, 106–7, 108–10, 111–12, 114, 115, 121
Proud Boys (*See also*: alt-right) 117–21, 207
punks 76, 105, 107, 109, 112, 120, 180, 279, 310, 368

queer 2, 12, 14–15, 17, 20, 51, 112, 149, 152–3, 215–30, 265
queer culture 12, 14–15, 20, 217–18, 220, 226
queer pornography (*See also*: porn/pornography, hipster pornography) 149, 152–3

race 4–5, 15, 19, 20, 29, 33, 139, 156, 176, 180, 184–6, 187, 189, 193, 196, 201, 207, 217, 219, 254, 256, 260, 264, 266, 267, 273, 294, 314, 317, 382–4
racism/racist 14, 20, 69, 78, 172, 173, 175, 178, 181, 185, 190, 201, 254, 266, 314, 383
Rancière, Jacques 238–9, 249, 287
retro 1, 7, 14, 70, 72, 75, 114, 151, 255, 264, 279
Rich in Faith 377, 380
Romania 19, 67–80, 188
Roșia Montană protests 68, 70, 78, 79
Ross, Kathleen (*See also*: Greif, Mark, Tortorici, Dayna) 2, 18, 87, 375
rural 6–7, 19, 57, 59, 76, 85–6, 88–9, 90–1, 92–4, 97, 169–70, 174, 179, 324–5

satire 17, 114, 121, 184, 204, 312, 375
Schiermer, Bjørn 8–9, 292–3, 323, 360, 375, 382
Selden Standard 86, 98–9
self-fashioning 3, 15–18, 19, 151, 158, 202
sensibility/sensibilities 9–10, 37, 87, 129, 168, 218, 237, 239, 240, 242, 243, 245–6, 249, 253, 322, 329, 330, 340, 359, 377, 386
sexism/sexist 14, 20, 254, 267
sexuality/sexualities (*See also*: gay, heteronormativity/heteronormative, heterosexuality/heterosexual, lesbian, LGBTQIA+, queer, straight) 4–5, 12, 147, 149, 153, 154, 159, 176, 180, 215, 217–18, 219, 220, 222, 225, 227, 255, 260, 267, 317, 364, 375, 385–6
Sherman, Cindy 222–3, 279
Simmel, Georg 106, 115–16
Simsek, Kara 16–17
sincerity 3, 9–10, 61, 183, 196
Solange 14, 20, 254–6, 260, 261, 265–6
South Africa 57 (*See also*: Johannesburg)
square/squares (*See also*: Mailer, Norman) 4, 168, 171–2, 173
stigma/stigmatize/stigmatized 107, 109, 116, 156, 176
straight 14, 20, 132, 146, 150, 175, 215–30, 292, 335
straight queer 20, 215–30
subculture/subcultural (*See also*: post-subculture) 1–2, 3, 7–9, 14, 16–18, 20–21, 30, 33, 35, 67, 79, 80, 87, 105, 106, 108, 114, 120–1, 132, 133, 139, 146, 154–5, 157, 159, 168, 215–16, 218, 220, 222–3, 224–30, 236, 254, 257, 264, 273–4, 290–1, 296, 322, 323, 325, 348, 357–9, 360–1, 362, 364, 367–8, 369–70, 373–87, 394, 396
subcultural capital (*See under*: capital)
suburban 5, 139, 174, 185, 190, 209, 324, 382
sustainability/sustainable 59, 86, 88–9, 92–3, 96, 99, 118, 392

taste 9, 16, 49–50, 69, 87, 111, 134, 138, 154, 158, 203, 205, 215, 218, 236, 239, 273, 281, 284, 290, 305, 308, 316, 318, 321, 325, 329, 340, 346, 349, 350, 359, 360, 370, 376–7, 380, 382, 384
aesthetic taste 87, 273, 376
hipster taste 9, 236, 346, 350, 376–77, 380
politics of taste 16, 218
Taylor, Timothy 172, 173, 177–8, 181
Thornton, Sarah 3, 16, 254

Toronto (*See also*: Canada) 168–9, 173, 175, 178–9
Tortorici, Dayna (*See also*: Greif, Mark, Ross, Kathleen) 2, 14, 18, 87, 114–15, 236, 333, 375
Trafford, Matthew J. 173, 175, 180–1
transgression/transgressional/transgressive/transgress 111, 146–8, 149–52, 153, 156, 159, 180, 187–8, 193, 199, 200–2, 204, 206–10, 212, 219–20, 223–4, 225, 227–8, 230, 259, 262, 384
transnational/transnationally 6–7, 18, 47, 105, 172, 173, 177, 317, 367

Unbreakable Kimmy Schmidt 236
urban/urbanities 1–2, 3, 5–7, 8, 10, 11–12, 18–19, 27–43, 48, 52, 55, 58, 67, 73, 77, 85–6, 87–9, 90–4, 97, 121, 129, 130, 132–3, 134, 136, 156, 167–72, 173, 174, 176, 179–80, 185, 238, 243–4, 246, 253, 276, 296, 310, 312, 330, 346, 357, 362, 376, 384

Varis, Piia (*See also*: Maly, Ico) 2, 323, 325, 328–9
Veblen, Thorstein 106, 111, 116
VICE Media 205, 206–9
vintage 1, 13, 31, 48, 53, 57, 68, 70–1, 72, 75, 79, 87, 91, 95, 109, 114–15, 151, 157, 215, 235, 240, 293, 294, 297–300, 322–3, 376

Wallace, David Foster 186
Warhol, Andy 226, 273, 276–7
white 1, 3–5, 11–13, 20–1, 28, 30, 33, 35–6, 40, 59, 71, 76–8, 85–6, 88–9, 92, 94–5, 97, 106, 108–9, 117, 139, 146, 170, 173, 176–7, 180–1, 183–96, 199–213, 216–18, 219–20, 221, 223, 230, 235, 238, 242–3, 248, 249, 253–4, 256, 257, 258–60, 261, 263–4, 265–6, 267, 276, 283, 294, 297, 313–14, 317–18, 331, 333–5, 357–9, 360, 362, 364–6, 367, 368, 370, 375, 382–3, 384, 387, 395, 398
  white hipster 4–5, 11, 28, 33, 40, 88, 139, 146, 170, 200, 206–8, 217–18, 219–20, 221, 223, 230, 259–60
  white male writer 20, 199–213
  "white Negro(es)" (*See also*: Mailer, Norman) 4–5, 30, 108, 200–1, 219–20, 257
  white supremacy/supremacist/superiority 62, 106, 108, 117, 207, 335, 370
white hipster (*See under* white)
whiteness 12–13, 20, 33, 110, 184–7, 188, 190, 191–2, 196, 200–1, 204, 209, 243, 254, 257, 258, 261, 263, 267, 357, 364–6, 369–70, 382–4
wilderness 5, 87, 110, 169, 170, 179, 186, 196, 297, 300
working class 11, 12, 32, 58, 74, 76, 108, 120, 131, 170, 179, 264, 322, 326, 334–5, 384–5
  working-class aesthetics 384–5
Whitman, Walt 117, 136, 228

yarn art 29, 34–6, 40, 42–3
yarn bombing 18, 27, 29, 31, 34, 35–7, 40, 42
Yeah Yeah Yeahs 254, 261–2
youth(s) 3, 9, 13–14, 20–1, 39, 70, 75, 146, 148, 153–4, 158, 194, 237, 240, 249, 274, 357–9, 360–1, 364, 366–7, 369, 374, 376–7, 378–9, 381, 384

Žižek, Slavoj 274, 283
Zukin, Sharon 28, 34, 37, 41, 43, 167

www.ingramcontent.com/pod-product-compliance
Lightning Source LLC
Chambersburg PA
CBHW060130280326
41932CB00012B/1479